Handbook of Multicultural Counseling

Editors

Joseph G. Ponterotto
J. Manuel Casas
Lisa A. Suzuki
Charlene M. Alexander

Foreword by

Thomas A. Parham

SAGE Publications
International Educational and Professional Publisher
Thousand Oaks London New Delhi

For information address:

SAGE Publications, Inc.
2455 Teller Road
Thousand Oaks, California 91320

SAGE Publications Ltd.
6 Bonhill Street
London EC2A 4PU
United Kingdom

SAGE Publications India Pvt. Ltd.
M-32 Market
Greater Kailash I
New Delhi 110 048 India

Printed in the United States of America

Library of Congress Cataloging-in-Publication Data

Main entry under title:

Handbook of multicultural counseling / edited by Joseph G. Ponterotto
  . . . [et al.].
        p.   cm.
    Includes bibliographical references and index.
    ISBN 0-8039-5506-5 (alk. paper). — ISBN 0-8039-5507-3
(pbk. : alk. paper)
      1. Cross-cultural counseling.   2. Multiculturalism—United States.
    3. Minorities—United States—Counseling of.   I. Ponterotto, Joseph G.
    BF637.C6H3174   1995
    158'.3—dc20   95-12874

This book is printed on acid-free paper.

95 96 97 98 99 10 9 8 7 6 5 4 3 2

Production Editor: Diane S. Foster   Typesetter: Christina Hill

Contents

Foreword

IMAGINE THE ANNOUNCEMENT of a historic event at which the great masters in the field of multicultural counseling are gathering to discuss the pressing counseling imperatives of our time. This text is your personal invitation to that event. Never before in the history of the multicultural counseling movement have so many of our best theorists, researchers, and practitioners lent their individual and collective expertise to a single project. Drs. Ponterotto, Casas, Suzuki, and Alexander are due tremendous congratulations for pulling together such a distinguished cast. You will be equally impressed with the expertise contained within the pages that follow.

My own frustration with the field of counseling focuses on the tangential way in which issues of diversity and multiculturalism are addressed. True enough, surveys indicate that 87% of programs offer at least one multicultural counseling course (Hills & Strozier, 1992), but how many of those programs offer more than one? Better still, how many have integrated culturally specific content into the entire curriculum? Few, I suspect, could pass that test. And yet that is precisely what our field needs: efforts that address issues of multicultural counseling in a comprehensive fashion.

In some respects, it seems as if our profession is caught in a state of inertia or a quandary about how to proceed with the diversity movement. Learning new theories and techniques that are culturally relevant is time-consuming, some complain. Others find it difficult to focus in on the one or two sources that would bring them up to speed. Still others see the necessity of learning about numerous cultural groups as too overwhelming a task. Clearly, the fields of counseling and (dare I say) clinical psychology in general, as well as multicultural counseling in particular, have been demanding a sourcebook that could speak to the complexity of the multicultural movement in a single volume. The *Handbook of Multicultural Counseling* may have come very close to filling that bill.

My frustration with the profession is tempered by my genuine excitement with this volume. It is truly unlike any other text I have ever seen or read. What excites me most about it is how it deviates from materials that are currently available in the field. The *Handbook* provides you, the reader, with an issue-oriented, problem-focused resource that presents a unique blend of historic and cutting-edge material. Rather than using chapters on specific populations to provide a general summary of the relevant counseling issues, the *Handbook* concentrates on specific challenges that confront counselors in the field.

As I travel across the United States, I am constantly asked about how to be more culturally sensitive and competent. Indeed, many if not most of us are searching for ways to operationalize culturally specific knowledge in our academic instruction, research methods, supervision and training, assessment, and counseling and therapy techniques. What is remarkable is that this text speaks to all of these domains. In addition, the book contains extensive coverage of models of ethnic identity development and also introduces the reader to multicultural issues in organizational development. This text is not only comprehensive but state-of-the-art as well, and I consider it a "must-have" resource for personal and institutional libraries.

Pardon me if my enthusiasm for this text is showing. Drs. Ponterotto, Casas, Suzuki, and Alexander have heard your pleas and mine for more tools that can help us cultivate the seeds of cultural sensitivity that have been planted throughout the fields of our profession. It is hoped that using this *Handbook* will make your personal tilling of those gardens more effective, efficient, and rewarding. It is a welcome addition to our profession, and those of us who have been struggling in the fields for years hail its arrival. Oh, by the way, a word of caution: Use of this *Handbook* may render your excuses for not being culturally competent null and void. Users are advised to be serious in their commitment to be transformed. After reading this, you will be expected to be accountable.

THOMAS A. PARHAM, PH.D.
Counseling Psychologist
Director, Counseling Center and
Career Planning and Placement Center
University of California, Irvine

REFERENCE

Hills, H. I., & Strozier, A. L. (1992). Multicultural training in APA-approved counseling psychology programs: A survey. *Professional Psychology: Research and Practice, 23,* 43-51.

Preface

MULTICULTURAL COUNSELING is at a crossroads. In 1991, Paul Pedersen called it a new "fourth force" in counseling, following the forces of the psychodynamic, behavioral, and humanistic movements. Although some would credit the women's movement as the fourth force, Pedersen's (1991) acknowledgment of the present and future impact of the multicultural emphasis in counseling is proving quite prophetic. It is important at this time to examine the current status of multicultural counseling and to provide a sense of direction for the field.

Recent surveys document the rapid growth of multicultural training in counseling curricula. The "multicultural counseling" course was projected to be the fastest growing new course offering in the 1991 to 1993 period (Hollis & Wantz, 1990), and its growth rate continues during the 1993 to 1995 period (Hollis & Wantz, 1994). Whereas in the late 1970s and early 1980s only a small percentage of counseling programs required a multicultural counseling course, recent surveys indicate that 42% to 59% (Hills & Strozier, 1992; Quintana & Bernal, 1995) require such a course and that most programs have one of more elective courses in the area.

As the number of courses and other training experiences in multicultural counseling has grown, so too has the amount of published literature on the topic. It appears that every year, more conference presentations, conceptual and research articles, and books appear on the topic. It is difficult, if not impossible, for the student, practitioner, or researcher to keep abreast of the literature. Given this challenge, the major goal of the *Handbook of Multicultural Counseling* is to provide, in one comprehensive treatise, a concise summary of the field's latest developments. By inviting contributions from many of the leading scholars in the area, as well as from newer emerging scholars in the field, we have sought to provide, under one cover, a synthesis of the field.

SIGNIFICANCE OF THE *HANDBOOK*

The *Handbook of Multicultural Counseling* is a valuable and unique contribution to the multicultural counseling literature for a number of reasons.

1. No currently available book in the field is as comprehensive as the *Handbook*. Unlike many edited books that serve basically as a collection of readings loosely tied together, the *Handbook* was conceptualized from its inception to be thorough and integrative. All major areas of multicultural counseling are covered: ethics, professional issues, research, theory, practice, and emerging trends.

2. As the counseling and counseling psychology professions work to embrace diversity, so too does the spirit of the *Handbook*. The book editors and the chapter contributors represent a broad spectrum of U.S. demography. Many racial/ethnic groups are represented among the contributors. Furthermore, the voices of both established senior scholars and lesser known junior scholars are represented.

3. Some scholars have criticized the profession's multicultural efforts as being strong in rhetoric but weak in action and support. The editors and authors of the *Handbook* are committed to sharing access to the profession. In support of this commitment, all royalties from the sale of the *Handbook* are being donated to support minority student scholarships in counseling. A subcommittee of editors and authors will oversee the application and award process.

CONTENTS OF THE BOOK

The *Handbook* has seven sections. Each section includes an introduction that serves as a "cognitive map" preparing the reader for the chapters that follow. Part I consists of three chapters that focus on history, ethics, and professional issues. Part II consists of eight chapters, all of which focus on theory and research in racial/ethnic identity development. Leading models of identity development are reviewed across major racial/ethnic cohorts. The four chapters that make up Part III focus on multicultural teaching, training, supervision, and assessment. Part IV presents three chapters focusing on practical aspects of multicultural counseling. Two major research reviews make up Part V of the *Handbook*. Finally, Parts VI and VII present nine chapters on selected emerging topics of emphasis in multicultural counseling.

Few can doubt the significance of multiculturism to the everyday work of counselors and other mental health professionals. We hope that the contents of the *Handbook of Multicultural Counseling* will stimulate much-needed discourse, debate, and research in the area.

JOSEPH G. PONTEROTTO
J. MANUEL CASAS
LISA A. SUZUKI
CHARLENE M. ALEXANDER

REFERENCES

Hills, H. I., & Strozier, A. L. (1992). Multicultural training in APA-approved counseling psychology programs: A survey. *Professional Psychology: Research and Practice, 23,* 43-51.

Hollis, J. W., & Wantz, R. A. (1990). *Counselor preparation 1990-1992: Programs, personnel, trends* (7th ed.). Muncie, IN: Accelerated Development Inc.

Hollis, J. W., & Wantz, R. A. (1994). *Counselor preparation, 1993-1995: Vol. 2. Status, trends, and implications* (8th ed.). Muncie, IN: Accelerated Development Inc.

Pedersen, P. B. (Ed.). (1991). Multiculturalism as a fourth force in counseling [Special issue]. *Journal of Counseling and Development, 70*(1).

Quintana, S. M., & Bernal, M. E. (1995). Ethnic minority training in counseling psychology: Comparisons with clinical psychology and proposed standards. *The Counseling Psychologist, 23,* 102-121.

Acknowledgments

PREPARING A BOOK with many chapters and numerous contributors, as is the case with the *Handbook*, requires teamwork and cooperation. We are indebted to the many authors who contributed their expertise and time to writing original and innovative chapters for no financial reward. It is the collective work of many individual authors that has made this comprehensive *Handbook* a reality.

Thomas A. Parham, a pioneer in the field of multicultural counseling, prepared the Foreword to this book, and we are most grateful to him.

We also want to acknowledge the strong support we received from another component of our team—Sage staff. Jim Nageotte and Marquita Flemming deserve a special mention for serving as catalysts for the project. Furthermore, we want to acknowledge Diane S. Foster, Christina Hill, Nancy Hale, Lenny Friedman, and Wendy Bernard, who have helped with production and marketing.

The *Handbook* editors gratefully acknowledge permission to reprint material from the following sources:

Counseling and Psychotherapy: A Multicultural Perspective by A. E. Ivey, M. Bradford, and L. Simek-Morgan, 1993, Boston: Allyn & Bacon. Copyright © 1993 by Allyn and Bacon. Pages 114-115 reprinted in Chapter 4 by permission.

"PT Conversation With Charles W. Thomas: Different Strokes for Different Folks" by J. A. E. Gardner and T. G. Harris, 1970, September, *Psychology Today*, pp. 48-53, 78-79. Brief excerpts are reprinted in Chapter 6 with permission from *Psychology Today*, Copyright (©) 1970 (Sussex Publishers, Inc.).

Bulletproof Diva: Tales of Race, Sex, and Hair by Lisa Jones, 1994, New York: Doubleday. Copyright 1994 by Doubleday. A brief excerpt is reprinted in Chapter 9, Table 9.2, with permission.

Using Race and Culture in Counseling and Psychotherapy: Theory and Process by J. E. Helms and D. A. Cook, in press, Fort Worth, TX: Harcourt Brace Jovanovich. A table is adapted as Table 9.3 in Chapter 9 by permission of Harcourt Brace Jovanovich.

An Analysis of Multiracial Change Efforts in Student Affairs by R. L. Pope, 1993, Doctoral dissertation, University of Massachusetts at Amherst, 1992, *Dissertation Abstracts International, 53-10,* 3457A. A figure is reprinted as Figure 15.1 in Chapter 15 by permission of copyright holder R. L. Pope.

"Cultural Identity Development and Family Assessment: An Interaction Model" by G. V. Gushue, 1993, *The Counseling Psychologist, 21,* 487-513. Tables are reprinted as Tables 29.1 and 29.2 in Chapter 29.

"Guidelines for Providers of Psychological Services to Ethnic, Linguistic, and Culturally Diverse Populations" by the American Psychological Association, 1993, *American Psychologist, 48,* 45-48. Copyright 1993 by the American Psychological Association. Reprinted in Appendix I by permission.

"Advisory Principles for Ethical Considerations in the Conduct of Cross-Cultural Research: Fall 1973 Revision" by J. L. Tapp, H. Kelman, H. Triandis, L. Wrightsman, and G. Coelho, 1974, *International Journal of Psychology, 9*(3), 240-249. Reprinted in Appendix II by permission of the International Union of Psychological Science.

"Multicultural Counseling Competencies and Standards: A Call to the Profession" by D. W. Sue, P. Arredondo, and R. J. McDavis, 1992, *Journal of Counseling and Development, 70,* 477-486. Copyright by the American Counseling Association. Reprinted in Appendix III with permission. No further reproduction authorized without written permission of the American Counseling Association.

PART I

Historical Perspectives
and Professional Issues

PART I OF THE *HANDBOOK* provides a historical perspective on the field and discusses some pressing issues confronting the profession. Morris L. Jackson begins Part I by taking the reader back to the roots of the multicultural counseling movement. By unearthing original and seminal articles, scouring historical association archives, and interviewing historically influential scholars, Jackson opens our discussion with a firm historical grounding. As a number of *Handbook* authors focus on helping counselors and clients acknowledge and respect their own racial/ethnic identity, so too does Jackson admonish us to understand and respect our professional roots.

In Chapter 2, Michael D'Andrea and Judy Daniels present a concise summary of current professional association activities in the multicultural area. Through their detailed account of a case study involving the American Counseling Association, D'Andrea and Daniels provide a model that other institutions and associations may follow.

In Chapter 3, Paul B. Pedersen takes an in-depth and critical look at the ethical guidelines of the counseling profession. Although some might consider research to be the cornerstone of the profession, some would argue that ethics serve as the guiding principle for service and research in multicultural counseling. Pedersen's constructive critique of our current ethical guidelines provides an interesting and important stimulus for discussion and debate.

1

Multicultural Counseling

Historical Perspectives

MORRIS L. JACKSON

MULTICULTURAL COUNSELING is counseling that takes place between or among individuals from different cultural backgrounds.

An examination of the literature reveals an absence of research related to the history of multicultural counseling. Graduate students, professionals, scholars, and practitioners have contributed to the growth and development of multicultural counseling without the benefit of a historical foundation. This chapter attempts to fill this literature void by providing a historical perspective of the multicultural counseling field.

Although such terms as *multiculturalism, cross-cultural communication,* and *cross-cultural intervention* are of relatively recent vintage, the phenomena they describe have been present throughout the course of human history. They were recognized in ancient Mediterranean civilizations from the new kingdom of pharaonic Egypt through the collapse of the Roman Empire (Thompson, 1989). Most of the discussions of these phenomena in the ancient sources are devoted to the great difficulties that arise from differences in cultures, including assumptions of cultural superiority not only by dominant political/military powers but also by conquered or colonized peoples. As Thompson showed, however, some dominant political/military powers went beyond lamenting the difficulties and made efforts both to acknowledge many cultural differences as legitimate and to deal effectively with the consequences of these differences.

It is noteworthy that Herodotus of Halicarnassus, who wrote an extensive history of the fifth-century wars between the Persians and the Greeks, is widely regarded as the father not only of history but also of anthropology (Lateiner, 1989). Herodotus traveled widely throughout the eastern Mediterranean basin, including Egypt and Mesopotamia, questioning both elites and commoners about the way they did things. He clearly took considerable delight in cultural variety and set forth the famous dictum "Custom is stronger than law" in order to explain why conquerors have so much trouble getting conquered peoples to adopt the conqueror's law. His account is a gold mine of information about how Persia managed to administer an empire that stretched from Egypt in the west to the Indus River Valley in the east, a territory that was home to hundreds of peoples, each of which saw itself as a distinct culture.

Multiculturalism has an established history. For centuries, people of different cultural backgrounds have recognized the existence of problems associated with communicating with people from other cultural backgrounds. American society is not unique in its concern over multicultural issues. The real issue is to what extent a society is willing to venture to ensure that the traditions, customs, values, and beliefs of a people different from the dominant majority will be recognized. The guidance and counseling movement must not ignore the rich multicultural past.

Ancient civilizations and American society share the understanding that groups from different cultural backgrounds do not necessarily relate effectively with each other even though they live in the same society. Immigrant groups have been arriving in the United States for years, bringing with them different cultural values. History and contemporary observations show that the ease and extent to which they assimilate depend on two important factors: race and cultural similarity to the dominant American racial group. The 1950s and 1960s were a period in American history that necessitated change and growth in the perspectives held by majority people concerning minority people and vice versa. People of diverse cultural backgrounds began to become more tolerant of each other. Society questioned whether many of the traditional values of American society, such as equality, freedom of expression, the right to vote, and education, were truly available for all.

METHOD OF RESEARCH

The history of multicultural counseling spans several decades. I examined several counseling and psychological journals and interviewed selected professionals who knew about the history of multicultural counseling. Reviewed for this chapter were the *Personnel and Guidance Journal*, now named the *Journal of Counseling and Development*, from 1952 to 1994; the *Journal of Non-White Concerns*, now named the *Journal of Multicultural Counseling and Development*, from 1972 to 1994; the *Journal of Consulting Psychology* from 1950 to 1970; the *Journal of Clinical Psychology* from 1950 to 1970; the *Journal of Negro Education* from 1950 to 1970; and the *Harvard Education*

Review from 1950 to 1970. The primary reference for this undertaking was the *Personnel and Guidance Journal.* The *Journal of Negro Education* and the *Harvard Education Review* were also consulted because they published articles by minority professionals during a period when it was difficult for them to find an outlet for their research. In addition, I reviewed the minutes of the American Personnel and Guidance Association (APGA) board of directors meetings for the years 1969 to 1974 and minutes of the APGA senate meetings for the years 1969, 1971, and 1974.

GENESIS OF THE
MULTICULTURAL COUNSELING MOVEMENT

Discussion of the history of multicultural counseling first necessitates discussion of the history of the American Counseling Association (ACA), as it is named today. This organization was called the American Personnel and Guidance Association (APGA) when it was officially established in 1952, changed its name to the American Association for Counseling and Development (AACD) in 1983, and changed its name again to the American Counseling Association in 1992 (Herr, 1985).

The guidance and counseling movement had its roots in the industrial cities of the Midwest and the eastern seaboard (Aubrey, 1977). During the first few decades of the 20th century, it was exclusively a vocational guidance movement; later it expanded to encompass psychological counseling as well. The early years of the profession were a time period in which African Americans and other minorities faced especially harsh discrimination and prejudice. Vocational counselors could not counsel minorities to enter the professions of their choice: It would be illogical for them to do so when discrimination routinely denied minorities access to those professions. Many vocational counselors resolved this difficulty by excluding minority clients altogether. Others matched minority clients to the types of employment they were most likely to be able to get, thus restricting the quality of the career guidance they provided (Aubrey, 1977).

During the 1940s and 1950s, African Americans and other minorities were not a significant part of the personnel and guidance movement. They did not hold key positions within the APGA during the 1950s, and they had no input in writing the association's by-laws or establishing its principles. The historical development of multicultural counseling was thus delayed by segregation, racism, discrimination, and prejudice. These factors affected institutions and organizations throughout the United States, and the American Counseling Association was not exempt from their influence.

In view of the prevalence of segregation during the 1940s and 1950s, when the APGA was first being established, it is easy to understand why Blacks and other minorities were not involved in building the foundation of the counseling profession. Even after laws were passed to address and rectify segregation, racism, discrimination, and prejudice continued to thrive. Segregation in schools, colleges, universities, and private organizations did not disappear overnight as a result of the passage of segregation laws. Nevertheless, the passage of desegregation laws in the 1950s and the movement toward integration in American society influenced the way the counseling profession provided counseling services to minorities. As Copeland (1983) indicated, the goal of counseling and guidance for minorities during the 1950s, in contrast to the present-day emphasis on group differences, was assimilation into mainstream America in the name of integration. Actually, integration was meant to be a two-way street, but minorities have always done most of the work to make the country a truly integrated society.

The melting pot notion has been a significant social science concept and political ideal of this country since its beginning. But the United States has never been a melting pot. Immigrant groups and minorities continue to maintain their unique cultural heritages through their churches, schools, civic associations, and residential enclaves. Thus, assimilation counseling proved to be ineffective for a large segment of the American population, as counselors worked with theories and techniques that were at odds with the cultural backgrounds of their clients.

EARLY WRITERS:
THE PRE-1960s ERA

A review of the counseling literature, most notably the *Personnel and Guidance Journal*, from the 1950s revealed few journal articles on counseling minority group clients. Three reasons appear to account for this shortcoming in the literature. First, it was difficult, if not impossible, for minority scholars to get their research published in professional journals. Racism was rampant throughout American society and was a major reason for excluding Black scholars from this opportunity. Second, the field of guidance and counseling was dominated by a small number of nationally known authors (Walsh, 1975). Third, research and writing were not popular activities before 1958 (Walsh, 1975). An analysis by Westbrook (1991) of articles on multiculturalism in the *Education Index* since 1950, covering 40 years, revealed very little interest in the topic during the 1950s, but an exponential increase in interest over the succeeding decades.

According to my own review of the *Personnel and Guidance Journal* from 1952 through 1959, five articles during this period addressed concerns of a multicultural clientele. A brief review of these articles is appropriate, for they seem to represent the earliest explorations of multicultural counseling. Murphy (1955) was one of the first professionals to publish an article on the importance of culture in the counseling environment. He challenged counselors by asking, "Should the counselor convey his own personal values to his client or should he restrict himself to techniques which enable him to assist the client to discover his own implicit values?" (p. 4). He also suggested that knowledge about the cultures of clients was more important for counselors than the skills and techniques they might learn.

Three years later, Augustine (1958) and Kiehl (1958) respectively discussed employment equality and opportunities for African Americans. These two authors were pioneers in their study of the counseling needs of African Americans. They addressed contemporary issues that affected the involvement of African Americans in the workplace, and challenged the status quo of discriminating against minorities who sought to improve their lot in life.

Augustine's (1958) study of the progress of Blacks from 1940 to 1950 indicated no significant progressive change in employment equality. Augustine postulated that Black youth were handicapped in their training and tended to concentrate in occupations that were low in prestige, income, and tenure security. Finally, he projected that by 1990 Black women would achieve equality at the professional level but Black men would be only 2.1% of all male professionals.

Kiehl (1958) reported that Black men had entered the engineering profession since 1899 and had experienced success in industry and government. He neglected to mention that very few Black Americans were able to receive the education and training required for this career. He recognized, however, that at present there was a surplus of White engineers and that society at large was not receptive to Black engineers. Thus, he pointed out that counselors faced a dilemma in advising Blacks who wished to enter the engineering profession.

One year later, Smith (1959), responding to the integration of schools in the South, suggested that more and more Black students would be facing the choice of whether to pursue careers and establish businesses in their own communities or whether to work in the larger community that was opening up opportunities for Black Americans. Before this point, working in the Black community had been the only option for most Blacks because of the pervasiveness of segregation and discrimination. But even with the expansion of opportunities created by integration, some Blacks might wish to work in their own communities to help their own people.

Oelke (1959) reviewed the performance of Black veterans on nine tests to determine the usefulness of these tests in guidance and industry. He reported a sparsity of information in the literature on the use of the tests, and concluded that test items should be modified to draw from the experiences of the cultural groups tested. It is obvious that he was addressing the cultural bias.

What these five articles had in common was their reference to culture, minority groups, and Blacks and their concern about the lack of scholarly attention to the topic. Their interest would set the stage for the arrival of the multicultural counseling movement in the 1960s.

Articles drawn from the *Journal of Clinical Psychology* during the 1950s also contained incipient multicultural themes. Heine (1950) provided psychotherapists with insight into two problems associated with therapy for minority group members. The first centers on the type of relationship the minority client can possibly have with a majority group therapist perceived to be a racist. Heine questioned the authenticity of the responses of minority group members in the therapeutic setting. The second concerns whether the majority group therapist can respond to the minority client as an individual instead of as a member of a minority group. Clearly, these two issues are still salient today. Research colleagues of Heine (1950)—most notably, Davis (1957), McCary and Tracktir (1957), and McCary (1956)—discussed at some length the significance of Blacks' results on tests that had been constructed for White people. They recommended that normative data be generated so that the studies conducted would provide more accurate results and the information produced would be more useful to therapists.

Articles from the *Journal of Consulting Psychology* during the 1950s contained information about race differences in intelligence test scores, and alluded to the importance of cultural factors and the impact of ethnocentric attitudes (Davidson, Gibby, McNeil, Segal, & Silverman, 1950; Mussen, 1953; Siegman, 1958; Sperrazzo & Wilkins, 1959).

An interesting pattern in the 1950s multicultural literature as a whole was that studies tended to focus on the significance of culture, not in the therapeutic relationship but in the administration of standard tests. A major concern was the comparison of Blacks and Whites on various measures of intelligence. Not until the 1960s does one begin to find research more concerned with the relationship of the therapist and the Black client.

THE 1960s

The 1960s was an era of revolution, change, and growth in the counseling profession. It was during this period that the multicultural counseling movement slowly began to establish itself. If the 1950s may be characterized as the decade of the birth of the multicultural counseling movement, then the 1960s are the decade of the movement's infancy. It was during the 1960s that American society began paying attention to the concerns of minorities. Leading the charge for the counseling profession to be responsive to all Americans were Black counseling professionals. According to T. Parham (personal communication, 1994), Black professionals in the field of psychology were at the same time formulating their own multicultural movement.

Several events during the 1960s made it easier for minorities to have their issues dealt with in the profession. The civil rights movement placed a spotlight on concerns that had been neglected in counseling members of minority groups. The passage of the Civil Rights Act in 1964 had a major effect on the multicultural movement in the counseling profession. America began to listen closely to its conscience and reflect on past mistreatment of members of minority groups. Race, prejudice, and discrimination were discussed openly as significant factors in the counseling relationship. The notion that minority group members were inferior to majority group members was questioned.

Thus, the multicultural movement gained general support because of Whites' new sensitization to racial issues, and in the counseling profession this sensitization took the form of concern over the profession's failure to provide "guidance for all"—that is, counseling that addresses the diverse needs of all the people who seek it.

In an earlier article, Robinson (1953) had stated that "guidance for all" was a principle that all guidance workers should use. A decade later, Hoyt (1967) was still saying that guidance for all was a goal toward which the counseling profession should strive. Copeland (1983) pointed out that although philosophically the counseling and guidance movement was supposed to serve everyone, in actuality it concentrated on the average homogeneous White American. Her forthright assessment and confession of the lack of the profession's full attention to the concerns of everyone was refreshing.

Aubrey (1977) stated that during the 1960s, the increased racial and cultural diversity of counselors and those being trained in counseling was beginning to make the profession more responsive to a diverse population. The 1960s empowered minorities to fight for their rights to receive equitable treatment in the counseling setting. It is noteworthy that special legislation was enacted at the 1966 APGA convention calling for guidance and counseling of persons who were "culturally disadvantaged" (Hoyt, 1967). The passage of special legislation to address the counseling concerns of people of color was an indictment of previous counseling practice and spoke to how far the multicultural counseling movement had come.

As Sue and Sue (1990) commented, the values of the profession of counseling mirror the values of the larger society. The counseling profession shares a historical bond of experiences with the larger society in terms of how and when it dealt with racism and discrimination (Atkinson, Morten, & Sue, 1979). Counseling and guidance in the United States did not grow in a vacuum from the factors shaping society. As society became more tolerant of cultural differences, so did the counseling profession.

During the 1960s the multicultural counseling movement took several steps forward in the area of research. Trueblood (1960), Phillips (1960), Wrenn (1962), Reed (1964), Boney (1966), Peterson (1967), Zaccaria (1967), Vontress (1966, 1967, 1968, 1969), and Grande (1968) began to discuss the necessity for counseling practitioners to pay attention to counseling issues of the culturally different and the culturally disadvantaged. Their writings paved the way for the myriad research articles that began to appear in the 1970s. The importance of culture and minority group membership and an emphasis on making some adjustments in one's counseling approach when working with nonmajority clients were central themes during the 1960s.

The 1960s also featured numerous multicultural pioneering activities within the APGA. At the 1969 APGA convention in Las Vegas, William Banks, now a professor at the University of California-Berkeley, spearheaded an effort to encourage the association to be more responsive to the concerns of the culturally different by presenting a petition to the association's senate calling for the establishment of an Office of Non-White Concerns. This was the beginning of the association's first Black caucus, about which McFadden and Lipscomb (1985) would later write. In 1972 it was established as the Association for Non-White Concerns (ANWC), and in 1985 its name was changed to the Association for Multicultural Counseling and Development. The small assembly of Black professionals in Las Vegas was responsible for the advancement of equitable treatment of all clients served by the profession.

The work of Black professionals in the 1960s was politically instrumental in keeping the multicultural counseling movement progressing and giving the ANWC its energy and impetus. The mission of the association was to be inclusive of all people of color and to ensure that the APGA provided adequate counseling and guidance for all (T. Parham, personal communication, 1994).

In the late 1960s and early 1970s three people of color were elected to the APGA's board of directors: Katherine Coles, Clemmont E. Vontress, and William Cash. Thelma Daley was the first African American and person of color elected as the president of the APGA and served from 1975 to 1976. These milestones are indicative of the increasing openness and responsiveness of the association to the concerns of people of color.

As the decade concluded, research in the multicultural counseling field began to provide some answers to the countless professionals who had been asking themselves the question, "How do I counsel a client who is culturally different from myself?" Counselor education, which had previously paid scant attention to the concerns of minorities, was criticized by minority writers (Atkinson, Staso, & Hosford, 1978). Black, Asian, Hispanic, and Native American counselors had understood how to counsel clients from their respective backgrounds, but many of these counselors had performed their counseling work in segregated settings. Once American schools were desegregated, cross-race counseling became more common and concerns about adequate cross-race counseling became more acute. The Black power movement and the movements of other disenfranchised groups in American society created an atmosphere in which different cultural groups felt empowered to proclaim that their counseling needs be met.

THE 1970s

According to Reynolds and Pope (1991), interest in multicultural and cross-cultural counseling issues grew substantially in the 1970s and generated a surge of innovative articles and research. In the early 1970s, Sue and Sue (1971) and Vontress (1971) discussed how mainstream psychology did not attend to the concerns of minorities. Counseling terms such as *culturally different* and *culturally disadvantaged* were prevalent in the literature and generally referred to domestic minorities. In addition, this decade witnessed a growing number of studies examining the effects of race in the counseling process.

Professional counselors in larger numbers were hungry for information that would sharpen their skills and strategies for working with minorities and fill the void in the literature. Researchers and scholars responded to this void by writing about counseling issues from a cultural perspective (Pedersen, Lonner, & Draguns, 1976; Sue & Sue, 1971; Vontress, 1971).

During the 1960s, the term *minority counseling* had been a popular term in the literature. Generally, minority counseling had involved a majority group counselor and a minority group member client. As the 1970s rolled in, the terms *cross-cultural* and *multicultural counseling* began to appear in the literature. These terms could describe interactions not only between majority group counselors and minority group clients but also between minority group counselors and majority group clients, or between counselors and clients who belonged to different minorities. By shifting the focus away from minority groups exclusively, these terms challenged majority group counselors to become aware of the role that their own cultural assumptions played in their interactions with clients. And whereas in the 1960s the primary minority groups receiving counselors' attention had been African American, Asian American, Native American, and Latino American, in the 1970s the term *minorities* expanded to include counseling of an increasing variety of racial and ethnic groups, as well as other groups of people who felt discriminated against or had experienced institutionalized oppression. Interest in the multicultural field soared as women, persons with disabilities, and other groups who experienced discrimination proclaimed their differences. During this period, society began to reexamine the ideal of assimilation and to explore the value of cultural diversity (Ornstein & Levine, 1982).

Multicultural/cross-cultural research and writing increased during the 1970s for several reasons. The first was the formation of the ANWC, which provided a platform for members to express and develop their views on working with clients from different cultural backgrounds. The knowledge gained from decades of same-race minority counseling could now be shared with both minority and majority colleagues. The second was the establishment of the *Journal of Non-White Concerns*, which offered minorities a medium for publishing their ideas on how to work with clients from various cultural backgrounds. A review of the early journals of the ANWC revealed a domination by only a few minority writers, primarily African Americans.

In 1970, Paul Smith was the editor of a special issue of the *Personnel and Guidance Journal* titled "What Guidance for Blacks." He was the first Black counseling professional to hold that position.

In 1975, the APGA expanded further and requested Derald Sue to become a guest editor of the same journal. As editor also in March 1977 and April 1978, Derald Sue provided the APGA membership with two special issues of the APGA journal that emphasized the concerns of a variety of cultural groups. Prior to these issues, most articles had exclusively addressed the counseling needs of African Americans. Sue is recognized for his vision of diversifying the ethnic representation of the journal.

Of particular importance to the multicultural counseling movement were two events. The first was the publication in 1971 of the *Guidance Monograph Series 6: Minority Groups and Guidance*. The series focused on counseling Blacks, Native Americans, Spanish-speaking students, and other neglected segments of the American population whose needs were not met by counselors. The second event occurred in Montreal in 1973. Paul Pedersen chaired a panel on cross-cultural counseling at the American Psychological Association. The result of this event was an edited book by Pedersen, Lonner, and Draguns, (1976), titled *Counseling Across Cultures*, that assembled professionals from a variety of cultural backgrounds and disciplines.

THE 1980s AND 1990s

The 1980s and 1990s witnessed unprecedented growth in the specialty of multicultural counseling. Professionals researched and wrote about diversity and multicultural counseling in record numbers. Ethnic groups not previously identified with the multicultural counseling movement sought to be culturally different. For example, individuals who for decades had concealed their Native American heritage now boldly professed to have an admixture of Indian blood (Cameron, 1992). During the early stages of the development of multiculturalism, professionals had researched and written about their own racial/ethnic groups, but the reverse began to happen in the 1980s and 1990s: Anglo American, African American, Native American, Latino American, and Asian American writers contributed to the literature in record numbers without confining themselves to their own cultural group. Further, in the 1990s, one is likely to observe a large percentage of Anglo Americans and a small percentage of people of color writing on international peoples of color. Two important questions before multicultural leaders are: "Should multicultural counseling include domestic minorities and international people or only domestic minorities?" and "Should counselors focus their attention on the historically underserved domestic minorities?" Implicit in these two questions is the issue of defining the boundaries of multicultural counseling. The debate on these two questions continues.

MONOLITHIC PERSPECTIVE OF COUNSELING

According to the *Merriam Webster's Collegiate Dictionary* (10th ed.), *monolithic* means "exhibiting or characterized by often rigidly fixed uniformity." The counseling field is uniform in that it was developed from a single point of view, namely, an Anglo-European perspective. This occurred because people of color were not originally participants in its decision-making bodies or professional practice.

Although the principle of "guidance for all" was meant to be inclusive, it did not actually extend to minority group members. Theories of counseling were developed at a time when minority group members were segregated and experienced discrimination and racism in schools, communities, workplaces, and society at large. Because minorities were not considered a part of mainstream society, theorists typically ignored the needs and cultural concerns of this segment of the American population. Consequently, the techniques and strategies that flowed from the operational theories reflected the implicit bias of a monolithic approach to client populations. According to Speight, Meyers, Cox, and Highlen (1991), many problems in the counseling field have arisen directly from attempts to view multicultural populations through a Eurocentric conceptual system.

In research as well, one finds evidence of a monolithic approach to client concerns. The journals reviewed for this chapter showed a consistent lack of attention to the issues affecting counseling clients from different cultural populations. Not until minority groups began to demand attention to their concerns did research begin to focus on minority populations. As Bradley (1978) noted, the innovations of the 1970s represented an attempt by the counseling profession to make some significant improvement in the services offered to minority clients.

THE SHIFT TO A PLURALISTIC PERSPECTIVE

Since the 1950s, when few writers were courageous enough to state the importance of working with minority clients, there has been a gradual increase in the amount of research that addresses the special needs of minority group members. Simultaneously, the counseling profession has come to recognize that the theories, techniques, strategies, and interventions taught and used by counselors have been inadequate for working with this population. In an attempt to shift from a monolithic to a pluralistic perspective of counseling, Davis (1978) explicitly stated that the available counseling tools and techniques may be inappropriate for clients from a different culture and that multicultural counselors must be creative and flexible in their counseling style. A pluralistic perspective in counseling urges researchers, scholars, students, teachers, and helpers to question the validity of the current theories, techniques, and strategies in use in the profession.

FUTURE DIRECTIONS

Multiculturalism has arrived in the counseling profession. With its arrival come the challenges of understanding unique cultural differences without repudiating the commonality of the human species.

Multicultural counseling in the United States faces numerous challenges. One is to determine how the term *multicultural* will be defined, for the concept has become inclusive of every group represented in the United States. Another is to identify ways to restructure counseling curriculums so that the numerous groups in the United States proclaiming their diversity will receive appropriate attention. Still another is to extend research beyond the handful of minority groups that have traditionally been studied.

Multiculturalism is here to stay. The questions facing the profession are: (a) What direction will this specialty of counseling take? and (b) Who will lead the multicultural movement? Lee (1989) suggested that the struggle for leadership of the multicultural counseling movement is entangled in the larger power struggle between people of color and the dominant White majority in the United States. The jury is still out on these issues.

REFERENCES

Atkinson, D. R., Morten, G., & Sue, D. W. (1979). *Counseling American minorities: A cross-cultural perspective.* Dubuque, IA: William C. Brown.

Atkinson, D. R., Staso, D., & Hosford, R. (1978). Selecting counselor trainees with multicultural strengths: A solution to the Bakke decision crisis. *Personnel and Guidance Journal, 56*(1), 546-549.

Aubrey, R. F. (1977). Historical development of guidance and counseling and implications for the future. *Personnel and Guidance Journal, 55*(1), 288-295.

Augustine, T. (1958). The Negroes' progress toward economic equality. *Personnel and Guidance Journal, 36*(9), 632-634.

Boney, J. D. (1966). Predicting the academic achievement of secondary school Negro children. *Personnel and Guidance Journal, 44*(1), 700-703.

Bradley, M. K. (1978). Counseling past and present: Is there a future? *Personnel and Guidance Journal, 57*(1), 42-45.

Cameron, S. (1992). *Multicultural counseling summit: A town meeting* [Videotape]. Alexandria, VA: American Counseling Association.

Copeland, E. J. (1983). Cross-cultural counseling and psychotherapy: A historical perspective. Implications for research and training. *Journal of Counseling and Development, 62,* 10-15.

Davidson, K. S., Gibby, R. G., McNeil, E. B., Segal, S. J., & Silverman, H. (1950). A preliminary study of Negro and White differences on Form 1 of the Wechsler-Bellevue Scale. *Journal of Consulting Psychology, 14*(1), 489-492.

Davis, J. (1957). The scatter pattern of a southern Negro group on the Wechsler-Bellevue Intelligence Scale. *Journal of Clinical Psychology, 13*(1), 298-300.

Davis, R. V. (1978). A paradigm and model for cross-cultural study of counseling. *Personnel and Guidance Journal, 56*(1), 463-466.

Grande, P. P. (1968). Attitudes of counselors and disadvantaged students toward school guidance. *Personnel and Guidance Journal, 46*(1), 889-892.

Heine, R. W. (1950). The Negro patient in psychotherapy. *Journal of Clinical Psychology, 10*(6), 373-376.

Herr, E. L. (1985). AACD: An association committed to unity through diversity. *Journal of Counseling and Development, 63*(1), 395-404.

Hoyt, K. B. (1967). Attaining the promise of guidance for all. *Personnel and Guidance Journal, 45*(1), 624-630.

Kiehl, R. (1958). Opportunities for Negroes in engineering. *Personnel and Guidance Journal, 37*(3), 219-222.

Lateiner, D. (1989). *The historical method of Herodotus.* Toronto: University of Toronto Press.

Lee, C. C. (1989, January). Editorial: Who speaks for multicultural counseling? *Journal of Multicultural Counseling and Development, 17,* 1.

McCary, J. L. (1956). Picture-frustration study normative data for some cultural and racial groups. *Journal of Clinical Psychology, 12*(3), 194-195.

McCary, J. L., & Tracktir, J. (1957). Relationship between intelligence and frustration-aggression patterns as shown by two racial groups. *Journal of Clinical Psychology, 12*(2), 202-204.

McFadden, J., & Lipscomb, W. D. (1985). History of the Association for Non-White Concerns in personnel and guidance. *Journal of Counseling and Development, 63,* 444-447.

Murphy, G. (1955). The cultural context of guidance. *Personnel and Guidance Journal, 34*(1), 4-9.

Mussen, P. H. (1953). Differences between the TAT responses of Negro and White boys. *Journal of Consulting Psychology, 17*(5), 373-376.

Oelke, M. C. (1959). Performance of Negro veterans on nine tests. *Personnel and Guidance Journal, 38*(1), 322-325.

Ornstein, A. C., & Levine, D. U. (1982). Multicultural education: Trends and issues. *Childhood Education, 58,* 241-245.

Pedersen, P., Lonner, W. J., & Draguns, J. G. (1976). *Counseling across cultures.* Honolulu: University of Hawaii Press.

Peterson, R. A. (1967). Rehabilitation of the culturally different: A model of the individual in cultural change. *Personnel and Guidance Journal, 45*(1), 1001-1007.

Phillips, W. B. (1960). Counseling Negro pupils: An educational dilemma. *Journal of Negro Education, 29,* 504-507.

Reed, H. J. (1964). Guidance and counseling. *Journal of Negro Education, 33,* 282-289.

Reynolds, A. L., & Pope, R. L. (1991). The complexities of diversity: Exploring multiple oppression. *Journal of Counseling and Development, 70*(1), 174-180.

Robinson, F. P. (1953). Guidance for all: In principle and in practice. *Personnel and Guidance Journal, 31*(1), 500-504.

Siegman, A. W. (1958). The effects of cultural factors on the relationship between personality, intelligence, and ethnocentric attitudes. *Journal of Consulting Psychology, 22*(5), 375-377.

Smith, P. (1959). Some aspects of Negro business. *Personnel and Guidance Journal, 37*(7), 511-512.

Speight, S. L., Meyers, L. J., Cox, C. I., & Highlen, P. S. (1991). A redefinition of counseling. *Journal of Counseling and Development, 70*(1), 29-36.

Sperrazzo, G., & Wilkins, W. L. (1959). Racial differences on progressive matrices. *Journal of Consulting Psychology, 23*(3), 273-274.

Sue, S., & Sue, D. W. (1971). Chinese-American personality and mental health. *Amerasia Journal, 2,* 39-49.

Sue, D. W., & Sue, D. (1990). *Counseling the culturally different: Theory and practice* (2nd ed.). New York: John Wiley.

Thompson, L. A. (1989). *Romans and Blacks.* Norman: University of Oklahoma Press.

Trueblood, D. L. (1960). The role of the counselor in the guidance of Negro students. *Harvard Educational Review, 30*(3), 252-269.

Vontress, C. E. (1966, Summer). The Negro personality reconsidered. *Journal of Negro Education, 35,* 210-217.

Vontress, C. E. (1967). The culturally different. *Employment Service Review, 10*(4), 35-36.

Vontress, C. E. (1968, Winter). Counseling Negro students for college. *Journal of Negro Education, 37,* 37-44.

Vontress, C. E. (1969). Counseling the culturally different in our society. *Journal of Employment Counseling, 6*(1), 9-16.

Vontress, C. E. (1971). *Counseling Negroes: Series 6. Minority groups and guidance.* Boston: Houghton Mifflin.

Walsh, W. M. (1975). Classics in guidance and counseling. *Personnel and Guidance Journal, 54*(4), 219-220.

Westbrook, F. D. (1991). Forty years of using labels to communicate about nontraditional students: Does it help or hurt? *Journal of Counseling and Development, 70,* 20-28.

Wrenn, C. G. (1962). The culturally encapsulated counselor. *Harvard Educational Review, 32,* 444-449.

Zaccaria, J. S. (1967). Guidance implications of concepts from the field of culture and personality. *Personnel and Guidance Journal, 45*(9), 907-910.

2

Promoting Multiculturalism and Organizational Change in the Counseling Profession

A Case Study

MICHAEL D'ANDREA

JUDY DANIELS

EVERY GENERATION INHERITS a unique set of challenges. Today, the counseling profession faces a major challenge regarding how it will respond to the cultural/racial/ethnic diversification of our contemporary society. This diversification is forging a new sociopolitical reality in which professional counselors will be called upon to work with very different types of client populations. These clients will present mental health professionals with unique developmental perspectives and personal concerns that are different from those presented by the individuals that most practitioners have typically been accustomed to serving in the past.

The changing contemporary social reality of which counseling professionals are a part demands a shift in many of the paradigms that have traditionally guided their work and professional identity. Certainly, numerous other political, economic, and social factors characterize the context that the profession must address to remain a viable and relevant force in our national mental health care system.

17

However, the ways in which the counseling profession responds to the diversification of society will reflect its moral sensitivity toward, respect for, and commitment to persons of different cultural, ethnic, and racial backgrounds within the United States and throughout the world. In short, multiculturalism represents the single most important test of the counseling profession's moral character, pragmatic viability, and professional relevance as we approach the 21st century (Daniels & D'Andrea, in press).

The terms *multiculturalism* and *multicultural counseling* are used repeatedly throughout this chapter. For clarification, in the context of the present discussion, *multiculturalism* relates to an individual's or an organization's commitment to increase awareness and knowledge about human diversity in ways that are translated into more respectful human interactions and effective interconnections. *Multicultural counseling* refers to a process in which a trained professional from one cultural/ethnic/racial background interacts with a client of a different cultural/ethnic/racial background for the purpose of promoting the client's cognitive, emotional, psychological, and/or spiritual development.

This chapter is designed to serve a fourfold purpose. First, we give a brief overview of the counseling profession's response to the multicultural movement over the past 30 years. Second, we discuss ways in which both individual racism and institutional racism are manifested in the reactions of many professional counselors toward multiculturalism. Third, we discuss an ongoing project aimed at advancing the principles of multiculturalism and reducing existing elements of racism within the profession. Fourth, we present a set of strategies for facing the long-term challenges that confront the counseling profession as it attempts to remain a viable and relevant force within the context of a rapidly diversifying society.

A HISTORICAL PERSPECTIVE

From Active Neglect to Benign Accommodation

Much of the profession's history has been characterized by what might be called "active neglect" in terms of addressing cultural, ethnic, and/or racial diversity in counseling training, practice, and research. *Active neglect* accurately describes the profession's lack of sensitivity and commitment for multicultural issues until rumblings of discontent were expressed in the mid-1960s. In 1965, the American Personnel and Guidance Association (APGA, now the American Counseling Association [ACA]) formally entered the era of multiculturalism by establishing the Human Rights Commission (Burn, 1992). One of the specific purposes of this commission was to assess and advocate for the needs of culturally unique groups and individuals. Four years later, the National Office of Non-White Concerns was created within APGA (Casas, 1984). Both of these actions followed in the wake of the civil rights movement, which catalyzed an increased awareness and concern throughout the United States regarding injustices perpetrated against persons of color.

As an increasing number of African Americans, Hispanic Americans, Asian Americans, Native Americans, and persons from other underrepresented groups (e.g., women, physically challenged persons, the elderly) increased their demands for respect and justice in the late 1960s and early 1970s, mental health professionals were further pressed to review and modify their professional standards and ethics. Recognizing the need to address their moral responsibility for providing effective professional services to persons from diverse backgrounds, psychologists and counselors attending the 1973 conference of the American Psychological Association (APA) in Vail, Colorado, developed the first set of ethical guidelines related to cross-cultural counseling (Paradis, 1981). This endorsement codified the notion that the counseling of culturally distinct persons by individuals who were not "trained or competent to work with such clients should be regarded as unethical" (Casas, Ponterotto, & Gutierrez, 1986, p. 347).

Four years later, the Association for Counselor Education and Supervision (ACES) followed the precedent set at the APA's Vail conference by recording its own organizational commitment to persons from diverse cultural, ethnic, and racial backgrounds. In a 1977 position paper, this national association "urged all persons involved in counseling to elevate the quality and availability of services to non-Whites" (Burn, 1992, p. 578).

The late 1970s and 1980s reflected a period in which numerous blue-ribbon committees were established to examine the serious lack of progress made within counseling training programs regarding racial, ethnic, and cultural matters (ACES Commission on Non-White Concerns [McFadden, Quinn, & Sweeney, 1978]; Austin Conference, 1975; Dulles Conference, 1978; National Conference on Graduate Education in Psychology, 1987; President's Commission on Mental Health, 1978 [Sue, 1990, 1991]).

Several other changes also occurring within APA during this period reflected an increased awareness of the need to expand the way psychologists and counselors traditionally worked with persons from diverse backgrounds. These changes primarily resulted from the efforts of numerous multicultural counseling advocates (the vast majority of whom were from non-White backgrounds) who consistently pressed for significant alterations in the way counseling practitioners and researchers conducted their work. Some of the APA's specific attempts to deal with the concerns raised by multicultural counseling activists included the establishment of the APA Office of Cultural and Ethnic Affairs in 1978, the Board of Ethnic Affairs in 1980, and the Society of Psychological Study of Ethnic Minority Issues (Division 45) in 1987.

Upon reviewing these changes, it could be argued that the advances made by the counseling profession in terms of promoting multicultural counseling in its own ranks have been both positive and frustrating. On a positive note, multiculturalism is increasingly becoming acknowledged as the "fourth force" in counseling and psychology (Pedersen, 1988, 1989, 1990). This has been largely due to a growing acceptance of the changing sociopolitical reality that characterizes our contemporary society. It is also due, in part, to a growing number of counseling practitioners who are becoming aware that it is in their best interests to acquire a broad range of multicultural counseling competencies if they are to remain professionally relevant and viable in the coming years.

Sue, Arredondo, and McDavis (1992) noted that it has been gratifying to observe the "increase in both the literature and training programs that address the need to develop multicultural awareness, knowledge, and skills" (p. 477). This point is underscored by the results of a 1977 curriculum survey indicating that less than 1% of the counseling psychology training programs in the United States at that time required multicultural courses in their training frameworks (McFadden & Wilson, 1977). In contrast, a recent national survey revealed that 89% of counseling psychology programs now offer a multiculturally focused course in their training format (Hills & Strozier, 1992). It is also important to point out that the numerous commissions and committees developed during the 1980s led to the formation of a number of multicultural counseling standards and competencies. One of the most comprehensive multicultural competency frameworks to be published to date is offered by Sue et al. (1992). This encompassing framework provides counseling trainers and practitioners with a clearly stated set of guidelines for working with persons of diverse cultural, ethnic, and racial backgrounds. Given the potential usefulness of these competencies for the preparation and development of the current and future generation of counselors, it is indeed frustrating and puzzling that no professional association has formally adopted Sue et al.'s framework as a part of its credentialing standards.

It is also important to note that all of the advancements mentioned above reflect various accommodations that the counseling profession has reluctantly been willing to make. These gains actually represent minimal common-sense changes that have had a relatively benign impact on the overall disposition of the profession.

Several experts have stressed that even the noticeable increases in the number of required multicultural counseling courses now being offered in training programs across the United States do not adequately address the challenges the profession faces as it prepares to enter the 21st century. In addition to the potential problems Reynolds discusses in Chapter 15 of this book regarding many of the cross-cultural counseling courses currently offered in counseling and psychology training programs, we have the following concerns:

1. The lack of integration of these courses into the overall curriculum
2. The tendency to develop multicultural counseling courses in a haphazard and fragmented manner without a strong conceptual framework linked to specific competencies
3. The reluctance of program chairpersons and faculty members to support the allocation of additional resources and personnel to promote students' multi-

cultural awareness, knowledge, and counseling skills once a single course in this area has been incorporated into the core curriculum

4. The tendency to present instructional services from a purely intellectual perspective without reference to the sociopolitical ramifications of counseling (i.e., the implications of oppression, discrimination, and racism) (Ponterotto & Casas, 1991; Sue & Sue, 1990; Sue et al., 1992)

Even if counseling training programs were willing to effectively address all of these concerns, the profession would still fall far short of developing the type of mental health service delivery system that adequately meets the needs of an increasingly diverse client population. In order to facilitate the establishment of such a system, a committed effort must be initiated among all training programs, practitioners, researchers, and the two dominant national counseling associations in the United States (i.e., the ACA [Association for Multicultural Counseling and Development] and the APA [Division 17]).

This effort should be guided by a greater willingness and commitment to institutionalize strategies within the profession that are specifically designed to help counseling practitioners, researchers, and trainers move beyond their own ethnocentric ways of thinking and behaving. A number of multicultural counseling advocates have recently discussed how the perpetuation of ethnocentrism in the counseling profession allows counselors and psychologists to maintain a host of biases that effectively impair the work they do within a pluralistic society (Atkinson, Morten, & Sue, 1993; Daniels & D'Andrea, in press).

Beyond reducing the effectiveness of counselors and psychologists who are currently called upon to work with clients from diverse backgrounds, the perpetuation of ethnocentrism represents a serious threat to the viability of the counseling profession (Daniels & D'Andrea, in press). To guarantee that the profession will remain a viable part of the United States' health care and educational systems in the next century, ACA and APA must take a greater lead in designing action plans that help reduce the current level of ethnocentrism that is manifested among many practitioners, researchers, and trainers in the field.

Clearly, this kind of proposal represents an ambitious undertaking, and one could offer many reasons that it simply cannot be done. However, we offer two reasons why such an initiative should be supported by both ACA and APA. First, working toward making the counseling profession more responsive to the unique psychological and personal needs of individuals from diverse cultural, ethnic, and racial backgrounds is the morally right thing to do. The fact that this kind of proposal has not been articulated and put forth by leaders (especially White leaders) in APA and ACA in the past raises serious questions about the ethical integrity of the profession's current and past leadership as it relates to the multicultural counseling movement.

Second, as has already been mentioned, the profession's viability and relevance in the future will largely depend on the manner in which it reflects a genuine commitment to multicultural counseling in its training programs, service delivery strategies, and research efforts today.

Having underscored the importance of creating systemic changes in the counseling profession at the present time, we now examine a major project that is currently underway to promote numerous organizational changes within the ACA. The goal of these changes is to create an organizational structure that is more responsive to the multicultural and developmental needs of those counseling practitioners, researchers, educators, and students who play a pivotal role in the present and future mental health care system in the United States.

Uncovering Institutional Racism in the Counseling Profession

For many persons in the field, the gains that were mentioned in the preceding section represent a signal that the counseling profession has made sufficient progress in the area of multicultural counseling. It is also readily noted, however, that a number of cross-cultural counseling advocates continue to express frustration and anger over the level of complacency that many White counseling professionals appear to manifest regarding the need to infuse multicultural considerations more formidably into the mainstream of the profession.

Their level of displeasure reached a peak at a recent national convention sponsored by the American Psychological Association. At this meeting Sue (1992) articulated his lack of patience over the continuing tendency of both APA and ACA to call for the development of more committees and commissions specifically charged with the responsibility of outlining additional multicultural counseling standards and competencies despite the work that has already been done in this area. As Sue stated,

> Given the time and expertise that has already been invested in developing a set of counseling competencies which have been approved by the Association for Multicultural Counseling and Development, it is time for this organization to embrace these standards and formally adopt them as guidelines that all counseling training programs in the United States are encouraged to follow.

In even more compelling terms, Parham (1992) presented his analysis of the reluctance of both APA and ACA to adopt the competencies outlined by Sue et al. (1992) and to move beyond their current level of support for the multicultural counseling movement:

> To make the types of changes that are necessary in order that the counseling profession will be able to meet the needs of an increasing number of clients from diverse cultural and racial backgrounds, the profession in general and its two national associations—the American Psychological Association and

the American Counseling Association—in particular, will have to learn to share more of its power and resources with persons who have traditionally been excluded from policy-making and training opportunities. However, if we are going to move in this direction, White counselors and organizational leaders are going to have to first be willing to confront the various forms of individual and institutional racism which have impeded this sort of progress up to this time. (Parham, 1992)

Most White counseling professionals would readily agree that the level of racism that exists in society negatively affects a large number if not all individuals and institutions in the United States in some way. However, it is interesting to note that almost none has come forward to discuss the ways in which this psychosocial pathology adversely affects the counseling profession. In attempting to clarify some of the ways in which individual and institutional racism imbues the profession, D'Andrea (1992) outlined several examples of how it is manifested in either the omission or the commission of specific actions/incidents in the field:

- Less than 1% of the chairpersons of graduate counseling training programs in the United States come from non-White groups (89% of all chairpersons in counseling training programs are White males).
- No Hispanic American, Asian American, or Native American person has ever been elected president of either the ACA or the APA.
- Only one African American person has been elected as president of APA.
- None of the five most commonly used textbooks in counselor training programs in the United States lists "racism" as an area of attention in its table of contents or index.
- A computerized literature review of journal articles found in social science periodicals over a 12-year period (1980-1992) indicated that only 6 of the 308 articles published during this time period that examined the impact of racism on one's mental health and psychological development were published in the three leading professional counseling journals (*The Counseling Psychologist*, *Journal of Counseling and Development*, and *Journal of Counseling Psychology*).
- All of the editors of the journals sponsored by ACA and APA (excluding one African American editor with the *Journal of Multicultural Counseling and Development*) are White.
- Despite more than 15 years of efforts invested in designing a comprehensive set of multicultural counseling competencies and standards, the organizational governing bodies of both ACA and APA have consistently refused to adopt them formally as guidelines for professional training and development.

D'Andrea (1992, 1993) concluded that the voices and opinions of minority practitioners, educators, and researchers continue to be seriously restricted, especially regarding the development and implementation of organizational policies and control of the dissemination of information generated by APA and ACA. Collectively, these acts of omission and/or commission represent ongoing examples of racism in the counseling profession.

The facts just listed suggest that our national counseling organizations need to be modified in many respects if they are to remain viable in a rapidly changing multicultural society. But if one mentions the need to create systemic changes in large organizations such as ACA and APA in order to bring multiculturalism into the mainstream of our profession, many persons respond with either confusion or cynicism about the possibility of ever making such changes.

This confusion and cynicism is often rooted in ignorance about the ways in which persons outside established organizational power structures (such as governing councils, advisory boards, and executive committees) can effectively stimulate changes within professional counseling associations. The following model of organizational change is therefore presented to give a basic understanding of some strategies that can stimulate systemic changes in professional institutions. This model consists of four fundamental strategies that we, in collaboration with several other multicultural counseling activists, are currently using to stimulate changes within the ACA.

1. *Mobilization Strategies* involve developing opportunities in which the rank-and-file members of our national organizations can meet to discuss the types of problems and barriers that prevent their associations from further advancing the spirit and principles of multiculturalism in the counseling profession.

2. *Education Strategies* involve providing opportunities for mental health professionals to increase their theoretical and practical understanding of multiculturalism and institutional racism, as well as providing instruction about organizational change processes. This component is important in that it facilitates an information-sharing process that is vital in creating organization change. In doing so, it also helps give direction and builds on the energy generated in the mobilization phase.

3. *Organizational Strategies* involve encouraging members of the organization to move toward designing specific demands/petitions that are intended to change the way in which a particular professional association typically operates. It is important to keep in mind that creating systemic change in any large professional association requires making recommendations and petitioning the organization's leadership for various modifications in its traditional way of operating. For organizations such as ACA and APA, this may include

   - Developing recommendations for implementing aggressive affirmative action policies when hiring persons in management positions at the national headquarters
   - Offering an organizational development plan that focuses on issues related to multiculturalism
   - Requesting access to vehicles that disseminate information about multicultural counseling issues to the general membership of the association (e.g., by agreeing to include a special column in the association's newspaper/newsletter)
   - Requesting that a specific percentage of programs selected for the association's annual national conventions target issues related to racism and multiculturalism

The process of institutionalizing multicultural changes within professional counseling associations requires that these kinds of recommendations be written in the form of a series of resolutions that are then circulated among the organization's members for their signatures of support.

4. *Institutionalizing Strategies* involve

- Submitting the resolutions/petitions that were signed by members of the association to the policy-making bodies within the association (e.g., the governing council, executive committees)
- Lobbying for their acceptance among persons who participate on these policy-making bodies
- Monitoring the actions (or lack of action) demonstrated by those persons who are responsible for formulating policies within the association (e.g., individual members on the governing council, executive committees) regarding the specific issues and demands that are outlined in the resolutions/petitions
- Developing a mechanism in which feedback can be provided to the general membership regarding the progress (or lack of progress) that was achieved as a result of petitioning the association's leaders for specific changes in the organization

The following section presents a case study describing how this model is currently being used to create systemic changes within the ACA. By utilizing the steps just outlined, the persons who have taken part in this effort hoped to stimulate a number of institutional changes that reflected greater sensitivity, respect, and commitment for the multicultural counseling movement within the profession. To help the reader understand the ways in which this framework was used, we first describe the various actions that were taken and then discuss how these specific actions corresponded to one or more of the steps described above.

A CASE STUDY APPROACH TO PROMOTING MULTICULTURALISM IN ACA

The Atlanta 1993 Summit: Dealing With Racism in the Counseling Profession

Acting upon Parham's (1992) earlier stated assertion that individual and institutional racism must be addressed if the multicultural counseling movement is to be more fully accepted into the mainstream of the profession, a number of counseling practitioners and educators affiliated with ACA began meeting in the summer of 1992 to discuss the possibility of convening a special summit meeting at the association's 1993 national convention in Atlanta, Georgia. The summit was tentatively entitled "Dealing With Racism in the Counseling Profession."

The idea to convene this special summit meeting was first publicly presented to members of the Western Region of the Association for Multicultural Counseling and Development during their 1992 regional conference in Sacramento, California. Formal endorsement for the Atlanta Summit came from the members of the Western Regional Executive Committee who were meeting during their 1992 annual conference in Sacramento, California *(Mobilization and Education Strategies)*.

Don C. Locke (North Carolina State University) and Michael D'Andrea (University of Hawaii) volunteered to coordinate the summit. As coordinators of this event, they agreed to be responsible for arranging the meeting, making sure the logistics were properly set up, and inviting persons to convene in Atlanta during the 1993 ACA national convention *(Mobilization Strategy)*. These tasks included securing a conference room during the ACA National Convention so that persons who were already planning to go to the convention could easily attend the summit, planning the agenda for the meeting, and inviting 38 nationally known leaders in the field of multicultural counseling to take part in an information-sharing *(Education Strategy)* and strategy-building session *(Organizational Strategy)*. When inviting these national leaders, the summit coordinators explicitly stated that the primary goal of the summit was to discuss various ways in which institutional racism continued to impede ACA from making a more substantial commitment to the multicultural counseling movement.

Despite experiencing the worst snowstorm to hit Atlanta in over 100 years (which led to the cancellation of some of the convention's activities), over 100 persons from across the United States who had heard about the summit meeting decided to attend and offer their input. Those in attendance included numerous African American, Hispanic American, Asian American, and Native American counseling practitioners, researchers, and educators from all parts of the United States (one participant who also attended the summit resided in Bolivia and had traveled to Atlanta to attend the national convention). Beyond this diverse representation of professionals, it was both surprising and gratifying to note that more than 40 persons attending the Atlanta summit were White counseling professionals and graduate students. Many of these individuals openly expressed much concern about the various ways racism was manifested in ACA and indicated their own willingness to work toward advancing the principles of multicultural counseling into the mainstream of the profession *(Mobilization and Education Strategies)*.

After a very stimulating discussion of these issues, the summit participants agreed to support four specific action strategies before adjourning. First, a five-person committee was selected from the summit participants to be responsible for meeting with the executive director, the current president, and the president-elect of ACA before the end of the convention. The purpose of this meeting was to report on the issues and concerns discussed in the summit and to request that these leaders support the call for an expanded forum that would cover the same theme at the 1994 ACA National

Convention in Minneapolis, Minnesota *(Organizational and Institutionalizing Strategies).*

A second committee was set up to coordinate a "public education campaign" within the association. This project involved having the committee members submit editorial statements for publication in ACA's monthly newspaper (the *Guidepost,* now known as *Counseling Today*). This strategy was deemed important so that the other 59,000 members of ACA might learn about the concerns expressed and action strategies developed during the summit *(Education Strategy).*

Finally, a third committee was designed to plan a mid-year National Multicultural Counseling Leadership Conference at the ACA Headquarters in Alexandria, Virginia, in August 1993 *(Mobilization, Education, Organizational, and Institutionalizing Strategies).*

The August 1993 National Multicultural Leadership Conference

The purpose of the August Multicultural Leadership Conference was threefold. First, it was designed to maintain the momentum created during the Atlanta summit by reconvening persons interested in further discussing ways of promoting the multicultural counseling movement in the profession *(Mobilization Strategy).*

Second, the conference planners invited representatives from the two major credentialing bodies in the counseling profession (the Council for the Accreditation of Counseling and Related Educational Programs [CACREP] and the National Board for Certified Counselors [NBCC]) to attend the National Leadership Conference. This was done so that the conference participants would have the opportunity to directly solicit their support to adopt the multicultural counseling standards and competencies outlined by Sue et al. (1992) into their professional credentialing standards *(Education, Organizational, and Institutionalizing Strategies).*

Third, ideas generated during the Atlanta summit were further discussed and summarized in the form of several resolutions to be submitted to the representatives of the ACA Governing Council for their review and future action *(Organizational and Institutionalizing Strategies).*

Although these resolutions were formally raised and discussed during their December 1993 meeting, they were all either tabled or rejected by the members of the ACA Governing Council at that time. The lack of support for these resolutions by the ACA leaders was not totally unexpected by many of the persons who participated in the Atlanta summit and the August Leadership Conference.

It did, however, confirm the belief that the goal of creating systemic changes aimed at infusing the principles and practice of multicultural counseling into the mainstream of the profession would require more time and an expanded effort. Ultimately, this translated into a more clearly recognized need to develop new strategies to mobilize and educate the ACA membership and leaders about the importance of infusing multiculturalism into all aspects of the counseling profession and our national association.

The 1994 Minneapolis Forum: Expanding Efforts to Create Organizational Changes Within ACA

Shortly after the August Leadership Conference, ACA President Beverly O'Bryant contacted the conveners of the Atlanta summit and indicated her commitment to support a 3-hour forum at the 1994 national convention in Minneapolis. This action was precedent setting for two reasons. First, it represented the first time the American Counseling Association formally sponsored a major event at its national convention that was specifically designed to address issues related to institutional racism in the counseling profession. Second, it marked the first time any major, national professional counseling organization endorsed an event to publicly discuss strategies aimed at creating a truly multicultural organizational climate within the association *(Mobilization, Education, and Organizational Strategies)*.

The responsibility for coordinating this event was delegated to several persons who acted as committee chairpersons during the Atlanta summit. These persons made up the National Planning Committee for the Minneapolis Forum. It was noted that this committee was well represented by women and men as well as individuals from diverse cultural, ethnic, and racial backgrounds. The committee members included Patricia Arredondo (Empowerment Workshops, Boston), Michael D'Andrea (University of Hawaii), Judy Daniels (University of Hawaii), Farah Ibrahim (University of Connecticut), Don C. Locke (North Carolina State University), Thomas Parham (University of California, Irvine), and Derald Sue (California School of Professional Psychology).

In discussing the theme of the Minneapolis forum, the planning committee members agreed that it should build on the issues discussed at the Atlanta summit and the National Multicultural Leadership Conference. It was unanimously agreed that the theme of the Minneapolis forum would be "Promoting Human Dignity and Development Through Diversity: Addressing Racism in the Counseling Profession." With this expanded theme in mind, the committee members proceeded to design the forum in such a way as to accomplish three main objectives.

First, they sought to establish a new tradition in the organization intended to publicly acknowledge and honor those persons whose life work embodies the spirit and principles of multiculturalism. With this in mind, the forum organizers submitted a national call through all of the ACA divisions and regional representatives for nominees for the First Annual Ohana Awards. The word *Ohana* is a Hawaiian term that means "extended and caring family"

(McDermott, Tseng, & Maretzki, 1980). By incorporating a Hawaiian tradition into the forum program, the organizers hoped both to honor those persons who are nationally respected for their work as multicultural counseling experts and to promote an awareness about a group of Native Americans who are frequently omitted from discussions about multicultural counseling and development (the Hawaiian people) *(Education Strategy)*.

Second, several counseling practitioners were asked to discuss ways in which they put multicultural counseling theory into practice in their communities. This segment of the forum provided the audience an opportunity to learn about practical counseling strategies and techniques that were found to be effective in work with a diverse client population *(Education Strategy)*.

Third, the forum organizers utilized half of the time allowed for the forum to encourage the audience to participate in ongoing efforts to create specific systemic changes within ACA that were aimed at promoting the principles of multicultural counseling into the profession. To increase their chances of achieving this objective, the planning committee members felt that it was important to:

1. Select speakers who would outline the ways in which various forms of institutional racism continue to impede ACA's ability to realize its potential to take a national lead in promoting the principles and spirit of multiculturalism in the counseling profession *(Education and Organizational Strategies)*.
2. Solicit direct input and support for a set of resolutions that would be presented to the members of the ACA Governing Council for future action *(Education, Organizational, and Institutionalizing Strategies)*.
3. Lead the audience in a "guided imagery" activity that involves having those in attendance at the forum take time to visualize something they could do to help promote the multicultural counseling movement in the profession. At the end of the guided imagery activity, members of the audience were asked to share their personal vision and plan of action with the rest of the forum participants. Several members of the audience eagerly stated specific actions they planned on taking upon returning to their communities after the convention *(Mobilization Strategy)*.

More than 600 persons who attended the Minneapolis Forum signed several resolutions that were presented during this historic meeting *(Education, Organizational, and Institutionalizing Strategies)*. The resolutions called upon the ACA's governing council, president, and president-elect to consider a variety of organizational changes to be implemented within the association, including:

1. The addition of a clause in the hiring policies for persons contracted by ACA to provide professional development workshops around the United States that would require all contracting agents to agree to "receive training in diversity issues relevant to the contracted topic by Master Counseling Trainers prior to

providing their professional development services for the American Counseling Association"

2. Organizational support to guarantee the ongoing inclusion of multicultural counseling training for ACA leaders, practitioners, researchers, and educators at all association regional meetings, annual Summit Leadership Conferences, and annual conventions in the future

3. An organizational mandate to provide two full-day multicultural professional development training workshops annually for members of the association's primary policy-making body (the governing council)

4. The addition of a new column in the association's monthly newspaper specifically designed to disseminate information about multicultural counseling to the 59,000 members of ACA

5. The establishment of a new tradition in which the president and executive director of ACA would make an annual report at the national convention regarding the progress the association has made in terms of placing persons from underrepresented groups in management positions within the organization

6. Support from ACA to sponsor another forum at the 1995 annual convention entitled "Promoting Human Dignity and Development Through Diversity: An Annual Report"

Shortly following this 1994 Minneapolis forum, members of the national planning committee met with ACA President Beverly O'Bryant and President-Elect Doris Coy to discuss the success of this major event and solicit their support for the resolutions. President O'Bryant indicated her full support to help institute the resolution calling for a new column in the association's newspaper entitled "Promoting Human Dignity and Development Through Diversity."

President-Elect Doris Coy agreed to have the members of the Minneapolis Forum National Planning Committee design and coordinate the opening session of the 1995 ACA National Convention (entitled "Promoting Human Dignity and Development Through Diversity: An Annual Report"). She also asked the members of the planning committee to serve as an advisory committee on issues related to multicultural and diversity counseling during her 1994-1995 presidential tenure.

ASSESSING THE IMPACT OF THE
ORGANIZATIONAL DEVELOPMENT MODEL

We evaluated the effectiveness of implementing this organizational development model by assessing if any concrete changes did in fact occur within ACA as a result of following this framework. Having conducted this evaluation, we noted that several changes have been institutionalized within ACA during the time the strategies described above were implemented (1992-1994). These changes are briefly described below.

First, the editors of the monthly newspaper published by ACA, entitled *Counseling Today*, agreed to include an ongoing column in all future editions that would specifically deal with issues related to multicultural and diversity counseling. The members of the organizational development project requested that the column be entitled "Promoting Human Dignity and Development Through Diversity." This was done to help provide a sense of continuity and to continue to build on the ideas generated at the 1994 Minneapolis forum.

Two of the members of the organizational development project agreed to act as co-editors for this column and accepted the responsibility of making sure that various issues related to multicultural counseling would be published in all future editions of the *Counseling Today* newspaper. This column first appeared in the August 1994 edition of *Counseling Today*.

Second, the ACA Governing Council approved two new policies during their September 1994 meeting that were directly related to the resolutions developed during the 1993 Multicultural Leadership Conference and distributed and signed by more than 600 ACA members who attended 1994 Minneapolis forum. The first policy change stated that a group of master multicultural counseling trainers would be identified to provide training to all the governing council members as well as the entire ACA headquarters staff during the 1995-1996 fiscal year. The second policy change stated that all persons contracted by ACA to provide professional development training services and/or workshops in the future must agree to discuss the ways in which the topic of their training relates to counseling persons from diverse cultural, ethnic, and racial backgrounds.

LOOKING TOWARD THE FUTURE

The diversification of our modern society is creating a sociopolitical reality that requires major alterations in the way the counseling profession and its national organizations operate. With this in mind, the members of the Minneapolis Forum National Planning Committee have developed a set of long-term goals that they hope to achieve by reducing the institutional barriers that currently block full acceptance of multiculturalism in the counseling profession. These goals include:

1. Establishing the principles of multicultural counseling as the centerpiece of the ethical standards of the counseling profession
2. Having the multicultural counseling standards and competencies that were outlined by Sue et al. (1992) institutionalized within national counselor education accreditation bodies (the Council for Accreditation of Counseling and Related Educational Programs [CACREP] and APA-approved counseling psychology program standards)

SUMMARY

This chapter has attempted to examine the history of the multicultural counseling movement from the 1960s to the present time. We have also provided an analysis of the types of barriers that continue to block the profession from taking the moral higher ground in terms of moving beyond its own cultural-centricity and institutional racism.

The case study presented in this chapter is offered as one example of the types of interventions necessary to facilitate the transformation of the counseling profession as it continues to grapple with the imminent challenges of a new age in human history—the Age of Reason, Respect, Acceptance, and Accommodation for human differences.

Although persons from different racial/cultural/ethnic backgrounds must continue to lead the way in promoting the spirit and principles of multiculturalism in the profession, it is imperative that White counseling professionals take a more active stand in advocating for the removal of the barriers that impede progress in this area. Together we can transform the profession, or together we will suffer the consequences of becoming an increasingly irrelevant entity in the national mental health care delivery system.

REFERENCES

Atkinson, D. R., Morten, G., & Sue, D. W. (Eds.). (1993). *Counseling American minorities* (4th ed.). Madison, WI: Brown & Benchmark.

Burn, D. (1992). Ethical implications in cross-cultural counseling and training. *Journal of Counseling and Development, 70,* 578-583.

Casas, J. M. (1984). Policy, training, and research in counseling psychology: The racial/ethnic minority perspective. In S. Brown & R. Lent (Eds.), *Handbook of counseling psychology* (pp. 785-831). New York: John Wiley.

Casas, J. M., Ponterotto, J. G., & Gutierrez, J. M. (1986). An ethical indictment of counseling research and training: The cross-cultural perspective. *Journal of Counseling and Development, 64,* 347-349.

D'Andrea, M. (1992, October). The violence of our silence. *Guidepost, 35*(4), 31.

D'Andrea, M. (1993, August). *Dealing with racism: Counseling strategies.* Paper presented at the annual meeting of the American Counseling Association, Atlanta.

Daniels, J., & D'Andrea, M. (in press). Ameliorating ethnocentrism in counseling. In D. W. Sue, A. Ivey, & P. Pedersen (Eds.), *A metatheory of multicultural counseling.* Honolulu: University of Hawaii Press.

Hills, H. I., & Strozier, A. L. (1992). Multicultural training in APA approved counseling psychology programs: A survey. *Professional Psychology: Research and Practice, 23,* 43-51.

McDermott, J. F., Tseng, W., & Maretzki, T. W. (1980). *Peoples and cultures of Hawaii: A psychocultural profile.* Honolulu: University of Hawaii Press.

McFadden, J., Quinn, J. R., & Sweeney, T. J. (1978). *Position paper: Commission on Non-White Concerns.* Washington, DC: Association for Counselor Education and Supervision.

McFadden, J., & Wilson, T. (1977). *Non-White academic training with counselor education and rehabilitation counseling, and student personnel programs.* Unpublished manuscript.

Paradis, F. E. (1981). Themes in the training of culturally effective psychotherapists. *Counselor Education and Supervision, 21*, 136-151.

Parham, T. (1992, August). *The White researcher in multicultural counseling, revisited—discussion and suggestions.* Paper presented at the annual meeting of the American Psychological Association, Washington, DC.

Pedersen, P. B. (1988). *A handbook for developing multicultural awareness.* Alexandria, VA: American Association for Counseling and Development.

Pedersen, P. (1989). Developing multicultural ethical guidelines for psychology. *International Journal of Psychology, 24*, 643-652.

Pedersen, P. B. (1990). The constructs of complexity and balance in multicultural counseling theory and practice. *Journal of Counseling and Development, 68*, 550-554.

Ponterotto, J., & Casas, M. (1991). *Handbook of racial/ethnic minority counseling research.* Springfield, IL: Charles C Thomas.

Sue, D. W. (1990). Culture specific strategies in counseling: A conceptual framework. *Professional Psychology, 24*, 424-433.

Sue, D. W. (1991). A conceptual model for cultural diversity training. *Journal of Counseling and Development, 70*, 99-105.

Sue, D. W. (1992, August). *Multicultural counseling research: Proposing an agenda for the 90s.* Paper presented at the annual meeting of the American Psychological Association, Washington, DC.

Sue, D. W., Arredondo, P., & McDavis, R. J. (1992). Multicultural counseling competencies and standards: A call to the profession. *Journal of Counseling and Development, 70*, 477-486.

Sue, D. W., & Sue, D. (1990). *Counseling the culturally different: Theory and practice* (2nd ed.). New York: John Wiley.

3

Culture-Centered Ethical Guidelines for Counselors

PAUL B. PEDERSEN

ETHICAL PRINCIPLES GENERATED in one cultural context cannot be applied to other substantially different cultural contexts without modification. In order to make those modifications, the counselor needs to distinguish between "fundamental" ethical principles, which are not negotiable, and "discretionary" aspects, which must be modified and adapted to each setting. The fundamental aspects are like hinges on a door, which make it possible for the door to swing open by remaining fixed in place. If the fundamental principles are compromised, the result will be a relativistic position in which justice is determined by whatever the common practice of a community may be. If the discretionary aspects are not modified, the result will be an absolutist domination by special interest groups that benefit from the status quo.

This chapter attempts to identify the ethical actions available to culture-centered counselors and the consequences of each alternative by leading the reader through the process of making ethical choices, from the general and abstract principles to the specific and practical applications. The first ethical act is to examine three comprehensive but contrasting perspectives of relativism ("to each his/her own"), absolutism ("mine is best"), or universalism ("we are both the same and different") typically found throughout the literature on ethics. The second ethical act is to examine the research on the cultural encapsulation and the exclusionary tendencies that have characterized professional counseling and that require meaningful change. The third ethical act is to look at alternative ethical guidelines that have been suggested to implement fair ethical judgments in multicultural settings. The fourth ethical act is to demonstrate the inadequacies of professional ethical guidelines now being used. The fifth ethical act is to shape the future direction of culture-centered ethical guidelines for ourselves and the profession of counseling.

RELATIVISM, ABSOLUTISM, AND UNIVERSALISM

All ethics are guided by one of three general perspectives: relativism, absolutism, or a dynamic universalism that accepts that all people are similar in some ways and dissimilar in others.

Berry, Poortinga, Segall, and Dasen (1992) contrasted relativism, absolutism, and universalism in a synthesis summary of the literature. The relativist position avoids imposing value judgments and allows each cultural context to be understood in its own terms. External descriptions of the group in the abstract or evaluations of group behavior by outsiders are not valid unless or until they are validated by the group's own internal criteria. There is little or no interest in similar patterns across cultures except at the most abstract level of analysis, and qualitative differences are fundamental to the group's identity. Valid comparisons across groups are not possible, and psychological interventions, assessments, and ethical guidelines must be based exclusively on internal group criteria. Ethical behavior would be judged by other members of the group without regard to the standards used by other groups outside this specific community. This approach has frequently been followed by anthropologists in studying cultural groups. Relativists believe in a context-bound measure of reality and discourage analysis of behavior by outside criteria.

Kierstead and Wagner (1993) divided relativism into categories. Relativism based on ethical egoism assumes that what is right for one person may not be right for anyone else. Relativism that is based on ethical nihilism assumes that there is no meaning to moral concepts. Cultural relativism assumes that right and wrong are determined exclusively by the culture of the individual. Relativism makes moral discourse difficult.

The absolutist position disregards problems of ethnocentrism and applies the same evaluative criteria across cultures in the same fixed and unchanging perspective. The importance of cultural context is minimized. Comparisons across groups are encouraged, and the same measures, strategies, theories, or ethical principles are applied in the same way regardless of cultural differences. The more powerful group defines and dominates the criteria by which ethical behavior is evaluated. Cultural differences between groups are disregarded, and cultural similarities to the dominant group are the primary criteria of judgment. Differences are typically described as deficits in intelligence, honesty, or right-mindedness as defined by the dominant and authoritarian group.

Historically, psychology has often focused primarily on narrowly defined absolute principles of human behavior without regard for cultural differences. Absolutists impose a single definition of reality on the plurality of cultural contexts.

The universalist position assumes that although psychological processes such as pleasure and pain may be universal in all cultures, the way those processes are manifested will be significantly different in each culture. The psychological processes of living may be the same but expressed in different ways. Comparisons are therefore possible across cultural groups by distinguishing the process from the manifestation. The application of psychological theories, measures, and ethical guidelines therefore requires understanding both the underlying, fundamental, and profound similarities and the essential and idiosyncratic differences. "Theoretically, interpretations of similarities and differences are made starting from the belief that basic psychological processes are panhuman and that cultural factors influence their *development* (direction and extent) and *deployment* (for what purposes and how are they used)" (Berry et al., 1992, p. 258). Universalists combine the search for culture-specific manifestations of difference with a search for fundamental similarities that link each cultural context with every other context.

Either the absolutist or the relativist position lends itself to easy answers in the search for ethical guidelines. The absolutist position imposes the criteria of the dominant culture on all of the other cultures without ambiguity, so that what is considered right in the dominant culture must be judged right elsewhere. The relativist position allows each group to generate its own internalized criteria for ethical judgment, so that the judgment of what is right in each culture will be different from the judgment in every other culture. The more difficult, more complex, and perhaps more accurate approach to generating ethical guidelines is the position that allows each group to manifest its own cultural identity of differences but at the same time acknowledges the common ground of psychological principles that connect each group with each other group. This is the position developed in this chapter.

RESEARCH ON MORAL/ETHICAL CHOICES

Positive guidelines are available through the "Guidelines for Providers of Psychological Services to Ethnic, Linguistic and Culturally Diverse Populations" (American Psychological Association [APA], 1993) and Ponterotto and Casas (1991). The negative consequences of cultural bias include encapsulation within a particular cultural framework and exclusion of those who are judged to be outsiders to the culture. The tendency to judge others by one's own standards is not always motivated by evil intentions, but the consequences of encapsulation and exclusion are hurtful and profoundly dangerous. Psychology has tended to escape the dilemma of focusing on similarities and differences at the same time. In the abstract, nomothetic, statistical aggregate, similarities and differences can be demonstrated without difficulty, but the more closely we approach the individual case the more difficult this balance of similarities and differences becomes.

The APA 1993 guidelines provide a sociocultural framework as the basis of ethical decision making (see Appendix I of this volume). They specify both the basic abilities and the research-based understanding essential to ethical decision making. Core abilities include (a) recognizing cultural diversity, (b) understanding the socioeconomic and psychological roles of culture, (c) understanding how socioeconomic and political factors influence cultural groups, (d) achieving self-awareness of sociocultural identity, and (e) understanding how culture shapes behavior. The research-based issues include (a) the impact of cultural similarity, (b) minority utilization of counseling, (c) relative effectiveness of counseling style, (d) the role of cultural values in treatment, (e) appropriate counseling and therapy models, and (f) competency in working with different cultures. Nine specific guidelines are provided to illustrate these examples of core abilities and the application of research-based knowledge. These general guidelines provide goals or objectives to which the culture-centered counselor can aspire in making ethical decisions.

Ponterotto and Casas (1991) did an excellent job of demonstrating the importance of underlying philosophical assumptions in the development of multicultural ethical guidelines. The failure to define philosophical assumptions leaves the provider open to accepting her or his own specific guidelines as appropriate, leading to encapsulation and exclusion. Individualistic values are presumed to be universally valid in the professional guidelines of the APA and the American Counseling Association (ACA), for example, and some guidelines show a systematic preference for the masculine perspective.

Philosophical premises that translate ethical theory into practice are identified by Ponterotto and Casas (1991). First, the principle of *altruism* guides counselors toward prevailing psychosocial problems and helps identify psychocultural strengths in each cultural group. Altruism shifts the focus of counseling interventions and research from the more abstract laboratory setting to field-based sites focused on real-world problems. Second, the principle of *responsibility* focuses on the relevance of what is done and the community involvement in the ethical decision. Responsibility requires counselors to be more reciprocal in their contacts with other cultures, being able to both teach and learn. Third, the principle of *justice* deals with the quality of fairness in ethical decisions. Justice does not tolerate exploitation by any one group or any other group for its own self-interest, intentionally or unintentionally. Fourth, the principle of *caring* is particularly important for counselors with a sense of vocation. Caring promotes trust and a personal investment in helping culturally different clients regardless of the consequences.

Philosophical principles can guide counselors toward a more purposive and intentional basis for making ethical decisions in multicultural settings. In the absence of philosophical principles, decisions must be made in a philosophical vacuum in which counselors impose those philosophical principles most familiar to them and mistakenly presume that they are maintaining a high level of ethical standards.

Wrenn (1962, 1985) described the dangers of cultural encapsulation among counselors seeking absolutist solutions to ethical problems. Culturally encapsulated counselors (a) define everyone's reality according to their own cultural assumptions, (b) minimize cultural differences, (c) impose a self-reference criterion in judging the behavior of others, (d) ignore proof that disconfirms their position, (e) depend on techniques and strategies to solve their problems, and (f) disregard their own cultural biases. A corresponding form of cultural encapsulation based on relativism would apply to counselors who (a) segregate each group's definition of reality from that of any other group, (b) minimize cultural similarities, (c) abstain from making judgments about behavior of other groups, (d) escape into a subjective and nonverifiable proof of their position, (e) disregard techniques and strategies used by other groups, and (f) embrace cultural biases. Neither form of encapsulation is acceptable, and a third alternative needs to be defined. Problems in the professional ethical guidelines for counselors have resulted from the confusion of distinction between fundamental and discretionary ethical principles.

There is increased pressure to acknowledge the importance of the consumer's cultural environment in a bottom-up, consumer-driven alternative to top-down theories and approaches to counseling. Pedersen (1994) documented the many different examples of professional counseling associations' inadequate attempts to mandate attention to cultural factors in the ethical practice of counseling.

Cultural encapsulation becomes most obvious in the process of exclusion, in which insiders are separated from outsiders. Some individuals or groups are judged to be outside the boundaries so that the normal rules of fairness no longer apply to them. Those who are excluded are nonentities, expendable and undeserving, so harm to them is acceptable if not perhaps appropriate and justified. Examples of exclusion range from discrimination to genocide, "ethnic cleansing," and other means of targeting victims who are then blamed for allowing themselves to become victims. Moral exclusion exists in degrees from overt and malicious evil to passive and apathetic unconcern.

Opotow (1990) listed the rationalizations and justifications that support moral exclusion, which help to identify otherwise hidden examples of moral exclusion in society. These examples include psychological distancing, displaced responsibility, group loyalty, and normalizing or glorifying of violence. In its subtle forms moral exclusion is so "ordinary" that it fails to attract attention at all and becomes an automatic response. It is possible to be exclusionary by what one says or does as well as by what one does not say or do. Moral exclusion is pervasive and not isolated in society. Usually moral exclusion depends on the psychological or social principles that define unacceptable attitudes. "As severity of conflict and threat escalates, harm and sanctioned aggression become more likely. As harm doing escalates, societal structures change, the scope of justice shrinks, and the boundaries of harm doing expand" (Opotow, 1990, p. 13).

CROSS-CULTURAL ETHICAL GUIDELINES

This section provides criteria-based points of reference on culture-centered ethics for judging and evaluating ethical guidelines. Tapp, Kelman, Triandis, Wrightsman, and Coelho (1974) developed excellent guidelines for cross-cultural research that are highly relevant to counseling and that are appended to this book. Shweder, Mahapatra, and Miller (1990) also provided an excellent critique of moral development described in the research literature and the suggestion of positive alternatives. Other research on unintentional racism by Goodyear and Sinnett (1984), LaFromboise and Foster (1989), and Ridley (1995) demonstrates that good intentions are not enough. Lonner and Ibrahim (1989) emphasized the importance of accuracy, Miller (1994) the importance of duty, Strike and Soltis (1985) the importance of consequences, and Murray (1993) the dangers of relying solely on science.

Tapp et al. (1974) studied ethical responsibilities of psychologists in research across cultures. Reporting to the APA Committee on International Relations in Psychology, they pointed out that a researcher's ethical obligation goes beyond avoiding harm to the subject to include demonstrations of how the research will enrich and benefit rather than harm the host country. Generally the benefit to the researchers is much clearer than that to the host culture providing data. Tapp et al.'s recommendation for collaboration with the host culture is also seldom observed. It is often difficult to translate psychological research into a traditional people's host culture in any meaningful way. Taft (1977) pointed out that

> most of us are so psychologocentric that we regard ourselves as having the right to mine our data from the places where we need it, providing we pay royalties to the natives (often, incidentally, in accordance with our own arbitrary concept of what is fair compensation) and provided we do not destroy the ecology irreparably. In the latter respect, we are often not really much more conscientious than is the typical multinational mining company. (pp. 11-12)

Tapp et al. (1974) collected data on ethical guidelines for cross-cultural research over several years. Several basic themes that exemplified principles or guidelines reappeared consistently:

1. Significant involvement of cross-cultural colleagues is correct, essential and desirable.
2. Criteria for informed and free consent must be determined in each cultural context.

3. The ultimate responsibility for making ethical judgment lies with the individual investigator, but it is incumbent upon the investigator to check with colleagues in and out of the culture.

4. One constant responsibility is to check the benefit of the research enterprise for science and society as well as subjects, students and scholars.

5. Advisory principles rather than a stringent ethical code can provide the necessary beginning for increased attention by individuals, institutions and national bodies.

6. Criteria for determining adequate, sufficient, or appropriate ethical standards of conduct can only be formulated through continuing exchange carried on by a trans-national group drawing from an even more diverse group of cross-cultural researchers. (p. 238)

The search for underlying principles or standards has been a recent theme in the psychological literature. Shweder et al. (1990) reviewed the adequacy of three culturally applicable theories of moral development. First, Kohlberg's cognitive developmental theory contends that a moral obligation originates in conventional or consensus-based obligations, and that obligations are rooted in convention at the lower stages but in natural law at the higher stages of development. Moral development therefore depends on the cognitive ability to construct a detached and impartial viewpoint to evaluate right from wrong. Second, Turiel's "social interactional" theory separates morality from convention. Moral obligation results from social experiences related to justice, rights, harm, and protecting the welfare of others. Third, a "social communication" theory that combines Kohlberg and Turiel's theories contends that moral obligation is based on the universal of a learned cultural context without depending on either consensus or conviction and without universals across cultures. A synthesis of these three alternatives differentiates between mandatory and discretionary features of moral obligation. Rationally based moral standards may be founded on universal principles of natural law, justice, and harm as mandatory features. Discretionary features of individualism, perceived rights, or the social contract each person has with every other person provide the flexibility to adapt and accommodate.

Bad ethical behavior is not always deliberate. Goodyear and Sinnett (1984) identified examples of how counselors might unintentionally violate ethical guidelines because of (a) misunderstanding, (b) lack of knowledge or special skills, (c) prejudiced attitudes that distort understanding, (d) inattention to consequences of counseling in the client's cultural context, or (e) apathy or disengagement from responsibility.

LaFromboise and Foster (1989) described other examples of institutionalized cultural bias in violation of ethical standards resulting in (a) underserving of minority populations, (b) minimizing of cultural issues in counselor education, (c) trivializing of culture in counseling texts, (d) getting around certification requirements for cultural awareness, (e) underrepresentation of minorities in counselor education programs, (f) inattention to culture in research about counseling, and (g) inadequate ethical guidelines for counselors.

Ridley (1995) documented how unintentional racism can occur. First, counselors may claim "color blindness" and state that they treat all clients equally regardless of their culture. Second, counselors may become so "color conscious" that all problems are perceived as cultural. Third, clients may transfer their good or bad feelings about others to the counselor. Fourth, counselors may transfer their good or bad feelings about others to the client. Fifth, counselors may misinterpret cultural ambivalence. Sixth, the client may appropriately respond to the counselor's own unexamined racism. Seventh, the counselor may misinterpret client nondisclosure.

Lonner and Ibrahim (1989) pointed out that accurate ethical assessment of a client's culture includes understanding (a) the client's worldview, (b) the client's culture-specific norm group, and (c) combined approaches for clinical judgment using standardized as well as nonstandardized methods. Even Kohlberg's measures of moral development may be culturally inappropriate. Segall, Dasen, Berry, and Poortinga (1990) concluded that Kohlberg's model of moral development reflects the values of an urban, middle-class group, and Gilligan (1982, 1987) further discovered a bias favoring the male viewpoint.

Miller (1994) argued that there is not one "universal morality of caring" but rather that alternative types of interpersonal moralities reflect the meaning systems of different cultural groups. She described both Kohlberg's superogatory view and Gilligan's morality of caring framework as culture bound. In her research comparing Americans and Hindus, Americans support an individually oriented interpersonal moral code stressing freedom of choice, individual responsibility, and a dualistic view of motivation, whereas Hindus support a duty-based interpersonal moral code stressing broad and socially enforceable interpersonal obligation and contextual sensitivity.

Strike and Soltis (1985) developed a taxonomy of consequentialist, nonconsequentialist, and rule utilitarian alternatives. Consequentialists, like utilitarians and hedonists, assume that the moral rightness of an action depends on its consequences. The problems with consequentialism are first that minorities are sometimes made to suffer for the greater good of the majority and second that the consequences may never be fully known. Nonconsequentialism assumes that each person's action is judged by his or her intention. The problem is that even good intentions can result in bad consequences (see Ridley, in press). Even well-intentioned racism can be hurtful. The rule utilitarian alternative is based on a reflective equilibrium, making respect for the person and human dignity a universal standard. In this more interactive mode, morality is judged both by its consequences and by the degree to which it treats every person or group with equal respect.

Due to scientific advancement and problems of bioethics, there is great urgency to clarify ethical obligations in multicultural social contexts.

The dominant model in bioethics assumes that moral reasoning proceeds downward, from fundamental principles to specific cases. This top-down model, deductivism, is flawed both as a description of moral reasoning, and

> as a prescription for how moral reasoning should be done. In recent years
> another model known as casuistry and based on case-centered moral reason-
> ing has emerged to challenge deductivism. (Murray, 1993, p. 185)

The case-centered approach to moral reasoning is grounded in applications
of morality as they apply to each case. This case becomes a source of moral
knowledge from which principles are generated; then principles become guidelines for interpreting new cases. Ethical guidelines are generated from accumulated experiences in making ethical decisions and not from timeless
abstract principles, however reasonable they may be.

PROFESSIONAL ETHICAL GUIDELINES

The weaknesses of both the APA and the ACA ethical guidelines are that
they lack explicit philosophical principles, assume a dominant culture perspective, and generally minimize or trivialize the role of culture in ethical
decision making. Explicit examples from the guidelines themselves as well as
six implicit assumptions are identified as sources of bias and exclusionary
judgment.

The initial ethical guidelines for the American Psychological Association
were derived empirically through a collection of more than 1,000 ethical cases
contributed by 7,500 APA members in 1948. The original ethical standards
were based on members' cases from which general principles were derived
(Griffith, 1992). The more recent revisions of the APA code of ethics, however,
have deemphasized aspirational language and emphasized minimal standards
of professional behavior.

> The minimal behavioral standards have been proposed as necessary and
> useful for adjudicating complaints of unethical conduct. Organizations strug-
> gling to articulate ethics, however, historically valued the primacy of their
> educational responsibilities. One can't help but wonder whether the age of
> trial lawyers, litigation and suits exploiting retributive justice has excessively
> influenced the document we are labeling as our code of professional ethics.
> (Griffith, 1992, p. 15)

The "Ethical Principles of Psychologists and Code of Conduct" (APA,
1992) tends to be more legal than aspirational in its framework. The code
presents itself in the preamble as providing a common set of values upon
which psychologists (including counselors) can build their professional work.
Each APA member is expected to supplement but not violate the code's values,
as he or she is guided by personal values, culture, and experience.

Principle A requires psychologists to maintain high standards of competence and work within the boundaries of their particular competence. "Psychologists are cognizant of the fact that the competencies required in serving,
teaching, and/or studying groups of people vary with the distinctive charac-

teristics of those groups" (APA, 1992, p. 1599). In those cases in which "recognized professional standards" are not specified, psychologists must protect the welfare of the client as best they can. Research on cultural bias in counseling (Pedersen, 1994) clearly demonstrates that counselors go beyond the boundaries of their competence in working with culturally different persons with few professional consequences. The lack of "recognized professional standards" for working with many different cultural groups makes it difficult to judge behavior as either following or violating Principle A.

Principle B requires psychologists to be honest, fair, and respectful of others by not making statements that are false, misleading, or deceptive. "Psychologists strive to be aware of their own belief systems, values, needs and limitations and the effect of these on their work" (APA, 1992, p. 1159). This principle does not prevent unintentional racism or many types of institutionalized racism by uninformed or naive professionals working in multicultural settings.

Principle C requires psychologists to uphold professional and scientific responsibility for their behavior and to adapt their methods to the needs of different populations. Psychologists are supposed to protect clients by monitoring their own and their colleagues' behavior. The lack of attention to multicultural issues in counseling and the tolerance for violation of the generalized guidelines that do exist demonstrate how this principle is being violated without consequences.

Principle D requires respect for people's rights, dignity, and worth.

> Psychologists are aware of cultural, individual, and role differences, including those due to age, gender, race, ethnicity, national origin, religion, sexual orientation, disability, language and socioeconomic status. Psychologists try to eliminate the effect on their work of biases based on those factors and they do not knowingly participate in or condone unfair discriminatory practices. (APA, 1992, pp. 1159-1160)

Although this principle urges meeting the needs of all clients inclusively, there are no guidelines on how that might be done.

Principle E is about concern for the welfare of others, including both human clients and animal subjects, to minimize harm. This principle deals with power differences and the tendency of the more powerful to exploit or mislead the less powerful. To the extent that multicultural relationships are defined by power differences, this principle seeks to protect the less powerful parties, although power is itself culturally defined.

Principle F emphasizes social responsibility to the community and society in general for contributing to human welfare, preventing suffering, and serving the interests of patients, clients, and the general public. Although the general principle is clear, the application of the abstract principle in practice is difficult.

The second part of the code reviews standards of behavior, restating the general principle and often implying that the same principle will be applied in the same way regardless of the cultural context. An example of this absolutist bias is in Standard 1.08 on human differences: "Where differences of age, gender, race, ethnicity, national origin, religion, sexual orientation, disability, language or socioeconomic status significantly affect psychologists' work concerning particular individuals or groups, psychologists obtain the training, experience, consultation or supervision necessary to ensure the competence of their services or they make appropriate referrals" (APA, 1992, p. 1601). It is hard to imagine any psychological service or intervention in which these differences would not be significant. This standard trivializes the importance of documented differences in its "conditional" language about culture. Standard 1.10 on respecting others also warns against "unfair discrimination" based on cultural membership, suggesting that discrimination as it is usually understood might not always be unfair. Standard 1.17 prohibiting multiple relationships and Standard 1.18 prohibiting barter with clients also disregard cultural patterns in less individualistic or money-driven groups.

The second standard relates to evaluation, assessment, or intervention. Standard 2.01 requires accurate assessment to be fully implemented, presuming that the counselor can interpret the client's behavior accurately in the client's cultural context. Standard 2.02 disregards research about implicit cultural biases in tests and measures. Standard 2.04 acknowledges that assessment techniques and norms may be biased, but this standard has had little effect on the practice of assessment.

There are several problems with the APA Ethical Principles. First, in the absence of more specific guidelines, the ambiguously stated standards tend to protect the status quo. Second, if the problem is not the principles but their appropriate application in practice, then this should be clarified in the standard on education and training rather than disregarded. Third, where cultural groups are mentioned, the assumption seems to be that the longer the list the more culturally sensitive the standard. The guidelines do not deal with the fundamental ethical issues of bias in the profession and rather are designed to protect the professional/provider against culturally different client/consumers.

The ACA's "Proposed Standards of Practice and Ethical Standards" (ACA, 1993), in a revision of the 1988 standards, also fails to guide the multicultural counselor. The weaknesses of the ACA standards are consistent with the limitations cited earlier in the APA guidelines. There are additional examples of a consistent cultural bias favoring an absolutist position (Ibrahim & Arredondo, 1990).

First, there is a bias toward an individualistic perspective, which would not be appropriate to collectivistic cultures. Collectivist cultures would have a difficult time excluding dual relationships (Standard of Practice [SP] 4), which might be desirable or even essential to appropriate caregiving. Also, separating the rights of individuals from the responsibility of the family (SP.13) will be difficult in family-oriented cultures. Even the primary obligation to respect the integrity and promote the welfare of clients (A.1) lends itself to an individualistic interpretation without further interpretative guidelines.

Second, there is a bias toward the culturally different client who must accommodate or adjust her- or himself to a majority culture standard of behavior. How does the provider know a client has been "adequately informed" (SP.2)? Is it necessary for the client not only to be informed but also to comprehend the information? In very private cultures, disguising the data source as advocated in SP.16 might not be sufficient to protect the client's sense of privacy. Is the usefulness of data more important than getting the client's permission? Who defines the limits in SP.18 of a counselor's competence? What constitutes an adequate continuing education? Does accuracy in SP.21 imply not only the accurate sending of an advertising message but also the accurate receiving and comprehension of that same message?

Third, there is an elitist bias favoring the more powerful care providers' obligation to protect the profession. In SP.24, limiting the use of the term *doctor* to counselor or "closely related" professions disregards the historical fact that disciplines other than counseling psychology have frequently been more responsive to multicultural populations' needs. The provider needs to accurately identify credentials to the client and verify that the client understands those credentials regardless of disciplinary background. In SP.43, "professional" counselors are obligated to see that students and supervisees get remedial attention when necessary, but the same obligation should apply to colleagues and peers or supervisors, who may also require remedial attention with regard to cultural sensitivity.

Fourth, there is an assumption that cultural issues can be dealt with in relatively simple and objective ways. In SP.34 the simple admonition to use assessment instruments "appropriately" is so general it has no meaning until the criteria of appropriateness are made clear. In SP.35, is merely informing the client about the nature and purpose of testing sufficient, or should the client also comprehend that information? Throughout the "Proposed Standards of Practice and Ethical Standards," the authors have tried to avoid controversy by becoming very general in their guidelines. The implicit assumption is that all colleagues of good will understand the guidelines in the same way, but this is a dangerous assumption. Cultural groups not addressed include language groups and physically disabled populations, which, by their omission, seem to be trivialized. There is frequent mention of "respecting differences" but no regard for "respecting similarities" at the same time, as though the liturgical acknowledgment of differences will protect the standards from criticism.

Fifth, there is an assumption of absolute standards for right and wrong behavior in a "one-size-fits-all" perspective. In SP.8 and later, there is a constant reference to "professional counselors," which either is redundant or suggests that the standard does not apply to "unprofessional counselors." The counselor who determines that he or she is unable to help a culturally different client should terminate contact. If the client determines that the counselor is unable to help, is termination also appropriate even if the counselor does not share the client's viewpoint? Do both counselors and clients have to be hopeful for counseling to be continued? In SP.36 the need to provide culturally appropriate interpretations of culturally biased tests is emphasized. If we begin with the assumption that all tests are to a greater or lesser extent biased, then compensating for that bias through skilled interpretation is extremely important, although not included in this standard. In SP.42 and elsewhere, counselors working through interpreters or across language barriers would be hard pressed to guarantee that the client's rights were protected. In SP.44 there is an implication that classes or course work should not contribute toward self-growth or require self-disclosure in order to be graded or evaluated. This standard seems to presume a scientific objectivity that minimizes subjective learning. In SP.47, cultures will differ on what they consider reasonable precautions to avoid causing injury. Who decides what is reasonable?

There is an underlying assumption throughout the ACA standards that what is good for the counselor is good for everyone. This "self-reference criterion" is dangerous. Client populations sometimes underutilize counseling— even good counseling—because it has a resocialization effect that alienates young people from their traditions. This may be true even though the effects of counseling are judged as "positive growth" by absolutist ethical standards. There also seems to be a bias toward the medical model and away from the educational model in the language used and the quasi-scientific implications. In many cultures the role of the teacher incorporates the counseling functions more adequately than the role of a doctor. It should be important to acknowledge the appropriate role of both medical and educational models from their different perspectives.

The International Association for Cross-Cultural Psychology has a statement on ethics adopted in 1978 that is still in force (Tapp et al., 1974), containing 13 advisory ethical principles: 6 regarding responsibilities to individuals and communities, 4 regarding collaborators and colleagues, and 3 regarding the discipline of psychology. Each advisory principle is amplified by a series of corollaries that operationalize the principles. The guidelines are purposefully constructed to specify ethical principles with examples and to guide the provider in applying the principles to ambiguous issues with regard to multicultural groups. Both cultural similarities and differences are fundamental and not peripheral to these carefully constructed guidelines and provide a constructive model combining the fundamental and universal, unchanging principles of ethics while suggesting discretionary aspects that can be modified to fit each situation. (The full ethics statement is provided in Appendix II of this book.)

ETHICAL GUIDELINES FOR THE FUTURE

The future must be guided by more adequate ethical guidelines that examine and clarify underlying philosophical assumptions, guide the counselor according to a relational view of responsibility, and validate the scientific nature of counseling. Counselors have a responsibility to interact meaningfully with the cultures of clients so that the methods used reflect ethical standards both explicitly and implicitly.

Even when the professional counseling association is well intentioned, it functions in a culturally encapsulated framework of assumptions that constrains equity. For any ethical standard to work, the basic underlying philosophical assumptions must be identified, challenged, and clarified so that counselors will be more intentional in their ethical decisions. Self-criticism by concerned professionals will assist in overcoming the dilemma of multicultural counseling and the implicit but fundamental assumptions that function as moral absolutes in the existing guidelines.

Ivey (1987) advocated a more relational view of ethics as negotiating between the client/consumer and the counselor/provider and the cultural context variables, all of which are constantly changing. Such a relational view would interpret standards of ethical behavior according to the consequences and according to the intention. Each ethical standard would be applied and interpreted differently in each cultural context, but it would be the same principle. Absolute standards that impose one viewpoint on all others would be unacceptable. A relational alternative would recognize the importance of absolute but abstract ethical principles and at the same time the multiplicity of applications in complex and dynamic cultural contexts to reflect both cultural similarities and cultural differences at the same time.

The ethical question speaks to the very scientific nature of counseling and psychology as a discipline. As a behavioral science, moral principles and ethical guidelines of counseling cannot be precisely validated. Ethical imperatives cannot be inferred from empirical data, but behavioral evidence can help identify empirical consequences.

> Natural science psychology, to be successful, must abandon two seductive myths: (a) Psychology is able to identify ethical principles that should guide humankind and (b) the logical gap between *is* and *ought* can be bridged by empirical evidence. In spite of these limitations, psychology can assist society in settling ethical disputes by revealing the empirical consequences of different policy choices, thus allowing society to make informed decisions as to which competing social policies to adopt. (Kendler, 1993, p. 1052)

Tapp (1986) reviewed her earlier research (Tapp et al., 1974) and found that the earlier guidelines applied as well now as they did then. Several issues remain particularly relevant today.

Psychology is a culture, an institution, and increasingly a socializing agent. Psychology transmits values about health and illness and must examine the underlying principles and assumptions that guide that socializing process. As psychology grows in influence it shapes the goals of behavior for the child, parent, country, and society. Increased reliance on psychological "remedies" influences the definition of health, maturity, autonomy, dependence, intelligence, aggression, and other important social constructs. Psychology has been given the responsibility of defining "healthy" growth and development. Because of this responsibility, psychology needs to become scientifically literate, socially sensitive, culturally aware, and humanely oriented. "It can manifest these dimensions in the way it courts scientific and social laws, shapes and sanctions ethical guidelines, seeks and applies knowledge in its multiplicity of settings" (Tapp, 1986, pp. 3-4).

Counseling psychology is interactive with culture in the socializing process. By neglecting cultural variables in the ethical guidelines, by defining culture narrowly to exclude social/political/economic factors, and by marginalizing the importance of culture in the teaching of psychology, the profession of counseling psychology has failed in its ethical obligation. The psychological impact of multiculturalism is not only indicated but required by special interest groups. Adequate ethical principles need to reflect this culturally expanded theoretical and empirical global context.

There is an equivalency in the ethics and methods of psychology. Cross-cultural psychology is both methodological and ethical in its application. Both ethics and methods are concerned with a procedure or style of conduct directed toward a beneficial goal. The best methodology must also demonstrate good ethical procedure. Interaction with consumers or providers, subjects or researchers, students or teachers, and citizens or leaders depends on the equivalence of ethics and methods. The cultural component provides guidance in sharing knowledge and creating trust through ethically sensitive principles and procedures.

If counseling psychologists disregard ethical issues across cultures and ignore the connection between culture and method, the result will be careless procedures, disconnected theory, and the isolation of counseling psychology from society. The counselor will then become a "sorcerer's apprentice, alien scientist, Blues-oriented practitioner, ivory-towered professor/teacher, research tourist, scientific imperialist and/or clinical colonist" (Tapp, 1986, p. 5). Multiculturalism must be more than the concern of cross-cultural counselors; it must extend to counselors generally.

REFERENCES

American Counseling Association. (1993, October). Proposed standards of practice and ethical standards. *Guidepost*, pp. 15-22.

American Psychological Association. (1992). Ethical principles of psychologists and code of conduct. *American Psychologist, 47*(12), 1597-1611.

American Psychological Association. (1993). Guidelines for providers of psychological services to ethnic, linguistic and culturally diverse populations. *American Psychologist, 48*, 45-48.

Berry, J. W., Poortinga, Y. H. Y., Segall, M. H., & Dasen, P. J. (1992). *Cross cultural psychology: Research and applications*. Cambridge, UK: Cambridge University Press.

Gilligan, C. (1982). *In a different voice*. Cambridge, MA: Harvard University Press.

Gilligan, C. (1987). Moral orientation and moral development. In E. F. Kittay & D. T. Meyers (Eds.), *Women and moral theory* (pp. 19-33). Totowa, NJ: Rowan & Littlefield.

Goodyear, R. K., & Sinnett, E. R. (1984). *Empathy: Development, training and consequences.* Hillsdale, NJ: Lawrence Erlbaum.

Griffith, R. S. (1992). New APA ethics code: Long on legalism, short on spirit. *National Psychologist, 1*(6), 15.

Ibrahim, F. A., & Arredondo, P. M. (1990). Ethical issues in multicultural counseling. In B. Herlihy & L. B. Golden (Eds.), *AACD ethical standards casebook* (4th ed., pp. 137-145). Alexandria, VA: American Counseling Association.

Ivey, A. E. (1987). The multicultural practice of therapy: Ethics, empathy and dialectics. *Journal of Social and Clinical Psychology, 5,* 195-204.

Kendler, H. H. (1993). Psychology and the ethics of social policy. *American Psychologist, 48,* 1046-1053.

Kierstead, F. D., & Wagner, P. A. (1993). *The ethical, legal and multicultural foundations of teaching.* Dubuque, IA: Brown & Benchmark.

LaFromboise, T. D., & Foster, S. L. (1989). Ethics in multicultural counseling. In P. Pedersen, J. Draguns, W. Lonner, & J. Trimble (Eds.), *Counseling across cultures* (3rd ed., pp. 115-136). Honolulu: University of Hawaii Press.

Lonner, W. J., & Ibrahim, F. A. (1989). Assessment in cross-cultural counseling. In P. Pedersen, J. Draguns, W. Lonner, & J. Trimble (Eds.), *Counseling across cultures* (3rd ed., pp. 229-334). Honolulu: University of Hawaii Press.

Miller, J. G. (1994). Cultural diversity in the morality of caring: Individually oriented versus duty-based interpersonal moral codes. *Cross-Cultural Research, 28*(1), 3-39.

Murray, T. H. (1993). Moral reasoning in social context. *Journal of Social Issues, 49*(2), 185-200.

Opotow, S. (1990). Moral exclusion and injustice: An introduction. *Journal of Social Issues, 46,* 1-20.

Pedersen, P. (1994). *Handbook for developing multicultural awareness* (2nd ed.). Alexandria, VA: American Counseling Association.

Ponterotto, J. G., & Casas, J. M. (1991). *Handbook of racial/ethnic minority counseling research.* Springfield, IL: Charles C Thomas.

Ridley, C. R. (1995). *Overcoming unintentional racism in counseling: A practioners guide to intentional intervention.* Thousand Oaks, CA: Sage.

Segall, M. H., Dasen, P. R., Berry, J. W., & Poortinga, Y. H. (1990). *Human behavior in global perspective: An introduction to cross-cultural psychology.* New York: Pergamon.

Shweder, R. A., Mahapatra, M., & Miller, J. A. (1990). Culture and moral development. In J. Stigler, R. A. Shweder, & G. Herdt (Eds.), *Cultural psychology: Essays in comparative human development* (pp. 130-204). New York: Cambridge University Press.

Strike, K., & Soltis, J. (1985). *The ethics of teaching.* New York: Teachers College Press.

Taft, R. (1977). Comments on the 1974 Tapp Report on the ethics of cross cultural research. *IACCP Cross Cultural Psychology Newsletter, 11*(4), 2-8.

Tapp, J. L. (1986, August). *Cross-cultural ethics revisited: Foster children in our parents' house or the alien in us!* Paper presented at the American Psychological Association meetings, Washington, DC.

Tapp, J. L., Kelman, H., Triandis, H., Wrightsman, L., & Coelho, G. (1974). Advisory principals for ethical considerations in the conduct of cross-cultural research: Fall 1973 Revision. *International Journal of Psychology, 9,* 231-349.

Wrenn, C. G. (1962). The culturally encapsulated counselor. *Harvard Educational Review, 32,* 444-449.

Wrenn, C. G. (1985). Afterward: The culturally encapsulated counselor revisited. In P. Pedersen (Ed.), *Handbook of cross-cultural counseling and therapy* (pp. 323-329). Westport, CT: Greenwood Press.

PART II

Theory and Models of Racial and Ethnic Identity Development

PART II OF THE *HANDBOOK* serves as the theoretical core for our discussion of multicultural counseling. Increasingly, research is documenting the relevance of racial and ethnic identity theory to the practice of counseling. Racial identity theory has stimulated extensive research in counseling, the results of which have fed back into modifications and developments of theory. The eight chapters that make up this section present the latest theoretical developments in models of racial/ethnic identity development for various groups in the United States.

Allen E. Ivey opens this section by introducing the term *multicultural counseling and therapy* (MCT) and emphasizing the perspective of psychotherapy as liberation. Building on the work of influential cultural identity theorists, Ivey guides us to a reconceptualization of the counseling relationship and counseling process. Through his presentation of cultural identity models and his case study, Ivey demonstrates that culture must be at the center of all counseling.

In Chapter 5, Sandra K. Choney, Elise Berryhill-Paapke, and Rockey R. Robbins present an insightful and comprehensive look at the acculturation process in American Indians. The authors convincingly state their preference for the acculturation construct in developing an accurate understanding of American Indian clients and their concerns. They review various acculturation models and present their own model, which is comprehensive, concise, and clear. The effects of acculturation on various mental health issues are explored, and concrete suggestions for research and counseling with American Indian people are provided.

William E. Cross Jr., is a pioneer in racial identity theory for African Americans. His Nigrescence model has stimulated more empirical research than any other extant identity model. In Chapter 6, Cross presents his latest conceptual developments on Black racial identity. Integrating his latest thinking with recent empirical findings, he presents an insightful and well-thought-out revision of his classic model.

The focus in Chapter 7 is on racial and ethnic identity development in Asian American persons. Reflecting on their own Asian American identity, Gargi Roysircar Sodowsky, Kwong-Liem Karl Kwan, and Raji Pannu present a comprehensive and enlightening picture of ethnic identity development in the large and varied Asian American community. Using a strong theoretical base for their discussion, the authors cover the relationship of ethnic identity to family dynamics and include revealing illustrations to highlight key points throughout the chapter.

J. Manuel Casas and Scott D. Pytluk address Hispanic racial and ethnic identity development in Chapter 8. Tapping into a diverse and interdisciplinary literature, the authors provide comprehensive and clear coverage of leading models of Hispanic ethnic identity, and they review recent and relevant research on the topic.

Chapter 9 turns to a focus on White racial identity development. Janet E. Helms, a leading theorist and researcher in racial identity, presents the latest developments of both her White identity model and her inclusive person-of-color (POC) identity conceptualization. She clarifies that her developmental models are best conceptualized as including various "statuses" rather than distinct "stages." Using detailed examples, Helms demonstrates the implications and utility of her model for the analysis of social relationships.

The topic of biracial identity development has received increasing attention in recent years. In Chapter 10, Christine Kerwin and Joseph G. Ponterotto highlight the rapid growth of the biracial population in the United States. The authors go on to review common identity myths regarding this population, examine leading models of biracial identity development, and present a new model based on their qualitative research.

This section closes with the contribution by Wayne Rowe, John T. Behrens, and Mark M. Leach, who present an integrative critique of current models of racial and ethnic identity development. The editors of the *Handbook* invited these chapter authors to read all the contributions in this section and then present an integrative and constructive perspective on identity theory. The authors also review a new model of White racial consciousness development that addresses many of the concerns expressed with previous models.

4

Psychotherapy as Liberation

Toward Specific Skills and Strategies in Multicultural Counseling and Therapy

ALLEN E. IVEY

COUNSELING IS in the midst of a revolution, but many counselors and therapists remain unaware that it is even happening. Specifically, we are learning that our present theories and techniques are bound up with a particular and necessarily limited cultural framework. Multicultural counseling and therapy (MCT), the product of many minds, is gaining increasing recognition. MCT shows us how individuals exist in contextual/cultural relationship. Although it draws on historical tradition, MCT provides a marked contrast to our individually focused educational backgrounds, as the term *culture-centered counseling* suggests.

Psychotherapy as liberation is part of the broader MCT framework. Drawing on many authorities in cultural identity theory (e.g., Cross, 1971; Helms, 1985, 1990; Jackson, 1975, 1990; Jackson & Hardiman, 1983; Sue & Sue, 1990), liberation psychotherapy focuses on helping clients learn to see themselves in relation not only to themselves but also to cultural/contextual influences, with special attention to the family. *Self-in-relation* replaces our traditional conception of the individual self (Miller, 1991).

As just one example of the importance of self-in-relation, consider the African American client who comes for therapy to seek stress management techniques to control his hypertension. We know that cognitive-behavioral techniques can be both emotionally and physically beneficial.

53

Liberation psychotherapists would support and utilize stress management but would consider these techniques insufficient. They would also consider it necessary to help this client examine his cultural context and consider how the constant barrage of racist acts in society contributes to his concerns. Similarly, women who are diagnosed as depressed or "borderline" need to be helped to see family and cultural issues of sexism as underlying much of their difficulty. Not helping clients see how their difficulties are the logical result of developmental, social, and contextual history constitutes a major failing of today's psychotherapy and counseling.

This chapter is also informed by Paulo Freire (1972), whose basic work inspired its title. Freire introduced the term *conscientizacào*, or the process of developing critical consciousness, stating that one of the major purposes in education (and counseling, by implication) is to liberate people to awareness of themselves in social context. Freire also offered some specific methods for generating critical consciousness that have practical implications for the counseling field. Ivey's (1986) developmental therapy helps provide even more specific suggestions for facilitating client cognitive/emotional liberating processes.

This chapter seeks to draw together theory and practice, reflection and action, in order to contribute to a new praxis in the field, one that is truly sensitive and fully based on cultural and contextual aspects of human development.

MULTICULTURAL COUNSELING AND THERAPY: FOUNDATIONS FOR A NEW WAY TO CONCEPTUALIZE THEORY AND PRACTICE

Liberation is a praxis: the action and reflection of [people] upon their world in order to transform it. (Freire, 1972, p. 66)

Multicultural counseling and therapy (MCT) offers a new conceptual frame for our theory, research, and practice. MCT demands that we reflect on the human condition in social context and work to change inhumane systems. No longer can we "blame the victim" by stating that personal issues are totally "in the person." As a liberating process, MCT seeks to inform the individual as to how the social and historical past, present, and future affect cognition, emotion, and action. In particular, the process of *conscientizacào*, defined by Paulo Freire (1972) as "learning to perceive social, political, and economic contradictions, and to take action against the oppressive elements of reality" (p. 19), is essential.

Psychoanalytic approaches have been criticized by Norman O. Brown (1959) for their abandonment of social context in favor of social adjustment and self-actualization. Brown stated that "human consciousness can be liberated from the parental (Oedipal) complex only by being liberated from its cultural derivatives, the paternalistic state and the patriarchal God" (p. 155). Humanistic and cognitive-behavioral theories have met with severe criticism for similar reasons. Lerman (1992) pointed out that humanistic theories have "failed to recognize that no person constructs their own reality without external influences" (p. 13). She criticized hallowed concepts such as self-actualization and autonomy as middle-class products that simply are not relevant to many cultural groups, especially those for whom power rests in others. It is difficult to be "self-actualized" while under the control of another cultural group. Though recognizing that cognitive-behavioral approaches do consider context, Kantrowitz and Ballou (1992) commented that "individuals are expected to improve their adaptive capacities to meet the environmental conditions, which serve to reinforce the dominant (male) social standards" (p. 79).

In effect, traditional counseling and therapy theory are White, male, Eurocentric, and middle-class in origin and practice. Therapy can be described as centrally concerned with maintaining the status quo. Feminist theory argues that patriarchy is a fundamental condition of psychological theory. The negative effects of the controlling patriarchal metaphor are well documented by the radical feminist Mary Daly (1973, 1978). She commented:

> In my analysis, racism is not exactly a "variation" of patriarchy. Rather, I see patriarchy as the root and core of all forms of oppression, including racism, sexism, classism, and speciesism. It would not be accurate to say that I "develop gender as the central issue." I find this kind of language inadequate to describe the atrocities against women and all oppressed beings on this planet. (Daly, personal communication, 1993)

Racism, a particularly virulent form of patriarchal domination, has been described by Fanon (1963) as a form of colonialism in which oppressors actually inscribe a mentality of subordination in the oppressed. This enables oppressors to use the labor and life of the oppressed for their own ends. In *The Wretched of the Earth* (1963), Fanon commented on how important it was for the oppressed to find their own voice and language to name and describe their condition. Asante (1987) also pointed out the importance of naming one's self as a way of learning new actions—"It is a liberating act, the intellectual equivalent of a slave's wave of good-bye to [the] master from the North side of the Ohio River" (p. 115).

The philosophers and theorists of contextualism operate in a very different world from traditional counseling and therapy theory. Hallowed words representing old solutions, such as *self-actualization, doing one's own thing*, and *individualism*, become new problems to be solved. In this frame of reference, traditional counseling and therapy, to paraphrase Eldridge Cleaver, is more problem than solution. Today even the most cursory review of the influential journals and texts still reveals a naive Eurocentric approach. The increasing influence of the multiculturalists is recognized, but they are still clearly a minority voice. All one has to do is look at the number of people attending multicultural presentations at an APA convention to know where the balance of power still lies. Cosmetically, things have indeed changed, but under the powder one still finds that old reality.

Despite these issues, the field seems to be moving toward a new view that is culturally meaningful and relevant. Many authors are clearly challenging the field by asserting that cultural issues need to take their place at the center of a totally redefined counseling and therapy (see Cheatham, 1990; Cheek, 1976; Fukuyama, 1990; Ivey, Ivey, & Simek-Morgan, 1993; LaFromboise & Low, 1989; Locke, 1990; Myers, 1988; Pedersen, Draguns, Lonner, & Trimble, 1989; White & Parham, 1990; Wrenn, 1962, 1985).

In the past few years, multicultural counseling and therapy (MCT) has come to be recognized as a new, major fourth force in the helping field (Pedersen, 1990). It is important to note that MCT is not going to be formed by one "famed" individual or a small group of key "gurus," as is the case for the popular individualistic therapies such as client-centered, cognitive-behavioral, and psychodynamic.

This chapter elaborates on possible methods, strategies, and techniques for MCT, with special attention to the issue of personal liberation. Philosophically, it is inspired by the radical contextualists Brown, Daly, Fanon, and Freire. Historically, it draws from the many experts who are forming the new MCT. Pragmatically, for organizing practice, it draws from Friere and the burgeoning literature on cultural identity theory (Cross, 1971, 1991; Hardiman, 1982; Helms, 1990; Jackson, 1975, 1990; Jackson & Hardiman, 1983; Ponterotto, 1988; Sue & Sue, 1991).

A general theoretical model based on Freire and cultural identity theory is presented, followed by specific skills and strategies oriented to the process of *conscientizacào* or development of critical consciousness. Finally, I briefly consider the place of traditional first-, second-, and third-force approaches to helping as reconsidered from the MCT frame of reference.

PSYCHOTHERAPY AS LIBERATION

Good theory manifests itself in good practice and promotes good research. It is vital that theory, practice, and research be integrated in praxis. At issue, however, is the definition of the "good," which naturally leads us to a search for truth. The "goods" and "shoulds" of our past history in counseling and therapy lie in the patriarchal concepts of individualism and domination. A psychotherapy of liberation cannot remain hierarchical, with firm distinctions between helper and helpee, counselor and client, and therapist and patient. The term *client colleague* will be used here to suggest the importance of generating a more mutual, culturally sensitive approach to counseling and therapy.

We often think of the helping professions as generous and giving. Freire (1972) stated that

> true generosity consists precisely in fighting to destroy the causes which nourish false charity. False charity constrains the fearful and subdued, the "rejects of life" to extend their trembling hands. True generosity lies in striving so that these hands—whether of individuals or entire peoples—need to be extended less and less in supplication, so that more and more they become human hands which work, and working, transform the world. (p. 29)

Taking these theoretical ideas into practice, Freire presented the concept of *co-intentional education*, in which problems are posed and two people work together intentionally. More concretely, feminist theory focuses on *self-in-relation* (Miller, 1991) and egalitarian relationships in which the client becomes a partner, exploring with the other. Developmental counseling and therapy (Ivey, 1986, 1991) talks about "co-construction of reality," in which two people work together to find new meaning and new ways of being. The person who "helps" may learn as much as the person being "helped."

"Liberating education consists in acts of cognition, not transferrals of information," and these acts of cognition become a dialogue between and among individuals (Freire, 1972, p. 67). A liberating psychotherapy will help individuals and groups become intentionally conscious of themselves and conscious of consciousness itself. Freire contrasted a "banking" education, in which "deposits" are made in the student, to a "problem-posing" education, in which teacher and student work together on presenting, discussing, and sometimes resolving contradictions and issues.

The cultural identity theorists are central to the elaboration of counseling and psychotherapy as a liberating process. These theories are liberating in that they focus on the expansion of consciousness—learning how to see oneself and others in relation to cultural context.

Cultural identity theory has its roots in the Black and African American consciousness movement of the 1960s and, more recently, the feminist, gay/lesbian, and other group liberation movements. The liberation that comes with consciousness of self-in-relation leads to a broader form of self-concept that Cross (1991) termed *reference group orientation (RGO)*. It could be argued that the RGO provided by the Black identity movement has done more for African American mental health than all other existing theories of human change put together. Feminist theory has done much the same for women, and the gay/lesbian movement for gays and lesbians.

Ivey and Payton (1994) traced the concept of cultural identity back to Plato:

> Meaning-making has been identified as a central aspect in the development of a cultural identity. Ivey (1986, 1991) has generated a developmental scheme of meaning-making based on Plato (Cornford, 1941/1982). The essence of this framework is Plato's observation in *The Republic* that the transition to enlightenment involves four levels of consciousness and that

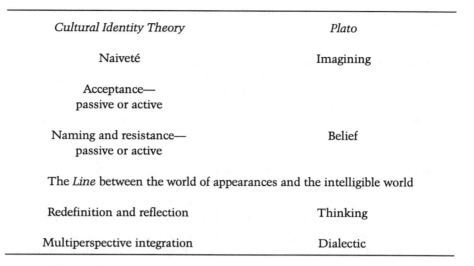

Cultural Identity Theory	Plato
Naiveté	Imagining
Acceptance— passive or active	
Naming and resistance— passive or active	Belief
The *Line* between the world of appearances and the intelligible world	
Redefinition and reflection	Thinking
Multiperspective integration	Dialectic

Figure 4.1. Cultural Identity Theory and Platonic Epistemology

each level builds on previous perceptions of reality, preparing the way for the next higher level. Ivey points out that the progressions of knowledge portrayed in the "Allegory of the Cave" may be construed as useful framework for the generation of cultural consciousness.

In connecting Plato to cultural consciousness, it may be helpful to recall that the prisoners in the Cave thought that the flickering shadows in front of them was "reality." As one prisoner was removed from his chains and taken out of the cave, he would eventually realize that what he saw in the cave was not reality, but only a perspective. However, as Plato soberly notes that if the former prisoner were returned to his fellows with news of the new truth, "they would kill him." The birth of consciousness is lonely and often fraught with real pain.

Cultural identity theory moves people from the cave of naive consciousness about self to awareness of self in relation to system. The parallels to the Platonic journey are not perfect, but do suggest that coming to a new view of reality may involve some difficulty. As Cornford notes, one moral of the allegory is drawn from the distress caused by too sudden passage "from naiveté to consciousness." (1941/1982, p. 227)

Cultural identity theory, then, enables us to frame counseling and psychotherapy as consciousness development, the generation of more complex cognitions and behaviors as one comes to see oneself in context. Although there are varying models within the cultural identity theory group, Ivey and Payton (1994) selected five stages of consciousness development as central. These are drawn from Freire (1972) and Jackson and Hardiman (1983), and Figure 4.1 presents them as they are related to Platonic epistemological constructs.

One seldom finds a "pure" type, and most people will be mixtures of stages. Jackson and Hardiman (1983) pointed out that each stage seems to have an entry point, a consolidation phase, and a time for exit as new data force the individual to accommodate to new perspectives. Parham (1989) noted that it is possible to cycle through the separate stages several times in a lifetime as one discovers new issues of identity and discrimination. Important in his discussion is an emphasis on circularity as contrasted with linearity and boundaries. Although Plato considered the "highest" forms of knowledge to be those involving the dialectic, the cultural identity theorists, and Parham (1989) in particular, remind us that each stage or level of consciousness has special value and need not ever be fully discarded. In short, a liberation psychotherapy must, of necessity, criticize hierarchical Platonic epistemology.

OPPRESSIVE OR REVOLUTIONARY ACTION?

Traditional therapy and counseling tend to be oriented toward oppressive action. Freire's diagram of oppressive action, shown in Figure 4.2, illustrates what occurs when a therapist acts on clients. Note that the language of therapy orients us as a dominant elite to act on clients or patients, and that whether we use humanistic, behavioral, or psychodynamic formats, we tend, as part of the action, to bring the client "back to reality." In this typical model, the client receives knowledge from the expert. Societal context is not considered, except perhaps as therapists and counselors as "experts" may define it.

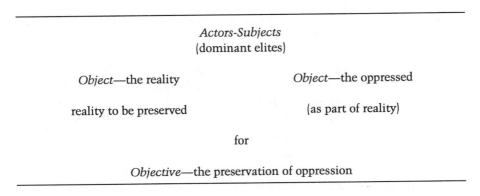

Actors-Subjects
(dominant elites)

Object—the reality   *Object*—the oppressed

reality to be preserved   (as part of reality)

for

Objective—the preservation of oppression

Figure 4.2. Freire's Conception of Oppressive Action
SOURCE: Freire, 1970, p. 131.

To put Freire's schema in concrete terms, consider the cognitive-behavioral therapist who meets with a Holocaust survivor or a Vietnam veteran who manifests clinical depression. Fairly effective treatment procedures can be

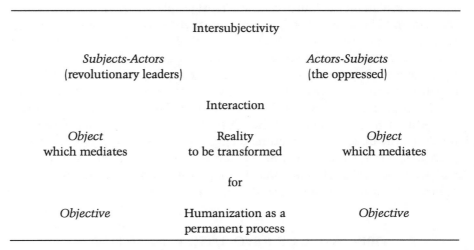

Figure 4.3. Freire's Conception of Revolutionary Action
SOURCE: Freire, 1970, p. 131.

established with this framework to help these clients feel better. Medication can also ease the process. Freire would term this type of therapy oppressive because it fails to inform the client colleague of how the depression is a logical result of developmental history and oppressive social conditions. Effective education and therapy seek to work with the client colleague in considering how oppressive conditions contribute to present reality. This *naming* of social context is very much a joint act between counselor and client colleague.

Freire also describes a conception of revolutionary action in which *intersubjectivity*—a framework of equality—surrounds the educator-student relationship (Figure 4.3). Feminist theory (e.g., Ballou & Gabalac, 1984) is the prime current example of how psychotherapy can become liberating rather than encapsulating. Note that the counselor or therapist works *with* the client in this model. Both learn together how they might transform reality: The interaction of the pair in the helping relationship replaces action of the therapy *on* the client in traditional helping models.

Psychotherapy as liberation demands two (or more) people working together to examine their relationship with each other *and* their social context. What is the impact of the social environment on individual thought and action? Armed with personal and contextual information, two (or more) people can work together to transform reality.

The Holocaust survivor and the Vietnam veteran learn how social contextual issues of anti-Semitism and society's denial of Vietnam contribute to their so-called emotional distress of *DSM-IV* diagnostic classification. In addition, client colleagues are encouraged to work toward attacking social conditions that may be causative of their issues. It is not enough to learn that one has been a victim; one can benefit from attacking the source of victimization. If the problem is not in the individual, we also need to attack external social/contextual stressors. Both therapists and clients can benefit from a therapy that also seeks to address environmental causes of individual distress.

CONSCIENTIZACÀO: HOW DOES ONE INTEGRATE THEORY WITH PRACTICE?

But how does one integrate theory with practice? It is useful to turn once again to Freire's integration of his theory with practice—praxis. Freire did not just theorize; he developed a comprehensive method that provides us with some specifics for counseling and therapy praxis. Chapter 3 (pp. 75-118) of *The Pedagogy of the Oppressed* (1972) outlines specifics of consciousness raising. The following paragraphs focus on his methods.

Freire might meet with a group of peasants over a campfire. The shared objective would be literacy training in which the peasants were to select and name the words they wished to learn. Reading education was focused on the peasants' life experiences. In this way, Freire was as much a learner as were his "students."

Freire and his students would identify objects in their natural and cultural surroundings. He stressed the importance of *codification*, a process in which themes of the culture were identified. He had the peasants identify things in their environment by questioning them about visual, tactile, and auditory stimuli. Counselors and therapists using the developmental counseling and therapy model (Ivey, 1986) would recognize this as sensorimotor questioning ("What are you seeing? Hearing? Feeling?"), in which direct experience is accessed as most fundamental. Neurolinguistic programming (Lankton, 1980) uses this type of questioning to help the client anchor present and past life experiencing. But Freire was using specifics of neurolinguistic programming long before this psychotherapeutic mode became popular. Although developmental counseling and therapy was generated independently of Freire, many of his concepts, particularly as related to contextual issues, have been integrated into its most recent methodology.

Freire followed codification of experience with naming. His groups would describe the events of their lives and name what they saw, heard, and felt. The named words of lived experience would serve as the foundation of their reading. In psychotherapeutic terms, we want to know the nature of direct experience and how the client names this experience.

It is here that cultural identity theory can be helpful in understanding what Freire was doing. The peasants and Freire were operating in a state of naiveté and were at a stage of passive acceptance of the conditions of life on a plantation (see Figure 4.1). In Platonic terms, they were "imagining" life rather than truly experiencing it. The act of naming experience enabled the peasants first to know what was happening and later to reflect on their condition.

For example, Freire might ask the peasants to describe what they saw, heard, and felt during a typical day. Then he might ask them to describe the life of the plantation owner as they saw, heard, and felt it. The words they used in these descriptions would be the foundation for literacy training. The concrete names the peasants used to describe their own lives and that of the plantation owner often presented a contradiction that might bring them to new and more forms of cognition and emotion about their lived experience. In short, the act of naming and identifying contradictions is essential to cognitive, emotional, and behavioral growth.

In the above example, the names given to life experience are primarily those of the client colleague. The names are not taken from a previously agreed-on theory developed by remote experts. The names also help the leader or counselor identify new ways to conceptualize experience.

If we extend these concepts to cultural identity theory, the task for varying cultural groups is first to identify experience as lived (what they see, hear, and feel) and then to name it and sometimes to act on it. As part of the experience, clients naturally reflect and redefine the meaning of their experience. These therapeutic and educational processes relate cultural identity theory, Platonic epistemology, and Freire's original thought, as shown in Table 4.1.

Table 4.1 illustrates that specific actions can be employed at each stage of consciousness to facilitate movement to the next level. Freire used many techniques similar to those used daily in counseling and psychotherapy, but his goal was equality and action in the system, not conforming individuals to the status quo. Institutional or environmental change as a result of naming also often was addressed by joint action of the leader and the group.

The goal of *conscientizacào* is critical consciousness—the client colleague's experiencing self, perhaps for the first time, and then beginning to see how self was constructed in a sociocultural relationship. Freire, Jackson and Hardiman, and the cultural identity theorists provide a diagnostic framework that can be used to design helping interventions and assess their effectiveness.

CASE EXAMPLE OF MCT THEORY IN PRACTICE

Assume you are working with a low-income Puerto Rican woman who suffers from *ataques de nervios*. These are best described as epileptic-like seizures that have an emotional base and function in Puerto Rican culture. American psychology originally pathologized these events as hysteria or thought them to be actually physical in origin (Rivera-Arzola, 1991). We now know that such events are a normal part of dealing with trauma and grief in

TABLE 4.1 Three Alternative Frames Compared as They Relate to Cognitive, Emotional, and Behavior Change

Cultural Identity Theory	Plato	Freire	Actions Needed to Produce Change to Next Level/Stage
Naiveté	Imagining	Magical consciousness (conforming)[a]	Describe life experience.
Acceptance		Naive consciousness	Name and note contradictions in experience with emphasis on contextual issues.
Naming and resistance	Belief	Beginning of critical consciousness (reforming)[a]	Encourage examination and reflection on contradictions in system. Major emotional change frequently occurs, often anger.
Redefinition and reflection	Thinking		Encourage examination of self and self-in-system. Emotional pride in self and culture.
Multiperspective integration	Dialectic	Critical consciousness (transforming),[a] conscientizacào	Continue emphasis of dialogic thought and co-investigation of reality and joint action to transform reality.

a. *Conforming, reforming,* and *transforming* are terms coined by Alschuler (1986) that are helpful in defining the changes that occur with critical consciousness.

Puerto Rican culture. The following passage is a direct quote from Cheatham, Ivey, Ivey, and Simek-Morgan (1993).

> The client colleague is a single parent, twenty-five years of age with two children. [As once was common in Puerto Rico,] she has been sterilized with only minimal information given to her before she gave consent. She has suffered physical abuse both as a child and in more recent relationships. The following is an example of how multicultural counseling and therapy might use cultural identity development theory to facilitate *conscientizacào* and the generation of critical consciousness.
>
> *Acceptance—diagnostic signs.* The client enters counseling hesitatingly as her *ataques de nervios* are increasing in frequency. A physician has referred the client to you believing that the fainting spells are psychological in origin as no physical reasons can be found. As you talk with the client, you discover that she blames herself for the failures in her life. She comments that she is "always choosing the wrong man," and she states she should have been sterilized sooner and thus fewer children would be born.
>
> *Acceptance—helping interventions and producing dissonance.* Your intervention at this stage is to listen, but following Freire (1972, pp. 114-116), you can seek to help her codify or make sense of her present experience. You use guided imagery as you help her review critical life events—the scenes

around sterilization, the difficulties of economic survival when surrounded by others who have wealth, and actual discrimination against Puerto Ricans in nearby factories. . . . Through listening and perturbing with dissonant images, the move to a more critical consciousness is begun. But, at the same time, your client colleague needs help. You may see that she has sufficient food and shelter, you may help her find a job. You may teach her basic stress management and relaxation, but especially you listen and learn.

Naming and resistance—Diagnostic signs. At this point, your client is likely to become very angry, for the responsibility or "fault" which she believed was hers is now seen as almost totally in the oppressive environment. Her eyes may flash as she talks about "them." An emotional release may occur as she becomes aware that the decision for sterilization was not truly hers, but imposed by an authoritarian physician. The woman is likely to seek to strike back wherever possible against those who she feels have oppressed her. In the early stages of naming, she may fail to separate people who have truly victimized her from those who have "merely" stood by and said nothing.

Naming and resistance—Interventions to help and to produce dissonance. Early in this stage, you are very likely to do a lot of listening. You may find it helpful to teach the client culturally-appropriate assertiveness training and anger management. There may be a delayed anger reaction to traditional sex roles. Later, this client may profit from reality therapy. However, the therapy must be adapted to her relational Puerto Rican heritage. You may support constructive action on her part to change oppressive situations. In the later stages of work with her, you may want to help her see that much of her consciousness and being depends on her *opposition* to the status quo and that she has given little attention to her own real needs and wishes. [At this point, identifying and naming contradictions between self and society may be especially important.]

Reflection and redefinition—Diagnostic signs. It gets very tiring to spend one's life in total anger toward society and others. The consciousness-raising theories find that at this stage that clients often retreat to their own gender and/or cultural community to reflect on what has happened to them and to others. Responsibility is now seen as more internal in nature, but keen awareness of external issues remains. You may note that the client colleague at this stage is less interested in action and more interested in understanding self and culture. There may be a great interest in understanding and appreciating her Puerto Rican heritage and how it plays itself out in North America.

Reflection and redefinition—Interventions to help and produce dissonance. Teaching clients the cultural identity development theories can be useful for them at this stage in that they help explain issues of development in culture. In addition, culturally appropriate theories such as . . . feminist theory may be especially helpful, although they are useful at all consciousness levels. Cognitive-behavioral, psychodynamic, and person-centered theories may be used if adapted to the culture and needs of the person. [The reflective consciousness is still considered a form of naive consciousness by Freire, as much of the emphasis is on the individual with insufficient attention given to systemic roots of difficulties.]

Multiperspective integration—Diagnostic signs. The client draws from all previous stages as appropriate to the situation. At times, she may accept situations, at other times be appropriately aggressive and angry, and later withdraw and reflect on herself and her relationships to others and society. She is likely to be aware of how her physical symptoms of *ataques de nervios* were a logical result of the position of women in her culture. She is able to balance responsibility between herself and society. At the same time, she does not see her level of *conscientizacào* as "higher" than others. She respects alternative frames of reference.

Multiperspective integration—Interventions to help and produce dissonance. You as helper may ask the client to join with you and your group to attack some of the issues that "cause" emotional personal and financial difficulty. The Puerto Rican woman may establish a family planning clinic with accurate information on the long-term effects of sterilization or she may establish a day-care center. The woman is clearly aware of how her difficulties developed in a system of relationships, and she balances internal and external responsibility for action. In terms of introducing dissonance, your task may require helping her with time management, stress management, and in balancing the many possible actions she encounters. You may also arrange to see that she has accurate feedback from others about her own life and work. [You do not merely encourage her to work to transform the system. You also work with her to facilitate the process. You and your client colleague are now working together to produce cultural change in oppressive conditions.]

[In summary,] MCT as presented here provides specific actions that can lead to critical consciousness and *conscientizacào*. The example here of a Puerto Rican woman could be changed to represent a middle-class woman, a gay male, or any of a variety of culturally distinct client colleagues. Particularly relevant for broader practice of counseling and therapy is Pfefferle's (1989) developmental concepts of the long-term psychological problems. She states that depressed clients typically see themselves as responsible for their problems in the early stages and only gradually move to awareness that depression was generated in a systemic context. Rigazio-DiGilio (1989) and Ivey and Rigazio-DiGilio (1990) found that systematic questioning of depressed clients led toward a critical consciousness. In this new state of awareness, the clients were able to balance responsibility for self and others in a more constructive fashion. (pp. 114-115; reprinted with permission)

The above discussion suggests that psychotherapy as liberation has much to offer individuals and the growth process. Our problem has been that we tend to focus too much of our efforts on the Platonic belief and thinking stages—thus our emphasis on behavior and cognition. We have given insufficient attention to sensorimotor reality and direct client experience, and, most seriously, we have failed to consider the systemic issues underlying the client colleague's world.

We have restricted counseling and psychotherapy unnecessarily in our search for self-actualization and individual change. No longer is it adequate to situate problems in the individual and then use our traditional humanistic, cognitive-behavioral, and psychodynamic strategies. The time has come to increase our attention to the direct experience of the individual through immediate sensorimotor reality and consider how that reality is affected by systemic contextual/cultural issues. Armed with this knowledge, we may or may not find it appropriate to utilize traditional techniques as we have in the past, but certainly our present techniques and strategies are inadequate in themselves for a new future.

Let us now turn to some specific verbal skills and strategies that may be useful to client colleagues and ourselves in the process of *conscientizacào* or raising critical consciousness.

THE SKILLS AND STRATEGIES OF *CONSCIENTIZACÀO*

Drawing on the above theoretical framework, Ivey (1993) defined specific skills and strategies that might be used in the process of *conscientizacào*— helping client colleagues and ourselves achieve critical consciousness. With each client colleague, the relationship needs to be more egalitarian and less hierarchical than what we usually associate with psychotherapy. It is important to note that the first task of *conscientizacào* is to identify where you and the other person are in terms of cultural identity and awareness of systemic issues. If you are not aware, then your opportunity to help your client colleague grow and develop is minimized. However, an aware client colleague can help you grow to increased awareness of the systemic issues of personal oppression underlying his or her personal distress.

Thus, the first task and strategy of gaining critical consciousness is to examine ourselves as contextual/cultural beings. A useful part of this process draws on cultural identity theory. Each of us needs to become fully aware of ourselves as racial and ethnic beings. Moreover, it is important that we expand our awareness of issues of gender, sexual preference, degrees of physical and emotional ability, spirituality, and socioeconomic issues. For some of our clients, the major issue may be sexual preference, with ethnic and religious concerns prominently intertwined. For other clients, the major issue may be gender or a physical challenge. Our multicultural identity has many facets.

Following are some specific skills and strategies that help client colleagues and ourselves move to new and more complete levels of multicultural understanding and action.

1. *Helping client colleagues first understand the self-in-relation more completely and then helping him or her move from naiveté or acceptance to naming and resistance.* For a client colleague who comes to us at the naive or acceptant level of cultural identity, we may anticipate a good deal of self-blame, an underlying depression or hopelessness, and a sense of futility. Moreover, this person may have a false consciousness and actively accept racist, sexist, or homophobic behavior—what some would term "playing host to the oppressor." To facilitate awareness and growth, one can use visualization exercises followed by naming the experience shown in the exercises. The client colleague can be asked, "What are you seeing? Hearing? Feeling?" Racist, sexist, homophobic, or other discriminatory experiences may be reviewed.

Ivey (1993) suggested some specific questions that may help the client colleague move from his or her present level or stage of consciousness to the next:

Moving from naiveté to examination of acceptant behaviors, feelings, and thoughts. Tell me about your life. Tell me about a time when you felt one-down, out of control, depressed/oppressed, or helpless. Tell me about the others in this situation?

Moving from acceptance to naming and resistance. What is your image of the situation? What are you seeing? Hearing? Feeling? Locate the feeling in a specific place in your body. What is your image of the other or the context? Use the same sensorimotor questions to elaborate the image and the bodily feelings which are associated. *How would you name that image, feeling, or experience?*

2. *Helping a client colleague expand their understanding of naming resistance and to move to the next stage or level.* We usually identify a client colleague as a person who has developed a well-defined anger at the system (although this anger may be injurious to health). We also tend to find that client colleagues at this level have identified their sense of self as built *in opposition* to the other: For example, African Americans are not White European Americans, women are not men, the differently abled are not able. The locus of control is often external rather than internal.

Some useful techniques that help individuals survive at this stage (and the previous stage) include listening carefully to the concrete details of the stories of oppression and presenting stress management and cognitive-behavioral therapy to help the person cope with "reality." Assertiveness training may be useful in helping the client colleague start work toward reforming the system. Also, it is important to start confronting the external locus of control, thus facilitating the development of a stronger sense of self-in-relation.

Some specific questions suggested by Ivey (1993) that facilitate movement to the next stage are:

Tell me a story of what happened. What happened first, next, and how did it end? Note the emphasis on linearity and cause and effect in story telling. (Here we are applying some basic principles of applied behavioral analysis and rational-emotive therapy) to client colleague images and stories so that they can understand them better. As a therapist, you can help your client colleague—"If you say X, then what is likely to be the consequence?" The skill of logical consequences may be useful as well.

After this review of the story, how would you name or think about the story now? Can you name your thought and feelings?

Have the client colleague tell several concrete stories in linear detail, then ask for reflection. As you look back on your story, what occurs for you? Can you name your thought and feelings?

3. *Helping a client colleague expand his or her understanding of reflection and redefinition and also to move to a dialogic, multiperspective stage or level.* Whereas the concrete naming and resistance stage tends to focus on action, this stage tends to emphasize reflective thought. Freire (1972, p. 75) discussed action and reflection as two parts of true praxis. Too extensive an emphasis

on action leads to "activism" with insufficient attention to the reasons and purpose of action. Too extensive an emphasis on reflection leads to "verbalism" with little or no action.

Reflective consciousness is an important part of cultural identity theory, and its obvious strengths and weaknesses have been well outlined by Freire. The cognitive, humanistic, and psychodynamic orientations are renowned for their verbalism and emphasis on thought as opposed to action. Behavioral psychology, of course, has received many attacks for insufficient attention to reflection. Small wonder that the cognitive-behavioral revolution is upon us, but even this approach has limitations in that it gives insufficient attention to experiencing the systemic issues faced in a multicultural society.

Reflection offers a time to build a sense of self-in-relation to cultural context and develop a stronger sense of internal locus of control. A woman, for example, may be expected to start defining herself uniquely as a woman rather than an opposition to men. A Latina/o will define her- or himself on the basis of personal and cultural norms.

Techniques useful in expanding self and cultural awareness are group consciousness-raising programs such as those widely used in the early stages of feminist or other cultural support groups. Traditional cognitive and behavioral psychological theories can be useful, but only if the theories are culturally shaped and adapted. Confrontation techniques within the interview and group are particularly important in that contradictions are identified. This is the basis of later true dialogical thought.

Characteristic questions useful at this time include:

- What is common to your stories? What are the patterns?
- How do you think about these stories, and how could you think about them differently?
- Which of your behaviors and thoughts are yours? Which of them come from your cultural surroundings and life history?
- How do family stories and family history relate to your conception of self? Of your cultural background? How the two relate?
- What parts of you are driven by internal forces and what parts by external forces? How can you tell the difference?
- Standing back, what inconsistencies can you identify?

4. *Continuing and expanding multiperspective integration.* Here we are looking for true praxis—the integration of thought and action. The individual or group here freely draws on and sees the value in all other stages and levels, but clearly sees self in social/family/historical context. The ability to take multiple perspectives on data is central to this stage, but this ability contains the seeds of a major problem, for it is easy for the individual or group to become bewildered by multiple possibilities and fail to act on new cognitions and emotions.

Supporting development at this stage are community and network efforts in which the individual or group seeks out new goals and actions. The individual at the multiperspective level will be able to see many points of view *and* take action, as appropriate to the situation. The transforming consciousness seeks to move toward action and to make a difference in the world.

Some questions that may help individuals and groups at the multiperspectival integration stage are:

- As you look back on all we've talked about and/or done, what stands out for you? How? Why? How do you/we put together all we've talked about? *These questions help individuals or groups look back and reflect on their own cognitive and emotional operations. These questions may also help reorganize old thought patterns, leading to a new perspective on old situations.*

- What rule(s) were you (or the other person or group) operating under? Where did that rule come from? How might someone else describe that situation (another family member, a member of the opposition, someone from a different cultural background)? How do these rules relate to us now?

- How might we describe this from the point of view of some other person, theoretical framework, or language system? How might we put it together using another framework?

- What does our family, our educational, or work history say about the development and operation of oppression?

- What shall we do? How shall we do it together? What is *our* objective and how can we work together effectively? Or, equally likely, the client colleague may wish to manage his or her own affairs and take action as a leader in his or her own right.

Perhaps the last question is the most important. It is the one that reminds us most specifically of the importance of integrating our thoughts with specific actions not only by ourselves, but also with others.

The questions above can be introduced, as appropriate, to any counseling or therapeutic situation. The goal is to help the client colleague see his or her issues in social and historical context. This is not to take responsibility for action away from individuals, but to help them understand that they are not alone in their issues and that full resolution of conflicting situations usually involves some action and awareness of social context. The stoic viewpoint—"It is not things but what we think of things that is important"—clearly does not hold here. Thought and action must become a unified whole.

You will also find that working systematically through these questions with a client colleague may result in beginning change in consciousness. We have become so enamored of individualistic psychology that even working carefully with questions of this type can result in major changes in thought patterns, which in turn can lead to new actions.

The egalitarian, dialogical aspect is also important in this framework. With clearly defined goals and specific techniques and questions, it would be all too easy to fall into a hierarchical client-counselor or patient-therapist model.

Thus, as often occurs in feminist therapy, goals should be established jointly with the client colleague, constant joint review of the value of each session should be undertaken, and goals should be jointly rewritten as needed. The dialogical therapist or counselor tends not to be formally wedded to a specific procedure, and all techniques and strategies are open to the client colleague's review and modification. In a sense, counseling and psychotherapy become less predictable when we join with client colleagues in co-constructing a new vision.

SUMMARY

Psychotherapy as liberation entails a radical revision of helping theory. The developmental psychology of cultural identity theory is basic to the framework, which focuses on self-in-context and self-in-relation. The individualism usually associated with traditional psychology is not eliminated, but is recognized for what it is—a cultural variant, most likely appropriate for those from a European American background. But even here, there is a question of excessive individualism. The failure of American and Western psychology to see the individual in cultural context suggests that considerable effort and thought needs to be given to revising our traditional modes of helping.

Humanistic, psychodynamic, and cognitive-behavioral theory have brought us many ideas and innovations. We need not discard them, but we need to review them anew as culturally derived phenomena. How can we adapt them to the culturally diverse future we all face?

Psychotherapy as liberation has been presented here as a beginning step toward integrating cultural identity theory more directly into helping practice. I hope that the ideas here may be useful in some small way toward a more culturally sensitive approach to the profession of helping.

REFERENCES

Alschuler, A. (1986). Creating a world where it is easier to love: Counseling applications of Paulo Freire's theory. *Journal of Counseling and Development, 64,* 492-496.

Asante, M. (1987). *The Afrocentric idea.* Philadelphia: Temple University Press.

Ballou, M., & Gabalac, N. (1984). *A feminist position on mental health.* Springfield, IL: Charles C Thomas.

Brown, N. (1959). *Life against death: The psychoanalytic meaning of history.* Middletown, CT: Wesleyan University Press.

Cheatham, H. (1990). Empowering Black families. In H. Cheatham & J. Stewart (Eds.), *Black families* (pp. 373-393). New Brunswick, NJ: Transaction.

Cheatham, H., Ivey, A., Ivey, M., & Simek-Morgan, L. (1993). Multicultural counseling and therapy. In A. Ivey, M. Ivey, & L. Simek-Morgan (Eds.), *Counseling and psychotherapy: A multicultural perspective* (pp. 92-123. Boston: Allyn & Bacon.

Cheek, D. (1976). *Assertive Black . . . puzzled White.* San Luis Obispo, CA: Impact.

Cornford, F. (Trans.). (1982). *The Republic of Plato.* Oxford, UK: Oxford University Press. (Original work published 1941)

Cross, W. (1971). The Negro to Black conversion experience. *Black World, 20,* 13-25.

Cross, W. (1991). *Shades of Black.* Philadelphia: Temple University Press.

Daly, M. (1973). *Beyond God the father.* Boston: Beacon.

Daly, M. (1978). *Gyn/ecology: The metaethics of radical feminism.* Boston: Beacon.

Fanon, F. (1963). *The wretched of the earth.* New York: Grove Wheatland.

Freire, P. (1972). *Pedagogy of the oppressed.* New York: Herder & Herder.

Fukuyama, M. (1990). Taking a universal approach to multicultural counseling. *Counselor Education and Supervision, 30,* 6-17.

Hardiman, R. (1982). *White identity development: A process oriented model for describing the racial consciousness of White Americans.* Unpublished doctoral dissertation, University of Massachusetts, Amherst.

Helms, J. (1985). Toward a theoretical explanation of the effects of race on counseling: A Black and White model. *The Counseling Psychologist, 12,* 153-165.

Helms, J. (1990). *Black and White racial identity.* Westport, CT: Greenwood Press.

Ivey, A. (1986). *Developmental therapy: Theory into practice.* San Francisco: Jossey-Bass.

Ivey, A. (1991). *Developmental strategies for helpers: Individual, family and network interventions.* North Amherst, MA: Microtraining.

Ivey, A. (1993, January). *Psychotherapy as liberation.* Presentation to the Round Table on Cross-Cultural Counseling, Columbia University, New York.

Ivey, A., Ivey, M., & Simek-Morgan, L. (Eds.). (1993). *Counseling and psychotherapy: A multicultural perspective.* Boston: Allyn & Bacon.

Ivey, A., & Payton, P. (1994). Towards a Cornish identity theory. In *Cornish Studies,2,* 151-163.

Jackson, B. (1975). Black identity development. *Journal of Educational Diversity and Innovation, 2,* 19-25.

Jackson, B. (1990, September). *Building a multicultural school.* Presentation to the Amherst Regional School System, Amherst, MA.

Jackson, B., & Hardiman, R. (1983). Racial identity development: Implications for managing the multiracial work force. In R. Vitvo & A. Sargent (Eds.), *The NTL managers' handbook* (pp. 107-119). Arlington, VA: NTL Institute.

Kantrowitz, R., & Ballou, M. (1992). A feminist critique of cognitive-behavioral theory. In M. Ballou & L. Brown (Eds.), *Theories of personality and psychopathology* (pp. 70-79). New York: Guilford.

LaFromboise, T., & Low, K. (1989). American Indian adolescents. In J. Gibbs & L. Hwang (Eds.), *Children of color* (pp. 114-147). San Francisco: Jossey-Bass.

Lankton, S. (1980). *Practical magic.* Cupertino, CA: Meta.

Lerman, H. (1992). The limits of phenomenology: A feminist critique of humanist personality theories. In M. Ballou & L. Brown (Eds.), *Theories of personality and psychopathology* (pp. 8-19). New York: Guilford.

Locke, D. (1990). A not so provincial view of multicultural counseling. *Counselor Education and Supervision, 30,* 18-25.

Miller, J. (1991). The development of women's sense of self. In J. Jordan, A. Kaplan, J. Miller, I. Stiver, & J. Surrey (Eds.), *Women's growth in connection* (pp. 11-26). New York: Guilford.

Myers, L. (1988). *Understanding an Afrocentric world view: Introduction to an optimal psychology.* Dubuque, IA: Kendall/Hunt.

Parham, T. (1989). Cycles of psychological Nigrescence. *The Counseling Psychologist, 17,* 187-226.

Pedersen, P. (1990). The multicultural perspective as a fourth force in counseling. *Journal of Mental Health Counseling, 12,* 93-95.

Pedersen, P., Draguns, J., Lonner, J., & Trimble, J. (1989). *Counseling across cultures* (3rd ed.). Honolulu: University of Hawaii Press.

Ponterotto, J. (1988). Racial consciousness development among White counselor trainees. *Journal of Multicultural Counseling and Development, 16,* 146-156.

Rigazio-DiGilio, S. (1989). *Developmental theory and therapy: A preliminary investigation of reliability and predictive validity using an inpatient depressive population sample.* Unpublished doctoral dissertation, University of Massachusetts, Amherst.

Rigazio-DiGilio, S., & Ivey, A. E. (1990). Developmental therapy and depressive disorders: Measuring cognitive levels through patient natural language. *Professional Psychology: Research and Practice, 21*, 470-475.

Rivera-Arzola, M. (1991). *Differences between Puerto Rican women with and without ataques de nervios.* Unpublished doctoral dissertation, University of Massachusetts, Amherst.

Sue, D., & Sue, D. (1990). *Counseling the culturally different* (2nd ed.). New York: John Wiley.

White, J., & Parham, T. (1990). *The psychology of Blacks.* Englewood Cliffs, NJ: Prentice Hall.

Wrenn, C. (1962). The culturally encapsulated counselor. *Harvard Educational Review, 32,* 444-449.

Wrenn, C. (1985). The culturally encapsulated counselor revisited. In P. Pedersen (Ed.), *Handbook of cross-cultural counseling and therapy* (pp. 323-329). Westport, CT: Greenwood Press.

5

The Acculturation of American Indians

Developing Frameworks for Research and Practice

SANDRA K. CHONEY

ELISE BERRYHILL-PAAPKE

ROCKEY R. ROBBINS

MANY COUNSELORS AND PSYCHOLOGISTS will have only limited opportunities to work with American Indian clients or to conduct scientific investigations with Indian populations. Some will believe that because of this they need not attempt to become effective counselors/therapists for Indian clients. Others will concede that attempts to become effective with American Indians are important but will state that such attempts should be left to psychologists who are themselves American Indian. The truth is that the number of Indian psychologists is so small that Indian clients are most likely to be treated by non-Indian counselors or psychologists.

With this in mind, we present information we believe useful for counselors and therapists who become involved in the helping process with American

AUTHORS' NOTE: The terms *American Indian*, *Indian*, and *Native American* are used interchangeably throughout the text of this chapter to denote those people indigenous to the continental United States. *Alaska Native* is used to broadly identify Eskimo and Aleut peoples of Alaska.

Indians as well as for those scholars who may choose to investigate issues pertaining to mental health service provision or mental health in general for American Indian populations. This information includes a brief demographic description of the U.S. American Indian/Alaska Native population, a rationale for the discussion of acculturation rather than racial identity, and an overview of historical and present-day acculturative influences. Information about the effects of acculturation on some of the more prevalent mental health issues of American Indians and on help-seeking behavior is also presented. Further, we critically review existing models of acculturation and offer an alternative model that attempts to address some of the deficits of earlier models. Finally, we include recommendations for counseling and research with American Indian individuals and groups.

DEMOGRAPHICS OF INDIAN COUNTRY

Census reports indicate that almost 2 million people identified themselves as American Indian/Alaska Native in 1990 (U.S. Bureau of the Census, 1991). These 2 million represented 542 tribal groups and spoke over 150 Indian languages. The median ages ranged from 18.8 years to 26.3 years on reservation lands, with those Indians living within tribal jurisdictional areas having slightly higher median ages (22.7 to 27.2 years) and those in Alaska Native villages slightly lower (16.8 to 25.0 years).

Although the total American Indian/Alaska Native population remains relatively small, certain regions of the country have been identified as areas of population density. For instance, 15.6% of Alaska's population is Alaska Native, and 8.9% of New Mexico's population, 8.0% of Oklahoma's population, and 5.9% of Arizona's population are American Indian. Cities with the largest Indian populations include Los Angeles with 87,487; Tulsa, Oklahoma, with 48,196; New York City with 46,191; Oklahoma City with 45,720, and San Francisco with 40,847 (Paisano, 1991). Just over one fifth (22.3%) of the total Indian population continues to live on over 300 existing reservation and trust lands, with another 15% living within tribal jurisdiction, Alaska Native villages, or tribal designated areas. The remainder, 62.3%, are divided among rural and urban areas. Social indicators suggest that American Indian/ Alaska Natives face higher poverty levels and lower educational attainment levels than do other groups regardless of their location (U.S. Bureau of the Census, 1991).

At the end of the 19th century, it was believed by many that American Indians and their cultures would vanish, but they have instead increased. From 1980 to 1990, the percentage increase of American Indians was higher than that of any other racial group. This growth rate indicates that although their numbers are small at present, American Indian and Alaska Native populations may eventually regain the numbers (around 5 million) that are estimated to have been in existence when the first European explorers made contact (Snipp, 1989).

RACIAL IDENTITY VERSUS ACCULTURATION

In conjunction with an increasing population, questions arise concerning ascribed and personal identity of Indian people. And indeed, for the American Indian adolescent, "Indianness," or the outward display of tribal attitudes, beliefs, customs, values, and appearances, may be the most important aspect of personal identity development (Red Horse, 1982).

Using Helms's (1990) definition of racial identity as the combination of reference group orientation, ascribed identity, and personal identity, the development of an "Indian" racial identity can be linked to the concept of Indianness. Tribal-specific customs and traditions reflecting attitudes and beliefs help tribal members define Indianness for their particular group.

Though belief sets are similar in certain aspects, they have unique qualities that help to distinguish one tribe from another (Locust, 1985). Thus, ideas of Indianness are heavily influenced by belief systems that are similar yet different. For example, in many tribes death is symbolized by an owl. Nonetheless, there are differences in the conceptual basis of death that supersede the representational similarities. The missing homogeneous worldview complicates the determination of a single description of Indianness or racial identity and makes its use as a defining concept problematic.

Besides this initial difficulty in the use of the concept of racial identity with American Indian people, problems related to environmental and religious influences arise. Indian people have always felt the influence of the physical environment (homeland) on customs and traditions. An ever-expanding Euro-American population, however, brought about relocation of tribal people in the early 1800s. The idea of Manifest Destiny created a situation in which Indian people were systematically stripped of their land and the sacred relationship they felt for it; traditional values were undermined. Immediately following relocation, rural or reservation life was the norm. During the 20th century, however, urban life became more common as American Indians moved to towns and cities in search of employment opportunities unavailable in rural areas or on reservations (Hanson, 1980). The progressive migration from virtually unlimited access to earth and sky to the confines of urban ghettos and high-rise apartments has subsequently been felt in the transmittal of tribal values from one generation to another. This change has also affected the manner in which these values are exhibited in tradition and customs modified to fit present-day realities. Those Indian people who remain on reservations or in rural areas tend to have different cultural values than do those who experience societal influences (i.e., economic, social, educational) that serve as catalysts for cultural change. An "Indian racial identity" cannot meaningfully address the cultural variations attributable to environmental factors any better than it is able to meaningfully address the preference for tribal over racial group (Indian) identification.

Finally, racial identity is susceptible to the influence of religion and spirituality because these influence individual belief systems. Early in the history of European and American Indian relations, attempts to Christianize the Indians began. These attempts were perceived as mostly successful and have resulted in a variety of religious denominations scattered throughout Indian Country. Those Indian people who failed to succumb to the tenets of Christianity continued to follow the "old ways." Today there are many who subscribe to the beliefs of Baptist, Methodist, Presbyterian, Episcopalian, Mormon, and Catholic religious denominations. Others adhere to combinations of traditional and Christian practices such as the Native American Church. There are also many who subscribe to pre-Christianization beliefs as exemplified by certain tribal societies, spiritual groups, and ceremonial activities. Differences in spiritual and/or religious beliefs can be vast and may provide parallel differences in the ways Indianness is conceived. A Christian Indian who was asked to tell what traditions, customs, and values exemplify Indianness might give a very different answer from that of one who followed the "old ways."

The influences of lifestyle (rural, reservation, and urban), missionary efforts, and a primary identification with the tribal over the racial group make speaking of racial identity for American Indian people difficult at best. Although Helms's definition may explain the racial identity attitudes of Black and, to a certain degree, White Americans, it lacks viability with people who identify themselves first and foremost as tribal members rather than "Indian."

Racial identity as a construct, then, may perpetuate the homogeneity myth about American Indians and fail to reflect cultural variations found among tribes. In fact, examination of the mechanics of culture and variations in values leads to the conclusion that the construct of racial identity is too general to apply to Indian people, who vary so greatly from tribe to tribe.

On the other hand, there remains the need for a means to assess individual differences in worldview that are attributable to culture. One method receiving much attention over the years is the assessment of acculturative status or acculturation. Acculturation refers to the degree to which the individual (in this case, the American Indian person) accepts and adheres to both majority (White/Euro-American) and tribal cultural values. It may be thought of as a response to Euro-American and traditional tribal societal values, norms, and mores across cognitive, behavioral, and affective domains.

Whereas racial identity implies a variety of complex processes based on ascription to a particular racial group in conjunction with other personal identity attributes (Helms, 1990), acculturation allows for a variety of personal group-oriented ascriptions. In this case, acculturation can allow for as many ascribed identity groups as there are tribal nations. Descriptions of acculturative status of individuals or groups of individuals need not define specific tribal traditions or spiritual influences, nor discuss the relevant differences between reservation, rural, or urban Indians, because acculturative status is a much broader measure of the unique social perspective of the individual.

ROOTS OF ACCULTURATION

When American Indians balked at slavery and religious conversion, the Spanish labeled them demonic and exterminated them from the Caribbean Islands. This policy was acceptable to other colonizing nations and resulted in the decimation of more than 90% of the American Indian population in North America during the first two centuries of colonization (Snipp, 1989). Deneven (cited in McLemore, 1991) contended that "the discovery of America was followed by possibly the worst demographic disaster in the history of the world" (p. 376).

Genocide and Removal

Initially, at least, racial genocide was seen as the simplest way to address the "Indian problem" in the United States (Ford, 1983; Richardson, 1981). As genocide gained less and less popularity, disputes over land, grazing, and hunting rights continued to grow in number and intensity. Enforced removal and relocation were thought to be the next best solution, considering the waning support for extermination. Removal and relocation would provide not only a simple resolution to many land title disputes but also a way to disrupt Indian culture through removal from the traditional homelands so important to customs, beliefs, and traditions.

Through the disruption of Indian culture, tribal organization and Indian family structure were expected to collapse, leaving a cultural vacuum into which White culture might insinuate itself. As captive nations, the tribes were expected to be absorbed into the greater White society as they adapted their culture by discarding it (Snipp, 1986). But as is often the case, what was expected did not occur. Indian culture is not dead, but has experienced many adaptations and modifications to fit new and unusual circumstances. For instance, burial customs of many tribes were greatly influenced by the experience of the tribes who were a part of the "Trail of Tears" (the removal of tribes from the southeastern United States to Oklahoma in the 1830s). As one Caddo elder revealed:

> Today, we put blankets on the caskets and I didn't know why. So I asked a friend of mine who is Cherokee and he said that we did it because on the Trail of Tears when somebody died the soldiers didn't let you have time to bury

them so you just had to throw a blanket over them on the ground. . . . You know, Caddos weren't on that Trail of Tears but we have that custom anyway.

Boarding Schools and Culture

As it became evident that neither extermination nor relocation was a viable method of complete cultural destruction and subsequent adoption of White cultural standards by Indians, other ideas presented themselves. Among these ideas was one relying on the power of education to change lives.

Most treaty agreements included provisions for the education of Indian youth through the establishment of rural schools and boarding schools (Debo, 1940/1986). Thus, the boarding school system was born and remained in vigorous effect for almost a century. The goal of the system was to remove Indian children from traditional settings and place them in new environments as far from home as possible. At school, children could be Christianized and made to accept the tenets of White society. Native language and customs were forbidden in overt attempts to weaken oral tradition and connections with tribal culture (Cross, 1986; Trennert, 1988). The detrimental effects of early boarding schools were intergenerational, affecting those who attended as well as those whose parents or grandparents attended (as in Dauphinais, 1993).

The Missionary Movement

Consistent with the federal policy of assimilation, traditional Indian spiritual/religious activities were outlawed in the late 1800s (Swinomish Tribal Mental Health Program, 1991, p. 31). With this legislation, missionaries renewed their zeal in the conversion of the Indian "pagan" and founded new missionary schools and religious outposts throughout the American West.

Many Indian people were eager converts. Some became so involved in the new religion that they discarded their previous spiritual beliefs and many social activities that were now considered unacceptable. Divisions within Indian communities along religious and social lines became evident, with accompanying recriminations common to both sides. Religious persecution from within and without the community, however, simply caused native spiritual activities to move underground (Swaney, 1993). Eventually, the Native American Church was organized to offer Indian people an alternative to formal Judeo-Christian ways of worship. However, it remained illegal to practice "native religions" until the federal government passed the American Indian Religious Freedom Act of 1978.

In sum, Christianization of the American Indian was more effective than any other assimilation effort. It produced desired changes in attitudes and behavior with the willing participation of Indian people that had been lacking in all other acculturation attempts.

Acculturation in the 1990s

"The task challenging Native communities is to retain their distinct cultural identities while preparing members for successful participation in a world of rapidly changing technology and diverse cultures" (Indian Nations at Risk Task Force, 1991, p. 1). This is no easy task, considering the continuing pressure placed on Indian people to discard those distinct identities for identities that are more familiar to the Euro-American majority. Indian people face acculturation on a daily basis, ranging from issues of national consequence, such as tribal sovereignty, to those of local interest, such as offering native language classes in elementary schools. Granted, acculturation is not an issue that imbues the thinking of all Indian people, but it remains a subliminal presence ready to erupt into consciousness at the slightest provocation.

The U.S. judicial system continues to contribute to the acculturative process. In many instances, untold harm is done to American Indian people because of the extreme ignorance of legal professionals in regard to cultural issues. Almost 20 years ago federal legislation assured American Indians that a concentrated effort would be made to keep their children in traditional settings. Yet even with the passage of the Indian Child Welfare Act of 1978, 25% to 35% of American Indian children (Kessel & Robbins, 1984) are still placed in non-Indian homes, where their exposure to Indian culture may be limited to specials on educational television and old John Wayne westerns. Because of this continuing practice, the loss of culture persists as "the younger generation is being reared without benefit of the wisdom and teachings of the elder generation" (BigFoot, 1993, p. 3).

Inexcusably, psychological services have contributed to the assimilation/acculturation process. According to Angie Debo (1940/1986), in the late 19th century and early 20th century, physicians frequently assessed many Indian mothers as "insane" and committed them, thereby enabling White families to adopt Indian children and gain Indian lands. Today, with less intentionality, many psychological assessments and treatments continue to ignore cultural differences between American Indians and Whites (Dana, 1986). Consequently, these assessments and treatments underserve and mis-serve American Indians. They also inadvertently promulgate highly detrimental misconceptions and stereotypes, not to mention encouraging questionable psychological services.

Mental health professionals

have long pondered the question, "What's wrong with the Indians? Why have Native Americans failed to adapt and flourish in Western society, after all they have had over 400 years to become fully acculturated?" Perhaps we are not finding the right answer because we have been asking the wrong question. A more revealing query may concern why Western society has not adjusted to Native American culture and learned to profit from much of what could be incorporated advantageously into a Western value structure? (Lamarine, 1989, pp. 16-17)

SOCIAL AND PSYCHOLOGICAL PROBLEMS
RELATED TO ACCULTURATION

Unemployment, alcoholism, and other social and psychological problems have undoubtedly had a detrimental effect on the American Indian. A 1990 report to the Senate Select Committee on Indian Affairs stated that American Indians, particularly adolescents, have more serious mental health problems than are reported for all race populations in the United States (U.S. Office of Technology Assessment [OTA], 1990). The report lists problems such as developmental disabilities, depression, suicide, anxiety, alcohol and substance abuse, self-esteem and alienation, running away, and dropping out of school as high-priority areas. Although exact causes remain unknown, it can be said with some certainty that Indian adolescents often have lives filled with stressors not shared by non-Indian adolescents.

In addition, it has been noted that American Indian adolescents may be extremely susceptible to high stress levels engendered by the developmental task of identity establishment, in that they may feel "particularly caught between two cultures" (U.S. OTA, 1990, p. 1). The clash of cultures has been noted to produce a unique sort of stress, acculturative stress, that is accompanied by physiological discomfort as one moves across cultures (Berry, Kim, Minde, & Mok, 1987). This discomfort may manifest itself in a variety of psychological as well as physical problems.

Posttraumatic Stress Disorder
(PTSD) and Acculturative Stress

Although PTSD has been more commonly associated with the trauma surrounding combat or physically violent situations, the disorder can develop in response to any extreme traumatic stressor involving direct exposure to or witnessing of an event that involves "actual or threatened death or serious injury, or other *threat to one's personal integrity* [emphasis added]" (American Psychiatric Association [APA], 1994, p. 424).

One of the most blatant examples of threat to personal integrity is the forced acculturation, racism, and discrimination continually experienced by tribal people in the United States. The product of these actions may be thought of as intergenerational PTSD. Further, it has been suggested that this societally induced form of stress exacerbates PTSD resulting from combat trauma experienced by American Indian combat veterans, particularly Vietnam veterans (Duran, Guillory, & Tingley, 1992).

Many Indian veterans viewed themselves as returning warriors and believed that by their participation in efforts to secure the safety and well-being of American mainstream society they would in some way experience greater tolerance and acceptance in the larger society upon their homecoming. They were unpleasantly surprised. "If they sought acceptance by Whites, they were disappointed. If they thought military service would bring them opportunity, they discovered that it had only lowered their status within the American mainstream" (Holm, 1992, p. 31). Although Vietnam veterans in general experienced this type of treatment and reacted with confusion and hurt, for Indian veterans it was simply "business as usual." The emotional detachment, diminished responsiveness to external stimuli, and hypervigilance were familiar to those whose lives had already been affected by the intergenerational aspects of forcible assimilation/acculturation.

Acculturation and Alcohol Abuse

In attempts to alleviate the sense of hopelessness and loss of identity engendered by intergenerational PTSD, acculturative stress, and other problems, alcohol has become a primary and destructive coping mechanism for Indian people (Berlin, 1987; Yates, 1987). Native Americans have higher rates of alcohol consumption than any other ethnic group in the United States (Weisner, Weibel-Orlando, & Long, 1984). Alcoholism, suicide, murder, accidental death and injury, assault, theft, social discord, unemployment, and divorce are epidemic in some Indian communities (Price, 1975). Due to the prevalence of alcoholism, fetal alcohol syndrome and fetal alcohol effect are becoming significant threats to the survival and functioning of future generations of American Indians (Streissguth, LaDue, & Randels, 1988).

A preponderance of studies suggest the influence of culture and acculturation on drinking patterns and habits. French and Hornbuckle (1980) claimed that the use and abuse of alcohol is directly related to the existence or nonexistence of social controls and corresponding cultural sanctions with regard to drinking in cultural environments. Price (1975) reported that drinking patterns differ among tribes and may be determined by the following factors: length of exposure time to alcohol, aboriginal controls, external controls, and internal controls. Hughes and Dodder (1984), however, suggested that American Indian college students' drinking patterns are quite similar to those of their White peers, although Indian students are more likely to have been arrested because of their drinking. In an investigation of urban Indian drinking styles, Weisner et al. (1984) found that family drinking models and psychological stress were the greatest predictors of drinking level. Their study also found that Indians considered to be "teetotalers" and "moderate drinkers" were those who were committed to Christian beliefs or to the preservation of traditionalism, ancestry, and culture. These findings suggest a relationship between drinking patterns and cultural values (Flores, 1986). Finally, "Indian people recognize the destruction by liquor of their youth, their health, and their cultures. . . . What makes the attainment of sobriety so difficult?" (Mail & Wright, 1989, p. 19).

Effects of Acculturation on Help Seeking

American Indian people face many issues amenable to psychosocial interventions. Unfortunately, reports consistently suggest that mental health services are underutilized because of such issues as lack of awareness of availability (Dinges, Trimble, Manson, & Pasquale, 1981), fear and mistrust (Dukepoo, 1980), and negative attitudes toward non-Indian psychologists (Manson & Trimble, 1982). Further, if services are sought, American Indians compared to non-Indians are almost twice as unlikely to return after the first session (Sue, Allen, & Conaway, 1981).

Important to the issue of service utilization and effective counseling with American Indians is the discrepancy in the assumptions Indians make about psychology and that psychology makes about them. LaFromboise (1988) suggested that although American Indians engaged in therapy may be opposed to the superimposition of Western biases on Indian behavior and beliefs, many well-intentioned psychologists believe that to be helpful they must encourage American Indians to create their own personal value system or to adjust to Western value systems. Others are unaware that Western psychological techniques and notions of health and well-being may undermine traditional values that some American Indians possess.

For many traditionally oriented Indian people, there is no separate concept for "mental health." A person is either in harmony or in disharmony, a condition that encompasses physical, emotional, environmental, and cognitive aspects of self (Locust, 1985) and that is viewed in the context of the community (Trimble & Hayes, 1984). However, the acculturated Indian client may not hold to these more traditional beliefs about health and unwellness. As LaFromboise et al. (1991) suggested, traditional Indian people's expectations about counseling may be quite different from those of urban Indians whose lifestyles are similar to their non-Indian neighbors'.

Family therapists have consistently viewed problems as occurring within the context of the family system. This fits well with the traditional Indian notion of extended family and the view of health and unwellness taken in the context of the community. In the late 1960s Attneave (1969) promoted network therapy as a means of working effectively with Indian people. Network therapy provides a framework from which to work with the individual along with his or her extended family and even the community. Attneave concluded that networking as a means of therapy is useful in most settings with Indian families, noting that "even in the socially isolating environment of our present metropolitan centers the vestiges of old networks and the seedlings of new ones can be found" (p. 209). Further, research has supported the viability of network therapy in a variety of cultural environments through evidence of positive counseling outcomes (Marshall, Martin, Thomason, & Johnson, 1991).

Empirical evidence concerning the differences in acculturative level and preferences for counselors, perceptions of counselor trustworthiness, and utilization of services has been plagued with inconsistency. Bennett, BigFoot, and Thurman (1989) found no support for the hypothesis that level of involvement in Indian versus White culture would affect preferences for various counselor attributes of American Indian adult clients. Similar results were found for American Indian college students (Bennett & BigFoot-Sipes, 1991). However, most analogue studies of Indian student populations produced opposite findings (BigFoot-Sipes, Dauphinais, LaFromboise, Bennett, & Rowe, 1992; Haviland, Horswill, O'Connell, & Dynneson, 1983; Johnson & Lashley, 1989). One difficulty with these and similar studies has been suggested to be the way in which acculturation was measured. In almost all instances, a single question asking the person to endorse one of four statements regarding involvement with Indian and White culture was the essential measurement. The reason for such a simple research design is the lack of adequate models and means of assessing acculturation that currently plagues both psychological research and practice with American Indians.

AMERICAN INDIAN ACCULTURATION MODELS AND MEASURES

Deficit Models of Acculturation

Measuring acculturation is not a new problem. As early as 1940, systematic attempts to quantify the degree to which Indian people had adopted various aspects of mainstream culture (as in Chief, 1940) were underway. Acculturation models began by assuming that American Indian culture evidenced deficiencies that could be corrected by their replacement with White cultural values. Today, models, for the most part, continue to promulgate this type of thinking. In fact, the "deficit model" approach asserts a naturally occurring, unidirectional movement from traditional culture to majority culture. This approach not only fails to address the movement toward retraditionalization evident today but also ignores the fact that particularly in the early part of this century, the unidirectionality of acculturation was forced, not naturally occurring. Further, accepting a deficits approach implies the superiority of White culture over Indian culture and uses this implication to invoke the concept of acculturative stress to explain dysfunctional behavior in more traditionally oriented Indian individuals, families, and communities.

Other problems experienced by acculturation models and measures are a failure to account for varying levels of acculturation (e.g., Chief, 1940; McFee, 1968; McShane & Plas, 1982; Wingert & Fifield, 1985), perpetuation of negative stereotyping of American Indians through suggestions of relationships between Indianness and psychopathology (as in Uecker, Boutillier, & Richardson, 1980), or promotion of one-way linear movement from Indian to White culture (Hobson, 1994; Stone, 1982; Zitzow & Estes, 1981). A dichotomous view of acculturation (that is, either Indian or White, with nothing

in between) avoids many of the complexities inherent in the study of acculturation status. But such a view also allows no means by which to account
for the variety of behaviors that may be the outward manifestations of the
adaptation and modification of Indian values to fit the demands of mainstream
American culture. Likewise, the promotion of unidirectional movement and
the correlation of Indianness with psychopathology are, respectively, limiting
and destructive to Indian people.

Models Accounting for Varying Levels of "Indianness"

Emergent patterns within acculturation research indicate a genre of models that appears to extend beyond the deficit model hypotheses of previous
work. For instance, Ryan and Ryan (1989) conceptualized the process of acculturation as occurring on five levels: traditional, transitional, marginal, assimilated, and bicultural. Similarly, Oetting and Beauvais's (1990) orthogonal
cultural identification theory suggested that individuals can be very bicultural,
be unicultural, have high identification with one culture and medium identification with another, or have low identification with both cultures.

These conceptualizations do not imply unidirectional movement, nor do
they view acculturation as dichotomous in nature. They do allow for a variety
of cultural positions and accompanying fluidity as the individual moves between traditional Indian and mainstream White culture. Unfortunately, they
focus primarily on acceptance or rejection of traditional values without a cor-
respondingly systematic focus on other aspects of acculturative behavior such
as spirituality, affect, or environmental influences.

Although conceptualization of the process of acculturation has expanded
an ever-evolving empirical knowledge base, research with American Indians/
Alaska Natives, as a whole, continues to explain this process inadequately. If
we go beyond previous models, we may begin to recognize that Indian people
have, in fact, developed flexible coping skills that allow them to participate in
a healthier process of living.

Acculturation From a Health Perspective

As has been shown, acculturation models can be misleading because they
are essentially imperfect small-scale replicas of reality. In presenting a new
model, the most we can hope for is that it is simple and can take into account
empirical evidence without too much tinkering. It is with an Indian sense of
humor that we go about building this new model, knowing that it is to some
extent an unavoidable reflection of a transient scientific and mainstream psychology and that its worth will be evidenced only by its capacity to help us
understand American Indian acculturation.

A health rather than a deficit approach is the underlying framework for
our model. Figure 5.1 presents a geometric depiction of the model as a series

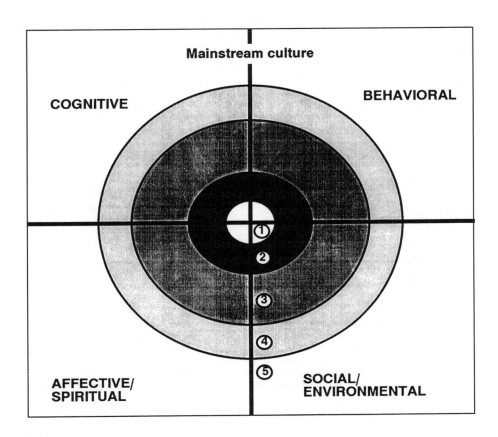

Figure 5.1. A Health Model Conceptualization of Acculturation

NOTE: 1 = traditional; 2 = transitional; 3 = bicultural; 4 = assimilated; 5 = marginal. Also, those considered to be marginal exhibit little or no adherence to the cultural values of either mainstream or Indian cultures but because of the enveloping nature of the mainstream are depicted within its boundaries.

of concentric circles (rather than a linear scale). The model itself represents the four areas of the human personality that are consistent with the major domains of the medicine wheel (a uniquely Indian means of conceptualizing the human condition based on four essential elements) and are widely applicable to psychology—namely, cognitive, behavioral, affective/spiritual, and social/environmental. Further, the way in which the majority culture envelopes the lives of American Indians is included. This is represented by the space outside the outer circle. Within the perimeters of each individual circle, different levels of acculturation may exist. No value judgments are placed on any level of acculturation, nor is any dimension of personality emphasized more than another. Responses unique to each level represent ways of coping developed according to the influences and demands of each individual's environment and the context or social situation in which responses occur.

TABLE 5.1. Establishment of Acculturative Levels Across Personality Domains

Domain	Acculturative Level[a]				
	1	2	3	4	5
Cognitive					
English	No	Some	Yes	Yes	Yes
Native language	Yes	Yes	Some	No	No
Understands White customs	No	Some	Yes	Yes	Some
Understands tribal customs	Yes	Yes	Yes	No	Some
Behavioral					
Acts in tribally appropriate ways	Yes	Yes	Yes	No	No
Acts appropriately for White culture	No	No	Yes	Yes	No
Participates in tribal social activities	Yes	Yes	Yes	No	No
Participates in White social activities	No	Some	Yes	Yes	No
Affective/Spiritual					
Embraces traditional spirituality or Indianized Christian religions	Yes	Yes	Some	No	No
Feels emotionally connected to tribe	Yes	Yes	Yes	No	No
Social/Environmental					
Socializes with other Indian people	Yes	Yes	Yes	No	No
Socializes with non-Indian people	No	Some	Yes	Yes	No
Chooses to live in Indian communities	Yes	Some	Some	No	No
Chooses to live in non-Indian communities	No	Some	Some	Yes	No

a. Within this category, 1 = traditional, 2 = transitional, 3 = bicultural, 4 = assimilated, and 5 = marginal.

Five levels of acculturation are described by the model. As in Ryan and Ryan's (1989) typology, these levels are traditional, transitional, bicultural, assimilated, and marginal. Table 5.1 provides elements from each personality domain as they are thought to apply to individuals within each acculturative level. The use of the term *some* in the table indicates that these elements may or may not be present or are only sometimes evident.

The major assumptions of this acculturation model are: (a) There are attributional strengths that can be identified within each level of acculturation or Indianness; (b) these attributes can function as coping skills given environmental demands and varying social contexts; (c) because the levels are not value laden, no one level is better or superior to another, and movement from traditional to assimilated levels is not a prerequisite to mental health and happiness; and (d) acculturation stress is not inevitable, although it can and does occur.

In our model, we assume an approach that avoids many of the problems found in other models. For instance, it does not confine itself to either a linear or a dichotomous perspective. It instead allows flexibility in individual responses to both White and traditional values, norms, and attitudes across cognitive, behavioral, social/environmental, and affective/spiritual domains, and offers a sense of fluid movement. An individual may conceivably have four different acculturative levels corresponding to the four personality domains. A person very "traditional" in all other respects may find that watching a grandson participate in Little League baseball is an enjoyable social activity. Thus, the acculturative level for the social/environmental domain might be more "transitional" than "traditional."

SUGGESTIONS FOR
PRACTICE AND RESEARCH

Counseling American Indians

The bulk of this chapter has been an attempt to illuminate issues surrounding the acculturation of American Indians. We have presented historical perspectives, related certain mental health issues, and have discussed models of acculturation. How then does this relate to the clinical practice of psychology? We believe that without an understanding of acculturation and the acculturative process, practitioners working with Indian people suffer a distinct disadvantage. It is extremely difficult to provide culturally appropriate services without knowledge of the culture or the ability to distinguish a culturally adaptive response from one that indicates psychopathology.

On the basis of our belief in the importance of acculturation, our social and professional experiences with Native people, and the literature with regard to counseling American Indians, we encourage those involved in the provision of mental health services to consider the points below when working with Indian clients.

1. Some Native Americans, particularly those with more traditional beliefs about health, may respond better to treatment if traditional healers are involved. Numerous studies point to this as an important consideration (e.g., LaFromboise, 1988; LaFromboise et al., 1991; Locust, 1985; Thomason, 1991).

2. As Attneave (1969) pointed out, the extended family has great potential for aiding positive therapeutic outcome. However, the counselor should be aware that using the Indian family in the counseling process will be somewhat different than when working with non-Indians. Sessions may occur outside the clinic or office setting. The Indian family may be less motivated to engage in "talk therapy" and more willing to be active agents of change.

3. Differences in communication styles (as in Dauphinais, Dauphinais, & Rowe, 1981), perceptions of trustworthiness (LaFromboise, Dauphinais, & Rowe, 1980), gender role definitions (LaFromboise, Heyle, & Ozer, 1990; Medicine, 1981), and social support networks including family relationships (as in Attneave, 1982) all provide major considerations when undertaking problem identification and treatment planning for American Indian clients.

4. Caution must be taken when employing standardized tests to assess American Indians. Life experience, cognitive structure, use of nonstandard English, differences in epistomologies, and economic hardship characterize the lives of many Indian people. A failure to take these into account can detrimentally

affect test results and assessments. Insensitive interpretations can contribute to American Indian students' dropping out of school, being denied placement opportunities, being indiscriminately referred, and eventually being relegated to low-paying jobs or even unemployment.

Understanding that there are tribal differences among Indian people and individual differences within the same tribe expressed in terms of acculturative level (Attneave, 1982) is important for all psychologists and counselors. Through such an understanding, perhaps stereotyping based on general assumptions can be avoided (Thomason, 1991).

Research

With respect to American Indians, the concept of acculturation permeates all areas of scientific investigation across many disciplines. It is probably one of the most potent within-group variables yet identified, as well as being one of the most difficult to conceptualize and to measure. We would, of course, suggest the continued examination of acculturation levels as a means of describing and explaining differences among Indian research participants. However, we also suggest that the following be considered:

1. Concerted efforts should be made to develop a means of measuring acculturation that accounts for the multifaceted nature of the process (i.e., across spiritual, cognitive, affective, and behavioral domains).
2. When thinking about the effects of acculturation, researchers should avoid making value judgments about the health status of any particular level of cultural response. All levels may be "healthy" or "unhealthy" depending on the situational context in which they are offered.
3. Group or individual "acculturative profiles" should be developed because defining a single acculturative level for any individual is an unreasonable goal given the possibility that a person may have cultural responses representative of differing levels for each domain.
4. The notion that acculturation is a naturally occurring unidirectional force should be discarded; in its place researchers must understand that although some degree of acculturation is indeed present in all Native people today, it represents the culmination of historic and current superimposition of values that are often alien to tribes and is not the natural result of cultural evolution.

With respect to particular topics for scientific inquiry, we offer the following:

1. Community-based research projects are much needed in Indian country. Indian communities today face many of the same emerging problems faced by other communities; however, the resources needed to solve these may be more limited. Researchers should collaborate with community leaders to design joint efforts that meet the needs of Indian people. For instance, it has been our experience that many of the community concerns center on youth. Youth suicide, gang violence, and alcohol and substance abuse have all been

identified as problems that are amenable to collaborative research and intervention.

2. Little is known about counseling process or outcome with American Indian clients, particularly adults. Preferences for counselors, attitudes and beliefs about counseling, the utility of particular counseling techniques, and methods for increasing service utilization are all areas that require further investigation.

3. Most research conducted to date with Native people has focused on identification of variables that are related to or that cause certain maladaptive behaviors (i.e., alcoholism, child abuse and neglect, depression and suicide). Research focusing on identification of variables related to adaptive functioning is minimal at best and is an area in which we see the need for increased activity.

4. Finally, a gratifying aspect of counseling/psychotherapy research conducted with Indian people is the acknowledgment by most investigators that Indians are not a homogeneous group. With this initial acknowledgment, we feel that American Indian mental health research is developing the potential to be of great assistance to Indian people.

REFERENCES

American Psychiatric Association. (1994). *Diagnostic and statistical manual of mental disorders* (4th ed.). Washington, DC: Author.

Attneave, C. (1969). Therapy in tribal settings and urban network intervention. *Family Process, 8,* 192-210.

Attneave, C. (1982). American Indian and Alaska Native families: Emigrants in their homeland. In J. R. McGoldrick & J. Giordano (Eds.), *Ethnicity and family therapy* (pp. 55-83). New York: Guilford.

Bennett, S. K., BigFoot, D. S., & Thurman, P. J. (1989, August). *American Indian client preferences for counselor attributes.* Paper presented at the annual meeting of the American Psychological Association, New Orleans.

Bennett, S. K., & BigFoot-Sipes, D. S. (1991). American Indian and White college student preferences for counselor characteristics. *Journal of Counseling Psychology, 38,* 440-445.

Berlin, I. N. (1987). Effects of changing Native American cultures on child development. *Journal of Community Psychology, 13,* 299-306.

Berry, J. W., Kim, U., Minde, T., & Mok, D. (1987). Comparative studies of acculturative stress. *International Migration Review, 21,* 491-511.

BigFoot, D. S. (1993, August). Child abuse and neglect in Indian communities. In S. K. Bennett (Chair), *Issues in the psychological treatment of American Indian families.* Symposium conducted at the annual meeting of the American Psychological Association, Toronto.

BigFoot-Sipes, D. S., Dauphinais, P., LaFromboise, T. D., Bennett, S. R., & Rowe, W. (1992). American Indian secondary school students' preferences for counselors. *Journal of Multicultural Counseling and Development, 20,* 113-122.

Chief, E. H. (1940). An assimilation study of Indian girls. *Journal of Social Psychology, 11,* 19-30.

Cross, T. L. (1986). Drawing on cultural tradition in Indian child welfare practice. *Social Casework, 67,* 283-289.

Dana, R. (1986). Personality assessment and Native Americans. *Journal of Personality Assessment, 50,* 480-500.

Dauphinais, P. (1993). Boarding schools: Fond memories of anguish and heartache. *Focus, 1,* 11-12.

Dauphinais, P., Dauphinais, L., & Rowe, W. (1981). Effects of race and communication style on Indian perceptions of counselor effectiveness. *Counselor Education and Supervision, 21*, 72-80.

Debo, A. (1986). *And still the waters run: The betrayal of the Five Civilized Tribes.* Norman: University of Oklahoma. (Original work published 1940)

Dinges, N. G., Trimble, J. E., Manson, S. M., & Pasquale, F. L. (1981). Counseling and psychotherapy with American Indians and Alaska Natives. In A. J. Marsella & P. B. Pedersen (Eds.), *Cross-cultural counseling and psychotherapy* (pp. 243-276). New York: Pergamon.

Dukepoo, P. C. (1980). *The elder American Indian.* San Diego, CA: Campanile.

Duran, E., Guillory, B., & Tingley, P. (1992). *Domestic violence in Native American communities: The effects of intergenerational post traumatic stress.* Paper presented at the Veteran's Administration conference on Post Traumatic Stress Disorder, Oklahoma City, OK.

Flores, P. J. (1986). Alcoholism treatment and the relationship of Native American cultural values to recovery. *International Journal of the Addictions, 20*, 1707-1726.

Ford, R. (1983). *Counseling strategies for ethnic minority students.* Tacoma, WA: University of Puget Sound. (ERIC Document Reproduction Service No. ED 247 504)

French, L. A., & Hornbuckle, J. (1980). Alcoholism among Native Americans: An analysis. *Social Work, 21*, 275-280.

Hanson, W. (1980). *The urban Indian* (Report No. RC014193). San Francisco: San Francisco State University. (ERIC Document Reproduction Service No. ED 213 587)

Haviland, M. G., Horswill, R. K., O'Connell, J. J., & Dynneson, V. V. (1983). Native American college students' preference for counselor race and sex and the likelihood of their use of a counseling center. *Journal of Counseling Psychology, 30*, 267-270.

Helms, J. E. (1990). *Black and White racial identity: Theory, research, and practice.* Westport, CT: Greenwood Press.

Hobson, B. T. (1994). *Cultural values and persistence among Comanche college students.* Unpublished doctoral dissertation, University of Oklahoma.

Holm, T. (1992). The national survey of Indian Vietnam veterans. In F. Montour & H. Barse (Eds.), *Report of the working group on American Indian Vietnam era veterans* (pp. 25-34). Washington, DC: Department of Veterans Affairs, Readjustment Counseling Service.

Hughes, S. P., & Dodder, R. A. (1984). Alcohol consumption patterns among American Indian and White college students. *Journal of Studies on Alcohol, 45*, 433-439.

Indian Nations at Risk Task Force. (1991). *Indian nations at risk: An educational strategy for action.* Washington, DC: U.S. Department of Education.

Johnson, M. E., & Lashley, K. H. (1989). Influence of Native Americans' cultural commitment on preferences for counselor ethnicity and expectations about counseling. *Journal of Multicultural Counseling and Development, 17*, 115-122.

Kessel, J., & Robbins, S. P. (1984). The Indian Child Welfare Act: Dilemmas and needs. *Child Welfare, 63*, 225-232.

LaFromboise, T. D. (1988). American Indian mental health policy. *American Psychologist, 43*, 388-397.

LaFromboise, T. D., Dauphinais, P., & Rowe, W. (1980). Indian students' perceptions of positive helper attributes. *Journal of American Indian Education, 19*(3), 11-16.

LaFromboise, T. D., Heyle, A. M., & Ozer, E. J. (1990). Changing and diverse roles of women in American Indian cultures. *Sex Roles, 22*, 455-476.

LaFromboise, T. D., Trimble, J. E., & Mohatt, G. V. (1991). Counseling intervention and American Indian tradition: An integrative approach. *The Counseling Psychologist, 18*, 628-654.

Lamarine, R. (1989). The dilemma of Native American health. *Health Education, 20*(5), 15-18.

Locust, C. (1985). American Indian beliefs concerning health and unwellness. *Native American Research and Training Center Monograph Series*, pp. 1-25.

Mail, P. D., & Wright, L. J. (1989). Point of view: Indian sobriety must come from Indian solutions. *Health Education, 20*(5), 19-22.

Manson, S. M., & Trimble, J. E. (1982). American Indian and Alaska Native communities: Past efforts, future inquiries. In L. R. Snowden (Ed.), *Reaching the underserved: Mental health needs of neglected populations* (pp. 143-163). Beverly Hills, CA: Sage.

Marshall, C. A., Martin, W. F., Thomason, T. C., & Johnson, M. T. (1991). Multiculturalism and rehabilitation counselor training: Recommendations for providing culturally appropriate counseling services to American Indians with disabilities. *Journal of Counseling and Development, 70,* 225-233.

McFee, M. (1968). The 150% man, a product of Blackfeet acculturation. *American Anthropologist, 70,* 1096-1107.

McLemore, S. D. (1991). *Racial and ethnic relations in America.* Boston: Allyn & Bacon.

McShane, D. A., & Plas, J. H. (1982). Wechsler scale performance patterns of American Indian children. *Psychology in the Schools, 19,* 8-17.

Medicine, B. (1981). The interaction of culture and sex roles in the schools. *Integrated Education, 19,* 28-37.

Oetting, E. R., & Beauvais, F. (1990). Orthogonal cultural identification theory: The cultural identification of minority adolescents. *International Journal of the Addictions, 25,* 655-685.

Paisano, E. L. (1991). *Major findings on American Indian and Alaska Native populations from the 1990 census.* Washington, DC: U.S. Bureau of the Census, Racial Statistics Branch.

Price, J. A. (1975). An applied analysis of North American Indian drinking patterns. *Human Organization, 34,* 17-26.

Red Horse, Y. (1982). A cultural network model: Perspectives for adolescent services and para-professional training. In S. M. Manson (Ed.), *New directions in prevention among American Indian and Alaska Native communities* (pp. 173-185). Portland: Oregon Health Sciences University.

Richardson, E. H. (1981). Cultural and historical perspectives in counseling American Indians. In D. W. Sue (Ed.), *Counseling the culturally different: Theory and practice* (pp. 216-255). New York: John Wiley.

Ryan, R. A., & Ryan, L. (1989). *Multicultural aspects of chemical dependency treatment: An American Indian perspective.* Unpublished manuscript, Turnaround Adolescent Treatment Program, Vancouver, WA.

Snipp, C. M. (1986). The changing political and economic status of the American Indians: From captive nations to internal colonies. *American Journal of Economics and Sociology, 45*(2), 145-157.

Snipp, C. M. (1989). *American Indians: The first of this land.* New York: Russell Sage.

Stone, S. A. (1982). *Native generations diagnosis and placement on the conflicts/resolution chart: A culturally specific methodology of alcohol treatment through the Native self-actualization process.* Unpublished manuscript.

Streissguth, A. P., LaDue, R. A., & Randels, S. P. (1988). *A manual on adolescents and adults with fetal alcohol syndrome with special reference to American Indians.* Seattle: University of Washington, Department of Psychiatry and Behavioral Sciences.

Sue, S., Allen, D. B., & Conaway, L. (1981). The responsiveness and equality of mental health care to Chicanos and Native Americans. *American Journal of Community Psychology, 6,* 137-146.

Swaney, G. (1994, August). American Indian issues in therapy. In S. K. Bennett (Chair), *Psychological issues in the treatment of American Indian families.* Symposium conducted at the annual meeting of the American Psychological Association, Toronto.

Swinomish Tribal Mental Health Program. (1991). *A gathering of wisdom.* Tacoma, WA: Author.

Thomason, T. C. (1991). Counseling Native Americans: An introduction for non-Native American counselors. *Journal of Counseling and Development, 69,* 321-327.

Trennert, R. A., Jr. (1988). *The Phoenix Indian school: Forced assimilation in Arizona, 1891-1935.* Norman: University of Oklahoma Press.

Trimble, J. E., & Hayes, S. (1984). Mental health intervention in the psychosocial contexts of American Indian communities. In W. O'Connor & B. Lubin (Eds.), *Ecological approaches to clinical and community psychology* (pp. 293-321). New York: John Wiley.

Uecker, A. E., Boutillier, L. R., & Richardson, E. H. (1980). "Indianism" and MMPI scores of men alcoholics. *Journal of Studies on Alcohol, 41,* 357-362.

U.S. Bureau of the Census. (1991). *1990 census count of American Indians, Eskimos, or Aleuts and American Indian and Alaska Native areas.* Washington, DC: Bureau of the Census, Racial Statistics Branch, Population Division.

U.S. Office of Technology Assessment. (1990, January). *Indian adolescent mental health: OTA special report* (Report No. OTA-H-446). Washington, DC: Author. (ERIC Document Report Service No. ED 324 177 RC 017 777)

Weisner, T. S., Weibel-Orlando, J. C., & Long, J. (1984). "Serious drinking," "White man's drinking," and "tee totaling": Drinking levels and styles in an urban American Indian population. *Journal of Studies on Alcohol, 45,* 237-250.

Wingert, J. L., & Fifield, M. G. (1985). Characteristics of Native American users of inhalants. *International Journal of the Addictions, 20,* 1575-1582.

Yates, A. (1987). Current status and future directions of research on the American Indian child. *American Journal of Psychiatry, 144,* 1135-1142.

Zitzow, D., & Estes, G. (1981). *Heritage consistence as a consideration in counseling Native Americans.* Aberdeen, SD. (ERIC Document Reproduction Service No. ED 209 035)

6

The Psychology of Nigrescence

Revising the Cross Model

WILLIAM E. CROSS JR.

THE APPEARANCE OF THIS BOOK marks the 25th anniversary of the date when the stages construct became part of the Black identity discourse. In September 1970, the still budding magazine *Psychology Today* published an interview between representatives of what, at the time, were two nascent social movements: Charles W. Thomas, speaking for the Black power or Black consciousness movement, and Jo Ann E. Gardner, speaking for the women's movement (Gardner & Harris, 1970). The moderator for the interview was T. George Harris, the magazine's editor, who, for much of the time, acted more like a referee, given Thomas's opening salvo: "I would be less than candid, Jo Ann, if I did not say that the woman's movement is a diversion. . . . It is an activist way to ignore racism. It is avoidance behavior" (p. 49). To this Jo Ann Gardner responded,

> That's a lie, Tom. . . . We are fighting for the same thing . . . but some black males are acting like white-sexist bastards. . . . They put forth the idea that black women should step back so that black men can step forward . . . and it scares me to death to see them adopt the worst crime of the white-male dominated society. (p. 49)

The battle would continue, but at one point Thomas found it relevant to note that "through our consultants we have identified about five stages that people go through in affirming their Blackness" (p. 78). Transcription of his follow-up comments captured in print, albeit inauspiciously, one of the earliest explications of the stages construct. Simultaneous with the publication of Thomas's more formal statement of his thesis (Thomas, 1971), which was based primarily on the behavior of Blacks living on the West Coast of the United States, there appeared from observers working with Blacks in Chicago (Cross, 1970, 1971), Pittsburgh (Milliones, 1973), Albany, New York (Jackson, 1976), and elsewhere (see Cross, 1991) Black identity development models that both replicated and in some instances surpassed the clarity of Thomas's statement. These models of metamorphosis are known today as Nigrescence models, reflecting the psychology of Nigrescence, or the *psychology of becoming Black.*

Within psychology, the viability of a construct is measured, to a large extent, by the volume and quality of research activity it generates, and by that yardstick alone, empirical research on various aspects of Nigrescence has contributed greatly to the past and present discourse on Black psychological functioning. In the realm of "minority psychology," few constructs have been as productive.

Spin-offs of the models are equally important to note. I still cherish a letter sent to me in 1987 by Dana G. Finnegan, a New York City therapist, that celebrated the publication of her new book, *Dual Identities,* which she coauthored with Emily McNally. As explained in Finnegan's letter, their clients often included chemically dependent gays and lesbians, and their text translated the stages of Nigrescence into the phases of both chemical recovery and the coming-out process. At the University of Massachusetts, the dean of the School of Education, Bailey Jackson, has guided doctoral students through the flowering of models applicable to Asian, Latin, and biracial populations, with his own Nigrescence model acting as a guide for these distinctive but related permutations. And somewhat ironically, a full circle, of sorts, has been drawn, in that Janet Helms (1990) and Rita Hardiman (1982) independently applied the stages construct to models depicting "White identity development."

As originally conceived, Nigrescence primarily mapped adult behaviors and beliefs, but Jean Phinney (1989, 1993) and others (Oetting & Beauvais, 1991) successfully extended the Nigrescence discourse to adolescent identity development. The connection between Nigrescence and early childhood development would, at first glance, seem remote. However, the types of racial socialization messages that Howard Stevenson and his associates at the University of Pennsylvania find embedded in communications between Black parents and their young children are remarkably similar to the three functions that Cross, Parham, and Helms (1991) linked to advanced Nigrescence (these identity functions will be discussed later in this chapter, when the reformulated Internalization stage is presented). Working at the other end of the spectrum, Thomas Parham (1989) showed that adults may experience multiple Nigrescence episodes. Nigrescence was thought to be a "one-time event" in the life of a person, noted Parham (1989), but even if a person has completed an original or baseline episode at an earlier point in the life span (say, for example, adolescence or early adulthood), the challenges unique to another period (middle age or late adulthood) may induce that person to re-cycle through some of the stages. When the new questions are resolved and their solutions internalized, a new plateau is reached, setting the stage for yet another re-cycling, should a new challenge or "encounter" surface in the future.

Equally significant is the growing awareness that Nigrescence is as much a historical as a contemporaneous process. The stages of identity change are found in Nat Turner's metamorphosis from a "safe" to a "rebellious" slave, in the racial awakening of the great W. E. B. DuBois while he was a student at Fisk University, in the identity processes of men and women joining the Marcus Garvey movement and the Harlem Renaissance in the 1920s and 1930s, in the unfolding of Blackness during the 1960s, and, more recently, in the layered-identity discourse linked to the Afrocentric movement. Note Alain Locke's famous comment, in 1925, about the metamorphosis of the "New Negro," for it could readily be mistaken as an excerpt from the 1968 anthology by LeRoi Jones and Larry Neal titled *Black Fire*, published 43 years later:

> In the last decade something beyond the guard of statistics has happened in the life of the American Negro and the three norns who have traditionally presided over the Negro problem have a challenge in their laps. The Sociologist, the Philanthropist, the Race-leader are not unaware of the New Negro, but they are at a loss to account for him. He simply cannot be swathed in their formulae. For the younger generation is vibrant with a new psychology; the new spirit is awake in the masses, and under the very eyes of the professional observers is transforming what has been a perennial problem into the progressive phases of contemporary Negro life. (Locke, 1925, p. 3)

RETHINKING NIGRESCENCE

Despite its usefulness as a psychohistorical construct, its value in delineating adolescent and adult behavior, and its capacity to provide some degree of guidance to other minority scholars, Nigrescence theory is in need of revision. On the one hand, findings from the general studies of Black identity, as well as research directly focusing on Nigrescence theory, confirm the theory's overall validity. In addition, the extant depictions of the middle stages (Encounter and Immersion-Emersion) seem to hold up well. On the other hand, empirical studies call into question a great deal about the original contours and dynamics of the first stage (Pre-Encounter) and advanced stages (Internalization, or Stages 4 and 5). To discover these gaps, we need to review the way Pre-Encounter and Internalization were originally depicted in the 1971 version of the model, note the contradictions revealed by empirical studies, and move to reframe these stages in a rewrite of the entire model (Cross, 1991).

PRE-ENCOUNTER AND INTERNALIZATION
IN THE 1971 MODEL

The 1971 Cross model consists of five stages, starting with the Pre-Encounter stage, which depicts the old identity or the identity to be changed; the Encounter stage, which defines the events and experiences that cause a person to feel the need for change; the Immersion-Emersion stage, which captures the point of transition between the old and emergent identities; and two final stages, Internalization and Internalization-Commitment, which outline behaviors, attitudes, and mental health propensities that accompany habituation to the new identity.

Keep in mind that Nigrescence models created a great deal of excitement because they allowed observers to trace the developmental stages Blacks traversed in moving from a self-hating to a self-healing and culturally affirming self-concept. Attention was immediately drawn to the emergent or new identity, and somewhat lost in the shuffle was the fact that all the models, including the Cross model, took as the point of departure the presumed self-hating and anti-Black characteristics of anyone operating at the Pre-Encounter level. A prototypical Pre-Encounter person is said to be at risk, in terms of his or her mental health or general personality (low self-esteem, high anxiety, lower levels of ego integration, etc.), and to show evidence, at the group identity level, of embracing a pro-American cultural stance that is assimilationist if not overtly anti-Black and anti-African.

We will move quickly to the advanced stages because the empirical research contests little about the original depictions of the middle or transition stages. In the original model, Stage 4 (Internalization) suggests that the person achieves self-healing and that this higher level of mental health is linked to his or her reconstituted cultural moorings. Black nationalist attitudes are said to become less hardened, making possible renewed contacts and friendships with select White people and coalition building with other persons of color. Although the term does not appear in the 1971 version, the description of Internalization favors a person who is not only pro-Black but multicultural. Thus, implicitly at least, there is a tendency to play down the continuance of a Black nationalist frame and to play up bicultural and multicultural beliefs. Lastly, running throughout the original model is the theme of ideological unity: People in the advanced stages are said to be united and less prone to ideological disputes.

Research Findings

A significant body of research is associated with the 1971 version of the model, and the findings have been the object of several comprehensive literature reviews (for example, see the excellent reviews by Cross, 1991; Cross, Parham, & Helms, in press; Helms, 1990; Ponterotto & Casas, 1991; Ponterotto & Pedersen, 1993). It should be added that the research laboratories headed by Joseph Baldwin at Florida A & M University, Howard Stevenson at the University of Pennsylvania, and Jerome Taylor at the University of Pittsburgh are playing an invaluable role in pinpointing the limitations of Nigrescence theory. From the research conducted to date, the following highlights are of significance to the current discussion:

1. The self-hatred dynamics of persons at the Pre-Encounter stage have been exaggerated: Research suggests that the Pre-Encounter stage incorporates bimodal trends in which some people, at this level, are classically self-hating, but the majority are not. The majority show low salience for race but apparently derive mental health benefits from group identity affiliations not necessarily connected to Black culture. What makes them Pre-Encounter oriented is not self-hatred trends, but the embracing of a worldview, value system, or general outlook on life that downplays the significance of race. They may accord importance not to "race" or "Blackness," but to their religion, professional status, social class position, or sexual orientation. On the other hand, research has confirmed that some Pre-Encounter types, albeit a minority, do show classic signs of self-hatred. The rewrite of the model must incorporate these bimodal tendencies and show that the driving force for Pre-Encounter is not necessarily confusion, self-hatred, and mental illness, but an identity that gives low salience to race. In addition, it must also show under what conditions self-hatred can be expected at Pre-Encounter.

2. In contradistinction to the 1971 model, which stressed self-healing and ideological unity, empirical findings suggest that very little personality or self-esteem change accompanies Nigrescence, and that rather than become unified, people in the advanced stages are quite divergent in their ideological perspectives. Given the continued spread of the Afrocentric movement in recent years, the original model is also deficient in that it underestimates the role Black nationalism plays in the lives of many who achieve Internalization. With these findings in mind, a rewrite of the model must show that at Internalization, (a) most change occurs within the person's worldview, value system, ideology, or reference group orientation, and not the general personality or personal identity component of the self-concept; (b) a great deal of ideological diversity may accompany advanced Blackness; and (c) rather than atrophying, Black nationalist tendencies may show sustained growth; consequently advanced identity development may be associated with nationalism, as it is with biculturalism or multiculturalism. What follows is a restatement of the model, inclusive of major changes in the first and advanced stages.

THE REVISED CROSS MODEL

Stage 1: Pre-Encounter

Nigrescence is a *resocializing* experience: That is, it is the transformation of a preexisting identity (a non-Afrocentric identity) into one that is Afrocentric. The focus of the Pre-Encounter stage is this preexisting identity or the identity to be changed. Of course, it is possible for a Black person to be socialized from early childhood through adolescence to have a Black identity. At adulthood, such persons are not likely to be in need of Nigrescence, although Parham (1989) extended the theory to include cyclical change across the life span. More to the point, although Nigrescence is not a process for mapping the socialization of children, it is a model that explains how assimilated as well as deracinated, deculturalized, or miseducated adolescents or Black adults are transformed, by a series of circumstances and events, into persons who are more Black or Afrocentrically aligned.

Attitudes Toward Race

Low-Salience Attitudes. Persons in the Pre-Encounter stage hold attitudes toward race that range from low salience or race neutrality, to anti-Black. Persons who hold *low-salience* views do not deny being physically Black, but consider this "physical" fact to play an insignificant role in their everyday life. Being Black and knowledge about the Black experience have little to do with their perceived sense of happiness and well-being and contribute little to their purpose in life. In a sense, Pre-Encounter persons place value in things other than their Blackness, such as their religion, their lifestyle, their social status, or their profession. Thus, they do have values and they do experience meaningful existence, but little emphasis is given to Blackness. As long as their Pre-Encounter attitudes bring them a sense of fulfillment, meaningful existence, and an internal sense of stability, order, and harmony, such persons will not likely be in need of any type of identity change, let alone movement toward Afrocentricity.

Some low-salience types have not given much thought to race issues, and appear dumbfounded and naive during such discussions. They often see personal progress as a problem of free will, individual initiative, rugged individualism, and the personal motivation to achieve. Others have taken a more conscious route toward neutrality and see themselves as having reached a higher plane (i.e., abstract humanism), beneath which lies, as they see it, the vulgar world of race and ethnicity. When pressed to give a self-referent, they may respond that they are "human beings [or Americans] who happen to be Black."

Social Stigma Attitudes. A variant of the low-salience perspective can be found in the Black person who, though sharing the low-salience orientation, also sees race as a problem or stigma. Thus, race, by default, is attributed some significance, not as a proactive force or cultural issue but as a social stigma that must be negotiated from time to time. The only "meaning" accorded race is its tie to issues of *social discrimination*; from this perspective, race is a hassle, a problem, a vehicle of imposition. Such people may have a surface interest in Black causes, not as a way of supporting Black culture and the exploration of Black history but as a way of joining with those who are trying to destroy the social stigma associated with Blackness. The need to defend oneself against Blackness as stigma can be found in Pre-Encounter persons who otherwise have very little knowledge of Black history and culture. Consequently, when you ask such people to define their Black identity, they invariably respond by telling you what it is like to be oppressed.

Anti-Black Attitudes. The extreme racial attitude pattern that is found within the Pre-Encounter Stage is anti-Blackness. There are some Blacks for whom being Black is very important, not as a positive force but as a negative reference group. Blackness and Black people define their internal model of what they dislike. They look out upon Black people with a perspective that comes very close to what one might expect to find in the thinking of White racists. Anti-Black Blacks loathe other Blacks, feel alienated from them, and do not see Blacks or the Black community as a potential or actual source of personal support. Their vision of Blackness is dominated by negative, racist stereotypes; conversely, they may hold positive racial stereotypes of White people and White culture. In viewing Black people as their own worst enemy, anti-Black Blacks often explain the "race problem" through the prism of some variant of the "victim-blame perspective." When in positions of leadership, anti-Black Blacks can be very effective in weaving an ideology that bashes Black leaders, Black institutions, Black studies, the Black family, and Black culture.

Pre-Encounter covers a broad range of attitudes, from low salience to low salience/Blackness as stigma, to the extreme of anti-Blackness/self-hatred. These major attitudinal markers of Pre-Encounter may be fused, to one degree or another, with other Pre-Encounter characteristics: varying levels of miseducation, a Eurocentric cultural frame of reference, "spotlight" or "race image" anxiety, a race-conflict resolution model that stresses assimilation-integrationist objectives, and a value system that gives preference to non-Afrocentric priorities.

Miseducation

In being formally educated to embrace a Western cultural-historical perspective, Pre-Encounter Blacks cannot help experiencing varying degrees of miseducation about the significance of the Black experience. In fact, Pre-Encounter Blacks are frequently "average" products of a formal education system that is extremely monoracial and monocultural (i.e., White and Western dominated) in its emphasis. One reason Nigrescence is such a ubiquitous theme in the discourse on Black identity is that it is difficult for any Black American to progress through the public schools without being miseducated about the role of Africa in the origin of Western civilization and world culture, and the role of Blacks in the evolution of American culture and history in particular. This miseducation does not automatically lead to self-hatred, but it most certainly can distort the intra-Black discourse on Black cultural-historical issues and/or Black challenges and problems. Thus, Pre-Encounter

Blacks do not oppose Black studies because of some unconscious anti-Black or self-hatred complex; rather, their cultural bias blinds them to the fact that there are other histories besides "American history" and other cultural experiences besides those of "Western civilization." The most damning aspect of miseducation is not necessarily poor mental health, but the development of a worldview and cultural-historical perspective that can restrict one's knowledge about, and one's capacity to advocate, the cultural, political, economic, and historical interests of Black people.

Anti-Black Blacks suffer from the type of extreme miseducation that, in fact, does result in self-hatred. They tend to have a very distorted interpretation of Black history and a very distorted image of the historical, cultural, economic, and political potential of Black people. They believe that Black people came from a strange, uncivilized, "dark" continent and that slavery was a civilizing experience. From their vantage point, there is nothing to be gained from the study of the slavery period, because "real" Black history begins at the end of the Civil War. Among poor Blacks, anti-Black Blacks actually develop the belief that Blacks somehow deserve the misery that comes with poverty. Extreme miseducation can result in a great deal of skepticism about the abilities and capacities of Black leaders, Black businesses, and Black professionals and an equal degree of romanticization and near-mystification of the capacities and talents of Whites. That is, if Blacks are thought to be intellectually inferior and technologically backward, Whites are seen as intellectually superior and as possessing mystical technological powers.

Eurocentric Cultural Perspective

A further extension of the miseducation concept is that Pre-Encounter persons have frequently been socialized to favor a Eurocentric cultural perspective. It is a perspective in which notions of beauty and art are derived from a White and decidedly Western aesthetic, as reflected in the content, themes, vehicles of emphasis, colorations, and modes of expression of numerous cultural and academic preferences. Afrocentricists frequently interpret the Pre-Encounter person's preference for Western art as an expression of self-hatred, but this is an error. In rare instances, some Pre-Encounter Blacks have been raised in a manner that leaves them nearly ignorant of the existence of perspectives other than Eurocentric cultural perspectives. However, most Pre-Encounter persons have been socialized to be *bicultural:* That is, they know about, and sometimes appreciate, both Black and White artistic expressions. However, the low-salience person in particular is likely to give higher status to Western art. For example, Pre-Encounter parents tend to socialize their children to place greater emphasis on "high culture," or "classical art forms" (e.g., ballet, classical music, modern dance), and seldom encourage them to consider taking classes in jazz, African dance, or Black literature. Although Pre-Encounter persons may personally enjoy Black music and art, they may depict them as "ethnic," "lowly," "less important," and something to be lost along the way toward acceptance and assimilation into the mainstream. Thus, it is not always the case that Pre-Encounter/low-salience Blacks lack knowledge or experience with Black art; rather, what separates them from people in more advanced states of Blackness are the attitudes they hold toward Black art forms and the priority and preferences they accord Western versus Black art.

It is important to stress that there is nothing offensive or surprising in the fact that many Blacks socialized in a Western society, such as the United States, England, or France, learn to appreciate and become intensely involved in Western art forms. As is well known, some of today's greatest performers and advocates of Western music and culture are Black people and other people of color. In September 1988, I was present at the National Conference of the New York Philharmonic Music Assistance Fund Program, which was attended by practically every active and retired Black musician employed with an American classical orchestra. In preparation for the conference, a number of the musicians were interviewed about their career development, and my presentation at one of the sessions involved a summary of the key issues and themes that were reflected in their transcribed interviews. Time and again it was clear that the musicians had developed a dual aesthetic, and, more important, given the point being made here, their appreciation of European art was in no way a marker of their dislike of African American music (e.g., jazz). However, when the appreciation of one art form is used as a rationale to reject, neglect, or even bash the other, we have a problem, and that is often what happens at the level of Pre-Encounter, at which one's identification with European music and culture may be employed as a measure of one's cultural correctness.

Anti-Black Blacks take this to the extreme and wrongly put White and Black art on the same continuum, with White art defining that which is positive, rational, and highly developed, and Black art connoting that which is exotic, emotional, and primitive. Thus, classical music, ballet, and Western theater define "good art," whereas jazz, the blues, and African dance are seen as interesting but less well developed, if not primitive and inferior, imitations of (White) classical artistic expression. In its more vulgar expression, anti-Black Blacks may even prefer light skin, "straight" hair, and European facial features.

Finally, it would be a mistake to think that this is solely a "problem of the Black middle class." Even in the inner city or "ghetto," where purer forms of Black expression can readily be found, one discovers the inner-city resident referring to the blues or jazz as something low, bad, or sexy. Sometimes such descriptions capture the Black urban resident's notion of what is earthy, funky, and soulful, but other times the terms connote a pejorative perspective toward Black art, life, and culture. The attitude that "fine" and "good art" is Western can be found in Pre-Encounter persons of varied socioeconomic standings.

"Spotlight" or Race Image Anxiety

Most Black people, with the exception of those who are anti-Black in perspective, manage to keep from internalizing extremely negative stereotypes that racist Whites have of Black people. But although Pre-Encounter Blacks do not believe in these stereotypes, they are often overly sensitive to the fact that many White people do give credence to such images. This can lead to a hypersensitivity toward racial issues in which one is constantly on the lookout for the portrayal of (negative) Black stereotypes. As a positive adaptation, this sensitivity can help the person flush out instances of social discrimination and racism. However, there is also the irony that this "sensitivity" to discrimination and stereotypes can also lead to an anxiety over things being "too Black." Even though a Pre-Encounter person may be married to a Black person, and even though he or she may live in a Black community, there are times when he or she feels that a situation is too Black oriented or "not integrated enough." Things are thought to get out of hand when Blacks act too loud or disorderly. I refer to this anxiety about being too Black as "Spotlight anxiety." It is an anxiety felt when the person is in the company of Whites, or when the situation is somehow construed as placing one in the "spotlight." It is a concern that may not be revealed in informal, all-Black circumstances. In this sense, it is almost as if the person accepts as natural all-Black situations that are "informal," but becomes nervous about formal or organized and "public" all-Black efforts. When Whites are around, the person may check him- or herself to determine whether he or she, or some other Black who is present, is acting "too Black" and failing to project the best race image. Although a great deal of pain and sorrow can be associated with such behavior, Pre-Encounter Blacks may exhibit instances of "Amos 'n' Andy" type humor, twisting their language and actions to fit a contrived notion of appropriate (Black) behavior.

Anti-Black Blacks are beyond any anxiety about the race's image; for them, the negative stereotypes White people hold in reference to Blacks are truth. They feel enslaved in a body and community they hate. They feel nothing but a sense of imposition, alienation, and inferiority, and their sense of Blackness is clearly that of a mark of oppression.

Assimilation-Integration

In being socialized to see the system as adequate, in suffering various degrees of miseducation about the origin of Black problems, and in having a basic faith in the system, Pre-Encounter Blacks are predisposed to accept a victim-blame analysis of Black problems and a race-conflict resolution perspective that stresses assimilationist-integration themes. In this perspective it is felt that if Blacks could "overcome" their own "self-made" problems and become a part of the system, as they think previously disadvantaged (White ethnic) groups have done, the race problem could be resolved. The message is generally framed with greater sophistication when articulated by well-educated Pre-Encounter Blacks. White racism is viewed as a surface-level problem, one that exists alongside the basic strengths and race-neutral opportunity structures and culture of the society. Once Blacks have managed to work through discriminatory obstacles, the onus is on them to prepare themselves in a fashion that will lead to acceptance by Whites. The emphasis is on one-way change, in which Blacks learn to fit in, and Whites are asked simply to stop discriminating. No real demands are placed on White attitudes, White culture, and White institutions, because, as stated previously, racism is thought to be a surface-level problem. Consequently, instead of having pluralistic notions of integration or concepts of multiculturalism, the Pre-Encounter Black is often wedded to an assimilationist vision of race-conflict resolution and social mobility. In fact, Pre-Encounter Blacks may oppose pluralistic and multicultural education as unnecessary, wasteful, remedial, or "inferior."

Value Structure and Value Orientation

In my original model I stressed that Pre-Encounter Blacks have radically different value structures (individualism versus communalism) and orientations (low versus high salience on Blackness) as compared to Blacks in the advanced stages. However, I now believe that although they hold radically different value orientations, Pre-Encounter persons do not necessary differ in their value structures from persons in advanced stages of Black identity development. People in Pre-Encounter often have affiliations with various secular, political, and religious organizations, and they have been known to demonstrate tremendous commitment and even militant dedication to certain issues, beliefs, and causes that go beyond merely thinking about oneself. These are the attributes I originally associated with Stage 4 or 5. In other words, the difference between persons at either extreme of the process, insofar as values are concerned, may not be at the level of value structure but at the level of value orientation. Pre-Encounter persons place priority on organizations and causes that have low race salience and or little nationalistic import, and Blacks who are deeper into Nigrescence stress activities and organizations for which race and Black culture are highly salient. However, at the value structure level of analysis, Pre-Encounter Blacks may be no less communalistic or more individualistic than Blacks in other stages.

Summary

Whether of the low-salience or anti-Black variety, the spectrum of Pre-Encounter attitudes and worldviews transcends social class boundaries. Class status may affect how Pre-Encounter attitudes are expressed, but the generic messages, priorities, or preferences embedded in both middle- and lower class Black expressions are generally equivalent. Thus, low salience can be found in both a middle-class Black professional for whom Blackness has little meaning and an inner-city resident whose primary vehicle for meaning and purpose in life is the Christian Church. At the more negative extreme of Pre-Encounter, the anti-Black Black can be the middle-class Black youth who has joined the ranks of a White-dominated, punk street group or the inner-city youth who, as a member of a "Black" street gang, pushes dope on other Black kids.

Pre-Encounter-oriented people can be rich or poor, light skinned or of ebony hue, living in Vermont or in Harlem, attending overwhelmingly White schools or all-Black institutions. The socialization of Pre-Encounter attitudes in Black people covers a multitude of situations and circumstances. As is the case with all the stages, Pre-Encounter is an attitude or perspective, not an inherited or divinely ordained trait, and people who come to share the same Pre-Encounter-oriented racial/cultural frame of reference do so through a variety of social experiences and circumstances, inclusive of instances of both success and oppression.

It would be a mistake to presume that Pre-Encounter is a form of mental illness. Although anti-Black Blacks may very well evidence poor mental health, the great majority of Pre-Encounter Blacks are probably as mentally healthy as Blacks in the more advanced stages of Nigrescence. The key factors that separate Pre-Encounter Blacks from those who are Afrocentric are not mental illness, but value orientation, historical perspective, and worldview. The complexity of the American economy means that there are all sorts of ecological niches within which Blacks are socialized, and each of these niches may support the growth of very particularistic worldviews, many of which are not framed by a racial or Afrocentric perspective. Pre-Encounter Blacks are part of the diversity of the Black experience and must be understood as such.

On the other hand, whenever life circumstances result in the social production of a Black person for whom "race" has limited personal salience or, in the case of the anti-Black Black, extremely negative personal salience, the scene has been set for a possible identity conversion experience.

Stage 2: Encounter

In most instances, the Pre-Encounter identity is the person's first identity, that is, the identity shaped by early development. This socialization involved years of experiences with one's family, extended family, neighborhood and community, and schools, covering the periods of childhood, adolescence, and early adulthood. It is a tried and fully tested identity that serves the person day in and day out. It helps the person feel centered, meaningful, and in control by making life predictable. Although we can tolerate and even come to enjoy a certain degree of change and variety in our external environment, it is almost impossible to imagine a world in which, at the beginning of each day, each person has to reconstruct his or her identity. Consequently, the predictability and stability functions of one's identity serve as filters against rapid and dramatic identity change. The person's identity filters incoming experiences so that the information "fits" into his or her current understanding of him- or herself and the world in which he or she lives. Therefore, any fully developed identity, let alone a Pre-Encounter identity, is difficult to change. Stage 2 of the Nigrescence process pinpoints circumstances and events that are likely to induce identity metamorphosis.

Because the person's ongoing identity will defend against identity change, the person usually has to experience some sort of encounter that has the effect of "catching the person off guard." The encounter must work around, slip through, or shatter the relevance of the person's current identity and worldview and, at the same time, provide some hint of the path the person must follow in order to be resocialized and transformed.

In many instances, it is not a single event that constitutes a person's encounter, but a series of smaller, eye-opening episodes, each of which chips away at the person's ongoing worldview. These small encounters have a cumulative effect: At a certain point, something happens to "break the camel's back," so to speak, and the person feels pushed toward Nigrescence.

If we look at the encounter more closely, we see that it entails two steps: first experiencing the encounter and then personalizing it. By this two-step analysis, I mean to split a hair. That is to say, one must make the distinction between being in the path or being the object of an encounter event or activity and actually personalizing it or being "turned around by it." An encounter must personally affect the individual in a powerful way. In the course of a year, let alone a lifetime, just about every Black person is exposed to information or some sort of racist situation that has the potential of an "encounter," but unless the person, for whatever reason, personalizes the encounter, his or her ongoing worldview or attitudes about "race" may go unchallenged. One last point: The encounter need not be negative, as in the case of a racist event; it may, instead, revolve around exposure to powerful cultural-historical information about the Black experience previously unknown to the person. Giving credence to (i.e., personalizing) this information may challenge the person to radically rethink his or her conception of Black history and Black culture. Even in such instances, however, a negative flavor to the encounter is often introduced, for it is almost inevitable that the person will quickly become enraged at the thought of having been previously miseducated by White racist institutions.

Although an encounter may eventually steer the person toward Nigrescence, the person's initial reaction may be one of confusion, alarm, anomie, and even depression. It can be a very painful experience to discover that one's frame of reference, worldview, or value system is "wrong," "incorrect," "dysfunctional," or, more to the point, "not Black or Afrocentric enough." However, such reactions are generally temporary. Somehow the person picks him- or herself up and begins to cautiously, and perhaps even fearfully, test the validity of his or her new perceptions. On the outside, the person is generally very quiet, but internally, a storm is brewing. The person will seek out new information or attend meetings in order to assess whether he or she should submit to metamorphosis.

The encounter brings with it a great deal of emotionality, and guilt, anger, and general anxiety may become energizing factors. The middle-class person may feel guilty for having denied the significance of race; the lower class person may feel guilt and shame for having degraded Blackness through street hustle and exploitation. Simultaneously, the person, regardless of class background, feels angry at those who are perceived as having "caused" his or her predicament—White people and all the White world. Furthermore, each person feels anxious at the discovery that there is another level of Blackness to which he or she should aspire. Inner-directed guilt, rage at White people, and the anxiety about becoming the right kind of Black person combine to form a psychic fuel or energy that powers the person into a frantic, determined, obsessive, extremely motivated search for Black identity. The Pre-Encounter person or "Negro" is dying, and the "Black American" or "Afrocentric" person is beginning to emerge.

Stage 3: Immersion-Emersion

The Immersion-Emersion stage addresses the most sensational aspects of Black identity development, for it represents the vortex of psychological Nigrescence. There is nothing subtle about this stage, and for good reason. It is during this period of transition that the person begins to demolish the "old" perspective, while simultaneously trying to construct what will become his or her new frame of reference. In moving from the Encounter to the Immersion-Emersion stage, the person has not changed; rather, he or she has merely made the decision to commit him- or herself to personal change. Consequently, upon entrance into the Immersion-Emersion stage, the person is more familiar with the identity to be destroyed than the one to be embraced. Because the person no longer wants to be governed by that which is most familiar—the self to be destroyed—the boundaries and essence of the old self are truncated, collapsed, and codified in very pejorative terms, images, and emotions. Any value or complexity once associated with the "old self" is now denied and made to appear useless. Yet the person is unfamiliar with the new self, for that is exactly what the person hopes to become. In effect, the new convert lacks knowledge about the complexity and texture of the new identity; consequently, he or she is forced to erect simplistic, glorified, highly romantic and speculative images of what he or she assumes the new self will be like. This state of "in-betweenness" can cause the person to be very anxious about whether he or she is becoming "the right kind of Black person." The person is in need of rather immediate and clear-cut markers that he or she is progressing in the right direction. This is why new converts are so attracted to symbols of the new identity (dress codes, hairstyles, flags, national colors, etc.), code phrases, "party lines," "ten-point programs," rigid ideologies, and either/or frames of analysis. It is a paradox of social change that the most dramatic displays of the new Black image are often exhibited by those who are the least at ease with the new identity (Cross et al., 1995). Framing the entire transition is a very dichotomized view of the world in which all that is White becomes evil, oppressive, inferior, and inhuman, and all things Black are declared superior—even in a biogenetic sense. If the absence of melanin is for White racists the marker of White superiority, during Nigrescence the inverse is true, and the presence of melanin becomes the marker of Black superiority. This demonizing of White people and White culture is often a major preoccupation of new converts. With this overview in mind, we can now follow the person through each step of the transition period.

Immersion

During the first phase of Immersion-Emersion stage, the person immerses him- or herself in the world of Blackness. The person attends political or cultural meetings that focus on Black issues, joins new organizations, drops membership in "Pre-Encounter" oriented groups, goes to Black rapping sessions, and attends seminars and art shows that focus on Blackness or Afrocentricity. Everything of value must be Black or relevant to Africanity, for the person is being swept along by "a sea of Blackness." The experience is an immersion into Blackness and a liberation from Whiteness. Phenomenologically, the person perceives him- or herself as being uprooted from the old self while drawn into a qualitatively different experience. This immersion is a strong, powerful, dominating sensation that is constantly being energized by rage (at White people and culture), guilt (at having once been tricked into thinking Negro ideas), and a developing sense of pride (in one's Black self, Black people, and Black culture). Superhuman and supernatural expectations are conjured concerning anything Black. The person accepts his or her hair and brown skin, and his or her very being is now "beautiful." That the person exists and is Black is an inherently wonderful thing. The person may spend a great deal of time developing an African and/or Black "urban" hairstyle, and such concerns are carried over to the person's style of dress. Converts give themselves African names or drop their "American" names, as did Malcolm X, and progeny are named after African heroes. Of course, an intense interest in "Mother Africa" becomes evident, and this is especially true of persons associated with the more contemporary variant of Nigrescence, the Afrocentricity movement. The label *Negro* is dropped as a self-referent, and preference is given to *Black*, *Black American*, *African American*, or *African*.

Black literature is passionately consumed, and in some instances people who never before had an interest in reading teach themselves to read and write. In fact, their new orientation causes them to process all types of information that focus on the Black and African experience (film, press, radio). In a related development, a person or group may decide that a new periodical, journal, newsletter, or television program is needed and may try to produce a new information outlet that does justice to the emerging Black/Afrocentric perspective. Like the Negritude movement in Africa, the American-based Afrocentric movement has resulted in an explosion in articles, books, newsletters, at least two journals, and, of course, any number of new organizations.

The new convert's attention may be drawn to issues other than political ones, and during the Immersion-Emersion stage, some may experience a creative burst in which they feel "driven" to write poetry, essays, plays, rap songs, novels, or literary "confessionals." A segment may turn to the plastic arts or painting. People who never before sought or experienced creative activity discover that they are able to express themselves in a totally new mode. Established artists speak of a radical shift in the direction of their art, as happened to LeRoi Jones (Imamu Amiri Baraka), Gwendolyn Brooks, and Don L. Lee (Haki Mutabiti). In explaining this change, these artists state that although they were born to a Black situation, their overall socialization and artistic training caused them to look for inspiration and content outside the Black experience. For example, some wanted to be "pure" and "free," creating art for art's sake, and others admitted that their artistic sensibility was once decidedly Eurocentric. With the realization of their Blackness, they were awakened to a vast and new world of rich colors, powerful dramas, irony, rage, oppression, survival, and impossible dreams!—and it is all there, within reach; the artist (or scholar) has simply to look in the mirror (those familiar with the Black 1960s will recall that the Black arts movement was one of the most powerful reflectors of Black identity change, as is equally true of today's Afrocentric movement).

Of course, the inspirational aspects of Nigrescence go beyond the world of Black art, and countless scholars from the 1960s have testified to the fact that the focus of their scholarly activities was radically transformed by what they learned and experienced from the Black movement. Such efforts continue today in the shaping and refinement of the Afrocentric movement, which is struggling to articulate a new frame of reference from which to approach the study of Black life in Africa and America.

During the immersion phase of Stage 3, the discourse between Black artists and scholars is generally guided by an aesthetic or analytic frame that incorporates values, methodologies, and interpretive schemes thought to be the exact opposite of those found in White art and scholarship. This belief is not so much explicated as declared. In speeches, papers, and articles offered by new converts, an inordinate amount of attention may be given to the description of what the new Blackness is not, whereas what it is may simply be affirmed and given little analysis. Later, when the convert has moved beyond the emotionality of early conversion, substantive and even radical concepts about Black (African) and White (European) history, culture, politics, and so forth may be discovered, researched, confirmed, and refined, but early attempts are too often laden with blatantly racist concepts.

For new converts, confrontation, bluntness, directness, and an either/or mentality may be the primary mode of communications with other people, Black or White. This communication style is associated with the much discussed "Blacker-than-thou" syndrome. As a prelude to passing judgment on whether a person has the "appropriate level of Blackness," the convert classifies Black people into neat groups or categories such as "Uncle Tom," "militant," or "Eurocentric" versus "Afrocentric," "together," "soulful," "middle-class," or "intellectual snob." Labeling and passing judgment on others help the person clarify his or her own identity, but this name calling, with its attendant ideological fractionation, can produce disastrous results, as in the California Black Panther versus "US" murders of the 1960s or the well-documented split between Malcolm X and the Nation of Islam. The more contemporary variant of Blacker-than-thou comes from the Afrocentricity movement, in which some converts see themselves as "more Afrocentric than others." They often describe Blacks who disagree with their perspective as insane, crazy, mentally ill, confused, unreliable, dangerous, and incapable of making a positive contribution to Black life. Often such converts mean well, as they merely seek the means of promoting greater consensus within the Black world, but their zeal for ideological "correctness" can lead to coercive, fascist tactics.

The name calling and Blacker-than-thou propensities are all part of the new convert's anxiety that his or her Blackness be "pure and acceptable." We can refer to this anxiety as *Weusi* anxiety. *Weusi* is the Swahili word for "Black," and *Weusi* anxiety is the anxiety the new convert experiences about being or becoming Black enough. Should the person be left to his or her own devices to work out all aspects of the identity crisis, such anxiety could lead to considerable personal chaos. Generally this is not the case, as most converts will seek and find the social support of others by joining certain organizations and groups. The groups joined provide a counterculture to the identity being replaced (the "Negro" or non-Afrocentric identity) by entangling the person in membership requirements, symbolic dress codes, rites, rituals, obligations, and reward systems that nurture and reinforce the emerging "new" (Black or Afrocentric) identity. This can lead to a great deal of conformity on the part of the new recruit. In fact, it is one of the paradoxes of conversion that while rebelling against the larger society, the new convert may willingly conform to a number of the demands of certain Black organizations. Again, we should keep in mind that the person's new identity is still emerging and has not been internalized; consequently, the person is anxious to be put in a position that allows him or her to demonstrate, in some fashion, that he or she is developing into the "right kind" of Black person.

Much that goes into the demonstration of one's level of Blackness takes place within the confines and privacy of Black organizations. The central themes of the Immersion-Emersion stage involve turning inward into Black-ness and withdrawing from everything perceived as being, or representing, the White world. Yet ironically, there also develops a need to confront the "man" as a means of dramatizing, concretizing, or proving one's Blackness. The con-frontation, especially for Black leaders, is a manhood (or womanhood) ritual— a baptismal or purification rite. Carried to its extreme, the impulse is to confront White people in authority, frequently the police, on a life-or-death basis. When this impulse is coupled with a revolutionary rhetoric or program, a paramilitary organization such as the Black Panthers may spring forth. For such people, no control or oppressive technique—including the threat of death—is feared. Consequently, Brothers and Sisters dream about or give a heavy rap about the need for physical combat, but daydreams and rhetoric are about as far as it goes. On the other hand, when warlike fantasies are in fact turned into participation in a paramilitary group such as the Black Panthers, the dreams of combat are sometimes actualized in the execution of planned attacks on the police. Far more often, however, Black paramilitary groups take on a defensive, provocative, ambivalent, "I dare you whitey" stance.

Most converts do not get involved with paramilitary activities. Instead, the episodes of hatred they may feel toward Whites during the Immersion-Emersion stage are worked through as daydreams or fantasies, such as the urge to rip off the first White person one passes on a particular day. During Immersion-Emersion, "Kill whitey" fantasies appear to be experienced by Blacks, regardless of age, sex, or class background. Persons who fixate or stagnate at this point in their development are said to have a "pseudo" Black identity based on the hatred and negation of White people rather than the affirmation of a pro-Black perspective, which includes commitment to the destruction of racism but not the random killing of Whites.

Finally, we note that during this transition period, the person experiences a surge in altruism. A constant theme of selflessness, dedication, and commitment to the (Black) group is evident; the person feels overwhelming love and attachment to all that is Black. The person's main focus in life becomes this feeling of "togetherness and oneness with the people." It is a religious-like feeling, and clusters of new converts can create an atmosphere in which Blackness or Africanity has a spiritual and religious quality.

Emersion

The first part of this transition stage is immersion into Blackness, an experience in which the person feels almost driven and compelled to act, think, and feel in a certain way. People are not "out of control" during immersion, but they often look back upon the episode as something akin to a "happening," as if Blackness were an outside force or spirit that was permeating, if not invading, their being. The second part of the stage is *emergence* from the emotionality and dead-end, either/or, racist, and oversimplified ideological aspects of the immersion experience. The person begins to "level off" and feel in control of his or her emotions and intellect. In fact, the person cannot continue to handle the intense emotional phases and concentrated affect levels associated with conversion and is predisposed to find ways to level off.

Frequently, this leveling off is facilitated by a combination of the person's own growth in conjunction with the person's observation that certain role models or heroes appear to be operating from the vantage point of a more advanced state of identity development. The first hint of this advanced state may be discovered during face-to-face interactions with role models who evidence a calmer, more sophisticated quality to their Blackness, or the person may infer it from having read *The Autobiography of Malcolm X*, in which Malcolm depicts moving beyond a rigid sense of Blackness as a consequence of his experiences in Mecca. The story of how one gets over the stage of Immersion is likely to differ from person to person, but however it occurs, it results in the discovery that one's first impressions of Blackness can be romantic and symbolic, rather than substantive, textured, and complex. In fact, the person may find him- or herself pulling away from membership in organizations whose activities seem designed to "help one feel immersed in Blackness" and toward memberships in, and associations with, groups or persons who are demonstrating a "more serious" understanding of, and commitment to, Black issues. When the grip of the immersion phase loosens, when the convert begins to comprehend immersion as a period of transition rather than an end state, and when the convert seems to understand that continued growth, perhaps of a less emotional nature, lies ahead, he or she has reached the end of the transition stage and is moving toward internalization of the new identity.

Negative Consequences of Transition

The previous paragraph depicts a person headed toward continued identity development. We should understand, however, that the volatility of the transition stage can very well result in regression, fixation, or stagnation as well as forward movement. The events of the Immersion-Emersion stage can inspire or frustrate an individual. Consequently, the degree of a person's continued involvement in Black affairs may prove significant or negligible. During the transition stage, the person embraces idealistic, if not superhuman, expectations about anything Black, in which case minimal reinforcement (when you are attracted to something, it does not take a great deal of reinforcement to sustain that interest) may carry the person over into advanced identity development (evolution into the next stage). On the other hand, prolonged or traumatic frustration and contesting of these expectancies may break the person's spirit and desire to change, in which case regression becomes a real possibility. For others, intense and negative encounters with White racists lead to their becoming fixated at Stage 3. In still a third scenario, people may give all the appearance of having grown beyond the boundaries of the Immersion-Emersion stage—that is, their behavior and attitudes suggest a great deal of internalization of the new identity—but for reasons that are not very clear, they cease involvement in the Black struggle. In effect, they "drop out." Let us examine more closely these three, more negative possibilities before moving on to a description of a person who internalizes the new identity and shows evidence of continued commitment to the struggle.

Regression. It bears repeating that the Immersion-Emersion stage is a period of transition, during which the old identity is at war with an emerging, new identity. Should a person's overall experience be negative and nonreinforcing to growth toward the new identity, he or she may become disappointed and choose to reject Blackness. With this choice, the pressure to change will sub-side, and the pull and grip of the old identity will reconstitute itself, resulting in regression toward the Pre-Encounter self-concept. Not only may the person reembrace the old, but he or she may do so with considerable enthusiasm, becoming almost reactionary in his or her disappointment with, and opposition to, the "Blackness" thing.

Continuation/Fixation at Stage 3. Individuals who experience particularly painful perceptions and confrontations will be overwhelmed with hate for White people and fixate at Stage 3. Even should they progress beyond the emotionalism of Stage 3, they may lock on to some variant of the "whitey as devil" philosophy. Distracting rage and hatred may be more a problem with Black people on the front lines of the most brutal and blatant forms of racism and poverty (life in the inner city and remote sectors of the rural South), whereas those who can move in and out of oppressive Black situations or who have greater access to insights that point to more progressive attitudes (college students, the Black middle class, Black scholars, securely employed working-class Blacks, etc.) will tend to escape the debilitating effects of reactionary hatred. The United States' recent swing to the radical right has provided fertile psychological soil for reactionary Black identities, ideologies, and organizations. More recently, Blacks of this persuasion have become totally exasperated with White America's willingness to allow the never-ending growth of the Black underclass, and for them, such White attitudes of neglect reflect an implicit, if not explicit, policy of genocide. Of course, Black reactionaries deny the historical and contemporary contributions of White progressives and White radicals, choosing to see any and all "Black" issues through the lens of a monoracial perspective.

Dropping Out. Another response to the Immersion-Emersion experience is "dropping out" of involvement with Black issues. The person does not regress to Pre-Encounter attitudes, as in the earlier example; in fact, the person may exhibit signs of having internalized the new Black identity (the concept of internalization will be discussed shortly). There seem to be two types of dropping out. In the first, the person seems exhausted by it all, perhaps seeing the "race problem" as insurmountable and without solution. Such persons may reengage with the race question at a later date, but for the time being, they withdraw from the discourse on race. In extreme cases, the person may become depressed and suffer from anomie. If the person enters Nigrescence with a vulnerable and unstable general personality, and the metamorphosis is particularly problematic and stressful, the person may experience a mental break-down. On the other hand, there are other, more psychologically healthy persons who drop out because, having achieved a "feel-good" attitude about their own personal, private, internal sense of Blackness, they move on to what they perceive are more important issues in life. They often refer to their Nigrescence experience as their "ethnicity phase."

Stage 4: Internalization

By working through the challenges and problems of the transition period, the person internalizes the new identity, which now evidences itself in naturalistic ways in the everyday psychology of the person. For the settled convert, the new identity gives high salience to Blackness, with the degree of salience being determined by ideological considerations. At one extreme are certain nationalists whose concern for race leaves little room for other considerations, but for others, Blackness becomes one of several (biculturalism) or many (multiculturalism) saliencies. From a psychodynamic point of view, the internalized identity seems to perform three dynamic functions in the everyday life of a person: (a) to defend and protect a person from psychological insults that stem from having to live in a racist society, (b) to provide a sense of belonging and social anchorage, and (c) to provide a foundation or point of departure for carrying out transactions with people, cultures, and human situations beyond the world of Blackness.

Internalization is not likely to signal the end of a person's concern with Nigrescence, for as one progresses across the life span, new challenges (i.e., new encounters) may bring about the need to re-cycle through some of the stages (Encounter through Internalization). Finally, the successful resolution of one's racial identity conflicts makes it possible for the person to shift attention to other identity concerns such as religion, gender and sexual preference, career development, social class and poverty, and multiculturalism.

Key Markers of Internalization

If Encounter and Immersion-Emersion usher in cognitive dissonance and its accompanying rollercoaster emotionality, then the Internalization stage marks the point of dissonance resolution, and the reconstitution of the person's steady-state personality and cognitive style. The person feels calmer, more relaxed, and more at ease with him- or herself. An inner peace is achieved, as *Weusi* anxiety (tension over being the right kind of Black person) is transformed into *Weusi* pride (Black pride) and *Weusi* self-acceptance (Black self-acceptance). The shift is from concern about how the person's friends see him or her ("Am I Black enough?"), to confidence in personal standards of Blackness; from uncontrolled rage toward White people, to controlled anger at oppressive systems and racist institutions; from symbolic, boisterous rhetoric, to serious analysis and "quiet" strength; from unrealistic urgency that can lead to dropping out, to a sense of destiny that enables one to sustain long-term commitment; from anxious, insecure, rigid, pseudo-Blackness based on the hatred of Whites, to proactive Black pride, self-love, and a deep sense of connection to, and acceptance by, the Black community.

In being habituated and internalized, Blackness becomes a backdrop for life's transactions. It can be taken for granted, freeing the person to concentrate on issues that presuppose a basic identification with Blackness. One *is* Black;

thus one is free to ponder matters beyond the parameters of one's personal sense of Blackness (organizational development, community development, problem solving, conflict resolution, institution building, etc.).

One of the most important consequences of this inner peace is that the person's conception of Blackness tends to become more open, expansive, and sophisticated. As general defensiveness fades, simplistic thinking and simple solutions become transparently inadequate, and the full complexity and inherent texture of the Black condition mark the point of departure for serious analysis.

Phenomenologically, the person perceives him- or herself to be totally changed, with both a new worldview and a revitalized personality. However, research findings show that Nigrescence tends to change the group identity or reference group component of the Black self-concept more than it does one's general personality. The person's personality is most certainly put under stress during Immersion-Emersion, and there is a great deal of emotionality associated with conversion, but with Internalization and the easing of internal psychological stress, the basic core of the person's personality is reestablished. For example, if a person was an effective (or ineffective) leader at Pre-Encounter, his or her leadership profile will go unchanged at Internalization. Likewise, this pattern is likely to be replicated in countless other examples: shy at Pre-Encounter, shy at Internalization; outgoing and gregarious at Pre-Encounter, outgoing and gregarious at Internalization; introverted and mildly uncomfortable around large groups at Pre-Encounter, introverted and uncomfortable in groups at Internalization; calm, rational, and deliberate at Pre-Encounter, calm, rational, and deliberate at Internalization; anxious and neurotic at Pre-Encounter, anxious and neurotic at Internalization; relatively normal and well balanced at Pre-Encounter, relatively normal and well balanced at Internalization. In fact, research suggests that during Immersion-Emersion, one's basic personality strengths act as a psychological cushion or relative backdrop of stability for the intense struggle taking place within the group identity level of the Black self-concept (conversely, personality weaknesses may make Nigrescence more stressful to the person, although the point being made here is that successful completion of Nigrescence rides on whatever are the person's extant personality strengths). At Internalization, when the dissonance surrounding reference group and worldview change has been resolved, the person is able to fall back on his or her basic personality attributes, which, though the person was greatly stressed, perturbed, and excited during Immersion-Emersion, helped him or her negotiate the group identity change in the first place.

For the fraction of people who were anti-Black at Pre-Encounter, Nigrescence may enhance their general level of self-esteem, but again, the person's characteristic personality attributes, beyond self-esteem, are likely to remain the same. As a form of social therapy, Nigrescence is extremely effective at changing the salience of race and culture in a person's life; however, it is not a process that lends itself to change in deep-structure personality dynamics.

What makes the person feel completely "new" are the changes experienced at the level of reference group orientation. In moving from Pre-Encounter to Internalization, the person has moved from a frame of reference in which race and culture had low salience to one characterized by high salience of Blackness in everyday life. With this change in salience comes membership in new organizations and changes in one's social network, one's manner of dress and personal appearance, one's self-referents, what one reads or views on television, how one socializes one's children, one's internal image of the capacity and efficacy of Blacks as a group, one's cultural and artistic preferences, one's historical and cultural perspective, the causes and social problems that engage one's activism, and perhaps even one's name. These types of changes define what is important in *adult life,* and that is why the person feels totally new. Left unnoticed to the person is the fact that his or her basic personality profile is the same as it was during Pre-Encounter.

Salience and Ideology

Although advanced Black identity development results in the person's giving high salience to issues of race and culture, not every person in Internalization shares the same degree of salience for Blackness, for this is likely to be determined by the nature of one's ideology. Persons who construct a strong nationalistic framework from their Immersion-Emersion experiences may continue along this ideological path at Internalization, whereas others may derive a far less nationalistic stance. The former can lead to total salience of Blackness, and the latter to less salience. For example, vulgar nationalists (persons who believe that Blacks and Whites are biogenetically different, with Blacks being of "superior" racial stock and Whites being an "inferior" mutation of Black stock) and traditional nationalists (persons who frame their nationalistic perspective with other than biogenetic constructs) may focus on race and culture in ways that in some instances border on the obsessive. The traditional nationalist presents the most healthy alternative, in that his or her frame of reference is subject to rational analysis and debate, whereas the vulgar nationalist's reactionary racism, which is usually steeped in an odd mixture of pseudoscientific myths, historical distortions, and outright mysticism, is beyond the pale of normal discourse. Although vulgar and traditional nationalists are African Americans by history and culture, both tend to stress the singularity of their cultural emphasis; in some instances, they may even deny that there is anything American or Eurocentric about their being. In this sense, their internalized Black nationalist identity, though far more sophisticated than the version espoused during Immersion-Emersion, carries with it, to varying degrees, themes of conflict on how to relate to the other half of their cultural-historical makeup.

Other Blacks reaching Internalization derive a bicultural reference group orientation from their Nigrescence experience. From their vantage point, Internalization is a time for working through and incorporating into their self-concept the realities of their Blackness as well as the enigmatic, paradoxical, advantageous, and supportive aspects of their Americanness. I especially like the way the Nigrescence theorist Bailey Jackson (1976) addresses this point:

> The individual [in Stage 4] also has a new sense of the American culture. The person is able to identify and own those aspects of the American culture that are acceptable (e.g., material possessions, financial security, independence, etc.) and stand against those aspects which are toxic (racism, sexism, war, imperialism, and other forms of oppression). The ownership of the acceptable aspects of the American culture does not preclude or override the ownership of Black culture. (p. 62)

Taking this a step further, others may embrace a *multicultural* perspective, in which case their concern for Blackness is shared with a multiplicity of cultural interests and saliencies. Consequently, the cultural identity of the Stage 4 person can vary from the monocultural orientation of the extreme nationalist to the identity mosaic of the multiculturally oriented Black person. Each ideological stance incorporates certain strengths and weaknesses, and there are times when the holders of one perspective may find themselves at odds with those who share another variant of Blackness. This means that Nigrescence may increase the salience of race and culture for all persons who successfully reach the advanced stages of Black identity development, but Internalization does not result in ideological unity. One can look upon this variability as ideological fractionation or as healthy ideological diversity.

Internalization and the Total Identity Matrix

The work of Internalization does not stop with the resolution of conflicts surrounding one's racial/cultural identity. Borrowing again from Bailey Jackson, we note that he believes Nigrescence should be viewed as a process during which a single dimension of a person's complex, layered identity is first isolated, for purposes of revitalization and transformation, and then, at Internalization, reintegrated into the person's total identity matrix:

> For the person who sees him/herself as a Black only or to view his/her Blackness completely separate from the other aspects of the person is seen as a dysfunctional fragmentation of self. While recognizing the necessity for the separation of the person's Blackness from other parts of him/herself in earlier stages as a strategy for making sense of that aspect of self, the person now needs to complete the developmental process by internalizing and synthesizing this new sense of Blackness. (Jackson, 1976, p. 42)

Jackson sees Internalization as the balancing and synthesis of Blackness with the other demands of one's personhood, such as one's sexual identity, occupational identity, spiritual or religious identity, and various role identities, aspects of which may be very race sensitive or, in other instances, race neutral.

Psychodynamics of Internalized Blackness

When discussing difficult social concepts, it is often helpful to vary one's approach. With this in mind, a slightly different perspective of the Internalized identity is revealed when one seeks an answer to the following question: "How does the internalized identity function in daily life?" That is to say, what psychodynamic functions evolve during Nigrescence, and how does each functional mode operate in everyday life? In a generic sense, one's identity is a cognitive maze or map that functions in a multitude of ways to guide and direct exchanges with one's social and material realities. Of course, Blacks function in two worlds, one Black and one White, and, as implied by our earlier commentary, this means that some of the identity functions and operations that are found in Blacks are no different from those that are evident in most Americans. On the other hand, the unique or "Blackness" part of Black identity (Cross, 1985; Cross et al., 1991) tends to perform three distinctive functions in everyday Black life: (a) to defend the person from negative psychological stress resulting from having to live in a society that, at times, can be very racist; (b) to provide a sense of purpose, meaning, and affiliation; and (c) to provide psychological mechanisms that facilitate social intercourse with people, cultures, and human situations located outside the boundaries of Blackness. A person may acquire these functions over the course of being socialized from childhood through early adulthood if his or her parents or caretakers have strong Black identities. Otherwise, the functions may unfold as part of his or her *resocialization* during Nigrescence. Let us take a closer look at each functional mode.

The Defensive Functions of Black Identity. Recall that people in the Pre-Encounter stage often give low salience to issues of race and Black culture and, in addition, may play down the existence of racism, so that they are psychologically unprepared to deal with racist situations. During Nigrescence, one of the first functional modes to evolve is the defensive or protective function of Blackness, which operates to provide a psychological buffer when the person encounters racist circumstances, especially those of a psychological nature (obviously, a psychological defense would be inadequate in the face of the threat of violence). In its most crude manifestation, during Immersion-Emersion, a siege mentality may be present in which the person sees all White people as racist dogs and all White institutions as racist to the core. The person is hypersensitive to racism and is "protected" by simply writing off all contact with Whites.

At the Internalization stage, the defensive function becomes much more sophisticated and flexible. Instead of the iron shield of Immersion-Emersion, it becomes a translucent filter that is often "invisible" or undetectable, allowing the person to process nonthreatening information and experiences without distortion. It seems to involve (a) an *awareness* that racism is a part of the American experience; (b) an *anticipatory set* recognizing that regardless of one's station in American society, one could well be the target of racism; (c) well-developed *ego defenses* that the person can employ when confronted with racism; (d) a *system-blame and personal efficacy orientation* in which the person is predisposed to find fault in the circumstances and not in the self; and (e) a *religious orientation* that prevents the development of a sense of bitterness and the need to demonize Whites.

The first two factors represent the heart of the protective capacity, for it is impossible to defend against something whose existence is denied or minimized. If one sees oneself as a special Negro who is beyond the reach of racism, then one will hardly be in a position to anticipate being the target of a racist. For a person with a Black identity and a well-developed defensive mode, racism is a given, and one understands that one may well be the focus of racism. The third factor refers to the behavioral and attitudinal repertoire one can employ in negotiating racist situations (withdrawal, assertion, counter-aggression, passivity, avoidance, etc.). The stronger, more mature, and more varied one's ego defenses, the greater one's capacity to handle a variety of racist configurations. Because Blacks frequently find themselves living in poor and degrading circumstances, the fourth factor helps one to maintain a sense of perspective and personal worth in the face of the stress that accompanies racism. In this way, the person is able to distinguish between that which is an extension of one's self-concept (what one deserves and what should be given credit), and that which is a reflection of the racist and oppressive system within which one must endure, survive, and struggle. Finally, the fifth factor, the spiritual and religious one, helps the person avoid becoming embittered and filled with hatred toward Whites. This is important because time and again, hatred originally directed toward Whites spills over and poisons aspects of Black-on-Black relationships. In a sense, the focus is kept on racism, as a form of human evil, rather than the demonization of White people, with its attendant hopelessness (one cannot negotiate with something perceived as the devil).

The defensive mode helps one to deal with the "hassle" of being Black. It operates to minimize the hurt, pain, imposition, and stigma that come when one is treated with disrespect, rudeness, and insensitivity. The defensive mode allows the person to maintain control and avoid overreacting, rather than being unduly hurt and caught off guard, so that he or she is able to pay more attention to who and what is instigating the problem.

There are two extremes to this modality (Cross et al., 1991). In one, the person may underplay the importance of racism, in which case the defensive function will be inadequately developed, and the person's identity will provide little protection against racism. In the other, the person may be overly sensitive or even paranoiac, "seeing" racism where it does not exist.

The Reference Group Functions of Black Identity. Most if not all human beings need to feel wanted, connected, accepted, and affiliated, although the group or groups from which one may derive a sense of well-being need not be those to which one is normally ascribed. As a case in point, many Blacks derive their sense of connection and affiliation from groups that have little to do with a nationalist or Black identity. Thus some Blacks gain personal fulfillment and happiness from being Christians, lawyers, doctors, gamblers, police officers, gays, or believers in obscure cults. Such people cannot be said to have a Black identity, because their sense of personal well-being is anchored in something other than their Blackness.

Having a Black identity means that the reference group functions of one's identity are grounded in one's Blackness. Being Black is important to one's well-being, one's purpose in life, and one's sense of connection to other Blacks. One's feeling of being wanted, accepted, appreciated, and affiliated is deeply rooted in Black people, Black culture, and the general Black condition. One's values, cultural preferences, artistic tastes, leisure activities, cooking styles and food choices, secular and religious musical tastes, church affiliation, organizational memberships, and social network or intimate friends are all influenced by one's perceived connection to Black people. In brief, some or a great deal of the meaning and hope one has for living a purposeful life is linked to one's perception of oneself as an African American.

This sense of Blackness is either muted or missing at Pre-Encounter, becomes an obsession during Immersion-Emersion, and continues as a singular concern (Black nationalism) or a concern mingled with other concerns (biculturalism or multiculturalism) at Internalization. In fact, at Internalization, one's reference group functions may take on a multidimensional character, as in the case of someone whose meaning in life synthesizes gayness, religiosity, and Blackness. However, whether it is mingled with other identities or singular, being Black plays an important reference group function in the daily life of the person.

At its best,

> The reference group functions of Black identity lead to the celebration of Blackness, the press to solve Black problems and a desire to promulgate Black culture and history. At its worst, it provides the basis for inhibiting, if not destructive, social conformity, ethnic chauvinism, reactionary cultural ideologies (biogenetically based ideologies), and a tendency to view as less than human, to one degree or another, those who are "not Black." Such negative and positive potential accompany any and all forms of nationalism, ethnicity or group affiliation, and is thus not unique to the Black experience; one can embrace a cultural perspective without being reactionary, but all biogenetically defined notions of culture are inherently reactionary. (Cross et al., 1991, p. 329)

Bridging or Transcendent Functions of Black Identity. The defensive and reference group functions combine to form the type of ethnic identity that is fairly typical of persons whose lives revolve around a particular culture, religion, or "race," and such people often show very little concern for experiences outside their own. In the case of Blacks, as long as one is operating (work, play, marriage, religion, etc.) in an all-Black or predominately Black human environment, the need to have, as part of one's identity, the functional skills and sensitivities that make one efficacious in interactions with non-Black peoples and cultures does not exist. However, it is one of the paradoxes of Black life that although Blacks are subject to what recently has been called "hypersegregation," it is nearly impossible for many, if not most, Black Americans to escape having to negotiate repeated and often enduring contacts, transactions, and communications with ethnic Whites, Asian Americans, Jews, Latinos, Cubans, Chicanos, American Indians, and, of course, White Protestants. In effect, another identity function that must be performed in the everyday life of many Black people is *bridging* and making connections to other experiences, groups, organizations, and individuals who make up the larger non-Black world within which the Black world is placed. Because the "Black-White" conflict is at the core of Nigrescence experience, the initial focus of bridging may be White society, White organizations, and the reestablishment of White friendships.

Bridging is often evident at the Pre-Encounter stage, but for the wrong reasons. There the focus is not bridging to share or fuse Blackness with Whiteness, and vice versa, as much as it is trying to get a handle on the essence of Whiteness as a vehicle for becoming the "right kind" of Black person. During Immersion-Emersion, bridging becomes muted or is destroyed. At Internalization, two trends may be present. Black nationalists may continue to discourage bridging to the White and other non-Black worlds, stressing instead the need to make connections and build bridges to and from Blacks in the diaspora (i.e., Pan-Africanism). For others, an initial concern for Pan-Africanism, Afrocentricity, and Blackness may actually be a prerequisite for bridging to worlds beyond Blackness.

Transracial and especially Black-White bridging activities can lead to conflicts within the Black community. Black nationalists may interpret bridging other than the Pan-African variety as a waste of limited time and resources; those involved in transracial connections may counter by stating that the Black condition is inherently bicultural, if not multicultural, and that meaningful change cannot take place without bridging. Other Blacks see any debate about "to bridge or not to bridge" as silly, because their workplace and community environments are decidedly multiracial and multicultural; consequently, they see the development of the bridging functions of Black identity as a necessity, not an option. Black women are quick to point out that the sexism of both White and Black men makes it absolutely necessary for them to bridge back and forth constantly between their Black identity and their gender, feminist, or womanist orientation. Finally, bridging adds a crucial element of flexibility to Black identity that allows one to better assimilate rapid culture and technological innovation (Cross, 1985; Cross et al., 1991). Black Americans, like all Americans, must be able to keep abreast of transformations in American society, and a rigid, provincial, identity structure cannot handle change. In this sense, bridging may be viewed as a metaphor for future change in Black identity.

It has been pointed out that bridging can be problematic in several ways (Cross et al., 1991). First, it involves the art of compromise; consequently, it is possible for one to make so many compromises that being Black ceases to have meaning. Second, it can facilitate the discovery of universals; however, Blacks can become so enchanted with "universal cultural trends" that interest in Blackness may be forsaken. In such instances, Blackness may come to be seen as a contradiction to humanism, rather than its expression as shaped, voiced, and codified by a particular sociohistorical experience (Cross et al., 1995).

In conclusion, the internalized Black identity functions to fulfill the self-protection, social anchorage, and transcendence or bridging needs of the individual African American. African Americans live in one of the most complex and demanding societies on earth; consequently, there should be little surprise in the discovery that the functional structure of Black identity is no less multidimensional.

Stage 5: Internalization-Commitment

It has already been mentioned, but it is worth repeating, that after developing a Black identity that serves their personal needs, some Blacks fail to sustain a long-term interest in Black affairs. Others devote an extended period of time, if not a lifetime, to finding ways to translate their personal sense of Blackness into a plan of action or general sense of commitment. Such people exemplify the fifth and final stage of Nigrescence: Internalization-Commitment. Current theory suggests there are few differences between the psychology of Blacks in the fourth and fifth stages other than the important factor of sustained interest and commitment, although to my knowledge there have been no empirical studies focusing on sustained commitment that follows Nigrescence. Consequently, other than repeating what has already been said about Internalization, a more differentiated look at Internalization-Commitment awaits the results of future research.

REFERENCES

Cross, W. E., Jr. (1970, April). *The Black experience viewed as a process: A crude model for Black self-actualization.* Paper presented at the 34th annual meeting of the Association of Social and Behavioral Scientists, Tallahassee, FL.

Cross, W. E., Jr. (1971). The Negro-to-Black conversion experience. *Black World, 20,* 13-27.

Cross, W. E., Jr. (1985). Black identity: Rediscovering the distinction between personal identity and reference group orientation. In M. B. Spencer, G. K. Brookins, & W. R. Allen (Eds.), *Beginnings: The social and affective development of Black children* (pp. 155-171). Hillsdale, NJ: Lawrence Erlbaum.

Cross, W. E., Jr. (1991). *Shades of Black.* Philadelphia: Temple University Press.

Cross, W. E., Jr., Parham, T. A., & Helms, J. E. (1991). The stages of Black identity development: Nigrescence models. In R. L. Jones (Ed.), *Black psychology* (3rd ed., pp. 319-338). Los Angeles: Cobb & Henry.

Cross, W. E., Jr., Parham, T. A., & Helms, J. E. (1995). Nigrescence revisited: Theory and research. In R. L. Jones (Ed.), *Advances in Black psychology* (pp. 1-69). Los Angeles: Cobb & Henry.

Finnegan, D. G., & McNally, E. (1987). *Dual identities*. Center City, MN: Hazelden.

Gardner, J. A. E., & T. G. Harris. (1970, September). PT conversation with Charles W. Thomas: Different strokes for different folks. *Psychology Today*, pp. 48-53, 78-80.

Hardiman, R. (1982). *White identity development*. Unpublished doctoral dissertation, University of Massachusetts at Amherst.

Helms, J. E. (1990). *Black and White racial identity*. Westport, CT: Greenwood Press.

Jackson, B. W. (1976). *The functions of Black identity development theory in achieving relevance in education*. Unpublished doctoral dissertation, University of Massachusetts.

Jones, L., & Neal, L. (1968). *Black fire*. New York: William Morrow.

Locke, A. (1925). *The new Negro*. New York: Boni.

Milliones, J. (1973). *Construction of the developmental inventory of Black consciousness*. Unpublished doctoral dissertation, University of Pittsburgh.

Oetting, E., & Beauvais, F. (1991). Orthogonal cultural identification theory: The cultural identification of minority adolescents. *International Journal of the Addictions, 25,* 655-685.

Parham, T. A. (1989). Cycles of psychological Nigrescence. *The Counseling Psychologist, 17*(2), 187-226.

Phinney, J. (1989). Stages of ethnic identity development in minority group adolescents. *Journal of Early Adolescence, 9,* 34-49.

Phinney, J. (1993). Three stage model of ethnic identity development. In M. E. Bernal & G. Knight (Eds.), *Ethnic identity: Formation and transmission among Hispanics and other minorities* (pp. 61-79). Albany: State University of New York Press.

Ponterotto, J. G., & Casas, J. M. (1991). *Handbook of racial/ethnic minority counseling research*. Springfield, IL: Charles C Thomas.

Ponterotto, J. G., & Pedersen, P. B. (1993). *Preventing prejudice: A guide for counselors and educators*. Newbury Park, CA: Sage.

Thomas, C. W. (1971). *Boys no more*. Beverly Hills, CA: Glencoe.

7

Ethnic Identity of Asians in the United States

GARGI ROYSIRCAR SODOWSKY

KWONG-LIEM KARL KWAN

RAJI PANNU

SINCE THE U.S. IMMIGRATION LAWS of 1965, Asians have become an increasing physical presence in the United States. Owing to a growing Asian critical mass and consequent ethnic pride, U.S. Asians are talking about the formation of their ethnicity in U.S. society. The attempts of Asians to say, "Hey, we're here, look at us, we're not going away" indicate how a U.S. ethnic group is reframing who they are. This represents the first envisioning and affirming of an Asian ethnic identity.

In this chapter, through illustrations and a social psychological framework, we reconfigure Asian identity images. We replace the popular media's one-dimensional identities of Miss Saigon, Mowgli the Jungle Boy, pot-bellied laughing Buddhas, chanting Hare Krishna devotees, cult-seeking Hindu yogis, exotic geishas, "gooks," bonsai gardeners, and the violent Bruce and Brandon Lee with multidimensional Asian ethnic identities. We also discuss the family's role in Asian ethnic identity.

U.S. society is too complicated to be called a melting pot—or even a goulash, a mosaic, or a tossed salad. It is a dynamic mixture of ethnic cultures

AUTHORS' NOTE: The first author dedicates this writing to "Hondo" Tarit Roysircar Sen, a second-generation Asian Indian, and to Roland Sodowsky, an eighth-generation Polish American.

and the dominant White culture, all in continuous firsthand contact, sometimes running parallel to each other and sometimes intertwining and interacting. Asian ethnic cultures, like the White culture, are contributing their respective characters to U.S. life, from food spices to fashions, art to politics, the sciences to the English language, and technological progress to health matters—thus defining, as a group, their distinctive ethnic identity.

Many Asian immigrants, as doctors, entrepreneurs, computer specialists, artists, executives, engineers, professors, skilled workers, and students, adopt the U.S. characteristics of optimism, ingenuity, and ambition; participate actively in the democratic political process; and watch baseball, basketball, and football. These same people are also culturally confident. Today many do not want to Anglicize their names. Asian adolescents are being encouraged by immigrant parents to attend Sunday meetings of Buddhist and Hindu clubs.

At the institutional level, Asians have provided some startling images. A striking mosque rises out of the cornfields of Perrysburg, Ohio. In urban metropolises, local theaters are showing popular films with names such as *The Joy Luck Club, M. Butterfly, Combination Platter, The Wedding Banquet,* and *Farewell My Concubine,* films written and/or directed by U.S. Chinese. U.S. Hindus are seen with their palms closed in prayer, holding a Vedic marriage in the Unitarian Church of Lincoln, Nebraska. New York's Asia Society is holding a touring show featuring visual artists who have emigrated from Vietnam, Thailand, and elsewhere in Asia.

At the individual level, the Chancellor of the University of California, Berkeley, a former candidate in the Los Angeles mayor's race, members of the U.S. Congress, cellists, violinists, fiction writers, editors, filmmakers, newscasters, news reporters, and owners of computer software companies are some talented Asians who are emerging as figures in White-dominated professional fields, denting myths about where Asians can typically be found. The "typical" American who goes to Japan today may be a third-generation Japanese American or the son of a Japanese woman married to a Californian serviceman.

On the U.S. cultural scene, Chinese, Tagalog, Korean, and Vietnamese are among the top 10 languages spoken in the United States by approximately 3 million Asians; Islam, Buddhism, and Hinduism are among the top five non-Christian religions, practiced by 1% of the population; 50% of U.S. Chinese and Indians eat ethnic foods at least once a week; and two recently founded Asian journals in English, *A Magazine: A Voice of Asian America* and the *Asian Pacific American Journal,* are holding Asian literature contests and publishing articles on such ethnic identity issues as sense of belonging to a particular culture of origin, biculturalism, immigration, language usage, generational statuses, cohesive families, religions, age cohorts, and gender.

In fact, ethnic identity has recently been recognized by the mainstream assessment tool, the *Diagnostic and Statistical Manual of Mental Disorders (DSN-IV)* (American Psychiatric Association, 1994, 4th ed.). The *DSM-IV* (1994) has exhorted mental health professionals to take into account the "cultural identity" of the individual: "Note the individual's ethnic or cultural reference groups. For immigrants and ethnic minorities, note separately the degree of involvement with both the culture of origin and the host culture (where applicable). Also note language abilities, use, and preference (including multilingualism)" (p. 843).

Unexpected Asian landmarks are the beginning features of a slowly developing photograph, clearly signaling the emergence of the ethnic identity of U.S. Asians, who form 37% of U.S. immigrants. Vietnamese, Filipinos, Chinese, and Indians constitute the largest numbers of current immigrants from Asia.

MULTIDIMENSIONALITY
OF ASIAN ETHNIC IDENTITY

Immigrating first-generation Asians are not identical to the people they left "back home," even though they are identified as "traditional." The fact that they immigrated, whether voluntarily or as political refugees, reveals their change- and risk-oriented personality. Their geographic and psychological mobility makes them different from their sedentary former country people. If there is a sufficient number of expatriates in one U.S. location, these individuals will group together to form an ethnic culture that runs parallel to the White dominant culture. The society formed is an ethnic and not a national culture because the immigrants are influenced simultaneously by U.S. White society. For instance, when newly emerging Asian religions face conflict with U.S. society, Asians subtly Americanize the internal operations of their religious organizations, incorporating temples and organizing boards; their lay leaders have more practical authority than the traditional holy men from their homeland. Although Sunday has no significance for Hindus, it is now the busiest day of worship and festivals in U.S. Hindu temples, showing that even "traditional" Hindus are not adhering to auspicious days and times determined by astrological almanacs. In *The Joy Luck Club* (Tan, 1989), the women who have monthly evening meetings to eat bean soup, play mah jong, discuss stocks and shares, tell stories about their tourist-like trips to China, and boast about their children's accomplishments write minutes of these meetings, which do not appear to be business meetings.

The second-generation Asian is different from the first-generation "traditional" immigrant. A college student, Maya Sen, who was born in the United States says that she is 100% Asian Indian and 100% American—which is statistically improbable but nonetheless true in her case. Maya is an individual but also a cultural being of the Asian Indian second generation. She has a good grade point average and plans to get a Ph.D., with the goal of eventually teaching Asian American studies or postcolonial literature. Maya's "traditional" parents, on the other hand, who immigrated in their late 20s and who symbolically feel a sense of belonging to their country of origin, India, may have tried to force Maya to choose between an Asian Indian ethnic identity and a White American identity.

What makes Maya different from her equally high-achieving White girlfriends is that she is determined to achieve something more than just a career: the creation of an ethnic identity out of conflicting cultural allegiances. Maya is determined to re-vision an identity out of the double-edged stereotypes that are a source of stress for many Asians. For instance, she needs to personally resolve her conflicting feelings about the stereotype that Asians are a model minority, resembling immigrating Jews of earlier generations or manifesting Garrison Keillor's tongue-in-cheek demographics of Lake Wobegon, where "all the children are above average." Perhaps fearing backlashes from other American minorities as well as White Americans who may resent her academic successes, Maya is trying hard to be a "regular" 100% American. But, at the same time, she does not see herself as American in terms of her cultural heritage. Her multicultural career interests indicate her need to express the more assertive political voice that her parents fearfully suppressed. As minorities, her parents believed that they needed to get ahead financially without seeking friendships in White society.

However, Maya may not agree to identify herself with those Asians "to whom no one would listen." Getting involved in Asian scholarship will enable her to locate herself in a professional network of Asians. It will provide a way to preserve some semblance of the "old" country folkways; otherwise she may end up feeling like a foreigner with no identity in the land of her birth. So perceiving oneself as 100% Asian Indian and 100% American is constructing the meaning that one must belong to both worlds or one will belong to neither. When first-generation parents talk about U.S. Whites, they tend to use the term *Americans*, leaving the impression that they are foreigners and always will be. The second-generation children refuse to accept the dichotomous choice of being either Americans or foreigners. They try to create a new self-definition: 100% Asian and 100% American—Asian American or U.S. Asian. Finding out how to be Asian on one's own terms rather than one's parents' terms can prove to be a difficult process.

An Asian Indian girlfriend of Maya's may not have Maya's "bridging philosophy." She may not have a clear understanding of the need to make cross-cultural connections and consequently may be less competent in relating to people from different societies. If she does begin the process of constructing her ethnic identity, the variety of cultural characteristics she will have to reassess and change may be intimidating. For instance, in her Asian Indian context, her identity is established by her family surname, which in turn affiliates her to a religion, caste, class, kinsmen/women, a particular type of diet, a language, and also a state in the "old" country.

The daughters of *The Joy Luck Club* (Tan, 1989) must understand how their lives have been molded by the "back home" and immigrant "entry" experiences of their Mainland Chinese mothers, experiences truly foreign to the second-generation daughters. By identifying with their first-generation mothers as well as drawing on their own experiences as second-generation daughters, the daughters are forced into deeper, more frequent, and more historical self-examinations than most young women of U.S. White culture.

June, one of the daughters of the Joy Luck Club, seems alone because she cannot identify easily with either her culture or the mainstream culture. She is confused by the values of her mother and her mother's friends, whom she calls "aunties"; they, in turn, see June and the other young women as

> daughters who grow impatient when their mothers talk in Chinese, who think they are stupid when they explain things in fractured English. They see that joy and luck do not mean the same to their daughters, that to these closed American-born minds "joy luck" is not a word, it does not exist. (p. 31)

Just as June does not know ethnic terms such as *joy luck*, many second-generation U.S. Asians do not know the Asian meanings of shame, guilt, filial piety, sacrifice for the family, bringing honor and praise to the family, and deference to older family members and the elderly. These concepts have important moral implications with regard to the interpersonal relationships of first-generation Asian immigrants, who perceive their sense of self, as related to their ethnic group, to be strongly tied to the family (for example, stating that "we are a Chinese family").

Thus, individuals who share the same ethnicity do not necessarily operate the same way in their respective ethnic identities. The differences between June and her mother go beyond the much-maligned generation gap; their communication is complicated by the immigrant identity of the mother and the Chinese American identity of the U.S.-born daughter.

Previously, assimilation in the United States was imposed by free public education, the Protestant work ethic, White middle-class neighborhoods, and the myth of the Eurocentric melting pot that, it was proposed, stirred and absorbed all cultures. The corollary to forced assimilation was forced segregation and/or ethnic groups' voluntary segregation. Today interethnic marriages—with Japanese Americans marrying non-Japanese Americans about 65% of the time—are occurring at triple the rate of two decades ago.

Interethnic marriage is not necessarily assimilation in the Eurocentric sense of the word. Those crossing the formerly impermeable boundaries of ethnicity, color, and religion may re-vision a shared future with a cross-cultural partner on the basis of a different set of commonalities, such as similar educational backgrounds, similar childhood suburban and soccer field experiences, a similar degree of comfort with the gender roles approved by the respective culture groups, or a love of similar pursuits. The decision to intermarry can also be a very personal one. At the same time, the Asian in the interethnic marriage is not negating his or her ethnic self, even though the person may be rejected by the parents or opposed by other ethnic members who have a definite preference for marriage within their ethnicity. The Asian partner is not losing an ethnic identity but rather is redefining, after marriage, how he or she sees the self as Asian. In the new multicultural family that is constructed, the Asian partner may infuse the Asian ethic that values the family above all else. The Asian retains select features of his or her Asian American ethnic identity (developed in the original immigrant Asian family) that are meaningful to him or her. The path taken in redefining one's Asian self is unique and personal for the Asian, just as it is for the White partner, who redefines who he or she is as a White person in the interethnic marriage.

The rise of interethnic marriages is paralleled by the increase in numbers of young Asian American activists who are gravitating toward dating and marrying members from their respective cultures for various reasons, such as their shared experience of growing up in two cultures, their wariness about fulfilling sexual stereotypes by getting into a relationship with a White person, and their belief that relationships are based on compatible value systems and tied to one's family, which are inextricably wrapped up in Asian cultures. Asian American activists who are deeply aware that the fight to take pride in their ethnic identity has been long and hard are going through an ethnic self-definition process different from that of Asian Americans who intermarry.

Because diversity breeds diversity, there are individual variations in degrees of ethnic identity held by the members of an ethnic group. In addition to the diversity in ethnic identity within one family, the whole family as a group may adopt different aspects of ethnic identity at home and in public. For instance, at work, in functional daily activities—such as shopping or dressing—and in English usage, all family members may manifest explicit U.S. White behaviors. On the other hand, at home the same members may show certain preferences for social life, religious activities, films, native language magazines/newspapers, and music that have explicit Asian features. Rather than being incongruent or inconsistent, the family may actually be coping with acculturative stress by adopting different sets of ethnic identity behaviors and slipping in and out of each with practiced ease and well-informed objectives.

The ethnic identity issues of children of interethnic marriages need to be understood. The United States is in the midst of a biracial/interethnic baby boom. Between 1968 and 1989, the percentage of children born to parents of different races more than tripled, from 1.0% of total births to 3.4%. According to the 1980 U.S. census (U.S. Bureau of the Census, 1980), there were approximately 2 million children living in biracial households. The largest proportion lived in Asian-White households, usually with Asian mothers and White fathers. In Los Angeles County in 1977, 60% of Japanese Americans married non-Japanese, and 49.7% of Chinese Americans and 34.1% of Korean Americans married out of their ethnic group. At the national level currently, the rates have probably since grown. In fact, among Japanese Americans, mixed-race births currently outnumber monoracial births: For every 100 births to two Japanese parents in the United States, there are 139 births to a Japanese and a non-Japanese parent.

A biracial and bireligious child—for example, a Japanese-Irish-Buddhist-Catholic-American child—will be perplexed when responding to affirmative-action-like traditional racial and ethnic categories of Black, Caucasian, Hispanic White, Hispanic non-White, Asian/Pacific Islander, and Native American. The biracial will probably check off the "Other" category because he or she cannot define him- or herself by any one particular racial or ethnic group. Forcing biracials to restrict themselves to one category or by even offering them the choice of more than one category (for example, by instructing them to check off as many racial and ethnic groups as applicable) cannot capture the multidimensionality of a biracial's ethnic identity. If biracials were asked to rate on a continuous scale their "Japaneseness" and then, separately, their "Whiteness," a more comprehensive profile of their ethnic identity might be obtained. They might rate themselves high on both, high on one and low on the other, or low on both.

Biracial/interethnic children may have greater difficulty figuring out their ethnic identity than U.S.-born Asian children whose parents are of the same ethnicity. Amerasians, born to G.I. fathers and Vietnamese mothers, are examples of biracial children who are unable to give a definitive answer as to how they identify—Vietnamese or American—or even where Vietnam is located or why they will not go back to Vietnam. There are many reasons for the identity confusions of Amerasians. They have been scorned by the society in Vietnam as illegitimate children of low-class "bar girls"/prostitutes and uneducated Americans. Some were abandoned by their mothers and their respective mothers' families. The Amerasians who have finally been able to immigrate to the United States are in their late adolescence and have little or no education, few skills other than streetwiseness, and a poor sense of cultural integrity. Although allowing them their political right to American citizenship, U.S. society has had little time for Amerasians because Vietnam is not a "feel-good" word. The additional weakness of inadequate English language skills makes it difficult for Amerasians to identify with the U.S. White reference group. Feeling like societal rejects of two cultures and being unable to affiliate themselves to a normative group could be accounting for the conduct problems that have been reported about recent Amerasian arrivals.

Some biracial Asian children may find that people feel comfortable making insensitive comments about Asians in front of them because they are considered safe or "one of us." Those who identify themselves strongly as Asians may feel indignation and pain about their "safe" status. Because of the ambiguity of their features, they may be told that they could "pass" for White. Even though "passing" could be easy for the biracial person, he or she may not be interested in doing it or in having a White ethnic identity. Biracial Asian Americans who are from two minority groups—for example, African/Asian Americans—raise even more complex ethnic identity issues within themselves as well as in other monoracial Asians.

At the personal level, biracial African/Asian Americans will need to decide how much they are Asian and how much African, especially if in childhood they were forced to disavow or neglect one of the two reference groups. If they want to identify more strongly with African Americans, they may experience tacit pressure from the African American group to prove their "Blackness." From their Asian group, they may experience racism. People who are biracial experience others' exaggerated emphasis on their physical appearance. They may have heard often in their childhood about "how good-looking biracial children are"; thus, they may have been given positive attention for physical attributes, but may have had a negative experience of a compliment that is only skin-deep.

As some biracial children mature into adults, they may go through the experience of considering themselves to be one race but realizing that others see them as another race, and they may have struggled with the mismatch between their self-identification and their perceived identification by others. On the other hand, some biracial children growing up in a middle-class White environment may not have even seen themselves as Asians or had conscious knowledge of themselves as Asians. However, they may "find" themselves in college when they are able to perceive their ethnic identity as multidimensional. The dilemma of biracial Asians may be that they had no adult role models when they were growing up. Their parents in the 1970s and 1980s may not have understood fully the impact of a biracial/interethnic heritage, and the Asian parents may not have consciously educated the children about their culture. Because ethnic identity is not cut and dried, biracial Americans need to define their multidimensional ethnic identity by networking and finding support within a multiethnic camp. They may perceive their identity as one of commonality and differences with monoracial U.S. Asians. They may draw strength and pride from this process of self-definition after having lived with an ambiguous ethnic identity through childhood and adolescence.

A THEORETICAL
CONCEPTUALIZATION OF ETHNIC IDENTITY

The multicultural constructs of racial, ethnic, and minority identity have received considerable attention in recent multicultural literature, both in theoretical conceptualizations (e.g., Atkinson, Morten, & Sue, 1993; Helms, 1990; Phinney, 1990; Rowe, Bennett, & Atkinson, 1994; Sabnani, Ponterotto, & Borodovsky, 1991; Smith, 1991) and in empirical inquiries (e.g., Bennett-Choney & Behrens, in press; Carter, in press; Helms, in press; Phinney, 1992). In fact, in a Delphi poll, 53 cross-cultural counseling experts who were asked about the future of cross-cultural counseling predicted a 30% increase in theoretical and empirical publications on racial, minority, and ethnic identity in the next 10 years (Heath, Neimeyer, & Pedersen, 1988). Several researchers have also considered identity constructs to be the most promising in multicultural counseling (Atkinson et al., 1993; Sue & Sue, 1990).

Even though racial, ethnic, and minority identities represent different, though related, constructs, they have been treated synonymously. Therefore, we attempt to delineate ethnic identity as an independent construct that may overlap to some degree with racial and minority identity. We specifically explore two overarching dimensions of ethnic identity: (a) the internal or invisible and (b) the external or visible.

Saliency of Ethnicity

The term *visible racial/ethnic group* has been noted in the literature (Cook & Helms, 1988). In Asian American student organizations, students who have straight black hair, dark, slanted eyes, and "ivory" skin identify themselves as Chinese, Japanese, Koreans, or Taiwanese— all of whom are members of a physically visible and identifiable racial stock (i.e., the Mongoloid race). We, the authors of this chapter, have experienced that we can identify members of our respective Asian groups when we see them in our daily work activities, and that we feel an urge to make eye contact with them. In an investigation of acculturation attitudes of Hispanics and Asian Americans, 13% of the participants indicated that they saw their ethnic identity in terms of their physical appearance (Sodowsky, Lai, & Plake, 1991).

Asians may be regarded as foreigners even if they are U.S. born because of their saliency. Ronald Takaki (1993), a professor of American history, reported an incident that illustrates this point:

> My driver and I chatted about the weather and the tourists. The sky was cloudy, and Virginia beach was twenty minutes away. The rearview mirror reflected a White man in his forties. "How long have you been in this country?" he asked. "All my life," I replied, wincing. "I was born in the United States." With a strong southern drawl, he remarked: "I was wondering because your English is excellent!" Then as I had done many times, I explained: "My grandfather came from Japan in the 1880's. My family has been here, in America, for over [a] hundred years." He glanced at me in the mirror. Somehow I did not look American to him; my eyes and complexion looked foreign. (pp. 1-2)

The concept of ethnic salience, however, offers a narrow perspective of ethnic identity and neglects the various social and psychological forces that constitute and maintain a person's identification with an ethnic group. Also, the increase of biracial/interethnic people in the United States, especially Asian biracial/interethnic people, can only be expected to rise and cause further intermingling, thus defying the identification of U.S. people by racial taxonomic groups.

In fact, Helms (in progress) recently argued that one cannot classify people in the United States according to genetic origins. She maintained that race-defining characteristics are chosen by the U.S. White dominant group, the group that holds the political power, and thus that race is sociopolitically defined. If we tend to notice members from our respective Asian ethnic groups in White surroundings, it is perhaps because we are "lone" minority individuals in U.S. White educational institutions. In our own ethnic gatherings or our country of origin, our cultural peers might not have "stood out" for us. Helms theorized that *sociorace* is a useful concept because it acknowledges that people are socialized according to the racial group they are assumed to belong to.

In summary, ethnic saliency does not necessarily tell us about the sense of attachment or belonging to one's ethnic group or about one's cultural heritage and values. Ethnic identity does.

Ethnic Identity: Definitions

Sue and Sue (1990) defined *culture* as all the customs, values, and traditions that are learned from one's environment. Sodowsky et al. (1991) stated that in a culture there is a "set of people who have common and shared values; customs, habits, and rituals; systems of labeling, explanations, and evaluations; social rules of behavior; perceptions regarding human nature, natural phenomena, interpersonal relationships, time, and activity; symbols, art, and artifacts; and historical developments" (p. 194).

Culture is a unifying influence. It combines the different aspects of life into a logical whole (Sodowsky et al., 1991) and therefore also integrates psychologically the members of a culture. Culture arouses "a sense of attachment or identification with the [ethnocultural] group by its individual members" (Berry, Poortinga, Segall, & Dasen, 1992). In fact, DeVos and Romanucci-Ross (1975) noted that it is this "*subjective* [italics added] symbolic or emblematic use of any aspect of culture . . . to differentiate [a group of people] from other groups that is central to the concept of ethnic identity" (p. 16). For instance, elderly Japanese seen early in the morning doing Tai Chi in the parks of New York City rather than doing toning and body conditioning in a dance studio are symbolically identifying with their culture of origin.

The sharing of a cultural heritage, a sense of social relatedness, and symbolic cultural ties define ethnic identity. According to Smith (1991), the ethnocultural group can be viewed as an ethnic reference group in which members

> share a common history and culture, . . . may be identifiable because they share similar physical features and values and, . . . through the process of interacting with each other and establishing boundaries with others, identify themselves as being a member of that group. Ethnic identity is the sum total of group members' feelings about those values, symbols, and common histories that identify them as a distinct group. Moreover, . . . a person does not belong to an ethnic group by choice; rather, he or she must be born into such a group and becomes related to it through emotional and symbolic ties. (pp. 181-182)

As can be seen from this description, unless one is physically removed from one's native group (as in the case of a South Korean infant adopted and raised by a U.S. White American family), both one's history and one's culture are environmental givens because one is born into an ethnic group whose members have a common history and cultural heritage. In addition, one's ethnic identity is based not only on overt physical features but also on a subjective sense of attachment to the various cultural values, assumptions, roles, and heritage shared by members of an ethnic group.

In an Asian American student association, there could be differences among individuals in one Asian ethnic group. A Japanese American student could strongly identify with the Japanese American ethnic culture and feel a strong sense of belonging with the members of the Japanese American group. This student might travel to Japan to discover cultural roots and might wish to marry only a Japanese American. This same student might not identify with the general "Asian American race" or with issues of racism. On the other hand, another Japanese American student might be less in tune with the specific Japanese American culture and its group membership. In the late 1980s, he or she might have been more concerned with joining the reparation movement to demand redress for the Japanese internment and might now be supportive of African Americans currently starting a movement for demanding similar reparations for slavery. A third Japanese American student might have a strong sense of ethnic identity as well as a strong need for activism against past and current forms of U.S. racism, so that the two multicultural strengths would interact with each other.

Helms agreed (1995) that cultural identification and racial identification may not be the same. The primary differences between racial identity and ethnic identity models are as follows. Racial identity is (a) based on a sociopolitical model of oppression, (b) based on a socially constructed definition of race, and (c) concerned with how individuals abandon the effects of disenfranchisement and develop respectful attitudes toward their racial group. On the other hand, ethnic identity (a) concerns one's attachment to, sense of belonging to, and identification with one's ethnic group members (e.g., Japanese, Vietnamese, Indian) and with one's ethnic culture; (b) does not have a theoretical emphasis on oppression/racism; but (c) may include the prejudices and cultural pressures that ethnic individuals experience when their ways of life come into conflict with those of the White dominant group.

If ethnic identity does address the influence of oppression, it is at the racial level rather than at the ethnic and cultural level. For instance, racism could be a source of acculturative stress and an obstacle to forming an attachment to one's ethnic group. Moritsugu and Sue (1983) commented that an ethnic person's minority status might predispose him or her to feelings of alienation, social isolation, heightened stress, and the risk of mental disorder. Thus, a discussion of ethnic identity cannot preclude the effects of racism on one's ethnic identity. Smith (1991) noted:

In racially pluralistic and ethnically pluralistic societies wherein race is the major determiner of one's status, ethnic identity development proceeds along racial lines and second along ethnic lines. Although one's ethnicity consti- tutes a major status or a superordinate identity, it may, depending on the situation, be considered secondary to race. . . . Race interacts with ethnicity, so that at any given point, either factor may assume pre-potency. (p. 187)

Members of a minority group may not have a common history and cul- tural heritage (for example, women or gays/lesbians across all racial and eth- nic groups in the United States) and consequently may not endorse an ethnic identity. Therefore, minority identity does not necessarily include ethnic iden- tity. Nevertheless, minority identity interacts with ethnic identity when an individual belongs to an ethnic group that is a minority group in a given society. Sue and Sue (1990) preferred to call the Minority Identity Development Model (MID) the Racial/Cultural Identity Development Model (R/CID) to emphasize the impact of minority and racist experiences on the identity of U.S. ethnic minorities.

ETHNIC IDENTITY:
A SOCIAL PSYCHOLOGICAL PHENOMENON

The ethnic identity process is a social psychological phenomenon. The social psychological approach provides relevant explanations to group inter- actions in pluralistic societies, in which salience, ethnicity, and out-group status have an impact on an ethnic individual's identity process. Isajiw (1990) noted:

[An] ethnic group is a phenomenon that gives rise to (1) social organization, an objective phenomenon that provides the structure for the ethnic commu- nity and (2) identity, a subjective phenomenon that gives to individuals a sense of belonging and to the community a sense of oneness and historical meaning. Ethnic identity can thus be defined . . . as a manner in which persons, on account of their ethnic origin, locate themselves psychologically in relation to one or more social systems, and in which they perceive others as locating them [i.e., the ethnic individuals] in relation to those systems. (p. 35)

Several assumptions about an individual's ethnic identity can thus be pro- posed. First, an individual is likely to be aware of his or her ethnic identity in a pluralistic society in which multiple social systems coexist. In U.S. society, these systems may be the various racial and ethnic groups, such as White, Black, Asian, Hispanic, American Indian, and Jewish American. The variety of social systems in a given society thus becomes a facilitative condition for an individual's ethnic identity to be formed and maintained. Berry, Kim, Minde, and Mok (1987) stated that in a monocultural society, the dominant group applies pressure on ethnic groups to assimilate, whereas in a multicultural society, the dominant society exerts less influence and may in fact be influenced to make some cultural changes by the diverse ethnic groups that run parallel to it. Berry et al. (1987) asserted that as a result, ethnic individuals in pluralistic societies may have better mental health than those in monistic societies.

Second, awareness of one's ethnic identity is likely to be heightened when social systems assume differential degrees of power status in a pluralistic society. When one is exposed to an immediate environment (e.g., school or work setting) in which one is an ethnic person, one is simultaneously confronted with two cultural groups (the dominant cultural group and one's ethnic group) whose respective value orientations may be different. Under such conflicting circumstances, not only does one develop a heightened sense of one's ethnic identity, but one needs to locate one's position, both socially and psychologically, with reference to the two social systems.

A corollary to the second assumption is Smith's (1991) view that an ethnic person engages in a process in which one comes to "terms with one's ethnic membership group as a salient reference group . . . [whose] standpoints or reference perspectives function to establish a person's goals and to regulate one's behavior" (p. 182), and develops emotional and symbolic ties with this group as well as psychological relatedness. Such a process can be further explained in light of the assertion that an individual's identity and self-concept are derived from a sense of group identification and belonging, and that an ethnic person identifies with a cultural reference group, whether his or her own ethnic group or the dominant group, to which a psychological relatedness is attached (Sherif, 1964; Tajfel, 1978).

Third, while the ethnic person is attempting to locate him- or herself socially and psychologically with respect to the dominant group, members of the dominant social system are also attempting to locate and develop their psychological relatedness to the ethnic person. However, the ethnic person is involved in an even more complex interactional process. The ethnic person, while trying to locate with reference to the dominant group, is simultaneously attempting to locate socially and psychologically with reference to an ethnic group. In addition, in the attempt to identify with an ethnic reference group, the person who lives in the dynamic context of a culturally pluralistic society perceives how members of the dominant group, his or her own ethnic group, and other groups are locating him or her in reference to their respective groups.

Hence the complex processes of ethnic identity are moderated by the extent to which (a) the ethnic person accepts or rejects the dominant group; (b) the members of the dominant social system show acceptance or rejection of the ethnic person; (c) the members of the person's ethnic group show acceptance or rejection of the ethnic person; (d) the ethnic person experiences a sense of belonging to his or her ethnic group; and (e) the ethnic person perceives how the members of the dominant group locate him or her in interethnic relations. Ethnic identity, therefore, is a process in which the ethnic person is constantly assessing the "fit" between the self and the different social systems in the environment (Spencer & Markstrom-Adams, 1990, p. 292).

Members of an ethnic group establish certain boundary lines within which the ethnic identity of the in-group is defined and consolidated, whereas that of the out-group is separated as incompatible and distinctive. Smith (1991) contended that "both minority and majority status[es] influence the process of ethnic identity" (p. 183). In other words, the reactive and interactive encounters of both the minority and majority groups affect the process of ethnic identity. Often the members of the ethnic minority group prefer to identify with the majority group. However, such identification is not always validated by prejudiced members of the dominant group or by members of the ethnic group, who may think that their ethnic fellow member has "sold out." Therefore, ethnic minority individuals living in a pluralistic society are often confronted with their ethnicity and accorded a minority status by Whites and their ethnic peers, as well as by themselves.

Because members of both the dominant group and minority groups have various degrees of psychological accommodation toward the other group, the ethnic individual often receives mixed messages regarding his or her ethnic identification, reinforcing it on some occasions and not reinforcing it on others, from both potential ethnic reference groups. In fact, Smith (1991) noted that it is easier to maintain a White identity than an ethnic identity:

> Whereas, the ethnic identity . . . of the majority group individual is continuously validated and reinforced in a positive manner by both his [her] membership group and the structure of the society's institutions, such is not the case for many ethnic minorities. Positive reinforcement frees the majority individuals to focus on aspects of life other than ethnicity. (p. 183)

Identification with one's ethnic group is considered by some scholars as crucial for positive mental health of the ethnic individual. More specifically, Smith (1991) stated:

> Acceptance of one's ethnic group as a positive reference group leads to positive self-esteem, whereas rejection . . . leads to self-estrangement and maladaptive psychological behavior. A sense of ethnic belonging is psychologically important for people, because it serves to anchor the individual's relatedness to others in society. An individual whose ethnic identity is anchored to his or her membership group stands greater chance of being psychologically healthy than one whose identity is marginal in relationship to his [her] actual membership group. (p. 186)

However, our view is that later generation ethnic and biracial people, such as third- and fourth-generation immigrants, could very well have a White identity (or the identity of an ethnic group different from their own), anchoring their relatedness to the U.S. White society (or an ethnic minority society different from their own). These individuals could also be psychologically healthy because they would not be marginal, but rather would have a clear sense of belonging to a reference group. The point is that one needs to have an ethnic sense of belonging (to any ethnic group) in order to prevent social alienation and self-estrangement.

According to Burke (1991), one derives the meaning of one's identity from traits shared with one class of people in a given society. Thus, the identity that one constructs represents a set of internalized meanings that one attributes to the self in a social position or role. An identity, then, serves as a standard or reference for who one is. The identity process represents a continuously operating and self-adjusting feedback loop that works by adjusting behaviors to reduce discrepancy and achieve congruence between the identity portrayed or given by the environment and the identity with its own set of meanings constructed by the person. As dissonance theory suggests, distress increases when the incongruence between the identity portrayed or given and one's personal construction grows, and this distress then activates behaviors to remediate the discrepancy. For example, if one receives the input that one is overly traditional (i.e., "too much of an ethnic person") or overly assimilated to White society, and if either of these messages does not match one's internalized standard of oneself, one may change one's behavior to change the discrepancy and thus one's ethnic identity distress. This reference to "internal" identity standards and "external" identity behaviors leads to a discussion of the components of ethnic identity.

Multidimensional Components of Ethnic Identity

Some operational variables have been empirically used when assessing ethnic identity. These variables (see Phinney, 1990) include (a) ethnic identification, which refers to how an ethnic person chooses to label his or her ethnic group membership (e.g., Hong Kong Chinese versus Chinese versus Chinese American versus Asian American); (b) a sense of belonging, which refers to the extent to which an ethnic person attributes importance to and is emotionally attached to his or her ethnic group (e.g., the amount of Japaneseness and the amount of Whiteness perceived in oneself); (c) positive and negative attitudes toward one's own ethnic group (e.g., ethnic pride versus hatred toward one's ethnic group); and (d) participation in ethnic activities and cultural practices (ethnic language usage, friendship patterns, religious affiliation, entertainment, media, food preferences, exogamy, and traditional customs). Variables lettered (c) and (d) have been extensively investigated in the acculturation literature (see Sodowsky et al., 1991).

Breton, Isajiw, Kalbach, and Reitz (1990) offered a social psychological framework to classify ethnic identity into components that include the ethnic identity variables identified by Phinney (1990). Isajiw (1990) noted:

> Locating oneself in relation to a community and society is not only a psychological phenomenon, but also a social phenomenon in the sense that the internal psychological states express themselves objectively in external behavior patterns that come to be shared by others. Thus, individuals locate themselves in one or another community internally by states of mind and feelings . . . and externally by behavior appropriate to these states of mind and feelings. Behavior according to cultural patterns is thus an expression of identity and can be studied as an indication of its character. (pp. 35-36)

Thus, Isajiw contended that ethnic identity can be divided into two aspects—external and internal—to characterize the interaction of the psychological with the social. Under these two overarching aspects, various components of ethnic identity are subsumed and can be identified.

External Ethnic Identity

According to Isajiw (1990), *external ethnic identity* refers to observable social and cultural behaviors. These behaviors are manifested in the areas of ethnic language, ethnic group friendship, participation in ethnic group functions and activities, ethnic media, and ethnic traditions. These behaviors are of interest to the acculturation literature (Sodowsky et al., 1991, for reviewed literature).

Internal Ethnic Identity

Internal ethnic identity has three dimensions: cognitive, moral, and affective. The *cognitive dimension* refers to the ethnic person's (a) self-images and images of his or her ethnic group, (b) knowledge of the ethnic group's heritage and its historical past, and (c) knowledge of the ethnic group's values. The *moral dimension*, which is considered the most central to subjective identity, refers to an ethnic person's "feelings of group obligations . . . [that] account for the commitment a person has to his [or her] group solidarity that ensues" (Isajiw, 1990, p. 36). The *affective* or *cathectic dimension* refers to an ethnic person's feelings of attachment to his or her own ethnic group. Two types of such feelings have been distinguished, both including a sense of security with one's ethnic group: (a) a sympathy and associative preference for same-ethnic-group members as against other-group members and (b) a comfort with cultural patterns of one's own ethnic group as against those of other groups (see Table 7.1).

Congruence/Incongruence of the Internal and External Dimensions

Separating ethnic identity into the complementary internal and external dimensions produces a complicated yet complete profile of an ethnic person. The internal and external dimensions compose the wholeness of ethnic iden-

TABLE 7.1 External and Internal Ethnic Identity and Their Respective Components and Variables

Components of Ethnic Identity Postulated by Isajiw (1990)	Int-Ext ID Variables Adapted From Breton et al. (1990)	Int-Ext ID Variables Adapted From Sodowsky et al. (1991)	Int-Ext ID Variables Proposed by Kwan & Sodowsky (1994)	Cultural Value Variables Proposed in This Chapter
I. EXTERNAL ASPECTS				
A. Ethnic Language				
1. Is the ethnic language the mother tongue?	Try to speak ethnic language with own ethnic friends	Language spoken well		
2. Knowledge of ethnic language	Provide opportunities for children to learn one's ethnic language	Language spoken with own ethnic group		
3. Ethnic language literacy		Language used in ideas and images		
4. Frequency of ethnic language use		Language used to express strong feelings		
		Language of one's dreams		
		Language one reads and writes		
B. Ethnic Group Friendship				
1. Exclusivity of in-group and out-group friends	Most social friends are from one's ethnic group	Have more majority than own ethnic friends		
2. Closeness of in-group and out-group friends				
C. Ethnic Group Functions				
1. Ethnic organization activities	Attend ethnic group gatherings			
2. Group-sponsored vacation activities	Vacation with own ethnic friends			
3. Nonethnic group activities	Know own ethnic group's members who are officials/leaders in community			
	Express views about own ethnic group's affairs in community			

(continued)

TABLE 7.1 Continued

Components of Ethnic Identity Postulated by Isajiw (1990)	Int-Ext ID Variables Adapted From Breton et al. (1990)	Int-Ext ID Variables Adapted From Sodowsky et al. (1991)	Int-Ext ID Variables Proposed by Kwan & Sodowsky (1994)	Cultural Value Variables Proposed in This Chapter
D. *Ethnic Media* 1. Ethnic radio/TV programs, newspaper	(Seek to) Listen/watch ethnic radio/TV program (Seek to) read ethnic newspapers, etc.		Pay attention to special events concerning one's ethnic group reported in the media	
E. *Ethnic Traditions* 1. Ethnic food 2. Celebration of ethnic holidays and events 3. Religious practice and nonreligious customs 4. Possess ethnic objects	Often eat own ethnic food Celebrate ethnic occasions and holidays Practice own ethnic religious/ nonreligious customs	Prefer own ethnic food Prefer own ethnic music, dances, etc. Adhere strictly to one's cultural values Eat own ethnic versus American food Wear ethnic clothes		
II. INTERNAL ASPECTS A. *Cognitive Dimension* 1. Self-images and images of one's group 2. Knowledge of one's group heritage and its historical past 3. Knowledge of one's group values	Rediscover one's ethnic heritage in U.S.	Believe one's group identity is represented by own ethnic group Believe oneself has more similarities to own ethnic group	Not bring shame to family Feel guilty if personal actions are self-satisfying but against family expectations Rarely make decision of which family disapproves Not disclose private issues to own ethnic group's members because of fear of social stigma Prefer children respect and obey parents rather than assert their own rights Seldom talk about oneself apart from family Perceive one's ethnic identity to be of one's ethnic group, whereas others perceive it to be American	Nonconfrontation or silence as a virtue Respect for older persons and the elderly Moderation in behaviors Devaluation of individualism Harmony between hierarchical roles Filial piety Structured family roles and relationships Humility Obedience High regard for learning

140

B. *Moral Dimension (Ethnic Group Obligation)*

1. How important it is to help people of own ethnic background
2. Importance attached to actual or potential children marrying into their own ethnic group
3. Extent of feelings of obligation to support own group's special causes and needs
4. Importance attached to actual or potential children learning ethnic language

Have a job that benefits oneself and one's ethnic members in U.S.
Hire one's ethnic members in U.S. into good positions
Wish children would marry one's ethnic group members
Support special causes and needs of one's ethnic group members in U.S.

Marrying within own ethnic group

Feel obligation to offer help to new ethnic group members in town
Try to help own ethnic group members who experience great difficulties

Modest about sexuality
Not demonstrative with heterosexual affection
Less need for dating
Strong sense of duty to family
Protect honor and face of family
Marrying within versus outside ethnic group
Importance attached to preserving the original religion.

C. *Affective/Cathectic Dimension*

1. Feelings of security with and sympathy and associative preference for members of own group as opposed to other groups
2. Feelings of security and comfort with the cultural patterns of one's group as opposed to cultural patterns of other groups or societies

Feel natural need to associate with one's ethnic group members in U.S.
Would like closest friends who are not relatives in U.S. to be one's ethnic group members

Proud of own ethnic group in U.S.
Friends one is close to are majority versus own ethnic group
People one trusts and turns to for help are majority versus own ethnic group
Trust in and seek help from family
Fear of being isolated by family

Have a sense of belonging to another ethnic group

141

tity. Although the external or behavioral could be reflective of the internal, Isajiw (1990) commented that the two should not be assumed to be interdependent.

In fact, a basic assumption of Breton, Isajiw, Kalbach, and Reitz's (1990) study is that "the retention of ethnic identity from one generation to another does not necessarily mean retention of both its aspects, or all the components of each aspect in the same degree" (p. 37). The internal and external aspects of ethnic identity may vary independently. In a similar vein, Rosenthal and Feldman (1992) noted that it is necessary to distinguish the "visible" and "invisible" elements of ethnic identity. Drawing an analogy from research on acculturation, they argued that the core or "invisible" elements of ethnic identity (e.g., cultural values) may be more resistant to change and may show less acculturation over time than the peripheral or "visible" elements (e.g., ethnic behaviors). Sodowsky and Carey (1987, 1988) also demonstrated that Asian Indians in the United States showed integration into the majority culture in terms of food, English language usage, clothes, and institutional behaviors, but a different acculturative mode in other areas (e.g., core cultural values), suggesting that "acculturation of a minority individual is best described by a composite profile rather than by a single score" (Sodowsky et al., 1991, p. 195).

The assumption that the internal and external aspects of ethnic identity vary independently has enabled Isajiw (1990) to postulate several forms of ethnic identity based on various combinations of the internal and external. A ritualistic ethnic identity, may be characterized by a high level of practice of ethnic traditions and a low level of corresponding feelings of group obligation. For example, a U.S.-born, second-generation ethnic person may be trained by immigrant parents to observe many religious rituals and traditional practices (external ethnic identity) but may not feel a moral commitment to or an associational preference for his or her ethnic group (internal ethnic identity). An ideological ethnic identity may be indicated by a high level of feelings of group obligation accompanied by a low level of practice of ethnic behaviors. A bicultural individual working in a professional capacity who has adopted many values, activities, and ways of living of the U.S. White society may be intellectually and philosophically drawn to network with and support his or her ethnic group (internal ethnic identity), but may not observe ethnic customs and habits (external ethnic identity). Ethnic rediscovery may be characterized by positive feelings for group obligations and a high level of practice of ethnic traditions. Later generation Asian individuals who try to discover their roots and undergo reverse acculturation may operate from this type of ethnic identity.

In an early study on acculturation from the perspective of ethnic identity, Clark, Kaufman, and Pierce (1976) contended that immigrants and their descendants may demonstrate selective acculturation: That is, these groups may acculturate more in some aspects (e.g., occupation and language use, which could be characterized as external ethnic identity) than in others (e.g., values and attitudes, which could be characterized as internal ethnic identity). Similarly, Cronin (1970) stated that immigrants showed differential acculturation in public versus private behaviors. Clark et al. (1976) compared three variables of ethnic identity—Acculturative Balance Scale (ABS), Traditional Orientation (TO), and Anglo Face (AF)—among individuals who represented three generational levels: first-generation immigrants (Japanese and Mexican Americans) and second- and third-generation descendants of immigrants in the United States. The three variables measured an ethnic people's relative knowledge of their ethnic culture and the contemporary American culture (ABS), the degree to which they acted in accordance with their ethnic traditions (e.g., language, citizenship, literacy, religious affiliation) (TO), and the strength of their sense of belonging and degree of participation in the dominant culture (AF). Although the three variables were not distinctly divided into the internal and external aspects of the ethnic identity, the researchers attempted to assess differential acculturation and the variation of the visible and invisible components of ethnic identity. The study revealed that few individuals have similar scores on the three components. In other words, it is possible for ethnic individuals to maintain a high level of traditional ethnic knowledge (internal ethnic identity) and ethnic behavior (external ethnic identity) while presenting an Anglo Face (a White identity), and vice versa.

Nonlinear Ethnic Identity Process

We hypothesize that the ethnic identity process follows a bidirectional system. Ethnic identity could be measured by assessing two dimensions: the degree of adoption of Whiteness and the degree of retention of one's Asianness (i.e., Japaneseness, Indianness, Chineseness). Modifying Berry's (1980) bidirectional acculturation model, we propose that an ethnic identity is a combination of "Yes" and/or "No" answers to two questions: "Is my ethnic identity of value and to be retained?" and "Is the White identity of the U.S. dominant society to be sought?" The first question measures one's identity grounded in one's ethnicity: that is, how one perceives oneself in the context of shared ethnic existence, values, and attachment. Does one see oneself as like or unlike others from one's ethnic origins? The second question measures one's identity grounded in the culture of U.S. White society and how one perceives oneself in the context of shared White existence and values and attachment to the White society. Four ethnic identity orientations occur, based on four combinations of "Yes" and/or "No" responses to the two basic ethnic identity questions (see Figure 7.1). According to a 2×2 design, the following four responses would be given: Yes, Yes (Bicultural Identity); Yes, No (Strong Ethnic Identity); No, Yes (Strong U.S. White identity); and No, No (Identity of Cultural Marginalization). We also propose that the four ethnic identity orientations allow for a nonlinear trend over time and across situations, so that (a) an individual with one ethnic identity orientation can move to another over time and/or across situations and (b) an individual can move back and forth among the four orientations, rather than heading in a linear manner from a strong ethnic

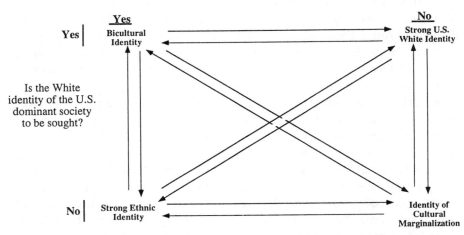

Is my ethnic identity of value
and to be retained?

Figure 7.1. Nonlinear Movement to Different Ethnic Identities Over Time and Across Situations, as Measured by Individuals' Response to Two Basic Ethnic Identity Questions

identity orientation to biculturalism and then toward a White identity orientation.

Take, for instance, a first-generation Asian Indian woman in the United States. She interacts with a social network of Asian Indian families in her city, feels a moral commitment to help new Asian Indian immigrants coming into her city, and visits her former hometown in India every 2 or 3 years. Her elderly parents have also recently immigrated to live with her in the United States. Thus, she endorses an Asian Indian ethnic identity orientation (choice of "Yes" to the first question). The same woman has received her university education in the United States and is an academician; she works closely with her White colleagues and has become a concerned citizen in her White middle-class neighborhood (choice of "Yes" to the second question). She also entertains in her home her White friends and colleagues. Thus, this woman has a bicultural identity orientation in her interpersonal interactions. In another context, this woman does not endorse a bicultural identity, but rather a strong ethnic identity orientation, saying "Yes" to the first question and "No" to the second question. Take, for example, her reactions to marriage and religious practices. Even though she came to the United States as a young single woman to get her university education in English language and literature, spent much time with U.S. White peers in the classroom and in doing research, obtained professional employment in the United States, and also sought U.S. immigration status, she chose to have an arranged marriage. Her parents and family elders chose a "suitable" bridegroom for her in India, a man she had never met prior to her wedding, and held a traditional Hindu wedding for the daughter in their hometown. Although this woman has now lived in the United States for a long time, she has not sought to convert to Christianity. Rather, she continues to observe Hinduism and in fact meets with a Hindu religion group weekly to sing Hindu hymns in the classical language, Sanskrit. This woman is in the forefront of organizing Hindu religious ceremonies in her city. In yet another context, the woman feels culturally marginal, not feeling a sense of belonging to either cultural group. With regard to gender role, she does not endorse subservience to males and authority figures, which is expected in her culture of origin; thus, she says "No" to the first question. She also says "No" to the second question because she does not philosophically agree with the political agenda of U.S. White feminists, and she feels that U.S. White feminists do not understand and therefore are not sensitive to racial and cultural issues of ethnic women.

The nonlinear ethnic identity process of this Asian Indian woman does not arise out of lability or instability. Rather, it arises out of the ethnic individual's adaptive principle of flexibility and openness to possibilities, which has been conditioned through exposure to the effects of the White society and her ethnic society, both societies being necessary for the formation of an ethnic identity.

As explained well by Helms (1995), ethnic identity is "a social identity based on the culture of one's ancestors' national or tribal group(s), as modified by the demands of the culture in which one's group currently resides" (p. 16). Thus, in conclusion, an ethnic individual does not have a one-dimensional or dichotomous cultural identity, either ethnic or White. Further, it is possible for a person to have different ethnic identity orientations because an ethnic person lives in diverse social and cultural contexts. However, one ethnic identity orientation may be predominant, but not exclusive, during one period of a person's life span. Finally, having to negotiate two ethnic identity orientations can make an ethnic individual's life complex and difficult because many options are available for the individual, and these put pressure on him or her to make many decisions. Such a cross-cultural life may, nonetheless, be rich, exciting, rejuvenating, and productive.

In her interpretation of the bidirectional acculturation model, Phinney (1990) conceptualized ethnic identity as the extent to which an individual acculturates to his or her native culture or the extent to which various Asian ethnic groups acculturate to their respective cultural heritage. This conceptualization is illustrated by the documentary *From Hollywood to Hanoi*, which is a reflection on the life of the Vietnamese filmmaker Tiana Thi Thanh Nga. The filmmaker, as a child, was brought out of Vietnam to the United States by her father in 1966 and told that she would never see Vietnam again. Her father taught her to hate the Viet Cong by threatening that Ho Chi Minh would come to tear her up if she did not have her dinner. With all neighborhood TVs tuned to the war "killing our boys there," the girl hated the "gooks" too. As a teenager, she wound up as a martial arts "cute girl," playing in Hollywood's generic Southeast Asian films, and also did such popular musical videos as *Karatecise, Lust in de Jungle,* and *Free as I Want 2B.* She picked up a Hollywood anglicized version of her name and kept it for a long time. She tried to be everyone; she tried to tune out the Vietnam war, but could not. So she had to go to Hanoi to seek the truth, to see for herself, and not to listen to rumors, even those within the Vietnamese American community. She went on a geographical, psychological, and cross-cultural journey of returning to a land that she and her family had abandoned politically, economically, and socially. So this is a story of growing up in American suburbs and going back: back to Ho Chi Minh City and then back again to the suburbs. The film shows how a person who was acculturated to U.S. White society developed a sense of ethnic identity through a process of reverse acculturation and finding her cultural self.

ETHNIC IDENTITY AND ASIAN FAMILIES

Culture, as sustained by ethnicity, significantly socializes family patterns, communication styles, relationship styles, and personality (Uba, 1994). Several authors have proposed that the cultural values of various U.S. Asian groups are markedly different from the cultural values of the U.S. White society: For example, Segal (1991) cited various authors who propose that most U.S. Asian groups focus on collective needs, interdependency, and conformity. Sodowsky, Maguire, Johnson, Ngumba, and Kohles (1994) and Ihle, Sodowsky, and Kwan (in press) found in studies on worldviews that White Americans, as compared to Chinese subjects, preferred an individualistic orientation in relationships and a focus on actualizing one's personal processes. These authors hypothesized that Asian families may have difficulty maintaining their sense of ethnic identity in a dominant culture that is vastly different from their own.

Asian Cultural Values

It is vital to briefly consider select core values that are important to many U.S. Asian groups. Explanations about personality, human development, behaviors, and motivations are provided by the religions of many Asian groups. Buddhism, Hinduism, Islam, Confucianism, Taoism, and Shamanism emphasize such personality traits as silence, nonconfrontation, moderation in behavior, self-control, patience, humility, modesty, and simplicity; all these traits are seen as virtues. These characteristics together point to an introspective, self-effacing personality, which could also be defined as an introverted type. In contrast, American psychotherapy appears to consider extraversion, sociability, self-confidence, and dominance as healthy traits.

Because of the belief that human nature is endowed with holy spirit, people are supposed to treat one another with religious respect. Other interpersonal attitudes considered morally good include selflessness, dedication, loyalty to others, and devaluation of individualism. In relationships with others, one is expected to practice charity, generosity, and self-sacrifice. Social harmony is achieved through structured family relationships that have clearly defined codes of behavior, including language usage, and hierarchical roles. Some of these formal relationships are those of father and son, husband and wife, older brother/sister and younger brother/sister, grandparent and grandchild, and uncle/aunt and nephew/niece. Extrafamilial relationships such as those between teacher and student, boss and employee, host and guest, and friend and friend are based on family relationship prototypes. Although most relationships are hierarchical, the person with seniority, due to sanctioned status, age, and/or male gender, is expected to manifest benign authority.

Family kinship is the basic relationship and the primary socializing agent, especially for teaching obedience and discipline. Informal social friendships and peer interactions are given less priority and are considered less influential, as is not the case in the U.S. White social system. Filial piety, especially that of the eldest son, is the cornerstone of morality. Family identity is characterized by the interdependence of individual members; by individual members' seeking the "honor" and "good name" of the family and protecting it from "shame"; and by reciprocal duties and obligations that take precedence over individual desires—such as duties of parents to children, when growing children need nurturance, education, and guidance, and, later in the family's history, duties of adult children to elderly parents.

Social control is obtained through family demands for obedience and fulfillment of obligations. If these behaviors are not observed, the principal techniques of punishment employed by the family are arousing moral guilt and making the morally reprehensible person "lose face" through social/public shame. The family practices a collective approach to shaming and disciplining the erring person. In U.S. White society, social control appears to be obtained through the expectations of individuals' voluntary self-discipline and personal accountability, and significant relationships, framed by democratic ideals, are supposed to feature equality, intimacy, love, and affection. An Asian society is situation centered, with a focus on the family and social self, and the society expects an individual's conformity to a situation's code of ethics. On the other hand, U.S. White society is individual centered and sees the person as an autonomous and free self, apart from others, who is responsible for his or her own direction. The family and society, in fact, exist to maximize the individual.

The Self as a Product of Ethnicity and Family

It appears that for many U.S. Asians the sense of self, with reference to the previously described cultural and religion-oriented values, is strongly tied to the family. McGoldrick (1982) theorized that it is through the family that culture is transmitted and that, as a result, ethnicity and family are strongly intertwined. Root (1985) and Sodowsky (1991) extended this conception by proposing that for the Asian client, family is an important aspect of cultural identity.

Therefore, if mental health practitioners wish to better serve Asians, they must understand cultural identity and its relationship to the family because both are at the core of the Asian self (Sodowsky, 1991). For instance, many U.S.-born Asians maintain a strong enough ethnic identity so that they refuse to place their elderly parents and grandparents in retirement/nursing homes. Instead, they accept their elderly into their homes despite the ensuing difficulties related to family leadership, cultural generation gaps, finances, space, privacy, food and eating habits, and sharing of time.

The following is a description of 19-year-old Dung and her family, the Le family. Dung and her 16-year-old brother, Khoi, have been in the United States for more than a decade, but her parents arrived only a few years ago, along with two more brothers and a sister. The arrival of her parents and her younger siblings, two of whom were born after Dung's departure to the United States, has left Dung torn between duty and freedom.

"It was strange," Dung says.

> It felt different. All of a sudden I had two parents who wanted to tell me what to do. Vietnamese parents are very different from American parents. I'm 19, and I can't go out without permission. My parents believe that girls don't do this and don't do that.
>
> But I respect my parents. It is my responsibility to take care of my brothers and sister. Every day I teach them English and help them with their homework. At home I'm Vietnamese, so I take care of my brothers and sister. In my culture girls do not speak with boys; they are supposed to be very quiet and not too friendly. I'm not supposed to date until after college.

"No problem," Dung adds, laughing, her speech punctuated with American adolescent slang. "I have lots of friends—my parents think I have too many friends . . . and I do go out with guys—but just as friends."

Had Dung been concerned with her personal autonomy, like many of her U.S. White adolescent peers, she might have expressed strong resentment against her parents. Not only could she have perceived her parents, whom she hardly knows—not having lived with them for 16 years—as excessively intrusive and controlling with "foreign" conventions and restrictions, but she could have also viewed them as cold-hearted and rejecting for having sent her, at age 10, on a lone voyage to the United States, with the injunction that she also take care of her 6-year-old brother. But when listening to Dung, one does not hear feelings of resentment of parents or opposition to familial obligations.

Acculturation Studies of Asian Ethnic Families

Family studies from acculturation perspectives could be interpreted as studies of ethnic identity. It is possible to place them in two categories: (a)

studies that seem to indicate familial conflict due to differences in acculturation within a family; and (b) studies that indicate that external aspects of
ethnic identity may be more easily modified by U.S. Asian families than internal aspects.

The Asian family system is vulnerable to emotional difficulty because of
the discrepant acculturation of its members. For example, Matsuoka (1990)
stated that Vietnamese American adolescents in their native culture form their
identity largely on the basis of familial relationships. But once they are exposed
to the U.S. White culture, they are attracted to the independence and autonomy given to White teenagers, and consequently may begin to rely increasingly
on White peers for their identity development. The diminishing use of the
family as a cultural base for the formation of their ethnic identity, as well as
of formal relationship ideals, religious values, and the collective spirit, may
contribute to both individual and familial difficulty. In general, it seems that
parents are afraid that children will lose a strong sense of their ethnic identity
(Segal, 1991), and that although the children are eager to identify with their
culture of origin, they are not quite as invested as their parents (Wakil, Siddique, & Wakil, 1981). In such parent-child cultural conflicts, parents may
react with rigidity and conservatism, and children with acting-out behaviors.
However, the parents and the children may not clearly understand the source
of the family's conflicts: ethnic identity differences in the family.

Siddique (1977) found that in Asian Indian families in Canada there was
an increase in mutual decision making between husbands and wives and an
increase in input from children regarding their career decisions. In addition,
parents let children participate in Western festivals. We have also observed
reductions in certain gender-specific cultural behaviors in the daily lives of
U.S. Asian families. Wives give their input to husbands on the purchase of
homes and vehicles and are involved in family financial matters outside the
home—for example, by communicating with banking, financing, and insurance organizations. With regard to children being listened to in certain matters,
there is the pragmatic realization that the children may be better informed
about the U.S. educational system and employment opportunities than the
immigrant parents. These White-acculturated behaviors suggest that external
aspects of ethnic identity may be amenable to change.

However, core values of culture, such as relationships with the opposite
sex and dating, may not be as subject to change (Wakil et al., 1981). We have
seen that many U.S. Asians are uncomfortable with the public display of het-
erosexuality because sexuality and sexual relationships are supposed to be
treated with modesty and a degree of formality. In future research, opposite-sex
relationships could be investigated in relation to internal ethnic identity.

In the few studies that do exist in which ethnic identity is considered a
developmental phenomenon (i.e., linear and not bidirectional), there does
appear to be a relationship between ethnic identity and family variables. As
part of a larger study on self-esteem, Phinney and Chavira (1992) found that

participants who had progressed developmentally in their ethnic identity tended to have higher scores on a family relations measure. Thus, they suggested that familial support may be an important prerequisite for minority youths, including Asians, to explore their cultures of origin. We would add to this observation that U.S. Asian parents who are highly critical of their children's acculturated behaviors, applying undue pressure on their children to observe family beliefs and religious ways, and imposing many sanctions and restrictions, may actually drive the children away from the ethnic culture. In fact, Rosenthal and Feldman (1992) indicated that feelings of ethnic pride were related to families marked by warmth, independence, and environments that were under control.

The above studies and arguments suggest that certain family environments may enhance one's sense of ethnic identity. Conversely, it seems equally probable that ethnic identity attitudes may influence relations with the family because, as previously mentioned, the family is a primary representation of cultural values and ethnicity. For example, one study examined how ethnic identity influences one's perceptions of one's family and familial roles. Sodowsky and Carey (1988) found that U.S. Asian Indian participants who designated themselves as Asian Indian or "mostly" Asian Indian tended to be aligned with traditional Asian Indian values. These participants also endorsed family items that were more traditional (e.g., preference for children not dating, respect for parental leadership). Thus, Sodowsky and Carey's research provided some support for the proposition that the extent to which one identifies with one's ethnic group influences one's adherence to cultural values that are linked to family structure or rules.

It seems that Phinney's (1990) developmental model can be used to generate research questions that focus on the relationship between ethnic identity types and the family. Phinney described the *moratorium stage* as one in which the individual has begun to explore his or her ethnicity, as evidenced by confused thoughts and feelings about the implications of ethnic group membership, and the *achieved-identity* stage as one in which the individual has completed ethnic identity exploration and emerged with a clear, secure understanding and acceptance of his or her own ethnic identity. Possible questions might be: (a) Do individuals in the moratorium stage or achieved-identity stage use their families to explore their cultural values more than individuals in Phinney's earlier two stages? (b) How does this cultural exploration via the family work? (c) What role does the family play in the development of the ethnic identity types? (d) Are families that have numerous achieved-identity members less vulnerable to acculturative stress?

As part of a larger study, Pannu and Helms (in progress) hypothesized that ethnic identity would be related to perceptions of familial acculturation and family functioning (variables of cohesion and family conflict) in a U.S. Asian Indian sample. Ethnic identity was thought to be important to examine because research has shown that Asian Indians have a strong commitment to the Indian culture that they left behind when they immigrated (Sodowsky & Carey, 1987). Contrary to predictions, ethnic identity did not predict perceptions of family functioning. However, ethnic identity was related to perceptions of familial acculturation. Specifically, Asian Indians who had actually explored their ethnic identity tended to perceive their family as Asian Indian acculturated (as opposed to being acculturated to U.S. White society). Pannu and Helms suggested that because the family is central to the cultural identity development of Asian Indians, participants who had actively searched for their ethnic identity may have used the family as a vehicle to explore what it meant to be Asian Indian.

Fernandez (1988) used the Minority Identity Development Model (MID) (Atkinson et al., 1993; the model was originally developed in 1979) to theoretically explore the possible influence of ethnic identity development on Southeast Asian family relationships. Fernandez outlined how each of the ethnic identity stages may be associated with different perceptions of one's family. She proposed that individuals in the Conformity stage may ignore ethnic familial responsibilities because they conform to U.S. White dominant cultural norms. In the Dissonance stage, individuals face information that shakes up their previous U.S. White conformity attitudes. They begin to feel conflict between the values of their culture of origin and U.S. White values. Thus, in this stage conflict between loyalty to the family versus personal desire for independence may be the key issue. Conversely, Southeast Asian adolescents in the Immersion stage may have strong familial ties and conform to familial roles. When in the Introspection stage, individuals struggle with their unequivocal bond to the ethnic group and their own personal autonomy. Fernandez proposed that as a result of this struggle, individuals who retain strong ties to the family without resolving issues of personal autonomy may become self-critical. Finally, Fernandez proposed that in the Synergetic Articulation and Awareness stage, individuals may maintain a close bond with the family and be happy with that commitment. On the other hand, individuals may not fulfill family commitments because of their desire for their own independence.

Pannu and Helms (in progress) speculated that it might be important to examine ethnic identity from the MID framework because it takes into account the sociopolitical construct of oppression of minorities by the White dominant group. Researchers could then begin to understand how oppression of ethnic groups, and not only of African Americans, may affect the identity attitudes and functioning of Asian families. We hypothesize that the more prejudice U.S. Asians experience, the more cohesive and supportive family members may be with each other and the more segregated and traditional an Asian family may become.

To summarize, the ethnic identity literature on Asian families, whether using an acculturation model or a linear developmental model, does indicate a relationship between ethnic identity and family relations.

SUMMARY

U.S. pluralism is not new. Many a small town has long known Chinese restaurants, Indian doctors, and Korean grocers. But now Asian ethnic cultures are crossing and paralleling each other and the U.S. White culture at great speed. The rising diversity of the United States is something more than cosmopolitan: It is a fundamental recoloring of the U.S. complexion and a revisioning of ethnic identities. The traditional metaphor for this was that of a mosaic. But the interaction is more fluid than that—more human and subject to revision. For instance, a Chinese American may say, "I am Chinese because I live in San Francisco, a Chinese city, and I want to tell you more about who I am." U.S. Asians are finally coming into their own. It is still very new—U.S. Asians defining an ethnic identity for themselves and having a voice.

REFERENCES

American Psychiatric Association. (1994). *Diagnostic and statistical manual of mental disorders* (4th ed.). Washington, DC: Author.

Atkinson, D. R., Morten, G., & Sue, D. W. (1993). *Counseling American minorities: A cross-cultural perspective.* Dubuque, IA: Brown & Benchmark.

Bennett-Choney, S., & Behrens, J. (in press). Development of the Oklahoma Racial Attitudes Scale—Preliminary Form. In G. R. Sodowsky & J. Impara (Eds.), *Multicultural assessment in counseling and clinical psychology.* Lincoln, NE: Buros Institute of Mental Measurements.

Berry, J. W. (1980). Acculturation as varieties of adaption. In A. M. Padilla (Ed.), *Acculturation: Theory, model, and some new findings* (pp. 9-25). Boulder, CO: Westview.

Berry, J. W., Kim, U., Minde, T., & Mok, D. (1987). Comparative studies of acculturative stress. *International Migration Review, 21,* 491-511.

Berry, J. W., Poortinga, Y. H., Segall, M. H., & Dasen, P. (1992). *Cross-cultural psychology: Research and applications.* New York: Cambridge University Press.

Breton, R., Isajiw, W. W., Kalbach, W. E., & Reitz, J. G. (Eds.). (1990). *Ethnic identity and equality.* Toronto: University of Toronto Press.

Burke, P. (1991). Identity process and social stress. *American Sociological Review, 56,* 836-849.

Carter, R. T. (in press). Exploring the complexity of racial identity attitude measures. In G. R. Sodowsky & J. Impara (Eds.), *Multicultural assessment in counseling and clinical psychology.* Lincoln, NE: Buros Institute of Mental Measurements.

Clark, M., Kaufman, S., & Pierce, R. C. (1976). Explorations of acculturation: Toward a model of ethnic identity. *Human Organization, 3,* 231-238.

Cook, D., & Helms, J. E. (1988). Visible racial/ethnic group supervisees' satisfaction with cross cultural supervision as predicted by relationship characteristics. *Journal of Counseling Psychology, 35,* 268-274.

Cronin, C. (1970). *The sting of change.* Chicago: University of Chicago Press.

DeVos, G., & Romanucci-Ross, L. (1975). *Ethnic identity.* Palo Alto, CA: Mayfield.

Fernandez, M. S. (1988). Issues in counseling Southeast Asian students. *Journal of Multicultural Counseling and Development, 16,* 157-166.

Heath, A. E., Neimeyer, G. J., & Pedersen, P. B. (1988). The future of cross-cultural counseling: A Delphi poll. *Journal of Counseling and Development, 67,* 27-30.

Helms, J. E. (1990). *Black and White racial identity: Theory, research, and practice.* Westport, CT: Greenwood Press.

Helms, J. E. (1995). The conceptualization of racial identity and other "racial" constructs. In E. Trickett, R. Watts, & D. Birman (Eds.), *Human diversity*. San Francisco: Jossey-Bass.

Helms, J. E. (in press). Toward an approach for assessing racial identity. In G. R. Sodowsky & J. Impara (Eds.), *Multicultural assessment in counseling and clinical psychology*. Lincoln, NE: Buros Institute of Mental Measurements.

Helms, J. E. (in progress). Socioracial groups in psychology: Terminology and assumptions. In J. E. Helms (Ed.), *The psychology of (socio)race: A tripartite perspective*.

Ihle, G. M., Sodowsky, G. R., & Kwan, K.-L. K. (in press). Worldviews of women: Comparisons between White-American clients, White-American counselors, and Chinese international students. *Journal of Counseling and Development*.

Isajiw, W. W. (1990). Ethnic-identity retention. In R. Breton, W. W. Isajiw, W. E. Kalbach, & J. G. Reitz (Eds.), *Ethnic identity and equality* (pp. 34-91). Toronto: University of Toronto Press.

Kwan, K. K. K., & Sodowsky, G. R. (1994). *Internal and External Ethnic Identity Measure*. Lincoln: University of Nebraska-Lincoln, Dept. of Educational Psychology.

Matsuoka, J. K. (1990). Differential acculturation among Vietnamese refugees. *Social Work, 35*, 341-345.

McGoldrick, M. (1982). Ethnicity and family therapy: An overview. In M. McGoldrick, J. K. Pearce, & J. Giordano (Eds.), *Ethnicity and family therapy* (pp. 3-30). New York: Guilford.

Moritsugu, J., & Sue, S. (1983). Minority status as a stressor. In R. D. Felner, L. A. Jason, J. N. Moritsugu, & S. S. Farber (Eds.), *Preventive psychology: Theory, research, and practice* (pp. 162-173). Elmsford, NY: Pergamon.

Pannu, R. K., & Helms, J. E. (in progress). *Asian Indian cultural identity and perceptions of family functioning*.

Phinney, J. S. (1990). Ethnic identity in adolescence and adulthood: A review of research. *Psychological Bulletin, 108*, 499-514.

Phinney, J. S. (1992). The multigroup ethnic identity measure: A new scale for use with diverse group. *Journal of Adolescent Research, 7*, 156-176.

Phinney, J. S., & Chavira, V. (1992). Ethnic identity and self-esteem: An exploratory longitudinal study. *Journal of Adolescence, 15*, 271-281.

Root, M. P. (1985). Guidelines for facilitating therapy with Asian American clients. *Psychotherapy, 22*, 349-357.

Rosenthal, D. A., & Feldman, S. S. (1992). The nature and stability of ethnic identity in Chinese youth: Effects of length of residence in two cultural contexts. *Journal of Cross-Cultural Psychology, 23*, 214-227.

Rowe, W., Bennett, S., & Atkinson, D. (1994). White racial identity models: A critique and alternative proposal. *The Counseling Psychologist, 22*, 129-146.

Sabnani, H. B., Ponterotto, J. G., & Borodovsky, L. G. (1991). White racial identity development and cross-cultural counselor training: A stage model. *The Counseling Psychologist, 19*, 76-102.

Segal, U. A. (1991, April). Cultural variables in Asian Indian families. *Journal of Contemporary Human Services, 72*, 233-242.

Sherif, M. (1964). Reference groups in human relations. In M. Sherif & M. O. Wilson (Eds.), *Group relations at the crossroads* (pp. 203-231). New York: Harper & Row.

Siddique, C. M. (1977). Structural separation and family change: An exploratory study of the immigrant Indian and Pakistani community of Saskatoon, Canada. *International Review of Modern Sociology, 7*, 13-34.

Smith, E. J. (1991). Ethnic identity development: Toward the development of a theory within the context of majority/minority status. *Journal of Counseling and Development, 70*, 181-188.

Sodowsky, G. R. (1991). Effects of culturally consistent counseling tasks on American and international student observers' perception of counselor credibility: A preliminary investigation. *Journal of Counseling and Development, 69*, 253-256.

Sodowsky, G. R., & Carey, J. C. (1987). Asian Indian immigrants in America: Factors related to adjustment. *Journal of Multicultural Counseling and Development, 15*, 129-141.

Sodowsky, G. R., & Carey, J. C. (1988). Relationships between acculturation-related demographics and cultural attitudes of an Asian-Indian immigrant group. *Journal of Multicultural Counseling and Development, 16,* 117-133.

Sodowsky, G. R., Lai, E. W. M., & Plake, B. S. (1991). Moderating effects of sociocultural variables on acculturation variables of Hispanics and Asian Americans. *Journal of Counseling and Development, 70,* 194-204.

Sodowsky, G. R., Maguire, K., Johnson, P., Ngumba, W., & Kohles, R. (1994). World views of White American, Mainland Chinese, Taiwanese, and African students: An investigation into between-group differences. *Journal of Cross-Cultural Psychology, 29,* 309-324.

Spencer, M. B., & Markstrom-Adams, C. (1990). Identity processes among racial and ethnic minority children in America. *Child Development, 61,* 290-310.

Sue, D., & Sue, D. W. (1990). *Counseling the culturally different: Theory and practice* (2nd ed.). New York: John Wiley.

Tajfel, H. (1978). *The social psychology of minorities.* New York: Minority Rights Group.

Takaki, R. (1993). *A different mirror: A history of multicultural America.* Boston: Little, Brown.

Tan, A. (1989). *The Joy Luck Club.* New York: Ballantine.

Uba, L. (1994). Families. *Asian Americans: Personality patterns, identity, and mental health.* New York: Guilford.

U.S. Bureau of the Census. (1980). *1980 census of population and housing.* Washington, DC: Government Printing Office.

Wakil, S. P., Siddique, C. M., & Wakil, F. A. (1981). Between two cultures: A study in socialization of children of immigrants. *Journal of Marriage and the Family, 43,* 929-940.

8

Hispanic Identity Development

Implications for Research and Practice

J. MANUEL CASAS

SCOTT D. PYTLUK

IN RECENT YEARS, the Hispanic population has received a greater amount of attention within the social science literature. Concomitant with such attention has been an increase in criticism directed at the quality and, from an applied perspective, the pragmatic value of this literature (see Casas, 1984). Along these lines, a major criticism has focused on researchers' failure to define accurately and/or describe the Hispanic samples used in their studies (see Ponterotto & Casas, 1991). More specifically, this criticism has focused on the prevailing tendency to use what Trimble (1990-1991) called "ethnic glosses" or overly general labels (e.g., Hispanics) to identify a specific racial/ ethnic group employed in a study while totally ignoring the extensive variables that serve to identify specifically and/or differentiate the diverse subgroups and individuals that make up such a group. For example, it is a well-documented fact (see Ponterotto & Casas, 1991) that the Hispanic population varies across numerous mutually nonexclusive and frequently interacting variables, including demographic variables (e.g., nationality, racial makeup, mean and median age, family size and composition, geographic distribution); sociohistorical variables (e.g., length of time in the United States, impetus for immigration to the United States, experiences with racism); sociopolitical variables (e.g., immigrant/citizen status, level of political participation); socioeconomic variables (e.g., educational attainment, labor force participation, individual and family income); and sociopsychological variables (e.g., acculturation level, actual and perceived power, self-entitlement, intragroup similarity and cohesion). (For further details relative to these variables, see Casas and Arbona, 1992.)

In recent years psychologists from diverse specializations have begun to direct greater attention to identifying and examining dynamic sociopsychological processes that may serve to differentiate the subgroups and/or individuals that make up the Hispanic population. Two such processes that a growing number of researchers believe must be understood and taken into consideration when working from a counseling perspective with such racial/ ethnic minority populations as the Hispanic and Asian American (populations that comprise a significant number of immigrants) are ethnic identity development, or enculturation, and acculturation.

In line with the position taken by such psychologists, this chapter directs selective attention to these psychosocial processes and, in particular, to the prevailing models that have been used to describe and explain them. It should be noted that major attention is directed to recently proposed models that to date have received little or no attention in the counseling psychology literature. For the sake of organization, the major variables and processes that are the focus of this chapter are sometimes addressed separately. However, this should in no way be interpreted as our taking the position that they are independent of one another. On the contrary, given the availability of information with respect to these variables (Bernal & Knight, 1993), it is our position that they are interactive. In presenting an overview, we direct specific attention to the implications of these processes vis-à-vis both the psychosocial functioning of Hispanic individuals and the provision of counseling services to such individuals. Furthermore, with respect to both ethnic identity development and acculturation, we put forth suggestions for future research.

In addition, it should be noted from the outset that although the ethnic identity models, including those describing the enculturation and acculturation processes addressed here, can be applied to any immigrant racial/ethnic group, they are generically discussed here solely in reference to those ethnic/ national groups that make up the Hispanic population of the United States. Such a focus should in no way be interpreted to mean that other racial/ethnic minority groups do not experience similar or complementary processes, as these groups also coexist with the dominant non-Hispanic White culture in the United States.

Finally, given our belief in the applicability of such models across cultures and ethnic groups, we have opted to use the generic term *Hispanic* to include individuals of diverse Hispanic-based national origins including Mexico, the countries of Central America (i.e., Guatemala, Honduras, Costa Rica, El Salvador, Nicaragua, and Panama), the Spanish-speaking countries of South America (i.e., Colombia, Venezuela, Peru, Chile, Ecuador, Uruguay, Paraguay, Argentina), the Spanish-speaking countries of the Caribbean (i.e., Cuba, the

Dominican Republic), and the U.S. territorial island of Puerto Rico. Having made this caveat, we alert the reader to the fact that in referring to works on ethnic identity, we have made an effort to retain the original terminology used by the various authors whose work is considered in this discussion.

MAJOR VARIABLES
AND PROCESSES DEFINED

The preponderance of the counseling-related research that has taken racial/ethnic identity into consideration has narrowly focused on its content (e.g., level of acculturation). In contrast, with the exception of the work of a few researchers (e.g., Atkinson, Morten, & Sue, 1993; Helms, 1990), much less attention has been given to its development or formation. However, in the past few years, a growing number of researchers (see Bernal & Knight, 1993) have taken the position that to understand accurately individuals from distinct racial/ethnic minority groups, one must understand both content and developmental variables and processes separately as well as interactively. Further, both need to be taken into consideration by counseling researchers and practitioners. Working from this perspective, we deem it necessary for the sake of edification and clarity to define these processes briefly before continuing.

Ethnic Identity

Relative to the definition of ethnic identity content and process, we rely on recent work conducted by Phinney (1993), who stated:

> It is important to clarify the distinction between the process of ethnic identity formation and what might be called the content of ethnic identity. Most research on ethnic identity has emphasized the content of ethnic identity, that is, the actual ethnic behaviors that individuals practice, along with their attitudes toward their ethnic group (Phinney, 1990). In contrast, our work has focused on the process of ethnic identity formation, that is the way in which individuals come to understand the implications of their ethnicity and make decisions about its role in their lives, regardless of the extent of their ethnic involvement. Content and process are likely to be related, in that the process of exploration may lead to more positive attitudes, but the two can be distinguished conceptually. (p. 64)

In her clarification of the two variables Phinney (1993) did not make direct reference to the role of enculturation and acculturation; however, to understand both ethnic identity and its developmental process one must take both enculturation and acculturation into consideration. Therefore, these two variables are also briefly defined.

Enculturation

Enculturation (i.e., ethnic socialization), according to Berry (1993), is the socialization process "by which developing individuals acquire (either by generalized learning in a particular cultural milieu, or as a result of specific instruction and training) the host of cultural and psychological qualities that are necessary to function as a member of *one's group*" (p. 272). In his work on enculturation, Berry developed a descriptive model that differentiates three types of culture transmission: vertical (influences stemming from one's parents), horizontal (those from one's peers), and oblique (those from other adults and institutions in one's own society). In essence, a child's ethnic identity develops through enculturation—a process in which parents in particular play a very significant role. According to Hurtado, Rodriguez, Gurin, and Beals (1993), the social/ethnic identity of the parents themselves serves as a mediating variable for determining what aspects of ethnicity are maintained by Mexican-origin persons and, in turn, what aspects are inculcated in their children. (For further details on Berry's model, see Berry, 1993.)

Acculturation

From both a sociological and a psychological perspective, the process of acculturation is defined as the product of culture learning that occurs as a result of contact between the members of two or more culturally distinct groups. From this definition, it is also presented as a process of attitudinal and behavioral change undergone, willingly or unwillingly, by individuals who reside in multicultural societies (e.g., the United States, Canada, and Israel) or who come in contact with a new culture due to colonization, invasions, or other political changes (Marín, 1992). In contrast to enculturation, which involves socialization into one's ethnic group, acculturation involves socialization into an ethnic group other than one's own. Researchers contend further that the psychological and social changes that may occur in the process of acculturation are dependent on the characteristics of the individual (e.g., level of initial identification with the values of the culture of origin), the intensity of and importance given to the contact between the various cultural groups, and the actual numerical balance between individuals representing the original culture and those who represent the new and more than likely larger majority culture. Finally, of utmost importance in understanding acculturation from a sociopsychological perspective is the fact that it is perceived to be an open-ended process. Because acculturation is such an important process affecting the development of ethnic identity, a later section of this chapter is devoted to its discussion.

Having defined these interactive ethnic-identity-related variables and processes, we contend that understanding them and giving them serious consideration when working with Hispanic individuals is of utmost importance if counseling researchers and practitioners are to interpret accurately the psychological makeup (e.g., beliefs, values, and attitudes) and behaviors of Hispanic individuals within an appropriate psychosocial context. Furthermore, we take the position that without such understanding, the educational and social service needs of all Hispanics cannot be effectively met (see Aboud & Doyle, 1993; Casas & Casas, 1994).

HISPANIC ETHNIC IDENTITY— CONTENT AND PROCESS: AN OVERVIEW

Ethnic Identity—The Content

According to Bernal, Knight, Organista, Garza, and Maez (in press), ethnic identity is a set of self-ideas specifically related to one's ethnic group membership. Instead of referring to the understanding of the ethnicity of others, ethnic identity refers directly to one's knowledge of personal ownership or membership in the ethnic group, and the correlated knowledge, understanding, values, behaviors, and proud feelings that are direct implications of that ownership (Knight, Bernal, Garza, & Cota, 1993). Relative to Hispanic ethnic identity, such ownership or membership might very likely be demonstrated by a strong adherence to such staunchly entrenched cultural values as giving primary importance to the family, or *familismo* (Sabogal, Marín, Otero-Sabogal, Marín, & Pérez-Stable, 1987); the need for social behaviors that promote smooth and pleasant social situations, or *simpatía* (Triandis, Marín, Lisansky, & Betancourt, 1984); the maintenance of personal respect, or *respeto*, in interpersonal relations (Marín, 1992); and cooperative approaches to learning (Duran, 1992).

In its ultimate essence, ethnic identity is an important and intricate part of the self-concept, whose development is influenced by the normative socialization processes that affect all persons in general, and by the intergroup phenomena resulting from the minority status of the ethnic individual (Knight, Bernal, Garza, & Cota, 1993). Because ethnic identity is a part of the self-concept and a product of a socialization process that can have its own uniqueness relative to each individual that is a part of an ethnic group, one should not expect it to be the same for all members of any respective ethnic group. Consequently, with respect to the Hispanic population, which, as noted above, varies across numerous demographic and social variables, one should expect a great deal of variance in reference to their identification as members of their generic ethnic group as well as in their cultural distinctiveness.

Although not yet thoroughly studied, the notion that the nature and degree of Hispanic ethnic identity plays a very important part in the way Hispanics manifest their ethnic culture on a daily basis (e.g., gender roles, child-rearing, and socialization practices) is supported by a small but growing body of literature (see Bernal & Knight, 1993; Bernal, Knight, Ocampo, Garza, & Cota, 1993). With specific attention directed to children, Bernal et al. (1993) contended that Mexican American children's variation in ethnic identity is probably associated with important characteristics of their behavioral and adaptational patterns. Thus, information relative to ethnic identity might be very helpful to counselors in their efforts to understand how and why Hispanic children adapt differentially to the variety of educational and social environments in which they find themselves. Such information could be of great assistance in helping counselors develop counseling interventions and educational strategies that are less challenging and more supportive of these children's cultural characteristics (Bernal et al., 1993).

Ethnic Identity—
The Developmental/Formative Process

Ethnic identity development or enculturation is a dynamic and continuously developing socialization process. Although researchers state that it is applicable to all persons, they also suggest that it has unique characteristics in reference to persons from racial/ethnic minority groups—in this case, Hispanics. Furthermore, though it is true that all persons undergo ethnic socialization (i.e., enculturation), a model of the socialization of Hispanics must take into account some important differences in their socialization as compared to that of persons from the dominant culture. More specifically, persons of all cultures experience enculturation: That is, they undergo the normative socialization experiences of their own specific culture. These enculturating experiences lead to the development of living skills, behavioral competencies, and values, as well as to a cultural identity. Similarly, Hispanic persons are enculturated by their families and community and develop appropriate values, skills, and, in turn, an Hispanic ethnic identity. For example, one would expect Hispanic children socialized in a traditional Hispanic family to develop preferences for learning cooperatively as well as for maintaining a high level of respect for their elders and, in particular, their teachers.

The unique aspect of the ethnic identity development process as it applies to Hispanics is that their ethnic identity is defined and formulated not only by their own cultural environment but also by both the dominant cultural group with which it is in contact and the nature of ethnic group/dominant group interaction (Berry, 1984). That is, the ethnic identity of Hispanic persons is continuously and differentially affected by the acculturation process. The differential impact of this process is fundamentally determined by the demographic and social characteristics of the community and work environments in which Hispanic persons exist. The more Hispanic the environments, especially in reference to the continued use of the Spanish language, the greater the likelihood that the acculturation process will have a weaker impact on the ethnic identity of Hispanic individuals. The reverse will be true for Hispanics living and working in predominantly non-Hispanic White environments.

ETHNIC IDENTITY
DEVELOPMENT MODELS

To provide an understanding of the dynamics inherent in the ethnic identity development process as it pertains to Hispanics, various models that focus on different aspects and stages of the process have been proposed. The most recent and/or frequently proposed models for use across diverse psychological disciplines are presented here to provoke thought with respect to future endeavors on the part of both counseling researchers and practitioners.

A Children's Ethnic
Identity Development Model

Focusing on the development of ethnic identity in children, Bernal et al. (1993) presented a model that is made up of five distinct components:

1. *Ethnic self-identification* concerns children's categorization of themselves as members of their ethnic group. Such identification requires that the children have an "own-ethnic-group category" with a corresponding label and distinguishing cues.
2. *Ethnic constancy* refers to the knowledge that children develop relative to the fact that their ethnic characteristics are permanent across time, settings, and transformations.
3. *Ethnic role behaviors* involve the children's engaging in the multitude of behaviors that reflect ethnic cultural values, styles, customs, traditions, and language.
4. *Ethnic knowledge* is the children's knowledge that certain role behaviors and traits, values, styles, customs, traditions, and language are relevant to their own ethnic group.
5. *Ethnic feelings and preferences* are children's feelings about their own ethnic group membership and their preferences for ethnic group members, behaviors, values, traditions, and language.

The types of cultural values and/or behaviors to which an Hispanic child might eventually subscribe include *familismo* (i.e., giving primary importance to one's immediate as well as extended family), patriarchal family structure (i.e., subscribing to traditional "masculine"/"feminine" values and behaviors), *respeto* (i.e., respecting individuals for their age and accumulated life experiences), cultural fatalism (i.e., a form of existentialism; a tendency to take life as it comes with a "resigned" mind-set), religiosity (i.e., a strong belief in the existence of a higher being and the need to follow prescribed formal practices to worship this being), belief in folk healing when in crisis, and a tendency not to separate physical from emotional well-being (Comas-Diaz, 1993). Adherence to these cultural values may have implications for counseling. For example, the religious focus given to endurance of human suffering and to self-denial might discourage a Hispanic individual from seeking counseling services in the first place. Also, the tendency not to separate physical and emotional well-being has implications for the type of help that might be preferred.

Bernal et al. (1993) contended that ethnic identity develops gradually in children. These researchers added that because *race* refers to inherited physical characteristics (i.e., characteristics that tend to be more visible and tangible) and *ethnicity* comprises factors such as behaviors, customs, beliefs, and values (i.e., characteristics that may be less tangible from a child's perspective), children's racial awareness probably develops earlier than ethnic awareness. Further research that tests this hypothesis would be welcome, especially with respect to Hispanic persons who may be biracial (Puerto Ricans, Hispanic persons from the Caribbean).

Three theoretical perspectives are used to explain the development of the five ethnic identity components contained in the model proposed by Bernal et al. (1993). These perspectives are social learning theory (Bandura, 1987), cognitive developmental theory (Flavell, 1985), and self-system theory (Harter, 1983). Using these three theories, Bernal et al. succinctly explained the development of ethnic identity in children, stating that children's information about their ethnicity and ethnic group membership is acquired from social learning experiences provided by their families, their communities, and the dominant society. As they grow older, and have greater freedom and wider opportunity for social contact, they learn increasingly complex information and integrate past learning with present learning. Through social cognitive processes, they make social comparisons and become aware of reflected appraisals relating to their ethnicity. With respect to stress-related phenomena, such children might be exposed to stereotypic beliefs regarding who they are and where they may or may not fit into the dominant social strata. Such beliefs might be associated with increased stress that would affect psychological well-being. Relative to cognitive development, Bernal et al. (1993) contended that

> cognitive developmental constraints may limit children's ability to grasp and incorporate the content of their ethnic identity. Furthermore, there may be differential maturation within the five components; e.g., children's self-identification as ethnic group members may precede children's understanding that their inherited ethnic characteristics are permanent. Harter's (1983) theory provides a developmental framework for self-descriptions that involve multiple domains (e.g., social competence, achievement competence) of the self and can be extended to children's view of their ethnic self. That is developmental changes in the nature of self-descriptions about the ethnic identity components may be similar to changes in other domains of the self. (pp. 34-35)

For instance, as a young Hispanic boy becomes an adolescent, his sex-role identity parallels his developing ethnic identity. His ethnic identity, then, might serve as the driving force that determines how staunchly he identifies with the male characteristics ascribed to traditional Hispanic culture (i.e., *machismo*).

A Social Cognitive Model

The social cognitive model, as presented by Knight, Bernal, Garza, and Cota (1993), takes into account both the enculturative process, which is undergone by all children regardless of their ethnicity, and the acculturation process (i.e., adaptation to the dominant culture), which is more specific to racial/ethnic minority children. This model includes five basic clusters of variables that interactively affect children's value-based social behaviors: (a) the broader social ecology (e.g., family background, family structure, and the sociocultural environment); (b) socialization by familial and nonfamilial agents (e.g., media, schools and peers); (c) children's self-concept (including but not limited to their ethnic, gender, familial, and school identity); (d) the immediate contextual features that activate specific identities to guide behavior; and (e) cognitive development (i.e., those abilities that moderate the abstraction and encoding of socialization rules presented by socialization agents, the nature and complexity of children's ethnic identity, and the enactment of internalized values in relatively novel situations).

From an overall perspective, this model entails mediating relationships among the aforementioned variables. According to Knight, Bernal, Garza, and Cota (1993), the social ecology in which a family is immersed determines the socialization processes and content that emanate from both familial and nonfamilial socialization agents. The information put forth by such agents affects the development of children's self-concept, which in its entirety encompasses their ethnic identity. The children's self-concept, in turn, plays an important part in determining their value-based social behaviors.

With respect to the cognitive development variable, the model proposes that such development and the socialization practices through which the socialization content is transmitted are causally linked to the timing of the development of ethnic identity and its respective behaviors. That is, children's cognitive abilities play a determining role relative to their abilities to abstract and encode socialization rules, to develop a complex ethnic identity that includes trait-level descriptors and values, and to enact those behaviors characteristic of ethnic values in novel situations (Knight, Bernal, Garza, & Cota, 1993).

Working from this model, in reference to Hispanics, Knight, Bernal, Cota, Garza, and Ocampo (1993) took the position that one would expect that recent Mexican immigrants who lived in a barrio with other Mexican immigrants would teach their children about Mexican culture as well as socialize them into this culture. These children would know about Mexican culture and probably self-identify as belonging to that ethnic group. Also, on the basis of this model, the children would probably engage in behaviors that were sanctioned by the culture: For example, they might be cooperative with other peers, have a high respect for authority, and speak Spanish (Knight, Bernal, Cota, et al., 1993). This example represents a highly ideal perspective, omitting part of the picture. While positive information with respect to Mexican culture is being absorbed, information from the dominant culture is also being taken in. This information often includes a negative/prejudiced view of Hispanics. Such dichotomous views can create internal conflicts for a child or adolescent who is beginning to "own" his or her ethnic identity. With a high respect for authority, for example, a Hispanic child might be likely to defer to a non-Hispanic White teacher who espoused prejudicial attitudes toward Hispanics. Such deference could very likely gnaw away at the psychological well-being of this child or adolescent. Further research is needed to better understand the implications of this type of scenario.

Racial Identity Development Models

Several racial identity development models proposed over the years by various counseling psychologists are also applicable for differentially explaining the ethnic identity development process (e.g., Atkinson, Morten, & Sue, 1983; Helms, 1990). Because some of these models are well covered in the other identity-focused chapters contained in this volume and because the models share theoretical and structural similarities, only the model proposed by Atkinson et al. (1983) is briefly presented here as a prototype. The reason for presenting any one of these models here is that a recently proposed adolescent-focused ethnic identity model (Phinney, 1993), which is described in this chapter, draws quite a bit from the racial identity development literature.

Early efforts to identify, define, and understand racial/ethnic identity development were mainly made by Black social scientists and educators (e.g., Cross, 1971; Jackson, 1975; Thomas, 1971); consequently, it is not surprising that the racial identity models originally proposed focused solely on the African American identity developmental experience. A major thrust of these models was to provide a mechanism by which to assess the attitudinal impact of such a process on the overall psychological development of African-American persons. The focus on race in the original models also reflects a very strong belief on the part of racial identity theorists that "even though Americans are members of many ethnic groups, the once biological and now social meanings and beliefs associated with racial group membership supersede ethnic group membership" (Carter & Qureshi, Chapter 12, this volume).

Regardless of such beliefs, more recent models (Atkinson et al., 1993), as evident in a number of chapters contained in this book, are much broader in scope and address the racial/ethnic and cultural development of persons from such diverse groups as Chinese Americans, Japanese Americans, Hispanics/Latino(a)s, gays, lesbians, and bisexuals. The major impetus for generalizing the basic tenets inherent in the identity models earmarked for African Americans is the fact that other minority groups, such as those mentioned above, have shared similar patterns of adjustment to racial, ethnic, and/or cultural oppression. Speaking to this point, Sue (1990) contended that "in the past several decades, Asian Americans, Hispanics, and American Indians have experienced sociopolitical identity transformations so that a 'Third World consciousness' has emerged with cultural oppression as the common unifying force" (p. 95).

One of the more generic identity models was developed by Atkinson et al. (1993) and is more inclusively called the "Racial/Cultural Identity Development Model" (R/CID). According to Atkinson et al., the R/CID model is intended to provide not a comprehensive theory of personality development but rather a framework to help counselors in their efforts to understand the attitudes and behaviors of persons from diverse racial, ethnic, and/or cultural backgrounds. In essence, the model, reflective of ego identity theory, identifies and defines five stages of development that oppressed people experience as they struggle to understand themselves in terms of their own culture, the dominant culture, and the oppressive relationship between the two cultures. Each stage of identity contains four corresponding beliefs and attitudes that may help counselors to better understand their minority clients. These attitudes/beliefs are believed to be an integral part of the minority person's identity and are manifest in how he or she views (a) the self, (b) others of the same minority, (c) others of another minority, and (d) majority/dominant individuals (Sue, 1990). The actual stages are as follows:

1. *Conformity.* Individuals in this stage unequivocally prefer dominant cultural values over those of their own culture, have a self-depreciating attitude, have a group-depreciating attitude toward others of the same minority, have a discriminatory attitude toward others of different minorities, and have a group-appreciating attitude toward the dominant group.
2. *Dissonance.* Individuals in this stage experience frequent conflict with respect to depreciating and appreciating attitudes toward the self, others of the same minority, others of different minorities, and the dominant group.
3. *Resistance and Immersion.* Individuals in this stage endorse minority-held views and reject the dominant society, have a self-appreciating attitude, have a group-appreciating attitude toward their own group, have conflicting feelings between empathy for other minorities and culturocentrism, and have group-depreciating attitudes toward the dominant group.
4. *Introspection.* Individuals in this stage experience uncertainty with the rigidly held group views of Stage 3 and attend more to notions of individual autonomy.
5. *Synergetic Articulation and Awareness.* Individuals in this stage have resolved the major conflicts confronted in Stage 4 and experience a sense of self-fulfillment with respect to cultural identity; have appreciative attitudes toward self, others of the same minority, and others of different minorities; and have a selective appreciation of the dominant group.

(For more detailed information relative to this model, see Atkinson et al., 1993.)

Certain aspects of this model that need to be understood by individuals who may want to use it when working with racial/ethnic minorities include the following:

1. Any and all persons from racial/ethnic groups that differ from the dominant Euro-American group can be identified at any one point of their personal history to be at any one stage in the model.

2. A person's life experiences and, in particular, the type of early contact (i.e., positive or negative) that is experienced with the dominant Euro-American cultural groups will determine the stage at which an individual may enter the developmental process. For example, if minority children experience negative interactions with Euro-American persons and very positive interactions from diverse individuals from their own racial/ethnic group, they may, from the onset, find themselves in the Resistance and Immersion stage of the model (i.e., Stage 3).

3. Given the ever-changing cross-racial/ethnic interactions that individuals can experience in their lifetime, it is quite possible for an individual to stay at one specific stage, move forward, or even move backward. A person at Stage 4 who is questioning his or her need to hold to staunch ethnocentric views may experience some very racially negative interactions with a person or persons from the dominant group and find him- or herself moving back to the resistant mind-set that characterizes Stage 3. For example, a Hispanic-identified adolescent girl might adhere to a highly traditional view of gender roles that might be challenged as "sexist" by a non-Hispanic feminist. Does this individual then revert back to a resistant mind-set that questions Anglo culture, or does this individual experience conflict around the extent of her adherence to the traditional Hispanic culture? Or does she maintain both values and behaviors relative to gender roles that might vary according to the situational context?

4. Adding to the complexity of the model, it should be noted that within any family, family members may find themselves at totally different stages. Needless to say, such an occurrence can contribute to a variety of family problems (see Szapocznik & Kurtines, 1980).

5. Finally, there are groups of ethnic/racial minority individuals whose developmental contexts further complicate the application of these models. Although Spanish-speaking immigrants are typically considered to make up a single racial group, it is notable that many Spanish speakers are also Black. The racial identity development process for such individuals requires the negotiation of a self-defined identity that might include Blackness as a racial component and Hispanicity as an ethnic component, with an externally (socially) imposed Black identity based solely on skin color. The manner in which such individuals develop and integrate their racial and ethnic identities from both internal and external sources of influence is undeniably complex and needs to be accounted for within any models of racial identity development.

Although this model has a strong following, we contend that racial identity models are limited from a developmental point of view in that they do not help to thoroughly understand the actual complex process of racial identity development. They focus solely on the development of identity in relationship to other groups and, in particular, the dominant majority, while giving no attention to enculturation or acculturation processes.

Ethnic Identity:
Crisis and Resolution Model

Challenging models like that proposed by Atkinson et al. (1983), Ruiz (1990) took the perspective that many studies addressing Chicano, Mexican American, and Latino ethnicity and identity formation are mostly empirical and are not directed to counselors who practice with these clients. He observed, further, that those models of cultural, racial, or ethnic minority identity development that do include implications for counseling are not tailored specifically for Chicano, Mexican American, and Latino clients. Thus, Ruiz described a Chicano/Latino ethnic identity model that attempts to fulfill this need by comprehensively describing the development, transformation, and resolution of ethnic identity conflicts.

Based on case histories that emerged out of counseling sessions with primarily Chicano, Mexican American, and other Latino university students, the model is founded on four premises:

(a) that marginality correlates highly with the concept of maladjustment (LeVine & Padilla, 1980); (b) that both marginality and the pressure to assimilate can be destructive to an individual (LeVine & Padilla, 1980); (c) that pride in one's own ethnic identity is conducive to mental health (Bernal, Bernal, Martinez, Olmedo, & Santisteban, 1983); and (d) that during the acculturation process, pride in one's own ethnic identity affords the Hispanic more freedom to choose (Bernal et al., 1983). (Ruiz, 1990, p. 32)

Five stages addressing ethnic identity conflicts, interventions, and resolutions make up this model. The first, (causal), second (cognitive), and third (consequence) focus on the development of ethnic identity conflicts.

In the causal period, variables such as parental messages or injunctions about ethnic identity either affirm, ignore, negate, or denigrate the family's ethnicity. Additional variables that contribute to ethnic conflict include the failure to identify with one's own ethnic group, rejections from that group, confusion, uncertainty, or a lack of familiarity with respect to one's culture (Bayard, 1978), and traumatic or humiliating events relative to one's ethnicity. Recommended counseling interventions include disaffirming and restructuring of the internalized negative injunctions related to ethnicity and cultivation of ethnic appreciation and pride.

Ruiz (1990) identified three faulty beliefs about ethnicity that are demonstrated by clients during the cognitive stage. These include the association of ethnic group membership with poverty and prejudice, the belief that assimilation is the only means to avoid poverty and prejudice, and the belief that life success is possible only through assimilation. Counseling interventions at this stage involve cognitive strategies aimed at deconstructing the faulty beliefs.

The consequence stage is characterized by a fragmentation of ethnic identity. The individual experiences intensifying ethnic identity conflicts and may even flee from his or her unwanted ethnic self-image. Concomitantly, the use of defense mechanisms to manage the conflicts increases.

During the fourth stage, the *working-through* stage, a typical client experiences distress caused by his or her inability to cope with ethnic conflict and a realization that an alien ethnic identity is no longer acceptable. He or she is therefore more willing to enter counseling than before and, if already in counseling, is more willing to disclose ethnic-identity-related concerns. This state is further characterized by a process of "dis-assimilation" (Hayes-Bautista, 1974), an increase in ethnic consciousness, a reclaiming and re-integration of disowned ethnic identity fragments, and a reconnection with ethnic continuity. According to Ruiz (1990), the initial phase of counseling should begin with the use of an ethnocultural assessment instrument followed by an eclectic use of interventions such as "ethnotherapy" focused on alterations of negative attitudes about race and ethnicity; "pluralistic counseling" directed toward a recognition of the client's culturally based beliefs, values, and behaviors (LeVine & Padilla, 1980; Padilla, 1981); and "ethnocultural identification" (Comas-Diaz & Jacobsen, 1987), which emphasizes coping with change in cultural values and transitional experiences, promoting the integration of the ethnocultural self, and using the client's natural support systems in the counseling process.

The final stage in this model, the *successful resolution* stage, is characterized by the client's greater acceptance of self, culture, and ethnicity, an improvement in self-esteem, and a sense that ethnic identity represents a positive and a success-promoting resource.

On the basis of this model, one could speculate that recent immigrant families might become strongly attached to traditional social and sex-role norms as a defense against the strong pressure to acculturate (Espin, 1993). More specifically, Espin (1993) contended that the traditional culture is idealized and "may become a symbol of the stable parts of personal identity and probably the strongest defense against any sense of identity loss that might be engendered by acculturation" (p. 283).

For example, recent immigrant parents who defensively attach themselves to tradition may pressure their more rapidly acculturating children to narrowly subscribe to the same set of beliefs. This scenario may result in conflict between the child and parents (Szapocznik & Kurtines, 1980) and within the child, who begins to question who he or she is in terms of ethnicity, as well as stress due to pressures from both the traditional parents and the host culture. With respect to practice, an understanding of such phenomena might help the counseling practitioner develop more effective prevention and intervention strategies.

Overall, the value of Ruiz's (1990) model is that it is based in clinical practice with Hispanic clientele. However, although it does provoke thought for the practitioner, it could benefit from empirical validation.

A Three-Stage Model of Ethnic Identity Development in Adolescents

Focusing on adolescents, Phinney (1993) suggested an integrated model of ethnic identity development that is based on existing models of ego identity and ethnic identity and on recent empirical studies with minority adolescents from several ethnic groups. This researcher directed her attention to adolescents because studies on ethnic identity have tended to ignore the adolescent population while primarily focusing on two areas: (a) Developmental psychologists have directed attention to the process by which children learn the label and the attributes of their own ethnic group (Aboud, 1987; Bernal, Knight, Garza, Ocampo, & Cota, 1990), and (b) social psychologists and sociologists have directed their attention to the characteristics that define ethnic identity in adult populations and the way that these characteristics are affected by contact with other groups (Berry, 1993; Phinney, 1990). According to Phinney (1993), the lack of attention given to adolescence is surprising given that identity formation is the central developmental task of adolescence (Erikson, 1968).

The actual model proposed by Phinney is congruent with the varied racial/ethnic identity development models discussed in the previous section (i.e., Atkinson et al., 1983; Cross, 1978; Helms, 1990). This congruence is based on the fact that Phinney's model is rooted in the ego identity development literature by sharing the idea that an achieved identity occurs through stages and is the result of a crisis, an awakening, and/or an encounter, which leads to a period of exploration or experimentation, and finally to a commitment or incorporation of one's ethnicity. Aside from focusing mainly on adolescents, Phinney's model differs from the others by reducing the number of stages contained in the model. She accomplished this reduction by suggesting that the encounter and exploration stages may not be separate stages but actually only one stage. This suggestion is based on her research with 10th-grade minority youth in which she found little evidence of any specific event or series of events that were emotionally intense or disruptive. According to Phinney (1993),

> Some subjects mentioned what sounded like encounter experiences, such as name calling and discrimination, but these did not necessarily lead to rethinking of the issues. It may be that an encounter experience is evident when individuals look back at the process of their own search, but that is not clear at the time it happens. Therefore, it may be more useful in empirical studies to consider encounter and exploration as a single stage. (p. 69)

Her model is therefore made up of the following three stages: (a) unexamined ethnic identity (i.e., individuals at this stage are not in the process of exploring ethnicity), (b) ethnic identity search (moratorium) (i.e., individuals in this stage are involved in exploring and seeking to understand the meaning of ethnicity for themselves), and (c) achieved ethnic identity (i.e., individuals at this stage are characterized by a clear and confident sense of their own ethnicity). For a detailed description and discussion of relevant research vis-à-vis this model, the reader is referred to Phinney (1993).

Although Phinney's attention to the adolescent is a step in the right direction, giving us a more comprehensive view of ethnic identity development for an age group that has been previously ignored, the model fails to address adequately the complexity of the overall developmental process an adolescent experiences. For example, a gay/lesbian/bisexual Hispanic adolescent may find him- or herself being marginalized from both the Hispanic and the gay/lesbian/ bisexual communities. The Hispanic community may ostracize such an individual on the basis of their perception that open lesbian/gay/bisexual identification might stigmatize, if not harm, the community. On the other hand, the gay/lesbian/bisexual community may be racist and exclude the individual. How does such a developmental situational context get internalized and managed by the gay/lesbian/bisexual Hispanic adolescent? How is his or her psychological well-being affected? How might a counselor intervene? Thus, a Hispanic individual must not only negotiate his or her ethnic identity in adolescence but also develop a sexual identity, a comfortable gender identity, and a general self-concept, all in dynamic interplay with one another. In addition, one cannot lose sight of the fact that while such identities are forming, these adolescents are also being influenced by the forces of acculturation and modernity (Ahsan & Khursheed, 1990; Hui, Drasgow, & Chang, 1983; Triandis, Bontempo, Leung, & Hui, 1990). Any theory of the development of the Hispanic individual in the United States needs to attempt to capture and highlight this complexity. Researchers in the field will then need to investigate the validity of such models employing already existing or new methodologies that are sensitive to the complex relationships among the variables described.

It is critical to add that there exists an interactive, mediating relationship between ethnic/social identity development and the acculturation process. More specifically, according to Hurtado et al. (1993), social/ethnic identity serves as a mediating variable for determining what aspects of ethnicity are maintained by Mexican-origin persons and then inculcated in their children.

ACCULTURATION—THE PROCESS:
A GENERAL OVERVIEW

The concept of acculturation appears as early as 1880; however, the definition that until recently has been most widely accepted was formulated by Redfield, Linton, and Herskovits (1936): "Acculturation comprehends those phenomena which result when groups of individuals having different cultures come into continuous first-hand contact, with subsequent changes in the original culture patterns of either or both groups" (p. 149).

Unfortunately, this definition largely confined the study of acculturation within the realm of anthropology and sociology. Furthermore, according to Marín (1992), although acculturation did not receive serious research attention within the realm of psychology until the 1970s (see Berry & Annis, 1974a, 1974b; Brislin, Lonner, & Thorndike, 1973; Olmedo, 1979), it is now generally accepted and largely defined as a multidimensional psychosocial phenomenon that is reflected in psychological changes that occur in individuals as a result of their interaction with a new culture (p. 237).

More specifically, as a psychosocial phenomenon, the construct of acculturation is perceived as the product of culture learning that occurs as a result of contact between the members of two or more groups. Working from this definition, acculturation is then presented as a process of attitudinal and behavioral change undergone, willingly or unwillingly, by individuals who reside in multicultural societies (e.g., the United States, Canada, and Israel), or who come in contact with a new culture due to colonization, invasions, or other political changes (Marín, 1992). Furthermore, researchers contend that the psychological and social changes that may occur in the process of acculturation are dependent on the characteristics of the individual (e.g., level of initial identification with the values of the culture of origin), the intensity of and importance given to the contact between the various cultural groups, and the actual numerical balance between individuals representing the original culture and those who represent the new and more than likely larger majority culture. Finally, as previously mentioned, of utmost importance in understanding acculturation from a sociopsychological perspective is the fact that it is perceived to be an open-ended process.

According to Marín (1992), the attitudinal and behavioral learning that occurs in the acculturation process may be perceived as occurring at three levels. The first level is the *superficial* one and basically involves the learning (and forgetting) of the facts that are part of one's cultural history or tradition. At this level, acculturating individuals might begin to forget the names of important historical figures, or other important historically related facts relative to their country of origin, while in turn learning prominent historical facts of the new country's culture in which they find themselves. The second level in the acculturation process is the *intermediate* one. At this level, the learning that can be expected to take place as a function of acculturation involves the more central behaviors that are perceived to be at the core of a person's social life. Such behavior could include language preferences and use. Furthermore, Marín contended that other possible indicators of this level of acculturation are ethnicity of friends, neighbors, and coworkers, ethnicity of spouse, names given to children, and preference for ethnic media in multicultural environments (p. 238). Finally, the third level is referred to as the *significant* level. At this level, the changes that take place occur in the individual's beliefs, values, and norms that make up those essential constructs that prescribe people's worldviews and interaction patterns. The changes that occur at this level tend to be more permanent and are reflected in the day-to-day activities of the acculturated individual. A number of examples of changes that occur at this level are aptly presented by Marín (1992) when he states:

> A number of studies have suggested that Hispanic cultural values encourage positive interpersonal relationships and discourage negative, competitive, and assertive interactions—what has been called the "simpatía" script (Triandis, Marín, Lisansky, & Betancourt, 1984). Acculturation pressures on Hispanics could be expected to change this social script so that it either becomes less central to the individual or it becomes a behavioral standard only when interacting with other Hispanics who have not been acculturated. Other group specific values and norms of Hispanics that could be changed as a function of acculturation are the significance of familialism (Sabogal, Marín, Otero-Sabogal, Marín, & Pérez-Stable, 1987) and collectivism (Marín & Triandis, 1985; Triandis, 1990). (p. 239)

It should be noted that although some cultural values and behaviors are easily modified through the process of acculturation, others remain quite strong across generations. For instance, with respect to *familismo*, Marín (1992) reported that Sabogal et al. (1987) found that although certain aspects of *familismo* (e.g., familial obligations, the power of the family as a behavioral referent) might be weakened through the acculturation process, other aspects might not (e.g., support received and expected from relatives).

ACCULTURATION MODELS

Although psychologists, sociologists, and anthropologists have sought to understand the acculturation process from a general perspective, they have also sought to identify sociopsychological and environmental models from which to better understand the evolution of the process itself. Until recently, the majority of models proposed took a bipolar perspective. That is to say, it was assumed that Hispanic individuals who came in contact with the majority non-Hispanic White culture would eventually assume the values, attitudes, and behaviors of this culture to the exclusion of their traditional culture. The bipolar models addressed in the literature that have historically received a significant amount of attention are the dominant majority model, the transitional model, the alienation model, the multidimensional model, and the bicultural model. It is beyond the scope of this chapter to examine each of these in detail. It should be noted, however, that the first three models identified above, the dominant majority model, the transitional model, and the alienation model, have been severely criticized due to their overtly or covertly supporting prejudicial attitudes toward individuals who are attempting to acculturate and/or assimilate to the dominant Euro-American society. Each of these models has at one point or another been adopted by American society as the appropriate belief regarding how groups arriving to the United States "should" fit in. The models that are currently receiving a great deal of attention by researchers and practitioners alike include the cultural adaptation model, the family biculturalism model, and the orthogonal cultural identification model (for details relative to these models, see Casas & Casas, 1994). The orthogonal cultural identification model deviates from the traditional bipolar perspective and as such merits discussion at this point.

ORTHOGONAL CULTURAL IDENTIFICATION MODEL

This model is based on orthogonal cultural identification theory, which contends that identification with different cultures is orthogonal in nature (Oetting & Beauvais, 1990-1991). In essence, this means that identification with any culture is essentially independent of identification with any other culture. In other words, identifying with one culture in no way diminishes the ability of an individual to identify with any other culture. This can be contrasted with all of the preceding proposed models of acculturation, which have viewed the individual along a continuum or continua between cultures. A benefit inherent in this model is that by its very nature it helps reduce the tendency to use "ethnic glosses" or overly generalized labels to identify persons from specific racial/ethnic groups. This model does so by stressing the individual's dynamic identification across diverse cultural dimensions rather than his or her simply being a static part of an ongoing process (Trimble, 1990-1991). The importance of this model lies in its emphasis on the identification of important cultural dimensions and variables that are attributes of the individual rather than simply on his or her racial/ethnic group.

Although Oetting and Beauvais's (1990-1991) contention that two cultures can maintain an orthogonal relationship within the same individual may be theoretically valid for certain values, attitudes, and behaviors within certain contexts, it may not be so for others. For instance, socioeconomic and political realities may require an immigrant Hispanic woman to abandon her traditional sex role by working outside the home while embracing this role when at home with her family. Given that she was enculturated into one culture first and then acculturated into another, she might be able to reconcile and/or integrate both cultural realities; however, her female child, being socialized by acculturating parents, might not be able to maintain such an orthogonal perspective. This child might develop a singular sex-role identity informed by each of the respective cultures without the degree of choice that her mother was able to exert. Further research is therefore needed to test the parameters within which an orthogonal relationship can exist across generations and settings.

From another theoretical perspective, there is a need to get beyond thinking about acculturation as a unidimensional variable as well as treating a similar score across individuals on an acculturation scale as having the same identical interpretation or meaning. Continuing to do so is to negate that individuals within any group have different social experiences, and process the "same" experience differently as a consequence of their structural positions within the group. For instance, for some Hispanics, ethnic socialization represents acceptance and pride in group membership; for others, a political acceptance of socially derogated patterns of behavior, and for still others, an unnecessary liability. (Hurtado et al., 1993, p. 139)

Unlike the ethnic identity theories and models, on which there is little research, the acculturation process has generated a significant amount of counseling-related research. The major areas that such research has addressed include the impact of acculturation on the counseling process (Atkinson, Casas, & Abreu, 1992; Atkinson & Matsushita, 1991; Atkinson, Thompson, & Grant, 1993), presenting problems (Cherpitel, 1992; Osvold, Lise, & Sodowsky, 1993; Williams & Berry, 1991), diverse attitudes (Hanassab, 1991; Leong & Tata, 1990; Marín, Marín, Otero-Sabogal, & Sabogal, 1989), behaviors and implications for counseling (Marín, Gamba, & Marín, 1992; Zimmerman & Sodowsky, 1993), diverse perceptions (Kunkel, 1990; Montgomery, 1992; Rick & Forward, 1992), achievement and academic performance (Barona & Pfeiffer, 1992; Gomez & Fassinger, 1994; Lese & Robbins, 1994), validation of acculturation measures (Orozco, Thompson, Kapes, & Montgomery, 1993; Sabnani & Ponterotto, 1992; Suinn, Ahuna, & Khoo, 1992), specific ethnic groups and implications for counseling (Heinrich, Corbine, & Thomas, 1990; Ramisetty-Mikler, 1993), and screening/diagnosis (Howes & DeBlassie, 1989; Negy & Woods, 1992).

To help strengthen our understanding of the acculturation process, new directions for research are suggested. For instance, there is a need to examine how sociopolitical variables influence the acculturation process. Do groups acculturate willingly, or do they feel compelled to acculturate? Is there a sociopsychological difference between those who do so willingly and those who feel compelled to do so? Is there a difference between what the two groups are willing to give up vis-à-vis their original culture?

In addition, according to Berry (1993), there has tended to be an implicit bias in the direction of acculturation research. More specifically, this research has usually limited itself to examining the changes in the so-called minority group as it gradually becomes more like the mainstream majority group. To truly understand the acculturation process, what is needed is research on the mutual influences that lead to changes in both groups in contact (Berry, 1993). According to Berry (1993),

> We cannot hope to understand the situation of an "ethnic minority" in a plural society unless we also understand the "ethnic majority," and their mutual relationships. Such an exclusive focus on the ethnic minorities gives us only part of what we need to know, and perhaps reinforces the implicit view that it is "they" who need "fixing" rather than "us"; this focus can also lead us to ignore the common fact that it is the relationship between "them" and "us" that should be of key scientific interest. (p. 279)

Given the important role that the acculturation process may play in the general realm of counseling, it behooves both practitioners and researchers to be aware that diverse measures to assess acculturation level do exist (Garcia & Lega, 1979; Olmedo, Martinez, & Martinez, 1978; Olmedo & Padilla, 1978; Suinn, Rickard-Figueroa, Lew, & Vigil, 1987). Furthermore, although the models that have been proposed to explain the acculturation process are deemed to be applicable across racial/ethnic groups, various researchers have addressed the need to develop separate measures for use with distinct racial/ethnic groups. For instance, researchers whose interest is the Hispanic/Latino population have recognized the need to have separate measures for use with distinct Hispanic/Latino ethnic/national groups (e.g., Cuban American and Mexican American) (Cuellar, Harris, & Jasso, 1980; Garcia & Lega, 1979). Likewise, Suinn et al. (1987) saw the need to develop a generic scale for use with Asian Americans. Although this scale appears to be applicable for use with Asian Americans in general (Suinn et al., 1987), Suinn et al. contended that future research may show that separate scales are necessary for use with the diverse ethnic/national groups that make up the Asian American population.

Readers who are interested in further examining the complex process of acculturation and identifying further directions for future research are referred to Hurtado et al. (1993).

SUMMARY

Wishing to move away from the deleterious practice of using ethnic glosses to describe very diverse populations, such as the Hispanic population, we have attempted to introduce the reader to the multiplicity of variables that contribute to such diversity. In particular, we directed attention to two of the major processes that a growing number of researchers contend must be understood and, in turn, taken into consideration in both research and clinical endeavors—ethnic identity development and acculturation. In addressing these two processes, we described the most current models, with special attention given to their application with Hispanics of diverse ages. In addition, we attempted to demonstrate how clinicians might use the models to better understand Hispanics and thus to plan more effective interventions.

More specifically, from a broad counseling perspective, what many researchers like Sue (1990) posited to be the value of the increased interest and work relative to ethnic identity and acculturation models is that (a) the models can help counselors avoid responding to the culturally different client from a stereotypic perspective by bringing to the fore within-group differences; (b) the implementation of the models has potential psychodiagnostic value (Helms, 1987); and (c) the models give emphasis and credence to the historical and sociopolitical influences that shape racial/ethnic minority identity. Finally, because many of these models are relatively new, we identified future directions for research.

In conclusion, although the ethnic identity and acculturation models presented here provide a framework from which to understand the respective identity and acculturation process, as a whole they fail to address, from a *dynamic* perspective, the affective and cognitive manifestations and their implications for an individual's psychological well-being and personality and/or characterological development from both a short- and a long-term perspective. Working from this vantage point, N. W. Zane (personal communication, August 13, 1994) took the position that variables like those discussed in this chapter should be considered from an interactive perspective. Such a perspective would supply the underpinnings for the formulation of a theory of personality development of the Hispanic individual in the United States that would be akin to the type of theory that already exists for the non-Hispanic individual. Efforts such as these would be at the "cutting edge" of the work needed to make the realm of multicultural counseling a substantive, practical, and theoretically driven discipline.

REFERENCES

Aboud, F. (1987). The development of ethnic self-identification and attitudes. In J. Phinney & J. M. Rotheram (Eds.), *Children's ethnic socialization: Pluralism and development* (pp. 32-55). Newbury Park, CA: Sage.

Aboud, F. E., & Doyle, A. B. (1993). The early development of ethnic identity and attitudes. In M. E. Bernal & G. P. Knight (Eds.), *Ethnic identity: Formation and transmission among Hispanics and other minorities* (pp. 47-59). Albany: State University of New York Press.

Ahsan, S. K., & Khursheed, A. (1990). Ethnicity, socioeconomic status, and socio-cultural modernity. *Social Sciences International, 6,* 18-22.

Atkinson, D. R., Casas, A., & Abreu, J. (1992). Mexican-American acculturation, counselor ethnicity and cultural sensitivity, and perceived counselor competence. *Journal of Counseling Psychology, 39,* 515-520.

Atkinson, D. R., & Matsushita, Y. J. (1991). Japanese-American acculturation, counseling style, counselor ethnicity, and perceived counselor credibility. *Journal of Counseling Psychology, 38,* 473-478.

Atkinson, D. R., Morten, G., & Sue, D. W. (1983). *Counseling American minorities.* Dubuque, IA: William C. Brown.

Atkinson, D. R., Morten, G., & Sue, D. W. (1993). *Counseling American minorities: A cross-cultural perspective* (4th ed.). Madison, WI: Brown & Benchmark.

Atkinson, D. R., Thompson, C. E., & Grant, S. K. (1993). A three-dimensional model for counseling racial/ethnic minorities. *The Counseling Psychologist, 21,* 257-277.

Bandura, A. (1987). *Social learning theory.* Englewood Cliffs, NJ: Prentice Hall.

Barona, A., & Pfeiffer, S. I. (1992). Effects of test administration procedures and acculturation level on achievement scores. *Journal of Psychoeducational Assessment, 10,* 124-132.

Bayard, M. P. (1978). Ethnic identity and stress: The significance of sociocultural context. In J. M. Casas & S. E. Keefe (Eds.), *Family and mental health in the Mexican American community* (pp. 109-123). Los Angeles: Spanish Speaking Mental Health Research Center.

Bernal, G., Bernal, M. E., Martinez, A. C., Olmedo, E. L., & Santisteban, D. (1983). Hispanic mental health curriculum for psychology. In M. C. Chunn II, P. J. Dunston, & F. Ross-Sheriff (Eds.), *Mental health and people of color: Curriculum development and change* (pp. 64-93). Washington, DC: Howard University Press.

Bernal, M. E., & Knight, G. P. (1993). *Ethnic identity: Formation and transmission among Hispanics and other minorities.* Albany: State University of New York Press.

Bernal, M., Knight, G., Garza, C., Ocampo, K., & Cota, M. (1990). The development of ethnic identity in Mexican-American children. *Hispanic Journal of Behavioral Sciences, 12,* 3-24.

Bernal, M. E., Knight, G. P., Ocampo, K. A., Garza, C. A., & Cota, M. K. (1993). Development of Mexican American identity. In M. E. Bernal & G. P. Knight (Eds.), *Ethnic identity: Formation and transmission among Hispanics and other minorities* (pp. 31-46). Albany: State University of New York Press.

Bernal, M. E., Knight, G. P., Organista, K., Garza, C., & Maez, B. (in press). The young Mexican American child's understanding of ethnic identity. In M. E. Bernal & P. C. Martinelli (Eds.), *Mexican American identity.* Encino, CA: Floricanto.

Berry, J. W. (1984, August). *Cultural psychology and ethnic psychology: A comparative analysis.* Presidential address presented at the 7th International Conference of the International Association of Cross-Cultural Psychology, Acapulco, Mexico.

Berry, J. W. (1993). Ethnic identity in plural societies. In M. E. Bernal & G. P. Knight (Eds.), *Ethnic identity: Formation and transmission among Hispanics and other minorities* (pp. 271-296). Albany: State University of New York Press.

Berry, J. W., & Annis, R. C. (1974a). Acculturative stress: The role of ecology, culture, and differentiation. *Journal of Cross-Cultural Psychology, 5,* 382-405.

Berry, J. W., & Annis, R. C. (1974b). Ecology, culture and psychological differentiation. *International Journal of Psychology, 9,* 173-193.

Brislin, R. W., Lonner, W. J., & Thorndike, R. M. (1973). *Cross-cultural research methods.* New York: John Wiley.

Casas, J. M. (1984). Policy, training, and research in counseling psychology: The racial/ethnic minority perspective. In S. D. Brown & R. Lent (Eds.), *Handbook of counseling psychology* (pp. 785-831). New York: John Wiley.

Casas, J. M., & Arbona, C. (1992). An examination of and recommendations relative to Hispanic career related issues: Research and practice. In D. Brown & C. Minor (Eds.), *Career development* (pp. 51-76). Alexandria, VA: National Career Development Association.

Casas, J. M., & Casas, A. (1994). The acculturation process and implications for education and services. In A. C. Matiella (Ed.), *The multicultural challenge in health education* (pp. 23-49). Santa Cruz, CA: ETR Associates.

Cherpitel, C. J. (1992). Acculturation, alcohol consumption, and casualties among United States Hispanics in the emergency room. *International Journal of the Addictions, 27,* 1067-1077.

Comas-Diaz, L. (1993). Hispanic/Latino communities: Psychological implications. In D. R. Atkinson, G. Morten, & D. W. Sue (Eds.), *Counseling American minorities: A cross-cultural perspective* (4th ed., pp. 245-263). Madison, WI: Brown & Benchmark.

Comas-Diaz, L., & Jacobsen, F. M. (1987). Ethnocultural identification in psychotherapy. *Psychiatry, 50,* 232-241.

Cross, W. E., Jr. (1971). The Negro to Black experience: Toward a psychology of Black liberation. *Black World, 20*(9), 13-27.

Cross, W. E., Jr. (1978). The Thomas and Cross models of psychological Nigrescence: A literature review. *Journal of Black Psychology, 4,* 13-31.

Cuellar, I., Harris, L. C., & Jasso, R. (1980). An acculturation scale for Mexican-American normal and clinical populations. *Hispanic Journal of Behavioral Sciences, 2,* 199-217.

Duran, R. P. (1992). Clinical assessment of instructional performance in cooperative learning. In K. F. Geisinger (Ed.), *Psychological testing of Hispanics* (pp. 137-156). Washington, DC: American Psychological Association.

Erikson, E. (1968). *Identity: Youth and crisis.* New York: Norton.

Espin, O. M. (1993). Psychological impact of migration on Latinas: Implications for psychotherapeutic practice. In D. R. Atkinson, G. Morten, & D. W. Sue (Eds.), *Counseling American minorities: A cross-cultural perspective* (4th ed., pp. 279-293). Madison, WI: Brown & Benchmark.

Flavell, J. H. (1985). *Cognitive development* (2nd ed.). Englewood Cliffs, NJ: Prentice Hall.

Garcia, M., & Lega, L. I. (1979). Development of a Cuban ethnic identity questionnaire. *Hispanic Journal of Behavior Sciences, 1,* 247-261.

Gomez, M. J., & Fassinger, R. E. (1994). An initial model of Latina achievement: Acculturation, biculturalism, and achieving styles. *Journal of Counseling Psychology, 41,* 205-215.

Hanassab, S. (1991). Acculturation and young Iranian women: Attitudes toward sex roles and intimate relationships. *Journal of Multicultural Counseling and Development, 19,* 11-21.

Harter, S. (1983). Developmental perspectives on the self-system. In E. M. Hetherington (Ed.), *Handbook of child psychology: Socialization, personality, and social development* (Vol. 4, pp. 275-385). New York: John Wiley.

Hayes-Bautista, D. E. (1974). Becoming Chicano: A "dis-assimilation" theory of transformation of ethnic identity. *Dissertation Abstracts International, 34,* 5332A (University Microfilms No. 74-4708, 283).

Heinrich, R. K., Corbine, J. L., & Thomas, K. R. (1990). Counseling Native Americans. *Journal of Counseling and Development, 69,* 128-133.

Helms, J. E. (1987). Cultural identity in the treatment process. In P. Pedersen (Ed.), *Handbook of cross-cultural counseling and therapy* (pp. 239-245). Westport, CT: Greenwood Press.

Helms, J. E. (Ed.). (1990). *Black and White racial identity: Theory, research, and practice.* New York: Greenwood Press.

Howes, R. D., & DeBlassie, R. R. (1989). Modal errors in the cross cultural use of the Rorschach. *Journal of Multicultural Counseling and Development, 17,* 79-84.

Hui, C. H., Drasgow, F., & Chang, B. (1983). Analysis of the modernity scale: An item response theory approach. *Journal of Cross-Cultural Psychology, 14,* 259-278.

Hurtado, A., Rodriguez, J., Gurin, P., & Beals, J. L. (1993). The impact of Mexican descendants' social identity on the ethnic socialization of children. In M. E. Bernal & G. P. Knight (Eds.), *Ethnic identity: Formation and transmission among Hispanics and other minorities* (pp. 131-162). Albany: State University of New York Press.

Jackson, B. (1975). Black identity development. *MEFORM: Journal of Educational Diversity and Innovation, 2,* 19-25.

Knight, G. P., Bernal, M. E., Cota, M. K., Garza, C. A., & Ocampo, K. A. (1993). Family socialization and Mexican American identity and behavior. In M. E. Bernal & G. P. Knight (Eds.), *Ethnic identity: Formation and transmission among Hispanics and other minorities* (pp. 105-129). Albany: State University of New York Press.

Knight, G. P., Bernal, M. E., Garza, C. A., & Cota, M. K. (1993). A social cognitive model of the development of ethnic identity and ethnically based behaviors. In M. E. Bernal & G. P. Knight (Eds.), *Ethnic identity: Formation and transmission among Hispanics and other minorities* (pp. 213-234). Albany: State University of New York Press.

Kunkel, M. A. (1990). Expectations about counseling in relation to acculturation in Mexican-American and Anglo-American student samples. *Journal of Counseling Psychology, 37,* 286-292.

Leong, F. T., & Tata, S. P. (1990). Sex and acculturation differences in occupational values among Chinese-American children. *Journal of Counseling Psychology, 37,* 208-212.

Lese, K. P., & Robbins, S. B. (1994). Relationship between goal attributes and the academic achievement of Southeast Asian adolescent refugees. *Journal of Counseling Psychology, 41,* 45-52.

LeVine, E. S., & Padilla, A. M. (1980). *Crossing cultures in therapy: Pluralistic counseling for the Hispanic.* Monterey, CA: Brooks/Cole.

Marín, G. (1992). Issues in the measurement of acculturation among Hispanics. In K. F. Geisinger (Ed.), *Psychological testing of Hispanics* (pp. 235-251). Washington, DC: American Psychological Association.

Marín, G., Gamba, R. J., & Marín, B. V. (1992). Extreme response style and acquiescence among Hispanics: The role of acculturation and education. *Journal of Cross-Cultural Psychology, 23,* 498-509.

Marín, G., Marín, B. V., Otero-Sabogal, R., & Sabogal, F. (1989). The role of acculturation in the attitudes, norms, and expectancies of Hispanic smokers. *Journal of Cross-Cultural Psychology, 20,* 399-415.

Marín, G., & Triandis, H. C. (1985). Allocentrism as an important characteristic of the behavior of Latin Americans and Hispanics. In R. Diaz-Guerrero (Ed.), *Cross-cultural and national studies in social psychology* (pp. 85-104). Amsterdam: Elsevier Science.

Montgomery, G. T. (1992). Acculturation, stressors, and somatization patterns among students from extreme south Texas. *Hispanic Journal of Behavioral Sciences, 14,* 434-454.

Negy, C., & Woods, D. J. (1992). Mexican-Americans' performance on the Psychological Screening Inventory as a function of acculturation level. *Journal of Clinical Psychology, 48,* 315-319.

Oetting, E. R., & Beauvais, F. (1990-1991). Orthogonal cultural identification theory: The cultural identification of minority adolescents. *International Journal of the Addictions, 25*(5A & 6A), 655-685.

Olmedo, E. L. (1979). Acculturation: A psychometric perspective. *American Psychologist, 34,* 1061-1070.

Olmedo, E. L., Martinez, J. L., & Martinez, S. R. (1978). Measure of acculturation for Chicano adolescents. *Psychological Reports, 42,* 159-170.

Olmedo, E. L., & Padilla, A. M. (1978). Empirical and construct validation of a measure of acculturation for Mexican Americans. *Journal of Social Psychology, 105,* 179-187.

Orozco, S., Thompson, B., Kapes, J., & Montgomery, G. T. (1993). Measuring the acculturation of Mexican Americans: A covariance structure analysis. *Measurement and Evaluation in Counseling and Development, 25,* 149-155.

Osvold, L. L., Lise, L., & Sodowsky, G. R. (1993). Eating disorders of White American, racial and ethnic minority American, and international women. *Journal of Multicultural Counseling and Development, 21,* 143-154.

Padilla, A. M. (1981). Pluralistic counseling and psychotherapy for Hispanic Americans. In A. J. Marsella & P. B. Pedersen (Eds.), *Cross-cultural counseling and psychotherapy* (pp. 299-306). Westport, CT: Greenwood Press.

Phinney, J. (1990). Ethnic identity in adolescents and adults: Review of research. *Psychological Bulletin, 108,* 499-514.

Phinney, J. S. (1993). A three-stage model of ethnic identity development in adolescence. In M. E. Bernal & G. P. Knight (Eds.), *Ethnic identity: Formation and transmission among Hispanics and other minorities* (pp. 61-79). Albany: State University of New York Press.

Ponterotto, J. G., & Casas, J. M. (1991). *Handbook of racial/ethnic minority counseling research.* Springfield, IL: Charles C Thomas.

Ramisetty-Mikler, S. (1993). Asian Indian immigrants in America and sociocultural issues in counseling. *Journal of Multicultural Counseling and Development, 21,* 36-49.

Redfield, R., Linton, R., & Herskovits, M. J. (1936). Memorandum for the study of acculturation. *American Anthropologist, 38,* 149-152.

Rick, K., & Forward, J. (1992). Acculturation and perceived intergenerational differences among Hmong youth. *Journal of Cross-Cultural Psychology, 23,* 85-94.

Rosenberg, M. (1970). *Conceiving the self.* New York: Basic Books.

Ruiz, A. S. (1990). Ethnic identity: Crisis and resolution. *Journal of Multicultural Counseling and Development, 18,* 29-40.

Sabnani, H. B., & Ponterotto, J. G. (1992). Racial/ethnic minority-specific instrumentation in counseling research: A review, critique, and recommendations. *Measurement and Evaluation in Counseling and Development, 24,* 161-187.

Sabogal, R., Marín, G., Otero-Sabogal, R., Marín, B. V., & Pérez-Stable, E. J. (1987). Hispanic familialism and acculturation: What changes and what doesn't? *Hispanic Journal of Behavioral Sciences, 9,* 397-412.

Sue, D. (1990). Culture-specific strategies in counseling: A conceptual framework. *Professional Psychology: Research and Practice, 21,* 424-433.

Suinn, R. M., Ahuna, C., & Khoo, G. (1992). The Suinn-Lew Asian Self-Identity Acculturation Scale: Concurrent and factorial validation. *Educational and Psychological Measurement, 52,* 1041-1046.

Suinn, R. M., Rickard-Figueroa, K., Lew, S., & Vigil, P. (1987). The Suinn-Lew Asian Self-Identification Acculturation Scale: An initial report. *Educational and Psychological Measurement, 47,* 401-407.

Szapocznik, J., & Kurtines, W. (1980). Acculturation, biculturalism, and adjustment among Cuban Americans. In A. M. Padilla (Ed.), *Acculturation: Theory, models, and some new findings* (pp. 139-160). Boulder, CO: Westview.

Thomas, C. W. (1971). *Boys no more.* Beverly Hills, CA: Glencoe.

Triandis, H. C. (1990). Toward cross-cultural studies of individualism and collectivism in Latin America. *Interamerican Journal of Psychology/Revista Interamerica de Psicología, 24,* 199-210.

Triandis, H. C., Bontempo, R., Leung, K., & Hui, C. H. (1990). A method for determining cultural, demographic, and personal constructs. *Journal of Cross-Cultural Psychology, 21,* 302-318.

Triandis, H. C., Marín, G., Lisansky, J., & Betancourt, H. (1984). Simpatía as a cultural script of Hispanics. *Journal of Personality and Social Psychology, 47,* 1363-1375.

Trimble, J. (1990-1991). Ethnic specification, validation prospects, and the future of drug use research. *International Journal of the Addictions, 25*(2A), 149-170.

Williams, C. L., & Berry, J. W. (1991). Primary prevention of acculturative stress among refugees: Application of psychological theory and practice. *American Psychologist, 46,* 632-641.

Zimmerman, J. E., & Sodowsky, G. R. (1993). Influences of acculturation on Mexican-American drinking practices: Implications for counseling. *Journal of Multicultural Counseling and Development, 21,* 22-35.

9

An Update of Helms's White and People of Color Racial Identity Models

JANET E. HELMS

THE CONSTRUCT OF RACE in psychology has been used in a variety of ways (cf. Betancourt & Lopez, 1993; Helms, 1994a, 1994b; Yee, Fairchild, Weizmann, & Wyatt, 1993), none of which is accurate according to basic standards of scientific practice. For example, Helms (1994a), extrapolating from Gotunda (1991), contended that the term has been used as a proxy for the following concepts: (a) differential sociopolitical and economic socialization, (b) biogenetic psychological characteristics inferred from the presence of observable "signs" commonly assumed to be racial in nature, and (c) differential cultural (e.g., values, beliefs, rituals) socialization.

Racial identity theory evolves out of the tradition of treating race as a sociopolitical and, to a lesser extent, a cultural construction. In such theories, racial classifications are assumed to be not biological realities, but rather sociopolitical and economic conveniences, membership in which is determined by socially defined inclusion criteria (e.g., skin color) that are commonly (mistakenly) considered to be "racial" in nature. Thus, racial identity theories do not suppose that racial groups in the United States are biologically distinct, but rather suppose that they have endured different conditions of domination or oppression.

AUTHOR'S NOTE: Shorter versions of this article were presented as the keynote address at the Psychology and Societal Transformation Conference, University of the Western Cape, South Africa, January 1994, and at a workshop, "Helms's Racial Identity Theory," at the Annual Multicultural Winter Roundtable; Teachers College-Columbia University, New York, NY, February 1994.

Originally, such theories or models were developed to explain the manner in which especially Black people (see Helms, 1990c, for an overview of these models), but occasionally members of other groups of color, adapted in an environment in which they were generally denied access to a fair share of societal resources, and in which innate racial inferiority was used as the justification for their maltreatment (Helms, 1990a). Subsequently, models have been developed to describe the adaptation of Whites as members of the ordained "superior" group (Hardiman, 1982; Helms, 1984, 1992) or to integrate existing models (Sabnani, Ponterotto, & Borodovsky, 1991).

Historically, the models used to describe the race-related adaptation of groups of color or Whites have proposed either typologies or linear stage-wise progressions. Typologies typically assign people to one or another of mutually exclusive personality categories (e.g., racist or nonracist), from which race-related behavior (in this case) is inferred. Duckitt (1992) criticized static approaches to investigating racial constructs in psychology, such as typologies, because of their theoretical sterility. In other words, typologies may describe categories of behavior, but not how they come to be or can be changed.

In general, stage models have the advantage of considering race-related adjustment as a dynamic process that can be modified. All of the racial adaptation stage models propose linear developmental processes, but they differ in the extent to which they consider stages to be mutually exclusive (i.e., "strong" stages) or interactive (i.e., "permeable" stages). My model (Helms, 1984) is commonly assumed to be a strong-stage model (e.g., Tokar & Swanson, 1991), although I intended my stages to be permeable (Helms, 1989).

Consequently, I (Helms, 1994a, 1994c) recently attempted to reformulate my model to address some of the dilemmas that occur when one uses a strong-stage model to conceptualize racial identity development. In doing so, I replaced the term *stages* with *statuses*, for reasons to be discussed subsequently. The purposes of this chapter are to elaborate and integrate my earlier discussions of racial identity theory and to suggest how statuses might be used to think about racial identity as a dynamic process.

In the service of these goals, I will (a) provide a rationale for the conceptualization of the developmental processes in terms of statuses rather than stages, (b) present general overviews and updates of the racial identity developmental process as it pertains to the various socioracial groups in the United States, and (c) discuss the implications of a thematic interpretation of the racial identity development process for the assessment of individuals and the analysis of interpersonal or social relationships (Carter & Helms, 1992; Helms, 1984, 1990a, 1990b, 1990e).

THE ORIGIN OF *STATUSES*

I (Helms, 1992; Helms & Piper, 1994) recently argued that the construct of stages has been inadequate for describing the developmental processes surrounding issues of race for the following reasons: (a) An individual may exhibit attitudes, behaviors, and emotions reflective of more than one stage (Helms, 1989; Parham & Helms, 1981); (b) to many researchers, *stage* seems to imply a static place or condition that the person "reaches" rather than the dynamic interplay between cognitive and emotional processes that racial identity models purport to address; and (c) neither theory nor measurement supports the notion of the various stages as mutually exclusive or "pure" constructs (Helms, 1989, 1990c).

I (Helms, 1984) presented a theoretical framework for considering the racial identity development of Blacks and Whites. I also proposed a counseling process interaction model that subsequently was expanded to describe other types of social interactions (Helms, 1990b, 1990d) as well as other groups of color (Helms, 1994a, 1994c, 1994d). In my original conceptualization, I used the language of racial identity stage theorists to explicate my constructs. However, I intended the term *stages* to mean mutually interactive dynamic processes by which a person's behavior could be explained rather than static categories into which a person could be assigned.

Draguns (personal communication, 1993) convinced me that my original use of *stages* was congruent with Freud's epigenic principle. Accordingly, resolutions of the developmental issues of earlier or more primitive stages leave their imprint on subsequent stages. Consequently, stages represent interactive themes rather than mutually exclusive categories. Despite advice to the contrary (Helms, 1989), theorists and researchers have tended to treat the stages within individuals as if they are mutually exclusive.

Consequently, given the propensity of recent scholars to locate the meaning of *stages* in the word rather than in the theorist's operational definition of the word, I (e.g., Helms, 1994a, 1994b, 1994c; Helms & Piper, 1994) capitulated and began substituting *status* (of the ego) for *stage* without intentionally changing the essential meaning of the concepts underlying either term. Ideally, such usage will encourage more conceptually complex analyses of people's expressions or manifestations of their racial identity than typically have occurred heretofore.

COMMON THEMES

In my version of racial identity theory, members of all socioracial groups, regardless of specific racial or ethnic group classification, are assumed to experience a racial identity developmental process that can be described by several statuses. However, the content of the statuses (formerly called *stages*) is assumed to differ between racial groups due to the power differences that have existed, and continue to exist, among socioracial groups in U.S. society. That is, the theory assumes differential socialization due to racial (rather than ethnic) classification as well as differential reactions to that socialization. With respect to management of racial stimuli within oneself as well as within one's

environment, statuses range from least developmentally mature or sophisticated to most mature or sophisticated. Maturation is triggered by a combination of cognitive-affective complexity within the individual and race-related
environmental stimuli (Helms, 1984, 1989).

Racial identity or identification with one's societally designated racial
group occurs in response to environments in which societal resources are differentially allocated on the basis of racial group membership. Usually, allocation of resources implies a hierarchy by which one group is assumed to be
entitled to more than its share of resources, whereas other groups are assumed
to be entitled to less than their share.

In U.S. society, "Whites" (rather than Caucasians) are members of the
entitled group, and it has been those characteristics (e.g., skin color) deemed
by them to indicate "Whiteness" that have permitted their members to have
access to entitled status (see Takaki, 1993, for a discussion of why *Caucasians*
and *Whites* are not synonyms in the United States). People of color, that is,
Native Americans, Blacks, Asians, and Latino/as of color, have tended to be
the deprived groups, though the nature of the deprivation may have varied
slightly depending somewhat on how and when a particular group entered the
collective societal awareness as a potential threat to the economic and political
status quo of the White majority (Takaki, 1993; Zinn, 1980).

Thus, the general developmental issue for Whites is abandonment of
entitlement, whereas the general developmental issue for people of color is
surmounting internalized racism in its various manifestations. In both circumstances, development potentially occurs by way of the evolution or differentiation of successive racial identity statuses, where *statuses* are defined
as the dynamic cognitive, emotional, and behavioral processes that govern a
person's interpretation of racial information in her or his interpersonal environments. Statuses give rise to schemata, which are behavioral manifestations
of the underlying statuses. It is schemata rather than the statuses per se that
paper-and-pencil racial identity attitude inventories (e.g., Helms & Carter,
1990) presumably assess.

As was true of racial identity stages, racial identity statuses are assumed
to permit increasingly more complex management of racial material, and a
person can use as many schemata as the ego has generated. Thus, persons
with more than one type of racial identity status potentially engage in increasingly more complex race-related behavior because they have more information-processing mechanisms by which to respond.

The statuses are assumed to develop or mature sequentially, as shown in
Tables 9.1 and 9.2, but are expressed according to level of dominance within
the individual's personality structure. Thus, maturity pertains not only to
whether a status has evolved within the ego (that is, is potentially accessible)
but also to whether it is strong enough to be called upon to assist the person
in coping with racial material. *Dominance* describes the status that most often
governs the person's racial reactions, whereas *accessibility* pertains to whether

TABLE 9.1 White Racial Identity Ego Statuses and Information-Processing
            Strategies (IPS)

Contact Status: satisfaction with racial status quo, obliviousness to racism and one's participation
in it. If racial factors influence life decisions, they do so in a simplistic fashion. IPS: Obliviousness.

Example: "I'm a White woman. When my grandfather came to this country, he was discriminated
against, too. But he didn't blame Black people for his misfortunes. He educated himself and got
a job; that's what Blacks ought to do. If White callers (to a radio station) spent as much time
complaining about racial discrimination as your Black callers do, we'd never have accomplished
what we have. You all should just ignore it."

Disintegration Status: disorientation and anxiety provoked by unresolvable racial moral dilemmas
that force one to choose between own-group loyalty and humanism. May be stymied by life
situations that arouse racial dilemmas. IPS: Suppression and ambivalence.

Example: "I myself tried to set a nonracist example [for other Whites] by speaking up when
someone said something blatantly prejudiced—how to do this without alienating people so that
they would no longer take me seriously was always tricky—and by my friendships with Mexicans
and Blacks who were actually the people with whom I felt most comfortable" (Blauner, 1993, p. 8).

Reintegration Status: idealization of one's socioracial group, denigration and intolerance for other
groups. Racial factors may strongly influence life decisions. IPS: Selective perception and negative
out-group distortion.

Example: "So, what if my great-grandfather owned slaves. He didn't mistreat them and besides,
I wasn't even here then. I never owned slaves. So, I don't know why Blacks expect me to feel
guilty for something that happened before I was born. Nowadays, reverse racism hurts Whites
more than slavery hurt Blacks. At least they got three square[meals]s a day. But my brother can't
even get a job with the police department because they have to hire less qualified Blacks. That
[expletive] happens to Whites all the time."

Pseudoindependence Status: intellectualized commitment to one's own socioracial group and
deceptive tolerance of other groups. May make life decisions to "help" other racial groups. IPS:
Reshaping reality and selective perception.

Example: "Was I the only person left in America who believed that the sexual mingling of the
races was a good thing, that it would erase cultural barriers and leave us all a lovely shade of tan?
. . . Racial blending is inevitable. At the very least, it may be the only solution to our dilemmas
of race" (Allen, 1994, p. C4).

Immersion/Emersion Status: search for an understanding of the personal meaning of racism and
the ways by which one benefits and a redefinition of whiteness. Life choices may incorporate
racial activism. IPS: Hypervigilance and reshaping.

Example: "It's true that I personally did not participate in the horror of slavery, and I don't even
know whether my ancestors owned slaves. But I know that because I am White, I continue to
benefit from a racist system which stems from the slavery era. I believe that if White people are
ever going to understand our role in perpetuating racism, then we must begin to ask ourselves
some hard questions and be willing to consider our role in maintaiing a hurtful system. Then,
we must try to do something to change it."

Autonomy Status: informed positive socioracial-group commitment, use of internal standards for
self-definition, capacity to relinquish the privileges of racism. May avoid life options that require
participation in racial oppression. IPS: Flexibility and complexity.

Example: "I live in an integrated [Black-White] neighborhood and I read Black literature and
popular magazines. So, I understand that the media presents a very stereotypic view of Black
culture. I believe that if more of us White people made more than a superficial effort to obtain
accurate information about racial groups other than our own, then we could help make this
country a better place for all peoples."

NOTE: Descriptions of racial identity statuses are adapted from Helms (1994a, 1994b). Racial identity ego
statuses are listed in the order that they are hypothesized to evolve.

TABLE 9.2 People of Color Racial Identity Ego Statuses and
Information-Processing Strategies (IPS)

Conformity (Pre-Encounter) Status: external self-definition that implies devaluing of own group and allegiance to White standards of merit. Probably is oblivious to socioracial groups' sociopolitical histories. IPS: Selective perception and obliviousness to socioracial concerns.

Example: "I think we ought to have a "multiethnic" racial category because I think it's unfair that Black people force you to be Black. I have a Black father and a White mother. So, what does that make me? I think racial tensions in this country would be a lot less if Black people didn't try to force people like me to be one of them."

Dissonance (Encounter) Status: ambivalence and confusion concerning own socioracial group commitment and ambivalent socioracial self-definition. May be ambivalent about life decisions. IPS: Repression of anxiety-provoking racial information.

Example: "I talked 'White,' moved 'White,' most of my friends were White. . . . But I never really felt accepted by or truly identified with the White kids. At some point, I stopped laughing when they would imitate Black people dancing. I distanced myself from the White kids, but I hadn't made an active effort to make Black friends because I was never comfortable enough in my 'Blackness' to associate with them. That left me in sort of a gray area" (Wenger, 1993, p. 4).

Immersion/Emersion Status: idealization of one's socioracial group and denigration of that which is perceived as White. Use of own-group external standards to self-define, and own-group commitment and loyalty is valued. May make life decisions for the benefit of the group. IPS: Hypervigilance toward racial stimuli and dichotomous thinking.

Example: "So there I was, strutting around with my semi-Afro, studiously garbling the English language because I thought that 'real' Black people didn't speak standard English, . . . contemplating changing my name to Malika, or something authentically Black" (Nelson, 1993, p. 18).

Internalization Status: positive commitment to one's own socioracial group, internally defined racial attributes, and capacity to assess and respond objectively to members of the dominant group. Can make life decisions by assessing and integrating socioracial group requirements and self-assessment. IPS: Flexibility and analytic thinking.

Example: "By claiming myself as African-American and Black, I also inherit a right to ask questions about what this identity means. And chances are this identity will never be static, which is fine with me" (Jones, 1994, p. 78).

Integrative Awareness Status: capacity to value one's own collective identities as well as empathize and collaborate with members of other oppressed groups. Life decisions may be motivated by globally humanistic self-expression. IPS: Flexibility and complexity.

Example: "[I think of difference not] as something feared or exotic, but . . . as one of the rich facts of one's life, a truism that gives you more data, more power and more flavor. . . . [You need a variety of peoples in your life] . . . so you won't lapse into thinking you're God's gift to all knowledge as North American Negro" (Jones, 1994, p. 80).

NOTE: Descriptions of racial identity statuses are adapted from Helms (1994c) and Helms and Piper (1994). Statuses are described in the order they are hypothesized to evolve. This table also appears in Helms and Cook (in press).

a status is strong enough to permit the person ever to react in the status-relevant manner.

In a sense, maturation is triggered by need. That is, as the person encounters personally meaningful racial material in her or his environments and is unable to cope with it effectively, new statuses, and consequently schemata, may begin to evolve. To the extent that a schema (or manner of behaving) works effectively in a person's environment and the person must be engaged in such environments, the underlying status becomes stronger. A schema is dominant when a person tends to use it primarily in many or most situations that the ego perceives as involving racial information. In other words, dominant schemata are those with a history of contributing to effective coping.

Thus, each time a person is exposed to or believes he or she is exposed to a racial event, the ego selects the dominant racial identity status to assist the person in interpreting the event. Once an interpretation is made, the schemata then respond in ways that are consistent with the dictates of the status and ideally protect the person's sense of well-being and self-esteem.

Secondary statuses are those that are present in the racial part of a person's personality constellation—that is, are potentially accessible under the "right" circumstances. If the dominant schema consistently does not work, then the person's coping strategy is to retrieve an earlier strategy, that is, a schema that has worked before. This process continues until the person finds a schema that permits her or him to function in or psychologically survive the racial situation. In the event that the person cannot resolve or leave threatening circumstances, then the ensuing discomfort may be the catalyst for strengthening existing statuses or developing new ones.

A reciprocal relationship exists between the statuses and the relevant schemata such that a status governs the quality of the expressed schema; and the schema strengthens the statuses that are effective in coping with intrapsychic and interpersonal racial material, but weakens the statuses when the elicited schema is not effective. If a status is consistently reinforced, it grows stronger, but if not, it withers away.

Most models of racial identity propose a maximum of six statuses (in other models, *stages* or *types*), and, as previously mentioned, the specific content or themes of these statuses vary according to the societally ascribed racial group membership of the person (see Helms, 1990a, 1990c, for overviews of these models). Moreover, the themes in society, and consequently the statuses and schemata, may change as the society changes.

So, for example, when racism was legal, themes related to clear separation of racial groups and differential allocation of resources were direct and explicitly acknowledged in society. Thus, it was not particularly unusual for people to acknowledge their own racial biases directly (Duckitt, 1992). However, as acceptance of the expression (as distinguished from possession) of personal racial biases became less socially acceptable, more subtle manifestations of such biases appeared (McConahay & Hough, 1976). Current debates over "political correctness" seem to be merely struggles over how best to express internalized racial reactions.

An implication of the flexible nature of societal environmental racial themes for racial identity theorists is that the statuses may have different thematic content depending upon the era in which the person is being racially socialized. The statuses may also have differing thematic content depending upon the person's racial membership group. However, the underlying cognitive-emotional information-processing strategy (IPS) may be consistent across eras. That is, for example, a person may rely on denial or obliviousness as her or his primary means of coping with race regardless of the era in which the person is socialized, but denial may "look" different in different eras. A person internalizes the racial societal messages that are available to him or her and processes them in the manner(s) that the ego (and society) permits.

WHITE RACIAL IDENTITY

My (Helms, 1984, 1990d, 1993a) theory describes the racial identity development process of White people. Helms and Piper (1994) defined *White people* as follows: "those Americans who self-identify or are commonly identified as belonging exclusively to the White racial group regardless of the continental source (e.g., Europe, Asia) of that racial ancestry" (p. 126). As a consequence of growing up and being socialized in an environment in which members of their group (if not themselves personally) are privileged relative to other groups, Whites learn to perceive themselves (and their group) as entitled to similar privileges. In order to protect such privilege, individual group members, and therefore the group more generally, learn to protect their privileged status by denying and distorting race-related reality and aggressing against perceived threats to the racial status quo. Consequently, healthy identity development for a White person involves the capacity to recognize and abandon the normative strategies of White people for coping with race.

As shown in Table 9.1, for White people, the maturation process of recognition and abandonment of White privilege begins with the ego's avoidance or denial of the sociopolitical implications of one's own and others' racial group membership (i.e., Contact status) and concludes with its capacity to strive for nonracist own-group membership and humanistic racial self-definition and social interactions (Autonomy status). Also, as shown in Table 9.1 (for Whites), I (Helms, 1993b, 1994c) argued that schemata are expressions of distinguishable information-processing strategies (IPS).

Thus, the information-processing strategies for responding to racial stimuli are as follows: (a) Contact—denial, obliviousness, or avoidance of anxiety-evoking racial information; (b) Disintegration—disorientation, confusion, and suppression of information; (c) Reintegration—distortion of information in an own-group-enhancing manner; (d) Pseudoindependence—reshaping racial stimuli to fit one's own "liberal" societal framework; (e) Immersion-Emersion—reeducating and searching for internally defined racial standards; and (f) Autonomy—flexible analyses and responses to racial material.

As previously discussed, the model describes the development or process by which the statuses come into being. Consequently, the highlights or distinguishable aspects of the statuses and related schemata are described. However, most individuals develop more than one status, and if multiple statuses exist, then they can operate in concert. That is, they may each influence a person's reactions to racial stimuli.

Thus, in Tables 9.1 and 9.2, although I have categorized the examples according to what appears to be the strongest status-schema theme, it seems to me that aspects of other statuses-schemata are present in virtually every instance. For example, in Table 9.1, the Contact segment is classified as *primarily* Contact because of the person's consistent obliviousness to and/or denial of the differential significance of her (and her grandfather's) Whiteness. However, the anger and out-group blaming for racial tensions that characterize the Reintegration status also waft through her comment. Similar blends of statuses can be found in the other examples as well, and presumably blends describe people's reactions more often than do "pure" statuses.

PEOPLE OF COLOR RACIAL IDENTITY

Table 9.2 summarizes the sequence by which the ego statuses as well as the correlated schemata become differentiated for people of color. In the United States, the term *people of color* refers to those persons whose ostensible ancestry is at least in part African, Asian, Indigenous, and/or combinations of these groups and/or White or European ancestry. Even a cursory overview of the history of race (rather than ethnic) relations in the United States (e.g., Takaki, 1993; Zinn, 1980) reveals that peoples of the so designated groups have been subjected to similar (but not necessarily identical) deplorable political and economic conditions because they were not perceived to be "pure" White.

One consequence of differential treatment of people according to their racial classification is that negative *racial* stereotypes of the affected groups of color become automatic societal themes that can be called upon to explain the circumstances of the deprived groups. Various historians (e.g., Takaki, 1993; Zinn, 1980) contend that many of the same racial stereotypes were used to control each of the visible socioracial and ethnic groups. Therefore, abandonment of internalized racism involves similar processes for each of the groups of color, regardless of the specific group to which they have been relegated.

Helms and Cook (in press) contended that overcoming internalized societal racial stereotypes and negative self- and own-group conceptions is a major component of racial identity development. Therefore, the central racial identity developmental theme of all people of color is to recognize and overcome the psychological manifestations of internalized racism. My model that explains the process by which this adaptation potentially occurs is a derivative of Cross's (1971) Negro-to-Black conversion model and Atkinson, Morten, and Sue's (1989) minority identity development model. Accordingly, the original or least sophisticated status and schema (i.e., Conformity) involve adapting and internalizing White society's definitions of one's group(s) either by conforming to the existing stereotypes of one's own group(s) or by attempting to become White. The most sophisticated status and schema (i.e., Integrative

Awareness) involve the capacity to express a positive racial self and to recognize and resist the multiplicity of practices that exist in one's environment to discourage positive racial self-conceptions and group expression.

The implicit information-processing strategies corresponding to the ego statuses shown in Table 9.2 are as follows: (a) Conformity—denial, minimization, and selective perception; (b) Dissonance—anxiety, ambivalence, or disorientation; (c) Immersion—hypersensitivity and dichotomous thinking; (d) Emersion—vigilance and energized collectivism; (e) Internalization—intellectualization and abstraction; and (f) Integrative Awareness—flexible analyses and responses to racial stimuli. Note that Immersion and Emersion are described as a single status in Table 9.2. I think that eventually it will be possible to distinguish them empirically as well as theoretically, although this is not the case at present.

Also apparent in the examples in Table 9.2 is the fact that racial identity themes may be blended in the individual's reactions to racial catalysts. As I argued with respect to White identity development, I do not think that most people express their racial identity in pure forms. Thus, the second example illustrates expression of both the Conformity and Dissonance statuses in that the speaker acknowledges his White cultural socialization and consequent greater familiarity with White people on one level (Conformity), but also is able to describe his lack of fit with either the Black or White socioracial group (Dissonance).

Nevertheless, each of the examples has a racial identity theme that seems to be stronger than the others, and to determine which is a person's strongest status, one would need to analyze the themes inherent in several samples of a person's race-related behavior. Themes that frequently occur presumably signal stronger underlying statuses; conversely, stronger statuses conceivably contribute to more consistent thematic expressions.

RACIAL IDENTITY IN
THE INTERPERSONAL ENVIRONMENT

Up to this point, racial identity development/expression has been discussed as an individual difference variable. Yet my (Helms, 1984, 1990a, 1990c, 1990d; 1994d) original rationale for offering a conceptual framework for discussing and studying racial factors was that such information would enable counselors and researchers to diagnose tensions in the environment and to intervene to resolve them in a manner compatible with the racial identity dynamics of the participants. Originally, *environment* referred to dyadic counseling or psychotherapy relationships (Helms, 1984). Subsequently, the concept of environmental context was elaborated to pertain to various forms of interpersonal relationships, including other types of "couples" (e.g., teacher-student) and group interactions (e.g., Helms, 1990a, 1990e, 1994d) in addition to global societal movements (Helms, 1989). Each of these types of relationships initially begins as interactions between individuals in response to particular overtly or covertly expressed racial events.

To encourage the goal of effective racial intervention, I proposed a racial identity interaction model. Basic premises of this component of my overall racial identity model are that (a) racial identity statuses structure people's reactions to one another as well as to external events, (b) people form harmonious or disharmonious alliances with one another based on the tenor of their expressed racial identity, (c) racial reactions occur within the context of direct or vicarious interpersonal activities, and (d) patterns of reactions within an interpersonal context can be classified according to quality.

Classification of the quality of interpersonal interactions allows one to predict the cognitive, affective, and behavioral themes that characterize the process. Diagnosis of the particular racial identity statuses governing participants' behaviors can make interventions potentially more relevant.

Events

The events that serve as catalysts for racial identity expression can be internal or external, subjective and not necessarily visible to independent observers or objective and available for others to react to and interpret. One role of racial identity ego statuses is assisting the person in managing interpersonal events, whether these events are internal-subjective or external-objective.

As is true with respect to intrapersonal adaptation, in interpersonal contexts, reciprocal relationships occur such that Person A uses a particular (presumably a dominant) schema to respond to Person B, who in turn interprets Person A's behavior by means of his or her own ego statuses and responds using the schemata available to him or her. Consider, for example, the excerpt of group dialogue shown in Table 9.3. In this dialogue, participants were responding to a question concerning their opinion as to whether White parents should be permitted to adopt African American and Native American children. Thus, the racial question is the objective event or catalyst that elicits the racial identity expressions.

Participants in this group were two White men (1 and 2), a White woman (the researcher-designated group leader), and an Asian woman. The White woman was randomly selected as the group discussion leader. In Table 9.3, Column 1 identifies the speaker, Column 2 is the person's comment, Column 3 is the speaking turn or response unit, and Column 4 classifies the comment according to racial identity theme.

Each separate response unit is an event, and a series of events involving the same two or more persons becomes an interpersonal relationship. In a group situation such as this, one actually finds several types of relationships: That is, each group member has some kind of relationship with each of the other group members, and the quality of this may change over the course of the interaction. I (Helms, 1984, 1990a, 1990b, 1990e) proposed that relationships or, for that matter, mutual reactions to events can be classified according

TABLE 9.3 Excerpt From a Group Discussion About Race

Participant	Comment	Response Unit No.	Racial Identity Theme
White Male 1	They might be, I mean, on the one hand, if a Black child were raised by White parents, um, the thing is with culture. I mean a lot of people make a really big thing about culture, and in some families that's very very important. But on the other hand, in a great number of families culture's really not important but Black and White, you know? It's just sort of regular every-day life, you know. The Black child might grow up with real strong sense of Black culture because he or she was interested in its own on his own initiative went out before his parents helped him out. And also have a firsthand account of White culture. He might actually come out ahead. He might get both. On the other hand, he might get neither if his parents aren't into. . . . I don't even think there is such a thing as a White culture but if he was raised by like Italian parents or something and he got a taste of Italian culture, suppose they weren't into that, he might not get any culture, you know, any background at all, he might just be . . . (Interrupted)	1	Contact
White Female 1	But see, that happens with any child . . . (Interrupted)	2	Ambiguous
White Male 1	But that's with anything. Like I, I personally, um, my parents are Ukrainian and they just came over they're first generation immigrants I'm the first one from here so consequently I got tons of Ukrainian culture, maybe more than I didn't want . . . (Group laughter, 3 seconds)	3 4	Contact
White Male 1	I got it shoved down my throat. But my children on the other hand, you know, more than likely the person that I marry won't be Ukrainian. How much culture that they'll actually get is, they might get a little sprinkling here and there, but I severely doubt that it's going to be even a twelfth of what I got. (Group laughter, 2 seconds)	5 6	Contact
White Male 1	I went to school there, I learned to speak the language, we always went to culture events, and that one happened because that's just me. What about my wife? I mean if my wife's not Ukrainian, you know, that's it. I mean, that's. . . . And I don't . . . I mean, that's it.	7	Contact
White Male 2	OK, we're coming down to the, here I'll round it off with, in a lot of cases it would be to the benefit of the children to be adopted by either a White or another kind of family, being that, uh, when they are brought up they're gonna have the idea that they are Black but they're going to have the White culture now.	8	Contact

TABLE 9.3 (Continued)

Participant	Comment	Response Unit No.	Racial Identity Theme
White Male 1	Right.	9	Contact
White Male 2	And I think . . .	10	Ambiguous
White Male 1	That might help them.	11	Contact
White Male 2	It's going to help them because, one, if they're growing up as children in that community they'll grow to have their friends that'll live there and they're going to be a part of the group, and I think that when children become older they're going to tend to overlook that he's Black this way, and he's not just gonna be, he's one of the guys, you know, he's one of our gang here, he's not a . . . you know, like a racial tensions. I think it'll take down that barrier, and I think it will actually help him to move up in the business world because they always are looking for educated responsible Black individuals to work in their corporations, and he won't have this idea that, oh, because I come from the slums I'm . . .	12	Reintegration/ Contact
Asian Female 1	You can't do it.	13	Conformity
White Male 2	Yeah, I can't do that. You're gonna have to make that job easier for me or something like this. He's gonna say, I can do that.	14	Reintegration
White Female 1	I don't know if I really agree with your reasoning. I mean I agree with you for saying that we should have this, they should be . . . (Interrupted)	15	Ambiguous
White Male 2	What I'm trying to say is that it's going to, take down that dumb train of thought that they seem to have that they can live on welfare, and uh, and yeah, I think it'll start a new race of superior Black race I guess. Not like, I don't know, superior race, but . . .	16	Reintegration
Asian Female 1	See, it's gonna take barriers away.	17	Conformity
White Male 2	Yeah, it'll take away the barrier that [they] believe in. It'll create a middle class of Black people instead of the, uh . . .	18	Reintegration/ Contact
Asian Female 1	For the traffing [sic] is a weird, you know, we say this [is] no problem, yeah, they can be adopted.	19	Conformity
White Female 1	I don't know, I very very strongly disagree with your whole attitude that they all come from the slums and that we need this better race of Black people, better than the old one. I don't think there's any, like (inaudible), but I agree with your final response.	20	Pseudo-independence/ Autonomy

NOTE: White Female 1 was the researcher-designated leader of this group. This table is adapted from Helms and Cook (in press). The group dialogue summarized in this table was made possible by a grant from the Fund for Dispute Resolution, 1775 M Street, Washington, DC 20010.

to one of four types (parallel, progressive, regressive, or crossed), where *type* means the predominant theme underlying most of the participants' reactions to shared racial identity events. The fourth type, crossed, now is considered to be a subtype of progressive or regressive interactions. Although I do not think that all relationships are exemplars of pure types, it should be possible in many instances to use observable dynamics to classify interactions.

Relationship Types

Participants in the four types of interactions may be of any racial classification, including White/White, person of color/person of color, and various cross-group combinations. The crucial characteristic in analyzing the nature of the relationship or interaction is not the racial classification of participants, but rather their expressed racial identity.

In *parallel* interactions, participants use schemata governed by the same ego statuses if they are of the same racial classification, or analogous statuses if they are of different racial classifications. The general impetus of this relationship is to maintain harmony and deny or avoid tensions. It is possible to do so because the participants in such interactions express similar racial attitudes and share assumptions about the racial dynamics in their environments. For those participants in Table 9.3 for whom the conversation is parallel, originally Contact is the expressed status (i.e., schema) that is dominant. However, as the interaction "progresses," it shifts to a Reintegration-Conformity alliance.

Thus, in the discourse shown in Table 9.3, there seems to be a sequence of parallel dyadic relationships (the White males, and White Male 2 and the Asian female) that eventually coalesces into a parallel coalition that includes everyone except the White female group leader. Notice, for example, that the males and the Asian female are able to finish each other's sentences (e.g., Response Units 8-11), even though the objective content of their sentences sometimes seems meaningless. They appear to anticipate one another's thoughts.

Also, as racial identity theory predicts, it is not so much the racial classification of discussants per se that determines the quality of the interaction, but rather the nature of their expressed racial attitudes. The Asian woman (a Pilipina), for example, is in coalition with White Male 2. This is especially surprising when one knows (from information she provided earlier in the discussion) that she was raised by Black adoptive parents.

In *regressive* interactions, the participant with the most social power operates relatively consistently from a more primitive or less sophisticated ego status than the person(s) with less social power. Ordinarily, social power is based on such factors as social role or status, numerical dominance, economic resources, and membership in the dominant group. Expressed and implicit tension and discord generally characterize such relationships thematically.

The group leader is in a regressive relationship with the other members of the group. Most of her comments appear to be consistent with an Autonomy-Pseudoindependence and possibly an Immersion-Emersion perspective, whereas her co-group members exhibit less sophisticated racial identity information-processing styles. Ordinarily, her leader status and White racial classification might be expected to give her social power in the group. However, her social power is compromised, probably because she is a female who is outnumbered by the White males in the group. In addition, as eventually becomes evident (Comment 20), her assumptions and beliefs about race are markedly different from those of the other group members, which generally leads to ostracism (Helms, 1990a, 1990b, 1990e, 1994d).

Notice how the other group members join forces to prevent her from speaking. This tension is typical of regressive relationships. As the excluded person, she eventually resolves the conflict by partially agreeing with a perspective that is not her own.

Progressive interactions are characterized by one or more participants of greater social power interpreting and responding to racial events from more sophisticated ego statuses than participants in the interaction of lower social power. Energy and growth-producing discourse are assumed to be general features of this type of interaction. Under other circumstances (e.g., more race relations training), the group leader in Table 9.3 might have turned this discussion into a progressive relationship. As it is, she does a good job of resisting the group pressure to conform to negative racial stereotyping, but it is not clear that anyone "grew" from this exchange.

Crossed interactions imply that the participants' manners of perceiving and reacting to racial material are directly opposed to one another. Consequently, such relationships tend to be antagonistic and short-lived.

In the example, one can perhaps infer from his interruption that the group leader is in a crossed relationship with the first male (Comments 2 and 3), but she actually self-diagnoses the crossed quality of her relationship with the second male ("I very very strongly disagree with your whole attitude").

SUMMARY

The racial identity model was originally proposed as a framework for promoting better psychotherapy relationships in the following ways: (a) The capacity to analyze clients' and therapists' racial reactions from a psychological rather than a demographic perspective could promote use of more relevant interventions for ameliorating race-related symptoms; (b) systematic analysis of the racial dynamics between persons could provide information about when, where, and what type of intervention is necessary to create a more healthy racial climate; (c) acknowledgment of race as a psychological characteristic of Whites as well as people of color should reduce the emphasis on changing clients who are people of color to adapt to White theorists' interpretations of such clients' "aberrant" behavior; and (d) such acknowledgment would permit replacing victim-blame perspectives with the capacity to promote modification of unhealthy racial identity development regardless of the racial classification of the person involved. I originally proposed (Helms, 1984, 1990d) and continue to believe that racial identity models will make it feasible to train therapists who can be responsive to intrapersonal as well as interpersonal racial dynamics both within and outside the therapy relationship.

However, racial identity models should also be useful for explaining racial discord in other types of societal relationships (e.g., parental, teacher-student). Gushue (1993) and Helms (1990a, 1990b, 1990e, 1994d) discussed racial identity and nontherapy (i.e., social) relationships in society in more detail. In addition, Table 9.3 perhaps illustrates how unfair racial policies can come into being. The participants in the laboratory discussion group were college students who someday could be responsible for making social policy for people of all racial classification groups. Regardless of whether you agree or disagree with their decision, notice how easily they were able to decide that it was acceptable for Whites to adopt Black (and Native American) children without ever really considering how Black people might interpret their decision.

The value of examining societal racial interactions using my models is that such situations may be rendered less mysterious and, thus, more manageable. Clearly, for example, if one knows that potential participants in a dialogue are crossed with respect to racial identity, then it is foolhardy to expect them to make peace without a peacemaker who can acknowledge the racial identity concerns underlying their various perspectives. Ideally, my model will allow people not only to mediate racial problems once they have occurred but to anticipate and resolve tensions before they become problems.

REFERENCES

Allen, A. (1994, May 29). Black unlike me: Confessions of a White man confused by racial etiquette. *Washington Post*, pp. C1, C2.

Atkinson, D. R., Morten, G., & Sue, D. W. (1989). A minority identity development model. In D. R. Atkinson, G. Morten, & D. W. Sue (Eds.), *Counseling American minorities* (pp. 35-52). Dubuque, IA: William C. Brown.

Betancourt, H., & Lopez, S. R. (1993). The study of culture, ethnicity, and race in American psychology. *American Psychologist, 48,* 629-637.

Blauner, B. (1993). "But things are much worse for the Negro people": Race and radicalism in my life and work. In J. H. Stanfield II (Ed.), *A history of race relations research: First generation recollections* (pp. 1-36). Newbury Park, CA: Sage.

Carter, R. T., & Helms, J. E. (1992). The counseling process as defined by relationship types: A test of Helms's interactional model. *Journal of Multicultural Counseling and Development, 20,* 181-201.

Cross, W. E., Jr. (1971). The Negro-to-Black conversion experience: Toward a psychology of Black liberation. *Black World, 20,* 13-27.

Duckitt, J. (1992). Psychology and prejudice: A historical analysis and integrative framework. *American Psychologist, 47,* 1182-1193.

Gotunda, N. (1991). A critique of "Our constitution is color-blind." *Stanford Law Review, 44*(1), 1-73.

Gushue, G. V. (1993). Cultural-identity development and family assessment: An interaction model. *The Counseling Psychologist, 21,* 487-513.

Hardiman, R. (1982). *White identity development: A process oriented model for describing the racial consciousness of White Americans.* Unpublished doctoral dissertation, University of Massachusetts, Amherst.

Helms, J. E. (1984). Toward a theoretical explanation of the effects of race on counseling: A Black and White model. *The Counseling Psychologist, 12*(4), 153-165.

Helms, J. E. (1989). Considering some methodological issues in racial identity counseling research. *The Counseling Psychologist, 17,* 227-252.

Helms, J. E. (1990a). Applying the Interaction Model to social dyads. In J. E. Helms (Ed.), *Black and White racial identity: Theory, research, and practice* (pp. 177-185). Westport, CT: Greenwood.

Helms, J. E. (1990b). Generalizing racial identity interaction theory to groups. In J. E. Helms (Ed.), *Black and White racial identity: Theory, research, and practice* (pp. 187-204). Westport, CT: Greenwood.

Helms, J. E. (1990c). An overview of Black racial identity theory. In J. E. Helms (Ed.), *Black and White racial identity: Theory, research, and practice* (pp. 9-32). Westport, CT: Greenwood.

Helms, J. E. (1990d). Three perspectives on counseling visible racial/ethnic group clients. In F. C. Serafica, A. I. Schwebel, R. K. Russell, P. D. Isaac, & L. B. Myers (Eds.), *Mental health of ethnic minorities* (pp. 171-201). New York: Praeger.

Helms, J. E. (1990e). *Training manual for diagnosing racial identity in social interactions.* Topeka, KS: Content Communications.

Helms, J. E. (1992). *A race is a nice thing to have.* Topeka, KS: Content Communications.

Helms, J. E. (1993a). I also said, "White racial identity influences White researchers." *The Counseling Psychologist, 21,* 240-243.

Helms, J. E. (1993b). *Toward a theoretical model for assessing racial identity statuses.* Paper presented at the Buros Institute Symposium on Multicultural Assessment, Lincoln, NE.

Helms, J. E. (1994a). The conceptualization of racial identity and other "racial" constructs. In E. J. Trickett, R. J. Watts, & D. Birman (Eds.), *Human diversity: Perspectives on people in context* (pp. 285-311). San Francisco: Jossey-Bass.

Helms, J. E. (1994b). How multiculturalism obscures racial factors in the psychotherapy process. *Journal of Counseling Psychology, 41,* 162-165.

Helms, J. E. (1994c). Racial identity and career assessment. *Journal of Career Assessment, 2,* 199-209.

Helms, J. E. (1994d). Racial identity in the school environment. In P. Pedersen & J. Carey (Eds.), *Multicultural counseling in schools* (pp. 19-37). Boston: Allyn & Bacon.

Helms, J. E., & Carter, R. T. (1990). Development of the White Racial Identity Attitude Inventory. In J. E. Helms (Ed.), *Black and White racial identity: Theory, research, and practice* (pp. 67-80). Westport, CT: Greenwood.

Helms, J. E., & Cook, D. A. (in press). *An introduction to using race and culture in counseling and psychotherapy.* Fort Worth, TX: Harcourt, Brace, & Javanovich.

Helms, J. E., & Piper, R. E. (1994). Implications of racial identity theory for vocational psychology. *Journal of Vocational Behavior, 44,* 124-136.

Jones, L. (1994, May). Mama's White. *Essence Magazine,* pp. 78, 80, 148.

McConahay, J. B., & Hough, J. C. (1976). Symbolic racism. *Journal of Social Issues, 32,* 23-45.

Nelson, J. (1993). *Volunteer slavery: My authentic Negro experience.* Chicago: Noble.

Parham, T. A., & Helms, J. E. (1981). The influence of Black students' racial identity attitudes on preference for counselor's race. *Journal of Counseling Psychology, 28,* 250-257.

Sabnani, H. B., Ponterotto, J. G., & Borodovsky, L. G. (1991). White racial identity development and cross-cultural counselor training: A stage model. *The Counseling Psychologist, 19*(1), 76-102.

Takaki, R. (1993). *A different mirror: A history of multicultural America.* Boston: Little, Brown.

Tokar, D. M., & Swanson, J. L. (1991). An investigation of the validity of Helms's model of White racial identity development. *Journal of Counseling Psychology, 38,* 296-301.

Wenger, J. (1993). Just part of the mix. *Focus, 21*(9), 3, 4.

Yee, A. H., Fairchild, H. H., Weizmann, F., & Wyatt, G. E. (1993). Addressing psychology's problems with race. *American Psychologist, 48,* 1132-1140.

Zinn, H. (1980). *A history of the United States.* New York: Harper & Row.

10

Biracial Identity Development

Theory and Research

CHRISTINE KERWIN

JOSEPH G. PONTEROTTO

THE TOPIC OF BIRACIAL IDENTITY DEVELOPMENT has received increasing attention in recent years (e.g., Root, 1992a). This interest has been spurred by demographic trends that indicate a rapid increase in the population and by the acknowledgment that there is little well-defined research and theory in the area.

This chapter provides an overview of issues, research, and theory in biracial identity development. We begin by defining important terms used throughout the chapter. Next, we present an update on demographic trends regarding interracial families and biracial individuals. Subsequently we move to a brief discussion of salient challenges faced by biracial persons and to common myths often associated with the population. A major portion of the chapter then reviews extant theories and models of biracial identity development. The chapter closes with recommendations for needed research in the area.

The reader should keep in mind that although this chapter focuses on the racial identity development of biracial individuals of Black/White parentage, references to other groups will also be provided. It is recognized, however, that different issues may be faced by interracial children due, in some part, to their family's racial composition (Keerdoja, 1984; Shackford, 1984). For example, children are likely to encounter different degrees of racial discrimination from White society depending, in some part, on their specific racial composition.

199

Keerdoja (1984) noted that children of White-Asian or White-Hispanic back-grounds assimilate more easily into White society than do children of Black-White unions, who, no matter what their percentage of Black heritage is or how light skinned they may be, are assigned to the Black community.

IMPORTANCE AND
COMPLEXITY OF RACIAL IDENTITY

The development of racial identity is important for members of minority groups and can also be seen as critical for individuals whose heritage includes more than one racial group. Ponterotto (1989) stated, "All racial/ethnic minority groups in the United States must negotiate some degree of biculturality, and as a result, the study of racial identity and acculturation issues is a must for all racial/ethnic minority focused research" (p. 270).

Development of racial identity would appear to be more complex for individuals with a multiracial heritage as compared to those with a monoracial background. Katz (1983) reported, "In large part, children develop both gender and racial identity by learning which group they are in and assuming that the 'other' group is different along most dimensions" (p. 68). Because there is a growing tendency for interracially married parents to encourage their biracial children to identify with both racial/ethnic groups (Barringer, 1989; Smolowe, 1993), many biracial children have before them the task of establishing a dual identity from the beginning of their lives.

It is often asserted that biracial individuals will encounter societal discrimination similar to that of monoracial minority group members (Brandell, 1988; Keerdoja, 1984; Shackford, 1984). Johnson (1992) stated, "The biracial child has a dual minority status both within the larger society as a member or partial member of a devalued racial group and often within the African American community due to perceived lack of 'full' affiliation" (p. 45). Keerdoja (1984) reported that although biracial children encounter the problems faced by most minorities, they also must figure out how to reconcile the heritages of both parents in a society that categorizes individuals into single groups.

TERMINOLOGY

It is important to define terms commonly found in the biracial identity literature. The following terms will be used throughout this chapter.

Bicultural

Buriel and Saenz (1980, cited in LaFromboise, Coleman, & Gerton, 1993) defined biculturalism as "an integration of the competencies and sensitivities associated with two cultures within a single individual" (p. 246). The bicultural model describes how members of minority groups learn two distinct behavioral repertoires, a process that is seen as adaptive for members of minority groups (cf. Cross, 1987; Valentine, 1971) and may have particular relevance for individuals whose racial heritage includes two or more groups.

Biracial

The term *biracial* is most often used to describe first-generation offspring of parents of different races. It most typically describes individuals of Black and White racial heritage (Sebring, 1985) but is not limited to this combination. The term *biracial* is consonant with terms such as *bicultural* and *bilingual* and is therefore preferred to terms such as *mixed* or *interracial* when referring to an individual. It most appropriately signifies the presence of two racial backgrounds in a nonjudgmental manner. Root (1992b) suggested a broader definition whereby the individual identifying as biracial might have a biracial parent or grandparent, for example.

Ethnicity

Jalali (1988) defined *ethnicity* as "the culture of [a] people [that] is thus critical for values, attitudes, perceptions, needs, modes of expression, behavior, and identity" (p. 10).

Interracial

The term *interracial* is most often used in connection with interracial marriage and/or interracial families. It refers to marriage between individuals of different races and/or a family unit that is made up of individuals having different racial backgrounds.

Multicultural

The term *multicultural* implies a sense of simultaneous loyalty to and embracing of more than one culture (i.e., not simply the presence of two or more races or cultures) (Williams, 1992).

Multiracial

Sometimes used interchangeably with *biracial, multiracial,* according to Root (1992b), more appropriately describes a person integrating two or more different heritages. It is inclusive of all individuals with more than one racial heritage and also "acknowledges that the suppression of multiracial heritage in this country may limit people's knowledge about their 'racial' roots" (Root, 1992b, p. 11).

Racial Identity

Sometimes used interchangeably with *ethnic identity, racial identity* refers to "the individual's acquisition of group patterns . . . one's sense of belonging to an ethnic group and the part of one's thinking, perceptions, feelings, and behavior that is due to ethnic group membership" (Rotheram & Phinney, 1987, p. 13). Rosenthal (1987) asserted that it "arises in interaction and is a function not only of the individual and his or her relation to the ethnic group but of that group's place in the wider social setting" (p. 160).

DEMOGRAPHIC TRENDS
RELATED TO MULTIRACIAL PERSONS

Interracial Marriage

In 1967, laws prohibiting interracial marriage (antimiscegenation laws) remaining on the books in 16 states were struck down by the U.S. Supreme Court (Brandell, 1988). State laws prohibiting interracial marriage typically regulated marriage specifically between Whites and people of other races (Perkins, 1994).

Twenty years after this Supreme Court ruling, there existed almost 1 million interracially married couples, representing an increase of 250% from 1967 to 1987 (Perkins, 1994). Smolowe (1993) estimated that the current number is well over 1 million marriages. *Time* magazine devoted a special issue to America's increasingly multicultural society, noting that interracial marriage has become increasingly common. In a survey that *Time* magazine conducted, 72% of those polled personally knew interracial married couples (Smolowe, 1993).

Children of Interracial Unions

According to federal statistics, about 1 million Americans (accounting for 3% of the total U.S. population) born in the 1970s and 1980s are of mixed racial heritage (Barringer, 1989). The increase in the birthrate of multiracial babies is 26 times higher than any other group (Smolowe, 1993).

Even given the above statistics, we may be underestimating the number of mixed-heritage individuals. Currently, the National Center for Health Statistics classifies children at birth according to their mother's race. The father's race, which may be the same as or different from the mother's, is ignored. Many writers focusing on issues associated with interracial families believe that these and other factors (e.g., the U.S. Census form currently has no specific category for multiracial individuals) converge to make the number of biracial or multiracial individuals in American society an underestimate.

Terry P. Wilson has been teaching a course entitled "People of Mixed Racial Descent" at the University of California at Berkeley since 1980. Encountering ever-increasing enrollment, Wilson reports a dramatic increase in the number of multiracial individuals and a corresponding increase in the number of individuals who identify themselves in this way. He stated that as recently as in the late 1970s, multiracial individuals largely identified racially with only one parent (Barringer, 1989).

MYTHS REGARDING BIRACIAL CHILDREN

This section will focus on prevailing myths in our society regarding biracial children and their families. It is important that counselors and educators have accurate, research-supported information on racial identity development. Unfortunately, several myths about biracial individuals have been presented in the media. "In a society in which racism is still prevalent, we can expect that interracial families will be confronted with prejudices and challenges" (Kerwin & Ponterotto, 1994, p. 10). Three common myths are presented below.

Myth 1: The Stereotype of the "Tragic Mulatto" or "Marginal Person"

A long-held notion is that biracial individuals are destined to have far-reaching problems due to their racial heritage. They are stereotyped as people who will be rejected at face value by all ethnic/racial groups and considered to be marginal but not actual members of these groups.

Some of the available literature on growing up biracial has reinforced this notion. One may find, for example, studies of individuals referred to mental health clinics for treatment. Unrepresentative single case studies from clinical samples reinforce the stereotype that any problem experienced by a biracial individual is necessarily related to his or her racial status.

Perhaps a more accurate representation of biracial identity is made by Wardle (1987), who spoke of the biracial youngster as one who may enjoy a "doubly rich heritage" (p. 56). Wardle warned against making assumptions about these individuals and urged that educators "recognize that interracial children are different from each *other*, just as all children are. No child should be stereotyped" (p. 56).

Myth 2: Biracial Individuals Must Choose to Identify With Only One Group

It has been widely believed that biracial individuals who are the offspring of one White parent and one parent of color should identify with only one racial/ethnic group, specifically with the group of the parent of color. The myth is that one has little choice but to adopt this identity because society will ultimately view the individual this way. This tendency is related to the anti-quated "one-drop rule," whereby a person with any amount of Black racial heritage would be designated as Black.

Acceptance of such a dictate would involve a biracial individual's ignoring the heritage(s) of one parent. It would also involve accepting membership in only one group, this one group not necessarily being of the individual's own choosing. These actions, we believe, could be detrimental to one's sense of self, in that an essential aspect of one's identity is being actively denied.

Myth 3: Biracial Individuals Do Not Want to Discuss Their Racial Identity

Kerwin, Ponterotto, Jackson, and Harris (1993) found that contrary to what some may expect, biracial youngsters do not mind inquiries about their heritage when such questions have a nonjudgmental tone. Biracial students told us that their teachers rarely asked about their backgrounds and rarely discussed issues such as race in the classroom. It should be noted, however, that many individuals perceive openness to discussion about race as acceptance.

Perceptions regarding such discussion may vary according to the groups involved. Kich (1992), for example, found that Japanese/White biracial adults reported that they felt scrutinized by constant questioning regarding their background in their youth. Kerwin (1991) found, however, that Black/White biracial children often felt supported and accepted by others who asked them about their heritage and were willing to enter into a discussion with them (with a nonjudgmental tone). It is unknown whether these differences are due to different groups' cultural norms regarding the social appropriateness of such discussion or to other factors such as physical appearance, time period, or geographic location.

MODELS OF BIRACIAL IDENTITY DEVELOPMENT

Future empirical work is needed to further explore issues relevant to the experiences of multiracial individuals. We believe that a theoretical foundation, although preliminary, would facilitate continuing empirical work in this area. We now turn to an examination of extant models of biracial identity development, concluding with a new framework that integrates current findings and available theoretical constructions.

Extant Models

Deficit Models

Deficit models of biracial identity development are usually exemplified by Stonequist's (1937) conceptualization of the "marginal personality." This deficit, perceived as having developed within the individual, was seen as arising from the supposed fact that persons with more than one group heritage could only be "marginal members" of these groups.

It has been argued that if marginality exists, the problem is not that of an individual's having a marginal personality. Rather, if and when marginality exists, it is a reflection of prejudice within the differing cultures and an internalization of such biases (Poston, 1990). The model of the marginal person is antiquated and prejudicial but continues to have some influence in popular culture.

Poston (1990)

Poston posited a "tentative" model of biracial identity development after recognizing the poor fit of existing models of racial identity development conceptualized for monoracial individuals. He reasoned that racial identity development would necessarily be different for biracial individuals due to the following factors:

1. The biracial individual may choose one group over the other at different stages of his or her life.
2. Monoracial identity models for minority group members include rejection of the minority culture followed by rejection of the majority culture. These stages may be different for biracial individuals because they have a stake in both cultures.
3. Monoracial identity development models do not include the possibility of integrating more than one racial/ethnic group identity into one's sense of self.
4. All models assume that the minority community will be completely accepting as the individual "immerses" him- or herself in the minority culture at a given stage.

Poston proposed a five-stage model of biracial identity development during which the individual develops *reference group orientation (RGO)* attitudes. Cross (1987) described RGO as a construct that encompasses one's group identity, including racial attitudes, racial self-identification, and racial preference. Although including one's racial identity, RGO attitudes specifically exclude personal identity constructs such as self-esteem and self-worth (see Cross, 1987, for extensive discussion of RGO).

Poston's initial stage, *Personal Identity*, occurs when a young person's sense of self is independent of group identity or RGO attitudes because these have not yet developed. Poston hypothesized that an individual lacking these attitudes would have an identity based primarily on personal identity constructs, such as self-esteem and self-concept, that develop within the context of the family.

The second stage, *Choice of Group Categorization*, occurs when the young individual perceives him- or herself as compelled to choose an identity, usually of just one ethnic/racial group. Individuals may feel pressured to make choices they would not otherwise make. According to Hall (1980), the pressure to choose one group over the other is related to issues such as one's immediate living and social situation, available peer groups, participation in cultural activities, family acceptance, and physical appearance. Poston thought it improbable for an individual to choose a multiracial identity at this second stage because having a multiple identity requires a cultural knowledge base and a level of abstract thinking beyond what is characteristically found for individuals at this developmental period.

During the third stage, *Enmeshment/Denial*, an individual has become enmeshed with one group and experiences guilt and self-hatred as well as rejection from one or more groups due to the choice made. Poston hypothesized that some case studies found in the psychiatric literature (see, for example, Gibbs, 1987) may be of individuals at this stage who have been unable to resolve issues such as guilt over disloyalty to one parent.

The fourth stage, *Appreciation*, is an emerging receptivity to one's multiple heritages and a resultant broadening of one's reference group orientation. Individuals may initiate exploration into their previously ignored heritage(s) through participation in cultural activities, for example.

Although individuals in the fourth stage still generally identify with one group, during the fifth stage, *Integration*, they perceive value in having a multiple identity. They continue to acquire knowledge regarding their multiple racial/ethnic identities and experience a sense of wholeness and integration.

Although Poston underscored the importance of numerous factors (e.g., family and peer groups) that ultimately affect identity choices, his model suggests that all biracial individuals will undergo confusion and resultant periods of maladjustment. Furthermore, Poston hypothesized that identity problems are experienced by multiracial individuals if outside prejudices become internalized and personal identity factors such as self-esteem are negatively affected. Poston noted that family and community support is essential, especially in the resolution of the denial of one parent's culture occurring during the Enmeshment/Denial stage. Hall (1980) reported that two thirds of multiracial adults interviewed had overcome the identity confusion they may have had and identified themselves as multiracial (i.e., reached the Integration stage).

Jacobs (1977, 1992)

Jacobs proposed three distinct stages of development in biracial identity formation. From interviews and doll-play instrument methodology with Black/White biracial children ranging in age from 3 to 8, he hypothesized the first two stages and projected a third stage that occurs beyond age 8. He later extended his research into the third stage through inclusion of 8- to 12-year-old children.

During Stage 1, *Pre-Color Constancy: Play and Experimentation With Color*, the child acquires the understanding that one's skin color is an enduring characteristic. In most cases, color is viewed as nonevaluative. However, it is posited that negative evaluations based on color may occur if negative experiences and/or low self-esteem preclude exploratory play with color.

During Stage 2, *Post-Color Constancy: Biracial Label and Racial Ambivalence*, the child becomes ambivalent about his or her own color, often rejecting one group and then the other. This is viewed as a necessary step so that "discordant elements can be reconciled in a unified identity" (Jacobs, 1992, p. 201) at a later stage. In addition to the attainment of color constancy, there is internalization of an interracial label, a term often provided by the family. The child may also construct his or her own label. Jacobs advocated the use of interracial labels and identified the provision of this label as a parenting style that facilitates a healthy self-concept for biracial children. Also during this stage is emerging awareness of societal discrimination based on race.

During Stage 3, *Biracial Identity*, the biracial child recognizes that racial group membership is not determined by skin color although it may be correlated with it. Rather, the child discovers that membership in racial/ethnic groups is determined by parentage. The biracial child identifies him- or herself as biracial not solely by the fact of his or her own skin color or that of his or her parents, but rather by the fact that one parent belongs to the social group of Black people and the other parent belongs to the social group of White people.

Kich (1992)

Kich developed his model on the basis of the findings of his dissertation, a qualitative study completed in 1982 involving Japanese/White adults aged 17 to 60. Kich reported that all 15 adults whom he interviewed traversed through three main stages during development of their biracial identity. This development was viewed as a lifetime process of "transitions from a questionable, sometimes devalued sense of self to one where an interracial self-conception is highly valued and secure" (p. 305). Kich (1992) reported that his clinical and anecdotal experiences had lent further validity to this stage model.

During Stage 1, *Awareness of Differentness and Dissonance* (ages 3 to 10), all biracial individuals, regardless of their specific racial makeup, experience a sense of being different. Although this sense of difference can be positively valued when dealt with within a secure family context, it may become a source of rejection from peers due to difficulty that others may have in understanding the biracial experience.

Biracial individuals interviewed by Kich reported that the awareness of difference often occurred

> during the earliest phases of their transition into peer and reference group contexts outside of the family (school, church, or community events). Looking different, with a name perhaps discrepant from appearance, and having parents or a birthplace that is noticed as "weird" or as "gaijin" (foreigner) increased the ways in which biracial people experience "not belonging." (Kich, 1992, p. 307)

During this initial stage, parental involvement in terms of developing a positive self-concept and provision of a positive interracial label is essential. Openness to discussion of racial and ethnic differences may be communicated verbally or via showing interest in differing cultural experiences such as foods, languages, and social contacts.

Stage 2, *Struggle for Acceptance,* occurs from age 8 through late adolescence or young adulthood. During this stage, individuals become more involved with friends, peers, and the wider community. These experiences further increase feelings that others perceive them and their families as different. Questions regarding one's background occur, and many individuals at this stage will list their parents' backgrounds (e.g., "My father is American and my mother is Japanese"). Kich (1992) stated, "They want to be known yet often are ashamed and outraged at being so persistently judged in their differences. . . . Maintaining a separation between family and social life can be used only temporarily as a defense against fears of rejection" (p. 310).

Kich (1992) found that some biracial individuals use a reference group orientation that does not involve race. They may focus instead on abilities or nationality, bypassing race and ethnicity. He stated, "Like all other adolescents, biracial youth struggle with finding an accepting place outside the home. But, unlike others, biracial and bicultural people do not find an easy or comfortable recognition, acceptance, and membership with others like themselves" (p. 312). Finally recognizing that the standard racial categories are limited, they begin to view their racial status as other than a personal problem.

A struggle with identification with one parent over the other also often occurs at the second stage. Kich believed that biracial children reared in single-parent families need to have some type of reconnection with the absent parent in order to lay the groundwork for the next stage, self-acceptance. This exploration typically occurs during high school or college. During this time, individuals may decide upon specific interracial labels and develop an awareness of the positive aspects of their multiple heritages.

Stage 3, *Self-Acceptance and Assertion of an Interracial Identity,* typically occurs after high school, often during transitions to or from college or work. The biracial individual achieves the "ability to create congruent self-definitions rather than be determined by others' definitions and stereotypes" (p. 314). The individual values and seeks out information regarding his or her cultural heritages while keeping in the forefront an awareness of also being an American. Finally, during this stage, the individual develops an openness to inquiries from others and an understanding that not all questions regarding racial background are intended negatively. The biracial individual recognizes that many people ask questions regarding race because of society's confusion regarding race.

LaFromboise, Coleman, and Gerton (1993)

LaFromboise et al. described the extant models of racial and ethnic identity development for single-heritage individuals and concluded that these models include the potential for individuals to become biculturally competent. They presented their bicultural "alternation model" in terms of second-culture acquisition such as that experienced by immigrant groups. This model can also be seen as relevant to individuals growing up in interracial/intercultural families.

The alternation model postulates that it is possible to gain competence in two cultures without losing one's original cultural identity or having to choose one culture over the other. The authors did not subscribe to the notion that developing competence in one culture necessarily leads to the loss of identification with another culture. The long-standing assumption that living in two cultures can only have negative impact, such as identity confusion and normlessness (i.e., "marginality"), was rejected. Conversely, LaFromboise et al. presented evidence that living in more than one culture is often perceived by individuals as beneficial. They believed that "the key to psychological well-being may well be the ability to develop and maintain competence in both cultures" (p. 402).

LaFromboise et al. also proffered the argument that any negative psychological impact from contact with two distinct cultures can be reduced via the development of bicultural competence. They viewed the presence of a strong personal identity as facilitative to the process of second-culture acquisition and bicultural competence. It may also be noted that the process of cultural acquisition was seen as an individualized process that varies in terms of its rate.

LaFromboise et al. suggested that in order to navigate two cultures effectively, individuals need to acquire competence in six dimensions:

1. Knowledge of cultural beliefs and values such as awareness of history, rituals, and everyday cultural practices
2. Positive attitudes toward the goal of bicultural competence and toward both groups with whom one has sufficient contact (but not necessarily equal regard)
3. The belief that one can live in an effective and satisfying way within more than one group
4. The ability to appropriately and effectively communicate verbally and nonverbally in each culture
5. Having a range of situationally appropriate behaviors and roles for each cultural group
6. Having a sufficient social support system providing a source of practical information

Williams (1992) and Stephan (1992)

Although not formal models of development, the empirical studies of Williams (1992) and Stephan (1992) have strong implications and are worthy of review. Williams conducted a study with 43 Amerasians, ages 16 through 35, who had lived at least six of their adolescent years in Japan (with U.S. military affiliation). Her four major developmental findings are:

1. Biracial Japanese/American individuals have a sense of holding something in common with other Amerasians as well as other racially mixed Americans.
2. They have an early awareness of racial differences, often due to others bringing it up to their attention.
3. The variable of physical appearance plays a role, but with unknown impact due to many individual differences.
4. Choice of a reference group is not always predicated on whether a particular community was accepting of the individual.

Stephan (1992) conducted two studies of biracial identity, one quantitative and one qualitative. In the first, Japanese-heritage Americans in Hawaii and Hispanic-heritage Americans in New Mexico (all college students) completed a questionnaire. In the second study, semistructured interviews were conducted with college students in Hawaii who identified themselves as having a mixed heritage.

Stephan found that although cultural exposure is usually extremely important, ethnic identity can develop without one's having been brought up with interaction with that group. Individuals may seek out information on their own or choose a particular group for other reasons (e.g., status, view that it would be one's accurate racial heritage, the influence of a friend).

Overall, Stephan found that dual-heritage individuals do not have difficulties in "expected" areas such as establishing a racial identity, reconciling differing cultural norms, or dealing with long-term effects based on rejection. She cited benefits of biracial status, including "increased contact with the members of one's heritage groups, enjoyment of the cultures of one's heritage groups, facility in languages spoken by one's heritage groups, and intergroup tolerance" (p. 62).

Kerwin-Ponterotto Model of Biracial Identity Development

The Kerwin-Ponterotto model of biracial identity development is based on the empirical findings reported in Kerwin (1991) and Kerwin et al. (1993). An attempt was made to integrate the findings of other empirical studies and the above-referenced models, drawing upon their similarities, into this model. It presents an integrated framework for viewing the complex process that many individuals go through in developing their own racial identity.

It is recognized that the eventual resolution of the steps toward a biracial identity formation is dependent on numerous personal, societal, and environmental factors. The actual resolution is also individual. For example, some adults may identify their public self as African American although they also hold a multiracial self-concept. This model consists of the following stages: Preschool, Entry to School, Preadolescence, Adolescence, College/Young Adulthood, and Adulthood.

Preschool. During this period (up to 5 years of age), racial awareness emerges. Parents interviewed by Kerwin (1991) reported that their biracial children noticed differences between their Black and White parents in hair texture and skin color from a very early age. This may be due, in part, to parents' own heightened sensitivity to their children's awareness. It is also possible that this development is enhanced for children reared in interracial families because of intrafamilial differences. The growing recognition of similarities and differences in people's appearance seems to be complex and variable but generally developmental in nature.

Goodman (1964) and others found that racial awareness generally develops in children between three and four years of age. McRoy, Zurcher, Lauderdale, and Anderson (1984) found that transracially adopted Black children had awareness of ethnicity as young as 3 years of age. By 7 years of age, all were aware of African Americans as a group, although their own major reference groups were White. Gunthorpe (1977) found that the majority of children (including White, Black, and biracial children) aged 3 to 5 recognized racial differences among dolls with varying skin tones.

Ramsey (1987) reported that the salience of race for categories used by children differs across situations and may also vary depending on the child's immediate milieu. Rotheram and Phinney (1987) stated, "Children's exposure to situations in which they are aware of their ethnicity will vary depending on their status as minority or majority group members, as well as on the degree of ethnic homogeneity or heterogeneity in their daily activities" (p. 16). Katz (1983) concurred that experiential factors, such as living in a racially homogeneous or heterogeneous environment, affect the rate of racial concept development.

It may be conjectured that some children reared in interracial families develop racial concepts relatively early due to their exposure to different racial groups. Payne (1977), for example, found a significantly higher level of racial awareness in biracial preschoolers than in White children. Conversely, children raised in some interracial families may experience denial of racial differences on the part of their parents, which may have a different effect on the development of racial awareness.

Entry to School. Katz (1983) contended that children enter school "with a fairly well-differentiated sense of self, together with some clearly defined notions about many social groups and their distinguishing characteristics" (p. 41). Upon entry to school, questions such as "What are you?" are asked of children, perhaps of multiracial children to a greater degree. The tendency to seek to classify others according to social categories appears to be universal, an attempt, perhaps, to simplify one's perceptual world at an early age (Katz, 1983). Children begin to use labels and/or descriptive terms to define themselves and their families in response to such inquiries.

Kerwin et al. (1993) reported that some children use descriptive terms for their actual skin color (e.g., "coffee and cream"), whereas others use a label (e.g., *interracial*) provided by their parents. This seems to depend, to some degree, on whether parents discuss racial labels with their children. Children provided with a label within the family typically use it to describe themselves and/or their families.

There are likely to be differences at this stage for biracial children depending on the degree of integration of their school environment as well as the availability of Black and White role models. These factors can also be seen to have great import in the development of realistic attitudes and nonstereotypical perceptions of members of different racial groups.

Preadolescence. Following awareness of skin color differences is increased awareness that physical appearance and perhaps language(s) spoken are also representative of group membership. There is an increasing recognition of one's own and others' group membership being related to factors such as skin color, physical appearance, language, and culture. At this stage, however, children tend to use labels representative of social groups by race, ethnicity, and/or religious background rather than terms that are simply physical descriptors.

Awareness that their parents belong to distinct racial/ethnic groups necessarily follows early racial awareness for biracial youngsters but may not occur until triggered by environmental circumstances such as a specific event. This may occur at any age but was typically found to occur during the preadolescent to adolescent period. Kerwin (1991) found that environmental factors seemed to trigger increased awareness for some children (e.g., incidents in which the child had dealt with racism, entry into an integrated environment for the first time, or, conversely, entry into a more segregated environment for the first time).

Adolescence. This may be the most challenging stage for biracial youngsters due to both developmental factors characteristic of this age group and societal pressures. Barringer (1989) wrote, "For people, particularly adolescents, who fall between the definitions, the search for a racial identity can be wrenching, often involving conscious or unconscious denial of one parent" (p. 22).

Kerwin (1991) found that adolescents perceived pressure from peers to choose one racial group over another. This appears to be related to Erikson's (1968) description of "in groupers" and "out groupers." Adolescents generally show a marked intolerance for differences. The pressure to identify with one group may also be related to difficulty in rejecting societal expectations. At this developmental juncture, it may be difficult for the biracial adolescent to resist pressure to conform with the expectations of others to identify solely with his or her parent of color. Proshansky (1966, as cited in Rotheram and Phinney, 1987) found that although older children are less prejudiced or at least demonstrate more socially acceptable attitudes than younger children, own-group preferences tend to increase with age.

Peer and societal pressure to choose a specific racial group may be neutralized by other RGO factors not related to race (e.g., sports teams, clubs, academic abilities and interests). For example, a 16-year-old biracial male described situations in his school in which peers increasingly grouped together on the basis of race. He further observed this tendency to occur more often with girls. He reported, "The boys all play sports together. And I think that's what brings us together. You know, we're all on a team. We all sit together. We all play games together and everything. So that kind of brings us together you know, Blacks, Whites, Hispanics, everybody" (quoted in Kerwin, 1991, p. 110).

On the other hand, dating during adolescence may bring racial issues to the forefront due to the reaction of others (especially parents of potential dating partners). For example, a biracial individual is likely to be perceived by monoracial Whites as belonging to a minority group, which will bring up issues associated with interracial dating (see, for example, Keerdoja, 1984; Norment, 1985; Shackford, 1984).

College/Young Adulthood. There may be a continuing immersion in one culture with a resultant rejection of the other. With the development of a more secure personal identity usually accompanying this stage, however, rejection of others' expectations and an acceptance of one's biracial and bicultural heritage is increasingly likely to occur.

Brody (1984) describes his own experience (having grown up with a single White mother) at this stage:

> After identifying totally with Whites for a while, I went through a period of rejecting the White race and trying to compensate for what I felt was lacking by totally immersing myself in Black culture (or what I thought was Black culture). This was no solution either. Eventually I came to accept myself as a product of both races and realized the futility of trying to fit anyone's expectations of me. (p. 15)

Depending somewhat on the individual's environmental circumstances and personal appearance, the multiracial individual may continue to overhear comments made by nonminority individuals that would not be said in front of someone clearly identifiable as a person of color.

If there is a successful working through of the above stages, at this point, and sometimes earlier, there will be a growing recognition of the advantages as well as the disadvantages associated with having a biracial heritage. Oftentimes, biracial individuals will have developed the advantage of "bicultural vision," which allows them to understand situations in a more in-depth and multifaceted way ("Bicultural Vision," 1994).

Adulthood. As the development of a biracial identity is viewed as a lifelong process, it can be seen that there needs to be a continuing integration throughout adulthood of the different facets making up one's racial identity. With the successful resolution of earlier stages, there will be a continuing exploration and interest in different cultures, including one's own. The integrated individual will find that he or she is able to function effectively in varying situations and understand different communities. An enhanced sense of self and "increased flexibility in interpersonal relations" may also be a consequence of "the resulting broader base of experience" (Adler, 1987, p. 58).

RECOMMENDATIONS FOR RESEARCH

Several research issues suggest avenues for future study in biracial identity development. The following list is considered suggestive rather than exhaustive in terms of further exploration of the complex issues involved in racial identity development.

Research Issue 1

Young children can develop bicultural competence provided they have opportunities and an open environment. During development, however, biracial adolescents report peer pressure to choose identification with only one racial group, usually that of their parent of color. In order to gain peer acceptance, they may feel the need to reject other groups and exclude others dissimilar to themselves. Future research efforts are needed to explore issues related to the effects of peer pressure during the adolescent period. It may be fruitful to explore the role of membership in groups such as clubs, sport teams, and religious organizations in providing an alternate reference group orientation. Gender differences should be examined.

Research Issue 2

A number of social and environmental variables affect the development of racial concepts and identity. There is a relationship between the cultural forces associated with one's living situation (e.g., integrated or nonintegrated neighborhood, schools) and the rate of development of racial awareness and racial identity. What is the interplay of these factors?

Research Issue 3

There appears to be a shift toward biracial individuals' choosing to identify as multiracial/multicultural individuals rather than conforming to society's expectation that they choose to identify with only one group. When and how did this shift occur, and how might this affect future generations of multiracial children?

Research Issue 4

Several researchers/writers in this area contend that biracial individuals who maintain a bicultural way of life find it beneficial and have an increased sense of self and identity. Future research could specifically examine the development of bicultural competence for biracial individuals.

Research Issue 5

What is the role of parents and educators in helping biracial children develop a healthy sense of identity? There appears to be some relationship between having an open dialogue with family and others, the use of an interracial label, and the perception of oneself as having both advantages and disadvantages associated with one's biracial heritage. Depending on one's specific heritage, appearance, geographic location, and other factors, there is also the possibility of increased exposure to prejudice and racist comments from different groups. How are biracial individuals best prepared to cope with the issues they are likely to face in our racist society?

SUMMARY

This chapter provides an overview of the issues, research, and theory in biracial identity development. We began with a discussion of the importance and complexity of racial identity for multiracial individuals. Demographic trends indicate that there is an increasing number of multiracial individuals, and there is a corresponding need for continued theory development and empirical research. Extant models of biracial identity development are reviewed. The Kerwin-Ponterotto model of biracial identity development was presented as an integrated framework for viewing the process by which individuals with more than one racial heritage develop their personal racial identity. Research recommendations were presented for further exploration of the complex issues involved in multiracial identity development.

REFERENCES

Adler, A. J. (1987). Children and biracial identity. In A. Thomas & J. Grimes (Eds.), *Children's needs: Psychological perspectives* (pp. 56-66). Washington, DC: National Association of School Psychologists.

Barringer, F. (1989, September 24). Mixed-race generation emerges but is not sure where it fits. *New York Times*, p. 22.

Bicultural vision. (1994, Spring). *Teaching Tolerance, 3*(1), 6.

Brandell, J. R. (1988). Treatment of the biracial child: Theoretical and clinical issues. *Journal of Multicultural Counseling and Development, 16,* 176-187.

Brody, H. (1984). Growing up in interracial families: Suggestions for single parents. *Interracial Books for Children Bulletin, 15*(6), 12, 15.

Cross, W. E., Jr. (1987). A two-factor theory of Black identity: Implications for the study of identity development in minority children. In J. S. Phinney & M. J. Rotheram (Eds.), *Children's ethnic socialization: Pluralism and development* (pp. 117-133). Newbury Park, CA: Sage.

Erikson, E. H. (1968). *Identity: Youth and crisis.* New York: Norton.

Gibbs, J. T. (1987). Identity and marginality: Issues in the treatment of biracial adolescents. *American Journal of Orthopsychiatry, 57,* 265-278.

Goodman, M. E. (1964). *Race awareness in young children.* New York: Collier.

Gunthorpe, W. W. (1977). Skin color recognition, preference and identification in interracial children: A comparative study. *Dissertation Abstracts International, 38,* 10-B. (University Microfilms No. 77-27, 946)

Hall, C. C. I. (1980). *The ethnic identity of racially mixed people: A study of Black-Japanese.* Unpublished doctoral dissertation, University of California, Los Angeles.

Jacobs, J. H. (1977). Black/White interracial families: Marital process and identity development in young children. *Dissertation Abstracts International, 38,* 10-B. (University Microfilms No. 78-3173)

Jacobs, J. H. (1992). Identity development in biracial children. In M. P. P. Root (Ed.), *Racially mixed people in America* (pp. 190-206). Newbury Park, CA: Sage.

Jalali, B. (1988). Ethnicity, cultural adjustment, and behavior: Implications for family therapy. In L. Comas-Diaz & E. E. H. Griffith (Eds.), *Clinical guidelines in cross-cultural mental health* (pp. 9-32). New York: John Wiley.

Johnson, D. J. (1992). Developmental pathways: Toward an ecological theoretical formulation of race identity in Black-White biracial children. In M. P. P. Root (Ed.), *Racially mixed people in America* (pp. 37-49). Newbury Park, CA: Sage.

Katz, P. A. (1983). Developmental foundations of gender and racial attitudes. In R. L. Leahy (Ed.), *The child's construction of social inequality* (pp. 41-78). New York: Academic Press.

Keerdoja, E. (1984, November 19). Children of the rainbow: New parent support groups help interracial kids cope. *Newsweek,* pp. 120-122.

Kerwin, C. (1991). Racial identity development in biracial children of Black/White racial heritage (Doctoral dissertation, Fordham University, 1991). *Dissertation Abstracts International, 52,* 2469-A.

Kerwin, C., & Ponterotto, J. G. (1994, May). Counseling multiracial individuals and their families—don't believe all myths. *ACA Guidepost,* pp. 1, 10-11.

Kerwin, C., Ponterotto, J. G., Jackson, B. L., & Harris, A. (1993). Racial identity in biracial children: A qualitative investigation. *Journal of Counseling Psychology, 40,* 221-231.

Kich, G. K. (1992). The developmental process of asserting a biracial, bicultural identity. In M. P. P. Root (Ed.), *Racially mixed people in America* (pp. 304-317). Newbury Park, CA: Sage.

LaFromboise, T., Coleman, H. L. K., & Gerton, J. (1993). Psychological impact of biculturalism: Evidence and theory. *Psychological Bulletin, 114,* 395-412.

McRoy, R. G., Zurcher, L. A., Lauderdale, M. L., & Anderson, R. E. (1984). The identity of transracial adoptees. *Social Casework: The Journal of Contemporary Social Work, 65,* 34-39.

Norment, L. (1985, September). A probing look at children of interracial marriages. *Ebony, 40*(11), 156-162.

Payne, R. B. (1977). Racial attitude formation in children of mixed Black and White heritage: Skin color and racial identity. *Dissertation Abstracts International, 38,* 6-B. (University Microfilms No. 77-27, 605)

Perkins, M. (1994, March 17). Guess who's coming to church? Confronting Christians' fear of interracial marriage. *Christianity Today,* pp. 30-33.

Ponterotto, J. G. (1989). Expanding directions for racial identity research. *The Counseling Psychologist, 17,* 264-272.

Poston, W. S. C. (1990). The biracial identity development model: A needed addition. *Journal of Counseling and Development, 69,* 152-155.

Ramsey, P. G. (1987). Young children's thinking about ethnic differences. In J. S. Phinney & M. J. Rotheram (Eds.), *Children's ethnic socialization: Pluralism and development* (pp. 56-72). Newbury Park, CA: Sage.

Root, M. P. P. (Ed.). (1992a). *Racially mixed people in America*. Newbury Park, CA: Sage.

Root, M. P. P. (1992b). Within, between, and beyond race. In M. P. P. Root (Ed.), *Racially mixed people in America* (pp. 3-11). Newbury Park, CA: Sage.

Rosenthal, D. A. (1987). Ethnic identity development in adolescents. In J. S. Phinney & M. J. Rotheram (Eds.), *Children's ethnic socialization: Pluralism and development* (pp. 156-179). Newbury Park, CA: Sage.

Rotheram, M. J., & Phinney, J. S. (1987). Introduction: Definitions and perspectives in the study of children's ethnic socialization. In J. S. Phinney & M. J. Rotheram (Eds.), *Children's ethnic socialization: Pluralism and development* (pp. 10-31). Newbury Park, CA: Sage.

Sebring, D. L. (1985). Considerations in counseling interracial children. *Journal of Non-White Concerns in Personnel and Guidance, 13*, 3-9.

Shackford, K. (1984). Interracial children: Growing up healthy in an unhealthy society. *Interracial Books for Children, 15*(6), 4-6.

Smolowe, J. (1993). Intermarried . . . with children. *Time, 142* (21), 64-65.

Stephan, C. W. (1992). Mixed-heritage individuals: Ethnic identity and trait characteristics. In M. P. P. Root (Ed.), *Racially mixed people in America* (pp. 50-63). Newbury Park, CA: Sage.

Stonequist, E. B. (1937). *The marginal man: A study in personality and culture conflict*. New York: Russell & Russell.

Valentine, C. A. (1971). Deficit, difference, and bicultural models of Afro-American behavior. *Harvard Educational Review, 41*, 137-157.

Wardle, F. (1987). Are you sensitive to interracial children's special identity needs? *Young Children, 42*(2), 53-59.

Williams, T. K. (1992). Prism lives: Identity of binational Amerasians. In M. P. P. Root (Ed.), *Racially mixed people in America* (pp. 280-303). Newbury Park, CA: Sage.

11

Racial/Ethnic Identity and Racial Consciousness

Looking Back and Looking Forward

WAYNE ROWE

JOHN T. BEHRENS

MARK M. LEACH

IF ACTIVITY in theory and model generation is any indication of the health of an academic field, then multicultural counseling and therapy (MCT) ought to be healthy indeed. And if we accept the relationship between health and longevity, then the area of racial/cultural/ethnic identity/acculturation may be close to achieving eternal life. As illustrated in the chapters in this section, modification and elaboration of earlier models, synthesis of previous models, and construction of essentially new models are taking place at an exhilarating pace.

The field of multicultural counseling is only now beginning to leave its infancy stage, but, as the appearance of this book attests, it has begun the development into a mature subset of behavioral science. At this point what we should expect are the very signs of vitality that may be seen in the preceding chapters. As an emerging academic specialty we are indeed healthy, vigorous, and, hopefully, maturing. Yet rather than be swept along with the existing momentum, we believe it would serve the field well to adopt a cautious stance from which to evaluate where we have been and where we are likely to be going.

This section has been given a jump-start by Allen E. Ivey, whose chapter (Chapter 4, "Psychotherapy as Liberation"), much like a good keynote speech, energizes us as it informs. Who wants to be associated with traditional counseling and therapy, which is "concerned with maintaining the status quo," when we can be part of MCT, which "has come to be recognized as a new, major force in the helping field"? Rather than reframing multicultural counseling by broadening the definition of *culture* (Pedersen, 1991), Ivey challenges us to see the process as a sociopolitical encounter. Personally, we agree wholeheartedly with the goals of MCT and admire the scholarly statement of a radical perspective. But we still are reticent to sign up because it seems to us that certain issues need further discussion.

For example, we are not comfortable with a situation in which the client colleague may be led to discover the "truth" as preconceived by the counselor, thus substituting one authoritarian system for another (albeit more egalitarian). Isn't the task essentially to bring the client to accept our worldview through a kind of Socratic process because we "know" that self-in-relation is good for him or her? Also, one wonders about how to implement interventions designed to activate the oppressed in organizational settings funded (or at least controlled) by the oppressor. Doesn't our innocence show at the interface of science and politics? It may be that these and other concerns will prove to be groundless. But MCT as liberation is on the table, and we now have the opportunity and the responsibility to discuss it.

Although the rapid development of theory is to be expected and may be a sign of vitality in developing areas, it is also associated with certain problems that we would do well to be aware of. For instance, the balance between theorizing and efforts directed at empirical confirmation needs to be considered. If empirical work is being conducted to the exclusion of theoretical refinement, there is the danger of stagnation. On the other hand, if theoretical formulations are being advanced with little attention paid to supporting empirical evidence, there is the danger that resources will be directed for an embarrassingly long time to concepts and paradigms that prove to be blind alleys. Because this area of multicultural counseling has recently been undergoing a kind of model formulation frenzy, it may be prudent to attend to the empirical support that exists for our theoretical models and to make sure that there is adequate evidence of model confirmation before we engage in model application.

Another problem likely to be associated with rapid model building is a kind of compartmentalization or lack of consensus regarding the concepts or terminology used by scholars who are working on closely related, even overlapping, topics. For example, there must be some confusion, particularly among nonspecialists, concerning the distinctions between terms such as *cultural identity*, *racial identity*, and *ethnic identity*. Some authors have approached the construct of identity by means of the associated concept of acculturation (Padilla, 1980), others from an egopsychoanalytic perspective

(Phinney, 1993), some from a social cognitive point of view (Knight, Bernal, Garza, & Cota, 1993), and so forth. The term *acculturation* is sometimes used exclusively to signify a process (Kaplan & Marks, 1990) and sometimes used to indicate a model, the process being labeled *second-culture acquisition* (LaFromboise, Coleman, & Gerton, 1993). How do the concepts of racial identity, ethnic identification, and acculturation relate to each other? These issues, of course, are not an exhaustive listing.

Birman (1994) suggested that issues of acculturation are more relevant for most immigrants and refugees, whereas issues relating to identity are more meaningful to their U.S.-born children and members of racial/ethnic minority groups who were born in the United States. Yet in the past, research conducted with American Indians, Hispanics, and Asian Americans focused mainly on acculturation, whereas racial identity was a concept more frequently applied to African Americans.

Even though cultural identity was recognized as significant, previous research with both Hispanic and Asian American populations emphasized acculturation as an explanatory concept. As would be expected, the instruments developed have mostly been measures of acculturation (e.g., Cuellar, Harris, & Jasso, 1980; Franco, 1983; Marin, Sabogal, Marin, Otero-Sabogal, & Perez-Stable, 1987; Montgomery & Orozco, 1984; Olmedo & Padilla, 1978; Suinn, Rickard-Figueroa, Lew, & Vigil, 1987). However, in their careful description of models of identity and acculturation related to the Hispanic population, Casas and Pytluk (Chapter 8, this volume) imply that racial/ethnic identity can be conceptualized as including both process and content aspects, the former associated with level of acculturation and the latter with identity development.

RACIAL/ETHNIC IDENTITY

As the previous chapters of this section indicate, there is a clear trend toward increased activity focused on identity development. In Chapter 4 of this volume, Ivey makes the point that identity theory is basic to the framework of multicultural counseling. Even though the chapter on American Indians is devoted to the authors' presentation of their model of acculturation, researchers (Moran, Fleming, Somervell, & Manson, 1994) at the National Center for American Indian and Alaska Native Mental Health Research have recently described a sophisticated measure of ethnic identification validated on over 2,000 American Indian adolescents. The revised Nigrescence theory of Cross is obviously related to investigations of Black identity that go back some 50 years (Burlew & Smith, 1991). Also, Kerwin and Ponterotto's chapter on biracial individuals (Chapter 10, this volume) synthesizes earlier models and presents a sequential model indicating the steps toward biracial identity formation. The chapter by Helms (Chapter 9) updates her approach to racial identity development for both Whites and non-Whites, and it is apparent in

Chapter 8, focused on Hispanics, that the recent work on identity development (Bernal & Knight, 1993) has had a significant impact. Finally, Sodowsky, Kwan, and Pannu (Chapter 7) feature Asians in the United States to illustrate the application of a comprehensive model of ethnic identity.

Sodowsky et al.'s model is an ambitious attempt to explain ethnic identity from a social psychological frame of reference. According to this point of view, one's identity is derived from a sense of identification and belonging to a group. People belong to many groups (e.g., gender, occupational, organizational, generational, ethnic/racial, regional) and therefore have many social identifications (Hogg & Abrams, 1990). The totality of these constitute one's identity. Ethnic identity is considered a function of how one locates one's membership in a reference group. This is based on the perception of relatedness that is self-accorded, accorded by the reference group members, and accorded by the dominant cultural group. The dimensions of ethnic identity are considered to be (a) self-identification, how one chooses to label one's group membership; (b) sense of belonging and attachment; (c) valence of feelings toward one's ethnic group (ethnic pride); and (d) participation in ethnic activities and practices. Sodowsky et al. also note that these variables can be distinguished in terms of being internal and external, in the sense of states of mind and behavior patterns, which they term the invisible and visible aspects of ethnic identity.

According to Bernal and Knight (1993), "Ethnic identity . . . is a psychological construct" that consists of "a set of self-ideas about one's own ethnic group membership" (p. 7). The dimensions along which these self-ideas vary include (a) self-identification, the terms used to identify oneself and the meaning of these labels; (b) knowledge of one's culture, such as the traditions, customs, values, and behaviors; and (c) preferences toward one's ethnic group, culture, ethnic group members, and the like.

We believe that the resemblance of these points of view, and the similar dimensions of Phinney's (1992) Multigroup Ethnic Identity Measure (even though derived from different theory), may be the faint glimmerings of a useful convergence. The recent work of Sodowsky, Bernal and Knight, and Phinney seems to mark a transition from earlier, more speculative theory making to a more solidly grounded approach. This could lead to a more precise understanding of identity as experienced by racial/ethnic minorities. As this conceptualization of identity is elaborated, it will be necessary to develop appropriate instruments with which to verify essential aspects of the model. In doing so it seems likely to us that two features will be incorporated: (a) the inclusion of both "invisible" and "visible" aspects of identity and (b) the independent appraisal of one's relation to the majority culture (Chapter 7, this volume), as proposed by a growing number of scholars (Berry, Trimble, & Olmedo, 1986; Leong & Chou, 1994; Mendoza, 1989; Oetting & Beauvais, 1991; Phinney, 1993; Sánchez & Fernández, 1993). Please stay tuned.

Chapter 9, updating Helms's earlier views on Black and White racial identity development, is if anything even more ambitious. Helms has now expanded upon her earlier work (Helms, 1990) to produce a general racial identity theory (RIT) with various processes described and with parallel statuses for people of color and for Whites. This revised theory again shows her innovative thinking and, if confirmed, would represent a great contribution to our understanding of how issues of race affect the behavior of Whites and non-Whites alike. However, we are concerned that this promise may not be realized because of the difficulties that may be encountered in attempting to validate key propositions.

Among the essential propositions that may not be amenable to testing are the following:

1. Racial identity development occurs by the evolution of racial identity statuses that are made up of the dynamic cognitive, emotional, and behavioral processes that manage racial stimuli.
2. The statuses develop sequentially but are not supplanted. Some residual from earlier or more primitive statuses leaves an imprint on subsequent statuses.
3. Statuses are expressed according to the level of dominance within the individual's personality structure, and dominance is determined as the status that most often governs the person's racial reactions.
4. Given a racial event, the ego selects the dominant racial identity status to assist the person in interpreting the event, and schemata then respond in ways that are consistent with the dictates of the status.
5. All statuses that have matured are present in the racial part of a person's personality constellation—that is, are potentially accessible under the "right" circumstances.

It may be that our concerns are unfounded and that the critical propositions of Helms's RIT can be objectively evaluated. But it seems to us that the constructs that support RIT are highly abstract, far removed from behavior, and perhaps difficult to operationalize, thus creating formidable barriers to objective inquiry. If it proves to be that the basic elements of the theory cannot be falsified, then Helms's RIT will need to be revised in order to be considered part of science.

An obviously related consideration concerns the measurement of RIT. At the time of this writing, it is not clear to us whether the Cultural Identity Attitude Scale (Helms & Carter, 1990b, cited in Kohatsu, 1994) will be the instrument used for future assessment of the identity development of people of color. Although it has begun to appear in some reports, we are not aware of any published data describing the scale and are consequently not yet able to evaluate its properties or the extent to which it may provide evidence supporting RIT.

WHITE RACIAL IDENTITY

A brief history, however, does exist for the assessment of White "identity," and we believe that significant problems have not been critically addressed.

To the best of our knowledge, only two instruments designed to assess White racial identity development (WRID) have appeared in the literature. The White Racial Consciousness Development Scale (WRCDS; Claney & Parker, 1989) was an innovative attempt to measure persons on the dimensions of Helms's 1984 WRID model and was developed before the White Racial Identity Attitude Scale (W-RIAS; Helms & Carter, 1990a) became readily accessible. However, the WRCDS has subsequently received little or no use in the published literature, probably because of the availability of the RIAS-W by the originators of the underlying theory and because of its inadequate psychometric properties (Bennett & Rowe, 1994).

In contrast, the RIAS-W has experienced increased use from the time of its introduction to the field. Paradoxically, at the same time that the RIAS-W appears to have become the measure of choice for WRID research, there seems to be growing recognition that it may have serious psychometric deficiencies. One problem that has appeared is that the Contact scale has occasionally produced unacceptably low reliabilities, ranging from .18 to .33 (Alexander, 1993; Davidson, 1992; Ottavi, Pope-Davis, & Dings, 1994; Sodowsky, Seaberry, Gorji, Lai, & Baliga, 1991). Also, given the reliabilities of the remaining scales, the interscale correlations involving Disintegration/ Reintegration and Pseudoindependence/Autonomy have often been so high that considering them to be separate scales may not be justified (Gilchrest, 1994; Grandner, 1992; Sodowsky et al., 1991; Tokar & Swanson, 1991).

Attempts to establish construct validity by demonstrating a predictable relationship with personality attributes, such as self-concept and moral development, or by other means frequently have been unsuccessful (Alexander, 1993; Bennett et al., 1993; Grandner, 1992; Haskins, 1992). Furthermore, factor analyses of the RIAS-W appear to indicate that the scales do not measure what they purport to measure (Alexander, 1993; Bennett, Behrens, & Rowe, 1993; Davidson, 1992; Swanson, Tokar, & Davis, 1994). For instance, Swanson and her colleagues found that the first factor consisted of 32 of the items from all five scales in a bipolar pattern of loadings focused on positive or negative attitudes toward African American people and culture.

The existing psychometric evidence would seem to suggest that the RIAS-W has four functional scales, two pairs of scales in which each member of the pair is empirically indistinct from the other, with the pairs being strongly negatively correlated with each other. When one considers that the content of the items from one pair (Disintegration + Reintegration) is generally negative in terms of responses to Blacks and racial issues, whereas the content of Pseudoindependence + Autonomy items emphasizes White nonracist attitudes, one is drawn to the conclusion that the RIAS-W may be essentially a one-dimensional, bipolar racism scale, accompanied by a certain amount of distracting measurement noise. It has also been argued (Rowe & Steward, 1994) that regarding the RIAS-W as a bipolar racism scale can account for many of the findings that previously appeared to support the Helms model.

Even though problems in the assessment of White "identity" come to attention as psychometric deficiencies, it is our opinion that the root lies at the conceptual level. It has been argued earlier (Rowe & Atkinson, 1995; Rowe, Bennett, & Atkinson, 1994) that White racial identity development models often are open to criticism because of the inappropriate use of the developmental concept, the use of an inappropriate parallel with minority identity development, and the use of the term *White racial identity*, when little attention is actually given to White identity. At issue here is whether a White person's sense of racial identity and a non-White person's sense of racial identity develop along similar pathways and whether, in fact, White identity models are about "identity."

Because of the inherent power inequities in society, it appears that the process of identity development should be different for members of the dominant and nondominant groups. As Phinney (1990) noted, "If the dominant group in a society holds the traits or characteristics of an ethnic group in low esteem, then the ethnic group members are potentially faced with a negative social identity" (p. 501). White people develop positive attitudes toward Whiteness as a result of the reinforcing aspects of the majority culture. But minority persons achieve positive attitudes toward their own group despite the denigration, both implicit and explicit, propagated by the dominant society. In addition, racial/ethnic minority persons develop attitudes toward Whites from the perspective of recognizing the oppressor; Whites do not develop attitudes toward non-Whites from such a perspective.

We think that even the term *White racial identity development* is a misnomer because the models actually provide little insight into the attributes of a White identity. Instead, they generally describe different levels of sensitivity to and appreciation of other racial/ethnic groups. Even though the stated purpose of these models is "to explain how Whites develop attitudes toward their racial-group membership" (Carter & Helms, 1990, p. 105), we believe they merely suggest that Whites are initially oblivious to racial issues and then develop certain views of racial/ethnic minorities that are then used to define White identity (Rowe & Atkinson, 1995).

The Helms (1990) model differs from others by including a stage (status) in which White people purportedly immerse themselves in reading biographies and autobiographies of nonracist Whites, participate in White consciousness-raising groups, or engage in other activities as they actively search for a new White identity. This appears contrary to our understanding of the social construction of Whiteness (Frankenberg, 1993). In our view, this focused self-exploration of the ontology of Whiteness may be observed on some college campuses, but seldom occurs with individuals in other environments in which this behavior is not structured.

Minority identity development models provide a framework with which to understand the development of positive attitudes toward oneself (positive identity) and one's racial/ethnic in-group. This seems reasonable because racial/ethnic minority people need to forge positive attitudes in a largely hostile cultural environment. On the other hand, White racial identity development models are more concerned with the development of attitudes toward out-group members. And this makes sense because our society has a positive view of the race with which they identify. It may be, that because of this, Whites do not ordinarily experience a clear sense of racial identity to the degree that racial/ethnic minority members do. For Whites the salient aspect is not their own difference that they must come to terms with, but rather the fact that some other people who populate their world are different.

Concerns such as these have led us to believe that existing models of White racial identity are unclear and may be misleading when applied to the counseling situation. Rather than looking at racial/ethnic identity and White identity as highly similar constructions, we have taken the position that, given the present state of knowledge, it would be better to step back from the amorphous construct of White racial identity and look at White racial attitudes. The undeniable reality is that White people say things and act in ways that seem to reflect a variety of attitudes toward racial/ethnic minorities. Rather than regarding these attitudes as a reflection of an underlying "racial identity," we chose to treat attitudes as the primary phenomena of interest. This approach resulted in the development of the paradigm of White racial consciousness (Rowe et al., 1994).

WHITE RACIAL CONSCIOUSNESS

White racial consciousness is conceived as the characteristic attitudes held by a person regarding the significance of being White, particularly in terms of what that implies in relation to those who do not share White group membership. For some people these beliefs may be clear and a significant factor in their conscious awareness. For others they may be vague and of little concern to how they construe their life experiences. Whatever the pattern of beliefs one may have regarding these issues, it is likely to be reflected to some extent in one's expressed attitudes, overt behaviors, and related affect, and it is from these observable manifestations that the person's type of "racial consciousness" can be inferred. Although we are aware that there is a less than perfect correlation between these phenomena, we have chosen to focus on attitudes because they may be considered relatively stable and are more readily available for assessment than either emotions or behavior.

Of course we recognize that *race* is a highly controversial term. As Ponterotto and Casas (1991) pointed out, "The biological emphasis on race is fraught with complexity and contradiction" (p. 10). We have been guided by a concept of race that includes both a social and a genetic component (Atkinson, Morten, & Sue, 1993). Therefore, we will define *White racial attitudes* to mean attitudes of Americans who consider themselves to be "White" toward racial/ethnic minority group members to the extent that they are identifiable and recognized as non-White.

Following the contemporary unidimensional approach to conceptualizing attitudes (Duckitt, 1992), attitudes are considered to be the affective orientation regarding the favorability of something. From this perspective, a person's attitude toward something comes about as the result of "the evaluative implications of his or her beliefs about [it]" (p. 12). Racial attitudes are considered to be related to behavior in the following manner. Information about racial matters and one's racial experiences interact, and the cognitive evaluation of this material leads to the affect inherent in racial attitudes. The specifics of any situation and the relevant social norms influence the racial attitudes and result in a conscious behavioral intention that, in turn, guides the subsequent behavior that we observe.

We take the position that attitudes are sometimes formed as the result of experience but are more frequently acquired through observation (Bandura, 1986). Moreover, although attitudes are often quite resistant to verbal persuasion, they frequently change as a result of direct or vicarious experience that is inconsistent or in conflict with previously held attitudes. The resulting lack of congruence (which we term *dissonance*) in one's cognitive schema is resolved in a particular way that is considered to be a function of one's innate attributes, learning history, and environmental influences. The attitudes of White people regarding racial/ethnic minorities are assumed to be acquired in the same manner as other attitudes and collectively constitute the construct we have labeled *White racial consciousness*.

It seems reasonable to believe that the particular set of attitudes held by a person would not be a random subset of the full array of possible attitudes, but would be related on some rational basis. To varying degrees, some attitudes are logically consistent or complementary, whereas others are inconsistent or contradictory. It is our position that the attitudes of Whites regarding racial/ethnic minorities, in fact, tend to cluster in relatively consistent conglomerations. We further believe that we can describe certain of these clusters of attitudes and from these descriptions derive labels for groupings of attitudes to indicate categories or types of White racial consciousness.

The use of the term *types* to refer to clusters of intercorrelated racial attitudes that characterize the beliefs of most individuals requires special comment. It is important to recognize that *type* refers to a describable set of attitudes and not an abstract personality configuration. We regard this approach as simply a means of classifying people according to the types of racial attitude profiles they hold. To say that a certain type of attitudes best characterizes a person is not to say that one is a certain type of person, with the implication that this attribute is a durable personality trait. We should try to avoid speaking of people as *being* a type, but the temptation is great to phrase it that way simply because it is easier (even though misleading).

Rather than proposing that there are various types of persons, we propose that there are various clusters or types of racial attitudes held by White people. We would expect that children would initially adopt attitudes similar to those of the sources that most influence them. However, as people reach adulthood

TABLE 11.1 Relationship Between Modes of Exploration/Commitment and Types of White Racial Consciousness

Exploration	Commitment	Status	Type
No	No	Unachieved	Avoidant
Yes	No	Unachieved	Dissonant
No	Yes	Unachieved	Dependent
Yes	Yes	Achieved	Conflictive
Yes	Yes	Achieved	Dominative
Yes	Yes	Achieved	Integrative
Yes	Yes	Achieved	Reactive

some retain the type of racial attitudes held earlier and others change their attitudes to become more characteristic of some other type. Although most people may be expected to hold some racial attitudes that are representative of more than one type, there is evidence (Behrens & Rowe, 1993a) that most people can be usefully classified by one of the types of White racial consciousness. And although the type characteristic of a person is relatively stable, it may change at any time as a result of direct or vicarious experiences perceived as conflicting with previous attitudes.

The categories or types of White racial consciousness that we have proposed (Rowe et al., 1994) were adapted from Phinney's (1990) stages of ethnic identity. In this model, exploration of one's ethnicity and commitment to one's ethnic group were the defining features of four categories of ethnic identity. We found that organizing White racial consciousness in terms of exploration of racial/ethnic minority issues and commitment to some position about these matters was a useful device, even though we do not accept the theoretical basis (Marcia, 1980).

As shown in Table 11.1, a person can present attitudes that show neither exploration nor commitment to racial/ethnic minority concerns, which we have termed *avoidant;* attitudes that indicate only commitment to some view but without personal consideration of alternatives, which we label *dependent;* or attitudes that emphasize exploration but withhold commitment to any point of view, which we call *dissonant.* Each of these types we consider to represent a status of unachieved White racial consciousness because the attitudes are not securely integrated into the belief structure of the individual. They lack one or both essential features: some exploration or reflection on matters relating to race/ethnicity, and commitment to some position or set of attitudes about these matters. Persons who present attitudes that do not indicate a lack of either exploration or commitment to racial/ethnic minority issues we regard as having an achieved White racial consciousness status, and we have identified categories that we have labeled *conflictive, dominative, integrative,* and *reactive.*

TYPES OF
WHITE RACIAL CONSCIOUSNESS

The statuses and types of racial attitudes identified by this conceptual model were recently described in some detail (Rowe et al., 1994), and interested readers are referred to that source. Below is an abbreviated description of the type of outlook that a person holding each type of attitude would hold. Each of the descriptions of types of attitudes is followed by a monologue that serves as a strong exemplar of that position.

Avoidant

Attitudes that indicate avoidance include a lack of consideration of one's own race as well as an avoidance of concern for racial/ethnic minority issues. For some people, the personal and social concerns related to racial/ethnic differences are somewhat aversive and something to be avoided or ignored. Whether they find these issues merely inconvenient or actually anxiety arousing, their preferred way of responding is to ignore, minimize, or deny the existence or importance of the problematic issue.

> Minority issues just aren't all that important to me. We just don't get involved in that sort of thing. I really am not interested in thinking about those things.

Dependent

Although people who are best characterized by dependent-type attitudes seem to have developed some kind of White racial consciousness, they have not personally considered alternative perspectives. Some people remain so dependent and unreflective in adulthood that they still look to significant others for what their opinions should be. The White racial attitudes of these people are held superficially and are not "owned" to the degree that these attitudes have been internalized by others.

> My thinking about minorities is mainly influenced by my (friends, family, husband/wife), so you could say I mainly learned about minorities from (them, him/her). That's why my opinion about minorities is pretty much the same as (theirs, his/hers).

Dissonant

People whose attitudes can be described as dissonant are clearly uncertain about what to think about issues dealing with racial/ethnic minorities. They lack commitment to attitudes they may express and are open to new information because of the confusion that they experience. They may be in this situation because of a lack of experience or information, but it frequently is

the result of the lack of congruence between their previously held racial attitudes and recent personal or vicarious experience. Dissonant attitudes are
often held by people who are in transition from one set of racial attitudes to
another.

> I used to feel I knew what I thought about minorities. But now my feelings
> are really mixed. I'm having to change my thinking. I'm not sure, so I'm
> trying to find some answers to questions I have about minorities.

Dominative

Dominative White racial attitudes are based on the premise that the majority society is entitled to dominate racial/ethnic minority peoples because
of an inherent superiority. Persons whose attitudes best represent this type
hold an ethnocentric perspective that presumes the cultural correctness of
their position and evaluates all others in terms of how close they approach
this standard. Any deficiency in matching any aspect of majority society is
seen as the result of defects in the personal qualities of racial/ethnic minority
people. Persons with such attitudes may tolerate relations with minority
people if they are in a superior role, but strongly disapprove of close personal relationships with them. Regardless of their station in life, they seem
to think they share in the credit for the accomplishments of outstanding
White people.

> The truth about minorities is that they are kind of dumb, their customs are
> crude, and they are pretty backward compared to what Whites have accom-
> plished. Besides that they are sort of lazy. I guess they just aren't up to what
> Whites are. I wouldn't want a family member, or even a friend of mine, to
> have a close relationship with a minority. You may have to work near them,
> but you don't have to live close to one.

Conflictive

People whose racial attitudes resemble conflictive-type attitudes will not
ordinarily support obvious discrimination toward racial/ethnic minorities but
are usually opposed to programs or procedures intended to reduce the effects
of discrimination. The conflict is between two traditional American values:
equality and individualism. Persons whose attitudes reflect the conflictive type
usually support issues that clearly involve the principle of fairness but are
likely to be opposed to any alteration of the status quo designed to remediate any currently inequitable situation caused by past discrimination. They
apparently think that things may not have been right at one time, but are
fine now.

> There should be equal chances to better yourself for everyone, but minorities
> are way too demanding. The media is always finding something they say is

unfair and making a big deal out of it. And the government is always coming up with some kind of program that lets them get more than they deserve. We shouldn't discriminate against minorities, but tilting things in their favor just isn't fair. Before, White ethnic groups didn't get a lot of government help, and the minorities of today shouldn't expect it either.

Integrative

People who hold integrative-type attitudes have a pragmatic view of racial/ethnic minority issues. Although their views are based on a sense of moral responsibility, their outlook is pragmatic in the sense that their actions are tempered by what effect they are likely to have. Those with integrated attitudes appear to have integrated their sense of Whiteness with a regard for racial/ethnic minorities. They value a culturally pluralistic society, are comfortable with their Whiteness, and are comfortable interacting with minority people. They apparently believe that racism can be overcome by goodwill, rational thought, and democratic processes.

> Integration is a desirable goal for our society, and it could significantly improve problems relating to prejudice and discrimination if people would keep an open mind and allow it to work. Race and culture is not a factor when I choose my personal friends. I'm comfortable around minority people and don't mind being one of a few Whites in a group. In fact, I wouldn't mind living next to minority people if their social class were similar to mine. I think we will need racial harmony for democracy to be able to function.

Reactive

People whose attitudes can best be described as reactive hold quite militant views in reaction to the racism that they recognize in American society. They tend to identify with minority groups and may romanticize the plight or issues relating to minorities. They may sometimes even seem to feel guilty about being White. Those who display reactive attitudes are often sensitive to situations that may involve discrimination. However, they may engage in paternalistic behavior and operate from an essentially White perspective. They apparently are affected by the inequities in our society and feel compelled to react against it.

> Our society is quite racist. It is really difficult for minority people to get a fair deal. There may be some tokenism, but businesses won't put minorities in the top positions. Actually, qualified minority people should be given preference at all levels of education and employment to make up for the effects of past discrimination. But they don't have enough power to influence the government, even though it's the government's responsibility to help minority people. It's enough sometimes to make you feel guilty about being White.

CHANGES IN
WHITE RACIAL CONSCIOUSNESS

Although achieved-status attitude types are considered to be relatively stable, they are always subject to change when information from direct or indirect learning experiences is inconsistent or in conflict with previously held attitudes. This perceived conflict between previous racial attitudes and one's experience may result in a lack of commitment or certainty regarding one's attitudes, the condition we term *dissonance.*

We believe that the experience of dissonance may be necessary for change from any one of the achieved-status attitude types to another. In the un-achieved White racial consciousness status, attitudes could change between those representing the avoidant and dependent types without dissonance occurring because these attitudes are not considered to be strongly held or internalized. But movement from the unachieved-status type to any of the achieved-status types should be associated with conflict and therefore be likely to produce dissonant-type attitudes during the transition. These propositions are admittedly based on our intuition and rational analysis, but, importantly, they are capable of verification.

MEASURING WHITE
RACIAL CONSCIOUSNESS

Measurement of the proposed attitudes will allow the investigation of propositions related to the hypothetical construct of White racial conscious-ness. To this end, the Oklahoma Racial Attitudes Scale (ORAS) is being de-veloped to provide a means for the empirical assessment of the model and a means by which practitioners, researchers, and educators involved in the train-ing of counselors and psychologists could assess the racial outlook of White persons with whom they work.

The preliminary form of the Oklahoma Racial Attitudes Scale (ORAS-P) was developed through six administrations of items over a 3-year period. After each administration, factor analyses and estimates of internal consistency were examined, and items were deleted or refined as the data appeared to require. Unexpected relationships between certain items occasionally sug-gested other aspects or dimensions of one of the types, and new items were therefore developed to be tested at subsequent administrations. Although it has admittedly been developed and normed exclusively with college students, the ORAS-P has been available to interested researchers since November 1993 and awaits broader applications. It consists of 42 items, each requiring a re-sponse on a 5-point scale anchored with *strongly disagree* and *strongly agree.* Ten items assess the unachieved statuses of White racial consciousness: avoidant (av), dependent (de), and dissonant (di). Thirty-one items make up the four scales measuring the achieved White racial consciousness statuses—

conflictive (C), dominative (D), integrative (I), and reactive (R)—and one item is not scored.

Adequate alpha coefficients and test-retest reliabilities along with factor analysis data have been reported (Choney & Behrens, in press), suggesting that the instrument appears to be measuring the types of attitudes described by the proposed model of White racial consciousness. These authors report the results of confirmatory factor analyses (CFA) using structural equations that support the appropriateness of the instrument as a measure of the underlying theory. Choney and Behrens (in press) discuss the difficulty of developing an instrument that measures racism as a multidimensional construct. While acknowledging the need for additional refinement, they note that no other measure of White racial attitude has been tested by CFA, which cannot be computed if a measure differs dramatically from its supposed structure. A detailed discussion of the development of the ORAS-P, scale reliabilities and intercorrelations, and the factor analysis procedures may be found in the monograph on minority assessment produced by the Buros Institute of Mental Measurement (Choney & Behrens, in press).

Following the scoring manual (Behrens & Rowe, 1993b), raw scores on the av, de, and di scales are reviewed, and subjects who appear to be characterized by an unachieved White racial consciousness status are so identified and removed from further analysis. T-scores are then computed for the remaining subjects on the C, D, I, and R scales. At present, we believe that it may be useful to classify people by the type of racial attitudes that best characterizes their outlook.

These scores are meaningful in terms of assessing the extent to which the types of White racial consciousness characterize the attitudes of each subject, *compared to the attitudes held by other members of the group tested.* Of course, individual assessment requires that appropriate reference group norms be available. We hope to be able to create a data bank that will be helpful to future users of the Oklahoma Racial Attitude Scale.

SUMMARY

Not only is the field of multicultural counseling and therapy thriving, but the area concerned with the impact of culture on the perceptions and behavior of people is undergoing a period of rapid change that holds great potential for important progress. We predict that the surge of model building will subside in the next decade as some concepts prove to have limited utility and as the consolidation of other views and the development of more convincing and comprehensive theoretical models takes place.

In regard to the racial outlook or awareness of Whites, we have presented an alternative paradigm. The paradigm of White racial consciousness makes no claim regarding a developmental sequence and focuses on attitudes rather than a hypothetical entity inferred from attitudes. It is our opinion that this approach is more justifiable conceptually and is likely to be more effective empirically. Whether this proves to be the case, however, remains to be seen. We encourage others to join in contributing to the answer. For further information regarding the ORAS-P or related matters, please contact one of the authors.

REFERENCES

Alexander, C. M. (1993). Construct validity and reliability of the White Racial Identity Attitude Scale (WRIAS). *Dissertation Abstracts International, 53,* 3799A.

Atkinson, D. R., Morten, G., & Sue, D. W. (1993). *Counseling American minorities: A cross-cultural perspective* (4th ed.). Dubuque, IA: William C. Brown.

Bandura, A. (1986). *Social foundations of thought and action.* Englewood Cliffs, NJ: Prentice Hall.

Behrens, J. T., & Rowe, W. (1993a). [Analysis of ORAS scoring program]. Unpublished raw data.

Behrens, J. T., & Rowe, W. (1993b). *Scoring the Oklahoma Racial Attitudes Scale-Preliminary Form.* Unpublished manuscript.

Bennett, S. K., Behrens, J. T., & Rowe, W. (1993, August). *The White Racial Identity Attitude Scale: Validity and factor structure.* Paper presented at the annual meeting of the American Psychological Association, Toronto.

Bennett, S. K., & Rowe, W. (1994). Assessing White racial identity: The White Racial Consciousness Development Scale (WRCDS). *Journal of Counseling and Development, 73,* 102-105.

Bernal, M. J., & Knight, G. M. (Eds.). (1993). *Ethnic identity: Formation and transmission among Hispanics and other minorities.* Albany, NY: SUNY Press.

Berry, J. W., Trimble, J., & Olmedo, E. (1986). Assessment of acculturation. In W. Lonner & J. Berry (Eds.), *Field methods in cross-cultural research* (pp. 291-324). Newbury Park, CA: Sage.

Birman, D. (1994). Biculturalism and ethnic identity: An integrated model. *Focus, 8*(1), 9-11.

Burlew, A. K., & Smith, L. R. (1991). Measures of racial identity: An overview and a proposed framework. *Journal of Black Psychology, 17*(2), 53-71.

Carter, R. T., & Helms, J. E. (1990). White racial identity attitudes and cultural values. In J. E. Helms (Ed.), *Black and White racial identity: Theory, research, and practice* (pp. 105-118). Westport, CT: Greenwood Press.

Choney, S. B., & Behrens, J. T. (in press). Development of the Oklahoma Racial Attitudes Scale-Preliminary Form (ORAS-P). In J. Impara & G. R. Sodowsky (Eds.), *Ninth Buros-Nebraska Symposium on Measurement and Testing: Multicultural Assessment.* Lincoln, NE: Buros Institute of Mental Measurement.

Claney, D., & Parker, W. M. (1989). Assessing White racial consciousness and perceived comfort with Black individuals: A preliminary study. *Journal of Counseling and Development, 67,* 449-451.

Cuellar, I., Harris, L. C., & Jasso, R. (1980). An acculturation scale for Mexican-American normal and clinical populations. *Hispanic Journal of Behavioral Sciences, 2,* 199-217.

Davidson, J. R. (1992). Evaluation of an education model for race/ethnic sensitive social work and critique of the White Racial Identity Attitude Scale. *Dissertation Abstracts International, 53,* 304A.

Duckitt, J. (1992). *The social psychology of prejudice.* New York: Praeger.

Franco, J. N. (1983). An acculturation scale for Mexican-American children. *Journal of General Psychology, 108,* 175-181.

Frankenberg, R. (1993). *White women, race matters: The social construction of Whiteness.* Minneapolis: University of Minnesota Press.

Gilchrest, G. G. (1994). Racial identity and cultural worldviews among ethnically diverse White college students: A quantitative and qualitative analysis. *Dissertation Abstracts International, 54,* 2804A.

Grandner, D. F. (1992). The relationship between White racial identity attitudes and moral development of college students. *Dissertation Abstracts International, 53,* 1055A.

Haskins, W. L. (1992). The relationship of self concept to stages of White racial identity attitudes. *Dissertation Abstracts International, 53,* 553B.

Helms, J. E. (Ed.). (1990). *Black and White racial identity: Theory, research, and practice.* Westport, CT: Greenwood Press.

Helms, J. E., & Carter, R. T. (1990a). Development of the White Racial Identity Inventory. In J. E. Helms (Ed.), *Black and White racial identity: Theory, research, and practice* (pp. 66-80). Westport, CT: Greenwood Press.

Helms, J. E., & Carter, R. T. (1990b). *A preliminary overview of the Cultural Identity Attitude Scale.* Unpublished manuscript.

Hogg, M. A., & Abrams, D. (1990). *Social identifications.* New York: Routledge.

Kaplan, M. S., & Marks, G. (1990). Adverse effects of acculturation: Psychological distress among Mexican American young adults. *Social Science and Medicine, 31,* 1313-1319.

Knight, G. P., Bernal, M. E., Garza, C. A., & Cota, M. K. (1993). A social cognitive model of the development of ethnic identity and ethnically based behaviors. In M. E. Bernal & G. P. Knight (Eds.), *Ethnic identity: Formation and transmission among Hispanics and other minorities* (pp. 213-234). Albany, NY: SUNY Press.

Kohatsu, E. L. (1994, August). *Racial identity attitudes: Implications and applications for Asian Americans.* Paper presented at the annual meeting of the American Psychological Association, Los Angeles.

LaFromboise, T. D., Coleman, H. L. K., & Gerton, J. (1993). Psychological impact of biculturalism: Evidence and theory. *Psychological Bulletin, 114,* 395-412.

Leong, F. T., & Chou, E. L. (1994). The role of ethnic identity and acculturation in the vocational behavior of Asian Americans: An integrative review. *Journal of Vocational Behavior, 44,* 155-172.

Marcia, J. E. (1980). Identity in adolescence. In J. Adelson (Ed.), *Handbook of adolescent psychology* (pp. 159-187). New York: John Wiley.

Marin, G., Sabogal, F., Marin, B. V., Otero-Sabogal, R., & Perez-Stable, E. (1987). Development of a short acculturation scale for Hispanics. *Hispanic Journal of Behavioral Sciences, 9,* 183-205.

Mendoza, R. H. (1989). An empirical scale to measure type and degree of acculturation in Mexican-American adolescents and adults. *Journal of Cross-Cultural Psychology, 20,* 372-385.

Montgomery, G. T., & Orozco, S. (1984). Validation of a measure of acculturation for Mexican Americans. *Hispanic Journal of Behavioral Sciences, 6,* 53-63.

Moran, J. R., Fleming, C. M., Somervell, P., & Manson, S. M. (in press). Measuring ethnic identity among American Indian adolescents. *Journal of Research on Adolescence.*

Oetting, E. R., & Beauvais, F. (1991). Orthogonal cultural identification theory: The cultural identification of minority adolescents. *International Journal of the Addictions, 25,* 655-685.

Olmedo, E. L., & Padilla, A. M. (1978). Empirical and construct validation of a measure of acculturation for Mexican Americans. *Journal of Social Psychology, 105,* 179-187.

Ottavi, T. M., Pope-Davis, D. B., & Dings, J. G. (1994). Relationship between racial identity attitudes and self-reported multicultural counseling competencies. *Journal of Counseling Psychology, 41,* 149-154.

Padilla, A. M. (1980). The role of cultural awareness and ethnic loyalty in acculturation. In A. M. Padilla (Ed.), *Acculturation: Theory, models, and some new findings* (pp. 47-84). Boulder, CO: Westview.

Pedersen, P. B. (1991). Multiculturalism as a generic approach to counseling. *Journal of Counseling and Development, 70,* 6-12.

Phinney, J. S. (1990). Ethnic identity in adolescents and adults: Review of research. *Psychological Bulletin, 108,* 499-514.

Phinney, J. S. (1992). The Multigroup Ethnic Identity Measure: A new scale for use with diverse groups. *Journal of Adolescent Research, 7,* 156-176.

Phinney, J. S. (1993). A three-stage model of ethnic identity development in adolescence. In M. E. Bernal & G. P. Knight (Eds.), *Ethnic identity: Formation and transmission among Hispanics and other minorities* (pp. 61-79). Albany, NY: SUNY Press.

Ponterotto, J. G., & Casas, J. M. (1991). *Handbook of racial/ethnic minority counseling research.* Springfield, IL: Charles C Thomas.

Rowe, W., & Atkinson, D. R. (1995). Misrepresentation and interpretation: Critical evaluation of White racial identity development models. *The Counseling Psychologist, 23,* 364-367.

Rowe, W., Bennett, S. K., & Atkinson, D. R. (1994). White racial identity models: A critique and alternative proposal. *The Counseling Psychologist, 22,* 129-146.

Rowe, W., & Steward, R. J. (1994). *Are we measuring racial identity or racism? Comment on Ottavi, Pope-Davis, and Dings (1994).* Unpublished manuscript.

Sánchez, J. L., & Fernández, D. M. (1993). Acculturative stress among Hispanics: A bidimensional model of ethnic identification. *Journal of Applied Social Psychology, 23,* 654-668.

Sodowsky, G. R., Seaberry, J., Gorji, T. N., Lai, E. W. M., & Baliga, G. (1991, August). *Theory of White racial identity: Qualitative and quantitative analyses of White psychology trainees' responses.* Paper presented at the annual meeting of the American Psychological Association, San Francisco.

Suinn, R. M., Rickard-Figueroa, K., Lew, S., & Vigil, P. (1987). The Suinn-Lew Asian Self-Identification Acculturation Scale: An initial report. *Educational and Psychological Measurement, 47,* 401-407.

Swanson, J. L., Tokar, D. M., & Davis, L. E. (1994). Content and construct validity of the White Racial Identity Attitude Scale. *Journal of Vocational Behavior, 44,* 198-217.

Tokar, D. M., & Swanson, J. L. (1991). An investigation of the validity of Helms's (1984) model of White racial identity development. *Journal of Counseling Psychology, 38,* 296-301.

PART III

Supervision and Training

EFFECTIVE PRACTICE in multicultural counseling requires adequate training and close clinical supervision. The four chapters that make up this section present the latest theory, research, and practical issues with regard to multicultural training and supervision.

Robert T. Carter and Adil Qureshi open this section (Chapter 12) by highlighting the diverse philosophies and approaches that form the foundation of training in multicultural counseling. To help clarify and make sense of the many approaches to training, the authors develop and present a concise organizational framework for classifying current and future training models and research. Carter and Qureshi then go on to apply their philosophically based framework to the extant training literature. The result is an enlightening and helpful framework that will guide training research for years to come.

Although counseling supervision has received extensive theoretical and research attention in the general counseling literature, there is a remarkable dearth of theory and research on multicultural-focused clinical supervision. In Chapter 13, Michael T. Brown and Joycelyn Landrum-Brown show that clinical supervision is not exempt from cross-cultural dynamics, and they demonstrate the potential impact of these dynamics on the supervisor-supervisee-client relationship. The authors successfully review and integrate an interdisciplinary literature to inform their original model of supervision.

Donald B. Pope-Davis and Jonathan G. Dings are the authors of Chapter 14, which focuses on the objective assessment of multicultural counseling competencies. The authors define and clarify the important multicultural competency construct, then go on to critically review three leading self-report measures of multicultural counseling competence. This chapter provides the most constructive and comprehensive psychometric critique currently available on such instrumentation. The chapter closes with guidelines for instrumentation use and with a candid discussion of the limitations of the instruments.

compare to uk?

As highlighted in the preface to this book, multicultural counseling courses are among the fastest growing in counseling curricula nationwide. There are many unanswered questions with regard to the structure, format, and content of the more "successful" multicultural course. In Chapter 15, Amy L. Reynolds highlights the challenges inherent in teaching the multicultural counseling course and presents practical guidelines and strategies for developing it. Essential to Reynolds' approach and perspective is a heavy emphasis on ethics in multicultural training and practice.

12

A Typology of Philosophical Assumptions in Multicultural Counseling and Training

ROBERT T. CARTER

ADIL QURESHI

OVER THE PAST THREE DECADES, counseling psychologists and other social scientists have begun to give more recognition to the influence of race and culture on human development and on psychological interventions in particular (Carter & Helms, 1992; Casas; 1985; Casas, Ponterotto, & Gutierrez, 1986; Copeland, 1983). More important, counseling and mental health training programs have begun to offer courses in what is often referred to as *cross-cultural counseling, diversity counseling,* or *multicultural counseling* (Bernal & Castro, 1994; Hills & Strozier, 1992). One major impetus for the addition of courses that focus on culture has been that the accreditation bodies of professional associations and state and national boards are calling on academic programs to attend to racial and cultural diversity in the training of mental health professionals (American Psychological Association, 1983, 1987, 1991a, 1991b; Aponte, 1992; Stricker et al., 1990). In addition, some scholars (e.g., Ibrahim & Arredondo, 1986; Myers, Wohlford, Guzman, & Echemendia, 1991) have argued that cross-cultural training is, for mental health professionals, an ethical imperative requiring the development of cross-cultural competencies (Sue, Arredondo, & McDavis, 1992). Pedersen (1991) proclaimed multiculturalism to be a "fourth force" in counseling and education. He suggested that the multicultural emphasis will revolutionize mental health in a manner similar to humanism's influence.

The purpose of this chapter is to reduce the confusion about the meaning attached to the concept of culture in mental health training that is evident in the literature concerning multicultural counseling competencies and training methods and approaches. The various approaches in the field are predicated on the theorists'/researchers' assumptions underlying their definition and understanding of culture. Assumptions and conceptions about culture are important because they circumscribe the types of knowledge, information, methods, and skills provided within the context of a particular approach.

However, it is unclear what scholars, researchers, and practitioners mean when they use terms such as *cross-cultural* or *multicultural*. It seems that the field referred to as *cross-cultural mental health* is driven by a number of unstated philosophical assumptions about the meaning of difference. What is missing in the literature is a way to understand the various philosophical assumptions that underlie approaches to understanding difference or the way the idea of culture is used and applied in psychology and counseling. Another purpose of this chapter is to offer a typology of assumptions that can be used to classify approaches of culture, training approaches, and methods. To accomplish this task, we reviewed the counselor education and training literature. We used Educational Resources Information Clearinghouse (ERIC), PsychLit, and *American Psychological Association Abstracts*, and culled articles from the following journals from 1980 to 1991: *Journal of Multicultural Counseling and Development, Journal of Counseling and Development, Journal of Counseling Psychology, The Counseling Psychologist, Journal of College Student Development*, and *Counselor Education and Supervision*. We tried to be as comprehensive as possible. If nothing else, the attempt to classify these assumptions into a system can serve as a guide for identifying assumptions that undergird conceptual approaches, training foci, and curricular emphasis. Further, it can guide research by providing a clearer sense of which philosophical assumption(s) are being taught or investigated.

Central to multiculturalism in counseling and mental health are approaches and methods used in training programs (Bernal & Padilla, 1982). Also, most mental health training includes explicitly or implicitly some type of orientation or set of assumptions about culture and race that each trainee is taught. Typically, this knowledge and, in some cases, these competencies, are developed so the trainee will be considered a competent mental health practitioner (Bernal & Castro, 1994).

The context for our typology is life and mental health practice in North America. It is not intended to include world cultures. It is therefore important to explore the historical background of the conception of culture in Western society, because American history is distinct from that of other countries. It is essential that any attempt to understand culture and difference in the United States considers the sociopolitical environment in which Americans have typically understood cultural difference. Also, the classifications are not mutually exclusive. In fact, we suspect that in some instances there is considerable overlap. Elements of one category can be found in another. Thus, the approaches derived from each philosophical system will also overlap in some cases. Nevertheless, we believe that the categories or types of assumptions will be of value.

Our discussion begins with a presentation on our assumptions about culture and race in the United States as manifested in efforts to define the concept of culture. This will be followed by a typology of philosophical assumptions, with a discussion of the counselor education and training literature that pertains to each type. We contend that although each approach has its strengths and weaknesses, a race-as-culture perspective is the most viable because it is historically and sociopolitically grounded. Nevertheless, each typology is discussed in terms of its advantages and disadvantages.

DEFINING *CULTURE*

One of the earlier definitions of culture in the social sciences was Tylor's, written in 1871: "Culture or civilisation . . . is that complex whole which includes knowledge, belief, art, law, morals, custom and any other capabilities and habits acquired by man as a member of society") (cited in Kroeber & Kluckhohn, 1952, p. 43).

For Tylor, social structure and socialization were the products of culture. Following Tylor's work is Kroeber and Kluckhohn's (1952) oft-cited effort to define *culture.* These scholars concluded after reviewing numerous definitions of culture that

> culture is . . . a set of attributes and products of human societies, and therewith of mankind, which are extrasomatic and transmissible by mechanisms other than biological heredity, and are as essentially lacking in subhuman species as they are in characteristics of the human species as it is aggregated in its societies. (p. 145)

Thus, the basic element of culture is the same for both definitions. That is, culture is seen as a human product transmitted through society by way of teaching and living. For most scholars, culture is a learned system of meaning and behavior that is passed from one generation to the next. According to LeVine (1982) and D'Andrade (1984), the early understanding of culture was predicated on traits and behaviors. Culture was seen to manifest itself in the way in which people behaved and lived. Other writers (Brislin, 1990; Johnson, 1990; Smedley, 1993; Sue et al., 1982) concur with the definition of culture as a system of meaning for a group that usually has specific geographic boundaries.

Smedley (1993) pointed out that culture and ethnicity, because they are learned, are fluid and flexible. Smedley noted in this regard that "individuals and groups can and do change their ethnic or cultural identities and interests through such processes as migration, conversion, and assimilation or through exposure to modifying influences" (p. 31). *Race,* however, though a term often

used to denote cultural groups, particularly in North America, has been associated with permanent attributes. Thus, an essential distinction between culture or ethnicity and race is the learned and fluid or flexible nature of the
former. However, racial classification has often been used to reflect culture or
degrees of civilization. The concept of "culture began by definitely containing the idea of betterment, of improvement toward perfection" (Kroeber &
Kluckhohn, 1952, p. 145). In the United States, from the 15th century to the
present, all cultures were in effect thought to exist on a phylogenetic racially
determined hierarchy in which White Europeans and Americans were at the
top and all other racial groups were ranked in descending order. Smedley (1993)
observed that "unlike other terms for classifying people . . . the term 'race'
places emphasis on innateness, on the inbred nature of whatever is being
judged. Whatever is inheritable is also permanent and unalterable, . . . whether
it be body size, . . . or color, or aggressiveness, fearsomeness, docility, dullness,
intelligence, or any other states of being" (pp. 39-40). Thus, in the United
States, Anglo-Saxon and now White American culture (Katz, 1985) is dominant and is compared against other cultures, usually on the basis of racial
designations. Implicit in the comparison was and is the notion that all other
racial and cultural groups are inferior to Whites (Kovel, 1984). During the
course of American history the concept of race was substituted for the concept
of culture.

Marger (1994) explained it this way: "At first, the justification for subjecting these groups to enslavement or to colonial repression lay . . . in their cultural primitiveness" (p. 32). It was the later development of

> scientific racism, however, that gave impetus to the view that European
> peoples were superior to non-Whites because of their racial inheritance.
> Eighteenth century scholars of various disciplines, including medicine, ar-
> chaeology, education, and anthropology, began to debate the origin of the
> human species. Darwin's idea of natural selection was now seen as a
> mechanism for producing superior human societies . . . and races. . . . With
> the scientifically endorsed belief that social achievement was mostly a matter
> of heredity. The colonial policies of the European powers were now justified.
> Native peoples of color were seen as innately primitive and incapable of
> reaching the level of civilization attained by Europeans. (pp. 32-33)

During the 19th and 20th centuries, as psychologists and educators raised
the specter of race exposed the power dynamics inherent in race relations, and
argued that people of color were not inferior, deviant, or deficit but rather
different culturally, the debate and dialogue in the mental health literature
began to shift from race and the experiences specifically associated with historically disenfranchised Americans (e.g., American Indian, African American, Hispanic American) to various cultural groups, generally defined. Some
scholars now argue that race as a cultural category should be rejected to avoid
the notion of biological or genetic differences/deficiencies (see Outlaw, 1990).
It may be accurate to reject the concept of biological race and replace it with

a cultural construct. Although some scholars consider a purely cultural approach to be appropriate, others who espouse nontraditional approaches in mental health believe that a historically grounded racial-cultural approach is more adequate. It may be that counseling/psychotherapy cannot become genuinely multiracial and multicultural or a fourth force in mental health until it recognizes its assumptions about difference and their implications. What is needed is a way to distinguish what approach is advocated or what assumptions about difference are implicit in terms such as *cross-cultural*, *multicultural*, or *diversity*. Our typology is offered as a way to clarify the meaning of such terms.

TYPOLOGY

An examination of the literature suggests that the philosophical assumptions underlying multicultural training approaches can be grouped into five types. These are *Universal* (e.g., Fukuyama, 1990; Ivey, 1987; Lloyd, 1987; Parker, 1987); *Ubiquitous* (e.g., Pedersen, 1977; Ponterotto, 1988; Sue et al., 1982); *Traditional* (e.g., Arredondo, 1985; Christensen, 1989; Copeland, 1982; Leong & Kim, 1991; Nwachuku & Ivey, 1991; Parker, Valley, & Geary, 1986; Ponterotto & Casas, 1987); *Race-Based* (e.g., Carney & Kahn, 1984; Corvin & Wiggins, 1989; McRae & Johnson, 1991; Ponterotto, 1988; Sabnani, Ponterotto, & Borodovsky, 1991; Sue, Akutsu, & Higashi, 1985); and *Pan-National* (e.g., Bulhan, 1985; Myers, 1988). The proposed classification (Table 12.1) is suggested as a mechanism for organizing our ideas and beliefs about training "cultural" competence in psychology. It should be noted that we are referring only to cross-cultural training in the United States. Although the typology includes perspectives that incorporate approaches that extend beyond the United States, the context for the categories and the classification system is the sociohistorical events that have led to the development of multicultural counseling in the United States. We also want to point out the difference between basic assumptions and the strategies used to teach about cultural difference. We believe that regardless of the strategies (i.e., approaches, content, and so forth) used by a professor or trainer, he or she works from basic and fundamental assumptions about the nature of cultural difference. It is possible for strategies to be mistaken for basic assumptions. Our typology is intended to highlight basic assumptions, not identify teaching strategies.

Universal

The Universal or Etic approach to culture holds that all people are basically the same as human beings; intragroup (within-group) differences are greater than intergroup (between-group) differences. It is espoused implicitly by traditional psychology theory and practice: That is, this assumption is equivalent to an individual difference viewpoint (Sue, 1980). Fukuyama (1990) suggested that "affirmation of human similarities through universal constructs" (p. 12)

TABLE 12.1 Summary of Classification System for Cross-Cultural Training Approaches and Methods

Type	Assumptions	Approach	Method
Universal	All people are basically the same; intragroup differences are greater than intergroup differences.	Affirm human similarities through universal constructs; focus on shared human experience.	Counselors should transcend construct of race.
Ubiquitous	All loci of identity or shared circumstance are constitutive of culture; people can belong to multiple cultures, which are situationally determined.	Make counselor comfortable with difference; foster cultural sensitivity.	Acknowledge and celebrate difference; increase awareness of others' cultures and expose stereotypes (e.g., sexism).
Traditional (Anthropological)	Culture equals country: It is determined by birth, upbringing, and environment and is defined by common experience of socialization and environment. Race as a social construct is ignored; culture is an adaptive phenomenon.	An individual's circumstances are superseded by the general culture; cultural membership circumscribes possible personality dynamics.	Trainee should experience new culture through exposure; use of cultural informants.
Race-Based	Race is the superordinate locus of culture; experience of belonging to a racial group transcends all other experiences; culture is a function of the values of the racial group and of the values, reactions, and institutions of the larger society.	Racial awareness; recognize the effect of racism and oppression; and foster racial identity development for all racial groups.	Trainee should learn about racism and their own racial identity development.
Pan-National	Culture is a function of a dynamic other than geosocial; racial group membership determines one's place in the distribution of power; culture is viewed globally.	Teach about the history of racial-cultural groups dating back to ancient times. Students should know the psychology of oppression and the history of imperialism and colonialism.	Teach trainees about how psychology of oppression and domination influences counseling process.

is a goal of counseling. She argued that "special populations" share certain themes that are relevant to the counseling situation, for example, "discrimination and oppression in society, identity development, etc." (p. 9). The universal approach does not deny the existence of culture as such; rather it calls for an intense focus on shared human experience while incorporating culture-specific knowledge.

Lloyd (1987) argued that training about specific cultures is contraindicated in that such knowledge gives rise to a homogeneous view of cultures, in effect forcing all members to fit a certain template. The Universal approach closely resembles the humanist vision of all people living in harmony, with group differences being of little or no relevance.

The main assumption underlying the Universal approach is that there is a human bond that supersedes all experience. On this basis, then, we are first and foremost human beings, and only secondarily does our experience and identity derive from other reference groups (e.g., ethnicity, race, gender). What is important is the uniqueness of the individual person. One should understand each person in the context of his or her various reference group identities.

Fukuyama (1990) and Lloyd (1987) noted that in practice a focus on cultural differences can result in the counselor's taking a client's culture for the client and not seeing the client as a unique individual but seeing him or her solely as culturally determined. They also noted that a culture-specific or emic focus may result in stereotyping and the use of separate standards for members of particular groups. Whereas Lloyd (1987) suggested that cross-cultural communication can be "enhanced by forgetting . . . cultural truths" (p. 166), Fukuyama (1990) and Parker (1987) promoted cultural awareness of both self and others. For Fukuyama (1990), "Many people belong to cultural groups that share similarities by 'being different.' . . . Members of . . . groups who do not fit within the dominant culture power structure experience various forms of discrimination, prejudice, or neglect" (p. 9). Fukuyama is not strictly a Universalist, for her focus on differences from the dominant culture power structure suggests that she sees many ways to be different culturally; however, it seems that difference is determined by how one does or does not fit into the dominant group. Thus, her proposed approach to multicultural counseling consists of universally applicable components.

Cultural sensitivity is required when one's approach to culture is general (as opposed to culture-specific; see below). Parker (1987) noted that "counselors should transcend the race, ethnicity, religion, and culture of their client's presenting problems and needs" (p. 179). Apparently, Parker assumes (a) that it is possible to transcend race, ethnicity, and culture (as opposed to avoiding, resisting, repressing, or denying them), and that effective therapy is a matter of going beyond the client's race, culture, or ethnicity without focusing on that of the counselor's; and (b) that focusing on domains of difference (i.e., differences within a superordinate cultural framework such as age, gender, or social class) is undesirable and/or that such a focus would detract from the counseling process. Implicit in this perspective seems to be the idea that domains of difference are unimportant aspects of psychosocial development.

Multicultural counselor training based on the Universal philosophical assumptions of culture would teach trainees about "special populations" from a unifying perspective, in an attempt to bring everyone together into the melting pot or salad bowl. The Universal approach would, perhaps ultimately, seek to do away with salient domains of difference or cultural difference (i.e., differences that emerge from and through being socialized within the framework of a particular group). Its aim seems to be to enable the counselor to overlook and not be affected by difference. The Universal perspective has the advantage of reminding us that humans have many characteristics and attributes in common and that all people are unique as individuals. Its disadvantage is that it downplays sociopolitical history and intergroup power dynamics by assuming that one group membership has no more meaning than any other.

Ubiquitous

The Ubiquitous approach is essentially a liberal position. It was perhaps stimulated or fostered by the definition of cross-cultural counseling offered by Sue et al. (1982), which states, "Cross-cultural counseling/therapy may be defined as any counseling relationship in which two or more of the participants differ with respect to cultural background, values, and lifestyle" (p. 47). One should note that Sue et al. did not define *culture* but essentially suggested that in cross-cultural counselor training, all types of differences might be considered cultural—a position recently endorsed by Pedersen (1991) in his argument for multicultural counseling as a fourth force. Virtually all forms of social or group identity and/or shared circumstances are constitutive of culture. Culture can be a function of affectional orientation, geography, income level, and so forth. People can belong, then, to multiple groups and cultures, which are situationally determined according to the specific group within which the individual is participating. A rationale for such a conception is that the above types of parameters are each constitutive of a distinct collective identity and based on common experience. The Ubiquitous approach would, for example, hold that there is a fundamental cultural difference between a gay White man and a straight White man, and that the therapeutic relationship must take this cultural difference and its consequences into account.

The assumption of the Ubiquitous approach is that any human difference can be considered cultural. It equates social group affiliations or domains of differences in a superordinate culture with distinct cultures. In this way, if a person develops a particular socially based identity such as class or age, then this, according to the Ubiquitous perspective, is culture. This view presumes that one's shared experience or identity cuts across superordinate cultural frameworks. Thus, all disabled people, gay people, or women or men share a culture that results from their reference group affiliation irrespective of their superordinate or dominant culture of origin. Choice is paramount vis-à-vis one's "cultural" identity. The choice is not so much whether one is or is not a member of a particular group, such as gay or middle-class, although it may be; what is more important is whether one chooses to have one's identity guided/informed/determined by the social reference group. Paradis (1981) noted that the development of unique identities is a function of consideration and selection of "those aspects of our culture and our ethnic/cultural heritage that we can integrate into our self-identities" (p. 136). The Ubiquitous approach has in part been promoted by people who have traditionally been socially outcast or simply ignored.

Margolis and Rungta (1986) shared with Fukuyama (1990) the position that "the psychological consequences of being 'different' are common across special populations, regardless of whether the individuals are members of an ethnic minority, homosexual, or disabled" (Margolis & Rungta, 1986, p. 143). These differences are problematic inasmuch as they render the counselor uncomfortable and thus inhibit him or her from effectively serving the culturally "different" client. The counselor training approach, then, is to make the counselor comfortable with and able to acknowledge cultural, socioeconomic, and other differences between counselor and client. As with Parker (1987), implicit in the Ubiquitous approach is pure agency: The individual simply chooses to transcend "culture"—that is, differences. Pedersen's (1977) "triad model" seeks to increase constructive change in the counseling process by fostering cultural sensitivity: that is, by increasing the counselor's ability to understand the client from the client's perspective, given the client's age, socioeconomic status, ethnicity, lifestyle, gender, and so forth. The crucial component seems to be a notion of efficacy: The culturally encapsulated counselor has difficulty effecting constructive changes.

Thus, training that uses this approach insists that differences be acknowledged and celebrated and that everyone's social identity be "accepted." By defining the various social group affiliations, or what we call "domains of difference," as "cultural," one legitimates them. This results in a focus on multiple group differences, which is buttressed by the concept of culture. The advantage of this perspective is that reference or social group differences of any kind will not be seen as pathology. Paradis (1981) proposed training objectives that aim to increase trainees' awareness of their own and others' cultures, as well as to excavate stereotypical and prejudicial attitudes associated with differences.

At the same time, the Ubiquitous approach can lead to avoidance and denial of groups' sociopolitical histories, intergroup power dynamics, and the relative salience of various reference group memberships. Although it is true that some authors (e.g., D'Andrea & Daniels, 1991; Margolis & Rungta, 1986; Paradis, 1981; Pedersen, 1977) address issues pertaining to counselor biases, none of them substantively addresses counselor participation in intergroup (biased) relations. Also ignored or minimized are the role and influence of the superordinate American culture. This view overlooks the fact that White men and women, though they may be different, nevertheless are so within the context of their superordinate cultural patterns. The Ubiquitous perspective would contend that both women and Blacks, for example, are in a sense equal in that they are members of oppressed "cultures." If all differences equal "cultural differences," *culture* loses much of its distinct meaning. In addition, the role and influence of superordinate cultural contexts are ignored. Although it is true that White women have been oppressed, as have Blacks, men and women from Black and White cultures are socialized according to each group's superordinate cultural framework or worldviews. Although both gender and race have been the basis of oppression, to equate the two is historically erroneous; it would seem that in some respects race supersedes gender in terms of oppression, an issue that has plagued feminism (Giddings, 1984). The Ubiquitous perspective promotes an ahistorical approach. Certain differences are different in kind, and therefore should not be put in the same category.

Traditional

The Traditional anthropological approach defines *culture* as country, which means a common language, kinship, history, mores, values, beliefs, rituals, symbols, epistemology, cultural artifacts, and so forth (Christensen, 1989; Copeland, 1983; Leong & Kim, 1991; Nwachuku & Ivey, 1991; Parker et al., 1986; Parker, Bingham, & Fukuyama, 1985). Culture, then, is not a matter of social differences or domains of difference; one is a member of a cultural group by birth, upbringing, and environment. Other domains of difference that may exist within a cultural group, such as social class or socioeconomic status, affectional orientation, gender, or educational level, are a part of the cultural experience but do not solely constitute the cultural experience, as is the case in the Ubiquitous definition of culture.

Rather, culture is the context in which the domains of difference find their unique expressions. For example, homosexuality varies considerably in terms of definition, status, and identity in accordance with its superordinate culture. Central to this definition of culture is common experience as a function of socialization and environment. Culture provides and limits the range of possible experiences. An individual's cultural (identity) development is, for the most part, a function of how the individual interprets his or her world according to the possibilities and limitations set forth by his or her culture. Thus, one interacts with external factors in a strictly adaptive manner.

The assumptions of the Traditional approach are that shared background is the basis of culture. Part of this is the notion that one's identity is related to worldview and thus "upbringing and life experiences" (Arredondo, 1985; Das & Littrell, 1989). As with cultural anthropology (Abu-Lughod, 1991), such a perspective can result in the very criticisms that Lloyd (1987) levied, namely, that individual clients are rendered "cultural others" to whom primarily differences are attributed. Leong and Kim's (1991) Intercultural Sensitizer basically provided a (cultural-behavioral) template from which to understand and interpret all aspects of an individual's situations, with virtually no acknowledgment of variation within cultural groups and no clear rejection of cultural determinism.

An individual's particular circumstances (e.g., socioeconomic status) are superseded by the general culture. Cultural membership is not a function of social affiliations or a within-culture reference group. Even if an individual eschews his or her culture and seeks to distance him- or herself from it, she or he is still guided by that culture. Basically, it is thought that one's cultural membership circumscribes the types of social and personality dynamics possible. Cultural norms, values, perceptual sets, and so forth develop in response to environmental contingencies. Culture is seen as free to adapt to constraints due to geographic and demographic boundaries. Hence, within a culture one may have different races, ethnic groups, and social arrangements.

Ideally, variability within cultures is acknowledged; however, ethnographic writings would suggest that, at least with regard to non-White populations, less variation within groups is recognized. Christensen (1989) is exceptional in this respect, in that she uses a stage model in which intragroup differences are acknowledged.

In regard to training, it is suggested that some "experience" of another culture is essential, the purpose of which is to give the trainee exposure to the new culture; the idea is that one person or family is representative of the entire group (see Howard, 1991). Nwachuku and Ivey (1991) spoke of using "cultural informants" (p. 91) as part of developing cultural knowledge, thus advocating a Traditional cultural approach to counseling.

Examples of the Traditional training are evident in other training approaches. A component of McDavis and Parker's (1977) ethnic minority counseling course involved "counseling ethnic minorities individually" by having students "view videotapes of the instructors demonstrating how to counsel ethnic minority clients" (p. 148) and "role play a counseling interview with an ethnic minority client" (p. 148). Parker et al. (1986), as part of their multifaceted cultural training approach, suggested the planning of multicultural actions that would consist of, at one level, some kind of direct contact with minorities. They suggested "spending the weekend in the home of an ethnic family, becoming a friend of a person from an ethnic minority group, or going on a date with an individual from an ethnic minority group" (p. 67). Apparently, the focus on cultural knowledge is based on the assumption that "theoretically, any human being can master any culture" (Herkovitz, cited in Das & Littrell, 1989). Proponents of the Traditional conception of culture tend to believe that it is possible to gain genuine empathy with or for a person from another culture.

Merta, Stringham, and Ponterotto (1988) proposed a simulated culture shock as a means of providing counselor trainees with "insight into the daily frustrations experienced by many people [racial-ethnic minorities]" (p. 242). In the same vein, Nwachuku and Ivey (1991), in their culture-specific approach, attempted to enable counselors to see client behavior through the client's cultural lenses and develop the counseling approach from this vantage point.

Proponents of the Traditional cultural approach assume that exposure to the culture or cultural knowledge is the primary key to effective cross-cultural counseling. Parker et al.'s (1986) Multifaceted approach, Parker et al.'s (1985) Ethnic Student Training Group, Leong and Kim's (1991) Intercultural Sensitizer, Nwachuku and Ivey's (1991) Culture-Specific approach all emphasize increasing knowledge about the other culture. In part, the Traditional cultural focus may stem from concern that such exposure is required as a way for trainees to develop comfort with the culturally different (Margolis & Rungta, 1986; Parker et al., 1986).

The Traditional view also teaches that ethnic/cultural prejudice is a function of erroneous individual beliefs (Das & Littrell, 1989; Parker et al., 1986). The concern about eliminating bias would follow from the Traditional approach's eschewal of any substantive discussion of sociopolitical (i.e., intergroup) power dynamics. The Traditional anthropological approach suggests that one is a member of a particular culture by accident of birth, not by any psychological choice process. One may choose how one takes up one's culture; however, one is in some way bound to that culture. Ideally, this approach would acknowledge variability in "lesser" domains of difference, with each culture having its own norms regarding sexuality, gender, and so on.

Christensen (1989) utilized a stage model that acknowledges majority and minority group dynamics, with an eye to power relations, discrimination, and the like. The Traditional approach does not define *culture* in terms of sociopolitical factors (for a critique of ethnology, see Clifford & Marcus, 1986). Thus, peoples who have lived in the United States for many generations are all deemed to be, first and foremost, Americans. In terms of training, then, little regard will be given to racial and cultural differences that obtain as a function of racism. Virtually no mention is made of superordinate cultural development in the face of intercultural dynamics. Thus it is feasible to have two different cultures coexisting in the same geographic-temporal space. Cultural anthropology tends to eschew discourse on race on the grounds that it is a "false" construct (i.e., biologically speaking). That race is also a social construct tends to be ignored by many who use the Traditional approach; Christensen (1989) defined *race* as "an arbitrary classification of populations conceived in Europe, using actual or assumed genetic traits to classify populations of the world into a hierarchical order, with Europeans superior to all others" (p. 275). Some scholars believe that race is central in cultural groupings in the United States. The value and sociopolitical history pertaining to the discourse on race are addressed in more detail below.

The advantage of the Traditional approach is that it reminds us that society's institutions reinforce the meanings of behavior, thought, and feelings learned through family. However, the disadvantage of this approach is that it deemphasizes similar processes that occur within a particular country or that evolve as a consequence of racism. The Traditional cultural anthropological perspective does not specifically address intergroup power dynamics.

Race-Based

The Race-Based approach holds that race is the superordinate locus of culture in the United States in that cultural groups are identified on the basis of racial categories. People are classified into races and consequently cultural groups by skin color, language, and physical features. Just as the Traditional anthropological definition subsumes the Ubiquitous one, the Race-Based subsumes the Traditional. Whereas Traditional cultural anthropology defines cultural boundaries according to national boundaries, the Race-Based perspective situates culture according to race and racist practices in the American context. The Race-Based approach does not reject the general approach to culture proffered by the Traditional perspective; however, in the final analysis, it defines *culture* interactively, with an eye to sociopolitical history and intergroup power dynamics. Race-Based researchers and theorists hold that the definitive aspects of culture—for example, cultural values (see Carter, 1995)—vary ultimately according to psychologically (i.e., racial identity) and socially grounded racial categories.

The Race-Based approach assumes that the experience of belonging to a racial group transcends/supersedes all other experiences in the United States. Because race is perhaps the most visible of all "cultural differences" and because of the history of racial segregation and racism that exists in the United States, race has been and continues to be the ultimate measure of social exclusion and inclusion. Race is relevant because it is visible. Visibility is of importance because it determines the rules and bounds of social and cultural interaction (Copeland, 1983; Kovel, 1984).

Proponents of the Race-Based approach understand culture to be a function of both race and ethnic background. Race in effect has become the marker or criterion for assigning cultural traits and characteristics. One's racial group in the United States is determined by skin color, physical features, and language, and the traits and attributes assigned by classification and group ranking have been and continue to be held as unalterable. This aspect of racial inferences is evident in the social sciences and in policy. Proponents of the Race-Based view believe that race as culture should not be seen as many ethnicities, culture in general, or diversities; it needs to be understood directly as the most significant difference—particularly because ethnicity and culture tend to be seen as more fluid and flexible than is true for race. Not to understand race in this way ignores American sociopolitical history and the fact that our society and culture are constructed on the basis of racial divisions. Virtually all Race-Based theorists share the contention that sociopolitical experiences and interactions between Whites and members of other races are important determinants of each group member's psychosocial development, particularly that of visible racial/ethnic group people (Carter, 1995 Copeland, 1982; Corvin

& Wiggins, 1989; Helms, 1990; McRae & Johnson, 1991; Midgette & Meggert, 1991; Ponterotto, 1988; Sabnani et al., 1991; Sue, 1991). For instance, these types of interactions influence one's racial identity development (Carter, 1995; Helms, 1990).

Racial boundaries have developed over hundreds of years, and as such have become deeply embedded in the social and psychological makeup of all Americans. One is Black, Red, Yellow, or White, and once one is so classified, historically ingrained ideas and assumptions about one's place in society begin to be applied. In most cases, the boundaries determine where one lives, what one is allowed to learn and consequently earn, and one's access to mental health institutions and services. For Black Americans, American Indians, Hispanic Americans, and some Asians, the social and psychological boundaries were established and enforced by law, and now many of these boundaries are maintained by tradition and custom (Marger, 1994; Wax, 1971; Zinn, 1980). It is essential that we find ways to understand race because it is so central to social order in our society. For instance, upon closer examination of social and historical trends, we find that over fairly short periods of time (usually a generation or two), ethnic group members become members of racial groups, and it is the racial category that is used to assign cultural traits. In this way, race remains salient in American life. Even though Americans are members of many ethnic groups, the once biological and now social meanings and beliefs associated with racial group membership supersede ethnic group membership. We are White, Black, Indian, Asian, and Hispanic.

Europeans' and later Americans' experiences with Indians and Africans were the seeds from which grew systems, laws, institutions, and customs written and tacit that etched color lines into American society. The color lines or racial divisions were formed well before the nation was born, and as such have become part of its socioeconomic and intellectual fabric. Our educational, social, political, moral, and economic systems are arranged to function in terms of color lines (Hacker, 1992; Thomas & Sillen, 1972). In order to maintain and sustain color lines, ideas and practices about the meaning and significance of race had to be developed and promulgated. Thus, was born a social and ideological racism that was and still is used to keep us divided (Fredrickson, 1988).

Some would argue that these historically based ideas were eliminated during the 20 years of struggle for civil rights, but others would say that racism and racial boundaries continue to be salient in American life. In fact, racial identity theory grew out of psychologists' efforts to explain and describe the social and psychological metamorphosis among Black people during the civil rights and Black power era. Black people transformed America and race relations. What was discovered during this period was that not every member of a racial group felt the same way about this group membership. Psychological differences within racial groups were proposed (see Cross, 1978, 1991; Helms, 1984, 1990). Racial identity involves one's psychological response to one's

Blackness, Whiteness, and so forth. Although models of racial identity have existed in the psychological literature for some time (Cross, 1978; Helms, 1984; Thomas, 1971), many of them have provided little insight into how racial identity may be applied to cross-cultural training, with the exception of Helms's (1984, 1990) and Carter's (1995) models for understanding race's influence in counseling. These theoretical frameworks have argued that individuals within particular racial groups (and for many cultural groups) may vary with respect to their psychological identification with their respective reference or racial group. Said another way, racial group membership per se is not an indication of how or whether a person identifies with a particular racial or cultural group.

Racial identity attitudes or statuses are composed of parallel attitudes, thoughts, feelings, and behaviors toward both oneself as a member of a racial group and members of the dominant racial group—in this case, Whites. The manner in which one's own racial identity is integrated into one's personality depends on numerous influences—family, community, society, one's own interpretive style, and the manner in which important peers validate, deny, or ignore this aspect of one's identity.

It would seem that either explicitly (e.g., Bowser & Hunt, 1981; Carter & Helms, 1992; Cook & Helms, 1988; Corvin & Wiggins, 1989; Helms, 1990; Katz, 1985; Sabnani et al., 1991) or implicitly (Carney & Kahn, 1984), White racism is seen to be perhaps the most important barrier to efficacious cross-racial counseling, and that effective training requires counselors to proceed through levels of racial identity development (see Cross, 1991; Helms, 1990). The stage models of racial identity contend, as McRae and Johnson (1991) pointed out, that intercultural effectiveness is in part a function of trainees' understanding of their psychological orientation toward their race. Inasmuch as one's identity is defined by oneself and others, the relative "level" of racial identity of counselor and client must necessarily affect the counseling situation (Carter, 1995).

The Race-Based approach makes explicit how untenable is the idea that it is possible to become sensitive to another's culture without first dealing with the overlay of race (Midgette & Meggert, 1991). For instance, Midgette and Meggert (1991) explicitly rejected the attempt to "feel" like someone of another racial group. They noted that "cultural knowledge" is not enough; indeed, some would argue that ethnographic work has helped to sustain the power differentials that obtain in the United States (see Clifford & Marcus, 1986). Ponterotto (1988) noted that the focus on cultural knowledge has "reinforced the ethnocentrically biased view that racial and ethnic minorities are in great need of study, as if they were mysterious, or very different from those of the majority culture" (p. 138). Corvin and Wiggins (1989) noted that "White racism is not the result of cultural differences, but the consequence of White ethnocentrism" (p. 106). The notion that racism is a function of cultural differences seems to reflect the Traditional approach that cultural knowledge, or intellectual and affective immersion in another culture, is sufficient for one to transcend, at least momentarily, one's own culture. The idea that racism is the consequence of White ethnocentrism and feelings of superiority shifts the focus from cultural knowledge to self-knowledge, from an external emphasis to an internal emphasis; racism is not so much a function of misinformation about other peoples as a function of misinformation about the self that leads to distortions about others.

The Race-Based approach assumes that intergroup power dynamics are important. It assumes that the White (or White-identified) counselor enjoys, consciously or not, the fruits of dominant group membership (McIntosh, 1989). Thus, the counselor has a vested interest in the status quo, a status quo that sees people of color as deprived, inferior, or deviant, and much less often as different (Midgette & Meggert, 1991; Ponterotto & Casas, 1991; Sue & Sue, 1990). Consequently, all people who are White identified seem to have no interest in working toward developing consciousness of the inequities inherent in the status quo, or in taking any action to effect any kind of social or psychological change (Prilleltensky, 1989). Hence proponents of the Race-Based approach stress consciousness raising about racism and racial identity development (Carter, 1990, 1995; Helms, 1990; Katz, 1985; McRae & Johnson, 1991).

The Race-Based approach holds that racism and racial identity should be the focus of cross-cultural mental health training. This means that training programs of this ilk focus on trainee racial identity and social, cultural, and institutional racism, particularly as it affects mental health services. Although attention may be paid to the specifics of cultural knowledge, this is secondary and perhaps responsive to the trainee's racial identity levels (Helms, 1990). The advantage of this perspective is that it considers the importance of sociopolitical and historical dynamics to current events. It also introduces psychological variability of racial groups, so that membership alone does not determine cultural affiliation. The disadvantage of this approach is that it requires a deeply personal and potentially painful journey and soul searching for any person, regardless of his or her race, to become aware of his or her racial socialization. This pain and discomfort, coupled with social sanctions against confronting race and racism at both personal and social levels, often operates as an obstacle to racial identity development.

It is difficult to address race as a social and personal issue because it tends to be treated as invisible in the social structure. The status quo cannot be ignored or passively accepted because racism is a contributing factor to poor mental health for all racial groups, including Whites. That race is definitive of culture is not specifically a view shared by all proponents of the Race-Based approach. Some authors (Christensen, 1989; Copeland, 1982; Corvin & Wiggins, 1989; Midgette & Meggert, 1991; Sue et al., 1982) recognize the deleterious effect of racism and/or oppression; however, few explicitly address the interactive and isolating effect of race on culture (Carter, 1995).

Pan-National

This approach views race in the global context as definitive of culture. Whereas the Race-Based approach conceives of culture as racially circumscribed in the context of American sociopolitical history, the Pan-National perspective holds that racial group membership determines culture regardless of geosocial contingencies. The Pan-National perspective has been developed by non-Europeans and, with few exceptions, deems European and American culture to be antithetical to non-European culture (Azibo, 1989, 1991; Baldwin, 1980; Bulhan, 1985; Myers, 1988; Myers, Speight, et al., 1991; Phillips, 1990).

One approach that seems to be based on the Pan-National assumption of difference is Afrocentrism, which views all Blacks as sharing the same basic biogenetic makeup. Afrocentric psychology seeks to return Blacks to their original or African self-consciousness, which derives from African spirituality and social theory (Azibo, 1989, 1991; Baldwin, 1980; Phillips, 1990). Because of the biogenetic determinacy of African self-consciousness, all peoples of Black African descent share the same basic psychosocial essence. The legacy of colonialism and slavery, however, has distorted, if not engulfed, African self-consciousness: "The European Worldview . . . is anti-African. It defines European people as the center of the universe at the exclusion of all other peoples" (Baldwin, 1980, p. 74). Myers et al. (1991) would describe it as a suboptimal conceptual system, one that "assumes the segmentation of two essential aspects of being—spirit and matter" (p. 56). Psychology, with its European roots, is seen as fundamentally inimical to the development and expression of African self-consciousness (Azibo, 1989; Baldwin, 1980). The objective of African psychology, therefore, is to facilitate the client's return to and expression of African self-consciousness (Phillips, 1990). Baldwin (1980) pointed out that such a role for the therapist is impossible given the status quo; he asserted that "we Black psychologists must first remove the alien Eurocentric self-consciousness from our own psyches that has so distorted our perception of our true role in the Black survival and liberation struggle of today." (p. 75).

Proponents of the psychology of oppression/liberation (e.g., Bulhan, 1985) focus on the role played by the imposition of European social theory on all non-European peoples. They would agree with Baldwin's (1980) contention that the European worldview has distorted African self-consciousness; however, a spiritually derived, biogenetic African personality is not part of the theory. Rather, the focus is on the role of oppression and violence arising from colonialism and slavery: "In situations of prolonged oppression, as found among [non-European people] in the diaspora, the oppressor had long obliterated the culture, language and history of the oppressed" (Bulhan, 1985, p. 189). The oppressed thus become fundamentally alienated from what Bulhan calls their "authentic biography," which is basically whatever is individual in the context of the sociopolitical dynamics that obtain. Authentic biography does not specifically represent a return to the original culture, as is the case for the Afrocentrists; indeed, it would seem that for Bulhan and Fanon, that would be impossible, inasmuch as for them culture is dialectical: "The dominant and dominated cultures coalesce with considerable regularity and intensity, one modifying the other and each losing in consequence its original character" (Bulhan, 1985, pp. 193-194). The psychology of oppression, as its name indicates, focuses on the relationship between oppression and psychosocial functioning and development. Culture is understood interactively, in that the cultures of the oppressor and the oppressed have developed in relationship to each other. Because of the violence of colonialism and slavery, and their legacies, oppressed non-European people or people of color are alienated from themselves and their cultures. Whites, on the other hand, have developed a culture based on violence. The upshot of this is a worldwide sociopolitical context that fundamentally alienates oppressed people. In this regard, "The paramount tasks of psychology and psychiatry are to unravel the relation of the psyche to the social structure, to rehabilitate the alienated, and to help transform social structures that thwart human needs" (p. 195). Psychological freedom is essentially unattainable given the status quo, and "fundamental social reconstruction" is necessary. Such reconstruction would allow for the attainment of "collective liberty," which would then serve as the basis for the "authentic biography" referred to above. The specific nature of culture and psychological expression that would develop is, of course, unknown and relatively unimportant; what is important is the attainment of the group upon which to restore "individual biographies and a collective history derailed, stunted, and/or made appendage to those others" (p. 275).

Bulhan (1985) expressed concern about the possibility of effective therapy given the historical power relationship between therapist and client. Exposing the power dynamics of this relationship is thus an important goal for the psychology of oppression/liberation, as well as "the empowerment of the collective and active engagement of victims" (p. 274).

A Pan-National training program would focus on thematizing and rejecting the anti-African (or Asian or Indian) power dynamics inherent in European psychology. It would attempt to enable trainees to understand and emancipate themselves from Eurocentric psychology as a requisite first step. Thus, scholars who teach and train from the Pan-National perspective advocate knowledge of ancient history and shared racially and culturally based characteristics and experiences. Both the psychology of oppression and Afrocentrism seek the empowerment of clients, but by different processes: Afrocentrism seeks to return the client to his or her biogenetic basis, but the psychology of oppression seeks the attainment of collective liberty, such that the expression and development of authentic biography is possible.

Afrocentric psychology assumes that personality is biogenetically determined, regardless of sociopolitical contingencies. The assumption of the biogenetic nature of African personality means that peoples of African descent are "the legitimate heirs of the human essence on this planet" (Baldwin, 1980, p. 75). Thus, culture is biogenetically given, and basic cultural values are constant unless distorted/encumbered by antithetical forces such as European culture. It is also assumed that a return to the original African self-consciousness is possible in the face of the domination of European culture. The psychology of oppression differs on both of these counts: African personality and culture are dialectically given, entirely in the face of European oppression. For Bulhan (1985), race is important in its sociopolitical context; it is not inherently determinative of anything (p. 253). Bulhan assumes that a psychology of liberation depends on social change; indeed, Franz Fanon, upon whose work Bulhan developed his, left his post as head psychiatrist and joined the Algerian liberation struggle. The worldwide oppressor-oppressed relationship between White and people of color is basically inimical to psychological health for all involved. Whereas Afrocentrism understands European culture as inherently being antithetical to African culture, the psychology of oppression understands European culture as having developed dialectically into a force that does violence to the cultures of all oppressed people. The Pan-National approach has the advantage of allowing for a broad and global understanding of race as it relates to oppression throughout the world and demonstrating how groups are connected by color and common experience. Its disadvantage is that when viewing racial oppression as the primary construct for cultural difference, one may overlook the role of other important reference groups such as religion and social class.

SUMMARY

We have attempted to understand the assumptions about culture in the context of multicultural counselor training. The discussion indicates that each of the five types of assumptions about culture, particularly as applied to multicultural counselor training, has important ramifications. It has not been our intent to suggest that any one approach is superior to any other (which does not mean we do not prefer one perspective); rather, we have sought to make explicit the underlying philosophical assumptions and what they mean and imply, in an attempt to provide a definitive picture of each approach. It is our hope that these typologies can serve as a basis from which to gain a clearer understanding of what some mean by their use of terms such as *culture, cross-cultural,* or *multicultural counseling.*

Several factors differentiate the various categories identified. In no specific order, they are: Does the conception of culture concern itself exclusively with intergroup differences, intragroup differences, or both? Does the conception of culture situate culture in ascribed (i.e., already given) or chosen loci of identity? Are multiple identities (cultures) possible within the conception of culture? Does the conception of culture thematize sociopolitical or power dynamics? Is culture understood as a self-contained construct, or is it deemed to develop dialectically or interactively? And finally, does the perspective on culture raise questions about the status quo? That is, does effective multi-cultural counseling one way or the other thematize social change?

The manner in which the different approaches address these questions implicates the philosophical assumptions upon which they are based, which in turn significantly influence the types of skills, information, and experiences promulgated by each of the approaches to multicultural counselor training. The Ubiquitous, Traditional, and Pan-National/Afrocentric perspectives tend to view cultural group membership (given their respective definitions of culture) as indicative psychosocially; within-group differences are not addressed, inasmuch as group membership implies shared experience and meaning. The Universal, Race-Based, and Pan-National/psychology of oppression perspectives tend to suggest that there is within-group variation, and that consequently group membership alone is not a sufficient index of culture and personality. Of course, even within the different categories there is variation. The Universal and Ubiquitous approaches view culture as chosen rather than ascribed: Individuals are free to identify with whichever domain of difference they choose, and thus multiple group membership is possible. The Traditional, Race-Based, and Pan-National approaches, on the other hand, suggest that cultural group membership is ascribed: One is born into a particular culture, and its influence is paramount regardless of chosen identity. On this score, a direct contrast between chosen and ascribed is impossible because the domains identified as "culture" are fundamentally different; however, some might argue that it is possible to extricate oneself from one's ascribed culture. Power dynamics, with few exceptions (e.g., Christensen, 1989), are of importance only in approaches that focus on race. Not surprisingly, these approaches have been propounded by scholars of color, who are subject to racism and thus have an interest in focusing on sociopolitical dynamics and social change. Only the Pan-National and the Race-Based approaches understand culture to be dialectically or interactively defined: that is, as a function, in part, of the relationship between oppressor and oppressed. According to the Race-Based approach, exclusion and isolation resulted in the maintenance of Indian, Asian, Hispanic, and African value orientations in the United States, but simultaneously exposure to or the inculcation of Euro-American culture resulted in distinct Indian, Asian, Hispanic, and Black American cultures. The Pan-National perspective focuses on how oppression results in the loss of a group's original culture and the subsequent development of a culture of oppression. The Traditional approach views culture as basically temporally and geographically adaptive: That is, culture changes in the face of technological and social development, as well as geographic contingencies (e.g., migration).

Another component of the typology is "knowing that vs. knowing how" (Johnson, 1987): The Universal, the Ubiquitous, and most of the Traditional approaches focus on cultural knowledge, whereas the Race-Based and Pan-National approaches tend to emphasize cultural self-awareness—that is, how one feels about one's own and other cultures.

It is our hope that the typology of philosophical assumptions will serve multicultural, cross-cultural counseling psychology in the United States by providing a way to exami ?e and develop training and research from each approach. Studies can investigate the merits of the various approaches by examining the ideas and methods of each. So, for example, studies can examine the effects in therapy or education of a Ubiquitous or Race-Based approach. Training programs can make their approaches to culture explicit by indicating whether they are Universal, Traditional, Ubiquitous, Pan-National, or Race-Based. Training methods can also be developed in accordance with the classification system and explicitly identified. It is hoped that as scholars and clinicians have debated the strengths and weaknesses of theories of human development and personality in psychology, the proposed classification system and typology can be used to stimulate debate and research in multicultural counseling psychology.

REFERENCES

Abu-Lughod, L. (1991). Writing against culture. In R. G. Fox (Ed.), *Recapturing anthropology: Working in the present* (pp. 137-162). Santa Fe, NM: School of American Research Press.

American Psychological Association. (1983). *Criteria for accreditation of doctoral training programs and internships in professional psychology.* Washington, DC: Author.

American Psychological Association. (1987). Resolutions approved by the National Conference on Graduate Education in Psychology. *American Psychologist, 42,* 1070-1084.

American Psychological Association, Office of Accreditation. (1991a, Summer). The nature, scope and implementation of Criterion II: Cultural and individual differences. *Capsule,* pp. 1-5.

American Psychological Association. (1991b). *Policies for accreditation governance: Final draft.* Washington, DC: Author.

Aponte, J. F. (1992). The role of accreditation in enhancing cultural diversity in psychology graduate and professional training programs. In S. D. Johnson & R. T. Carter (Eds.), *Addressing cultural issues in an organizational context: Proceedings of the Tenth Annual Winter Roundtable on Cross-Cultural Counseling and Psychotherapy* (pp. 73-80). New York: Columbia University, Teachers College.

Arredondo, P. (1985). Cross-cultural counselor education and training. In P. B. Pedersen (Ed.), *Handbook of cross-cultural counseling and therapy* (pp. 281-290). Westport, CT: Greenwood Press.

Azibo, D. A. (1989). African-centered theses on mental health and a nosology of Black/African personality disorder. *Journal of Black Psychology, 18,* 173-214.

Azibo, D. A. (1991). Toward a metatheory of the African personality. *Journal of Black Psychology, 17,* 37-45.

Baldwin, J. A. (1980). The psychology of oppression. In M. Asante & A. Vandi (Eds.), *Contemporary Black thought* (pp. 95-110). Beverly Hills, CA: Sage.

Bernal, M., & Castro, F. G. (1994). Are clinical psychologists prepared for service and research with ethnic minorities? Report of a decade of progress. *American Psychologist, 49,* 797-805.

Bernal, M., & Padilla, A. (1982). Status of minority curricula and training in clinical psychology. *American Psychologist, 37,* 780-787.

Bowser, B. P., & Hunt, R. G. (Eds.). (1981). *Impacts of racism on White Americans.* Beverly Hills, CA: Sage.

Brislin, R. W. (Ed.). (1990). *Applied cross-cultural psychology.* Newbury Park, CA: Sage.

Bulhan, H. A. (1985). *Franz Fanon and the psychology of oppression.* New York: Plenum.

Carney, C. G., & Kahn, K. B. (1984). Building competencies for effective cross-cultural counseling: A developmental view. *The Counseling Psychologist, 12,* 111-119.

Carter, R. T. (1990). The relationship between racism and racial identity among White Americans: An exploratory investigation. *Journal of Counseling and Development, 69,* 46-50.

Carter, R. T. (1991). Cultural values: A review of empirical research and implications for counseling. *Journal of Counseling and Development, 70,* 164-173.

Carter, R. T. (1995). *The influence of race and racial identity in psychotherapy: Toward a racially inclusive model.* New York: John Wiley.

Carter, R. T., & Helms, J. E. (1992). The counseling process as defined by relationship types: A test of Helms' interactional model. *Journal of Multicultural Counseling and Development, 20,* 181-201.

Casas, J. M. (1985). The status of racial- and ethnic-minority counseling: A training perspective. In P. B. Pedersen (Ed.), *Handbook of cross-cultural counseling and therapy* (pp. 267-274). Westport, CT: Greenwood Press.

Casas, J. M., Ponterotto, J. G., & Gutierrez, J. M. (1986). An ethical indictment of counseling research and training: The cross-cultural perspective. *Journal of Counseling and Development, 64,* 347-349.

Christensen, C. P. (1989). Cross-cultural awareness development: A conceptual model. *Counselor Education and Supervision, 28,* 270-287.

Clifford, J., & Marcus, G. E. (Eds.). (1986). *Writing culture: The poetics and politics of ethnography.* Berkeley: University of California Press.

Cook, D. A., & Helms, J. E. (1988). Visible racial/ethnic group supervisees' satisfaction with cross-cultural supervision as predicted by relationship characteristics. *Journal of Counseling Psychology, 35,* 268-274.

Copeland, E. J. (1982). Minority populations and traditional counseling programs: Some alternatives. *Counselor Education and Supervision, 21,* 187-193.

Copeland, E. J. (1983). Cross-cultural counseling and psychotherapy: A historical perspective, implications for research and training. *Personnel and Guidance Journal, 62,* 10-15.

Corvin, S. A., & Wiggins, F. (1989). An antiracism training model for White professionals. *Journal of Multicultural Counseling and Development, 17,* 105-114.

Cross, W. E. (1978). The Thomas and Cross models of psychological Nigrescence: A review. *Journal of Black Psychology, 5*(1), 13-31.

Cross, W. E. (1991). *Shades of Black.* Philadelphia: Temple University Press.

D'Andrade, R. G. (1984). Cultural meaning systems. In R. A. Shweder & R. A. LeVine (Eds.), *Culture theory: Essays on mind, self, and emotion* (pp. 88-122). Cambridge, UK: Cambridge University Press.

D'Andrea, D., & Daniels, J. (1991). Exploring the different levels of multicultural counseling training in counselor education. *Journal of Counseling and Development, 70,* 78-85.

Das, A. K., & Littrell, J. M. (1989). Multicultural education for counseling: A reply to Lloyd. *Counselor Education and Supervision, 29,* 7-15.

Fredrickson, G. M. (1988). *The arrogance of race.* Middletown, CT: Wesleyan University Press.

Fukuyama, M. A. (1990). Taking a universal approach to multicultural counseling. *Counselor Education and Supervision, 30,* 6-17.

Giddings, P. (1984). *When and where I enter: The impact of Black women on race and sex in America.* New York: Bantam.

Hacker, A. (1992). *Two nations: Black and White, separate, hostile, unequal.* New York: Scribner.

Helms, J. E. (1984). Toward a theoretical explanation of the effects of race on counseling: Black/White interactional model. *The Counseling Psychologist, 12*(4), 153-165.

Helms, J. E. (1990). *Black and White racial identity: Theory, research, and practice.* Westport, CT: Greenwood Press.

Hills, H. I., & Strozier, A. L. (1992). Multicultural training in APA-approved counseling psychology programs: A survey. *Professional Psychology: Research and Practice, 23*(1), 43-51.

Howard, G. S. (1991). Culture tales: A narrative approach to thinking, cross-cultural psychology, and psychotherapy. *American Psychologist, 466,* 187-1197.

Ibrahim, F. A., & Arredondo, P. M. (1986). Ethical standards for cross-cultural counseling: Counselor preparation, practice, assessment, and research. *Journal of Counseling and Development, 64,* 349-351.

Ivey, A. (1987). The multicultural practice of therapy: Ethics, empathy, and dialectics. *Journal of Social and Clinical Psychology, 5,* 195-204.

Johnson, S. D., Jr. (1987). Knowing that versus knowing how: Toward achieving expertise through multicultural training for counseling. *The Counseling Psychologist, 15,* 320-331.

Johnson, S. D., Jr. (1990). Toward clarifying culture, race, and ethnicity in the context of multicultural counseling. *Journal of Multicultural Counseling and Development, 18*(1), 41-50.

Katz, J. H. (1985). The sociopolitical nature of counseling. *The Counseling Psychologist, 13,* 615-625.

Kovel, J. (1984). *White racism.* New York: Columbia University Press.

Kroeber, A. L., & Kluckhohn, C. (1952). Culture: A critical review of concepts and definitions. *Papers of the Peabody Museum of American Archaeology and Ethnology, 48.*

Leong, F. T. L., & Kim, H. H. W. (1991). Going beyond cultural sensitivity on the road to multiculturalism: Using the Intercultural Sensitizer as a counselor training tool. *Journal of Counseling and Development, 70,* 112-118.

LeVine, R. A. (1982). Properties of culture: An ethnographic view. In R. A. Shweder & R. A. LeVine (Eds.), *Culture theory: Essays on mind, self, and emotion* (pp. 67-87). Cambridge, UK: Cambridge University Press.

Lloyd, A. P. (1987). Multicultural counseling: Does it belong in a counselor education program? *Counselor Education and Supervision, 26,* 164-167.

Marger, M. N. (1994). *Race and ethnic relations* (3rd ed.). Belmont, CA: Wadsworth.

Margolis, R. L., & Rungta, S. A. (1986). Training counselors for work with special populations: A second look. *Journal of Counseling and Development, 64,* 642-644.

McDavis, R. J., & Parker, M. (1977). A course on counseling ethnic minorities: A model. *Counselor Education and Supervision, 16,* 146-149.

McIntosh, P. (1989, July/August). White privilege: Unpacking the invisible knapsack. *Peace and Freedom,* pp. 10-12.

McRae, M. B., & Johnson, S. D., Jr. (1991). Toward training for competence in multicultural counselor education. *Journal of Counseling and Development, 70,* 131-135.

Merta, R. J., Stringham, E. M., & Ponterotto, J. G. (1988). Simulating culture shock in counselor trainees: An experiential exercise for cross-cultural training. *Journal of Counseling and Development, 66,* 242-245.

Midgette, T. E., & Meggert, S. S. (1991). Multicultural counseling instruction: A challenge for faculties in the 21st century. *Journal of Counseling and Development, 70,* 136-141.

Myers, H. F., Wohlford, P., Guzman, L. P., & Echemendia, R. J. (Eds.). (1991). *Ethnic minority perspective on clinical training and services in psychology.* Washington, DC: American Psychological Association.

Myers, L. J. (1988). *Understanding an Afrocentric world view: Introduction to an optimal psychology.* Dubuque, IA: Kendall/Hunt.

Myers, L. J., Speight, S. L., Highlen, P. S., Cox, C. I., Reynolds, A. L., Adams, E. M., & Hanley, C. P. (1991). Identity development and world view: Toward an optimal conceptualization. *Journal of Counseling and Development, 70*(1), 54-63.

Nwachuku, U. T., & Ivey, A. E. (1991). Culture-specific counseling: An alternative training tool. *Journal of Counseling and Development, 70,* 106-111.

Outlaw, L. (1990). Towards a critical theory of "race." In D. L. Goldberg (Ed.), *Anatomy of racism* (pp. 58-82). Minneapolis: University of Minnesota Press.

Paradis, F. E. (1981). Themes in the training of culturally effective psychotherapists. *Counselor Education and Supervision, 21,* 136-151.

Parker, W. M. (1987). Flexibility: A primer for multicultural counseling. *Counselor Education and Supervision, 26,* 176-180.

Parker, W. M., Bingham, R. P., & Fukuyama, M. (1985). Improving cross-cultural effectiveness of counselor trainees. *Counselor Education and Supervision, 24,* 349-352.

Parker, W. M., Valley, M. M., & Geary, C. A. (1986). Acquiring cultural knowledge for counselors in training: A multifaceted approach. *Counselor Education and Supervision, 26,* 61-71.

Pedersen, P. B. (1977). The triad model of cross-cultural counselor training. *Personnel and Guidance Journal, 55,* 94-100.

Pedersen, P. B. (1991). Introduction to the special issue on multiculturalism as a fourth force in counseling. *Journal of Counseling and Development, 70,* 4.

Phillips, F. B. (1990). NTU psychotherapy: An Afrocentric approach. *Journal of Black Psychology, 17,* 55-74.

Ponterotto, J. G. (1988). Racial consciousness development among White counselor trainees: A stage model. *Journal of Multicultural Counseling and Development, 16,* 146-156.

Ponterotto, J. G., & Casas, J. M. (1987). In search of multicultural competence within counselor education programs. *Journal of Counseling and Development, 65,* 430-434.

Ponterotto, J. G., & Casas, J. M. (1991). *Handbook of racial/ethnic minority counseling research.* Springfield, IL: Charles C Thomas.

Prilleltensky, I. (1989). Psychology and the status quo. *American Psychologist, 44,* 795-802.

Sabnani, H. B., Ponterotto, J. G., & Borodovsky, L. G. (1991). White racial identity development and cross cultural training: A stage model. *The Counseling Psychologist, 19,* 76-102.

Smedley, A. (1993). *Race in North America: Origin and evolution of a world view.* Boulder, CO: Westview.

Stricker, G., Davis-Russell, E., Bourg, E., Duran, E., Hammond, W. R., McHolland, J., Polite, K., & Vaughn, B. E. (Eds.). (1990). *Toward ethnic diversification in psychology education and training.* Washington, DC: American Psychological Association.

Sue, D. W. (1991). A model for cultural diversity training. *Journal of Counseling and Development, 70,* 99-105.

Sue, D. W., Arrendondo, P., & McDavis, R. J. (1992). Multicultural counseling competencies and standards: A call to the profession. *Journal of Multicultural Counseling and Development, 26*(2), 64-84.

Sue, D. W., Bernier, J. E., Durran, A., Feinberg, L., Pedersen, P., Smith, E. J., & Vasquez-Nuttall, E. (1982). Position paper: Cross-cultural counseling competencies. *The Counseling Psychologist, 10,* 45-52.

Sue, D. W., & Sue, D. (1990). *Counseling the culturally different: Theory and practice* (2nd ed.). New York: John Wiley.

Sue, S. (1980). Issues in Asian American psychology curriculum. *Journal of the Asian American Psychological Association, 5,* 6-11.

Sue, S., Akutsu, P. D., & Higashi, C. (1985). Training issues in conducting therapy with ethnic-minority-group clients. In P. B. Pedersen (Ed.), *Handbook of cross-cultural counseling and therapy* (pp. 275-280). Westport, CT: Greenwood Press.

Thomas, A., & Sillen, S. (1972). *Racism and psychiatry.* New York: Brunner/Mazel.

Thomas, C. (1971). *Boys no more.* Beverly Hills, CA: Glencoe.

Wax, M. L. (1971). *Indian Americans: Unity and diversity.* Englewood Cliffs, NJ: Prentice Hall.

Zinn, H. (1980). *A people's history of the United States.* New York: HarperCollins.

13

Counselor Supervision

Cross-Cultural Perspectives

MICHAEL T. BROWN

JOYCELYN LANDRUM-BROWN

CLINICAL SUPERVISION is an essential element of therapist training, but research in the area lacks maturity (Russell, Crimmings, & Lent, 1984). In addition, we believe that a particularly timely evolution in the field would be theoretical and empirical development with respect to cross-cultural issues. If supervision is the act of overseeing the development of therapeutic competence in a fellow clinician (see Holloway, 1992; Loganbill, Hardy, & Delworth, 1982), then the articulation, examination, and management of factors affecting supervisory and counseling relationships or the criteria against which therapeutic competence is to be determined would seem to be of critical importance. Cross-cultural dynamics have been clearly implicated as features of a wide range of other relationships, including counseling relationships (see Atkinson, Morten, & Sue, 1993). Furthermore, competence in treating culturally diverse others is currently viewed as an essential component of therapeutic competence (American Psychological Association, 1980; Casas, 1984; Pedersen, 1991; Sue et al., 1982; Sue & Sue, 1990).

We assert that clinical supervision is not likely to be exempt from cross-cultural dynamics. A supervisor's cultural frame of reference, or worldview, is likely to influence, for example, the therapeutic choices made by supervisees and their supervisors. Furthermore, we argue that worldview conflicts between supervisees and supervisors may be reflected in the evaluation of the trainee, in the quality of the supervisory relationship, and in each party's therapeutic approach.

Little attention has been paid to clinical supervision, however. A number of special journal issues have been published on cross-cultural counseling and multicultural counselor education (see Bradley, 1987; Hines & Garcia-Preto, 1992; Pedersen, 1991; Savickas, 1993; Smith & Vasquez, 1985), but even when education and training issues have been addressed (e.g., *Journal of Counseling and Development*'s special issue in 1991), scant attention is given to intercultural dynamics in supervision. Consequently, we know very little about the science and practice of cross-cultural clinical supervision.

Attempting to fill the current knowledge vacuum, we first review extant theory and research with respect to cross-cultural counseling in order to identify variables and issues potentially relevant to clinical supervision. Next, we examine the status of contemporary theories of clinical supervision with respect to cross-cultural issues. In closing, we propose needed conceptual and empirical directions for the field of clinical supervision.

Before proceeding, however, we would like to present our position on two points of definition. Literally speaking, the term *multicultural supervision* alludes to the study and practice of supervision in and for different cultures. Multicultural supervision would involve the study of different cultural patterns of supervision as pertaining to its content, process, and outcomes. The term *cross-cultural supervision*, on the other hand, refers to supervision contents, processes, and outcomes pertaining to the client-counselor-supervisor triad in which at least one of the parties in the triadic relationship is culturally different from one or both of the other parties. Although some persons may be inclined to use the terms interchangeably, we believe that the latter term is more appropriate for the field of supervision. Supervision scholarship is likely to be concerned with the effect of cross-cultural encounters for supervision and counseling process and outcome. Just as a client's cultural characteristics affect counseling process and outcome with a culturally dissimilar counselor, the cultural characteristics of each person of the supervisory triad may affect the content, process, and outcome of clinical supervision.

CROSS-CULTURAL DIMENSIONS

The Supervisory Constituents

Before identifying the possible cross-cultural factors that might affect clinical supervision, it is helpful to first identify the different relationships germane to the supervisory process. It seems clear to us that the supervisory process consists of at least three parties: the client, the counselor-supervisee, and the supervisor. Holloway and colleagues (Holloway, 1992; Holloway & Dunlap, 1989) presented a useful scheme for identifying the various aspects of supervision and their interrelationships but failed to directly identify the client as

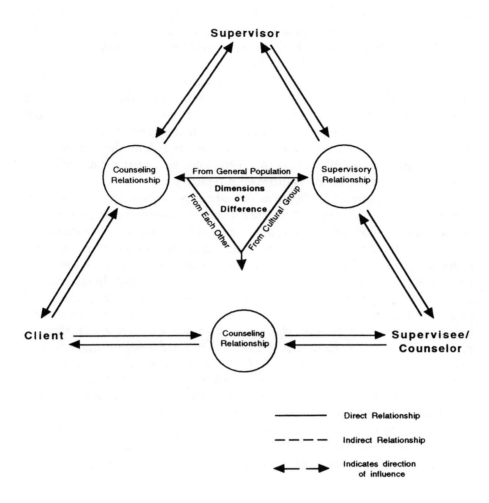

Supervisor

Counseling Relationship

Supervisory Relationship

From General Population

Dimensions of Difference

From Each Other

From Cultural Group

Client

Counseling Relationship

Supervisee/ Counselor

—————— Direct Relationship

— — — Indirect Relationship

◄— —► Indicates direction of influence

Figure 13.1. Supervisory Triad

a party to the process. Those authors indicated that the cultural values of the supervisor and the supervisee affect the supervisory relationship as well as the supervisory process. We agree with Holloway and Dunlap and contend, further, that the cultural characteristics of the supervisor, supervisee, *and* the client affect counseling and supervisory contents, process, and outcomes. We present our own schema for these characteristics and their interrelations in Figure 13.1.

As depicted in the figure, the supervisor directly influences the attitudes, knowledge, and skills of a supervisee through his or her own attitudes, knowledge, and skills. The supervisor also indirectly influences the supervisee through his or her personal characteristics, modes of relating, and nature of concerns brought to supervision (not shown in Figure 13.1); these elements can affect how a supervisor is perceived by the supervisee and, as a consequence, can influence supervisor-supervisee interactions. In addition, the supervisor indirectly influences the client through his or her influence on the supervisee's performance as counselor.

The supervisee, as clinician, directly influences the attitudes, knowledge, and skills of the client. The supervisee also indirectly influences the client (not shown in Figure 13.1) and the supervisor through his or her personal characteristics, modes of relating, and nature of concerns brought to supervision; as expressed earlier, these elements can affect how the supervisee is perceived by the supervisor and the client and, as a result, can influence trainee-client and supervisee-supervisor interactions.

The client indirectly influences the attitudes, knowledge, and skills of both the counselor/supervisee and the supervisor through his or her personal characteristics, modes of relating, and nature of concerns brought to counseling; these influence the perceptions of the client that are held by the counselor/supervisee and supervisor. We contend that the attitudes, knowledge, and skills of all supervisory parties, as well as their personal characteristics, modes of relating, and concerns, can reflect or express cultural influences. We propose, therefore, that all parties to the supervisory process bring to it a number of cross-culturally relevant features that influence the process. For example, supervisor and supervisee perceptions and conceptualizations regarding a client and his or her concerns are influenced by the client's cultural characteristics and the supervisor's and supervisee's own cultural frames of reference; these perceptions and conceptualizations may come in conflict with each other as a function of worldview differences between the supervisor and supervisee. We believe that it is impossible to accurately construe the supervisory process without alluding either to the client-counselor/supervisee-supervisor triad or to the influence of their worldview perspectives.

Dimensions of Difference

Cross-culturally relevant characteristics of the client, counselor/supervisee, and supervisor can be classified along three major dimensions of difference: differences from the general population, differences from one's cultural group, and differences from either or both of the other parties in the supervisory process. (We would like to acknowledge the work of Gottfredson, 1986, in identifying and classifying career choice risk factors potentially affecting the career development of "special groups." Our dimensions of difference are similar to two of the three risk factor categories articulated by Gottfredson.) Those differences may pose significant barriers to effective supervision that are identical to those to effective counseling (see Atkinson et al., 1993), such as client anger and resistance, counselor defensiveness, counselor overidentification, supervisee resistance, poor counselor development, supervisor countertransference, and supervisor patronization. The barriers can affect the quality of interpersonal relations, the nature of the counseling and supervisory process, and the effectiveness of the counseling and supervisory enterprise.

Differences From the General Population

Differences between each member of the supervisory triad and members of the general population (that is, European Americans) are probably the most discussed as characteristics that might influence psychological processes and perspectives; these differences include language system or dialectical differences (verbal and nonverbal), social and/or economic status differences and associated value systems, educational differences, and differences due to cultural isolation. To the extent that any supervisory triad member differs on any salient feature from the general population, the content, process, and outcome of supervision can be negatively affected. In addition, to the extent that supervision and counseling theory are predicated upon an understanding of "the general population," the use of those theories may be inappropriate for understanding and managing cross-cultural dynamics in clinical supervision. For example, traditional counseling and supervisory roles in Western societies rely heavily upon verbal interaction and rapport (see Atkinson et al., 1993; Sue, 1981). The more the parties in the supervisory process, particularly those in direct communication given in Figure 13.1, can understand one another, the more effective one can expect verbal-based approaches to be. It is important to note that even when persons appear to be using the same language system, they may not be using it in a similar fashion or attributing similar meanings to similar words, terms, gestures, and nuances. The quality of interaction among supervisory constituents is influenced by similarities and differences in language systems. In addition, the extent to which supervisory constituents value verbal communication should affect the quality of supervisory and counseling interactions.

Some differences in values and interaction styles between parties in the supervisory process and those from the general population are due to social status or economic status differences. We have separated social status from economic status because of the observation that persons who may not differ economically from the general population, at least in terms of net family income, may differ quite significantly in terms of social status. Such persons may harbor significant levels of resentment or sensitivities that surface when these persons encounter the social status imbalances characteristic of counseling and supervisory encounters. Value differences associated with economic status differences may also be reflected in people's appointment-making and -keeping behavior, attitudes toward sexual and substance-taking behavior, and attitudes toward counseling and supervision (see Sue, 1981).

Relatedly significant educational differences between the client, the counselor/supervisee, and/or the supervisor from the general population of European Americans can affect their perspectives and approaches with regard to the whole range of human concerns and conditions (see Sue, 1981). As already alluded to, such differences can affect the contents and processes associated with supervision and counseling, resulting in radically different outcomes than have been typical or characteristic.

A supervisor, supervisor/counselor, and client may come from cultural groups that may experience different degrees of separation and oppression than are experienced in the general society. Those experiences shape one's general views and rules about life and how to approach living in it: In other words, the experiences influence one's level of acculturation. Culture-based perspectives may be so fundamentally different that effective supervision involving the supervisory parties is obstructed. Cultural differences may be reflected in assessed levels of acculturation, perceptions of oppression and unfair discrimination, confidence in societal institutions (like counselor training and supervision), and worldviews.

One or all of the supervisory parties may also differ from the general population in terms of ethnicity and/or race. Although such differences may not betoken psychological content or process differences, they can affect the perception of such differences, reflecting biases, stereotypes, and "isms" (namely, racism and ethnocentrism) that are sure to affect the supervisory process adversely. People hold values associated with racial/ethnic physiognomy (e.g., skin color, hair texture and length, size of visible body parts). The biases of supervisory constituents regarding perceived racial classification and perceived values associated with racial physiognomy are expected to influence both the counseling and supervision relationships just as they do broader social relationships.

Other possible areas of difference between supervisory parties and persons from the general population include ethnic or racial identity, nationality, urbanicity, geographic origin, and occupational and economic background. Few of these issues have been investigated with respect to counseling processes and outcomes and virtually none of them has been studied with respect to supervisory processes and outcomes.

Consider, also, that the extent to which the supervisor and supervisee value the therapeutic approaches of Western societies will influence their approaches to treating clients. Clearly, the more that members of the supervisory triad are found to differ from the general norm, the more likely that one can anticipate process and outcome difficulties in the counseling and supervisory relationships.

The main point of this section is that, given the etic perspectives of contemporary psychology, supervision science is currently constructed to address characteristics most represented in the general population of counselors/supervisees and supervisors. We reiterate that the extent to which any member of the supervisory triad differs from the general population of European Americans can affect the content, process, and outcome of clinical supervision; we would suspect that the effect would most likely be a negative one. There is a need for research designed to test our assertion.

Differences From One's Cultural Group

The field of applied psychology is recognizing more and more that members of various ethnic or racial groups differ from one another in psychologically meaningful ways. To the extent that any party to the supervisory relationship differs from others of his or her ethnic or racial group, knowledge, experience, and attitudes with respect to relevant ethnic or racial groups may not generalize to that party. The three relationships in the supervisory process (i.e., supervisor-supervisee/counselor, counselor/supervisee-client, and supervisor-client) can be seriously affected by misperceptions and wrongly applied culturally specific knowledge and experience.

Ethnic and racial group members may be found to differ from one another on the following dimensions: ethnic or racial identity, facility with English and the language of one's ascribed ethnic or racial group, traditionality of interests and concerns, cultural values orientation, mental ability, nationality, migration history, migration status, reservation residential status, tribal identification, occupational and economic background both here and in country of origin, and urbanicity. Although level of acculturation was presented earlier as a "between-ethnic-group" dimension, it is important to consider that persons within an ethnic or racial group can differ on this variable. Each of these dimensions may affect how members within a group perceive problems and how they engage in relationships with others who are either within or outside of their ethnic or racial group. For the purpose of illustration, consider the possible interaction between an African American client in Cross's (1971; Parham, 1989) Encounter stage, an African American counselor in the Immersion stage, and a European American supervisor possessing attitudes associated with Helms's (1990) Contact stage. The Encounter and Immersion stages are two of five stages of Cross's Black racial identity development theory, and the Contact stage is the first of five stages of Helms's White racial identity development theory. A complete discussion of these stages has been provided by Atkinson and Thompson (1992), Cross (1978), and Helms (1990). Briefly, however, Black racial identity theory proposes that African Americans advance through a series of stages in developing racial consciousness and in perceiving racial injustice. The Encounter stage is described as the stage when an African American, first cautiously and then resolutely, searches for a Black identity, typically as a result of some direct encounter with racism. The Immersion stage represents the phase of development at which the African American immerses him- or herself in everything that is perceived as relating to Blackness. White racial identity development theory posits that Whites advance from a stage of first acknowledging racism to developing as nonracist persons; during the Contact stage, a White person first becomes consciously aware that Blacks exist as culturally unique from Whites.

In the scenario depicted in the previous paragraph, the supervisor may find him- or herself at a loss to understand the client's perceptions of racism, be afraid of the counselor/supervisee's anger about the client's encounter with racism and his or her tendency to direct the client toward militancy, and be defensive with respect to the supervisor/counselee's charges that the counselor is racist (for a more complete discussion of cross-racial identity counseling interactions, see Atkinson & Thompson, 1992, and Helms, 1990).

Differences From Others in the Supervisory Process

To the extent that members of the supervisory process differ from one another on salient between-group and within-group dimensions identified above, they may encounter difficulty in identifying problems and goals for counseling and supervision. They may also confront challenges to developing effective working alliances. For example, some authors (see Codina & Montalvo, 1994) have noted the insecurity and low self-esteem that some Chicanos and Latinos experience because of their lack of facility with Spanish and the negative reactions of other Chicanos and Latinos to this "inadequacy." All of the between-group and within-group dimensions of difference identified earlier can challenge the understanding of supervisory triad members about one another, the manner in which they may interact with one another, the subject matter of focus in supervision and counseling, and the outcomes associated with both supervision and counseling.

Worldview Congruence Model

Another useful means of construing the impact of "dimensions of difference" is through use of the "worldview congruence model." *Worldview* is defined as the way an individual perceives his or her relationship to the world (e.g., nature, other people, animals, institutions, objects, the universe, God) (Sue, 1981). The concept of worldview is used to illustrate how different individuals and cultural groups tend to experience the world in different ways. Worldviews are learned ways of perceiving one's environment and, as a result, can become salient factors in shaping the way that individuals perceive and respond to individuals and events in their environment.

The concept of worldview has been used by researchers (Myers, 1991; Nichols, 1976; Nobles, 1972) to discuss how interpersonal conflicts are often a result of conflicts on eight worldview dimensions: psychobehavioral modality, axiology, ontology, ethos, epistemology, logic, concept of time, and concept of self. We define this conflict as worldview incongruence. Table 13.1 describes positions on the eight worldview dimensions.

Our worldview congruence model illustrates how worldview conflicts come into play in supervisor, counselor/supervisee, and client triadic relationships. Worldview incongruence is not a static variable. It is dynamic in that it can vary according to relationship pairs, situations, worldview dimensions,

TABLE 13.1 Worldview Positions

Worldview Incongruence		
Worldview Dimensions	**Example Worldview Positions**	
Psychobehavioral Modality	Doing vs. Being vs. Becoming	
Axiology (Values)	Competition vs. Cooperation Emotional Restraint vs. Emotional Expressiveness Direct Verbal Expression vs. Indirect Verbal Expression Seeking Help vs. "Saving Face"	
Ethos (Guiding Beliefs)	Independence vs. Interdependence Individual Rights vs. Honor & Protect Family Egalitarianism vs. Authoritarianism Control & Dominance vs. Harmony & Deference	
Epistemology (How One Knows)	Cognitive vs. Affective Processes, vs. Cognitive & Processes "Vibes," Intuition Affective	
Logic (Reasoning Process)	Either/or Thinking vs. Both/and Thinking vs. Circular	
Ontology (Nature of Reality)	Objective vs. Subjective vs. Spiritual & Material Spiritual Material	
Concept of Time	Clock-Based vs. Event-Based vs. Cyclical	
Concept of Self	Individual Self vs. Extended Self	

and time constraints. Given the supervisory triad, there exist only five logical patterns of conflict and/or complements possible; we call these patterns *worldview congruence situations*. Figure 13.2 highlights the five basic worldview congruence situations for the supervisory triad. Clients, counselors, and supervisors may alternatively complement and conflict with each other on

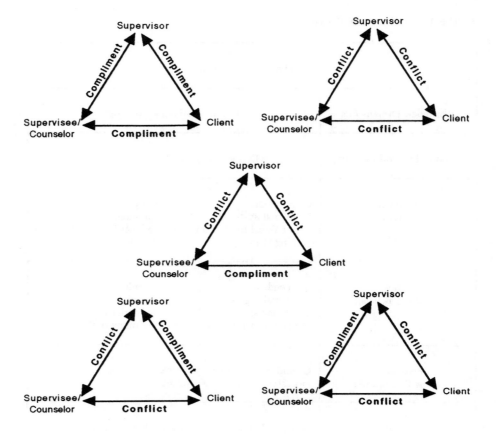

Figure 13.2. The Five Possible Worldview Congruence Scenarios for the Supervisory Triad

each of the eight worldview dimensions, resulting in the possibility of 40 potential scenarios (5 worldview situations × 8 worldview dimensions).

Worldview conflicts within the triadic relationship may result in distrust, hostility, and resistance. Although it is not always necessary for all parties in the relationship to have congruent worldviews, it is critical that the supervisor and counselor/supervisee be aware of potential worldview incongruities that might disrupt the therapeutic and supervisory process. Knowledge of one's own worldview perspectives is an initial step, with assessment of the worldviews of the other parties in the triadic relationship as a secondary step.

Given the possibility of cross-cultural worldview conflicts, supervisors and supervisee/counselors may find it helpful to gain an understanding of their worldview and how worldview conflicts play a role in the therapeutic and supervisory relationship. In Figure 13.3, we illustrate five worldview congruence positions that could occur in one supervisory triad.

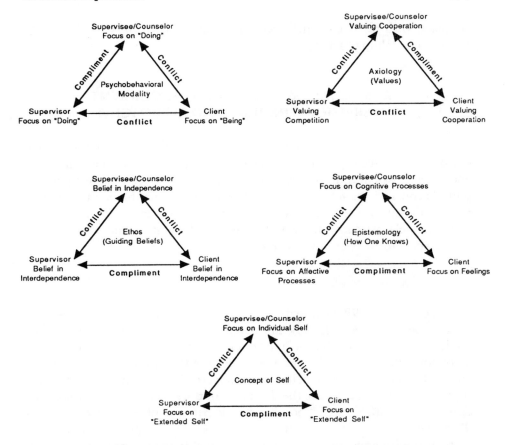

Figure 13.3. Possible Worldview Positions in One Supervisory Triad Occurring on Five Worldview Dimensions

As one can see, in terms of Triad 3, for the ethos worldview dimension, the worldview incongruence occurs for belief in independence versus belief in interdependence. For the supervisor, it would be helpful to help the supervisee learn to identify the ways in which this conflict might affect therapy. It would also be helpful for the supervisor to assist the supervisee/counselor in increasing his or her awareness of how his or her belief in independence might influence their therapeutic approach and intervention choices.

In the example given in Triad 2, for the axiology worldview dimension, the worldview incongruence arises because the supervisor values "seeking help," whereas both the supervisee/counselor and client value "saving face." In this case, it might be necessary for the supervisor to help the supervisee identify how valuing "saving face" might play out in the counseling relationship by exploring a parallel process in the supervisory relationship. It might also be necessary for the supervisor to examine with the client the ways that collusion with the client might occur in regard to both the client's and the counselor's valuing "saving face."

CROSS-CULTURAL RELEVANCE OF CURRENT SUPERVISION THEORIES AND APPROACHES

Quite a few models of supervision exist but only one addresses cross-cultural issues (see Loganbill et al., 1982), and, unfortunately, that one model addresses cross-cultural concerns superficially. What we have done up to this point is consider the relevant cross-cultural dimensions that are likely to influence the supervision process. We now review the major classes of supervision models currently offered in the published literature and critique them with respect to cross-cultural issues.

Psychodynamic Models

As Holloway (1992) pointed out, models of supervision first paralleled the major schools of psychotherapy. The psychoanalytic school presented the first model of supervision. The supervisory process is highly dogmatic in nature, involving psychoanalysis for the supervisee, intensive work on self-awareness and understanding, and modeling of the supervising analyst. The goal of the supervisory process is to use the dynamics of the supervisor-supervisee relationship to "work through" nontherapeutic patterns of relating with others (Russell et al., 1984). Consistent with psychoanalytic approaches to psychotherapy, the supervisory process imposes a rigid frame for interpreting client and supervisee behaviors and attitudes. The supervisory process would seem to require the supervisee to abandon personal perspectives and background experiences in favor of those expounded and modeled by the supervisor/ analyst. Furthermore, the culture-bound nature of interpretation limits the introduction of cultural specific information pertinent to either the client or the counselor-supervisee. Psychoanalytic approaches, among many others, emphasize that most problems, in both content and process, are a function of intrapsychic rather than societal forces within the client (in the case of counseling) and/or the counselor/supervisee (in the case of supervision) (see Atkinson et al., 1993; Sue, 1981; Sue & Sue, 1990; Sue & Zane, 1987). The cultural imposition that occurs as an inevitable result of psychotherapeutic supervision is viewed as appropriate and essential to supervisee development.

Observational Supervisory Methods

The ability to directly observe the behaviors of therapist/supervisee and client appears to have generated more contemporary approaches to supervision (Holloway, 1992). The major focus of these approaches is the operationalization of Rogers's (1957) and Truax and Carkhuff's (1967) facilitative conditions. Those conditions are predicated upon a view of human beings as positive, growth-directed beings who would develop appropriately if the conditions were present. The objective of phenomenological approaches such as the approach of Rogers is to train the supervisee to create and effectively communicate the therapeutic conditions. The use of direct observational methods led to the description of discrete counseling behaviors (i.e., microskills) that are used to train supervisees/counselors.

Ivey (1987) indicated, however, that the appropriateness of various counseling behaviors is likely to be dependent upon the cultural perspective of the client. We would add that the appropriateness of counseling and supervision behaviors is dependent upon the cultural perspectives of all parties to the supervisory process. It is possible, therefore, that cultural conflict between the supervisor and supervisee can surface with respect to microskills usage, such as the use of direct confrontation or self-disclosure (see Sue, 1981). Furthermore, to the extent that observational approaches to supervision are based on phenomenological approaches such as person-centered psychotherapy, they are flawed by the same cultural biases that plague other talk-oriented, intrapsychic-oriented approaches. Also, there is a lack of empirical evidence supporting the relationship between exhibiting high levels of facilitative behavior and positive therapeutic outcome (Russell et al., 1984); it may be that unexplored cultural dimensions mediate the relationship.

Group Supervision

As Holloway (1992) pointed out, group supervision approaches represent another evolution in the development of supervisory models. Group supervisory approaches rely on the multiple feedback of additional parties to the supervisory process, though the focus has chiefly been on increasing the self-awareness of a counselor/supervisee's interpersonal style and behavior. To the extent that group supervision can be utilized to elicit alternate cultural perspectives concerning counseling *and* supervisory relationships (Gibbs, 1985), it could be a very effective supervisory approach. The usefulness of group supervision as a means of increasing the cultural relevance of supervision is probably positively correlated to the degree of cultural heterogeneity present in the group.

Behavioral Models

Behavioral theories have been the source for several more approaches to supervision (e.g., Jakubowski-Spector, Dustin, & George, 1971). Common to these approaches, according to Russell et al. (1984), is the identification of specific skills and behaviors that make up each stage of the counseling process, and the application of learning principles to the reinforcement of those skills and behaviors and to the extinguishing of inappropriate behaviors. The major criticism of behavioral approaches to supervision is that they appear to oversimplify the counseling process (Russell et al., 1984), ignoring some of the interaction dynamics that characteristically surface in cross-cultural encounters, such as client cultural restraints on self-disclosure or counselor denial of culturally dissonant components of client problems (Atkinson et al., 1993).

Cross-Theoretical Models

There exist other models of supervision based upon theories of counseling such as rational-emotive therapy (see Wessler & Ellis, 1983), client-centered therapy (see Patterson, 1983), and social learning theory (see Hosford & Barmann, 1983). However, these have been criticized for providing few directions for research and practice, and for being inconsistent with the observation that supervisors do not practice supervision in the same way as they practice counseling (Holloway, 1992). Holloway (1992) pointed out that, over time, recognition that the practice of psychotherapy is different from that of teaching psychotherapy has given rise to "cross-theoretical" models of supervision. These models, according to Russell et al. (1984), incorporate knowledge of individual differences, social role theory, and instructional psychology. There are two major cross-theoretical approaches (Holloway, 1992): social role models and developmental models.

Social Role Models

Holloway (1992) observed that a number of supervisory approaches (i.e., Bernard, 1979; Littrell, Lee-Borden, & Lorenz, 1979) emphasize a set of roles for the supervisor that establish certain expectations and attitudes about what functions a supervisor will perform. Supervisor actions that are consistent with role expectations will promote behavioral consistency and certainty for the supervisee/counselor. These approaches have already been criticized for their lack of specificity (Russell et al., 1984) and for the lack of research testing the models (Holloway, 1992; Russell et al., 1984). What has yet to be established, on either a conceptual or an empirical level, is the possible role of between-group and within-group cultural variables in shaping or mediating the formation of efficacious expectations and attitudes.

Expectations and attitudes are products of a person's cultural perspective. If a supervisor engages in a role that interacts unfavorably with that expected by a supervisee, there can be conflict. Given that supervisors and therapist trainees rely upon their social power to influence the attitudes and behaviors of supervisees and clients, respectively (see Strong, 1968), how the influencers' roles are perceived by those they hope to influence can affect their perceived credibility and attractiveness; such perceptions will ultimately affect their ability to exert their influence.

Developmental Models

Several models present clinical supervision as a process possessing sequential and qualitatively distinct stages through which the supervisor and the supervisee/counselor pass (Littrell et al., 1979; Russell et al., 1984). These models represent the latest development in the evolution of supervisory models and theories. They generally assume that formal training is necessary for a supervisee's skills to improve, which is a cultural bias in itself. Supervisees, for example, may believe that they need an *academic credential* in order to practice counseling and psychotherapy, but they may not believe that traditional approaches to counseling and psychotherapy training will enhance their repertoire of therapeutic skills. Quite to the contrary, they may actually believe that current training approaches will rob them of the ability they have developed prior to entry into the training program.

Developmental models of supervision have been influenced by theorists such as Chickering (1969) and Erikson (1963), who proposed models of universal psychosocial development chiefly predicated on studies of people in Western societies. The first of two categories of these supervisory models (see Russell et al., 1984) proposes clearly defined stages of supervisee development, often predicated upon a trainee's position in the training hierarchy (namely, prepracticum, practicum, and internship), in which specific issues or developmental tasks must be resolved before progressing. Supervisory models that fit in this category include Hogan's (1964), Littrell et al.'s (1979), and Stoltenberg's (1981) models. Common to these notions is the assumption that novice counselors need more structure and instruction than experienced counselors. We believe that cultural conflict and misunderstanding are most likely to surface in the earliest stages of the supervisory process because of the power differential in the supervisor-supervisee roles as described by the models. If not handled properly, we believe the early stages of supervision along the lines of those models will result in cultural oppression for both the client and the counselor. Such oppression is unlikely to be experienced by a trainee in the last stages of those models because if the supervisee/counselor has survived up to that point, the trainee is likely to be a well-indoctrinated (culturally assimilated) entity, and because the models allow a more collegial relationship between the supervisor and supervisee to engage in a mutually growthful experience.

A second category of developmental supervisory models exists that incorporates a step-by-step, cyclical process of conflict resolution and skill mastery of various issues encountered in professional training. The models of Ekstein and Wallerstein (1972), Delaney (1972), and Loganbill et al. (1982) are examples of this second group of models. These models allow for much more mutuality in the relationship between the supervisor and the supervisee for joint problem solving than occurs in the early stages of the first category of developmental supervision models. Indeed, one model (Loganbill et al., 1982) explicitly identifies the issue of respect for individual differences for skill mastery and conflict resolution, though it is the only such model that does so. Nonetheless, the Loganbill et al. model ignores the influence of supervisor and supervisee cultural backgrounds on clinical supervision. Instead, the model focuses solely upon the importance of a trainee's acquiring counseling skills and facilitative attitudes with respect to a client's cultural frame of reference.

Neither category of supervision model explicitly articulates the potential interaction between clients, counselors/supervisees, and supervisors of different racial, ethnic, and cultural characteristics. Nor does either address the salient cross-cultural dimensions and dynamics to which focus should be given in supervision. We argue that a new development in supervisory model building is needed that explicitly addresses the cultural characteristics of all supervisory parties, the dynamics of their interaction, and the process of working through cross-cultural dilemmas in supervision and counseling.

NEEDED CONCEPTUAL
AND EMPIRICAL DIRECTIONS

Current Studies

Only two studies could be located in the published psychological literature in which the role of cultural and racial characteristics in supervision was investigated. In the first study, Vander Kolk (1974) found that Black supervisees anticipated less supervisor empathy, respect, and congruence than White supervisees. In the second study, Cook and Helms (1988) studied the responses of four racial/ethnic groups—Asian, Black, Hispanic, and Native American—concerning factors affecting the quality of cross-cultural clinical supervision. They found that supervisor liking and conditional liking were related positively to satisfaction with supervision. Especially noteworthy were findings that supervisees' perceptions of their supervision relationships with largely White supervisors varied according to their race/ethnicity. Furthermore, only two of five relationship dimensions (supervisor's liking and emotional discomfort) were rated positively.

A third study (Ladany, Pannu, & Brittan, 1994) is currently unpublished but presents findings worthy of note. Offered as a test of Helms's (1990) model of racial identity interaction in the context of counselor supervision, the authors investigated the influence of racial identity interaction and racial matching on supervisory working alliance and the supervisee's perception of the supervisor's influence on his or her cross-cultural competence. Notwithstanding numerous methodological shortcomings, findings appeared to indicate that racial identity was related to supervisory alliance and the supervisee's perception of the influence of the supervisor on his or her cross-cultural competence. The three sets of findings suggest that additional empirical study and conceptualization concerning cross-cultural supervision are warranted, but the call has yet to be heeded.

Current Conceptualizations in Cross-Cultural Counseling

Much has been written about the culture-bound nature of counseling and psychotherapy (Atkinson et al., 1993; Casas, 1984; Sue, 1981; Sue & Sue, 1990; Sue & Zane, 1987), but little has been written addressing the culture-bound nature of the supervision process. Of those who have addressed cross-cultural issues in training and education (e.g., D'Andrea & Daniels, 1991; Hunt, 1987; Leong, 1993; Leong & Kim, 1991; Locke, 1990; McRae & Johnson, 1991; Parker, Valley, & Geary, 1986; Ponterotto & Casas, 1987; Swanson, 1993), most writers have delineated the structure of counseling training as well as the needed training experiences necessary for producing multicultural competence. Regarding training structures, writers have argued for the presence of racially and ethnically diverse faculty and students, an articulated commitment to addressing training issues with respect to multicultural populations, modification of the core curriculum to ensure appropriate conceptual and experiential preparation to conduct effective therapy with diverse others, and contact with diverse client groups. With respect to needed training experiences, writers have addressed the need to develop trainee knowledge, skill, and attitudes relevant to counseling across cultures. In order to accomplish this, most writers have argued for trainee assessment of cultural attitudes and knowledge, expanding the knowledge base through reading ethnic literature and taking classes in ethnic studies, developing culturally sensitive attitudes through various self-awareness programs, and expanding social and counseling contact with ethnically and racially diverse others.

Very few writers have presented a discussion of possible cross-cultural issues in clinical supervision. Peterkin (1983) and Morgan (1984) wrote about their experiences supervising pastoral care and psychiatric trainees, respectively. Both of the authors spoke about the language barriers that surfaced, even in supervising individuals using "English." They also addressed the success they experienced with their supervisees when they forthrightly addressed the role of cultural differences in their supervisory sessions in shaping their views of the client, supervisee, and the counseling and supervisory processes. Morgan suggested that cultural and racial differences in supervision might pose problems that exceed those encountered in counseling because the supervisee may not be as free to escape the hierarchical and, possibly, oppressive environment of the supervisory relationship, whereas clients can quit counseling altogether. Holiman and Lauver (1987) discussed the use of co-counseling, direct observation, and video recording to examine culture-based difference in perceptions of clients. The authors emphasized that their approach would be useful in exploring counselor perception filters; they appeared to assume that supervisor perceptual filters would not require exploration.

Brinson and Kottler (1993) did not address counselor supervision per se, but they did address a number of issues surfacing in cross-cultural mentoring that we believe generalize to the supervisory relationship. The following issues were highlighted as sociocultural factors impeding cross-cultural mentoring and could, in our opinion, impede the supervisory process: issues of trust, managing power relations, the unwillingness of the "underling" to express a need for help, the readiness to believe that the trainee/mentee is judged and treated differently, feelings of isolation, and cross-cultural misunderstandings. None of these issues has been addressed in existing supervisory models.

Because of the nature of ethnic and race relations in the United States, it is reasonable for racially and ethnically different others to approach one another cautiously. That caution is likely to be at high levels in supervisory relationships, in which European Americans are more likely to be the supervisors and racial and ethnic others are more likely to be the supervisees. Hence specific power dynamics will need to be carefully managed: paternalism and oppression on the part of the supervisor and internalized racial oppression (Landrum & Batts, 1985; Landrum-Brown, 1990) on the part of the supervisee. Internalized racial oppression is the conscious and unconscious psychological response exhibited by individuals to racism. It is characterized by psychosocial reactions to internalized stereotypes and other negative messages regarding one's racial distinctness, and is exhibited in the following ways: system beating, blaming the system, denial of racial heritage, avoidance and rejection of Whites and Eurocentric systems, and lack of understanding of the political and psychosocial significance of race and racism. For example, "system beating," as described by Landrum and Batts (1985) and Landrum-Brown (1990), would include psychosocial reactions such as manipulation of others or the system through guilt, games, and illicit activities; acting out anger and aggression; playing dumb; clowning; and being "invisible." As it pertains to cross-cultural supervision, system beating might involve the client's acting out in ways that would perpetuate racial stereotypes to avoid therapeutic intervention; for example, a client might take on a "bad nigga" role in order to frighten his or her counselor and take control over the therapy session. For a counselor/supervisee it might involve manipulating the supervisor's guilt regarding racism in order to avoid certain training experiences. Effective supervision of these circumstances would be to appropriately identify the behavior as acting out or manipulative and to facilitate the counselor's understanding of how the behavior is playing out in the therapeutic process, possibly as resistance.

Because of the determination and focused persistence often necessary for racially and ethnically diverse others to move successfully up the academic ladder, and also because of the pride that is likely to result from this success, many non-European Americans may find it difficult to ask for and receive help. They may believe that to do so will simply feed into the negative stereotypes that they have been fighting all along. Ironically, the failure experiences that often result from not asking for or accepting help feed the very stereotypes that the individual is seeking to avoid.

Relatedly, supervisees of a different race or ethnicity may be particularly sensitive and resistant to corrective feedback. When this sensitivity is added to the sense of isolation and "fishbowlism" that many non-European Americans may experience in their graduate training programs, it is easy to see how cultural misunderstandings can become significantly problematic to the supervisory relationship and lead to the unconscious but systematic filtering out of such persons from the profession. Unfortunately, more racial and ethnically diverse persons are needed in the profession.

Supervisees may wish to maintain their cultural consciousness as well as what they may believe to be the cultural relevance of their therapeutic approaches. They may resist supervisory interventions in order to protect those approaches. Research and theory have yet to show how the cultural relevance of therapeutic and supervisory approaches is to be evaluated and developed.

What is urgently needed is an expansion of current supervisory models to incorporate the intercultural dynamics embodied in Figure 13.1. A logical starting place might be an integration of our supervisory process model with Loganbill et al.'s (1982) developmental model of supervision. For example, Loganbill et al.'s discussion of the assessment of the supervisee could be greatly expanded to address the cultural interplay between the supervisee/counselor, supervisor, and client; Loganbill et al. discussed only the dynamics of the supervisor-supervisee interaction and failed to frame it as a possible cross-cultural encounter. As another example, Loganbill et al.'s discussion of the supervisee developmental issue of respect for individual differences focused only on the counselor's need to appreciate client differences in backgrounds, values, and physical appearance. They failed to see that supervisors have these same issues with respect to both the client *and* the supervisee/counselor.

Important Research Variables

Recently, Holloway (1992) reviewed the research literature on supervision and determined that it could be organized around the following themes: individual and cultural characteristics of the participants, domain-specific expectations and goals, supervisory relationship, teaching objectives and strategies, evaluation, and institutional factors. We will discuss some needed research directions in each of these areas with respect to cross-cultural issues.

Individual and Cultural Characteristics

We were unable to locate any study that examined the impact of a supervisor's ethnicity, race, or cultural characteristics on important supervision variables. As Figure 13.1 shows, dimensions of difference are expected to interact with those of the supervisee/counselor and client to affect the supervisory process. Investigators have sought to determine ideal supervisor characteristics, the impact of supervisor experience and theoretical orientation, and the influence of supervisor gender. It is still unclear, however, whether supervisor race/ethnicity and/or cultural characteristics affect how a supervisor is perceived by supervisees. Further, the impact of supervisor race/ethnicity and cultural characteristics is unexplored for a number of important dependent variables: supervisor satisfaction, supervisee satisfaction with supervision, preferences for interpersonal power bases, interpersonal influence and attraction, supervisee evaluations, supervisor effectiveness, and role expectations.

With the exception of two studies (Cook & Helms, 1988; Vander Kolk, 1974), investigations of the role of ethnicity/race and cultural characteristics of the supervisee have not appeared in the published literature with respect to the supervisory process. A number of important questions have yet to be asked and answered. Are there preferences for certain types of supervisees? How are culturally different supervisees perceived and evaluated by their supervisors? Do those perceptions interact with supervisor characteristics? These are a few of many questions currently unexplored by supervisory investigators. In addition, there is a need to study whether supervisee ethnicity, race, and cultural variables, either alone or in interaction with cognitive characteristics and experience level, influence the typical supervisee variables: supervisory needs, acquisition of counseling skills, in-session cognitions, reactions to supervisory style, supervisory problems or issues, supervisee ratings, evaluations of supervisee, preference for supervisory activities, satisfaction with supervision, and role expectations. Again, it should be noted that supervisee characteristics may be found to interact with supervisor and client characteristics on those supervisee variables.

The possible influence of matching supervisor and supervisee characteristics on trainee satisfaction and performance has been studied, but not with respect to ethnicity, race, and cultural characteristics. Possible additional dependent variables in such studies could be interpersonal influence and attraction, supervisory satisfaction, acquisition of counseling skills, evaluation of supervisee, and evaluation of supervisor.

Given the model of the supervisory process depicted in Figure 13.1, it will not escape the reader that client characteristics affect the counseling relationship with the counselor/supervisee, and may influence the supervisory relationship. However, the possible influence of client characteristics on supervision has generally escaped empirical scrutiny. Such a state of affairs is surprising, given the general assertion by the profession that the counseling relationship needs to become more culturally relevant to multicultural others. Because of the role of supervision in shaping the architecture of counseling, it makes sense that client cultural and racial characteristics might influence the content and process of counseling and, as a consequence, be found to influence the content and process of clinical supervision. An important line of future research would be to investigate the possible effect of client characteristics, particularly cultural characteristics, on clinical supervision. We venture that those characteristics might be found to interact with those of the counselor/supervisee and supervisor.

Because of the likely interactions among the worldview perspectives of client, counselor/supervisee, and supervisor, we suggest that an examination of the impact of cultural congruence between supervisory constituents on supervisory content, process, and outcome variables might be a useful area of inquiry.

Other Areas of Study

In the area of counselor/supervisee and supervisor role expectations and goals, it has yet to be investigated whether culturally different others hold different role expectations and goals for counseling and supervision. Do culturally different others approach the supervision activity in a different way?

The quality and characteristics of the supervisory relationship have been the chief outcome measure for many supervision studies (Holloway, 1992), but, of the few measures of supervision in existence, none have incorporated aspects of intercultural dynamics. Furthermore, none have been applied to the evaluation of cross-cultural supervision. An interesting issue for study might be the evaluation of supervision in cases in which the client is ethnically, racially, and/or culturally dissimilar from the counselor/supervisee and/or supervisor: Does supervision in these circumstances tend to be evaluated differently from supervision in which the client is not dissimilar? In addition, it has yet to be studied whether supervisee skill and learning are affected by cross-cultural dynamics of the supervisory process. Finally, we have no data concerning whether the quality of cross-cultural supervision encounters is different from homocultural supervision encounters; a study in this area might utilize content analysis of supervision transactions.

Might the training objectives and strategies of supervision vary according to the cross-cultural dynamics incorporated in the supervisory process? Might different strategies differ in effectiveness depending upon the cultural characteristics of the constituents of the supervisory process? These are two questions that come to our minds as we consider the area of supervision research concerning supervisory objectives and strategies.

Supervision research focusing on evaluation has not yet incorporated cross-cultural competence in trainee or supervisor performance evaluations. Consistent with some of the research in the area, trainees' cross-cultural competence in both counseling and supervision needs to be evaluated, along with that of the supervisor in supervision. However, although strides have been made with respect to counselor cross-cultural competence (see, for example, D'Andrea, Daniels, & Heck, 1991), no such innovations appear to have been made with respect to supervision.

Finally, if organizational variables associated with the training program affect supervision (Holloway, 1992), then it follows that the climate of the training institution with respect to cultural diversity affects the cross-cultural dynamics of counseling and supervision. To date, the influence of organizational variables on supervision has rarely been studied, and the role of cultural diversity has not been studied at all.

REFERENCES

American Psychological Association, Education and Training Committee of Division 17. (1980, September). *Cross-cultural competencies: A position paper.* Paper presented at the annual meeting of the American Psychological Association, Montreal.

Atkinson, D. R., Morten, G., & Sue, D. W. (1993). *Counseling American minorities: A cross-cultural perspective.* Madison, WI: Brown & Benchmark.

Atkinson, D. R., & Thompson, C. E. (1992). Racial, ethnic, and cultural variables in counseling. In S. D. Brown & R. W. Lent (Eds.), *Handbook of counseling psychology* (2nd ed., pp. 349-382). New York: John Wiley.

Bernard, J. M. (1979). Supervisor training: A discrimination model. *Counselor Education and Supervision, 19,* 60-68.

Bradley, R. W. (Ed.). (1987). Special section: Discussion on multicultural counseling. *Counselor Education and Supervision, 26*(3), 162-191.

Brinson, J., & Kottler, J. (1993). Cross-cultural mentoring in counselor education: A strategy for retaining minority faculty. *Counselor Education and Supervision, 32,* 241-253.

Casas, J. M. (1984). Policy, training, and research in counseling psychology: The racial/ethnic minority perspective. In S. D. Brown & R. W. Lent (Eds.), *Handbook of counseling psychology* (pp. 785-831). New York: John Wiley.

Chickering, A. W. (1969). *Education and identity.* San Francisco: Jossey-Bass.

Codina, G. E., & Montalvo, F. F. (1994). Chicano phenotype and depression. *Hispanic Journal of Behavioral Sciences, 16,* 296-306.

Cook, D. A., & Helms, J. E. (1988). Visible racial/ethnic group supervisee's satisfaction with cross-cultural supervision as predicted by relationship characteristics. *Journal of Counseling Psychology, 35*(3), 268-274.

Cross, W. E., Jr. (1971). The Negro-to-Black conversion experience. *Black World, 7,* 13-27.

Cross, W. E., Jr. (1978). The Cross and Thomas models of psychological Nigrescence. *Journal of Black Psychology, 5,* 13-19.

D'Andrea, M., & Daniels, J. (1991). Exploring the different levels of multicultural counseling training in counselor education. *Journal of Counseling and Development, 70*(1), 78-85.

D'Andrea, M., Daniels, D., & Heck, R. (1991). Evaluating the impact of multicultural training. *Journal of Counseling and Development, 70,* 143-150.

Delaney, D. J. (1972). A behavioral model for practicum supervision of counselor candidates. *Counselor Education and Supervision, 12,* 46-50.

Ekstein, R., & Wallerstein, R. S. (1972). *The teaching and learning of psychotherapy* (2nd ed.). New York: International Universities Press.

Erikson, E. H. (1963). *Childhood and society* (2nd ed.). New York: Norton.

Gibbs, J. T. (1985). Can we continue to be color-blind and class-bound. *The Counseling Psychologist, 13*(3), 426-435.

Gottfredson, L. S. (1986). Special groups and the beneficial use of vocational interest inventories. In W. B. Walsh & S. H. Osipow (Eds.), *Advances in vocational psychology: Vol. 1. Assessments of interests* (pp. 127-198). Hillsdale, NJ: Lawrence Erlbaum.

Helms, J. E. (Ed.). (1990). *Black and White racial identity: Theory, research, and practice.* Westport, CT: Greenwood Press.

Hines, P. M., & Garcia-Preto, N. (Eds.). (1992). A special issue: Multicultural practice. *Families in Society, 73*(6), 323-384.

Hogan, R. A. (1964). Issues and approaches in supervision. *Psychotherapy: Theory, Research, and Practice, 1*, 1739-1741.

Holiman, M., & Lauver, P. J. (1987). The counselor culture and client-centered practice. *Counselor Education and Supervision, 26*(3), 184-191.

Holloway, E. L. (1992). Supervision: A way of teaching and learning. In S. D. Brown & R. W. Lent (Eds.), *Handbook of counseling psychology* (2nd ed., pp. 117-214). New York: John Wiley.

Holloway, E. L., & Dunlap, D. M. (1989, April). *The power of involvement in the supervision relationship.* Paper presented at the annual meeting of the American Education Research Association, Boston.

Hosford, R. E., & Barmann, B. (1983). A social learning approach to counselor supervision. *The Counseling Psychologist, 11*(1), 51-58.

Hunt, P. (1987). Black clients' implications for supervision of trainees. *Psychotherapy: Theory, Research, and Practice, 24*(1), 114-119.

Ivey, A. E. (1987). Cultural intentionality: The core of effective helping. *Counselor Education and Supervision, 26*(3), 168-172.

Jakubowski-Spector, P., Dustin, R., & George, R. L. (1971). Toward developing a behavioral counselor education model. *Counselor Education and Supervision, 10*, 242-250.

Ladany, N., Pannu, R., & Brittan, C. S. (1994, August). *Supervisory racial identity interaction, the supervisory alliance, and cultural competence.* Paper presented at the annual convention of the American Psychological Association, Los Angeles.

Landrum, J., & Batts, V. (1985, August). *Helping Blacks cope with and overcome the personal effects of racism.* Paper presented at the annual meeting of the American Psychological Association, Los Angeles.

Landrum-Brown, J. (1990). Black mental health and racial oppression. In D. S. Ruiz (Ed.), *Handbook of mental health and mental disorder among Black Americans* (pp. 113-132). New York: Greenwood Press.

Leong, F. T. L. (1993). The career counseling process with racial-ethnic minorities: The case of Asian Americans. *Career Development Quarterly, 42*(1), 26-40.

Leong, F. T. L., & Kim, H. H. W. (1991). Going beyond cultural sensitivity on the road to multiculturalism: Using the Intercultural Sensitizer as a counselor training tool. *Journal of Counseling and Development, 70*(1), 112-118.

Littrell, J. M., Lee-Borden, N., & Lorenz, J. (1979). A developmental framework for counseling supervision. *Counselor Education and Supervision, 19*, 129-136.

Locke, D. C. (1990). A not so provincial view of multicultural counseling. *Counselor Education and Supervision, 30*, 18-25.

Loganbill, C., Hardy, E., & Delworth, U. A. (1982). A conceptual model for supervision. *The Counseling Psychologist, 10*, 3-43.

McRae, M. B., & Johnson, S. D., Jr. (1991). Toward training for competence in multicultural counselor education. *Journal of Counseling and Development, 70*(1), 131-135.

Morgan, D. W. (1984). Cross-cultural factors in the supervision of psychotherapy. *Psychiatric Forum, 12*(2), 61-64.

Myers, L. J. (1991). Expanding the psychology of knowledge optimally: The importance of world view revisited. In R. L. Jones (Ed.), *Black psychology* (3rd ed., pp. 15-28). Berkeley, CA: Cobb & Henry.

Nichols, E. (1976, November). *The philosophical aspects of cultural differences.* Paper presented at the conference of the World Psychiatric Association, Ibadan, Nigeria.

Nobles, W. (1972). African philosophy: Foundation for Black psychology. In R. L. Jones (Ed.), *Black psychology* (1st ed., pp. 18-32). New York: Harper & Row.

Parham, T. A. (1989). Cycles of psychological Nigrescence. *The Counseling Psychologist, 17*, 187-226.

Parker, W. M., Valley, M. M., & Geary, C. A. (1986). Acquiring cultural knowledge for counselors in training: A multifaceted approach. *Counselor Education and Supervision, 26*(1), 61-71.

Patterson, C. H. (1983). A client-centered approach to supervision. *The Counseling Psychologist, 11*(1), 21-26.

Pedersen, P. B. (Ed.). (1991). Multiculturalism as a fourth force in counseling [Special issue]. *Journal of Counseling and Development, 70*(1).

Peterkin, J. (1983). A White Australian woman's reflections on supervising Black students in America. *Journal of Pastoral Care, 37*(2), 98-102.

Ponterotto, J. G., & Casas, J. M. (1987). In search of multicultural competence within counselor education. *Journal of Counseling and Development, 64*, 430-434.

Rogers, C. (1957). Training individuals to engage in the therapeutic process. In C. R. Strother (Ed.), *Psychology and mental health* (pp. 76-92). Washington, DC: American Psychological Association.

Russell, R. K., Crimmings, A. M., & Lent, R. W. (1984). Counselor training and supervision: Theory and research. In S. D. Brown & R. W. Lent (Eds.), *Handbook of counseling psychology* (pp. 625-715). New York: John Wiley.

Savickas, M. L. (Ed.). (1993). A symposium on multicultural career counseling [Special issue]. *Career Development Quarterly, 42*(1).

Smith, E. M. J., & Vasquez, M. J. T. (Eds.). (1985). Cross-cultural counseling. *The Counseling Psychologist, 13*(4), 531-684.

Stoltenberg, C. (1981). Approaching supervision from a developmental perspective: The counselor complexity model. *Journal of Counseling Psychology, 28*, 59-65.

Strong, S. R. (1968). Counseling: An interpersonal influence process. *Journal of Counseling Psychology, 15*, 215-224.

Sue, D. W. (1981). *Counseling the culturally different.* New York: John Wiley.

Sue, D. W., Bernier, J. E., Durran, A., Feinberg, L., Pedersen, P., Smith, E., & Vasquez-Nuttall, E. (1982). Position paper: Cross-cultural counseling competencies. *The Counseling Psychologist, 10*, 45-52.

Sue, D. W., & Sue, D. (1990). *Counseling the culturally different: Theory and practice.* New York: John Wiley.

Sue, S., & Zane, N. W. S. (1987). The role of culture and cultural techniques in psychotherapy: A critique and reformulation. *American Psychologist, 42*, 37-45.

Swanson, J. L. (1993). Integrating a multicultural perspective into training for career counseling: Programmatic and individual interventions. *Career Development Quarterly, 42*(1), 41-49.

Truax, C. B., & Carkhuff, R. R. (1967). *Toward effective counseling and psychotherapy: Training and practice.* Chicago: Aldine.

Vander Kolk, C. J. (1974). The relationship of personality, values, and race to anticipation of the supervisory relationship. *Rehabilitation Counseling Bulletin, 18*, 41-46.

Wessler, R. L., & Ellis, A. (1983). Supervision in counseling: Rational-emotive therapy. *The Counseling Psychologist, 11*(1), 43-50.

14

The Assessment of Multicultural Counseling Competencies

DONALD B. POPE-DAVIS

JONATHAN G. DINGS

IN RECENT YEARS, mental health researchers have stressed the importance of counseling professionals' meeting the needs of clients who are culturally different (Pope-Davis & Ottavi, 1994; Sue & Sue, 1990). Concern about this issue has stimulated counselors and educators to provide more focused multicultural training and preparation so that future counseling professionals can appropriately respond to an emerging culturally diverse population (Pedersen, 1988; Sue & Zane, 1987). In support of this notion, recent ethical guidelines for psychological practice with ethnic, linguistic, and culturally diverse populations (American Psychological Association, 1993) have strongly encouraged professionals to become multiculturally competent. These guidelines include standards for psychologists and counselors to become culturally aware, knowledgeable, and skilled in working with culturally diverse populations. However, the general inclusion and implementation of multicultural counseling competencies appears to be occurring slowly (Sue & Sue, 1990) and is in need of a more focused approach.

Concern regarding multicultural counseling competencies was initiated with the publication of a multicultural position paper by Sue et al. (1982). These authors described multiculturally competent counselors as those who have moved from being culturally unaware to being aware and sensitive to their own cultural issues and to the ways that their own values and biases affect culturally diverse clients. Multiculturally competent counselors also consider factors such as the impact of the sociopolitical system on people of color in the United States, have knowledge and information about particular cultural groups, and are able to generate a wide range of appropriate verbal/ nonverbal responses to client needs. Overall, multiculturally competent counselors are comfortable with differences that exist between the counselor and client in race and beliefs and are sensitive to circumstances that may suggest referral of the clients to members of their own race or culture (Sue et al., 1982; Sue, Arredondo, & McDavis, 1992). Other researchers have supported these multicultural counseling competencies in counseling practice, research, and training (Casas, Ponterotto, & Gutierrez, 1986; Ibrahim & Arredondo, 1986), as well as with instructional training materials that address multicultural counseling issues (Pope-Davis, Prieto, Reynolds, & Vazquez, 1994; Pope-Davis, Reynolds, & Vazquez, 1992).

Although these are all necessary and appropriate steps in the right direction, what is lacking in this discussion is the important role that counselor training must play if multicultural competencies are to become a permanent part of the profession. At issue are three general concerns:

1. What counseling abilities are necessary to work effectively in multicultural counseling situations?
2. What assessment tools are available to measure the success of training programs in imparting these abilities to counselors?
3. What are the limitations of these resources?

THE CONSTRUCT: MULTICULTURAL COUNSELING COMPETENCIES

Multicultural counseling competencies are centered on (a) understanding the different experiences of members of various cultural groups, (b) understanding the barriers to communication across cultures that exist as a result of these differences, and (c) possessing a specific set of abilities that can potentially make a counselor culturally skilled. Cultural groups, in the broadest sense, can be considered predominantly in terms of racial and ethnic differences and similarities, as well as in terms of differing regional and national origin, socioeconomic status, sexual orientation, gender, language, and so on. In using the word *cultural* with regard to multicultural counseling competencies, the emphasis is not on any specific differences (e.g., the counseling of African American clients by White American counselors), but rather on the effects of multicultural barriers, and on understanding the different experiences of other cultural groups.

The construct of multicultural counseling competencies must be distinguished from that of counseling competencies. Some combination of aware-

ness, knowledge, and skills attributed to successful counselors, such as positive regard for others (Rogers, 1951), an ability to communicate effectively, and an understanding of various counseling techniques and strategies, is a necessary but insufficient basis for success in multicultural counseling. Likewise, a sophisticated understanding of the role of culture in individuals' lives and the effect of communication style differences among culturally diverse groups on interaction across cultures are very useful in communicating with individuals of different cultural backgrounds, but are not sufficient as a basis for successful multicultural counseling. A construct related to cultural awareness, racial identity, may also be important to the extent that possessing self-understanding in terms of one's own racial identity plays a role in attaining multicultural counseling competencies. The importance of racial identity in this process is suggested in the counselor training model proposed by Sabnani, Ponterotto, and Borodovsky (1991), as well as by research documenting a relationship between White racial identity development and multicultural counseling competencies among counseling graduate students (Ottavi, Pope-Davis, & Dings, 1994).

COMPONENTS OF
MULTICULTURAL COUNSELING COMPETENCIES

One important description of the construct of multicultural competencies is provided by Sue et al. (1982). Written under the joint authorship of many of the most eminent multicultural counseling scholars in the field, this chapter delineates several characteristics of the multiculturally competent counselor: four beliefs/attitudes descriptors, three skills descriptors, and three knowledge descriptors. These competencies focus on awareness of self and others, sensitivity, general counseling knowledge, knowledge of certain cultural groups distinct from one's own, and skill at verbal and nonverbal communication. Although useful beginnings of a description of multicultural counseling competency, these competencies need further clarification. Too much is left to the reader in trying to discern, for example, what counts as being "able to exercise institutional intervention" on a client's behalf. This description of multicultural counseling competencies appears to overestimate some readers' ability to augment the words on the page in interpreting the 11 characteristics, leaving the conception of the construct a bit too general.

With continued interest in multicultural counseling competencies, an updated and greatly expanded description was recently published (Sue et al., 1992). In this revised edition, 31 attitudes/beliefs, skills, and knowledge competencies are delineated within a framework of three "proposed cross-cultural competencies and objectives": "counselor awareness of own cultural values and biases," "counselor awareness of clients' world view," and "culturally appropriate intervention strategies" (pp. 484-486; also see Appendix III of this volume). Statements of 9 proposed attitudes/beliefs, 11 knowledge components, and 11 skills provide a specific description of what a multiculturally competent counselor should feel, know, do, and have already done. The set of values, awarenesses, and sensitivities delineated under the heading of attitudes and beliefs within each proposed competency describes an open-minded counselor who has made efforts to understand him- or herself in the broader context of a culture, both as a person and as a counselor. Knowledge is described specifically, but in a manner that goes beyond listing requisite facts. Making this kind of list would require an oversimplification of a complex understanding or else a nearly endless task. The competent counselor must understand *how* "race, culture, ethnicity, and so forth may affect personality formation, vocational choices, manifestation of psychological disorders, help-seeking behavior, and the appropriateness or inappropriateness of counseling approaches" (p. 485). Skills are explained mostly in behavioral terms of communicating effectively and obtaining or having obtained assistance and training from fellow counselors and other sources of information on multicultural counseling. For some competencies, this dimension overlaps with the other two both in content and in its focus—for example, "Culturally skilled counselors are not averse to seeking consultation with traditional healers and religious and spiritual leaders and practitioners in the treatment of culturally different clients when appropriate" (p. 486). This example reads very much like an attitude description. However, it could readily be reworded into behavioral terms by substituting *seek* in place of *are not averse to seeking*. Wording aside, some degree of conceptual overlap between skills, attitudes/beliefs, and knowledge is unavoidable. If the complex activity of multicultural counseling could be thoroughly described by presenting a list of mutually exclusive components, then it would be little more than a conglomeration of simple activities.

In many instances, this most recent list of competencies provides a state-of-the-art delineation of multicultural counseling competencies, including specific descriptions of knowledge, skills, and attitudes/beliefs of the multiculturally competent counselor. The descriptors contained in this list strike a reasonable balance between attempting to detail every imaginable aspect of competence and the generalities of the earlier effort (Sue et al., 1982), yielding a substantive basis for training and research. Finally, this list does not include a fourth dimension of multicultural counseling competency proposed by Sodowsky, Taffe, Gutkin, and Wise (1994), that of a multicultural counseling relationship. According to Sodowsky et al., this dimension is best defined as the ability to develop a personal (therapeutic) interaction between a counselor and a client from a different culture. This construct includes "the counselor's interactional process with the minority client, such as the counselor's trustworthiness, comfort levels, stereotypes of the minority client, and world view" (p. 142).

INSTRUMENTS DESIGNED TO ASSESS
MULTICULTURAL COUNSELING COMPETENCIES

There are currently three self-report measures of multicultural counseling competencies: the Multicultural Awareness-Knowledge-Skills Survey (MAKSS) (D'Andrea, Daniels, & Heck, 1991); the Multicultural Counseling Inventory (MCI) (Sodowsky et al., 1994); and the Multicultural Counseling Awareness Scale (MCAS-B) (Ponterotto, Rieger, Barrett, & Sparks, 1994; Ponterotto, Sanchez, & Magids, 1991). A fourth instrument, the Cross-Cultural Counseling Inventory (CCCI) (Hernandez & LaFromboise, 1985), was designed for use by supervisors in evaluating counselors' multicultural counseling competencies; a revised edition (CCCI-R) has been developed (LaFromboise, Coleman, & Hernandez, 1991).

In this chapter, the MAKSS, MCI, and MCAS-B will be examined at some length. Because it is designed for evaluation of counselors by their supervisors, the CCCI-R has a decidedly different focus from the self-report measures and is better evaluated by comparison with other instruments used by supervisors in rating counselors' competencies, rather than by comparison with three self-report measures. The CCCI-R was also developed much earlier than the other instruments and has amassed a comparatively large amount of validity-related evidence, giving it a relatively advantageous position in any comparison across all four instruments. Finally, the CCCI-R is a single-factor scale providing a global measure of multicultural counseling competencies, whereas the MAKSS, MCAS-B, and MCI are multifactor instruments yielding three, two, and four scales, respectively. Each of the self-report measures was developed with explicit reference to the Sue et al. (1982) multicultural counseling competency position paper, suggesting a common standard on which they can be compared. A general overview of the three instruments is presented in Table 14.1. They share the purpose of assessing multicultural counseling competencies and were all designed for use with counselors and students in counseling programs.

Multicultural Awareness-
Knowledge-Skills Survey (MAKSS)

Instrument Development

The MAKSS is a 60-item instrument containing three scales of 20 items each. Eight additional questions are included to identify the participant and gather demographic information. As the instrument's name implies, the three scales are Awareness, Knowledge, and Skills. Items 1 through 20 are Awareness scale items, 21 through 40 are Knowledge scale items, and 41 through 60 are Skill scale items. A 4-point rating system is employed, with responses ranging

TABLE 14.1 A Comparison of the Multicultural Awareness Knowledge and Skills Survey (MAKSS), the Multicultural Counseling Inventory (MCI), and the Multicultural Counseling Awareness Scale-B Revised (MCAS-B)

Property	MAKSS	MCI	MCAS-B
Item sources	Instructional objectives	Literature review	Literature review
Subscales	Awareness Knowledge Skills	Awareness Knowledge Skills Relationship	Awareness Knowledge/Skills (and untested Social Desirability)
Scale development	A priori, theory driven; "confirmed" by questionable use of F.A., small N	F.A. driven, with concern for interpretation; best half of original items.	Card-sort and F.A. driven; somewhat selective among items
Scale type	4-point rating (mixed types)	4-point rating	7-point rating
Reliability	Adequate	Adequate	Adequate
Validity evidence overall	Minimal	Superior	Approaching adequacy for one scale, little for the other
Interpretation	Rather unclear; no normative data given	Fairly straight-forward; more normative data needed	Complicated by scaling and factor structure concerns; more normative data needed
Scoring	Addition of scale items	Average of scale items	Addition of scale items

from *very limited* (1) to *very good* (4) for the majority of items, including all items on the Skills scale; *very limited* (1) to *very aware* (4) for three items on the Awareness scale; and *strongly disagree* (1) to *strongly agree* (4) for the remainder of the instrument. Within each scale, points are added together to form a scale score ranging from 20 to 80. Reverse scoring is employed for seven negatively worded items (11 through 16, and 38), most of which are contained in the Awareness scale.

Awareness

Two examples are as follows: "At this point in your life, how would you rate your understanding of the impact of the way you think and act when interacting with persons of different cultural backgrounds?" (*very limited* to *very aware*). "Ambiguity and stress often result from multicultural situations because people are not sure what to expect from each other" (*strongly disagree* to *strongly agree*).

Knowledge Scale

Two general formats are used, examples of which are: "At the present time, how would you rate your own understanding of the following terms: *ethnicity* (*very limited* to *very good*); *cultural encapsulation* (*very limited* to *very good*)." "In the early grades of schooling in the United States, the academic achievement of such ethnic minorities as African Americans, Hispanics, and Native Americans is close to parity with the achievement of White mainstream students" (*strongly disagree* to *strongly agree*).

Skill Scale

Outright self-ratings are employed throughout this scale, for example: "How would you rate your ability to conduct an effective counseling interview with a person from a cultural background significantly different from your own?" (*very limited* to *very good*). "How well would you rate your ability to identify the strengths and weakness of psychological tests in terms of their use with persons from different cultural/racial/ethnic backgrounds?" (*very limited* to *very good*).

Reliability and Interscale Correlation

Reported Cronbach's alpha reliabilities are .75, .90, and .96 for the Awareness, Knowledge, and Skills scales, respectively (D'Andrea et al., 1991, p. 145). Pretest and posttest interscale correlations are presented in Table 14.2. These suggest that related but not identical dimensions are being measured.

Validity-Related Evidence

Of the three scales, Skills is the most straightforward and readily discerned. All items begin with "How well would you rate your ability to . . ." and conclude with a description of a desirable multicultural counseling ability. This scale depends on the quality and integrity of each respondent's self-reported self-perceptions, and is in addition sensitive to response set by virtue of the absence of reverse-scored items.

Both Awareness and Knowledge are more subtle in their approach, each including a variety of response categories and at least one reverse-scored item. Knowledge includes 8 items that essentially could have been presented in the form of a true-false test and 12 items on which respondents report the extent to which they perceive themselves to understand a given term. One difficulty with this latter format is that as a counselor gains greater insight into a given concept, such as racism (Item 23), he or she may develop an appreciation of

TABLE 14.2 Intercorrelations of MAKSS Subscales and Reliabilities

Variables	1	2	3	4	5	6
1. Knowledge (Pretest)	.90[a]					
2. Awareness (Pretest)	.45	.75[a]				
3. Skills (Pretest)	.51	.32	.96[a]			
4. Knowledge (Posttest)						
5. Awareness (Posttest)				.32		
6. Skills (Posttest)			.11	.48		

SOURCE: Data extracted from D'Andrea et al., 1991.
a. Reliabilities.

the depth and complexity of the concept from the standpoint of which his or her understanding seems somewhat lacking and is thereby rated lower. For the novice, who has learned about racism briefly without a certain depth of understanding, a definitional understanding may seem deserving of the highest rating. In this regard, the 12 "self-rating" items of the Knowledge scale seem somewhat less dependable indicators of knowledge relative to the 8 seemingly true-false items. Overall, this scale would probably benefit from having a greater percentage of its items reverse-scored.

The Awareness scale's relatively low reliability (.75, in comparison with .90 and .96 for Skill and Knowledge, respectively) can be explained in a somewhat positive light by noting the variety of item and response formats and the large number of reverse-scored items it contains. Whereas the other two scales are sensitive to response sets, the Awareness scale changes from item to item. In terms of content, it asks for a self-rating outright only six times. Because this scale is placed first, carryover effects from Knowledge items are avoided. However, after initial presentation of all or most of the Awareness scale items, it would prove useful to this instrument as a whole to mix the order of presentation of items across subscales to guard against the effects of response sets.

No indicators of impression management or self-deception (Paulhaus, 1991) are provided in this instrument, which is somewhat of a weakness for a self-report measure in the affective domain. The instructions promise that test results will be confidential and that the respondent will not be subjected to adverse consequences (e.g., a poor grade, in the context of a training program) in an apparent attempt to dissuade test takers from responding in a socially desirable fashion. Its success in this regard is unknown.

Criterion-related validity evidence is based upon a few relatively small samples that are made up of two racial groups (one sample is mostly Asian, the other mostly White). Graduate students in counselor education programs make up the samples, which is consistent with the purpose of the instrument noted by its authors: to provide a means of evaluating the success of training programs. As reported by the authors, two separate investigations with differing samples yielded essentially similar results: statistically significant increases in MAKSS scores for the treatment group receiving relevant training (t test yielding $p < .01$ for each scale), the absence of statistically significant differences within the control group (t test, $p = .05$), and statistically significant difference scores between treatment and control groups on each scale (Mann-Whitney Wilcoxon Rank Sum Test, $p < .02$). In a third investigation, a treatment-group-only design yielded statistically significant increases in all scales (t test, $p < .01$). These results provide some evidence of criterion-related validity in that relevant experience has the expected outcome of an increased score on each scale of the MAKSS.

The use of intact groups without random assignment to treatment and control groups in the first two studies (as noted by the authors as well, D'Andrea et al., 1991, p. 147) and small numbers of participants ($N = 11$ in the control group for the second study) raise some concern about the statistical soundness of these results and their generalizability to the larger population of counseling graduate students. Although these limitations appear to reflect the practical reality of working with populations of counseling students at a given institution, the study of a greater range and number of institutions should be undertaken. Statistical information describing graduate students' performance should be presented as well. Mean scores, for example, would provide a potentially useful point of reference for users wishing to make a norm-referenced interpretation on the basis of MAKSS results.

Evidence related to construct validity is presented by the authors predominantly in the form of factor analysis results employing a small sample ($N = 90$) and an analysis strategy whereby each factor was considered individually against alternatives to a one-factor solution (i.e., the 20 items making up a given scale were analyzed separately from the other 40). Although this procedure yielded very favorable results for the Knowledge and Skills scales and somewhat mixed but relatively favorable results for the Awareness scale, a far stronger case for construct validity could have been made by pooling the three scales' items and finding support for a three-factor solution employing the particular items selected for each scale. Item-scale correlations could also be provided as additional evidence related to construct validity. Some favorable construct validity evidence resides in the internal consistency reliability figures presented above as well.

The authors' primary claim to content validity resides in the derivation of their items from specified instructional objectives (D'Andrea et al., 1991, p. 144, as derived from Sue et al., 1982). This procedure is not described in adequate detail to be evaluated fully as evidence related to validity. Secondary evidence of content validity is presented by the authors in the form of having found a matching MCAS Awareness scale item for 18 of 20 MAKSS Awareness items. Again, the procedure for determining what counts as a match is not presented in any detail (e.g., agreement of a certain number of expert judges), making evaluation of this evidence nearly impossible. In any case, this evidence of content validity is somewhat weakened by the fact that the MAKSS Awareness scale has only begun to amass favorable evidence related to validity.

In summary, there is a need for far more validity-related evidence to be presented in support of this instrument. Currently existing evidence of validity is somewhat thin by most standards, although some of this is the result of small sample sizes. Additional data collection is necessary, as is a revised statistical approach to construct validity. It would be worthwhile to show that the various scales on this instrument are appropriately correlated with similar measures of multicultural counseling skills, awareness, and knowledge, not as highly correlated with similar but distinct constructs such as general multicultural awareness and general counseling skills, and negatively correlated with racism, ethnocentrism, and other attitudes that are opposite those of a multiculturally skilled counselor.

Multicultural Counseling Inventory (MCI)

Instrument Development

This instrument was developed "in order to operationalize some of the proposed constructs of multicultural counseling competencies" (Sodowsky et al., 1994, p. 139). The authors reviewed the counseling literature to determine the qualities of a multiculturally skilled counselors, and presented a detailed list of these qualities (Sodowsky et al., 1994). From this list and several qualities reflecting general skills, a large pool of items was generated and administered to a large ($N = 604$) sample of psychology graduate students and members of three professional counseling associations from the same midwestern state. Participants were asked to "indicate how accurately each statement describes you when working in a multicultural counseling situation" by using a 4-point rating scale ranging from *very inaccurate* to *very accurate* or by checking a "do not know" option. Several open-ended questions were included in which participants were asked to describe their multicultural counseling strengths and weaknesses, as well as their reactions to the questionnaire.

After the elimination of a single item on the basis of more than 20% of the respondents' endorsing "do not know," pair-wise item correlations were examined using factor analysis. A four-factor solution was chosen on the basis of a scree plot of the eigenvalues and factor interpretability. Following a Varimax rotation, items that failed to load on a given factor at .33 or higher, or that failed to meet criteria (Sodowsky et al., 1994), were dropped. The remaining items were examined to arrive at the following names for the four dimensions: Multicultural Counseling Skills (11 items), Multicultural Awareness (10 items), Multicultural Counseling Knowledge (11 items), and Multicultural Counseling Relationship (8 items).

Skills Scale

As described by the authors, the Skills scale includes items "referring to success with retention of minority clients, recognition of and recovery from cultural mistakes, use of nontraditional methods of assessment, counselor self-monitoring, and tailoring structured versus unstructured therapy to the needs of minority clients" (Sodowsky et al., 1994, p. 141), as well as items referring to general counseling skills. Sample items: "I monitor and correct my defensiveness (e.g., anxiety, denial, minimizing, overconfidence)"; "I use several methods of assessment (including free response questions, observations, and varied sources of information and excluding standardized tests)"; "I am able to be concise and to the point when reflecting, clarifying, and probing" (answered with five other Skills items at the end of the inventory, in response to the changed directions: "When working with all people").

Awareness Scale

The Awareness scale is made up of items reflecting "proactive multicultural sensitivity and responsiveness, extensive multicultural interactions and life experiences, broad-based cultural understanding, advocacy within institutions, enjoyment of multiculturalism, and an increase in minority case load" (Sodowsky et al., 1994, p. 142). Sample items: "When working with international students or immigrants, I have knowledge of legalities of visa, passport, green card, and naturalization"; "I enjoy multicultural interactions as much as interactions with people of my own culture."

Knowledge Scale

This scale refers to "culturally relevant case conceptualization and treatment strategies, cultural information, and multicultural counseling research" (Sodowsky et al., 1994, p. 142). Sample items: "I include such issues as age, gender roles, and socioeconomic status in my understanding of different minority cultures"; "I use the natural support system (e.g., family, extended kin, friends, elders, and folk healers) of minorities in a differentiated and specific manner."

Relationship Scale

The Relationship scale refers to aspects of "the counselor's interactional process with the minority client such as the counselor's trustworthiness, comfort level, stereotypes of the minority client, and world view" (Sodowsky et al., 1994, p. 142). Sample items: "I perceive that my race causes the person to mistrust me"; "I have feelings of overcompensation, oversolicitation, and guilt that I does not have when working with majority clients"; "I am confident

TABLE 14.3 Intercorrelations of MCI subscales, With Reliabilities on Diagonal

Variables	1	2	3	4
1. Knowledge	.80	.21	.41	.41
2. Skill		.81	.21	.39
3. Awareness			.80	.18
4. Relationship				.67

SOURCE: Data extracted from Study 2 sample used in Sodowsky et al., 1994.

that my conceptualization of client problems does not consist of stereotypes and biases."

Reliability and Intercorrelation of Scales

Scale internal consistency reliabilities (Cronbach's alpha) and correlations are reported in Table 14.3. These suggest that related but not identical constructs are being measured and that items within each scale perform consistently, particularly when scale length is taken into account.

Validity-Related Evidence

As a check on scale interpretability, graduate students who had recently completed a series of multicultural counseling lectures and readings were asked to evaluate the accuracy of each dimension name and the completeness with which the items included sampled the named domain. Seventy-five to 100% of the 14 raters agreed with the names selected, and 100% agreed that the content coverage was adequate and representative within each domain.

Graduate students from the same university were also asked to rate the performance of a videotaped counselor demonstrating either a "culturally consistent counseling perspective" (Sodowsky et al., 1994, p. 140) or a discrepant perspective. Significant differences in the expected direction were obtained at the $p < .001$ level for the initial MANOVA and for subsequent ANOVAs on each scale and the total scale. These results constitute criterion-related evidence of validity, as do the results of a further study employing a pretest-posttest approach to assess the effect of a multicultural counseling course taken by 42 master's and doctoral students. Significant increases were found at the .005 level for the total scale and every scale except for Relationship, which yielded a small, nonsignificant increase.

An examination of discriminant validity was provided in the original study by comparing scores of participants who indicated that more than 50% of their work was in multicultural services with the scores of those who indicated that less than 50% of their work was in multicultural services. Because only 82 participants fell into the former group, an equal number was selected at random from the latter group (i.e., the remainder of the sample). After significant MANOVA results ($p < .001$), ANOVAs were performed on each scale and the total scale, yielding significant differences in the expected direction for the total scale ($p < .001$), the Awareness scale ($p < .001$), and the Relationship scale ($p < .02$). ANOVAs for Skills ($p < .06$) and Knowledge ($p < .13$) approached but failed to achieve statistical significance at the .05 level, yielding small differences in the expected direction—that is, with participants having more than 50% of their work in multicultural services demonstrating higher scores.

Sodowsky et al. (1994) reported results of a study of factor stability using responses from 300 counselors from a random sample of university-affiliated counseling centers nationwide. These results were compared with the original study, yielding similar reliabilities and slightly lower interscale correlations. These data yielded favorable results in terms of "factor congruence" (Gorsuch, 1983) and in terms of confirmatory factor analysis, with a four-factor, oblique solution yielding a goodness-of-fit index of .84.

In a criterion-referenced context, meaningful interpretation relies to a great extent on the user's ability to place a meaning upon a score that accurately reflects the manner in which the respondents have answered the questions. In this regard, the MCI is both strong and weak. It is strong in that these averaged scale scores deliver a result ranging from 1.0 to 4.0 that can be referenced by each point of the rating scale employed. A 3.0 indicates that the participant considers the counseling descriptors in that scale to be, on the average, a "somewhat accurate" description of himself or herself when working in a multicultural counseling situation. The MCI appears somewhat weak, however, in terms of the range of responses endorsed with regard to the distinction among the highest scores on the rating scale: *Somewhat accurate* and *very accurate* leave relatively little room between them. Given the nature of counseling, if the behaviors referenced in the item stem are ones that counselors have used or experienced in a multicultural counseling situation, a rating lower than 3 seems relatively unlikely. A rating lower than 2 seems very unlikely unless the item describes a practice or approach to which the respondent is philosophically or pragmatically opposed, or that is genuinely unknown to the respondent (and the respondent is entirely honest in this self-evaluation). The question of whether an adequate range is included is further raised by the scores found in the ANOVA comparisons: Only the Awareness scale yielded a difference bigger than .2 (with differences reported only to the tenths place, a .7 difference was recorded) or a score outside the range of 3.1 to 3.5 (2.4 was the "less than 50% work" group mean score on Awareness).

To the extent that construct-related evidence of validity can be considered in component parts, this instrument is adequate. Its content-related evidence of validity seems good for an instrument of its type, although not quite sufficient by the standards applied to standardized tests. Criterion-related evidence of validity is mostly favorable but somewhat lacking in quantity; future research should provide some needed additional information in this regard, although preliminary evidence has been obtained suggesting that MCI scores are not influenced by social desirability (Sodowsky et al., 1994). Construct-related evidence is favorable as well. In general, its items focus more explicitly on behaviors than on attitudes relative to the other instruments considered in this study. In this regard, the MCI may provide the most behaviorally based assessment of self-reported multicultural counseling competencies.

Multicultural Counseling Awareness Scale-Form B: Revised Self-Assessment (MCAS-B)

Instrument Development

The MCAS-B was developed from a pool of items written by the authors to assess awareness, skill, and knowledge. One hundred and thirty-five items were generated from an examination of the counseling literature, with a particular concentration on several noted authors. Seventy items remained after the authors combined, revised, or eliminated redundant or unclear items. Three independent card sort procedures were employed to provide a check on the classification of items as representing awareness, skill, or knowledge, with the result that two categories of items (knowledge and skills combined, and awareness) emerged rather than the original three. In order to counteract potential difficulties associated with response sets, about half of the awareness items were then converted to negatively scored items. These 70 items were then presented to five external experts ("published researchers in multicultural counseling," Ponterottó et al., 1991, p. 9), who rated each favorably on the basis of clarity and domain appropriateness. A 7-point rating scale was decided upon, with descriptors at 1 (not at all true), 4 (somewhat true), and 7 (totally true), and the instructions, "Using the following scale, rate the truth of each item as it applies to you."

Pilot testing used a purposefully diverse sample (N = 126) made up of undergraduate and graduate counseling students and practicing counselors from the greater New York City area, in addition to 10 experts in multicultural counseling. An examination of the resulting statistical characteristics of the items in each scale and factor analysis, as well as item content specifications, led to the adoption of two scales for the instrument: a Knowledge/Skills scale and an Awareness scale. Item analysis was used to eliminate skewed items (means above 6.25 or below 1.75), range-restricted items (responses falling on less than 6 of the 7 scale points), low item-total correlation items (less than .2), low factor loadings (i.e., less than .35), and multiple high-factor-loading items (greater than .35). After addition of an awareness item and three "social desirability" items, the revised version of the MCAS-B contained 14 Awareness items and 28 Knowledge/Skills items. As for the impact of Awareness subscale revisions on the instrument, confirmatory factor analysis conducted by Ponterotto et al. (1993) on a pool of four samples of counselors and counseling students (total $N = 414$) was found to provide only limited support for the two-factor model.

Knowledge/Skills Scale

The Knowledge Skills scale employs 28 items related to general counseling knowledge and specific multicultural counseling knowledge. Sample items: "I am familiar with the research and writing of Paul B. Pedersen and I can discuss his work at length spontaneously"; "I am aware of the individual differences that exist within members of a particular ethnic group based on values and beliefs, and level of acculturation"; "I am aware of certain counseling skills, techniques, or approaches that are more likely to transcend culture and be effective with any client."

Awareness Scale

The Awareness scale is made up of 14 items measuring counselors' awareness of multicultural issues. Ten are reverse-scored. Sample items: "I am aware that the use of standard English with a lower-income or bilingual client may result in misperceptions of the client's strengths and weaknesses"; "I feel that different socioeconomic status backgrounds of counselor and client may serve as an initial barrier to effective cross-cultural counseling."

Social Desirability Cluster

One of the three items in the Social Desirability cluster, "I am familiar with the research and writing of Michael Santana-Devio and I can discuss his work at length spontaneously," is evidently designed to examine impression management (Paulhaus, 1991) in that the person named is fictitious. This seems reasonable, given the large number of items worded in the same exact way for important authors in the Knowledge/Skills scale. The nature of the remaining items is not as clear, and the three-item Social Desirability cluster has not been piloted adequately to provide unambiguous interpretations, as noted by Ponterotto et al. (1991). The cut score suggested by Ponterotto et al. for invalidating the results of the questionnaire, 15 out of a possible 21, should probably be revised downward. On the fictitious author item noted above, any response other than "1" (*not at all true*) would appear to suggest an outright lie on the part of the respondent.

Reliabilities and Interscale Correlations

For the original sample used by the authors, each scale and the instrument as a whole (not including the social desirability items and the additional Awareness item) demonstrated adequate coefficient alpha reliabilities: Awareness,

.78; Knowledge/Skills, .93; total instrument, .92. Awareness and Knowledge/ Skills evidenced a small, positive (.14) and large, positive (.97) correlation with the total score, respectively, and a moderate positive correlation with each other (.37). This correlation suggests that the scales measure different constructs, and the reliabilities indicate consistency within each scale before the adjustments are made to the awareness scale.

Validity-Related Evidence

A regional sample consisting of graduate students and practicing counselors from the greater New York City area was augmented by a sample of 10 experts on multicultural counseling in providing evidence related to discriminant validity. Statistically significant differences were observed on the Knowledge/Skills scale, with higher scores being obtained by non-White ethnic group members relative to Whites, doctoral students relative to master's students and bachelor's degree students, master's students relative to bachelor's degree students, multicultural workshop/seminar attendees relative to nonattendees, and those who had explicit multicultural course work relative to those having none. However, no such differences were found on the Awareness scale. Similar results have been obtained in more recent studies employing the revised scales. Pope-Davis, Reynolds, and Dings (1994) found moderate correlations of Knowledge/Skills with multicultural course work, workshop hours, and supervision in a sample of counseling interns ($N = 112$). A statistically significant but low correlation ($r = .18$) was found for Awareness and supervision. Similarly, Pope-Davis, Dings, and Ottavi (1995) found moderate correlations between Knowledge/Skills and multicultural course work and workshop hours for a sample of practicing counselors ($N = 126$). In this study, Awareness exhibited a moderate negative correlation with age, and gender exhibited a moderate correlation with each scale. Correlations from both studies are presented in Table 14.4.

Ponterotto et al. (1993) found evidence of convergent and divergent validity in comparing MCAS-B subscales with a measure related to multicultural knowledge and skills (a self-report adaptation of the Cross-Cultural Counseling Inventory-Revised) and a measure related to awareness (New Racism Scale [NRS]; Jacobson, 1985). Correlations of .44 and .16 ($N = 68$) of this version of the CCCI-R with Knowledge/Skills and Awareness, respectively, were reported. These correlations were in the predicted direction, because the CCCI-R is more a measure of knowledge than awareness. Correlations of .16 and .49 ($N = 42$) for the Knowledge/Skill and Awareness scales were found with the NRS. They also were in the expected direction, in that both the MCAS Awareness scale and the NRS measure bias. Ponterotto et al. also found no significant correlations between the Marlowe-Crowne Social Desirability Scale (Crowne & Marlowe, 1960) and each of the MCAS-B scales: .22 with Knowledge/Skills, and .00 with Awareness ($N = 45$). As for the impact of Awareness subscale revisions on the factor structure of this instrument and

TABLE 14.4 Intercorrelations of MCAS Scales and Demographic and
Educational Variables

Variables	1	2	3	4	5	6	7	8
1. Knowledge/Skills	—							
2. Awareness	.39***	—						
3. Gender	.34***	.39***	—					
4. Age	−.09	−.35***	.06	—				
5. Year in program	−.12	−.36***	.22***	.64***	—			
6. MC workshop hours	.40***	.09	.20*	.06	.05	—		
7. MC course work	.32***	.11	.23**	−.16*	.30***	.33***	—	
8. MC supervision	.05	.07	.03	.18*	.04	.07	−.10	—

SOURCE: Data extracted from sample used in Pope-Davis, Dings, & Ottavi, 1995.
NOTE: MC = multicultural counseling. Knowledge/Skills and Awareness are subscales of the Multicultural Counseling Awareness Scale (MCAS).
* = $p < .05$; ** = $p < .01$; *** = $p < .001$.

the tenability of its two-factor approach to self-reported multicultural counseling competency, confirmatory factor analysis conducted by Ponterotto et al. (1993) on a pool of four samples of counselors and counseling students (total $N = 414$) was found to provide only limited support for the two-factor model.

As a newly developed instrument, the MCAS-B is still in the process of having validity evidence gathered. The usefulness of the instrument and the possibility of future revisions may be better considered after the results of factor analysis are replicated in future studies, particularly with regard to obtaining more encouraging confirmatory factor analysis results than those of Ponterotto et al. (1993), and if favorable validity-related evidence is obtained in general. The Awareness scale is at present of questionable value overall and remains to be validated more extensively in terms of experimental and correlational results, unless the nature of the construct awareness is deemed not to vary across groups of counselors. Some items appear to contain either two clauses or two objects as a result of using the word *and*, with the implication that respondents may be responding to either or both of these stimuli.

Although the authors based their adoption of the two-scale structure on the confluence of results from the card sort procedures and a factor analysis, the combination of Knowledge and Skills into a single scale does raise some face validity concerns regarding meaningful interpretation of the scale. And even though the authors explicitly did not adopt the Sue et al. (1982) delineation of competencies (or any other) as their sole theoretical model in instrument building, and were therefore not particularly bound by a priori concerns in scaling, the combination of knowledge and skills suggests that one dimension is being measured, not two. One possibility in this regard is that until it can be demonstrated that counseling skills are being evaluated by these items, the authors should consider dropping *skills* from the scale name. The usefulness of the total scale as distinct from the Knowledge/Skills scale is questionable, given their extremely high correlation. Ponterotto et al. (1993) recommended that their findings be interpreted cautiously and noted the need for additional and more rigorous testing.

The unique contribution of the MCAS-B lies in an effort to assess social desirability, although additional items and pilot testing are needed before this scale can be used effectively. The weaknesses detailed above generally undermine interpretability of the Awareness scale, whereas relatively favorable results are obtained for the Knowledge/Skills scale despite conceptual and interpretation difficulties arising from the combination of Knowledge and Skills.

COMPARISONS ACROSS INSTRUMENTS

Comparisons Involving MAKSS

Of the three self-report instruments, the MAKSS relies most heavily on the literature, employing a content-consideration-driven method of scaling. The absence of a statistical selection process for determining the items that ultimately make up each subscale and the relative dearth of validity-related evidence for this instrument are important weaknesses. Given these limitations, the most likely use for the MAKSS is in examining student performance relative to course work objectives in cases in which the course used for this comparison shares the content upon which MAKSS items and scales were based. It would be useful to have additional information such as a table of specifications in determining just how well the subdomains of knowledge, awareness, and skills are represented in the MAKSS relative to the MCI and MCAS-B. Considering the relative weakness of the awareness scales of the other two instruments, the other potential uses of the MAKSS rest with the possibility that it may have an awareness scale as good as that of the other instruments. However, it must be stressed that a greater amount of validity-related evidence is required before this possibility can be evaluated scientifically.

On its face, the MAKSS appears to be more like the MCAS-B than the MCI in terms of item content, given its focus on self-perceptions of feelings and beliefs rather than behaviors. The only empirical comparison involving this instrument examined the MAKSS and the MCI, finding a moderate correlation between the full scales of each instrument (as noted by Sodowsky et al., 1994).

TABLE 14.5 Means, Standard Deviations, and Minimum and Maximum
Self-Ratings for MCI and MCAS Scales

	Mean	SD	Min.	Max.
MCAS Scale				
Total	218.15	23.33	168	273
Knowledge/Skills	131.79	20.01	81	182
Awareness	86.36	6.62	63	98
MCI Scale				
Total	3.12	.28	2.56	3.72
Skills	3.45	.29	2.86	4.00
Knowledge	3.23	.38	2.18	3.91
Awareness	2.71	.53	1.40	3.80
Relationship	2.89	.44	1.88	3.88

SOURCE: Data extracted from sample used in Pope-Davis & Dings, 1994.

Comparison of MCI and MCAS-B

Pope-Davis and Dings (1994) presented descriptive and correlational data
from an administration of both instruments to a sample of 92 interns. Means,
standard deviations, and minimum and maximum ratings for MCI and
MCAS-B scales are reported in Table 14.5. The mean of interns' ratings is
above the midpoint for each MCI scale, most markedly for Skill, for which
the mean is 3.45. This can be interpreted in the context of the 4-point rating
scale to suggest that the interns consider the statements in the Skill scale, for
example, to be about evenly divided, on the average, between "somewhat accurate" and "very accurate" descriptions of their counseling behaviors. Not
surprisingly, scale standard deviations appear to reflect greater range of scores
and centrality of mean scores, with greater variability being evidenced by the
scales' having means closer to the midpoint (2.5), excepting total score. For
the MCAS-B, interns' means were far above the midpoint for each scale, with
midpoints equal to 49, 98, and 147 for Awareness, Knowledge/Skill, and total
score, respectively. The Awareness scale exhibited the least central mean score,
as well as the smallest standard deviation and range. Interpretation of these
scores is somewhat less clear than for the MCI, with the Awareness mean of
86.36 suggesting that the interns consider the Awareness statements, on
average, to fall between 6 and 7 on the scale (from 1, *not at all true*, to 7, *totally
true*). The three-item Social Desirability scale was included in the questionnaire to maintain its integrity, but not used to remove any completed questionnaires, as no participant obtained a Social Desirability score high enough
to be excluded from this study on the basis of the cut score suggested by
Ponterotto et al. (1993).

Interscale correlations, with reliabilities on the diagonal (in boldface)
and disattenuated correlations above the diagonal (in italics) are presented in

TABLE 14.6 Intercorrelations of MCAS and MCI Subscales, With Reliabilities on Diagonal and Disattenuated Correlations Above Diagonal

Variables	1	2	3	4	5	6	7	8
1. MCAS Knowledge/Skill	**.90**	.47	.70	.33	.65	.09	.63	1.07
2. MCAS Awareness	.38	**.71**	.32	.47	.28	.10	.35	.76
3. MCI Knowledge	.58	.24	**.76**	.54	.72	.21	.95	.68
4. MCI Skill	.27	.35	.41	**.76**	.34	.56	.88	.39
5. MCI Awareness	.54	.21	.55	.26	**.77**	.25	.95	.64
6. MCI Relationship	.07	.07	.15	.40	.18	**.67**	.72	.10
7. MCI Total	.55	.31	.77	.71	.77	.55	**.86**	.64
8. MCAS Total	.96	.61	.56	.33	.53	.08	.56	**.90**

SOURCE: Data extracted from sample used in Pope-Davis & Dings, 1994.

Table 14.6. On the basis of the observed reliabilities and correlations, several conclusions can be put forward about the performance of the MCI and the MCAS-B for this sample of interns. First, coefficient alpha reliabilities indicate that each scale performs adequately with regard to internal consistency. Even the lowest coefficient alpha, .67 for MCI Relationship, is acceptable for a scale of its length, although a longer version of this eight-item scale would be preferable if appropriate items could be obtained. Second, the observed interscale correlations within each instrument are fairly comparable to those obtained in previous studies, suggesting that each instrument is not performing in an unusual manner for the current sample. Two unrelated MCI interscale correlations are somewhat low (Skill with Awareness, $r = .26$, and Knowledge with Relationship, $r = .15$), and the single MCAS-B interscale correlation, $r = .38$, is an almost exact replication of the .39 correlation reported by Pope-Davis, Reynolds, and Dings (1994) and the .37 correlation noted by Ponterotto et al. (1991).

Because the interscale correlations within the instruments and the internal consistency of each scale suggest that there are no substantial difficulties within any of the scales or for either instrument as a whole, it is reasonable to examine observed interscale correlations across instruments as indicators of the comparability of the constructs being measured by each scale employing a multitrait multimethod approach (Campbell & Fiske, 1959). In contrast to the pattern of similarity among same-name and shared-name scales across instruments, the scale intercorrelations suggest that different constructs are being measured at every level. For the Awareness scales, the disattenuated correlation of .28 indicates that they share less than 10% of their variance.

MCAS-B Knowledge/Skills has its highest disattenuated correlation (.70) with MCI Knowledge, showing that only about half of their variance is shared. In addition, a disattenuated correlation of practically the same magnitude (.65) is found between MCAS-Knowledge/Skill and MCI Awareness. In other words, for this sample, MCAS-B Knowledge/Skill is about as similar to MCI Awareness as it is to MCI Knowledge, which is also about as similar as MCI Awareness and Knowledge are to each other. In any case, this level of disattenuated correlation indicates that the scales are not nearly similar enough to be judged to be measuring the same construct. Approximately the same level of relationship is observed between the two total scores, suggesting that the differences in the construct being measured are more pervasive than a matter of a single scale differing. Finally, the disattenuated correlation of 1.07 between MCAS-B Total and MCAS-B Knowledge suggests that there is little value in considering these scores separately, and the disattenuated correlation of .33 between MCAS-B Knowledge/Skill and MCI Skills indicates a low degree of relationship.

The task of explaining the differences between these two instruments is a more complicated matter than examining a table of correlations, but would be easier if both instruments had already accumulated a substantial quantity of evidence related to validity for use in assessing multicultural competency. With a larger sample, confirmatory factor analysis and related techniques might be used to cast light on the statistical performance of individual items in each scale and in the broader context of both instruments. Yet given the differences evidenced in interscale correlations, the use of factor analysis is not likely to inform this inquiry beyond providing a somewhat more detailed indication of which items provide the most promising source of a complex explanation of the differences between the MCI and MCAS-B. Given this sample and such recently developed instruments, the most parsimonious explanation of these differences can be found in the nature of the items that make up their scales. In terms of scale content, MCAS-B items focus more on thoughts and attitudes than on behaviors and experiences relative to MCI items. In addition to the items noted above in the instrument section, one may consider the following: "I am sensitive to circumstances (personal biases, stage of ethnic identity) that may dictate referral of the minority client to a member of his or her own race/culture," from the MCAS-B Knowledge/Skills Scale; "I make referrals or seek consultations based on the clients' minority identity development," from the MCI Knowledge scale. These items sample very similar content, but each asks the question from a different perspective: The former requires a self-report of perceived sensitivity, whereas the latter requires a self-report of perceived behavior. To the extent that counselors are able to make more accurate assessment and self-reports of their behaviors than their attitudes, the MCI appears to be tapping into an aspect of multicultural counseling competency that may be more readily amenable to self-report than the aspect examined by the MCAS-B.

UTILIZATION OF INSTRUMENTS

In considering how best to evaluate the attainment of multicultural counseling competencies, a single overarching question emerges: Is self-report the best way to measure this construct? For knowledge assessment, more direct methods, such as a multiple-choice or essay achievement test, seem more appropriate. For skill, performance assessment by a supervisor is a logical source of rich information about a counselor's ability to work across cultural barriers. For awareness, any number of possibilities seem as good as direct self-report. For example, criterion-keyed responses to various statements seem capable of eliciting a less transparent measure of awareness. Yet at the same time, the question of how best to assess multicultural counseling competencies is driven by pragmatic concerns and the context of the counseling profession.

Because paper-and-pencil tests are easily and inexpensively administered and scored, assessment of multicultural counseling competencies has been developed in this way. It seems probable that more meaningful results than those of any self-report could be obtained through careful evaluation of counselors' performance in multicultural counseling sessions and feedback from clients, but such a measurement procedure may require a great deal of effort in development and a presumably skilled evaluator and knowledgeable client in most situations. This twin difficulty may be difficult to overcome, having been dealt with only at a most general level by the CCCI-R (LaFromboise et al., 1991), a supervisory rating rather than a performance assessment per se, and a unidimensional measure at that. Less expensive measures yielding multidimensional information have been preferred for evaluating graduate students and are typically the only means by which it is feasible to conduct multi-institution, multiregion studies of counseling program outcomes (see Pope-Davis, Reynolds, Dings, & Nielson, 1995).

Another reason for the popularity of self-report measures is that measuring multicultural counseling competencies in an achievement-oriented fashion would seemingly violate the ethos of counseling psychology: that self-understanding, particularly with regard to sensitive issues such as prejudice and racism, is a fundamental component of every counselor's personal and professional development. Self-report seems a natural measure of self-understanding, and to substitute an achievement measure might be insensitive to the value placed on self-understanding. This seems to be true despite the extent to which licensure examinations for counselors abound.

From this perspective, it seems likely that self-report will continue to dominate the assessment of multicultural counseling competencies. With widespread use of some self-report measures, graduate student norms may be established, providing an indication of which aspects of multicultural counseling competencies need further attention in the development of individual counselors or in the improvement of training programs that undertake self-study. In this regard, counselor training may benefit in the long run. Instruments such as the CCCI-R and other evaluations of counseling performance may still be used in smaller studies in which it is possible to devote such resources to data collection.

LIMITATIONS OF SELF-REPORT MEASURES

Those researchers, psychologists, and counselors wishing to examine multicultural counseling competencies need to consider the limitations inherent in self-report measures and the lack of validity-related evidence amassed for the instruments considered in this chapter. Using self-report measures raises the possibility that participants may assess anticipated rather than actual behaviors or attitudes, that they may select socially desirable responses, and that they may have interpreted items differently than intended by the authors. Tendencies to respond in these ways may be further increased in cases in which the participant is specifically identified rather than anonymous or random, or in which there is something of great personal/professional importance at stake in the outcome. Such measures, however, would be inappropriate for licensure. With regard to validity-related evidence, it is worth noting that the measures reviewed in this chapter are still relatively new measures under development and that they are not all equal. The MCI has amassed a more convincing body of evidence supporting its use, although even it could profit from revisions such as the addition of a social desirability scale.

Two additional cautions are in order regarding the use of these instruments in evaluating counseling training outcomes. First, the conceptual foundation upon which an instrument is built should match in some fundamental sense the foundation of the training program being evaluated. Second, given the dearth of validity-related evidence for these self-report measures, it is unclear not only what each instrument measures but also to what extent two measures can be considered in any way interchangeable, even if both appear to have a reasonable degree of match with the conceptual underpinning of a curriculum.

SUMMARY

If the counseling profession is to respond appropriately to the needs of an emerging diverse society, it must begin to examine ways in which it provides clinical and educational training for the next generation of mental health professionals. The multicultural counseling measures discussed in this chapter provide a beginning point. Given the complexity of multicultural counseling, more varied ways of assessment are greatly needed. In addition, assessment tools need to be developed that give clients the opportunity to provide feedback regarding the multicultural competencies of counselors. The latter may perhaps be the best indictor of how culturally skilled the profession has become.

REFERENCES

American Psychological Association. (1993). Guidelines for providers of psychological services to ethnic, linguistic, and culturally diverse populations. *American Psychologist, 48*, 45-48.

Campbell, D. T., & Fiske, D. W. (1959). Convergent and discriminant validation by the multitrait-multimethod matrix. *Psychological Bulletin, 56*, 81-105.

Casas, J. M., Ponterotto, J. G., & Gutierrez, J. M. (1986). An ethical indictment of counseling research and training: The cross-cultural perspective. *Journal of Counseling and Development, 64*, 347-349.

Crowne, D. P., & Marlowe, D. (1960). A new scale of social desirability independent of psychopathology. *Journal of Consulting Psychology, 24*, 349-354.

D'Andrea, M., Daniels, J., & Heck, R. (1991). Evaluating the impact of multicultural counseling training. *Journal of Counseling and Development, 70*, 143-150.

Gorsuch, R. L. (1983). *Factor analysis.* Hillsdale, NJ: Lawrence Erlbaum.

Hernandez, A. G., & LaFromboise, T. D. (1985, August). *The development of the Cross-Cultural Counseling Inventory.* Paper presented at the 93rd annual convention of the American Psychological Association, Los Angeles.

Ibrahim, F. A., & Arredondo, P. M. (1986). Ethical standards for cross-cultural counseling: Counselor preparation, practice, assessment, and research. *Journal of Counseling and Development, 64*, 349-352.

Jacobson, C. K. (1985). Resistance to affirmative action: Self-interest or racism. *Journal of Conflict Resolution, 29*, 306-329.

LaFromboise, T. D., Coleman, H. L. K., & Hernandez, A. (1991). Development and factor structure of the Cross-Cultural Counseling Inventory—Revised. *Professional Psychology: Research and Practice, 22*, 380-388.

Ottavi, T. M., Pope-Davis, D. B., & Dings, J. G. (1994). Relationship between White racial identity attitudes and self-reported multicultural counseling competencies. *Journal of Counseling Psychology, 41*, 149-154.

Paulhaus, D. L. (1991). Measurement and control of response bias. In J. B. Robinson, P. R. Shaver, & L. S. Wrightsman (Eds.), *Measures of personality and social psychological attitudes* (pp. 17-59). San Diego: Academic Press.

Pedersen, P. (1988). *A handbook for developing multicultural awareness.* Alexandria, VA: American Counseling Association.

Ponterotto, J. G., Rieger, B. P., Barrett, A., Harris, G., Sparks, R., Sanchez, C. M., & Magids, D. (1993, September). *Development and initial validation of the multicultural counseling awareness scale.* Paper presented at the Ninth Buros-Nebraska Symposium on Measurement and Testing: Multicultural Assessment, Lincoln, Nebraska.

Ponterotto, J. G., Rieger, B. P., Barrett, A., & Sparks, R. (1994). Assessing multicultural counseling competence: A review of instrumentation. *Journal of Counseling and Development, 72*, 316-322.

Ponterotto, J. G., Sanchez, C. M., & Magids, D. M. (1991, August). *Initial development and validation of the Multicultural Counseling Awareness Scale (MCAS-B).* Paper presented at the annual convention of the American Psychological Association, San Francisco.

Pope-Davis, D. B., & Dings, J. G. (1994). An empirical comparison of two self-report multicultural counseling competency inventories. *Measurement and Evaluation in Counseling and Development, 27*, 93-102.

Pope-Davis, D. B., Dings, J. G., & Ottavi, T. M. (1995). The relationship of multicultural counseling competency with demographic and educational variables. *Iowa Psychologist, 40*(1), 12-13.

Pope-Davis, D. B., & Ottavi, T. M. (1994). Examining the association between self-reported multicultural counseling competencies and demographic and educational variables among counselors. *Journal of Counseling and Development, 72*, 651-654.

Pope-Davis, D. B., Prieto, L., Reynolds, A. L., & Vazquez, L. A. (1994). *Multicultural counseling: Issues of diversity. A training video.* Iowa City: University of Iowa, Audiovisual Center.

Pope-Davis, D. B., Reynolds, A. L., & Dings, J. G. (1994). Multicultural competencies of doctoral interns at university counseling centers: An exploratory investigation. *Professional Psychology: Research and Practice, 25,* 466-470.

Pope-Davis, D. B., Reynolds, A. L., Dings, J. G., & Nielson, D. (1995). Examining multicultural counseling competencies of graduate students in psychology. *Professional Psychology: Research and Practice.*

Pope-Davis, D. B., Reynolds, A. L., & Vazquez, L. A. (1992). *Multicultural counseling: Issues of ethnic diversity. A training video.* Iowa City: University of Iowa, Audiovisual Center.

Rogers, C. (1951). *Client-centered therapy.* Boston: Houghton Mifflin.

Sabnani, H. B., Ponterotto, J. G., & Borodovsky, L. G. (1991). White racial identity development and cross-cultural counselor training: A stage model. *The Counseling Psychologist, 19,* 72-102.

Sodowsky, G. R., Taffe, R. C., Gutkin, T. B., & Wise, S. L. (1994). Development of the Multicultural Counseling Inventory: A self-report measure of multicultural competencies. *Journal of Counseling Psychology, 41,* 137-148.

Sue, D. W., Arredondo, P., & McDavis, R. J. (1992). Multicultural counseling competencies and standards: A call to the profession. *Journal of Counseling and Development, 70,* 477-486.

Sue, D. W., Bernier, J. E., Durran, A., Feinberg, L., Pedersen, P., Smith, E. J., & Vazquez-Nuttall, E. (1982). Position paper: Cross-cultural counseling competencies. *The Counseling Psychologist, 10,* 45-52.

Sue, D. W., & Sue, D. (1990). *Counseling the culturally different: Theory and practice* (2nd ed.). New York: John Wiley.

Sue, S., & Zane, N. (1987). The role of culture and cultural techniques in psychotherapy: A critique and reformulation. *American Psychologist, 42,* 37-45.

15

Challenges and Strategies for Teaching Multicultural Counseling Courses

AMY L. REYNOLDS

DESPITE GROWING ATTENTION focused on cultural differences over the past two decades, counseling and psychology training programs have only minimally infused multicultural issues into their philosophy and curriculum (Hills & Strozier, 1992; LaFromboise & Foster, 1992; Sue, Arredondo, & McDavis, 1992; Wyatt & Parham, 1985). For at least the past decade, ethical and accreditation standards have asserted the need to identify multicultural counseling as a core component of counseling and psychology training programs (Altmaier, 1993; Burn, 1992; Casas, Ponterotto, & Gutierrez, 1986; LaFromboise & Foster, 1992). Criterion II, which is one of the primary American Psychological Association (APA) accreditation standards, requires that programs incorporate multiculturalism in four areas: (a) faculty recruitment and promotion, (b) student recruitment and evaluation, (c) curriculum, and (d) field training (Altmaier, 1993). Rickard and Clements (1993) reported a recent trend toward more negative accreditation judgments from the APA Committee on Accreditation based on some programs' lack of compliance with Criterion II. A growing number of psychologists believe that "professionals without training or competence working with clients with diverse cultural backgrounds are unethical and potentially harmful" (Sue et al., 1992, p. 480).

These ethical concerns have led to increased visibility of the issue of multicultural counseling competencies. Within counseling psychology, there have been extensive efforts to explore and delineate the multicultural competencies necessary for effective practice. In the early 1980s the field of counseling psychology first specified what multicultural knowledge, awareness, and skills were needed by counseling professionals (Sue et al., 1982). Since the early 1980s, there has been a growing interest in and development of multicultural competencies research and instrumentation. To date, at least four multicultural counseling competence assessment tools have been developed and are currently in various stages of validation and research (D'Andrea, Daniels, & Heck, 1991; LaFromboise, Coleman, & Hernandez, 1991; Ponterotto, Rieger, Barrett, & Sparks, 1994; Ponterotto et al., in press; Sodowsky, Taffe, Gutkin, & Wise, 1994). This research and the availability of assessment instruments (a) encourage greater depth and complexity in the study of multicultural counseling, (b) provide training programs with the necessary information to more effectively train future practitioners, and (c) create opportunities for future research.

In addition to the focus on multicultural counseling competencies, the multicultural counseling literature is increasingly attending to research on multicultural training in counseling and psychology training programs. The response of the counseling programs to multicultural initiatives has been identified as strong yet uneven (Casas et al., 1986; Hills & Strozier, 1992; Ponterotto & Casas, 1987; Ridley, 1985; Ridley, Mendoza, & Kanitz, 1994; Wyatt & Parham, 1985). Although the single multicultural counseling course (i.e., an overview multicultural counseling course that attempts to address cultural group knowledge or multicultural counseling skills and awareness) is still the most common format utilized (Ridley, Mendoza, & Kanitz, 1994), there is a wide variability in the type and depth of training (Ponterotto & Casas, 1987). Although there has been some literature exploring the specifics of multicultural training and teaching in counseling and psychology, there has been little empirical research that evaluates the effectiveness of the various training efforts and teaching strategies used (D'Andrea et al., 1991; Ponterotto & Casas, 1987).

According to D'Andrea et al. (1991), there is little consensus about the most necessary and effective types of training. Much of the research published on multicultural training focuses on the design or the effects of a single training program effort, which does not necessarily generalize to other programs or aid faculty in developing their own multicultural training programs (Brooks & Kahn, 1990; D'Andrea et al., 1991; Lefley, 1986; McDavis & Parker, 1977; Mio, 1989; Parker & McDavis, 1979; Parker, Valley, & Geary, 1986). In order for the multicultural training efforts of counseling programs to be effectively assessed, it is vital that evaluation tools be developed and strengthened (Brooks & Kahn, 1990). Because "research on multicultural counseling and training is still in its infancy, providing little empirical data to guide program developers in making decisions" (Ridley, Mendoza, Kanitz, Angermeier, & Zenck, 1994, p. 128), many counseling programs have been using untested multicultural training efforts.

This chapter will explore the challenges to implementing a multicultural training emphasis in a counseling program and offer some suggestions to combatting barriers. General teaching strategies and specific design considerations for creating a multicultural counseling course are examined. Finally, ethical considerations in multicultural training are addressed, and the need for more research on multicultural training and teaching is emphasized.

CHALLENGES TO CREATING
MULTICULTURAL TRAINING PROGRAMS

Although there has been increasing support for the need to integrate multicultural issues in counseling and psychology training programs, there are numerous challenges or barriers to teaching multicultural counseling. Many of these are due to institutional, departmental, and/or programmatic lack of information, confusion, neglect, or resistance. On the college or departmental level, there is often a lack of support and funding for multicultural courses and initiatives (D'Andrea & Daniels, 1991). Examples of systemic barriers include ineffective recruiting strategies for students and faculty of color, lack of encouragement or reward for multiculturally oriented scholarship, and absence of backing for the expansion or development of a counseling or psychology curriculum by either including multicultural courses or integrating multicultural issues into all courses.

There is much that counseling programs can do to incorporate multicultural issues into their curriculum and philosophy even without institutional support; however, because of the realities of higher education and how faculty are promoted, new courses are approved, and funding is distributed, institutional resistance will affect a counseling program's efforts toward integrating multiculturalism. Therefore, working for institutional change is crucial to creating change at both the programmatic and interpersonal level (LaFromboise & Foster, 1992; Sue, 1991).

According to D'Andrea and Daniels (1991), faculty need to "make specific institutional changes to guarantee that students receive multicultural counseling training in a systematic manner" (p. 82). Such efforts may help to unify the faculty and model for the students the program's commitment to multiculturalism. Examples of how to work for institutional change include initiating college-wide committees that examine the inclusion of multicultural issues into the curriculum; ensuring that individuals who support multiculturalism are involved with personnel, hiring, and curriculum committees; working to change the criteria for faculty promotion and tenure; and encouraging the development of an institutional multicultural awareness education program for faculty and staff. These strategies will bring together and unify individuals committed to multiculturalism from all types of programs, departments, and offices across campus.

Although institutional support for multicultural initiatives is very important, programmatic efforts are even more crucial to making advances in multicultural training. Multicultural training must become the responsibility and commitment of the entire training program as a whole rather than the vision or effort of an individual faculty member (Hills & Strozier, 1992; LaFromboise & Foster, 1992; Midgette & Meggert, 1991). According to Midgette and Meggert (1991), "individual educators must examine their role in influencing these changes" (p. 136). There are many ways that multicultural training efforts are not supported at the programmatic level. For example, assistant and adjunct professors are more likely to be the faculty responsible for implementing multicultural training efforts (Hills & Strozier, 1992), which means the burden of changing the curriculum becomes the responsibility of those with the least power in the program and the institution. It is vital that counseling program faculty openly discuss and reach consensus on their commitment to multicultural training and that all faculty take an active role, particularly senior faculty (Hills & Strozier, 1992; Ridley, Mendoza, & Kanitz, 1994).

If an individual faculty member takes on the role of multicultural expert for a training program, none of the other faculty members will need to develop his or her own multicultural counseling or training skills. This makes it difficult for a program to move beyond the single-course approach and toward a more integrated curriculum. According to Ridley, Mendoza, Kanitz, Angermeier, and Zenck (1994), "a more inclusive and programmatic approach to teaching will have important effects on students and faculty" (p. 140). This approach is clearly preferable to making multicultural course work an elective, which serves only those students and faculty who are interested in expanding their multicultural sensitivity and skills.

Increasingly, multicultural experts are asserting that "counselor training programs have undergone very few changes to facilitate actual curricula and pedagogical strategies" (Midgette & Meggert, 1991, p. 139). Midgette and Meggert contended that one of the primary reasons for so little change may be the "lack of qualified counselor educators to provide culturally competent skills and experience necessary for ethical and professional practice" (p. 138). Many faculty currently in counseling programs did not receive any multicultural training while pursuing their doctorates unless they specifically sought out continuing education at professional conferences. According to Ridley, Mendoza, and Kanitz (1994), "Little has been written about the development, implementation, availability, or effectiveness of multicultural retraining for trainers" (p. 248).

Another significant barrier to the incorporation of multicultural initiatives comes directly from the students themselves. For many students, learning multicultural counseling sensitivity and skills creates discomfort, fear, ambivalence, and varying degrees of resistance. Some researchers have specifically identified these concerns as related to racial identity or as part of the developmental process in creating multicultural awareness (Ottavi, Pope-Davis, &

Dings, 1994; Ponterotto, 1988; Sabnani, Ponterotto, & Borodovsky, 1991).
Although many may assume that negative reactions are a problem of White
students, people of color and members of other oppressed groups may also be
resistant to learning multicultural counseling skills, knowledge, and awareness (Ridley, Mendoza, & Kanitz, 1994). As with White students, resistance
on the part of the students of color and other oppressed groups may be due to
issues of cultural identity, developmental issues, and other related variables.

Despite the realities of these challenges to creating multicultural training
programs, many counseling programs are making strides in their efforts. According to Margolis and Rungta (1986), "The counseling profession has always
been sensitive to human rights movements that have evolved in the larger
society" (p. 642). Historical commitment to human rights and individual differences has helped to ensure that multicultural issues stay on the agenda of
counseling programs. Notwithstanding the existence of institutional or programmatic barriers, the literature that explores the range of teaching strategies
available to develop or enhance multicultural awareness, knowledge, and skills
continues to expand multicultural training possibilities.

TEACHING STRATEGIES

There are multiple ways of structuring and infusing multicultural learning
in a counseling program. Copeland (1982) identified several multicultural program designs: (a) separate course, (b) area of concentration model, (c) interdisciplinary approach, and (d) integration model. These program designs, in
addition to the workshop and traditional program designs specified by Ridley,
Mendoza, and Kanitz (1994), offer a wide array of choices for program faculty
to consider when designing their multicultural training program. Although
there is no conclusive research supporting the choice of one design over another, many multicultural experts have expressed some consistent opinions.
Although the single-course approach is the most common, it is also the most
frequently criticized because it does not offer enough depth, may lead to stereotyping about specific cultural groups, and does not encourage generalization
or integration of multicultural awareness, knowledge, and skills (LaFromboise
& Foster, 1992; Margolis & Rungta, 1986; Wyatt & Parham, 1985). According
to Midgette and Meggert (1991), "Offering a separate course in multicultural
counseling does not meet minimum requirements to fulfill most standards"
(p. 136).

Conversely, some experts point to the integration approach as the best for
multicultural training because it encourages integration and generalization of
multicultural skills and sensitivities across counseling competencies and
knowledge bases such as testing, ethics, groups, and career counseling
(Copeland, 1982; LaFromboise & Foster, 1992). But Ridley, Mendoza, and
Kanitz (1994) suggested that the integration approach "may not be adequate
in providing intensive, in-depth training that may be the goal of some pro-

grams" (p. 273). Instead, they proposed that counseling programs combine a variety of the designs in order to accentuate their strengths and minimize their weaknesses. For example, program faculty could offer a required multicultural counseling course in addition to integrating multicultural issues throughout all of their courses and offering electives for specific courses (e.g., counseling lesbians, gays, and bisexuals; Blacks and mental health).

There is "strong evidence that the best training experience uses a multifaceted approach" (Lewis & Hayes, 1991, p. 119). LaFromboise and Foster (1992) argued for the inclusion of multicultural emphasis within the scientist-practitioner training model. The scientist-practitioner approach focuses on the acquisition of clinical and research skills through didactic course work, hands-on research and clinical experience, and modeling and mentoring (LaFromboise & Foster, 1992). More research is needed in order to affirm or challenge the various opinions of multicultural experts regarding the best way to train counselors and psychologists in multicultural competencies.

Many multicultural experts view the purpose and goals of multicultural training differently. According to D'Andrea and Daniels (1991), the purpose of multicultural training is to "stretch counselors' awareness, extend their knowledge, and expand their repertoire of counseling competencies" (p. 79). Midgette and Meggert (1991) contended that the "goal of cross-cultural training is to increase a counselor's intentionality through increasing the person's purposive control over the assumptions that guide his or her behavior, attitudes, and insights" (p. 138). On the basis of their diverse teaching philosophies and strategies, different experts propose unique and sometimes overlapping processes or theoretical models to conceptualize multicultural counseling or training (LaFromboise & Foster, 1992; Ridley, Mendoza, & Kanitz, 1994). Developing an understanding of one's own philosophy and attitudes about multicultural training as well as the range of possible teaching strategies available is necessary before an appropriate multicultural training approach is chosen.

One of the most common types of training concentrates on increasing the multicultural awareness or cultural sensitivity of the participants. This model typically focuses on developing tolerance and/or acceptance of cultural differences, incorporates a wide range of activities and exercises, and is often used on college campuses, in business and industry, and in community organizations. A second type of multicultural training centers on unlearning oppression and sensitizes participants to the realities of racism, sexism, heterosexism, and other forms of oppression. Contrary to the first type of training, which may be conceptualized as the "can't we all just get along" type of sensitivity training, the oppression-focused model of training may confront the worldviews and perceptions of participants, challenge notions of power and the status quo, and examine the issue of cultural diversity from a sociopolitical framework.

A third and final type of multicultural training, and one that is often used within the counseling profession, focuses on enhancing the multicultural attitudes, knowledge, and skills of the participants. This type of training is appropriate for a work or training setting in that it helps participants work more effectively across cultural differences. A multicultural-competency-based training effort may incorporate either of the previously described types of training as part of expanding the cultural awareness and sensitivity of the trainees.

Determining which type of training focus is appropriate is not a simple decision. It must be based on the values, goals, and worldview of the program faculty and individual educator. According to many experts, a developmental approach to multicultural training is preferable (Carney & Kahn, 1984; Christensen, 1989; Lopez et al., 1989). Developmental theories provide guidelines for structuring the learning environment. Multicultural training may be guided by general developmental concepts or by specific training models that offer general approaches and sometimes even specific activities (Carney & Kahn, 1984; Lopez et al., 1989; Sabnani et al., 1991). An example of a general developmental concept that may be used in the design of multicultural training efforts is the notion of challenge and support (Sanford, 1963). Developmental theorists believe that a balance of challenge and support is needed in order to facilitate learning (Sanford, 1963). Too much challenge causes trainees to withdraw because they feel overwhelmed. Too much support leads to complacency and detachment because there is nothing testing or challenging the trainees.

In order to be successful, multicultural trainers must understand these theoretical constructs, know about multicultural resources, and be able to use that information to match the developmental needs of the trainees. It is important to note that there are some potential problems or concerns with the developmental approach. If a trainer or educator is too focused on the model and how it predicts behavior and is not attentive to the individual trainees, then often the trainees may be forced to fit the model. Whatever training model is used, it must be used after gathering extensive and meaningful information on the trainees and designing the instruction approach and methods to meet their needs. Regardless of the method chosen, it is important to acknowledge that "cultural diversity training . . . is a complex and longterm problem" (Sue, 1991, p. 104).

COURSE DESIGN CONSIDERATIONS

Because the data and literature on multicultural training in counseling programs and evaluation of such efforts are lacking, there are some pedagogical challenges that affect how programs design and create their training efforts. One major challenge often centers around the content of the course. As delineated by Ridley, Mendoza, and Kanitz (1994) and others, the various definitions of *multiculturalism* affect how a multicultural course or training effort is structured. Some experts define *multiculturalism* exclusively around racial and ethnic issues and fear that broader definitions weaken the efforts to eradicate racism from the counseling profession (Helms, 1994; Locke, 1990). Others adopt a broader definition that expands the definition of *culture* to include such areas as gender, socioeconomic status, sexual/affectional orientation, and national origin (Pedersen, 1988; Speight, Myers, Cox, & Highlen, 1991). Although there are pros and cons to both approaches, "'universal' and 'focused' multicultural approaches are not necessarily contradictory" (Sue et al., 1992, p. 478). Therefore, it may be useful to focus multicultural training on race while also incorporating other aspects of difference throughout the curriculum.

There are also varying opinions regarding the best ways to teach multicultural sensitivity and counseling skills. According to Ridley, Mendoza, and Kanitz (1994), the range of teaching strategies for a multicultural counseling course includes didactic methods, experiential exercises, supervised practical/internships, reading assignments, writing assignments, participatory learning, modeling/observational learning, technology-assisted learning, introspection, and research. Although the various experts may have diverse teaching preferences, there is little research that examines the strength of some teaching designs over others (D'Andrea et al., 1991).

A final pedagogical challenge centers on faculty and student diversity and its effect on the course. Although there has been minimal research exploring the effects of the diversity of the students and faculty on the actual training experience, the experience and outcome of multicultural training could quite easily be affected by their diversity. A classroom that consists of predominantly White students or has no openly lesbian, gay, or bisexual students creates a different type of environment and dialogue as students and faculty explore these issues. The effect of classroom and program diversity on multicultural training needs further research so we have a better understanding of what is needed for the optimal educational environment.

According to some multicultural experts, "No one training model seems to encompass all the necessary components in a way that can be evaluated as effective" (McRae & Johnson, 1991, p. 132). Concerns about the "cookbook approach" to multicultural training have been widely expressed (see Ridley, Mendoza, & Kanitz, 1994; Speight et al., 1991). Because each class is unique in its makeup and each program different in its history, philosophy, and approach to multicultural issues, it is important that faculty members who are planning to teach multicultural courses develop their own philosophy, style, and training approach. Utilizing someone else's course design without reviewing its appropriateness and fit for one's own students and teaching style could potentially pose problems for the trainees because their unique needs and concerns may not be considered or incorporated. In order to effectively teach multicultural counseling and related courses, it is vital that faculty understand the various design components that may be incorporated in a multicultural course.

Rather than recommending a specific multicultural training design to be used, I will discuss the central design elements useful to consider for multicultural training. According to Reynolds (1993a), there are six central design elements: (a) content—information oriented, (b) cognitive—worldview or cognitive filter, (c) affective—emotions or feelings, (d) experiential—hands-on activities, (e) skills, and (f) process—interpersonal dynamics oriented and focused on the here and now. Reynolds (1993a) recommended that all of these design elements be addressed sometime during the training and education of counseling students.

It is vital that a component of multicultural training include some cultural-specific content and information. Although many have expressed concerns about the dangers of focusing on cultural group differences (e.g., that it can lead to stereotyping), it is vital that individuals understand that cultural differences exist and that they vary on an individual basis. Other content information that is significant for individuals to know and understand includes core theoretical constructs such as acculturation, oppression, prejudice, racial identity, and other forms of cultural identity.

A cognitive focus is also important because it involves examining and challenging the worldview or cognitive filter one uses to make sense of the world. In teaching, one should offer experiences that encourage exploration of the contradictions embedded in the trainees' own experiences and ways of viewing the world. Such cognitive approaches can facilitate the development of new perspectives and encourage individuals to expand their frame of reference. Myers (1993), in her work on belief systems analysis in which individuals examine the optimal versus suboptimal nature of their worldview, encourages an epistemological and cognitive approach to multicultural education and self-awareness.

Affective learning is just as important as cognitive learning; however, many academic programs appear more likely to emphasize cognitive and content learning. Teaching focused on examining and possibly changing deeply rooted feelings and attitudes is less common and less frequently discussed in the literature. Despite the difficulty in achieving, or at least measuring, multicultural awareness, cultural self-awareness is a vital first step toward cultural sensitivity (Ridley, Mendoza, Kanitz, Angermeier, & Zenck, 1994; Sue et al., 1992). In order to encourage affective learning, developing an effective environment or atmosphere is key. Belief and values are thought to be best explored through "introspection and reflective self-evaluation" (Sue et al., 1992, p. 138). In order to explore feelings and values honestly, there is a need for an environment based on trust and openness. Traditional grading and evaluation are a challenge to creating an environment in which students feel comfortable taking the risks necessary to expand their cultural awareness. Alternative grading policies such as pass/no pass might help alleviate some barriers to risk taking. A variety of interventions are needed to access and encourage emotional learning (e.g., simulation games, experiential learning).

Experiential or hands-on activities are another key mode of learning in groups. These activities show the importance and centrality of feelings and thoughts. They encourage self-awareness, which is a major source of content for many experience-based designs or interventions. Direct experiential contact with culturally diverse groups has been emphasized in the multicultural counseling literature. Some experts believe that such contact allows individuals to move beyond facts or knowledge about a cultural group and that depth of experiential contact is related to enrichment of cross-cultural sensitivity and integration and generalization of multicultural knowledge and understanding (LaFromboise & Foster, 1992; Margolis & Rungta, 1986).

Many counseling programs also emphasize the importance of skills in their multicultural training. According to Sue and Sue (1990), "Becoming culturally skilled is an active process that is ongoing, and that is a process that never reaches an end point" (p. 146). Some multicultural experts believe that the "current status of multicultural training continues to focus much of its attention on 'knowing that' and only some of its attention on 'knowing how'" (McRae & Johnson, 1991, p. 133). Teaching students culturally responsive interventions is a vital and necessary aspect of multicultural training.

A final design component involves process or interpersonal dynamics, including focusing on the here and now. Although there is no research that examines the use of these six design components in multicultural course work, it is likely that the process focus or even attention to group dynamics in the context of multicultural teaching and training is the least common. LaFromboise and Foster (1992) argued for a social-learning approach in which modeling and interaction with others are emphasized as part of the learning process.

The use of these design components is strongly influenced by one's worldview or philosophy about multicultural issues, how change occurs, and one's teaching style. In addition to being familiar with these components, it also may be useful to be aware of the multicultural education literature, which is filled with theories and examples about how to increase cultural sensitivity (Banks, 1994). Much of this literature can be adapted to meet the needs of a counseling curriculum. Exploring alternative literature outside of the counseling profession encourages creativity and increases the number of teaching tools and strategies. According to Copeland (1982), "Innovative training materials must be implemented" (p. 193).

The Multicultural Change Intervention Matrix (MCIM), developed by Pope (1993), is an example of an alternative conceptual model that was created from a higher education and organizational perspective but can be used in any educational environment. The MCIM is based on the concepts of systemic planned change and multicultural organization development (MCOD)—principles that provide a framework for codifying and understanding the range of multicultural interventions and activities that may be used to address multicultural issues (Pope, 1993).

The MCIM consists of two major dimensions. One dimension identifies three possible targets of intervention: (a) individual, (b) group, and (c) institution. Because of this range of targets, the MCIM can be used to conceptualize change within individuals or groups of students or faculty in a program as well as change within a department or institution. The second dimension of the matrix differentiates between levels of intervention: (a) first-order change and (b) second-order change. Watzlawick, Weakland, and Fisch (as cited in Lyddon, 1990) explored first- and second-order change within a family systems context. Lyddon expanded their work and applied it to a broader counseling context. He described first-order change as essentially "change without change"—that is, a change within the system that does not create change in the structure of the system. Second-order change is "change of change," or any change that fundamentally alters the structure of a system.

According to Lyddon (1990), changing the internal state of an individual, group, or institution, including even changing a group's membership, without altering its basic structure still maintains the coherence of the system and is considered first-order change. When change occurs that actually creates a transformation in the actual definition or makeup of the group or structure of the individual or institution, it is considered second-order change.

As shown in Figure 15.1, the MCIM offers six different ways to perceive and structure multicultural change efforts. By increasing one's understanding of the range of targets and goals that may be used in multicultural training, one can more easily expand the types of activities, strategies, and tools considered. Through exploration of the six cells of the MCIM, more multicultural training options can be considered. Although much of the description of these possible change efforts is taken from the work of Pope (1993), additional information about applications in a counseling or academic context has been included.

Cell A change efforts (first-order change—individual) typically involve education at the awareness, knowledge, or skill level. This type of educational effort is often focused on content, such as information about various racial or other cultural groups. Possible examples might include offering information on cross-cultural communication, sharing data on the presenting concerns or treatment outcomes of various racial groups, describing the economic and social conditions of a particular cultural group, or giving an antiracism presentation.

A Cell B change effort (second-order change—individual) is education aimed at the cognitive restructuring level, suggesting worldview or paradigm shifts. Kuhn's concept of paradigm shift (as cited by Kuh, 1983) is described as a "radical change in the way in which the world is viewed" (p. 1). According to Pope (1993), such worldview or paradigm shifts require more intensive, interactive, or experiential emphasis than mere sharing of information about various people of color groups (i.e., awareness). Often these interventions are more process oriented and challenge an individual's underlying assumptions. A possible example might include a prolonged, extensive, and periodic consciousness-raising workshop that is individually focused and experientially oriented (i.e., the individual is obliged to examine belief/thought systems—to be introspective and self-challenging).

A Cell C change effort (first-order change—group) is a change in the composition of the group in which members of underrepresented groups are added

TARGET OF CHANGE	TYPE OF CHANGE	
	1ST-ORDER CHANGE	2ND-ORDER CHANGE
INDIVIDUAL	A Awareness	B Paradigm Shift
GROUP	C Membership	D Restructuring
INSTITUTION	E Programmatic	F Systemic

Figure 15.1. The Multicultural Change Intervention Matrix
SOURCE: From Pope, 1993. Reprinted with permission.

but there is no change in the goals or norms of the group. Cell C focuses on diversity in terms of numbers without examining the interpersonal and structural dynamics of a group. An example of such a change is the traditional recruitment effort that increases the number of students of color without altering the environment or examining and modifying programmatic philosophy or curriculum.

Cell D change efforts (second-order change—group) might involve total reformation and restructuring of a counseling program with a new mission, goals, and members. This type of change demands examination of group makeup, values, and goals prior to changing the group. It requires involving the new members in this self-examination and planning process. An example would be hosting a retreat for all counseling students and faculty to reexamine and reformulate the philosophy, values, and goals of the counseling program, including multicultural training efforts. Rather than adding a few multicultural goals, this approach demands a reexamination of the entire philosophy and purpose of a counseling program.

A Cell E change effort (first-order change—institution) involves a programmatic intervention aimed at the institution or department that addresses multicultural issues but does not alter the underlying values and structure of the institution. Creating a new faculty position or responsibility within a program to address the concerns of students of color or developing a multicultural counseling course is an example of a change effort that may not alter the institutional dynamics, values, or priorities. Adding a multicultural course to the curriculum of a counseling program without changing how students are evaluated throughout the program will probably not create institutional or programmatic change.

A Cell F change effort (second-order change—institution) requires more intrusive means in which underlying institutional values, goals, and evaluation are directly examined and then linked to multicultural values and efforts. Examples include requiring goal-directed multicultural initiatives within all counseling courses that link the outcome of those initiatives to student evaluation and faculty promotion decisions on individual multicultural competencies.

The six cells of the MCIM are separate and unique; however, their relationship with each other is fluid and dynamic. For example, awareness work is an important part of creating a paradigm shift within an individual. Or programmatic efforts may be a necessary precursor to the development of systemic change. According to Pope (1994), the dotted lines between the various cells are meant to depict that interconnection and encourage the use of all six levels and targets of multicultural interventions. The relationships between the various cells have yet to be studied, and the research examining the philosophical assumptions of the MCIM must be undertaken. Because the MCIM is still a relatively new model, there is much exciting research to be completed. Although the dualistic nature of our society might encourage readers to assume that second-order change is "better" than first-order change because it creates long-term and structural transformation, it is vital that all six types of change efforts be seen as a valuable and necessary part of the multicultural training process.

The MCIM offers an alternative framework in which to conceptualize multicultural training. It emphasizes exploring change at the individual, group, and institutional level, as some multicultural experts argue is necessary in order to truly infuse multiculturalism in a counseling program (LaFromboise & Foster, 1992). The MCIM can be used to design the goals and activities of an individual course or to restructure an entire counseling curriculum. The first step in using this matrix would be as a tool to conceptualize and assess the type and level of multicultural training efforts currently being used in a counseling program. Once the initial assessment is completed, faculty can identify what types of training are typically missing and what can be done to expand and enhance their multicultural initiatives.

According to Pope (1993), utilizing a method of systemic planned change efforts, such as the MCIM, to create multicultural change not only may assist with the necessary goal setting but also may identify methods of implementation. Much of the multicultural training offered in counseling programs typically focuses solely on changing individual students without examining whether the faculty or program itself also might need to change. Without information that examines the targets and levels of multicultural training, it is increasingly difficult to make informed and effective decisions about what interventions will help create multiculturally competent counselors.

Whether or not one decides to use a conceptual framework such as the MCIM to develop a multicultural training program or counseling course, there are many design considerations that need to be explored. The first rule of design is that the primary focus should be on the person rather than the subject matter. It is always more important to focus on students and how they learn than to focus merely on the content. In actuality, the richest resource for learning, and therefore design, resides in the learners themselves. This perspective is consistent with the underlying philosophy of many counseling programs that emphasize the importance of counselors' understanding themselves before they can help others.

When considering what instructional strategies to select, there are many important issues for faculty to consider. As a teacher, will you be more instructor centered or learner centered? As you teach, is the individual or group the focus of your interventions? Is self-instruction more important than group learning? Do you feel more comfortable with didactic, experiential, or vicarious learning? How do you incorporate issues such as level of risk and level of learner experience? How important is learner motivation to your teaching strategy? Is your approach more active or passive? Do you believe that multicultural education and change need a long or short time to occur? Do you believe in emphasizing feelings, thoughts, or behaviors? How personal do you believe multicultural training can or should become? All of these questions are important to consider when planning a multicultural counseling class.

In addition to answering those questions, it is important to consider the steps in the planning process. One of the first steps necessary is to identify the explicit learning goals or targets of your course (e.g., knowledge, skills, awareness, cognitive levels). It is also necessary to identify the implicit learning goals, such as assumed skills or level of competence. In order to identify these goals, assessment of the students is vital. Once you have gathered data on the students, it is possible to plan the learning activities most appropriate to the explicit and implicit teaching goals and the developmental competencies or levels of the students. For example, what are the students' capacities for perspective and risk taking? What is their capacity for personal reflection and self-knowledge? It is important to check for balance and variety to suit the diverse learning differences and preferences. Teachers must also assess anxiety levels, unattended needs, and students' perception of the relevance of the goals and activities chosen. Finally, because continuity is important, teachers must identify bridges and build connections between course sessions or sections. For a more detailed conceptual model to use in developing a multicultural training program, read Ridley, Mendoza, and Kanitz (1994).

ETHICAL CONSIDERATIONS IN TRAINING

Prior to becoming involved in multicultural training, faculty and other trainers must strongly consider the ethical implications of their work. Ethics and multicultural training belong together, yet are rarely linked. The assumption is that reliance on personal ethical standards is sufficient for public protection; however, an actual ethical code, created by multicultural trainers and educators, is strongly needed (Reynolds, 1993b). The absence of ethical directives is partially due to the fact that multicultural training in counseling is a relatively new area that is still unfolding. There have been no attempts to regulate the quality of work that is done, even though such regulation is desperately needed. Many programs and departments, especially those who do not have faculty members with multicultural expertise, may be so eager for assistance and trusting of those who volunteer their teaching services that they do not consider the possible ethical ramifications of multicultural training.

Over the past decade a variety of articles and chapters have been written on the ethics of multicultural counseling and training (see Ibrahim & Arredondo, 1986; Paradis, 1981). Initially, the literature focused on the need to incorporate the need for multicultural competence within professional ethics statements and codes and the ethical need to infuse multicultural training within the curriculum. More recently, efforts are being focused on what ethical concerns, beyond competence, are within multicultural counseling (Burn, 1992; Casas et al., 1986; LaFromboise & Foster, 1989).

Many types of ethical violations can occur within a multicultural training context, such as faculty members' considering themselves experts even though they do not have the proper training background or experiences, or a department or program's claims to emphasize multicultural training when it has only one multicultural counseling course or one faculty member competent in multicultural issues. A final and very important ethical issue centers on the type of design and interventions chosen by a faculty member. Inappropriate choices can actually be harmful on both an individual and group level.

Although just specifying the ethical concerns in multicultural training could be the topic of a lengthy article, it does seem important to highlight the range of ethical issues (see Pedersen, Chapter 3, this volume). Faculty competence is primary and most central to the issue of multicultural training. It is vital that all counseling faculty members be retrained so that they may adequately address multicultural issues in their classroom and in their advising and dissertation mentoring. Faculty need exposure to many important areas, including but not limited to (a) training design, so that they understand how best to design their classes; (b) group work, because group dynamics often play out strongly in multicultural training settings; (c) a systems perspective, so they understand how to deal with diversity issues on an organizational or institutional level; (d) cultural diversity content, including some specific cultural and group differences, along with how racism, sexism, and other forms of oppression work; and (e) an awareness of how multicultural issues affect the counseling process.

In order to be effective in the classroom, it is vital that faculty members' have personal and work experiences that have exposed and sensitized them to working in a multicultural context. Cultural diversity and sensitivity is not something that can be learned from books. Faculty also need personal experiences to truly understand and be able to relate effectively to a diverse audience about these issues. Self-reflection and personal work are vital components to being effective and competent as a multicultural trainer and educator. According to Midgette and Meggert (1991), "Counselor educators and supervisors have not achieved enough personal insight and knowledge themselves to help students develop into culturally competent practitioners" (p. 140). There is little data available on the attitudes and abilities of counseling faculty to effectively teach multicultural course work because the majority of the literature has focused on the students (Midgette & Meggert, 1991). Until there is more information on the multicultural awareness and skills of counseling faculty, there will be a lack of understanding of what needs to change in order to achieve the goals and values of our profession, which is demanding faculty who are multiculturally competent.

SUMMARY

Although multicultural counseling and the issues of cultural groups historically underserved by the counseling profession have been explored in the literature for almost three decades, the literature exploring the teaching of multicultural issues in counseling and psychology is still in its infancy. Counseling, as a profession, must move beyond emphasizing the need to incorporate multicultural issues as one of its core issues and generate effective strategies to ensure that those competencies are being developed.

Understanding the challenges and barriers, both individual and systemic, that interfere with a counseling program's ability to infuse multicultural issues throughout its curriculum is vital to making strides in multicultural training. Devising strategies to deal with these barriers is an important step; however, there is not enough information on the effectiveness of multicultural training strategies. Conceptual models that offer more coherent explanations and pragmatic options are necessary. As Ridley, Mendoza, and Kanitz (1994) contended, a systematic examination of a program's philosophy, goals, and specific training strategies will assist counseling programs in their efforts to become more multiculturally sensitive.

There is a strong need for more research in the area of teaching and training of multicultural counseling. The minimal data gathered offer little definitive direction for counseling faculty wanting to develop or enhance the multicultural competencies of their students. Evaluation of multicultural teaching efforts is necessary so that counseling faculty can make informed decisions regarding how and what they will teach. Many multicultural experts believe that evaluation is critical to improve the quality of multicultural training (D'Andrea & Daniels, 1991; Ridley, Mendoza, & Kanitz, 1994). According to Ridley, Mendoza, and Kanitz (1994), there are three barriers to effective evaluation of multicultural training: (a) lack of clear training objectives, (b) inadequate outcome measures, and (c) problems with research design strategies.

In addition to the challenges involved in the teaching of multicultural counseling skills, little, if any, multicultural training focuses on the broader roles and responsibilities of counselors and psychologists. According to Ridley, Mendoza, & Kanitz (1994), "Training focused on professional development in other roles, such as administrator, supervisor, mentor, and consultant, is at best informal and in most cases nonexistent" (p. 247). Multicultural issues must be woven into the very fabric of our definition of what it means to be a counselor or psychologist. Multicultural competencies should become as central to the field of counseling as empathy and other basic communication skills.

None of these vital changes can occur until all counseling faculty make a genuine commitment to multicultural issues. The first step is the most important—counseling faculty must make a commitment to examine their own values and biases and seek out the training and retraining necessary for them to be multiculturally competent. Although multicultural counseling is a valuable specialization, it should no longer be acceptable for those faculty members who do not specialize in multicultural issues to ignore their responsibility to develop multicultural competencies. These issues must be integrated into the philosophy, outcome expectations, and syllabus of every course of every counseling training program in the United States. Until this level of commitment is reached, we are doing a disservice to our core values and ethics as a profession.

REFERENCES

Altmaier, E. M. (1993). Role of Criterion II in accreditation. *Professional Psychology: Research and Practice, 24,* 127-129.
Banks, J. A. (1994). *Multiethnic education: Theory and practice* (3rd ed.). Boston: Allyn & Bacon.
Brooks, G. S., & Kahn, S. E. (1990). Evaluation of a course in gender and cultural issues. *Counselor Education and Supervision, 30,* 66-76.
Burn, D. (1992). Ethical implications in cross-cultural counseling and training. *Journal of Counseling and Development, 70,* 578-583.
Carney, C. G., & Kahn, K. B. (1984). Building competencies for effective cross-cultural counseling: A developmental view. *The Counseling Psychologist, 12,* 111-119.
Casas, J. M., Ponterotto, J. G., & Gutierrez, J. M. (1986). An ethical indictment of counseling research and training: The cross-cultural perspective. *Journal of Counseling and Development, 64,* 347-349.
Christensen, C. P. (1989). Cross-cultural awareness: A conceptual model. *Counselor Education and Supervision, 28,* 270-289.
Copeland, E. J. (1982). Minority populations and traditional counseling programs: Some alternatives. *Counselor Education and Supervision, 21,* 187-193.
D'Andrea, M., & Daniels, J. (1991). Exploring the different levels of multicultural counseling training in counselor education. *Journal of Counseling and Development, 70,* 78-85.
D'Andrea, M., Daniels, J., & Heck, R. (1991). Evaluating the impact of multicultural counseling training. *Journal of Counseling and Development, 70,* 143-150.
Helms, J. E. (1994). How multiculturalism obscures racial factors in the therapy process: Comment on Ridley et al. (1994), Sodowsky et al. (1994), Ottavi et al. (1994), and Thompson et al. (1994). *Journal of Counseling Psychology, 41,* 162-165.
Hills, H. I., & Strozier, A. L. (1992). Multicultural training in APA-approved counseling psychology programs: A survey. *Professional Psychology: Research and Practice, 23,* 43-51.
Ibrahim, F. A., & Arredondo, P. M. (1986). Ethical standards for cross-cultural counseling: Counselor preparation, practice, assessment, and research. *Journal of Counseling and Development, 64,* 349-352.

Kuh, G. D. (Ed.). (1983). *Understanding student affairs organizations* (New Directions for Student Services No. 23). San Francisco: Jossey-Bass.

LaFromboise, T. D., Coleman, H. L., & Hernandez, A. (1991). Development and factor structure of the Cross-Cultural Counseling Inventory—Revised. *Professional Psychology: Research and Practice, 22,* 380-388.

LaFromboise, T. D., & Foster, S. L. (1989). Ethics in multicultural counseling. In P. B. Pedersen, W. J. Lonner, & J. E. Trimble (Eds.), *Counseling across cultures* (3rd ed., pp. 115-136). Honolulu: University of Hawaii Press.

LaFromboise, T. D., & Foster, S. L. (1992). Cross-cultural training: Scientist-practitioner models and methods. *The Counseling Psychologist, 20,* 472-489.

Lefley, H. P. (1986). Evaluating the effects of cross-cultural training: Some research results. In H. P. Lefley & P. Pedersen (Eds.), *Cross-cultural counseling for mental health professionals* (pp. 49-71). Springfield, IL: Charles C Thomas.

Lewis, A. C., & Hayes, S. (1991). Multiculturalism and the school counseling curriculum. *Journal of Counseling and Development, 70,* 119-125.

Locke, D. C. (1990). A not so provincial view of multicultural counseling. *Counselor Education and Supervision, 30,* 18-25.

Lopez, S. R., Grover, K. P., Holland, D., Johnson, M. J., Kain, C. D., Kanel, K., Mellins, C. A., & Rhyne, M. C. (1989). Development of culturally sensitive psychotherapists. *Professional Psychology: Research and Practice, 20,* 369-376.

Lyddon, W. J. (1990). First- and second-order change: Implications for rationalist and constructivist cognitive therapies. *Journal of Counseling and Development, 69,* 122-127.

Margolis, R. L., & Rungta, S. A. (1986). Training counselors for work with special populations: A second look. *Journal of Counseling and Development, 64,* 642-644.

McDavis, R. J., & Parker, M. A. (1977). A course on counseling ethnic minorities: A model. *Counselor Education and Supervision, 17,* 146-149.

McRae, M. B., & Johnson, S. D. (1991). Toward training for competence in multicultural counselor education. *Journal of Counseling and Development, 70,* 131-141.

Midgette, T. E., & Meggert, S. S. (1991). Multicultural counseling instruction: A challenge for faculties in the 21st century. *Journal of Counseling and Development, 70,* 136-141.

Mio, J. S. (1989). Experiential involvement as an adjunct to teaching cultural sensitivity. *Journal of Multicultural Counseling and Development, 17,* 38-46.

Myers, L. J. (1993). *Understanding an Afrocentric world view: Introduction to an optimal psychology* (2nd ed.). Dubuque, IA: Kendall/Hunt.

Ottavi, T. M., Pope-Davis, D. B., & Dings, J. G. (1994). Relationship between White racial identity attitudes and self-reported multicultural counseling competencies. *Journal of Counseling Psychology, 41,* 149-154.

Paradis, F. E. (1981). Themes in the training of culturally effective psychotherapists. *Counselor Education and Supervision, 21,* 136-151.

Parker, W. M., & McDavis, R. J. (1979). An awareness experience: Toward counseling minorities. *Counselor Education and Supervision, 21,* 312-317.

Parker, W. M., Valley, M. M., & Geary, C. A. (1986). Acquiring cultural knowledge for counselors in training: A multifaceted approach. *Counselor Education and Supervision, 26,* 61-71.

Pedersen, P. (1988). *Handbook for developing multicultural awareness.* Alexandria, VA: American Association of Counseling and Development.

Ponterotto, J. G. (1988). Racial consciousness development among White counselor trainees: A stage model. *Journal of Multicultural Counseling and Development, 16,* 146-156.

Ponterotto, J. G., & Casas, J. M. (1987). In search of multicultural competence within counselor education programs. *Journal of Counseling and Development, 65,* 430-434.

Ponterotto, J. G., Rieger, B. P., Barrett, A., Harris, G., Sparks, R., Sanchez, C. M., & Magids, D. (in press). The Multicultural Counseling Awareness Scale (MCAS): A self-report assessment instrument. In G. R. Sodowsky & J. C. Impara (Eds.), *Multicultural assessment.* Lincoln: University of Nebraska-Lincoln, Buros Institute of Mental Measurements.

Ponterotto, J. G., Rieger, B. P., Barrett, A., & Sparks, R. (1994). Assessing multicultural counseling competence: A review of instrumentation. *Journal of Counseling and Development, 72,* 316-322.

Pope, R. L. (1993). An analysis of multiracial change efforts in student affairs. (Doctoral dissertation, University of Massachusetts at Amherst, 1982). *Dissertation Abstracts International, 53-10,* 3457A.

Pope, R. L. (1994). *Multicultural organization development: Implications and applications for student affairs.* Unpublished manuscript.

Reynolds, A. L. (1993a, February). *Design methods and issues in cultural diversity training.* Presented at the Teachers College Cultural Diversity Training in Higher Education: Issues and Concerns, New York, NY.

Reynolds, A. L. (1993b, February). *Ethical considerations in cultural diversity training.* Presented at the Teachers College Cultural Diversity Training in Higher Education: Issues and Concerns, New York, NY.

Rickard, H. C., & Clements, C. B. (1993). Critique of APA accreditation Criterion II: Cultural and individual differences. *Professional Psychology: Research and Practice, 24,* 123-126.

Ridley, C. R. (1985). Imperatives for ethnic and cultural relevance in psychology training programs. *Professional Psychology: Research and Practice, 16,* 611-622.

Ridley, C. R., Mendoza, D. W., & Kanitz, B. E. (1994). Multicultural training: Reexamination, operationalization, and integration. *The Counseling Psychologist, 22,* 227-289.

Ridley, C. R., Mendoza, D. W., Kanitz, B. E., Angermeier, L., & Zenck, R. (1994). Cultural sensitivity in multicultural counseling: A perceptual schema model. *Journal of Counseling Psychology, 41,* 125-136.

Sabnani, H. B., Ponterotto, J. G., & Borodovsky, L. G. (1991). White racial identity development and cross-cultural counselor training: A stage model. *The Counseling Psychologist, 19,* 72-102.

Sanford, N. (1963). Factors related to the effectiveness of student interaction with the college social system. In B. Barger & E. E. Hall (Eds.), *Higher education and mental health* (pp. 8-26). Proceedings of a conference, University of Florida, Gainesville.

Sodowsky, G. R., Taffe, R. C., Gutkin, T. B., & Wise, S. L. (1994). Development of the Multicultural Counseling Inventory: A self-report measure of multicultural competencies. *Journal of Counseling Psychology, 41,* 137-148.

Speight, S. L., Myers, L. J., Cox, C. I., & Highlen, P. S. (1991). A redefinition of multicultural counseling. *Journal of Counseling and Development, 70,* 29-36.

Sue, D. W. (1991). A model for cultural diversity training. *Journal of Counseling and Development, 70,* 99-105.

Sue, D. W., Arredondo, P., & McDavis, R. J. (1992). Multicultural counseling competencies and standards: A call to the profession. *Journal of Counseling and Development, 70,* 477-486.

Sue, D. W., Bernier, J. E., Durran, A., Feinberg, L., Pedersen, P., Smith, E. J., & Vasquez-Nuttall, E. (1982). Position paper: Cross-cultural counseling competencies. *The Counseling Psychologist, 10,* 45-52.

Sue, D. W., & Sue, D. (1990). *Counseling the culturally different: Theory and practice.* New York: John Wiley.

Wyatt, G., & Parham, W. (1985). The inclusion of culturally sensitive course materials in graduate school and training programs. *Psychotherapy, 22,* 461-468.

PART IV

Practical Strategies for Practice

ONE CRITICISM LEVELED with regard to multicultural counseling is that there is more information on theory and research in the field than there is on the competent and proficient *practice* of counseling within and between cultures. Part IV of the *Handbook* addresses this criticism by presenting three chapters with a highly pragmatic and practitioner emphasis.

Linda Berg-Cross and Ruby Takushi Chinen open this section in Chapter 16 with a concise review and integration of three leading training models that serve as the foundation for their original and popular "Person-in-Culture Interview" (PICI). The authors present thorough guidelines and descriptive case vignettes to demonstrate the utility and face validity of the well-thought-out, semistructured PICI interview.

In Chapter 17, Ingrid Grieger and Joseph G. Ponterotto highlight the challenges of multicultural counseling given the great within-group heterogeneity common to American racial/ethnic client populations. The authors highlight key constructs in the practice of multicultural counseling and present an organizational framework replete with "real" case examples that serves to help the practicing counselor address and understand the role of culture in counseling.

Charlene M. Alexander and Lynn Sussman close this section in Chapter 18 with a look at nontraditional interventions in counseling. Specifically, the authors concentrate on the use of "creative arts" common to the lives of racial/ethnic minority individuals yet often ignored by the counseling profession, and demonstrate how these art forms can be used in building relationships and intervening with culturally different clients.

16

Multicultural Training Models and the Person-in-Culture Interview

LINDA BERG-CROSS

RUBY TAKUSHI CHINEN

THERE IS A GROWING RACIAL and ethnic divisiveness apparent in many communities, college campuses, and corporations across the United States. Each cultural group wants to maintain its identity, get respect for its uniqueness, and socialize future generations to honor their heritage. Unfortunately, respect and knowledge about other cultures are not keeping pace with the pride and possessiveness one feels for one's own particular heritage. Intergroup animosities are being fueled by deep ethnic identifications and shallow appreciations for the lifestyles of other groups (Berg-Cross & Zoppetti, 1991). Strong emotional ties with ancestral groups are also creating friction with the sociopolitical needs and developmental patterns of the planet that stress greater and greater interdependence, interaction, interrelatedness, and common values. Historical pushes to homogenize are being resisted by conservative, intragroup cultural pride. The blossoming of expanded social contacts that has long characterized the American experience is in danger of being replaced by insulated, alienated subgroups who resist all but the most superficial types of coexistence (Berg-Cross, Starr, & Sloan, 1993).

The combined effects of polarizing group interests and reactions against cultural homogenization are fueling racial and ethnic divisiveness. There is a great need for effective tools that allow therapists, trainers, and educators to reach out to a culturally diverse group of clients. Ethnic minority students are an increasing proportion of the college population and will soon represent over 25% of all college students (U.S. Dept. of Education, 1988), yet traditional mental health services are often ineffective or unresponsive to their needs (Sue & Morishima, 1982). Ethnically different students are under particular stress; the normal stresses of adolescence are compounded with problems such as immigrant status, generational conflicts over acculturation, prejudice, and discrimination. In response to an increase in racist incidents on campus, many counseling centers have sought to provide cross-cultural awareness training to peer counselors (Vohra, Rodolfa, DeLaCruz, Vincent, & Bee-Gates, 1991).

Within the community, frequent moves, lack of upward mobility, inadequate family support, and an inability to meaningfully relate to cultural institutions (e.g., schools, churches, civic groups) have increased the need for mental health services among adult men and women. Mental health workers are often unfamiliar with the cultural context of the many different clients with whom they work (Young & Marks, 1986). Workshops on "diversity" often create as many stereotypes as they dispel and leave counselors with little idea of how to gain rapport or tailor an intervention more effectively.

The need for cross-cultural sensitivity and the search for training are apparent not only on college campuses or in mental health settings. The field of international management has become painfully aware of the high financial cost of cross-cultural insensitivity, and managers have been sent scurrying in search of further training (Black & Mendenhall, 1990; Crump, 1989; Evans, Hau, & Sculli, 1989; Li, 1992). A recent article in the *Washingtonian* (Ferguson, 1994) poked fun at diversity training with the title "Chasing Rainbows: Dale Carnegie Meets the New Age—and Business Is Buying It Big-Time." The author argued that diversity or sensitivity training is a lucrative, unregulated field run by shrewd, possibly only minimally trained consultants. Clearly, the mental health professions must respond to criticisms such as these by supporting formal incorporation of cross-cultural training into curricula and by becoming more visible and available for consultation to organizations and management.

Heath, Neimeyer, and Pedersen (1988) noted the increasing need for cross-cultural sensitivity in our rapidly changing society and predicted an improvement in cross-cultural counseling training over the next decade (see also Hills & Strozier, 1992; Kanitz, Mendoza, & Ridley, 1992; Ponterotto & Casas, 1987). Short-term improvements in cross-cultural sensitivity are possible even when students are not aware that cultural diversity is a goal. For example, Goldberg, Kestenbaum, and Shebar (1987) found that by creating a nurturing, diversified classroom setting, understanding between Jews and Arabs was increased even though they were brought together for joint professional training without an overt diversity focus. Clearly, however, greater changes can be obtained with a more overt, directed focus, and the importance of such sensitivity in mental health professionals makes formal inclusion of cross-cultural concepts in training essential.

Over the past 5 years, three different models have been generated to structure cross-cultural training and to help mental health workers create a productive, cohesive workforce. The first focuses on six program designs intended to incorporate multicultural training in mental health curricula (Ridley, Mendoza, & Kanitz, 1992). The second was developed to provide cultural diversity training to business and industry (Sue, 1991). The third offers cross-cultural training exercises tailored to the specific needs of an organization (Brislin, 1989). A brief review of the models will help place programs and exercises into a proper perspective. By using the Ridley et al. (1992) format model, the Sue (1991) content model, and the Brislin (1989) technique model, institutions and training programs can reconceptualize their multicultural training efforts and design more inclusive, appropriate programs geared toward their own particular needs. The Person-in-Culture Interview (PICI) and suggested additional exercises will then be described as training tools that can be used in each of the training models presented.

MODELS OF
CROSS-CULTURAL TRAINING

Mental Health Training and Curriculum Design

At the level of mental health training and curriculum, six program designs for multicultural training have been described by Ridley et al. (1992). These range from programs that do not recognize the role of culture in the counseling process to those that use culture as the basis for all conceptualizations and interventions. The first of the six program designs, the *traditional program design*, typically views existing counseling models as appropriate for persons of all cultural backgrounds, and therefore makes few cross-culturally sensitive modifications in the training curricula. Faculty believe that the laws governing human behavior are fundamentally similar and that culture does not influence those processes (laws can include basic psychological principles as diverse as classical conditioning and nonconditional acceptance).

The second program option, the *workshop design*, does not alter the traditional curriculum but incorporates a multicultural training module into a program of study. Often the workshops occur on a regular basis over the year or during a few intense weekends of study. The third type of training program is the *separate course design*. Here, a single course is developed that covers academic and clinical approaches to a variety of subgroups in the community. An example is the course described by Parker, Valley, and Geary (1986) that addressed cultural knowledge and multicultural community experience.

The *interdisciplinary cognate* approach is a far more intensive multicultural approach. It uses diverse disciplines (psychology, anthropology, political science, sociology, etc.) to understand how culture influences human behavior.

This approach can be presented within a workshop or separate-course format. An example is the multiethnic group experience described by Hurdle (1990), in which a traditional psychology course in interpersonal group therapy theory is used as a context for helping social work students understand the importance of cross-cultural issues. The *subspecialty* model puts increased emphasis on multicultural knowledge by requiring a number of different courses and experiences that lead to cross-cultural competency.

In the *integrated program design*, multicultural theory is woven into every aspect of the training program. Every assessment procedure, diagnosis, and treatment is viewed within particular cultural contexts. For example, Fukuyama (1990) described a universal transcultural model of training that addresses all forms of oppression, challenges all faculty to include diversity concepts in courses, and encourages cooperation with other disciplines. Specific research, clinical, and institutional suggestions for developing an integrated program design are also offered by LaFromboise and Foster (1992). Their suggestions range from institutional modifications that demonstrate a commitment to ethnic diversity among tenured faculty and administration to support of inclusion of cross-cultural issues in courses and research programs (e.g., inclusion of ethnicity as a demographic variable).

Although the Ridley et al. (1992) six-curricula model of training was developed to understand counseling programs, it can be used by industry to redefine the various levels at which their own diversity programs are operating. For example, in a subspecialty model, the Employee Assistance Program (EAP) worker would be given the opportunity to assess cultural conflicts at all levels of the organization. In an integrated program design, cultural sensitivity would be woven into recruitment, benefits packages, training, job specifications, and job evaluation.

Cultural Diversity Training for Business and Industry

Sue (1991) described a model for cultural diversity training that was developed initially for business and industry but that is also applicable to mental health training. It provides the educator or consultant with a framework for assessing the specific training needs of a program or organization. The first dimension is the *functional focus*, or area of concern that the organization seeks to address. For instance, management may wish to focus their energies on the recruitment, retention, or promotion/advancement of qualified minority candidates. The second dimension is those *barriers to diversity* encountered in an organization. These barriers are described as (a) differences in communication or leadership style, (b) interpersonal discrimination or prejudice, and (c) systemic structural or policy barriers. The third dimension is the specific *competencies* that are desired: for example, positive beliefs/attitudes toward minority groups, increased knowledge of different cultures, or improved communication skills. These three dimensions form a matrix that the multicultural educator or consultant can use to identify appropriate interventions for the organization.

Specific Training Exercises for Corporations

Once an area of need has been identified with the Sue model, specific training exercises can be used. Richard Brislin (1989) proposed a model for generating the specific cross-cultural training techniques to be used by corporations. In this technique model, there are three levels of trainee involvement (low, moderate, and high) and three targets of training (learning by cognition, affect, and behavioral enactments). This three-by-three matrix leads to nine different approaches to cross-cultural training. A brief description of each follows:

1. *Low-involvement exercises with a target on cognitions:* This type of training includes lectures from experts and assigned readings.
2. *Moderate-involvement exercises with a target on cognitions: Attribution training* is the most popular teaching modality of this type. In attribution training, participants learn to analyze problems from the viewpoint of people of another culture. Brislin, Cushner, Cherrie, and Yong (1986) prepared 100 critical incidents that help people understand the way the host culture interprets common interpersonal conflict situations. A sample incident follows:

> *Learning the Ropes*
>
> Helen Connor had been working in a Japanese company involved in marketing cameras. She had been there for two years and was well respected by her colleagues. In fact, she was so respected that she often was asked to work with new employees of the firm as these younger employees "learned the ropes." One recent and young employee, Hideo Tanaka, was assigned to develop a marketing scheme for a new model of the camera. He worked quite hard on it, but the scheme was not accepted by his superiors because of the industry wide economic conditions. Helen Connor and Hideo Tanaka happened to be working at nearby desks when the news of the nonacceptance was transmitted from company executives. Hideo Tanaka said very little at that point. That evening, however, Helen and Hideo happened to be at the same bar. Hideo had been drinking and vigorously criticized his superiors at work. Helen concluded that Hideo was a very aggressive Japanese male and that she would have difficulty working with him again in the future. Which alternative provides an accurate statement about Helen's conclusion? (Brislin et al., 1986, p. 448)

Readers then choose one or more of the following explanations: (a) Helen was making an inappropriate judgment about Hideo's traits based on behavior that she observed [correct answer]; (b) because, in Japan, decorum in public is highly valued, Helen reasonably concluded that Hideo's vigorous criticism in the bar marks him as a difficult coworker; (c) company executives had failed to tell Helen and Hideo about economic conditions, and consequently Helen should be upset with the executives, not Hideo; (d) Helen felt that Hideo was attacking her personally (p. 448). The rationale for each "correct" answer is contained in one of 18 thematic essays that provide a conceptual framework for the understanding and analysis of cross-cultural interaction.

3. *High-involvement experiences with a target on cognitions:* Most multicultural theory courses fall under this category, using concepts and models from the behavioral and social sciences to understand broad areas of cross-cultural misunderstanding. Typical of the issues covered here is Argyle's (1986) work on the seven areas most likely to lead to cross-cultural confusion: bribery, nepotism, gifts, buying and selling, eating and drinking, punctuality, and relations with the opposite sex. Through study, the rules governing complex, confusing, or difficult-to-understand social interactions across a variety of cultures become contextually understandable and appreciated.

4. *Low-involvement exercises with a target on affect:* Attending musical or theatrical productions from another culture arouses an emotional understanding of the culture. Also, this type of training includes hearing firsthand the experiences of people, such as the training participants, who have already worked within the culture.

5. *Moderate-involvement exercises with a target on affect:* Many workshops in the United States focus on this model of training: The participants are taught self-awareness through discussions of prejudice, racism, and values.

6. *High-involvement exercises with a target on affect:* Experiences in this category include role playing and simulations of negotiation with the culturally different others.

7. *Low-involvement exercises with a target on behavior:* Here, participants see videotapes or live models who demonstrate appropriate, culturally relevant behaviors.

8. *Moderate-involvement exercises with a target on behavior:* Most typical in this category are field trip assignments that demand new behaviors of the participant.

9. *High-involvement exercises with a target on behavior:* This module includes extended experiential encounters with another person or culture. The Person-in-Culture Interview, to be described, falls into this category.

CROSS-CULTURAL TRAINING AND THE PERSON-IN-CULTURE INTERVIEW

The proposed Person-in-Culture Interview (PICI) is a training device that gives therapists, peer counselors, and business managers a way to approach and dismantle multiple barriers to cross-cultural understanding. It is a simple tool that can be incorporated into any of the models described above.

Rationale for the Person-in-Culture Interview

In clinical settings, a number of factors can create therapeutic obstacles when the therapist is from a different cultural background than the client. Such factors include different communication patterns, different values, different explanations concerning the causes and solutions of problems, and different social and interpersonal needs (Young & Marks, 1986). Attempts to overcome these barriers have traditionally relied on learning the values and lifestyles that typify various cultures and then changing one's own behavior to be sensitive to these cultural factors. These culturally related obstacles to productive and mutually satisfying communication are also present in businesses and large organizations.

Cross-cultural counseling approaches, such as those developed by Ibrahim (1985) and Kluckhohn and Strodtbeck (1961), have stressed the importance of understanding the worldview and values of a client's culture. These models rely on universal values that exist on a continuum; each cultural group is seen as emphasizing different aspects of these values. For example, the five cultural dimensions found in Kluckhohn and Strodtbeck's model are (a) beliefs about human nature (good, bad, mixed), (b) relations of human nature (scientific, supernatural, harmony), (c) activity orientation (doing, being, becoming), (d) time orientation (past, present, future), and (e) relational orientation (individualistic, collateral group, lineal group). Therapists try to understand how various cultural groups express their values along these continua.

Unfortunately, the more one deals with individuals from a particular culture, the more apparent it becomes that most people, though displaying expected culturally bound behaviors and attitudes, have many core values and life-guiding perceptions different from their cultural stereotype. In the real world, errors of stereotyping can indeed become more problematic than errors of cultural insensitivity. Instead of communicating more effectively, cultural knowledge devoid of personal knowledge inevitably leads to stereotyping and an inability to relate empathically.

Besides cultural knowledge, a variety of cross-cultural training approaches are geared toward developing one-on-one skills that help individuals bridge cultural differences. For instance, development of racial consciousness in the therapist has emphasized increased knowledge of self (Merta, Stringham, & Ponterotto, 1988), experiential involvement with other cultures has proved successful as a way to increase credibility with culturally different clients (Mio, 1989), structured learning and behavioral approaches have stressed modeling, role playing, and reinforcement to foster therapist-client comfort, and interpersonal process recall has emphasized self-confrontation and mutual recall through feedback as a path for mutual understanding (Pedersen, 1982).

The PICI (reproduced in Table 16.1) is designed to provide a cross-cultural experience that is sensitive to cultural issues without stereotyping any particular individual. It is a one-on-one, open-ended, 24-item interview with the goal of birthing a deep human encounter between individuals with culturally different backgrounds by asking each party to share his or her worldview with the other. The interview is constructed so that both cultural and idiosyncratic values will be spontaneously revealed in the course of the interview. It is an exercise that allows the interviewer to become cognizant of the important cultural experiences in a person's life as well as the unique personal visions that shape the sense of self. The interviewee shares both the cherished cultural values and the personal, hard-to-reveal values that have been forged from the

TABLE 16.1 The Person-in-Culture Interview

Flip a coin to see who will be the first person to ask the questions. After the first interview round, switch roles. All sharing during this exercise should be kept confidential. No one should disclose information they are uncomfortable sharing. Good luck and have fun.

1. (For workshop participants) What are the most enjoyable activities in your life? What types of activities, interactions, and thoughts are most rewarding?
   (For clients in a mental health setting) What would be the best (most pleasurable) part about getting rid of your problem?

2. (For workshop participants) What are the most enjoyable activities for the other members of your family? Are there different activities, interactions, and thoughts that are most rewarding?
   (For clients) Why would your family be happy to have you get rid of this problem? (What would be most pleasurable for them?)

3. (For workshop participants) In general, what types of experiences are particularly painful for you?
   (For clients) In what way do your current problems create pain for you?

4. (For workshop participants) What types of experiences have been most painful for the other members of your family?
   (For clients) In what way do your current problems create pain in your family?

5. Describe your most embarrassing experience in the past year and in your life, or describe what might be an embarrassing situation.

6. What kinds of things make you angry? Or how would someone be able to tell that you are angry?

7. How do the different members of your family express anger?

8. Do you have enough money to eat well?

9. Does your family have enough money to eat well?

10. Do you feel safe where you live?

11. Does your family feel safe where they live?

12. Name situations in which you feel safe.

13. What about the rest of the family? What types of things make them feel safe?

14. What types of things make you feel important?

15. How do the people in your family get that feeling of importance and self-esteem?

16. What types of things make you feel that you are living life to the fullest?

17. If you "fit in" at home and in your community, tell what a normal day would be like. What type of normal day are you striving for?

18. Each little community has certain images of a successful person. In what ways would your community judge you to be successful or unsuccessful?

19. Draw me a "psychological map" of where you are in the center of the universe. Who are the people closest to you (psychologically)? Who are the people most distant from you? Draw a straight line between you and each person with whom you have good communication. Draw a dotted line between you and the people in your map with whom you have dysfunctional, aversive, or strained communications. Draw a zigzag line between you and those people with whom communication is infrequent.

20. Draw me a totem pole of the important people in your life. Put the weakest person on the bottom. Put the most powerful person on the top. Pretend the totem pole is 100 feet high and people can be placed on any of 100 steps—each one foot higher than the next. People can share "steps" on the totem pole. Be sure to include yourself and anyone in the community or elsewhere who is very important in your life.

21. What are your religious beliefs?

22. On a day-to-day basis, how do you learn new things? Who gives you new information? How do you go about learning new information?

23. What are your feelings about death?

24. How can your life be more meaningful?

25. What types of things do you feel you are responsible for on a day-to-day basis as a human being? What types of things do you feel your family is responsible for? What types of things do you think your society/community is responsible for?

interaction between the megaculture, a specific subgroup, and a unique personality.

The PICI has been developed to train therapists in cross-cultural understanding, to help build a therapeutic alliance with culturally different clients, and to increase racial and ethnic tolerance among community leaders, and it can be easily adapted for use as a nonclinical exercise in all types of cross-cultural training programs. It provides for learning about a particular culture while fostering a broader expertise in communicating with any person from a different cultural background (Johnson, 1987).

Structure and Content of the Person-in-Culture Interview

The PICI is a 24-item, open-ended interview that a therapist can give a client or any two people can give to one another in a structured context with the goal of furthering cultural understanding. The PICI uses a traditional interview format so that it can be incorporated into any usual intake interview, or it can be modified for use as an exercise in nonclinical training situations. The philosophy behind the interview format is that there are basic needs in all human beings and that the method by which those needs are met is culturally derived. When one asks about basic drives, culturally relevant issues are likely to emerge. The PICI Interview is based on the four major motivational theories of our time: psychodynamic psychology, humanistic psychology, family (systems) psychology, and existential psychology. Questions are generated from each theory in a direct manner (to be discussed in detail below).

During the PICI training workshops, participants are told to pair off and give each other the interview. Participants are further instructed to pair off in such a way that they are interviewing someone who appears to be very different from themselves. Invariably, these interviews are profound learning experiences and sometimes lead to intense interpersonal bonding. The effect is similar to a group encounter session, although here the time together is brief (1 to 2 hours) and very intimate (one on one). We have been struck most of all by the genuine respect that the individuals have for one another after a PICI exercise. In therapy sessions, clients often remark that they feel the therapist really "knows" them after the interview.

The PICI process relies on individuals' being open to communicating with a "trusted stranger" about a variety of intimate topics. Some cultural groups that value privacy might be expected to have great difficulty or discomfort during the interview. Although it is our experience that this does not happen, it may be helpful to use the PICI among peers in an effort to minimize the difficulty a participant may have in discussing personal matters with an authority figure. Of course, in both situations, we urge people not to answer with any information they would not feel comfortable sharing. Our experience is still limited to urban, educated populations, and undoubtedly there are a number of situations in which the PICI would be contraindicated. Until we have more experience, we need to safeguard every participant and terminate the exercise if a person appears unduly distressed or uncomfortable.

The following section contains the 25 questions and a sampling of the range of responses one gets from various ethnic minorities. The individuals quoted throughout this chapter are all students or friends of students at Howard University in Washington, DC.

Psychodynamic Questions

All people try to increase the amount of pleasure they experience and decrease the amount of pain that they feel. This assumption has been the cornerstone of both Freudian psychodynamic theory and Skinnerian behavioral theory. Of course, neither of these theories assumes that people are conscious of what pleasures they are motivated to obtain and/or what pain they are motivated to avoid. However, the conscious representation of these needs reflects culturally acceptable derivatives and hence would be ideally suited for our needs. Besides seeking pleasure and avoiding pain, psychodynamic theory postulates that all human beings have enormous needs to deal with feelings of shame and anger (Strachey & Freud, 1985). The following seven questions are intended to help us understand how an individual reflects on culturally appropriate and personally meaningful expressions of basic psychodynamic drives:

1. (For workshop participants) What are the most enjoyable activities in your life? What types of activities, interactions, and thoughts are most rewarding? (For clients in a mental health setting) What would be the best (most pleasurable) part about getting rid of your problem?

2. (For workshop participants) What are the most enjoyable activities for the other members of your family? Are there different activities, interactions, and thoughts that are most rewarding?
   (For clients) Why would your family be happy to have you get rid of this problem? (What would be most pleasurable for them?)

3. (For workshop participants) In general, what types of experiences are particularly painful for you?
   (For clients) In what way do your current problems create pain for you?

4. (For workshop participants) What types of experiences have been most painful for the other members of your family?
   (For clients) In what way do your current problems create pain in your family?

5. Describe your most embarrassing experience in the past year and in your life, or describe what might be an embarrassing situation.

6. What kinds of things make you angry? Or how would someone be able to tell that you are angry?

7. How do the different members of your family express anger?

Typical of the range of responses one obtains in response to this set of questions are the following answers in response to Question 5, "During the past year, can you remember any experiences that were particularly embarrassing for you?" Notice how the Russian woman feels shame about her professional persona and inferior as an immigrant with an accent. Similarly, the African American feels shame when he is perceived as incompetent, but the story has the added tension of perceived racism.

Zelda, age 37, Russian

For me, it was embarrassing, my job at the Harbour Country Day School. In Leningrad, I taught English for 10 years. There, when I spoke with an accent, made a mistake or used a word incorrectly, no one cared. Here, I teach ESOL [English as a Second Language], and I got terribly embarrassed the first few months. For the first 4 or 5 months I was afraid to open my mouth around the other teachers. I felt so embarrassed teaching English without speaking English better than I do. Every teacher and secretary spoke better than I. I was even embarrassed teaching the children who did not speak English.

And I remember that when people asked me what I taught, I would tell them that I taught social studies. I couldn't make myself say that I was teaching English—so I would say social studies.

Then after a while, I felt that I speak much better when I am not in the school. I didn't have the complex then—when I didn't have people around me who I knew, I didn't have to compare my speech with theirs.

Charlie, age 28, African American Graduate Student

Well, I teach a psychology course and my students are predominantly Caucasian. I pride myself on having everything in order. One day I gave a particular syllabus to the class. I hadn't had time to proof it. I got to class late—and I have a Caucasian male in class who had had trouble dealing with me. I was 10 minutes late to the first class and he was like making it very clear . . . "Are we going to have this the rest of the term? You came in here sort of late. I knew you said you got caught on the bridge—whatever bridge that is . . . and I'm just wondering if this is how it's going to be." That is how he got started.

There was a mistake with the date and the name of the textbook. And it was embarrassing because I have a tremendous amount of composure and it was hard for me to remain composed in that situation without jacking him up. Because I knew it was full of prejudice.

On the question "When you get angry, how do you express it?" an African American describes using a cultural musical outlet to express himself, and a Russian mother describes how her anger, exacerbated by the stress of acculturation, is expressed as scapegoating of her son.

Sean, age 24, African American

If it is spontaneous anger, I usually say the traditional four-letter words. But if someone made me angry and I had time to reflect on it, I usually go down in my basement and play on some African drums. My wife can tell when I am angry because I play very loudly.

Laura, age 32, Russian

Since we came to the United States it is much harder for me to control my temper. It seems as though I am always shouting at my son. At home, I don't ever remember yelling. I feel like I am a different person—like I have lost all my patience.

Humanistic Needs

Humanistic theories of human development state that human beings have basic needs that are hierarchically arranged: Until the needs at the bottom are met, higher needs are not experienced. Once the basic needs are met, however, the next level of needs emerges with the same intensity and need of satisfaction as was experienced with the more basic needs. The following 11 questions ask about satisfaction of needs based on Maslow's hierarchy (Maslow, 1968):

8. Do you have enough money to eat well?
9. Does your family have enough money to eat well?
10. Do you feel safe where you live?
11. Does your family feel safe where they live?
12. Name situations in which you feel safe.
13. What about the rest of the family? What types of things make them feel safe?
14. What types of things make you feel important?
15. How do the people in your family get that feeling of importance and self-esteem?
16. What types of things make you feel that you are living life to the fullest?
17. If you "fit in" at home and in your community, tell what a normal day would be like. What type of normal day are you striving for?
18. Each little community has certain images of a successful person. In what ways would your community judge you to be successful or unsuccessful?

Questions 8 to 12 tend to deliver universal answers, at least in the urban centers where we have been using the questionnaire. The following are responses to "What makes you feel safe?"

Zelda, age 21, Russian

That I won't get robbed. That there is always someone home. That we always know each other's schedule.

Tar, age 23, Sudanese

That I have enough money to eat. And that I am safe and that my family is safe from harm.

Linda, age 19, Maryland

Knowing that my family is alive and well.

Some of the most culturally revealing answers occur to Question 14. A student from Ghana feels important due to her family identification and family achievements; an African American gathers importance by being an intellectual mentor to his children and being financially able to buy them toys; a male student from Sudan feels most important when the family seeks out his opinion.

Paro, age 26, Ghana

It is most important that I'm a member of this family. Bearing that last name. I feel comfortable with myself. And I feel proud of my achievement in terms of getting the money to fund my education. When I worked full time and wasn't going to school, I did a good job. Everything I did, I feel I did well. I excelled and the members of my family excelled.

I am an Arozneyerg and I am proud to be a member of this family. I can share with them and they with me. When my sister does this and that, it makes me feel so proud. We gloat in each other's glory in a way.

John, age 30, African American

It is very important to me to take my kids out and let them know that I am in charge. Like if we go to a museum, I try to explain what each of the exhibits is about. My 6-year-old is very inquisitive and keeps on asking me questions. I usually try to give her complete answers. Since I am more informed than most people about such things, often other patrons will stop and listen and ask questions themselves. Also, it is very important to me to have enough money in my pocket so that when I am in Toys R Us with the kids, I can just take out the money and buy them what they want.

John, age 25, Sudan

Usually I feel most important when people ask my opinion before they make a decision—an important decision in the family. The effort you make to know someone's opinion is very important. It is OK not to follow their advice, but you must listen to it. For example, when you get married it is very important to ask members of the family if they agree to the marriage and to hear all their opinions. There will be hurt feelings and bad relations if they are not consulted in the very beginning.

Question 16 asks, "What types of things make you feel you are living life to the fullest?" (self-actualization question). Like many of the other questions, this one produces a mixture of unique responses, culturally rooted responses, and universal responses.

Paul, age 20, African American

I would want to have high self-esteem. I would like to financially be able to do the things that I want. And I would like to have someone that I care about to share my free time.

Lana, age 32, Ghana

In the morning, I would go to work. It would be a professional job that I liked and where I could use my education. Then in the evening, I would like to be able to come home and share time with my family and neighbors.

Miriam, age 23, Russian

For me, first of all it is important that I like my job. That I can stay on the phone when I have free time and that I have some friends and people with whom I can communicate. That I can go different places is very important—that I can read magazines, newspapers and have the opportunity to go to the theater.

Family Psychology

Although this field is still in its infancy, empirical research has continually found two basic dimensions that characterize families: how power is distributed among the family members, and cohesiveness within the family (Figley, 1989). The following two questions will help individuals share information about how their family is organized.

19. Draw me a "psychological map" of where you are in the center of the universe. Who are the people closest to you (psychologically)? Who are the people most distant from you? Draw a straight line between you and each person with whom you have good communication. Draw a dotted line between you and the people in your map with whom you have dysfunctional, aversive, or strained communications. Draw a zigzag line between you and those people with whom communication is infrequent.

20. Draw me a totem pole of the important people in your life. Put the weakest person on the bottom. Put the most powerful person on the top. Pretend the totem pole is 100 feet high and people can be placed on any of 100 steps—each one foot higher than the next. People can share "steps" on the totem pole. Be sure to include yourself and anyone in the community or elsewhere who is very important in your life.

Stereotypes are broken in the examples below: An African American puts his grandfather as the most powerful person in the family, a student from Ghana cannot differentiate the members of her family on this dimension, and a musician from New York puts his boss as the most important person in his life.

Charlie, age 28, African American

One hundred for my grandfather, 75 for my son (age 6), 50 for my mom, 30 for my aunt and uncle, 0 for society.

Student, age 28, Ghana

I think of the community as my family. I don't think I can do it because I cannot think of anyone as being most important and anyone as being the weakest. Because I don't look at it that way.

If we talk about sharing respect and listening to everyone, I can do that. I can put father and mother on the top and go down from the first sibling to the youngest sibling. Not that I wouldn't show my younger brother respect, but if I had to listen to someone, I would be obliged to listen to my older brother first. Not that my younger brother isn't important, but things just have to go from father to mother to first sibling, all the way down to the youngest.

Piano Player, age 33, New Yorker

At the top, 80 is my boss. My parents are maybe a 50. And around 30 are my friends.

Existential Psychology Questions

Existential psychologists feel that people have a need to confront the most basic philosophical issues of their existence. Existentialism is the oldest and most radical of the healing arts and has been used by many therapists to transcend cultural and national boundaries in their quest to understand and treat a particular client (Vontress, 1988). The following five sets of questions are derived from the basic questions posed by existential psychology (Yalom, 1985):

21. What are your religious beliefs?
22. On a day-to-day basis, how do you learn new things? Who gives you new information? How do you go about learning new information?
23. What are your feelings about death?
24. How can your life be more meaningful?
25. What types of things do you feel you are responsible for on a day-to-day basis as a human being? What types of things do you feel your family is responsible for? What types of things do you think your society/community is responsible for?

Responses to death are some of the most unique and personally revealing in the interview:

Mina, age 23, Ghana

I am very scared of death. I'm especially afraid of death because I am so far away from home and my parents are getting older. It's something you know is going to happen one day, but you wish it wouldn't happen. I don't live in constant fear, but it is something that bothers me. I don't know how I will handle it. I've experienced very few deaths. I had an aunt die when I was quite young, and I remember I did not handle that well. I pray harder each day, "God keep them." But at the same time I have to be realistic. I know someday one of them is going to die.

Rose, age 29, African American

I had a relative that had a stroke—my mother. Everyone in the family looked to me because I am the most sensitive about how to handle these things. I can honestly say that I'm very comfortable about death. In fact, I call it entering the transition. I'm very comfortable with it. But if it were very close to me, someone in my nuclear family, I'm not sure how I would handle it because it would alter my life so dramatically. The only reason I personally fear death is that my children are little and still need my guidance every day.

Although the PICI tends to be a serious and emotional encounter between people, many have moments of infectious humor and witty life observations. Consider the following response to the question "What is the responsibility of the community?"

Leaf, age 27, Nigerian

I feel that the community is responsible not just for their own sons and daughters but for any child in the community. In my country, everyone looks after each child in the community. If a child is fighting or crying, you go out and find out what happened—even if it is not your child.

Or let us say you sit and do not get up on the bus for a person older than you—you get a knock on your head—even if you do not know the person. If you know who it is and go home and tell your mother, she will call and thank the person for disciplining you. But I notice it is different here. You can't say anything to anyone's child. It is none of your business and you'll get a lawsuit!

ADDITIONAL EXERCISES

In organizational settings, it is useful to include a set of statements that allow participants to explore their style of relating within an organization. Although many such questionnaires exist, the FIRO-B (Schutz, 1977) and the Involvement Inventory by Heslin and Blake (1973) are applicable to most work settings. Both scales need to be taken and scored beforehand. The Involvement Inventory is in the public domain and is reproduced here so readers can easily incorporate it into the PICI. It examines three Platonic types of orientations:

philosophers (oriented toward ideas), warriors (oriented toward getting things done and dealing with objects), and hedonists (oriented toward having a good time and dealing with people). Although it is not designed specifically for the workplace, it is a reliable and valid test that has held up over time and reveals three patterns central to a diversified work place (affective involvement with people, behavioral involvement in accomplishing tasks, and cognitive involvement with ideas). Note that the three areas explored mirror the three types of multicultural training explicated by Brislin (1989).

The instrument consists of a set of 102 statements that the subjects endorse as 1 = *disagree*, 2 = *unsure, probably disagree*, 3 = *unsure, probably agree*, or 4 = *agree*. Items with reversed statements such that agreement indicates low involvement are scored as 1 = *agree*, 2 = *unsure, probably agree*, 3 = *unsure, probably disagree*, and 4 = *disagree*. Items 1 to 39 indicate Affective involvement, 40 to 74 indicate Behavioral involvement, and 75 to 102 indicate Cognitive involvement. The totals of the three scales *A*, *B*, and *C* can be summed for an overall involvement score. Tables 16.2 through 16.4 list the inventory questions and scoring procedures.

After the PICI is completed, participants take a break and reconvene to discuss their work styles. Participants are given their scores on the three subscales of the inventory and are asked to use their scores to help initiate a discussion of the following three groups of questions:

1. How important is it to you to get personally involved with the people at work? How important is it to you to feel close to the people at work? How cautious are you about personally disclosing information about yourself at work?
2. Are you pragmatic about going ahead with the information on hand, or are you more of an idealist or a worrier who wants to cover additional bases before committing yourself to a course of action?
3. Do you like to be a follower or leader at work? Do you like to work on long-term projects or smaller, time-limited tasks?

After the discussion of the Involvement Inventory, training workshops or seminars may choose to close and summarize the day's training events with an additional informal exercise geared toward facilitating self-disclosure and sharing of personal experiences in a larger group setting. One easy, popular task consists of asking trainees to prepare a collage of themselves to present to all the other participants. Each person is provided with a large brown paper bag, scissors, glue, and a variety of colorful magazines. Participants are asked to decorate the outside of the bag with visual images that represent how they believe others see them. The inside of the bag is filled with images that represent the more private, personally held views of the self. Upon completion of the exercise, participants present to the group as much or as little of both the inside and outside of the paper bag collage as they desire and, when possible, indicate how experience with the PICI has affected the images presented.

TABLE 16.2 The Involvement Inventory

Directions: Indicate your level of agreement with each statement by placing a check in the appropriate space on the answer sheet. Do not spend a lot of time on any one item. Respond with your initial reaction.

1. I like to get close to people.
2. I find it easy to express affection.
3. When I become angry, people know it.
4. When I am happy, I like to shout and whoop it up.
5. I am the kind of person who would shout a friend's name across a crowded room if I saw him/her come in the door.
6. I know I would stand up in a group and call a liar a liar.
7. I enjoy the shoulder to shoulder contact with other people in a crowded elevator.
8. The wise thing for a person to do is argue his/her case with a policeman who has pulled him/her over for speeding.
9. In nonwork situations I like to flirt with someone I find attractive even if I'm not serious.
10. I am an expressive person.
11. I prefer dogs to cats.
12. I have struck up a conversation with another person while waiting for an elevator.
13. The thought of participating in one of these "sensitivity training" groups where people tell each other exactly how they feel really appeals to me.
14. If someone is driving down the street and sees a friend walking in the opposite direction, they should honk the car horn and wave.
15. It is a thrill to walk into a party alone with a large group already there.
16. I like to dance the latest dances at a party.
17. If I am required to have continual close contact with someone who has irritating habits, I would bring them to her/his attention.
18. After I have been reading for some time, I have to spend some time talking with someone, otherwise I feel lonely.
19. If I were emotionally attached to someone, I could sing a song or say a poem to him/her.
20. I get nervous when people get personal with me.
21. I am able to hide my feelings when I feel sad or angry.
22. People consider me a serious person.
23. When I am angry, I become quiet.
24. I never am wholly relaxed with other people.
25. I wish I were more relaxed and free-wheeling in my dealing with my friends.
26. I have never spoken harshly to anyone.
27. If a friend of mine was concerned about something that she/he was embarrassed to speak about, I would probably let her/him work it out herself/himself.
28. I become embarrassed when the topic of conversation touches on something the other person wants to avoid.
29. If someone challenged something I said in a decidedly hostile manner, I would probably break off the conversation at the first convenient opportunity.
30. It is best to forget an unpleasant person.
31. I get as much kick out of watching an exciting game of football or basketball as I do playing a game.
32. Even though I may want to, I feel nervous about putting my arm around the shoulder of a friend.
33. There are many times when I have held back from saying what I knew I should say because I didn't want to hurt someone's feelings.
34. If a person does something to hurt a friend, he/she should do something to make it up to him/her rather than mentioning or apologizing for the hurt.
35. If I were riding on a train and the car I was in had only one of a pair of seats empty, I would go on to another car looking for a double seat that was empty so that I wouldn't have to sit with someone.
36. I am never quite sure how to handle it when someone flirts with me.

TABLE 16.2 (Continued)

37. In a social situation, if a good looking person puts their arm around another person in a friendly manner while talking, they should disengage themselves at the first appropriate chance.
38. When people tease me in a group, I often do not know what to say in response.
39. I prefer watching television to sitting around and talking.
40. I always have at least four projects going at once.
41. I am the one who gets others going and in action.
42. I tend to take charge in my groups and direct the others.
43. I like to take risks.
44. I would rather build something than read a novel.
45. I have a very strong need to run things and organize things, even though doing so cuts into time I might devote to other activities.
46. I love to repair things.
47. I love to work with my hands building things.
48. I have strong "arts and crafts" interests.
49. I do good work with my hands.
50. Nothing is quite so enjoyable as winning in competition.
51. I enjoy persuading people.
52. I enjoy playing competitive athletics.
53. It would be fun to try to make a radio using only a very basic blueprint.
54. As an accomplishment, I get a bigger kick out of the Space Shuttle than out of the Theory of Relativity.
55. Even though I may delegate tasks to people who are helping me, it makes me nervous to do so because I know if I want it done right, I should do it myself.
56. I find that I work faster than most people I know.
57. I have always enjoyed constructing model airplanes, ships, cars, and things like that.
58. I prefer to follow and let someone else take the lead.
59. I like to keep my risk low.
60. I prefer to be involved in an activity that another person rather than myself has organized.
61. I doubt that I could produce and market a product successfully.
62. I would rather read a play than make something.
63. I wouldn't know where to begin if I had to build something like a fireplace.
64. I avoid taking chances.
65. I would rather play solitaire than build a birdhouse.
66. I prefer to join a group that is already well established, rather than join a new one.
67. For me the greatest joy is in finding out about things rather than in doing things.
68. Life is so short that we should spend more time enjoying it and less time rushing around doing various projects.
69. I average more than seven hours of sleep a night.
70. I prefer to stick with one task until it is done before taking on another task.
71. I find it more gratifying to work out a successful compromise with the opposition than to compete with and defeat them.
72. When I am bored, I like to take a nap.
73. True contentment lies in coming to a harmonious adjustment with life rather than continually trying to "improve" it.
74. I envy the people in some religious orders who have time for peaceful contemplation and well-organized daily routine.
75. I love to try to spot the logical flaw in TV commercials.
76. You take a big chance if you don't listen to more than one version about something.
77. I would not hesitate to write to any source or official to get the information I need on some problem.
78. I try to read two or three versions of a problem I am trying to understand.
79. I enjoy debating issues.
80. I enjoy analyzing two opposing views to find where they differ and where they agree.

(Continued)

TABLE 16.2 (Continued)

81. When someone tells me something that does not sound quite right, I often check his/her source.
82. My acquaintances turn to me for new slants on the issues of the day.
83. I have more information about what is going on than my associates.
84. It is almost always worth the effort to dig out the facts yourself by reading a number of viewpoints on an issue.
85. I don't believe that any religion is the one true religion.
86. I don't believe in life after death.
87. It is a good idea to read one or two foreign newspapers as a check on our Associated Press and United Press International dominated newspapers.
88. Governmental response to such things as air pollution, water pollution, pesticide poisoning, and population explosion leads one to believe that it does not have the public welfare as its main interest.
89. It is fun to search far and wide to gather in all of the appropriate information about a topic to be evaluated.
90. I like a friendly argument about some issue of the day.
91. If people were forced to describe me as either short-tempered or overcritical they would probably say that I am overcritical.
92. I have trouble finding things to criticize in something I read.
93. Most of what I read seems reasonable to me.
94. I wish someone would put out a book of **known facts** so that people would know what is right these days.
95. I don't like to argue ideas.
96. You should take the expert's word on things unless you know for sure that they are wrong.
97. I would rather read a summary of the facts in an area than try to wade through the details myself.
98. I get almost all of my news information from television.
99. As with most people, 95 percent of my opinions come from personal acquaintances.
100. Once I have made up my mind on an issue, I stick to it.
101. If people were forced to describe me as either selfish or narrow-minded, they would probably say that I am narrow-minded.
102. Most of my acquaintances would describe me as productive rather than as individualistic.

SOURCE: Heslin & Blake, 1973. Slight modifications have been made to update the items.

SUMMARY

Multicultural sensitivity in the mental health profession and in the business world is a growing need in our rapidly changing society. The Person-in-Culture Interview (PICI) is a flexible interview that is designed to provide a cross-cultural experience that celebrates differences and is sensitive to the cultural histories of each party involved. It is designed to help participants explore both the broad worldviews that a cultural group may hold and the individual expression of those views. Users of the interview can look to the training models described in this chapter to reconceptualize their specific multicultural training needs. It is hoped that users of the PICI will adapt and expand the PICI format to further cross-cultural understanding in the developing mental health profession and in their own communities and offices.

TABLE 16.3 Involvement Inventory Answer Sheet

	Disagree	Unsure, Probably Disagree	Unsure, Probably Agree	Agree		Disagree	Unsure, Probably Disagree	Unsure, Probably Agree	Agree		Disagree	Unsure, Probably Disagree	Unsure, Probably Agree	Agree
1.	—	—	—	—	35.	—	—	—	—	69.	—	—	—	—
2.	—	—	—	—	36.	—	—	—	—	70.	—	—	—	—
3.	—	—	—	—	37.	—	—	—	—	71.	—	—	—	—
4.	—	—	—	—	38.	—	—	—	—	72.	—	—	—	—
5.	—	—	—	—	39.	—	—	—	—	73.	—	—	—	—
6.	—	—	—	—	40.	—	—	—	—	74.	—	—	—	—
7.	—	—	—	—	41.	—	—	—	—	75.	—	—	—	—
8.	—	—	—	—	42.	—	—	—	—	76.	—	—	—	—
9.	—	—	—	—	43.	—	—	—	—	77.	—	—	—	—
10.	—	—	—	—	44.	—	—	—	—	78.	—	—	—	—
11.	—	—	—	—	45.	—	—	—	—	79.	—	—	—	—
12.	—	—	—	—	46.	—	—	—	—	80.	—	—	—	—
13.	—	—	—	—	47.	—	—	—	—	81.	—	—	—	—
14.	—	—	—	—	48.	—	—	—	—	82.	—	—	—	—
15.	—	—	—	—	49.	—	—	—	—	83.	—	—	—	—
16.	—	—	—	—	50.	—	—	—	—	84.	—	—	—	—
17.	—	—	—	—	51.	—	—	—	—	85.	—	—	—	—
18.	—	—	—	—	52.	—	—	—	—	86.	—	—	—	—
19.	—	—	—	—	53.	—	—	—	—	87.	—	—	—	—
20.	—	—	—	—	54.	—	—	—	—	88.	—	—	—	—
21.	—	—	—	—	55.	—	—	—	—	89.	—	—	—	—
22.	—	—	—	—	56.	—	—	—	—	90.	—	—	—	—
23.	—	—	—	—	57.	—	—	—	—	91.	—	—	—	—
24.	—	—	—	—	58.	—	—	—	—	92.	—	—	—	—
25.	—	—	—	—	59.	—	—	—	—	93.	—	—	—	—
26.	—	—	—	—	60.	—	—	—	—	94.	—	—	—	—
27.	—	—	—	—	61.	—	—	—	—	95.	—	—	—	—
28.	—	—	—	—	62.	—	—	—	—	96.	—	—	—	—
29.	—	—	—	—	63.	—	—	—	—	97.	—	—	—	—
30.	—	—	—	—	64.	—	—	—	—	98.	—	—	—	—
31.	—	—	—	—	65.	—	—	—	—	99.	—	—	—	—
32.	—	—	—	—	66.	—	—	—	—	100	—	—	—	—
33.	—	—	—	—	67.	—	—	—	—	101.	—	—	—	—
34.	—	—	—	—	68.	—	—	—	—	102.	—	—	—	—

TABLE 16.4 Involvement Inventory Scoring Sheet

1. The A scale (Affective or feeling involvement with people) includes items 1 through 39. Items 1 through 19 are weighed differently than items 20 through 39. Draw a line under item 19 on the scoring sheet. Add the checks in each column for items 1 through 19 and place the sum in the spaces below. Multiply each column total by the multiplier beneath it. Add the four products across and put the total in the blank designated (A).

$$\underline{\hspace{3em}} \quad \underline{\hspace{3em}} \quad \underline{\hspace{3em}} \quad \underline{\hspace{3em}}$$

    ×1   ×2   ×3   ×4

____ + ____ + ____ + ____ = ____ (A)

Draw a line under item 39. Add the checks in each column for items 20 through 39 and proceed as you did with items 1 through 19 (notice that the multipliers are reversed from those for items 1 through 19).

    ×4   ×3   ×2   ×1

____ + ____ + ____ + ____ = ____ (a)

2. The B scale (Behavioral involvement in accomplishing tasks) includes items 40 through 74. Draw a line under item 57. Proceed with the scoring as above.

    ×4   ×3   ×2   ×1

____ + ____ + ____ + ____ = ____ (B)

Draw a line under item 74 and proceed as above.

    ×4   ×3   ×2   ×1

____ + ____ + ____ + ____ = ____ (b)

3. The C scale (Cognitive involvement with analyzing pronouncements encountered) includes items 75 through 102. Draw a line under item 91 and proceed with the scoring as above.

    ×4   ×3   ×2   ×1

____ + ____ + ____ + ____ = ____ (C)

Total the remaining columns and proceed as above.

    ×4   ×3   ×2   ×1

____ + ____ + ____ + ____ = ____ (c)

4. Obtain scale scores by adding the totals for each two-part scale. Then obtain the total involvement score by adding the three scale scores.

    A + a = ____

    B + b = ____

    C + c = ____

    Total involvement score = ____

REFERENCES

Argyle, M. (1986). Conceptual framework for the development and evaluation of cross-cultural orientation programs. *International Journal of Intercultural Relations, 10,* 197-213.

Berg-Cross, L., Starr, B. J., & Sloan, L. (1993). Race relations training on college campuses: Goals and techniques for the 90's. *Journal of College Student Psychotherapy, 8,* 151-177.

Berg-Cross, L., & Zoppetti, L. (1991). Person-in-Culture Interview: Understanding culturally different students. *Journal of College Student Psychotherapy, 5,* 224-232.

Black, J. S., & Mendenhall, M. (1990). Cross-cultural training effectiveness: A review and a theoretical framework for future research. *Academy of Management Review, 15,* 113-136.

Brislin, R. (1989). Intercultural communication training. In M. K. Asante & W. Gudykunst (Eds.), *Handbook of international and intercultural communication* (pp. 441-457). Newbury Park, CA: Sage.

Brislin, R., Cushner, K., Cherrie, C., & Yong, M. (1986). *Intercultural interactions: A practical guide.* Beverly Hills, CA: Sage.

Crump, L. (1989). Japanese managers—Western workers: Cross-cultural training and development issues. *Journal of Management Development, 8,* 48-55.

Evans, W. A., Hau, K. C., & Sculli, D. (1989). A cross-cultural comparison of managerial styles. *Journal of Management Development, 8,* 5-13.

Ferguson, A. (1994, April). Chasing rainbows: Dale Carnegie meets the New Age—and business is buying it big-time. *Washingtonian,* pp. 35-42.

Figley, C. (1989). *Treating stress in families.* New York: Brunner/Mazel.

Fukuyama, M. A. (1990). Taking a universal approach to multicultural counseling. *Counselor Education and Supervision, 30,* 6-17.

Goldberg, A., Kestenbaum, S., & Shebar, V. (1987). Jerusalem, Arabs and Jews: What can group work offer? *Social Work With Groups, 10,* 73-83.

Heath, A. E., Neimeyer, G. J., & Pedersen, P. B. (1988). The future of cross-cultural counseling: A Delphi poll. *Journal of Counseling and Development, 67,* 27-30.

Heslin, R., & Blake, B. (1973). The involvement inventory. In J. Jones & J. Pfeiffer (Eds.), *The 1973 annual handbook for group facilitators* (pp. 87-94). La Jolla, CA: University Associates.

Hills, H. I., & Strozier, A. L. (1992). Multicultural training in APA-approved counseling psychology programs: A survey. *Professional Psychology: Research and Practice, 23,* 143-151.

Hurdle, D. E. (1990). The ethnic group experience. *Social Work With Groups, 13,* 59-69.

Ibrahim, F. A. (1985). Effective cross-cultural counseling and psychotherapy: A framework. *The Counseling Psychologist, 13,* 625-638.

Johnson, S. D., Jr. (1987). Knowing that versus knowing how: Toward achieving expertise through multicultural training for counseling. *The Counseling Psychologist, 15,* 320-331.

Kanitz, B. E., Mendoza, D. W., & Ridley, C. R. (1992). Multicultural training in religiously-oriented counselor education programs: A survey. *Journal of Psychology and Christianity, 11,* 337-344.

Kluckhohn, F. R., & Strodtbeck, F. L. (1961). *Variations in value orientations.* Evanston, IL: Row, Peterson.

LaFromboise, T. D., & Foster, S. L. (1992). Cross-cultural training: Scientist-practitioner model and methods. *The Counseling Psychologist, 20,* 472-489.

Li, L. C. (1992). The strategic design of cross-cultural training programmes. *Journal of Management Development, 11,* 22-29.

Maslow, A. (1968). *Toward a psychology of being.* New York: Van Nostrand Reinhold.

Merta, R. J., Stringham, E. M., & Ponterotto, J. G. (1988). Simulating culture shock in counselor trainees: An experiential exercise for cross-cultural training. *Journal of Counseling and Development, 66,* 242-245.

Mio, J. (1989). Experiential involvement as an adjunct to teaching cultural sensitivity. *Journal of Multicultural Counseling and Development, 17*, 38-46.

Parker, W. M., Valley, M. M., & Geary, C. A. (1986). Acquiring cultural knowledge for counselors in training: A multifaceted approach. *Counselor Education and Supervision, 26*, 61-71.

Pedersen, P. (1982). The intercultural context of counseling and therapy. In A. J. Marsella & G. M. White (Eds.), *Cultural conceptions of mental health and therapy* (pp. 333-358). Boston: Kluwer.

Ponterotto, J. G., & Casas, J. M. (1987). In search of multicultural competence within counselor education programs. *Journal of Counseling and Development, 65*, 430-434.

Ridley, C. R., Mendoza, D. W., & Kanitz, B. E. (1992). Program designs for multicultural training. *Journal of Psychology and Christianity, 11*, 326-335.

Schutz, W. (1977). *FIRO-B*. Palo Alto, CA: Consulting Psychologist Press.

Strachey, S., & Freud, A. (Eds.). (1985). *Standard edition of the complete psychological works of Sigmund Freud*. New York: Norton.

Sue, D. W. (1991). A model for cultural diversity training. *Journal of Counseling and Development, 70*, 99-105.

Sue, S., & Morishima, J. (1982). *The mental health of Asian Americans*. San Francisco: Jossey-Bass.

U.S. Department of Education, National Center for Educational Statistics. (1988). *Total enrollment in institutions of higher education*. Washington, DC: Author.

Vohra, S., Rodolfa, E., DeLaCruz, A., Vincent, C., & Bee-Gates, D. (1991). A cross-cultural training format for peer counselors. *Journal of College Student Development, 32*, 82-84.

Vontress, C. (1988). An existential approach to cross cultural counseling. *Journal of Multicultural Counseling and Development, 16*, 73-83.

Yalom, I. (1985). *Existential psychotherapy*. New York: Basic Books.

Young, R. A., & Marks, S. E. (1986). Understanding attributional processes in cross cultural counseling. *International Journal of the Advancement of Counseling, 9*, 319-326.

17

A Framework for Assessment in Multicultural Counseling

INGRID GRIEGER

JOSEPH G. PONTEROTTO

COUNSELING IS a highly complex and interactive process. Providing mental health services to someone who is similar to the counselor in terms of values, attitudes, beliefs, culture, life experiences, and religion is challenging enough; counseling someone who differs from the counselor on these and other characteristics presents an even greater challenge. It is clear that as the demography of the United States continues to shift, counselors will increasingly work with clients who have backgrounds and cultural experiences highly dissimilar to their own (Atkinson, Morten, & Sue, 1993; Sue, Arredondo, & McDavis, 1992).

Successful counseling requires an accurate assessment of the client's concerns, which includes an in-depth understanding of the factors that influence the client's experience, perception, and presentation of her or his problems. Furthermore, comprehensive assessment entails viewing the client as a unique individual, as a social unit within a family, and as a member of a cultural group (Ponterotto & Casas, 1991).

There is a perception among multicultural specialists, however, that the majority of counselors are not adequately trained to conduct accurate clinical assessments of clients who represent culturally diverse (particularly non-White, non-middle-class) groups (e.g., Dana, 1993; Highlen, 1994; Sue & Sue, 1990). Recent national surveys support the concern that training curricula in counseling and related psychological disciplines are not keeping pace with the changing nature of population demographics (e.g., Allison, Crawford, Echemendia, Robinson, & Knepp, 1994; Bernal & Castro, 1994; Hills & Strozier, 1992; Quintana & Bernal, 1995; Rogers, Ponterotto, Conoley, & Wiese, 1992; Suarez-Balcazar, Durlak, & Smith, in press).

Changing client demographics and the less than adequate state of multicultural training in counseling curricula speak to the need for increased attention to diversity issues. The focus of this chapter is on assessing clients as unique individuals and as members of an influential family and cultural group. It is our premise that in order to help clients, counselors must understand the client's orientation to and experience of the counseling process.

We have two primary goals for this chapter. First, we will review two constructs—worldview and acculturation—that the literature and our own clinical experience have highlighted as central to counseling assessment in a heterogeneous society. We summarize these constructs briefly and present preferred references for more elaborate discussions of the topics. Second, we provide a pragmatic framework for conceptualizing salient foci for the assessment process. Integrated throughout this section are brief case summaries taken primarily from the clinical practice of the senior author and her supervisees.

THE WORLDVIEW
AND ACCULTURATION CONSTRUCTS

Worldview

One of the most popular constructs in the multicultural counseling literature is that of "worldview." There is consensus in the counseling profession that to understand a client's frame of reference for the counseling process, and to meet the client's needs and expectations in therapy, the counselor must accurately assess the client's worldview (Carter, 1991; Ibrahim, 1991; Ibrahim, Ohnishi, & Wilson, 1994; Sodowsky & Johnson, 1994; Sue & Zane, 1987).

Ibrahim et al. (1994) perceived worldview as the "lens" through which people interpret their world. According to these authors, worldview is a culturally based variable stemming from the socialization process. The assessment of worldview is a necessary step in understanding the client's frame of reference for the counseling process.

Perhaps the most comprehensive presentation of the worldview construct was put forth by Dana (1993). His view parallels that of Ibrahim et al. (1994), but is more expansive and inclusive. Dana (1993) dissected worldview into two components—group identity (e.g., nature of cultural heritage) and individual identity (e.g., self-concept)—that form the basis of one's values, beliefs, and language. These characteristics in turn provide the foundation for one's perceptions of counseling services (e.g., needs), service providers (e.g., personal qualities), and service delivery (e.g., process and style of counseling).

Dana's (1993) comprehensive conceptualization of worldview sheds light on the process of counseling assessment in an increasingly heterogeneous society. An accurate assessment entails inquiry into the client's individual, group, and cultural identity, into his or her values, beliefs, and language, and into his or her perceptions of the helping process. A very well-organized model for conducting such an assessment is provided in Ibrahim et al. (1994).

Readers should be aware that there are numerous instruments of both paper-and-pencil (e.g., "Scale to Assess World View"; Ibrahim & Kahn, 1987; Ibrahim & Owens, 1992) and semistructured format (e.g., Berg-Cross & Chinen, Chapter 16, this volume; Ibrahim et al., 1994; Jacobsen, 1988; Washington, 1994) that assess aspects of worldview. It would be helpful to the reader to review the contents of these instruments in order to understand the scope of the worldview construct.

Acculturation

Another established construct in psychology generally, and multicultural counseling specifically, is acculturation. Acculturation has been defined as "a multi-dimensional and psycho-social phenomenon that is reflected in psychological changes that occur in individuals as a result of their interaction with a new culture" (Marin, 1992, as cited in Casas & Casas, 1994, p. 25). Acculturation theory and research has focused on groups made up of a significant number of past and present immigrants, particularly Asian Americans and Hispanic Americans (Casas & Casas, 1994; Ponterotto & Pedersen, 1993). To some degree, the concept of acculturation has been applied to American Indians (e.g., Choney et al., Chapter 5, this volume). When focusing on intra-cultural variation in African Americans and White Anglo Saxon Americans, the construct of racial identity has been more often applied (Ponterotto & Pedersen, 1993).

Interest in acculturation and ethnic identity has spawned rigorous research into the objective measurement of these constructs. We would estimate that there are now roughly 50 distinct instruments measuring dimensions or levels of acculturation and racial/ethnic identity development. Listings, descriptions, and/or comprehensive psychometric critiques of these instruments can be found in Dana (1993), Paniagua (1994), Ponterotto and Casas (1991), and Sabnani and Ponterotto (1992).

The availability of reliable and valid measures of acculturation and ethnic identity has facilitated research on the relationship of these constructs to measures of mental health. Collectively, the results of this research indicate that levels of acculturation and ethnic identity development are related to clients' attitudes toward Western-type mental health services and to levels of mental health functioning. The findings do vary somewhat from study to study, most likely due to sampling and instrumentation variability, and therefore, the

reader is cautioned to review the findings of specific studies carefully before
drawing definitive conclusions. Research reviews on the relationship between
racial/ethnic identity and acculturation to mental health criteria can be found
in Atkinson and Thompson (1992), Goodstein (1994), Leong and Chou
(1994), and Ponterotto and Pedersen (1993).

AN APPLIED
FRAMEWORK FOR ASSESSMENT

Much of the literature on worldview and acculturation has been theoretical
and empirical in nature. What would be helpful to counselors at this time is
the application of these constructs to actual clinical situations. Therefore, this
section of our chapter delineates those aspects of worldview and acculturation
that most directly affect the counseling process and also offers illustrative case
vignettes.

Drawing from the worldview and acculturation literature reviewed in this
chapter and from our own clinical experience, we have identified six components of worldview and acculturation that are useful to examine in the context
of counseling assessment. These components are the client's level of psychological mindedness (defined as familiarity with the Western middle-class conception of the term), the family's level of psychological mindedness, the
client's/family's attitude toward counseling, the client's level of acculturation, the family's level of acculturation, and the family's attitude toward
acculturation.

Throughout our discussion of these components, we integrate brief summaries of the real-life cases of Tsui-Ling, Mary, Marisol, Diane and Akeem,
Tarik, Indira, and Angela. Although these cases are based upon actual histories, the names and some identifying information have been changed for
obvious reasons of confidentiality.

In presenting our worldview and acculturation perspectives, we define
multicultural or *cross-cultural* to include differences based upon race, ethnicity, and nationality. Although narrow in scope, our definition fits the range of
cases soon to be described. Readers shall note, however, that much broader
and inclusive definitions of *multicultural* have been put forth (e.g., Pedersen,
1991). Within our definition fall worldview differences between and within
White ethnic groups. This chapter, unlike the others in the *Handbook*, does
incorporate White ethnic cohorts into the discussion and includes case
vignettes representative of such groups. The reader is cautioned not to generalize from the cases presented to the entire cultural group under discussion.
Most of our examples focus on traditional (less acculturated) clients and families, and therefore the case interpretations may not be at all representative of
more highly acculturated individuals from the noted cultural group.

In keeping with the intended spirit of this portion of the *Handbook*, which
calls for an applied and pragmatic focus, we have refrained from citing

numerous references in this particular section. It is our hope that this decision will facilitate the smooth flow of the six components and accompanying case vignettes.

Client's Level of
Psychological Mindedness

The client's worldview profoundly affects the level of psychological mindedness that he or she brings to the counseling situation (Midgette & Meggert, 1991). Conceptualizing one's problems from a psychological point of view and having the construct of emotional disturbance as a part of one's interpretive lens generally assumes a Western Eurocentric worldview. To the extent that the client's background diverges significantly from one that is Eurocentric, it is likely that even basic psychological constructs will not be within his or her cultural frame of reference.

A poignant example of this distinction centers on the construct of depression. Most middle-class Americans, inclusive of highly acculturated immigrants, possess a worldview that conceptualizes depression in terms of emotional symptoms and consequences. These individuals, therefore, usually exhibit a certain degree of psychological mindedness with regard to the depression construct. By contrast, consider a client from traditional Eastern society (e.g., Asian cultures) in which a translated term for *depression* is not even in the lexicon of the culture. Although some researchers believe that a "core illness" of depression is universal (Singer, 1975), the clinical manifestations of the disorder and the acknowledgment and experience of the symptoms vary so much between Western and Eastern cultures that some scholars regard the construct as a disorder of the Western world (e.g., Marsella, 1978) without universal applicability (see integrative discussion by Fernando, 1988).

The implication of this example is that the counselor cannot assume the client is psychologically minded with regard to Western-established mental health constructs. The following case involves the construct of depression and illustrates the need for the counselor to probe the client's worldview and to assess her level of psychological mindedness, particularly with regard to framing the problem and determining appropriate psychotherapeutic goals.

Tsui-Ling, an international student from Taiwan, is a 28-year-old married woman who came to a university counseling center with the presenting complaint of feeling unmotivated to complete her dissertation and, in general, not having the requisite energy to engage in her academic work. Her goal for counseling was to learn strategies and techniques for improving concentration and for working more efficiently.

However, once she had completed an in-depth intake, it became apparent to the counselor that Tsui-Ling was suffering from a major depressive episode that was probably precipitated by a miscarriage late in the second trimester. This occurred while she was visiting with her family at home in Taiwan. Upon her return to the United States, she exhibited what were, from a Western point of view, typical signs of depression: fatigue, lack of energy, loss of motivation, inability to concentrate, loss of enjoyment in most activities, feelings of hopelessness and sadness, loss of appetite, and sleep disturbance. However, for Tsui-Ling, the conceptualization of this concern in terms of a personal or psychological issue was not within her frame of reference. Further, in discussing her family history, Tsui-Ling reported that her father had taken his own life. When questioned about why this had happened, her explanation was that he had taken his life in order "to save face." Further exploration revealed that her father probably had suffered from severe depression that had persisted for years. He had experienced classic signs of depression and hopelessness, and yet the cultural framing for his suicide was that he was "saving face."

In Tsui-Ling's traditional Chinese culture, psychological mindedness was virtually nonexistent. The concept of depression was not known to her. When asked how her family and community responded to the miscarriage that she had suffered on her visit, she responded that they took very good physical care of her. Upon returning from the hospital, she was put to bed; she was brought various broths and nurturing foods; women sat with her and carefully watched over her physical condition for several days. The miscarriage was framed as an event that had only physiological, but certainly no emotion or psychological, ramifications.

Because of the nurturing that Tsui-Ling's mother, sisters, and other women in her community had provided, she did in fact feel better physically. Therefore, she was even more puzzled when she continued to feel fatigued, dispirited, and unmotivated, even upon her return to the United States. The notion of the loss of the fetus as having strong emotional sequelae was not within her worldview.

Similarly, in trying to understand her father's suicide, Tsui-Ling focused on a business reversal that had occurred within the year prior to his death and concluded that he had felt embarrassed about that and had therefore ended his life. The idea that he had been suffering from a long-standing depression and that he probably committed suicide more as a result of his emotional disturbance was something that she was not culturally able to conceptualize.

For this client, an important part of the therapeutic process was to educate her about psychological constructs such as depression and about the emotional fallout of significant life events, particularly those that appear to be primarily medical in nature. Tsui-Ling came to understand that her miscarriage was not simply a physiological phenomenon in need of physical and medical support, but that it had profound emotional consequences as well. By altering her worldview, Tsui-Ling was able to understand her lack of motivation, fatigue, and poor concentration on a psychological level. It became clear to her that she was not simply dealing with an academic problem; rather, she was able to appreciate that there was a grieving process and an emotional working through that she needed to experience as well. Further assessment revealed that, like her father, Tsui-Ling had been struggling with depression much of her life and that it had been exacerbated by the miscarriage. A medication evaluation was recommended, and ultimately both counseling and medication were helpful in alleviating Tsui-Ling's long-term dysthymic disorder.

Had the counselor accepted the client's initial goal of improving academic efficiency without considering how her cultural frame of reference affected her level of psychological mindedness, the counseling process would have been of little or no use to this client. Of course, in general, counselors should, and do, realize that the client's presenting concern is often not what most needs to be worked on. However, particular attention must be paid to problem conceptualization and goal setting in cases such as Tsui-Ling's, in which the client's worldview precludes psychological mindedness.

Family's Level of Psychological Mindedness

Closely related to the client's level of awareness of psychological constructs and his or her ability to conceptualize problems psychologically is, of course, the family's level of psychological mindedness. In the example given above, no members of this family had conceptualized their problems as psychological in nature, and therefore, they had provided no basis for the client to do so. Sometimes, as the client's level of psychological understanding and sophistication increases, he or she can bring that back to family members, who may or may not be receptive to expanding their worldview in this direction.

Even when we examine some American cultural or ethnic groups, it is clear that differences may emerge with regard to psychological mindedness. For example, in some traditional Irish American families, thinking about problems in a psychological manner is foreign and unacceptable (see discussion by McGoldrick, 1982). There is a cultural value on stoicism, on keeping a stiff upper lip, and on not "feeling sorry" for oneself. In a family of this background, an individual who is depressed and trying to express that as a psychological or emotional phenomenon may receive very little support. That is not to say that members of a traditional Irish American family are not caring or not empathic; rather, their worldview does not value psychological and emotional phenomena. Thus, for traditional family members, the suggestion to "pull yourself together and stop feeling sorry for yourself" is not meant to be callous and unfeeling; rather, it is meant to be useful advice. There is a belief that people can "snap out of it" if they choose to do so, and that by being productive and getting to work, they can distract themselves from whatever is bothering them.

For a client from a background in which the family does not believe in emotional disturbance or psychological explanations for unhappiness, entering the therapeutic process may be conflictual. This client may not feel he or she has permission to talk about his or her pain, to receive help, or to focus on what is happening emotionally. He or she may view the therapeutic process as self-indulgent and self-pitying and may feel uncomfortable knowing that this is a process that his or her family would not respect. For a client of this background, preliminary work will need to be done that gives the client permission to be there in the first place; if this is not resolved, the client is likely to experience ongoing conflict about his or her presence in the therapeutic situation.

A particularly stark and dramatic example of the points delineated above is the case of Mary, a client who came to counseling complaining of severe depression that had persisted over several years. She is a 19-year-old college sophomore from an Irish American family; she has six siblings. Mary reported that her parents had had a conflictual and at times violent relationship until her mother developed cancer and died a year earlier. She described their fighting as having been constant and as having gone on for as long as she could remember; because of her parents' religious beliefs, divorce was out of the question. Since her mother's death, Mary's father had hardly mentioned her. Although Mary and her siblings missed their mother, there had been little open grieving within the family.

Mary's relationship with her father was very stormy and, in fact, the incident that precipitated her decision to come to counseling was an argument that had escalated into physical violence in which she had been severely beaten. Since that incident, a week prior to her first visit, Mary had felt angry and more hopeless than ever.

The family's attitude toward Mary was that she was spoiled, that she felt sorry for herself, and that being beaten was a natural consequence of talking back to Dad. By now, she should have "known how he was." Although Mary had an older brother who had been hospitalized for depression and had attempted suicide on several occasions, a sister who had been seeing a psychiatrist for several years, and two other siblings who had all but severed ties with the family, her father was puzzled about why his children needed professional help and why they could not simply function within the family structure. He was particularly puzzled because the family was quite affluent: The children had a nice home in which to live and all of their material comforts taken care of, and thus had no reason to be unhappy. If only his children would stop feeling sorry for themselves and stop talking back to him, everything would be fine in the father's view.

When Mary first came into counseling, discoloration from two Black eyes and from other facial bruises was still evident. For the week prior to her first visit, she had lived in her home with evidence on her face of having been severely battered, but no one had commented upon it. Mary had requested counseling in high school, but her parents had seen it as unnecessary. Even now, Mary was unsure whether she was making "too big a deal about things" and whether she really should be in counseling. In fact, it was a professor who recognized that something was terribly wrong and urged her to get professional assistance.

The first step in the therapeutic process was to assure Mary that her pain was real, worthy of exploration, and in need of professional intervention. In a very short time, Mary was able to recognize that denial was all-pervasive in her family and that every family member had participated in it. Even her siblings who were in intensive treatment themselves never discussed with other family members why they had sought it and seemed to be very ambivalent about needing professional help. For Mary, it was a courageous decision to acknowledge her pain, explore her family's role in contributing to her pain, and fully commit herself to the psychotherapeutic process. (For a more comprehensive overview of counseling Irish Americans, the reader is referred to McGoldrick, 1982 and McGoldrick & Pearce, 1981.)

Client's/Family's Attitudes
Toward Helping and Counseling

Related to level of psychological mindedness is the attitude of the client and the family toward seeking help, particularly for emotional problems and particularly outside of the family. To cite other examples from American ethnic groups, it is not uncommon in Italian American or in Hispanic American families that even if a problem is acknowledged as being emotional or psychological, it is still not acceptable to talk to somebody outside of the family about it (see related discussion of Rotunno & McGoldrick, 1982). Speaking to a "stranger" about one's feelings, and particularly about one's feelings as they involve other family members, is seen as a serious violation of the family's privacy. It is understood that whatever goes on in the family needs to stay in the family; one does not air one's "dirty linen" in public. Again, this is not meant to suggest that members of Italian American or Hispanic American families are uncaring or unfeeling; rather, there is a belief that the family can manage whatever distress an individual is feeling and alleviate it within the family. If someone outside the family is to be spoken to, the obvious person is the parish priest, who usually has a close relationship with the family, rather than a professional helper.

For the less acculturated Italian American or Hispanic American client, like the Irish American client, preliminary work needs to be done to raise that client's comfort level in speaking to somebody outside of the family about his or her personal concerns. It is not uncommon for a client from this background to say, "My parents would kill me if they knew I was talking to you about this" or "No one in my family would believe that I'm even saying these things to a stranger." This is a client who probably needs extra assurance about confidentiality and about the legitimacy of having an objective listener provide help and feedback. Thus, particular sensitivity is needed on the part of the counselor in order to appreciate the level of conflict that the client may be experiencing simply by being present in the counseling situation.

For example, Marisol presented at a community mental health center because of anxiety regarding her parents' marriage. She is a 25-year-old single woman whose family immigrated to the United States from the Dominican Republic when she was 4 years old. Her mother suspected that her father, a successful businessman, was having an affair with a woman who worked in his office. Marisol's mother confided her suspicions and fears to her, but would not confront her husband directly. Marisol worked in her father's office and believed her mother's suspicions were true, but also did not confront her father about them. Marisol's mother could think about and talk about little other than her marital situation, engaging Marisol in these discussions for hours at a time on a daily basis. Her mother knew that she herself was in tremendous emotional pain and recognized that her daughter was suffering as well. Nevertheless, Marisol was clear that her mother would be absolutely horrified to know that she was discussing her family situation with someone outside of the family, despite her mother's level of psychological understanding and her openness about sharing her own thoughts and feelings.

Marisol needed a great deal of reassurance about the confidentiality of the therapeutic relationship. She also needed to work through her feelings about "betraying" her family before she would deal directly with her own pain and anxiety. If the counselor had ignored the intensity of the personal conflict that this client experienced by being in counseling, the psychotherapeutic process could not have proceeded. In addition, it was important for the counselor to understand gender roles and expectations within the traditional Latino family. Sensitivity to the consequences of the family's challenging the father precluded confrontation as an early and obvious response within this family.

Client's Level of Acculturation

It almost goes without saying that the more acculturated a client is in terms of middle-class mainstream American values, the more comfortable he or she is likely to be in the therapeutic situation. We need to be mindful, always, that the roots of psychotherapy are White, European, and Western in origin: The more closely clients fit those demographics, the more comfortable they are going to be with the process, and, conversely, the more they deviate from those demographics, the greater their level of distrust is likely to be.

The first example of the impact of acculturation on levels of trust involves a cross-cultural couple, Diane and Akeem. Diane is a 35-year-old African American woman from Chicago; Akeem is a 36-year-old Black man from Ghana. The couple entered counseling at Diane's urging to discuss issues that were primarily of concern to her. Among her concerns were Akeem's lack of verbal communication with her, his insistence on socializing only with other people from Ghana, and his secretiveness, as Diane viewed it, about some of his business dealings and travels. Akeem was puzzled by Diane's unhappiness, primarily because his behavior as a husband was absolutely appropriate from his cultural perspective. Furthermore, although seeking counseling was a reasonable and relatively comfortable strategy for Diane, for Akeem it was entirely foreign and uncomfortable. Having an initial interview with a White female counselor appeared to be quite comfortable for Diane, who assumed that the counselor shared her cultural (i.e., American) perspective about marital values and expectations. For Akeem, a White female counselor heightened his sense of discomfort and distrust of the counseling process. Inviting an African American male counselor to serve as co-therapist with this couple was a critical first step in allowing Akeem to begin to engage in the counseling process. It was also important to educate Akeem about what counseling was, what function it might serve for him, and how it might help his marriage. Several sessions were spent on this educational process, on learning more about Akeem's culture in general and about his cultural values and assumptions about marriage in particular. Over time, the couple was able to acknowledge that a basic assumption upon which their relationship was founded—that their shared racial background also meant shared basic values and expectations—had been naive. Akeem had grossly underestimated Diane's "Americanness," and Diane had not understood how different many aspects of Akeem's values, expectations, and worldview were from her own. The sense of safety that eventually prevailed in the counseling setting allowed both of them to speak openly about their fears, wishes, and expectations and to renegotiate important aspects of their relationship.

A second, and unfortunate, example involves Tarik, a 42-year-old Black man from Ethiopia. Tarik became despondent about the death of his father in Ethiopia and particularly about his not being at home at the time of his father's death or for the funeral. Tarik confided in a coworker that in the weeks since his father's death, he had felt so terrible that he had had thoughts of killing himself. His colleague took him to a community mental health center to see a counselor, which Tarik agreed to very reluctantly. The counselor, a White male, assessed Tarik's emotional and mental status and concluded that although he was certainly depressed and grieving, he did not appear to be an immediate danger to himself. Nevertheless, he asked Tarik to return the next day and explained the need for contact while Tarik was so acutely depressed. When Tarik did not return the next day, the counselor called his home, leaving a message with Tarik's wife that consisted of his name and a request that Tarik call. When Tarik did call back, he expressed a great deal of anger that the counselor had called him at his home. He had not shared his distress with his wife, had no intention of doing so, and was angry that his privacy had been breached, albeit unintentionally. It would have been useful for the counselor to explore, even more than with a client of his own cultural background, whether the client's wife was aware of what he was experiencing, how he would feel if she did become aware of it, and whether he might be contacted at home under any circumstances. For this client, being placed in a position in which he was forced to share more with his wife than was in his previous realm of experience was so uncomfortable that he refused to continue in counseling. The call to his home, rather than being viewed as a sign of caring on the part of his counselor, was viewed as a violation of a marital boundary that exacerbated his distrust of the counseling process.

Family's Level of Acculturation

It is not accurate to assume that the family's level of acculturation is identical to that of the client. In fact, varying levels of acculturation are often a point of conflict and a focus of concern for therapy. It is not unusual for a client to be highly acculturated into mainstream American life and values and for the family to be almost entirely unassimilated. Family members may choose not to learn English and to retain their language of origin exclusively. They may choose to live in neighborhoods that are made up entirely of members of their own ethnic, national, or religious group and generally to arrange their lives in such a way that they have very little contact with the mainstream culture. To the extent that parents and other family members are unacculturated and the client wishes to become acculturated, the level of conflict between the client and his or her family will obviously rise. The family's level of acculturation will influence not only their attitude toward the client seeking help in counseling but also their attitude toward every aspect of the client's life.

It is not uncommon for first-generation American college students to experience this type of conflict and to deal with cultural or bicultural strain. Often it is their desire to become as acculturated as possible and to be viewed as "American." They often choose to speak English and to adopt American modes of dress, speech, and socializing. They often have the expectation that they be allowed to date, go out unchaperoned, have a number of romantic partners, and essentially be allowed to live the "typical" American young person's life. Often this runs contrary to the family's expectations. For the Anglo counselor, it is very important to appreciate what the impact of giving the client "permission" to make choices about assimilation and following the mores and customs of mainstream America might be in terms of exacerbating tensions in the family.

An example of bicultural strain involves Indira, an 18-year-old high school senior who came to the counselor requesting information about birth control. Indira was born in India and immigrated to the United States when she was 8 years old. She was not allowed to date or, in fact, to be out of her house except for school-related activities. Nevertheless, she had contrived ways to spend time with boys and at this point had decided to become sexually active. When questioned by her counselor about her family's cultural background, Indira reported that her parents were traditionally Indian, speaking their native language in their home, eating traditional foods, associating only with members of their extended family, and visiting India every summer. When questioned about her parents' attitude toward dating and marriage, Indira reported that her parents planned to arrange a marriage for her with someone who was probably raised in India, or, at the very least, was from a traditional Indian background. Indira went on to explain that virginity was a key expectation in the arranged marriage and that, in fact, if the groom came to suspect that his bride was not a virgin, he had a duty to report that to the bride's parents and to terminate the marriage. Further exploration revealed that Indira was not opposed to an arranged marriage.

It became clear to the counselor that simply providing information and resources about birth control and even exploring the client's own feelings about sexuality were not sufficient in this situation. Given the low level of acculturation of this client's family, any decisions that the client made about her own sexual behavior had to be carefully considered in terms of the long-term cultural consequences. This client, although wishing to live the life of an Anglo teenager, ultimately saw herself as not disappointing her parents' long-term marital expectations for her. Therefore, she needed to come to the realization that in some ways enjoying the freedoms of the Anglo teenager and young adult might not serve her well in the long run.

Family's Attitude Toward Acculturation

There may or may not be a difference between the family's level of acculturation and the family's attitude toward their children's becoming acculturated. For example, often parents from India, Asia, or the Middle East choose a low level of acculturation for themselves and would prefer a low level of assimilation for their children as well. It is expected that children will retain the language of their native country as well as traditional patterns of dating, friendship, and affiliation. This means that parents often will not allow their children a great deal of freedom to explore American culture or to interact socially with American peers. On the other hand, for parents of European origin, for example, in Italian American families, it is not uncommon for the older generation to have a low level of acculturation—that is, to retain the Italian language, to interact exclusively with other people who are family members or who are from the same region of Italy, and to have as little contact as possible with mainstream American life (see related discussion of Rotunno & McGoldrick, 1982). However, often these parents, though they would like their children to retain knowledge of the Italian language and appreciation for their culture, are less restrictive in terms of their children's dating, assimilating, and adopting some American norms and values. Thus, children of European descent will often experience some pressure to retain their culture of origin, but will probably encounter parental attitudes that are less prohibitive and less punitive when they venture into the mainstream culture. These parents, though not choosing to acculturate themselves, seem to have an appreciation that it could be advantageous for their children to become acculturated to a certain degree.

In the previous example involving a client from India, her family's level of acculturation was low and their attitude toward their children's acculturation was very negative. They did everything they could to keep their children at home, to forbid their contact with non-Indian peers outside of school, and to preserve their traditional way of life. They saw no value in their children's becoming acculturated; in fact, they viewed acculturation as threatening their traditional way of life. As noted above, parents of Middle Eastern, Asian, and traditional Hispanic backgrounds hold similar views. Females, especially, are carefully monitored, chaperoned, and given very little personal freedom by highly acculturated American standards. Furthermore, the restrictions on their personal freedom are not negotiable. Thus, it is important that the counselor understand that for these clients "separation/individuation" issues are not simply a matter of renegotiating parental boundaries and expectations. Rather, they are issues with profound consequences for disconnection with the family, should the client choose to pursue them.

By way of contrast with the previous case, Angela, an Italian American woman, entered counseling because she was frustrated by her parents' overprotectiveness. Angela's parents were born in Italy and immigrated to the United States shortly before her birth. As a 22-year-old college senior who lived at home, Angela believed that she had a right to come and go as she pleased within reason, and she was planning to move out of her house upon college graduation. Angela's parents, who spoke Italian almost exclusively and associated only with members of their extended family, could not understand why Angela would want to leave home, where Mom did everything for her, or why anyone needed to go out regularly or to stay out past midnight. In fact, Angela had a 35-year-old brother who, despite having a high-paying job, continued to live at home, rarely dated, and stayed at home almost every evening. Angela's parents considered her brother's behavior to be normal and even exemplary and Angela's wishes to have more personal freedom and to leave home at age 22 to be aberrant.

On the other hand, they were proud of Angela's college education and even of her popularity with her peers, and they accepted her having had a number of boyfriends over the years. They were unhappy when her boyfriends had not been Italian, but they made no threats to her about the consequences of continuing these relationships. Angela requested assistance with helping her family understand her need for greater freedom and autonomy without their personalizing it. She did not believe that her parents would disown her or reject her if she continued to come home late or even if she moved out. Rather, she wanted to lower the level of conflict at home and to find a way to leave on good terms with her parents. She wanted her parents to understand that the choices she was making were a normal part of the acculturation and maturation process. She believed that with better communication and with less anger on her part, her parents would come to accept her lifestyle more comfortably.

After a few sessions, Angela was able to tell her parents that she was seeing a counselor and why. It was suggested that she invite her parents into counseling for a few sessions in which a male counselor who was fluent in Italian would serve as a co-therapist. Angela's parents agreed, with trepidation, and did come to a greater understanding about Angela's need for autonomy. The presence of an Italian male counselor who was fluent in Italian certainly made the situation more comfortable for Angela's parents and enhanced the credibility of the therapeutic process.

SUMMARY

This chapter has highlighted the need for attention to culturally sensitive counseling assessment and intervention. Counselors of all races and backgrounds will increasingly be called upon to assist clients who possess markedly different worldviews. One's worldview will influence one's understanding of the traditional Western counseling process, one's willingness to see a counselor, one's level of psychological mindedness, one's comfort with self- and family disclosure, and one's expectations for the counselor-client relationship. Clearly, a worldview assessment should be a key aspect of any client assessment and problem/goal conceptualization.

We close this chapter with three summary statements/recommendations regarding multicultural assessment. It is our hope that the chapter contents and the statements that follow will stimulate some thought and offer some useful insights for counseling in an increasingly heterogenous society.

First, national survey research cited at the beginning of this chapter documents that the majority of counseling and related training programs operate from a Eurocentric bias. Although this training emphasis may equip students for work with middle-class White Americans and highly acculturated immigrants, a knowledge gap exists for assessing more culturally diverse clients (see particularly the recent survey by Allison et al., 1994). It is likely to be a number of years before training programs, collectively, are adequately preparing practitioners for multicultural practice. In the interim, it is the ethical responsibility of the individual practitioner/researcher to engage in self-study for multicultural competence (see Pedersen, Chapter 3, this volume, and the Appendices at the end of this volume).

Second, the research literature has highlighted the centrality of the worldview and acculturation constructs to multicultural counseling (refer back to the eight chapters that constitute Part II of this book). These constructs highlight differences not only between cultures but also within cultures. It is important that the case vignettes presented in this chapter and others of the *Handbook* not be seen as representative of the entire cultural, racial, ethnic, or gender group under study. For example, it is likely that the worldview of a fourth-generation Mexican American or Italian American will be more similar to that of a White middle-class Protestant than to that of a first-generation counterpart from the same ethnic group. Assessing level of acculturation through paper-and-pencil and (preferably) semistructured interview protocols will guide the counselor in assessing the client's worldview regarding counseling services.

Third, although the case studies in this chapter have focused primarily on racial, ethnic, and national groupings, other variables need to be included in a counseling assessment. Gender, gender identity, religious identity, and sexual orientation also affect worldview and subsequent expectations for the counseling process. Multicultural assessment must acknowledge the multiple identities and affiliations of the client. One of the more useful and comprehensive formats for such an assessment is presented by Ibrahim et al. (1994).

Finally, it is hoped that the myriad variables that an increasingly diverse client population brings to the counseling relationship will be viewed by the counselor as an opportunity to be challenged in rich and exciting ways. Just as women within the counseling profession and as clients have challenged the patriarchal assumptions at the heart of early psychoanalytic theory and practice, so today's ethnically and racially diverse counselors and clients continue to invite close scrutiny of psychology's Eurocentric roots and careful assessment of its cross-cultural applicability. The multicultural perspective thus invites a freshness of response and an openness of spirit on the part of the counselor. Diversity challenges the counseling profession to continuous growth, fluidity, and evolution; it defies stagnation.

REFERENCES

Allison, K. W., Crawford, I., Echemendia, R., Robinson, L., & Knepp, D. (1994). Human diversity and professional competence: Training in clinical and counseling psychology revisited. *American Psychologist, 49,* 792-796.

Atkinson, D. R., Morten, G., & Sue, D. W. (Eds.). (1993). *Counseling American minorities: A cross-cultural perspective* (4th ed.). Dubuque, IA: William C. Brown.

Atkinson, D. R., & Thompson, C. E. (1992). Racial, ethnic, and cultural variables in counseling. In S. D. Brown & R. W. Lent (Eds.), *Handbook of counseling psychology* (2nd ed., pp. 349-382). New York: John Wiley.

Bernal, M. E., & Castro, F. G. (1994). Are clinical psychologists prepared for service and research with ethnic minorities? Report of a decade of progress. *American Psychologist, 49,* 797-805.

Carter, R. T. (1991). Cultural values: A review of empirical research and implications for counseling. *Journal of Counseling and Development, 70,* 164-173.

Casas, J. M., & Casas, A. (1994). The acculturation process and implications for education and services. In A. C. Matiella (Ed.), *The multicultural challenge in health education* (pp. 23-49). Santa Cruz, CA: ETR Associates.

Dana, R. H. (1993). *Multicultural assessment perspectives for professional psychology.* Boston: Allyn & Bacon.

Fernando, S. (1988). *Race and culture in psychiatry.* London: Croom Helm.

Goodstein, R. (1994). *Racial and ethnic identity and their relationship to self-esteem.* Unpublished doctoral dissertation, Fordham University at Lincoln Center, New York, NY.

Highlen, P. S. (1994). Racial/ethnic diversity in doctoral programs of psychology: Challenges for the twenty-first century. *Applied and Preventive Psychology, 2,* 91-108.

Hills, H. I., & Strozier, A. L. (1992). Multicultural training in APA-approved counseling psychology programs: A survey. *Professional Psychology: Research and Practice, 23,* 43-51.

Ibrahim, F. A. (1991). Contribution of cultural worldview to generic counseling and development. *Journal of Counseling and Development, 70,* 13-19.

Ibrahim, F. A., & Kahn, H. (1987). Assessment of world views. *Psychological Reports, 60,* 163-176.

Ibrahim, F. A., Ohnishi, H., & Wilson, R. P. (1994). Career assessment in a culturally diverse society. *Journal of Career Assessment, 2,* 276-288.

Ibrahim, F. A., & Owens, S. V. (1992, August). *Factor analytic structure of the scale to assess world view.* Paper presented at the annual meeting of the American Psychological Association, Washington, DC.

Jacobsen, F. M. (1988). Ethnocultural assessment. In L. Comas-Diaz & E. E. H. Griffith (Eds.), *Clinical guidelines in cross-cultural mental health* (pp. 135-147). New York: John Wiley.

Leong, F. T. L., & Chou, E. L. (1994). The role of ethnic identity and acculturation in the vocational behavior of Asian Americans: An integrative review. *Journal of Vocational Behavior, 44,* 155-172.

Marsella, A. J. (1978). Thoughts on cross-cultural studies on the epidemiology of depression. *Culture, Medicine, and Psychiatry, 2,* 343-357.

McGoldrick, M. (1982). Irish families. In M. McGoldrick, J. K. Pearce, & J. Giordano (Eds.), *Ethnicity and family therapy* (pp. 310-339). New York: Guilford.

McGoldrick, M., & Pearce, J. K. (1981). Family therapy with Irish Americans. *Family Process, 20,* 223-244.

Midgette, T. E., & Meggert, S. S. (1991). Multicultural counseling instruction: A challenge for faculties in the 21st century. *Journal of Counseling and Development, 70,* 136-141.

Paniagua, F. A. (1994). *Assessing and treating culturally diverse clients.* Thousand Oaks, CA: Sage.

Pedersen, P. B. (1991). Multiculturalism as a generic approach to counseling. *Journal of Counseling and Development, 70,* 6-12.

Ponterotto, J. G., & Casas, J. M. (1991). *Handbook of racial/ethnic minority counseling research.* Springfield, IL: Charles C Thomas.

Ponterotto, J. G., & Pedersen, P. B. (1993). *Preventing prejudice: A guide for counselors and educators.* Newbury Park, CA: Sage.

Quintana, S. M., & Bernal, M. E. (1995). Ethnic minority training in counseling psychology: Comparisons with clinical psychology and proposed standards. *The Counseling Psychologist, 23,* 102-121.

Rogers, M. R., Ponterotto, J. G., Conoley, J. C., & Wiese, M. J. (1992). Multicultural training in school psychology: A national survey. *School Psychology Review, 21,* 603-616.

Rotunno, M., & McGoldrick, M. (1982). Italian families. In M. McGoldrick, J. K. Pearce, & J. Giordano (Eds.), *Ethnicity and family therapy* (pp. 340-363). New York: Guilford.

Sabnani, H. B., & Ponterotto, J. G. (1992). Racial/ethnic minority instrumentation in counseling research: A review, critique, and recommendations. *Measurement and Evaluation in Counseling and Development, 24,* 161-187.

Singer, K. (1975). Depressive disorders from a transcultural perspective. *Social Science and Medicine, 9,* 289-301.

Sodowsky, G. R., & Johnson, P. (1994). World views: Culturally learned assumptions and values. In P. Pedersen & J. C. Carey (Eds.), *Multicultural counseling in schools: A practical handbook* (pp. 59-79). Boston: Allyn & Bacon.

Suarez-Balcazar, Y., Durlak, J. A., & Smith, C. (in press). Multicultural training practices in community psychology programs. *American Journal of Community Psychology.*

Sue, D. W., Arredondo, P., & McDavis, R. J. (1992). Multicultural counseling competencies and standards: A call to the profession. *Journal of Counseling and Development, 70,* 477-486.

Sue, D. W., & Sue, D. (1990). *Counseling the culturally different: Theory and practice* (2nd ed.). New York: John Wiley.

Sue, S., & Zane, N. W. (1987). The role of culture and cultural techniques in psychotherapy: A critique and reformulation. *American Psychologist, 42,* 37-45.

Washington, E. D. (1994). Three steps to cultural awareness: A Wittgensteinian approach. In P. Pedersen & J. C. Carey (Eds.), *Multicultural counseling in schools: A practical handbook* (pp. 81-102). Boston: Allyn & Bacon.

18

Creative Approaches to Multicultural Counseling

CHARLENE M. ALEXANDER

LYNN SUSSMAN

ALTHOUGH THERE APPEARS to be a consensus in the counseling literature that the traditional counselor role does not adequately serve members of racial/ethnic minority populations, there is little written that provides counselors with the skills necessary to integrate multicultural issues into the counseling relationship (Lee & Richardson, 1991). When skills are provided, they tend to perpetuate rather than transcend the three most frequently cited barriers to multicultural counseling: language differences, class-bound value differences, and culture-bound value differences that exist between counselor and client (Atkinson, Morten, & Sue, 1989). For example, Sue et al. (1982), in a position paper on cross-cultural counseling competencies, stated that a multicultural counselor:

1. must be able to generate a wide variety of verbal and nonverbal responses.
2. must be able to send and receive both verbal and nonverbal messages accurately and "appropriately."
3. is able to exercise institutional skills on behalf of his/her client when appropriate. (p. 46)

AUTHORS' NOTE: The authors dedicate this chapter to their respective children, Celeste M. Alexander and Joshua Meyer Daube.

But how does one develop a large repertoire of verbal and nonverbal skills? In other words, how does one acquire what one is not aware of? The counselor's role as we know it has also been criticized for being too intrapsychic and having a Eurocentric developmental approach. Atkinson, Morten, and Sue (1993) suggested alternative roles that can be used instead of or in addition to the traditional counselor role, such as that of facilitator of self-help programs for the client. In all of these suggestions for developing a multicultural counseling relationship, verbal communication is crucial to building rapport and enhancing the interaction between counselor and client. We believe that additional approaches can be used to transcend counselors' reliance on traditional culture-bound means of communication—that is, language. These approaches can be gleaned from an in-depth exploration of the culture of the client.

Training programs have defined the specific knowledge, skills, and awareness that counselors need to become multiculturally competent, yet they still ignore the client's contribution to the relationship. Clients who perceive counselors as culturally responsive also see them as more credible sources of help and disclose more to them than to counselors perceived as culturally insensitive (Atkinson et al., 1993). We believe that if clients perceive counselors as being aware of the creative expressions of their culture and not afraid to use them, their perception of counselors' expertness, attractiveness, and trustworthiness could be further enhanced.

However, counselors are frequently at a loss concerning how to use this knowledge in creative, constructive ways with clients and students alike. Creative expression is not introduced as a viable means of communication or rapport building in training programs. In our graduate training, reference was never made to the possible value of using dance or literature as means of attaining multicultural knowledge, skills, or awareness.

The purpose of this chapter is to present some creative approaches that can be used with culturally diverse clients. These approaches focus specifically on the use of culturally relevant ways of communicating and celebrating racial/ethnic differences and similarities that clients can find engaging. In no way are we suggesting that the following approaches should be used with all clients and counselors or under all circumstances. Rather, they should be thought of as ways to augment the traditional counselor role. We hope that the following provides food for thought in terms of the way that helping professionals communicate with culturally diverse clients.

ETHICAL CONSIDERATIONS

Our "creative" approach to multicultural counseling may challenge traditionally held beliefs of ethical guidelines and may be uncomfortable to engage in initially. Atkinson et al. (1989) suggested that when adapting alternative roles, the counselor should be more actively involved in the client's life experiences, and that this may involve "the counselor moving out of his/her office into the client's environment" (p. 271). However, the American Psychological Association (1993), in their "Guidelines for Providers of Psychological Services to Ethnic, Linguistic, and Culturally Diverse Populations" (see Appendix I, this volume), suggested that "psychologists' practice [should] incorporate an understanding of the client's ethnic and cultural background" (p. 46). We further believe that ethically appropriate practice should be considered within the cultural context in which it occurs.

For example, there may be times when counselors are asked to expand their role/boundaries in which they traditionally work in order to facilitate a more effective intervention. The counselor's guiding principles in deciding when an intervention is appropriate must always be that the intervention does not cause any harm to the client, and that in consultation with colleagues, it is determined that the benefits of the intervention clearly outweigh any potential risks to the client. There is support for extending client-counselor boundaries and inviting counselors to reconceptualize their work with culturally different clients.

USE OF MUSIC IN COUNSELING

Music has been used therapeutically in the counseling relationship. It has been proven beneficial as a tool in relaxation training, and as a way of helping clients to identify different relaxing or anxiety-provoking stimuli. The music used has been generally termed *classical*, meaning of European American origin. We believe that it is time to broaden the definition to include music of other cultures.

Music can also be used to help clients/students problem-solve around issues of racial identity of racial conflict. For example, calypso music contains themes of racial identity and has historically reflected the local and international social climate at any given time. Thus it can become a mechanism for students and clients to problem-solve around racial identity issues. Specifically, some calypso musicians strive to promote themes of "internalization" (see Helms, 1990), and students and clients from Caribbean cultures can be invited to construct calypso music that reflects their stage of racial identity development, allowing counselors to have further insight into their development.

Music can also be used as a way to help minority students feel welcome on predominantly White college campuses. Minority students have reported positive feelings at having seen and heard culturally relevant material on college campuses (Alexander, Collins, & Saul, under review). College campuses can use music as a way to facilitate minority students' transition to college. Music videos can be placed in the student commons area as a way of introducing students to cultural diversity and building cultural awareness.

Clinic offices can also use a variety of cultural music in their waiting rooms. Readers of this chapter may have on occasion found themselves bopping along to music played in some department store and subsequently spending more time in that store. This is no accident, and one could investigate changes in client referrals as a result of introducing the music of a given culture to the counseling setting. Counselors can also encourage clients to write music as a way of expressing their feelings.

USE OF DANCE IN COUNSELING

As with music, dance can also be used as a form of self- or group expression. At the annual meeting of the American Counseling Association, the "Electric Slide" became a form of group harmony. The dance is easy to learn and allows for group participation, individuals from differing racial/ethnic backgrounds can participate, and there is a definite sense of accomplishment at the end of the dance. One of the authors used this at a new student orientation program with approximately 200 students attending. The dance was used as a way of breaking the ice and reducing some of the tension and anxiety around participating in a multicultural program. The dance becomes a metaphor for entering a new culture: the need to pay attention and observe the "rules" of the dance or culture before engaging in it, the need to not be afraid to make mistakes initially, and, in this instance, the joy of a shared experience. Multicultural educators can then encourage the group to talk about how it felt to enter the dance, what prevented them from participating, and how they felt at the end of the dance. One student talked about not wanting to appear foolish because of his lack of dance expertise and his consciousness of possible ramifications of entering a new culture for people of his own culture (i.e., "wanna-be a home-boy"). Counselors can use this as a way of defining cultural similarity at the beginning of a training program or course on diversity. Each participant can be encouraged to add his or her personal style to the dance—for example, by an extra leg lift or hip action; in so doing, each individual sees what he or she brings to that culture. The same can also be applied to other dances, such as the samba or merengue.

USE OF FOOD IN
MULTICULTURAL COUNSELING

In *Ethnic and Regional Foodways in the United States: The Performance of Group Identity*, Kalcik (1985) wrote that "for old and new ethnic groups in America, foodways—the whole pattern of what is eaten, when, what, how, and what it means—are closely tied to individual and group ethnic identity" (p. 38). Food is therefore an additional marker of ethnic identity. It is important for counselors to note that foodways are extremely resistant to change, despite pressure from the majority culture, because food is our earliest introduction to culture and therefore the last to be changed.

Kalcik (1985) also described the ways that traditional foods and the manner in which food is consumed form a link to the past and ease the shock and discomfort of entering a new culture. For instance, immigrants to the United States may open stores so that they have access to ethnic ingredients and open restaurants so they have easier access to foods that take time to prepare.

Food is one way in which the acculturation process is expressed by members of different ethnic groups. Newly arrived ethnic groups or individuals to the United States will either try to maintain their traditional foodways by eating foods similar to those of their country of origin or give in to outside pressure and quickly adopt the food habits of the new country. Both outcomes are geared toward trying to adapt to a new lifestyle—either by attempting to maintain ties with the old country or by attempting to speed up the process of acculturation (Kalcik, 1985).

One can learn much from the manner in which food is eaten and prepared in a particular racial/ethnic minority household. Besides being one way to celebrate ethnic and group identity, it has been shown to be related to factors such as age of the cook (are there children in the household?), socioeconomic status, and urbanization (e.g., the ability to obtain ingredients more readily and year round). For example, in some African American households, ensuring that meats are appropriately cleaned before preparation is essential. This was a central issue for a client in an inpatient facility who eventually refused to eat the food prepared for her. One can imagine the varied assessments attributed to this behavior. In some cultures it is customary to offer a guest a refreshment. This may consist of coffee and a sweet or a liqueur in the Greek American culture, for example. In some cultures it is considered impolite not to accept this welcomed offer. The counselor's gesture of offering a client a cup of coffee or cold drink when appropriate can encourage the formation of a therapeutic alliance between two culturally different people.

The same could be said about the Japanese culture and its relationship with tea. When one of the authors worked as a counselor at a small Japanese-affiliated university located in a small Northeast town in the United States, both the foreign student advisor, who was American, and the Japanese student advisor, who was Japanese, set up teapots in their offices and would routinely offer tea to students. This simple gesture was a way of connecting the Japanese students to their country of origin while at the same time supporting them in their struggle to adjust to the demands of living in a new country. This same foreign student advisor also encouraged the bookstore to sell Japanese food products. This was especially meaningful to the students, given that the nearest Japanese grocery store was not within easy access. She also found a supplier of Japanese-style rice, which the cafeteria served.

In African cultures, it is customary to share food off the same plate as a sign of closeness. Counselors can use this as a way of building closeness with a client. Counselors can discuss with clients the different ways their families celebrate certain traditional holidays. The celebration of Kwanzaa by African American families or Passover by Jewish American families revolves around the consumption and preparation of food. Very often, festivals and holidays are a time when racial/ethnic groups will link people with their past and present by serving foods that are associated with their cultural heritage (Kalcik, 1985). For example, if an African American client is struggling with issues of racial identity development, the counselor can teach the client directly about the foods eaten during Kwanzaa.

Perhaps there are ways to use food as a means of forging alliances with members of different racial/ethnic minority groups outside of the traditional counseling relationship. The ultimate goal of this type of activity would be to encourage the members of your community to view the counseling center as an integral part of the community, one dedicated to helping its citizenry. For instance, counseling centers could invite community members to a holiday celebration where ethnic foods could be served.

Potluck dinners are another way to share the ethnic diversity of the counseling staff and are often organized on college campuses as a way of celebrating student diversity.

USE OF ART IN
MULTICULTURAL COUNSELING

Some of the meaning that we ascribe to our experiences is idiosyncratic; other meaning is shaped by the process of acculturation and socialization and results in the formation of shared meaning. The creation of art is an endeavor that is both social and highly personal (Wadeson, 1980).

Art does not rely on verbalization and therefore can be an ideal form of self-expression between a counselor and a client from different cultural backgrounds. For instance, in the experience of one of the authors as a counselor, reliance on other means of communication with newly arrived Japanese students was helpful at times. Students came to our office looking for assistance because most often they were feeling homesick. Although we were limited in the type of assistance that we could provide, we would attempt to communicate with one another by using pictures from magazines and drawing pictures. A happy face or a frown communicated the same message in both cultures. Attempts to empathize with the concerns of these students prior to making a referral led to credibility in that community.

We are suggesting that art can be used in the counseling relationship as a way to learn more about one's culture and/or worldview. This is very different than suggesting that one engage in the process of art therapy. For instance, clients who are struggling with acculturation or ethnic identity issues may be encouraged by their counselor to interview various members of their family across generations in order to learn stories about their cultural heritage as a way of linking them to their past (see Borodovsky & Ponterotto, 1994). A counselor could encourage a client to make a collage that links his or her current lifestyle, attitudes, and beliefs to his or her cultural heritage.

USE OF PLAY IN COUNSELING

Counselors at times need to engage children in counseling. The traditional approach has been to use games such as puzzles, building blocks, or computer games. We would like to suggest using games familiar to the child's culture. For example, some African American children in urban settings play a form of jump rope called Double Dutch. The game involves children turning two ropes in opposite directions at the same time while the two children at the end verbally support the child in the middle. For example, the children turning the rope might chant, "Go Tania. . . . Go Tania. . . . Jump higher. . . . Jump higher." Children usually report feeling a great sense of accomplishment at the end of the game.

Hopscotch is another children's game that can be used by counselors. One does not need a group of children to play this game; it can be played individually, with the counselor looking on or with the counselor engaging in the game as well. The object of the game is to successfully complete a number of "hops" in a specified sequence. A degree of balance and accuracy is involved. The child is reinforced for each successful attempt and completion of the sequence.

Hand-clapping games are also popular with some children. Typically these involve a repetition of complex hand slapping while the two parties involved invent rhymes as the game goes along. Rhymes can center on current events or on events in the child's life. Counselors can direct the game by participating as the second party and use the information obtained in this fashion to gain further insight into the world of the child.

USE OF FOLKTALES IN COUNSELING

The use of folktales is another creative way to infuse multiculturalism into the counseling relationship. Folktales reflect the client's culture and can be helpful in providing counselors with a glimpse of the types of problems faced by their client as well as problem-solving skills available to him or her. In addition, culturally relevant storytelling may facilitate a therapeutic alliance between a culturally dissimilar client and counselor because it provides the counselor with the opportunity to start where the client is and not vice versa.

Although we generally tend to think of folktales as intended for children, some stories were originally meant to be heard by children and adults, and others were meant for adults alone. In addition, folktales were often told in families or village groups (Cole, 1982). These stories were shared orally because they were created prior to the development of a written language. The content of the stories was subject to change depending on the storyteller's interpretation and the setting in which they were told (Lester, 1969). Because of the unique relationship that often formed between the storyteller and listener, folktales "express the wishes, hopes, and fears of many people rather than the concerns of a particular writer, and they deal with universal human dilemmas that span differences of age, culture, and geography" (Cole, 1982, p. xvii).

In an anthology of folktales collected from around the world, Cole (1982) identified several themes common to many of the stories. For instance, some stories address the theme of childhood development—what it is like for children to go from childhood to adolescence to adulthood. Often these children are disadvantaged in some way: perhaps because they are the youngest of several siblings or not particularly bright. Another theme, according to Cole (1982), is that of the magical helper—the person who grants wishes to the story's hero or heroine.

Although many of the world's tales share common themes, folktales also communicate culturally specific values, customs, and wisdom in a language that is familiar to a particular group. In addition, folk- and fairytales are culture-specific because they provide us with a glimpse of the types of problems faced by people living in a particular culture and their means of coping and problem solving. For instance, Native American folktales communicate this group's appreciation and relationship to the Earth and its animals. Native Americans believe that the Earth is a member of one's family and should be respected and cherished and not controlled (Bruchac, 1991; Caduto & Bruchac, 1991). Caduto and Bruchac (1991) wrote that "to the native people of North America, what was done to a frog or a deer, to a tree, a rock or a river, was done to a brother or a sister" (p. xviii). These beliefs are passed down from one generation to the next through experience and storytelling. Native American folktales are meant to teach as well as to entertain. Bruchac (1991) wrote that if a child misbehaves, he or she will be told a story rather than punished because "striking a child breaks that child's spirit, serves as a bad example and seldom teaches the right lesson. But a story goes into a person and remains there" (p. i).

African American folktales originated when Africans were brought to North America against their will to be slaves. They were torn from their families and culture back home and forced to speak English. One way of coping with their experience of oppression was to make up stories that incorporated "memories and habits from the old world of Africa" (Hamilton, 1985, p. x). In these stories, animals were used to portray people in their new environment. Slaves were often portrayed by weaker animals such as the rabbit. However, weaker animals were often endowed with special talents or powers that gave them the ability to outsmart the larger and stronger animals.

In addition to promoting cultural understanding, folktales have been shown to promote personality development in studies conducted with racial/ethnic minority children, adolescents, and adults. For instance, a study conducted by Costantino, Malgady, and Rogler (1986) examined the effectiveness of exposing high-risk Puerto Rican children to *cuento* therapy. In general, folktales attempt to transmit values in the form of a message or moral. Used therapeutically, these stories can be presented in such a way as to facilitate and motivate adaptive functioning. Costantino et al. (1986) wrote: "By presenting culturally familiar characters of the same ethnicity as the children, the folktales serve to motivate attentional processes; to model beliefs, values and behaviors with which children can identify; and to model functional relationships with parental figures" (p. 640). Costantino et al. tested two types of *cuento* therapy and compared the results to both art/play therapy and no therapy. One version of *cuento* therapy utilized original Puerto Rican *cuentos* and the other version adapted *cuentos* to reflect themes consistent with American culture. The results of the study indicated that the adapted *cuento* therapy was effective in reducing trait anxiety in first-grade children as compared to the other treatments, and that both *cuento* therapies improved WISC-R Comprehension and reduced aggressive behavior. The authors also pointed out that participant attendance was high and attrition was extremely low, and attributed this to the fact that the therapists used in the study were bilingual and bicultural, that therapy protocols were bilingually presented, and that the children's mothers and children enjoyed sharing stories.

Given that the literature indicates that racial/ethnic minority members do not benefit from traditional counseling and tend not to use mental health services despite apparent need, the use of folktales and folklore may be one way to make counseling more attractive to members of these groups.

SUMMARY

Counselors have been struggling to delineate the "how to" of multicultural counseling, and although some direction has been provided in the literature, much is left unsaid or left up to the imagination. What we have attempted to illustrate is that counselors can tap into the minority client's everyday life to aid in the therapeutic process. In no way is this intended to be an exhaustive list of all possible interventions, but it is intended to stimulate counselors to explore different aspects of a client's life often ignored by counselors.

REFERENCES

Alexander, C., Collins, L., & Saul, K. *Diversifying the environment: Use of techniques to enhance cultural awareness.* Unpublished manuscript.

American Psychological Association. (1993). Guidelines for providers of psychological services to ethnic, linguistic, and culturally diverse populations. *American Psychologist,* 48(1), 45-48.

Atkinson, D. R., Morten, G., & Sue, D. W. (Eds.). (1989). *Counseling American minorities: A cross-cultural perspective* (3rd ed.). Dubuque, IA: William C. Brown.

Atkinson, D. R., Morten, G., & Sue, D. W. (Eds.). (1993). *Counseling American minorities: A cross-cultural perspective* (4th ed.). Dubuque, IA: William C. Brown.

Borodovsky, L. G., & Ponterotto, J. G. (1994). A family-based approach to multicultural career development. In P. Pedersen & J. C. Carey (Eds.), *Multicultural counseling in schools: A practical handbook* (pp. 195-206). Boston: Allyn & Bacon.

Bruchac, J. (1991). *Native American stories.* Golden, CO: Fulcrum.

Caduto, M. J., & Bruchac, J. (1991). *Keepers of the animals: Native American stories and wildlife activities for children.* Golden, CO: Fulcrum.

Cole, J. (Ed.). (1982). *Best-loved folktales of the world.* Garden City, NY: Doubleday.

Costantino, G., Malgady, R. G., & Rogler, L. H. (1986). Cuento therapy: A culturally sensitive modality for Puerto Rican children. *Journal of Consulting and Clinical Psychology, 54*(5), 639-645.

Hamilton, V. (1985). *The people could fly: American Black folktales.* New York: Knopf.

Helms, J. E. (Ed.) (1990). *Black and White racial identity development: Theory, practice, and research.* Westport, CT: Greenwood Press.

Kalcik, S. (1985). Ethnic foodways in America: Symbol and the performance of identity. In L. K. Brown & K. Mussell (Eds.), *Ethnic and regional foodways in the United States: The performance of group identity.* Knoxville: University of Tennessee Press.

Lee, C. C., & Richardson, B. L. (Eds.). (1991). *Multicultural issues in counseling: New approaches to diversity.* Alexandria, VA: American Counseling Association.

Lester, J. (1969). *Black folktales.* New York: Richard W. Barron.

Sue, D. W., Bernier, J. E., Durran, A., Feinberg, L., Pedersen, P., Smith, E., & Vasquez-Nuttall, E. (1982). Position paper: Cross-cultural counseling competencies. *The Counseling Psychologist, 10*, 45-52.

Wadeson, H. (1980). *Art psychotherapy.* New York: John Wiley.

PART V

Research Reviews

CHAPTERS 19 AND 20 make up Part V of the *Handbook* and consist of major reviews of empirical research in multicultural counseling. In Chapter 19, Donald R. Atkinson and Susana M. Lowe review the empirical literature since 1970 to answer three important questions: (a) Do counselor-client dyads that are matched for ethnicity produce more favorable outcomes? (b) Does multicultural training of counselors result in better clinical outcomes for ethnic minority clients? and (c) Does research support the utility of modifying traditional forms of counseling when working with ethnic minority clients? The authors are systematic and rigorous in their review procedures, and the integrative conclusions provide insightful information for all counselors and trainers.

In Chapter 20, Frederick T. L. Leong, Nicole S. Wagner, and Shiraz Piroshaw Tata review an extensive and interdisciplinary body of literature in order to examine racial and ethnic variations in help-seeking behavior. Among the enlightening results of this review are the following common themes: (a) All groups examined have a need for mental health services, (b) there is great within-group heterogeneity when it comes to mental health attitudes and behaviors, and (c) all minority groups are in need of culturally responsive services if they are to benefit from counseling. The empirical research review is rigorous and comprehensive, and the authors provide many excellent suggestions with regard to current mental health practices.

19

The Role of Ethnicity, Cultural Knowledge, and Conventional Techniques in Counseling and Psychotherapy

DONALD R. ATKINSON

SUSANA M. LOWE

AFTER REVIEWING the literature published in the 1970s and 1980s on psychotherapeutic services and treatment practices for ethnic minority populations, Sue and Zane (1987) concluded that

> investigators have been remarkably consistent in offering recommendations or suggestions for improving the relationship between therapists and ethnic-minority clients . . . (a) more ethnic therapists who presumably are bilingual or are familiar with ethnic cultural values should be recruited into the mental health field, (b) students and therapists should acquire knowledge of ethnic cultures and communities, and (c) traditional forms of treatment should be modified because they are geared primarily for mainstream Americans. (pp. 37-38)

These three recommendations, which can be found over and over again in the literature on multicultural counseling, have resulted in a number of changes at the service delivery, academic training, and professional policy levels. At the service delivery level, counseling services have been urged to hire bilingual/bicultural counselors to work with ethnic minority clients (Sue & Zane, 1987). At the training level, academic programs have been urged to provide courses in multicultural awareness, knowledge, and skills (Ridley, Mendoza, & Kanitz, 1994).

At the professional policy level, the influence of these recommendations is reflected in the American Psychological Association's (APA's) "Ethical Principles of Psychologists and Code of Conḋ ̣ct" (1992), *Accreditation Handbook* (1986), and "Guidelines for Providers of Psychological Services to Ethnic, Linguistic, and Culturally Diverse Populations" (1993). Although the Ethics Code (APA, 1992) is silent about the need for more ethnic psychologists, Standard 1.10 does state that "psychologists do not engage in unfair discrimination based on age, gender, race, ethnicity, national origin, religion, sexual orientation, disability, socioeconomic status, or any basis proscribed by law" (p. 1601). The recommendation that students and therapists acquire knowledge of cultures is reflected in the General Principles of the Ethics Code, which specify that psychologists are "aware of cultural, individual, and role differences, including those due to age, gender, race, ethnicity, national origin, religion, sexual orientation, disability, language, and socioeconomic status" (Principle D: Respect for People's Rights and Dignity, p. 1599). The influence of the recommendation that treatment be modified for ethnic minorities can be found in both the General Principles, which state that "psychologists are cognizant of the fact that the competencies required in serving, teaching, and/or studying groups of people vary with distinctive characteristics of those groups" (Principle A: Competence, p. 1599), and Standard 2.04, which specifies that "psychologists attempt to identify situations in which particular interventions . . . may not be applicable or may require adjustment in administration . . . such as individuals' gender, age, race, ethnicity, national origin, religion, sexual orientation, disability, language, or socioeconomic status" (p. 1603).

Similarly, the recommendations cited by Sue and Zane (1987) are reflected in Criterion II of the APA *Accreditation Handbook* (1986). Criterion II implies that ethnic minority psychologists should be recruited into the field and that all students should be provided knowledge of ethnic cultures by stating that

> social responsibility and respect for cultural and individual differences are attitudes which must be imparted to students and trainees and be reflected in all phases of the program's operation: faculty recruitment and promotion, student recruitment and evaluation, curriculum, and field training. Social and personal diversity of faculty and students is an essential goal if the trainees are to function optimally within our pluralistic society. (p. 4)

The recommendations that students and therapists should acquire knowledge of ethnic cultures and that psychological treatment should be modified for ethnic minorities are reflected in the Criterion II statement that "programs must develop knowledge and skills in their students relevant to human diversity such as . . . ethnic and racial backgrounds" (p. 4). There is evidence that Criterion II serves as more than just an aspirational guideline. Rickard and Clements (1993) pointed out that noncompliance with Criterion II increasingly has served as the underlying rationale for negative judgments by the APA Committee on Accreditation. Furthermore, the chair of the Committee on Accreditation has implied that site visitors will be encouraged by the committee to place even more emphasis on Criterion II in the future (Altmaier, 1993).

The Guidelines (APA, 1993) speak most directly to the recommendation that treatments be modified to meet the needs of ethnic minorities. They state, among other things, that psychological service providers "need knowledge and skills for multicultural assessment and intervention" (p. 45), "recognize ethnicity and culture as significant parameters in understanding psychological processes" (p. 46), "consider not only differential diagnostic issues but also the cultural beliefs and values of the client and his/her community in providing intervention" (p. 46), and "become familiar with indigenous beliefs and practices and . . . respect them" (p. 47).

Thus, it seems obvious that the three recommendations for "improving the relationship between therapists and ethnic-minority clients" (p. 37), for which Sue and Zane (1987) found almost unanimous agreement in the cross-cultural literature of the 1970s and 1980s, have had an important impact on service delivery, academic training, and professional policy in the 1990s. However, although there is almost unanimous professional support for these recommendations among scholars specializing in multicultural counseling, no one has yet conducted an extensive review to determine the research support for these recommendations. After three and a half decades of research on cross-cultural issues in counseling, it seems appropriate to ask if there is empirical support for training more ethnic therapists, acquiring knowledge of ethnic cultures, and modifying traditional forms of treatment.

The purpose of this chapter is to review the cross-cultural counseling research literature published since 1970 to determine if there is support for the three recommendations identified by Sue and Zane (1987) and to develop guidelines for future research that could have implications for policy, training, and practice. More specifically, this chapter reviews research that has implications for the following questions: (a) Are counselor and client dyads that are matched for ethnicity associated with more favorable counseling process and outcome than are ethnically mismatched dyads? (b) Is counselor training in ethnic cultures associated with more favorable counseling process and outcome for ethnic minority clients than no training in ethnic cultures? and (c) Is there empirical support for modifying traditional forms of therapy when working with ethnic minority clients?

Wherever possible, this review has drawn on the findings of earlier reviews in order to make our task more manageable. For those variables for which no earlier review was available or for those studies that were missed in earlier reviews or published subsequent to the earlier reviews, we present our own analysis of the original research. To make the findings most relevant to counselors and counseling psychologists, and to keep it manageable, the review focuses on counseling process and outcome studies and therefore draws most heavily upon professional counseling journals.

RESEARCH SUPPORT FOR
RECRUITING MORE ETHNIC COUNSELORS

Research relevant to the recommendation that "more ethnic therapists who presumably are bilingual or are familiar with ethnic cultural values should be recruited into the mental health field" has compared the effectiveness of ethnically and linguistically similar counseling dyads to ethnically and linguistically dissimilar dyads. This body of research includes studies of both counseling process (preference for counselor ethnicity, perceptions of counselor credibility, other process variables) and outcome (utilization and treatment outcome).

Counseling Process Research

Preference for Counselor Ethnicity

Two types of research methodology have been used to assess participant preference for counselor ethnicity, simple choice methodology and paired-comparison methodology. In the simple choice methodology, participants are asked to simply make a choice between counselors of two ethnicities (e.g., between an Asian American counselor and a European American counselor) or between an ethnically similar counselor or an ethnically dissimilar counselor. In the paired-comparison methodology, participants make numerous forced choices between an ethnically similar counselor and a menu of other counselor characteristics (e.g., a counselor of the same sex, a counselor with a dissimilar personality, an older counselor).

Studies Using Simple Choice Methodology. Early research on preferences for counselor ethnicity focused on African American preferences for either an African American (Black) or a European American (White) counselor. For the most part, the initial studies ignored within-group or individual differences among research participants. In one of the first reviews of this research, Harrison (1975) concluded that although the research results were mixed, Black clients tended to prefer a Black counselor. A subsequent review by Sattler (1977) also concluded that "all things being equal, many Black subjects prefer Black therapists to White therapists" (p. 267). Two later reviews by Atkinson (1983, 1985) provided further evidence that African Americans prefer ethnically similar counselors. A dissertation study not reviewed earlier found that

Black community college students preferred a Black counselor over either a White or a Hispanic counselor (Greene, 1982). More recently, Bernstein, Wade, and Hofmann (1987) reported that both Black and White participants in their study preferred a Black female counselor regardless of type of problem presented.

The results of three studies published since these earlier reviews suggest that African American preferences for counselor ethnicity are a function of Black racial identity development (Helms & Carter, 1991; Morten & Atkinson, 1983; Reed, 1988). One study reported that the racial identity of participants was not significantly related to preferences for a Black counselor (Ponterotto, Anderson, & Grieger, 1986). In general, however, it appears that African Americans immersed in proBlack racial identity prefer a Black counselor, whereas those at the Internalization (or equivalent) level of racial identity development base their preference on factors other than counselor race.

Past reviews have revealed a paucity of studies examining the preferences for ethnically similar counselors by members of racial/ethnic groups other than African Americans. Atkinson (1983) found only two studies involving Hispanics; no evidence of a preference effect was found in either study. In his later review, Atkinson (1985) cited a study in which Mexican Americans with a strong commitment to Mexican culture expressed a preference for ethnically similar counselors, a finding that was subsequently replicated by Sanchez and King (1986). Greene's (1982) previously unreported dissertation found that Hispanic community college students preferred a Hispanic counselor over either a White or a Black counselor. A recent article by Lopez, Lopez, and Fong (1991) included a comprehensive review of the research on Mexican American preference for ethnically similar counselors. All six of the counselor preference studies in this review concluded that Mexican Americans prefer a counselor from the same ethnic background. Lopez et al. also reported findings from three of their own studies, all three of which concluded that Mexican Americans clearly prefer an ethnically similar counselor. Two of these three studies included participant's level of acculturation as a variable of interest. One of the two studies found acculturation to be related to preferences for counselor ethnicity; middle- and high-acculturated Mexican American college men more often preferred a counselor of the same ethnic background than did low-acculturated students. This latter outcome appears to conflict with the earlier findings that Mexican Americans with a strong commitment prefer an ethnically similar counselor over an ethnically dissimilar counselor. However, it is conceivable that Mexican Americans who score high on unidimensional measures of acculturation are at the same time highly committed to Mexican American culture.

Only a few studies employing the simple choice methodology have examined either American Indian or Asian American preferences for ethnically similar counselors. In his 1983 review, Atkinson cited one study examining American Indian preference and another assessing Vietnamese preference for an ethnically similar counselor. Both reported no preference effect. Atkinson (1985) updated the earlier review with one study in which Native American college students indicated a strong preference for Native American counselors (Haviland, Horswill, O'Connell, & Dynneson, 1983). In a more recent article, Johnson and Lashley (1989) reported that strong commitment to Native American culture was directly related to preference for an ethnically similar counselor. Korsgaard (1990) found that Asian American participants who were Asian identified (low in acculturation) were more likely to choose an Asian counselor than were Western identified (high in acculturation) participants. Moreover, subjects chose an Asian counselor when the problem was relevant to Asian culture and a Caucasian counselor when the problem was relevant to Western culture.

Studies Using Paired-Comparison Methodology. A series of four paired-comparison studies provide additional evidence that when given a choice between an ethnically similar counselor and an ethnically dissimilar counselor, the majority of American Indians (Bennett & BigFoot-Sipes, 1991), Asian Americans (Atkinson, Poston, Furlong, & Mercado, 1989), Blacks (Atkinson, Furlong, & Poston, 1986; Ponterotto, Alexander, & Hinkston, 1988), Mexican Americans (Atkinson et al., 1989), and Whites (Atkinson et al., 1989; Bennett & BigFoot-Sipes, 1991) will express a preference for an ethnically similar counselor. However, these studies also documented that the majority of ethnic minority participants often rank preferences for other counselor characteristics (most notably similar attitudes and values, similar personality, more education, and older) higher than they do preference for an ethnically similar counselor. With regard to within-group differences, some evidence was found that African Americans (Ponterotto et al., 1988) and American Indians (Bennett & BigFoot-Sipes, 1991) who reported a strong commitment to their ethnic culture were more likely to prefer an ethnically similar counselor than those who expressed a weak cultural commitment. However, no differences in African American preference rankings based on cultural commitment were found by Atkinson et al. (1986), nor were differences based on racial identity development found by Ponterotto et al. (1988).

Summary of Preference for Counselor Ethnicity Studies. For both the simple choice and paired-comparison methodologies, there is consistent and strong evidence that, other things being equal, ethnic minority participants prefer an ethnically similar counselor over an ethnically dissimilar counselor. As might be expected, it is equally clear that not all ethnic minority individuals make their choice of a counselor solely on the basis of an ethnic schema. The results of the paired-comparison studies suggest that when asked to compare preference for counselor ethnicity to preference for other counselor characteristics, many ethnic minority participants prefer counselors who have similar attitudes and values, have more education, are older, or have similar personalities over a counselor who is ethnically similar to them. Several within-group variables examined in both the simple choice and the paired-comparison studies may help explain individual differences in preferences for counselor characteristics within an ethnic group. In particular, acculturation, cultural commitment, and racial identity development all appear to be related to preference for counselor ethnicity.

Ratings of Counselor Credibility

To the extent that counseling can be conceptualized as an interpersonal influence process (Strong, 1968), the ability of the counselor to influence the client assumes a paramount role in the counseling process. Earlier research in social psychology has documented that in any source-receiver communication, the ability of a source to influence a receiver is a function of perceived source credibility (expertness and trustworthiness) and attractiveness (Simons, Berkowitz, & Moyer, 1970). Building on the earlier social psychology research, counseling researchers have used counselor credibility and attractiveness (often combined into a single construct, counselor credibility, due to high correlations among expertness, trustworthiness, and attractiveness) as either an independent or a dependent variable in studies of counseling process. In addition to maximizing the counselor's ability to influence the client, it is argued that ethnic minority clients are more likely to utilize counseling services if they perceive the counselor to be a credible source of help. A recent study by Akutsu, Lin, and Zane (1990) lends support to this argument. These researchers found that counselor credibility was a strong predictor of utilization intent among both Chinese and Caucasian students.

Of interest to the current review are those studies in which ethnic minority participants have rated the perceived credibility of ethnically similar and dissimilar counselors. Atkinson (1983) reported 11 studies that assessed perceived counselor credibility, only 2 of which found a significant effect for counselor-client ethnic similarity. An update of this review revealed additional conflicting results regarding an ethnicity similarity effect for perceived counselor credibility (Atkinson, 1985).

Recent studies examining Mexican American ratings of perceived counselor credibility have also reported mixed or negative findings. In a review of 12 studies with Mexican American participants, Lopez et al. (1991) distinguished "choice method" (preference for counselor ethnicity) from "judgment method" (perceived counselor credibility) research and concluded that "a judgment approach typically does not find evidence that Mexican Americans prefer ethnically similar counselors" (p. 488). In the same article, Lopez et al. reported the results of their own study in which Mexican Americans rated a Mexican American therapist as more competent to help them than they did an Anglo-American therapist. However, two recent studies found that neither Mexican American high school students (Hess & Street, 1991) nor Mexican

American college students (Atkinson, Casas, & Abreu, 1992) rated counselor credibility differentially on the basis of counselor ethnicity (Anglo American versus Mexican American), regardless of their level of acculturation.

Research with African American participants published since the earlier reviews has also produced conflicting results. Shipp (1986) reported that Black participants rated a Black counselor more expert, trustworthy, and attractive than a White counselor. Conversely, a study assessing Black high school students' perceptions of counselor attractiveness (defined as friendliness, sociability, warmth, and trustworthiness) found no evidence that Black counselors were perceived as more attractive than Caucasian counselors (Goldberg & Tidwell, 1990). However, these conflicting findings may be the result of sampling African Americans at divergent stages of Black racial identity development. There is some evidence that when clients are allowed to choose whether they see an African American or Caucasian counselor, African American participants rate African American and Caucasian counselors equally credible (Wade & Bernstein, 1991). It can be hypothesized that an ethnic similarity effect is neutralized in this situation because clients at the Immersion/ Emersion stage choose African American counselors, whereas clients at the Pre-Encounter stage choose European American counselors. Cultural mistrust may also account for differences in preferences for counselor race by African Americans. Watkins and Terrell (1988) reported that Black participants with high levels of cultural mistrust had diminished expectations about the trustworthiness and expertise of White counselors. Similar findings were reported in a replication of this study that also examined Black expectations about counselor trustworthiness and expertise when seeking help for various types of problems (Watkins, Terrell, Miller, & Terrell, 1989). Blacks who were highly mistrustful rated White counselors as less credible and less able to help with general anxiety, shyness, feelings of inferiority, and dating difficulties than Black counselors.

Research has provided tentative support for the hypothesis that Asian Americans perceive an ethnically similar counselor to be more credible than a Caucasian counselor, although credibility ratings may be influenced, in part, by level of acculturation or generation since immigration. Two studies reported that Asian Americans, regardless of acculturation level, rated an ethnically similar counselor as more credible than a Caucasian American counselor (Atkinson & Matsushita, 1991; Giuffreda, 1986). Gim, Atkinson, and Kim (1991) also reported that Asian American college students perceived an ethnically similar counselor to be more credible and culturally competent than a counselor who was ethnically dissimilar. However, Murakawa (1987) reported that although second-generation Asian Americans perceived an Asian therapist as more credible than a Caucasian therapist, among third-generation Asian Americans there was no significant ethnicity effect.

Summary of Counselor Credibility Studies. Although more recent studies continue the pattern of conflicting results, there is growing evidence that ratings of perceived credibility for ethnically similar and dissimilar counselors are related to within-group differences. The review of research in this section leads to the tentative conclusion that for *some* individuals within each of the ethnic minority groups, counselor similarity/dissimilarity is an important factor in determining perceived counselor credibility. This conclusion agrees with our own personal and clinical experience and appeals to common sense.

Other Process Variables

The 1983 review by Atkinson indicated that studies on counseling process variables (which included credibility) were almost evenly divided between those that found an ethnic similarity effect and those that did not. Atkinson (1985) concluded that process research published since the earlier review continued this same pattern of conflicting results. A few additional studies were found in the current review that have examined the relationship between counselor ethnicity and process variables other than preference for counselor race or perceived counselor credibility.

Greene, Cunningham, and Yanico (1986) reported that Black college students expected Black counselors to be more helpful than White counselors. An analogue study of peer counseling by Berg and Wright-Buckley (1988) revealed that both Black and White subjects liked Black interviewers more than they did White interviewers and had more positive impressions of them, although this effect was mitigated by confederate self-disclosure. Interestingly, however, both Black and White participants disclosed more intimately with White interviewers than they did with Black interviewers. Wade and Bernstein (1991) found that counselor-client ethnic similarity did not influence African American client perceptions of counselor empathy and positive regard.

Two other counseling process studies were found that were not included in earlier reviews. Franco and LeVine (1980) reported that counselor ethnicity as identified in a portfolio description was not a factor in either Chicano or Anglo students' willingness to seek counseling. In a survey of five distinct ethnic groups (Black American, American Indian, Latino American, Filipino American, and multiethnic individuals) regarding their suggestions for improving counseling, availability of an ethnically similar counselor was ranked 10th out of 11 suggestions (Atkinson, Jennings, & Liongson, 1990). However, some evidence was found that the unavailability of an ethnically similar counselor was more often a reason why participants strongly committed to their ethnic culture never sought counseling than it was for participants who were bicultural or strongly committed to mainstream culture.

Summary of Other Process Variables. The five studies of counseling process variables other than preference for counselor ethnicity and perceived counselor credibility published since Atkinson's (1985) review have produced somewhat mixed findings. However, the results of two of these studies do suggest that Black participants have more favorable impressions of Black counselors than of White counselors, thus reinforcing an ethnic similarity effect. Furthermore, one study found evidence that citing the unavailability of an ethnically similar counselor as a reason for not previously seeking help was a function of cultural commitment. This latter finding reinforces the need to take within-group diversity into account when examining the effects of counselor-client ethnic similarity on counseling process variables.

Counseling Outcome Research

Unfortunately, very few studies relating the ethnic similarity effect to treatment outcome have been reported in the counseling psychology literature. Two reviews by Atkinson (1983, 1985) concluded that the research assessing counselor-client ethnic similarity on counseling outcome had produced mixed findings. However, research published subsequent to these two reviews has produced much stronger evidence of an ethnic similarity effect.

Several studies not covered in the earlier reviews have examined the relationship between counselor-client ethnic similarity and some measure of utilization. Terrell and Terrell (1984) reported that Black clients with high levels of cultural mistrust were more likely to terminate counseling with a White counselor after the first session than they were with a Black counselor. Further, Wade and Bernstein (1991) found that Black clients who were assigned a Black counselor were less likely to drop out of counseling over the course of three sessions than were Black clients who were assigned to a White counselor. However, a study by Reed (1988) found no evidence that those Black clients who preferred a Black counselor and were assigned to one were less likely to terminate counseling prematurely than Black clients who preferred a Black counselor but were not assigned to one.

The strongest support for an ethnic similarity effect on counseling outcome is provided by three studies of archival data in mental health centers. Flaskerud (1986) examined the case records of 300 clients (50 Blacks, 50 Mexican Americans, 50 Filipinos, 50 Vietnamese, 100 Whites) in four public community mental health agencies and found that both ethnic and language similarity between therapist and client were predictive of dropout status. Those clients who matched with their therapist on the basis of language and/or ethnicity were less likely to drop out of therapy within four sessions or less (without their therapist's consent) than were clients mismatched for language and/or ethnicity.

Two major studies supported by the National Institute of Mental Health provide substantial evidence of a relationship between ethnic similarity between therapist and client and treatment utilization. In an analysis of archival data on 1,746 Asian clients seen in Los Angeles County mental health facilities between 1983 and 1988, Flaskerud (1991) reported that Asian clients who were matched with ethnically similar therapists had lower dropout rates than

Asian clients who were seen by ethnically dissimilar therapists. Furthermore, Asian clients who were matched with their therapists on the basis of either language or ethnicity were seen for significantly more sessions than those who were mismatched on these variables. In a similar review of archival data gathered by the Los Angeles County Department of Mental Health between 1984 and 1988, Sue, Fujino, Hu, Takeuchi, and Zane (1991) reported that "for all groups except for African Americans, ethnic match [between therapist and client] resulted in substantially lower odds of dropping out than for unmatched clients" (p. 536). They also found that therapist-client ethnic matching was a predictor of length of treatment for Asian American, African American, Mexican American, and White clients. Both ethnic match and language match were found to be predictive of better outcomes (as measured by therapist ratings on the Global Assessment Scale) for Asian American clients. Ethnic match alone was related to positive treatment outcome for Mexican Americans.

Summary of Outcome Studies

Although there is a limited number of studies in the counseling psychology literature linking counselor-client ethnic similarity with outcome variables for traditional counseling psychology clients, three major archival studies of patients at mental health facilities provide substantial evidence that treatment outcomes are enhanced by matching therapist and client on the basis of language and ethnicity. As with the process research reviewed earlier, common sense suggests that ethnicity matching may be more important for some clients than for others. Unfortunately, only one of the studies on client outcome included a within-group variable in the research design. The study by Terrell and Terrell (1984) points to cultural mistrust as an important client variable that is worthy of further examination in research relating counselor-client matching on ethnicity and treatment outcome.

RESEARCH SUPPORT FOR
ACQUIRING KNOWLEDGE OF ETHNIC CULTURES

No studies were found that directly relate to the second recommendation for which Sue and Zane (1987) found almost universal support, namely, that "students and therapists should acquire knowledge of ethnic cultures and communities" (p. 38). Although one study was identified that demonstrated the efficacy of training in multicultural skills (Wade & Bernstein, 1991), none was uncovered that assessed whether teaching counselors about specific ethnic cultures results in improved counseling with ethnic minority clients.

Teaching counseling trainees about specific ethnic cultures and communities is intuitively appealing, but it can also be argued that knowledge of cultures and communities could have a detrimental effect. Sue and Zane (1987) noted that although insufficient knowledge of an individual's cultural background is problematic, teaching counselors about specific cultural values and behaviors may increase the risk that counselors will stereotype their ethnic minority clients by assuming they should manifest these values and behaviors. Obviously, research is desperately needed that assesses whether including cultural content in the curricula of training programs actually results in enhanced counseling services, process, and outcome for ethnic minority clients. More research is also needed that examines the efficacy of training in multicultural skills such as those assessed by Wade and Bernstein (1991).

RESEARCH SUPPORT FOR
MODIFYING CONVENTIONAL FORMS OF TREATMENT

Three bodies of counseling research have implications for the recommendation that "traditional forms of treatment should be modified because they are geared primarily for mainstream Americans" (Sue & Zane, 1987, p. 38). (In order to avoid confusion in the use of the word *traditional*, we apply the term *conventional* in reference to psychological techniques practiced in North America and the term *traditional* in reference to psychological techniques practiced in the client's ancestral culture.) The first body of research compares the effectiveness of selected conventional counseling techniques with particular ethnic groups. This approach assumes that counselors need to modify their forms of treatment by selecting the conventional techniques that are most congruent with the needs and experiences of a particular ethnic minority population. The second type of research examines the effectiveness of responding to cultural content as a means of building rapport with ethnic minority clients. This approach assumes that counselors need to modify the content of counseling, not necessarily the counseling strategies that they use. The third area of research examines how the healing/helping beliefs and strategies indigenous to the client's culture might be used to enhance counseling process and outcome. This approach assumes that counselors need to modify counseling treatment by incorporating principles and helping strategies from the client's culture.

Identifying Conventional Counseling Strategies
That Are Effective With Ethnic Minority Clients

A number of studies have compared the effectiveness of directive and non-directive counseling techniques with ethnic minority client populations. A few additional studies have examined the effectiveness of counselor self-disclosure and other conventional techniques with ethnic minority participants.

Directive Versus Nondirective Counseling Techniques

In this section we included studies in which the researchers identified the techniques being compared as directive and nondirective. We also exercised our own subjective judgment as to what constituted "directive" and "nondirective" techniques by labeling probes and closed questions as directive techniques and affective, facilitative, empathic, and reflective responses as nondirective techniques. The majority of these studies have used client perceptions of counselor credibility as the dependent variable.

There is fairly strong evidence that Latinos expect counseling to be a directive process and that they prefer a directive style of counseling to a nondirective style. A survey by Kunkel (1990) indicated that Mexican American college students who identified closely with Mexican culture expected counseling to be more directive than did their Anglo-oriented or bicultural counterparts. Four counseling analogue studies revealed that Latinos also rate a counselor more positively and are more willing to see a counselor who uses a directive approach than a counselor who uses a nondirective approach. LeVine and Franco (1983) found that Mexican American females were more willing to seek counseling services when a male counselor's style was described as directive than when it was described as nondirective. Pomales and Williams (1989) reported that Hispanic students (mostly Puerto Ricans, some Mexican Americans), regardless of their level of acculturation, rated directive counselors as more knowledgeable about psychology and more willing to help than nondirective counselors; the students were also more willing to see the directive counselor. Ponce and Atkinson (1989) found a similar main effect for counseling style in a study examining Mexican American college students' perceptions of counselor credibility; participants gave counselors with a directive counseling style more positive ratings than those with a nondirective style regardless of participant level of acculturation. Borrego, Chavez, and Titley (1982) reported that both Mexican American and Anglo American undergraduates were more willing to return for a second interview when the counselor used probing techniques than when the counselor used reflecting techniques.

There is also fairly consistent evidence that Asian Americans prefer a directive counseling style. After reviewing 12 studies on Asian American mental health, Leong (1986) concluded that directive counseling approaches are more consistent with the Asian values of respect for authority figures and low tolerance for ambiguous situations than are nondirective approaches. Two published studies and one unpublished dissertation appearing since Leong's (1986) review all reported that Asian Americans rated counselors as more credible when they demonstrated a directive style of counseling versus a nondirective style (Atkinson & Matsushita, 1991; Exum & Lau, 1988; Giuffreda, 1986). One study published subsequent to Leong's (1986) review contradicted these findings for Asian Americans. Akutsu et al. (1990) reported that empathy was the sole significant predictor of Chinese college students' perceptions of counselor credibility. However, the authors of the latter study noted that the directiveness condition in their experiment may have included behaviors that are inconsistent with Asian American cultural values (e.g., "presenting forceful opinions"). That not all directive techniques are viewed with equal favor by Asians was documented by Merta, Ponterotto, and Brown (1992). These researchers found that "high acculturated [Asian] foreign students rated authoritative peer counselors higher in overall effectiveness, whereas low-acculturated foreign students rated collaborative peer counselors higher" (p. 214).

One study was found in which American Indian high school students served as participants in an assessment of directive versus nondirective counseling styles. Dauphinais, Dauphinais, and Rowe (1981) reported that American Indian students perceived a counselor with a directive style as more credible than one with a "facilitative" style. Two studies compared African American, European American, and Latino preferences for directive and nondirective counseling styles. Anderson (1983) examined Black, White, and Mexican American preferences for directive versus nondirective counseling and reported no significant effect for counseling style. In another multiethnic study, Folensbee, Draguns, and Danish (1986) found that Anglo Americans, Black Americans, and Puerto Ricans rated counselors who used affective responses higher in credibility than counselors who responded with closed questions.

Counselor Self-Disclosure Versus
Nondisclosure as Counseling Strategies

The few studies that have been conducted on counselor self-disclosure as a technique with ethnic minority participants have produced mixed results. In an analogue study, Berg and Wright-Buckley (1988) reported that Black females liked peer counseling interviews more and formed more positive impressions of the peer interviews when the interviewer disclosed intimately than when there was no intimate disclosure. The authors also found that intimately disclosing White interviewers elicited more intimate self-disclosure by both Black and White subjects than did Black interviewers. In another analogue study, Wetzel and Wright-Buckley (1988) reported that intimate self-disclosure by White therapists resulted in a slight decrease in the number of Black females' self-referents and intimacy of self-disclosure. On the other hand, intimately disclosing Black therapists induced significantly increased participant intimate disclosure and self-referents.

Borrego et al. (1982) reported no differences in willingness to self-disclose by Mexican American and Anglo American students when the counselor utilized a disclosing interview technique. No studies examining the strategy of counselor self-disclosure with Asian American or American Indian clients were found.

Evaluating Other Conventional Counseling Techniques

Three studies have examined the effectiveness of other conventional counseling techniques with ethnic minorities.

On the basis of Neuro-Linguistic Programming principles, Sandhu (1984) exposed 60 male Choctaw adolescents to counselors who either mirrored or did not mirror their nonverbal behaviors. The results indicated that the participants rated as most empathic those counselors who demonstrated the mirroring condition.

Comas-Diaz (1981) assigned 26 Puerto Rican women identified as depressed to a behavior therapy group, a cognitive therapy group (modified to include elements of learned helplessness), or a control condition. After five treatment sessions, women in the two therapy groups showed a significant reduction in depression compared to the control group; there were no significant differences between the two therapy groups.

Rodriguez and Blocher (1988) exposed Puerto Rican women in a special college admissions program to a modified Adkins Career Choice Modular Program (identified by the authors as the type of structured, specific, and task-oriented career program that is needed by educationally disadvantaged populations), a conventional college career discussion program, or a placebo control group. Although participants in both treatment groups made more positive changes in career maturity and locus of control than did those in the control group, no significant differences were found between the participants in the two treatment groups.

Summary of Research on Conventional Counseling
Strategies That Are Effective With Ethnic Minority Clients

With the exception of the Akutsu et al. (1990) and Folensbee et al. (1986) studies, both of which found support for a nondirective technique, and the Anderson (1983) study, which found no effect for counseling style, the results of research on directive versus nondirective counseling have been remarkably consistent: American Indians, Asian Americans, and Latinos perceive counselors using directive counseling techniques as more credible and approachable for help than counselors utilizing nondirective or facilitative approaches.

The case for counselor self-disclosure and other selected techniques is less compelling. The four studies examining self-disclosure as a counseling strategy and the three studies on other conventional counseling techniques yielded no consistent pattern of results.

Culturally Responsive Versus Nonresponsive Counseling

One way of modifying conventional forms of treatment is redirecting the focus of counseling by responding to cultural content in the counseling session.

Recently several studies have examined the effects of culturally responsive and culturally nonresponsive counseling on ethnic minority clients' perceptions of counselor credibility and cultural competence. Cultural responsiveness in this context refers to counselor responses that acknowledge the existence of, show interest in, demonstrate knowledge of, and express appreciation for the client's ethnicity and culture and that place the client's problem in a cultural context.

Four studies examining African American perceptions of counselors who utilize a culturally responsive approach have revealed that this approach is rated more positively than a culturally nonresponsive approach. Pomales, Claiborn, and LaFromboise (1986) reported that Black college students rated culture-sensitive counselors (counselors who acknowledged and showed interest in the role of culture or race in the client's problem) as more culturally competent than culture-blind counselors (counselors who minimized the importance of culture or race and shifted focus to other factors), regardless of the students' level of racial identity development. Indirect support for culturally responsive counseling also was provided by Wade and Bernstein (1991). These researchers reported that Black clients rated counselors who had received sensitivity training (aimed at attending to the client's values and articulating the client's problem within a cultural framework) higher on credibility and more positively on several relationship measures than counselors who had not completed the training. Clients of counselors who received sensitivity training also returned for more follow-up sessions and expressed greater satisfaction with counseling than those who were assigned to counselors who had not received additional training. Further, Thompson, Worthington, and Atkinson (1994) reported that Black university students engaged in more depth of self-disclosure and reported greater willingness to make a self-referral when exposed to a counselor with a cultural content (attending to racial aspects of students' concerns) orientation than when exposed to a counselor with a universal content (ignoring racial aspect of students' concerns) orientation. Poston, Craine, and Atkinson (1991) examined the effects of counselor dissimilarity confrontation (i.e., White counselor self-disclosure regarding ethnic difference with client) and client cultural mistrust on Black clients' willingness to self-disclose. Although failing to reach a conventional level of statistical significance, counselor self-disclosure was positively correlated with client willingness to self-disclose.

Two studies examining the effects of cultural responsiveness were found in which Asians and Asian Americans served as participants. Gim et al. (1991) reported that culture-sensitive counselors (who acknowledged the importance of ethnicity and cultural values to the client) were rated higher in credibility and cultural competence than culture-blind counselors (who ignored ethnicity and cultural values). Sodowsky (1991) found that counselors portrayed as being culturally consistent with Asian culture were rated by Asian Indian students attending an American university as more expert and trustworthy than culturally discrepant counselors.

Counselor responsiveness to cultural content was also found to affect Mexican American ratings of counselor credibility and cultural competence. Atkinson et al. (1992) reported that culturally responsive counselors (acknowledging the role of Mexican-American culture and ethnicity in the client's concern and demonstrating knowledge of Mexican-American culture) received higher ratings for cultural competence than culturally unresponsive counselors (ignoring the portion of the client's comments linked to culture), regardless of client acculturation or counselor ethnicity.

Summary of Culturally Responsive Versus Nonresponsive Counseling

The results of these studies provide a clear-cut case for cultural responsiveness as a counseling strategy for building credibility with ethnic minority clients. There is also evidence that culturally responsive counseling results in greater client willingness to return for counseling, satisfaction with counseling, and depth of self-disclosure.

Indigenous Beliefs and Techniques

Sue and Zane (1987) suggested that in order to build credibility with culturally different clients, counselors need to conceptualize client problems in a manner that is consistent with the client's belief system and adopt methods of resolving the problem that are compatible with the client's culture. This implies that conventional forms of treatment can be modified by adapting mental health attributions and helping strategies from the client's culture to conventional counseling treatments. Included in this section are two types of studies: (a) studies assessing the mental health beliefs and attributions in a culture that could inform the development of culturally appropriate techniques and (b) studies evaluating techniques that are based on or taken from the client's culture.

Two studies were found that attempted to identify the mental health beliefs and attributions of Asians or Asian Americans. A study by Luk and Bond (1992) found that Hong Kong Chinese college students hold both internal and external attributions about the causes of mental health problems (acknowledging both environmental/hereditary factors and social-personal factors) but primarily internal attributions for curing the problems. The authors concluded that although the research participants "believed that a problem was caused by an interaction of external and internal factors, . . . [they also believed that] the patients themselves had the chief responsibility for taking remedial measures, including that of engaging the resources of their interpersonal network" (p. 155).

Narikiyo and Kameoka (1992) compared the attributions of mental illness and judgments about help seeking of Japanese American and White American college students. They reported that Japanese Americans were more likely than White Americans to "attribute mental illness to social causes, to resolve problems on their own, and to seek help from family members or friends or both" (p. 363). The authors concluded that "even among seemingly acculturated Japanese Americans, cultural values may continue to influence beliefs about mental illness and help seeking" (p. 368).

On the basis of the assumption that Mexican Americans place greater emphasis on family decision making than do conventional counselors (who may emphasize individual choice over family choice), Atkinson, Winzelberg, and Holland (1985) exposed Mexican American women being seen at a Planned Parenthood agency to counselors reflecting either a family choice or individual choice philosophy for family planning. No differences were found in the ratings of counselor credibility for a counselor expressing an individual choice versus a counselor expressing a family choice philosophy regarding locus of control for family planning.

Schinke et al. (1988) examined the efficacy of a conventional substance abuse prevention program that included culturally meaningful examples and a bicultural focus for American Indian adolescents. These researchers reported that participants receiving the prevention program scored more positively on measures of substance use knowledge, attitudes, and interactive skills, and on self-reported use of tobacco, alcohol, and drugs, than did participants in the no-intervention control group.

One study actually compared a helping technique from the indigenous culture to conventional counseling. Costantino, Malgady, and Rogler (1986) randomly assigned 210 Puerto Rican third-grade students identified as having behavior problems to original *cuento* therapy (using Puerto Rican folktales to model adaptive behavior), adapted *cuento* therapy (adapted to provide bicultural folktales), art/play therapy, and no therapy. The two versions of *cuento* therapy significantly reduced participants' trait anxiety relative to traditional therapy and no therapy, increased Comprehension subtest scores on the WISC-R, and decreased observer-rated aggression.

Summary of Research on
Indigenous Beliefs and Techniques

The two studies of Asian mental health attributions indicate that both Hong Kong Chinese and Japanese Americans make external attributions about the causes of mental health problems but internal attributions about the resolution of these problems. However, only the Narikiyo and Kameoka (1992) study provided evidence that Asian Americans assign greater responsibility for resolving problems to the client than do European Americans. Further, only the study by Costantino et al. (1986) provided evidence that a helping technique taken from the client's culture is more effective than conventional (art) therapy.

DISCUSSION

Research Support for Recruiting More Ethnic Counselors

This review provides strong evidence that, in general, ethnically similar counseling dyads are associated with more positive counseling process and outcome than are ethnically dissimilar counseling dyads. Other things being equal, *most* ethnic minority clients prefer an ethnically similar counselor over an ethnically dissimilar counselor, and *some* ethnic minority clients assign higher credibility to an ethnically similar counselor, express greater willingness to see an ethnically similar counselor, and benefit more from therapy with an ethnically similar counselor than an ethnically dissimilar counselor. In our judgment, these findings provide unequivocal support for the recruitment, training, and hiring of more ethnic minority counselors.

Further evidence of the need for more ethnic minority counselors is provided by the U.S. Bureau of the Census (1992) projections for population growth through the year 2050. American Indians, Asian Americans and Pacific Islanders, Blacks, and Hispanics made up 24.3% of the population in the 1990 census. Using median projected birth and immigration rates, the Bureau of the Census anticipates that these groups will constitute 28.4% of the population by the year 2000 and 47.3% by the year 2050. These data add a sense of urgency to the recommendation that more ethnic minorities be recruited into the counseling profession. Dramatically larger numbers of ethnic minority counselors will need to be trained in the next 50 years if the rapidly increasing numbers of ethnic minorities are to receive optimal mental health services in the future.

It is also evident from this review (and it makes intuitive sense) that not all ethnic minority clients will prefer or benefit most from an ethnically similar counselor. A growing body of research indicates that preferences for counselor ethnicity, ratings of counselor credibility, and utilization of counseling services are related to characteristics that distinguish clients within ethnic groups. Client within-group variables that have been found to interact with ethnic similarity between counselor and client include cultural mistrust and stage of racial identity development for African Americans; cultural commitment for American Indians; acculturation, cultural commitment, and generation since immigration for Asian Americans; and acculturation and cultural commitment for Latinos. It may be premature, however, to conclude that the reactivity of these variables is restricted to the particular ethnic groups with which they have been associated to date. Although acculturation probably makes the most sense as a variable of interest for groups that have recently immigrated to the United States, cultural mistrust, racial/ethnic identity development, and cultural commitment may have application across all four ethnic minority groups. For example, the Cultural Mistrust Inventory (Terrell

& Terrell, 1981) was designed to be used with African Americans specifically, but the underlying construct appears to be applicable with other ethnic minority groups. Furthermore, a number of other within-group variables that correlate ethnic client responsiveness to counselors and counseling may be worthy of investigation (e.g., Casas and Pytluk, Chapter 8, this volume, suggest that client "modernity" may be another within-group variable worthy of future research).

In noting the consistency with which investigators recommended the recruitment of more ethnic therapists into the mental health field, Sue and Zane (1987) observed that this recommendation assumes that ethnic therapists will be bilingual or familiar with ethnic cultural values. Interestingly, these therapist qualities have not been directly addressed in the vast majority of studies examining counselor ethnicity or ethnic similarity between counselor and client as independent variables (the one exception found in this review is the study by Flaskerud, 1991). Although it may be safe to conclude that most ethnic minority counselors trained in the United States are proficient with the English language and knowledgeable about mainstream culture, it is obvious that great diversity exists in their bilingual ability, cultural knowledge, cultural practice, and cultural commitment related to their ancestral culture. These differences in language ability, cultural knowledge, cultural practice, and cultural commitment may play an important role in counseling process and outcome with ethnic minority clients. Bilingual ethnic counselors, for example, may be more effective with bilingual, ethnically similar clients than are monolingual ethnic counselors. Similarly, ethnic counselors who express their knowledge of and/or commitment to their ethnic culture may be more effective with ethnically similar clients who are culturally committed than are ethnic counselors who withhold this knowledge and/or commitment.

The failure of past research to take counselor language, counselor cultural commitment, and other within-group variables for the counselor into account is a serious limitation of multicultural research to date, and may reflect psychology's penchant for attributing therapeutic success to client characteristics while ignoring therapist characteristics. Only recently have some multicultural counseling researchers (most notably Janet Helms, 1990, and her colleagues) begun to take individual differences among counselors into account by including the racial identity development of the counselor as an independent variable in the research design. However, this design sophistication has not generalized to research with other ethnic groups. The most glaring omission is the failure of past research with American Indians, Asian Americans, and Latinos to include European American counselors' racial awareness or attitudes toward ethnic minorities in the design. For the most part, past research has skirted the obvious issue of counselor racism and has focused instead on client "mistrust" of counselors. It is important that future research attend to counselor variables that may influence ethnic minority client perceptions of trust and other counseling process variables.

Most of the research reviewed on counselor ethnicity either identified the ethnically dissimilar counselor as a European American (in one form or another) or left the counselor's ethnicity undefined. When research participants are given an ethnically dissimilar counselor as a preference or rating, it is often unclear whether they are assuming that the counselor will be European American. An ethnically dissimilar counselor could be a member of an ethnic minority group other than that to which the research participant belongs. If one of the factors influencing ethnic minority perceptions of counselors is mistrust of European Americans, there may not be the same degree of mistrust of counselors from other minority groups due to a perception of shared oppression. On the other hand, although it is often assumed that ethnic minority counselors find it easier to build rapport with a client from another ethnic minority group than do European American counselors, this hypothesis has yet to be tested empirically. It is hoped that future research on counselor-client ethnic similarity/dissimilarity will be expanded to include the situation in which the counselor and client represent different ethnic minority groups.

Research Support for Acquiring Knowledge of Ethnic Cultures

It is somewhat disconcerting that no studies were found in which the efficacy of teaching counselors about specific ethnic cultures and communities was examined. Teaching counselor trainees about specific ethnic cultures and communities is intuitively appealing, but it can also be argued that knowledge of cultures and communities could have a negative effect. Sue and Zane (1987) noted that although insufficient knowledge of an individual's cultural background is problematic, teaching counselors about specific cultural values and behaviors may increase the risk that counselors will stereotype their ethnic minority clients by assuming they should manifest these values and behaviors. Thus, research is needed that assesses whether including cultural content in the curricula of training programs actually enhances or detracts from counseling process and outcome for ethnic minority clients. Although the studies of cultural responsiveness reviewed earlier provide some evidence that counselors who are knowledgeable about the client's culture are perceived favorably by the client, these studies were not designed to evaluate the effectiveness of instruction in ethnic cultures and communities. Several lines of research evaluating instructional effectiveness are possible. For example, one line of research might focus on counselor behavior by examining *if* and *how* counselors utilize knowledge of ethnic minority cultures in counseling. Assuming that counselors do modify their behavior as a result of learning about ethnic minority cultures, another line of research might look at counseling process to determine if knowledge of ethnic minority cultures affects client attitudes and behavior. A third line of research might look at the effects of counselor knowledge of culture on counseling outcome. In the absence of such research, we cannot be sure that courses designed to provide information about specific cultures and communities are having the positive effect they are intended to have.

Research Support for Modifying Conventional Forms of Treatment

In general, the research support for modifying conventional forms of treatment is much more equivocal than the research support for recruiting ethnic counselors. The strongest support for modifying conventional treatment was found in the research on culturally responsive versus nonresponsive counseling. All seven studies reviewed found some evidence (six found statistically significant evidence) that ethnic minority participants perceive culturally responsive counseling more positively than culturally nonresponsive counseling. The results of these studies suggest that counselors should be aware of, show recognition of, demonstrate knowledge of, and express interest in the client's ethnic identification and cultural background and how both may or may not relate to the client's problem. In order to be responsive to the client's culture and its potential relevance in counseling an individual, it is important to assess preferences for counselor characteristics, client acculturation or cultural commitment, and level of cultural mistrust during the intake process. Precounseling assessments would provide a context for counselors (regardless of whether the assigned counselor was matched according to the client's preferences) to respond sensitively to the client. We believe that further research in the areas of counselor responsiveness and precounseling assessment of cultural content will help define the cultural sensitivity construct, a construct that has generated a wide variety of definitions and descriptions (Ridley, Mendoza, Kanitz, Angermeier, & Zenk, 1994).

Some support was also found for adopting helping strategies from the client's ancestral culture, although only a few studies were found in this area. The identification of mental health beliefs and attributions associated with specific cultural groups appears to be a promising line of research, given Sue and Zane's (1987) observation that a client's problem must be conceptualized in a manner that is consistent with the client's belief system. It is hoped that more research on mental health attributions and culture as well as more research on indigenous helping strategies will be forthcoming in the future.

Although our review reveals consistent evidence that American Indians, Asian Americans, and Latinos prefer a directive approach, the research on directive versus nondirective counseling styles to date has failed to demonstrate that ethnic minorities have a stronger preference for directive counseling than do European Americans. In fact, the few studies that have compared the reactions of ethnic minority and European American participants to directive and nondirective techniques (Akutsu et al., 1990; Anderson, 1983; Borrego et al., 1982) have found no evidence of an ethnicity effect. Thus, the expectation and preference for a directive counseling style found among ethnic minorities may represent a generalized expectation and preference for a directive counseling style, regardless of the client's ethnicity. Additional research is needed to compare preferences for directive and nondirective counseling styles within ethnic groups and across various ethnic groups, including European Americans, to determine if the preference for directive counseling is disproportionately present among ethnic minority groups or merely reflective of a general preference for a directive counseling style. Research is also needed to determine if treatment outcome, regardless of client ethnicity, is in any way related to receiving a preferred or disliked counseling style.

The studies on counselor self-disclosure and other conventional counseling techniques are few, and those that have been published have produced mixed results. Even the studies that did produce the hypothesized results offer little support for the efficacy of a selected counseling strategy with a particular ethnic group. The two self-disclosure studies that included both African American and European American participants found no difference in their response to counselor self-disclosure. The positive findings for Neuro-Linguistic Programming mirroring with American Indians are interesting but may simply reflect individual differences, not cultural differences, because no comparison was made to other ethnic groups. Although Puerto Rican women exposed to the experimental treatments in Comas-Diaz's (1981) and Rodriguez and Blocher's (1988) studies made greater criterion gains than those assigned to a control group, no evidence was found in either study to support the superiority of one treatment over another. In order to demonstrate the efficacy of a selected counseling strategy with a particular ethnic population, future research needs to produce evidence that at least one strategy is more effective with one ethnic population than another. Merely demonstrating that one strategy is more effective than another with a single ethnic population in the absence of compelling evidence to the contrary with another ethnic population provides little support for matching treatment strategies to client ethnicity. Another problem is that ethnicity is often confused with culture. The assumption underlying the matching of treatment strategies to ethnic clients is that cultural values and behaviors may fit one counseling strategy better than another. Selecting participants on the basis of ethnicity alone provides no assurance that they hold the values or behave in ways consistent with their ancestral culture. Future research on the use of these techniques with ethnic minorities should incorporate client within-group variables, such as acculturation and cultural commitment, as measures of involvement in the participant's ancestral culture.

SUMMARY

Of the three recommendations for which Sue and Zane (1987) found almost unanimous agreement in the multicultural literature, subsequent research has provided strong support for one and moderate support for another, while a third has received no research attention. This review found strong support in the form of both process and outcome research for the recruitment of ethnic counselors. With respect to the recommendation that conventional forms of treatment should be modified to meet the needs of ethnic minority clients, unequivocal evidence was found that counselors who are culturally responsive are perceived more favorably by ethnic minority clients than are counselors who ignore the client's culture. Evidence was found that ethnic minorities respond more favorably to directive than to nondirective counseling techniques, but it is questionable whether this reaction is unique to ethnic minorities. No research was found that directly assessed the effectiveness of teaching counselors about ethnic cultures and communities.

REFERENCES

Akutsu, P. D., Lin, C. H., & Zane, N. W. S. (1990). Predictors of utilization intent of counseling among Chinese and White students: A test of the proximal-distal model. *Journal of Counseling Psychology, 37,* 445-452.

Altmaier, E. M. (1993). Role of criterion II in accreditation. *Professional Psychology: Research and Practice, 24,* 127-129.

American Psychological Association. (1986). *Accreditation handbook.* Washington, DC: Author.

American Psychological Association. (1992). Ethical principles of psychologists and code of conduct. *American Psychologist, 47,* 1597-1611.

American Psychological Association. (1993). Guidelines for providers of psychological services to ethnic, linguistic, and culturally diverse populations. *American Psychologist, 48,* 45-48.

Anderson, J. W. (1983). The effects of culture and social class on client preference for counseling methods. *Journal of Non-White Concerns, 11,* 84-88.

Atkinson, D. R. (1983). Ethnic similarity in counseling psychology: A review of research. *The Counseling Psychologist, 11,* 79-92.

Atkinson, D. R. (1985). A meta-review of research on cross-cultural counseling and psychotherapy. *Journal of Multicultural Counseling and Development, 13,* 138-153.

Atkinson, D. R., Casas, A., & Abreu, J. (1992). Mexican-American acculturation, counselor ethnicity and cultural sensitivity, and perceived counselor competence. *Journal of Counseling Psychology, 39,* 515-520.

Atkinson, D. R., Furlong, M. J., & Poston, W. C. (1986). Afro-American preferences for counselor characteristics. *Journal of Counseling Psychology, 33,* 326-330.

Atkinson, D. R., Jennings, R. G., & Liongson, L. (1990). Minority students' reasons for not seeking counseling and suggestions for improving services. *Journal of College Student Development, 31,* 342-350.

Atkinson, D. R., & Matsushita, Y. J. (1991). Japanese American acculturation, counseling style, counselor ethnicity, and perceived counselor credibility. *Journal of Counseling Psychology, 38,* 473-478.

Atkinson, D. R., Poston, W. C., Furlong, M. J., & Mercado, P. (1989). Ethnic group preferences for counselor characteristics. *Journal of Counseling Psychology, 36,* 68-72.

Atkinson, D. R., Winzelberg, A., & Holland, A. (1985). Ethnicity, locus of control for family planning, and pregnancy counselor credibility. *Journal of Counseling Psychology, 32,* 417-421.

Bennett, S., & BigFoot-Sipes, D. S. (1991). American Indian and White college student preferences for counselor characteristics. *Journal of Counseling Psychology, 38,* 440-445.

Berg, J. H., & Wright-Buckley, C. (1988). Effects of racial similarity and interviewer intimacy in a peer counseling analogue. *Journal of Counseling Psychology, 35,* 377-384.

Bernstein, B. L., Wade, P., & Hofmann, B. (1987). Students' race and preferences for counselor's race, sex, age, and experience. *Journal of Multicultural Counseling and Development, 15,* 60-70.

Borrego, R. L., Chavez, E. L., & Titley, R. W. (1982). Effects of counselor techniques on Mexican-American and Anglo-American self-disclosure and counselor perception. *Journal of Counseling Psychology, 29,* 538-541.

Comas-Diaz, L. (1981). Effects of cognitive and behavioral group treatment on the depressive symptomatology of Puerto Rican women. *Journal of Consulting and Clinical Psychology, 49,* 627-632.

Costantino, G., Malgady, R. G., & Rogler, L. H. (1986). Cuento therapy: A culturally sensitive modality for Puerto Rican children. *Journal of Consulting and Clinical Psychology, 54,* 639-645.

Dauphinais, P., Dauphinais, L., & Rowe, W. (1981). Effects of race and communication style on Indian perceptions of counselor effectiveness. *Counselor Education and Supervision, 21,* 72-80.

Exum, H. A., & Lau, E. Y. (1988). Counseling style preference of Chinese college students. *Journal of Multicultural Counseling and Development, 16,* 84-92.

Flaskerud, J. H. (1986). The effects of culture-compatible intervention on the utilization of mental health services by minority clients. *Community Mental Health Journal, 22,* 127-141.

Flaskerud, J. H. (1991). Effects of an Asian client-therapist language, ethnicity and gender match on utilization and outcome of therapy. *Community Mental Health Journal, 27,* 31-42.

Folensbee, R. W., Jr., Draguns, J. G., & Danish, S. J. (1986). Impact of two types of counselor intervention on Black American, Puerto Rican, and Anglo-American analogue clients. *Journal of Counseling Psychology, 33,* 446-453.

Franco, J. N., & LeVine, E. S. (1980). Effects of examiner variables on reported self-disclosure: Implications for group personality testing. *Hispanic Journal of Behavioral Sciences, 7,* 187-197.

Gim, R. H., Atkinson, D. R., & Kim, S. J. (1991). Asian-American acculturation, counselor ethnicity and cultural sensitivity, and ratings of counselors. *Journal of Counseling Psychology, 38,* 57-62.

Giuffreda, M. H. (1986). *The effects of counselor race, counseling approach, problem type and level of acculturation on Asian Americans' perceptions of counselor credibility and utility.* Unpublished doctoral dissertation, The Catholic University of America, Washington, DC.

Goldberg, B., & Tidwell, R. (1990). Ethnicity and gender similarity: The effectiveness of counseling for adolescents. *Journal of Youth and Adolescence, 19,* 589-593.

Greene, C. F., Cunningham, J., & Yanico, B. J. (1986). Effects of counselor and subject race and counselor physical attractiveness on impressions and expectations of a female counselor. *Journal of Counseling Psychology, 33,* 349-352.

Greene, C. J. (1982). *A study of community-college students' initial counselor preferences based on the nature of the personal problem and on the age, ethnicity, and sex of the counselor and student.* Unpublished doctoral dissertation, University of San Francisco.

Harrison, D. K. (1975). Race as a counselor-client variable in counseling and psychotherapy: A review of the research. *The Counseling Psychologist, 5,* 124-133.

Haviland, M. G., Horswill, R. K., O'Connell, J. J., & Dynneson, V. V. (1983). Native American college students' preference for counselor race and sex and the likelihood of their use of a counseling center. *Journal of Counseling Psychology, 30,* 267-270.

Helms, J. E. (1990). *Black and White racial identity: Theory, research, and practice.* Westport, CT: Greenwood Press.

Helms, J. E., & Carter, R. T. (1991). Relationships of White and Black racial identity attitudes and demographic similarity to counselor preferences. *Journal of Counseling Psychology, 38*, 446-457.

Hess, R. S., & Street, E. M. (1991). The effect of acculturation on the relationship of counselor ethnicity and client ratings. *Journal of Counseling Psychology, 38*, 71-75.

Johnson, M. E., & Lashley, K. H. (1989). Influence of Native-Americans' cultural commitment on preferences for counselor ethnicity and expectations about counseling. *Journal of Multicultural Counseling and Development, 17*, 115-122.

Korsgaard, C. (1990). *Acculturation: Intragroup differences in the choice of gender and ethnicity of a counselor in an Asian-American population.* Unpublished doctoral dissertation, California School of Professional Psychology, San Diego.

Kunkel, M. A. (1990). Expectations about counseling in relation to acculturation in Mexican-American and Anglo-American student samples. *Journal of Counseling Psychology, 37*, 286-292.

Leong, F. T. L. (1986). Counseling and psychotherapy with Asian-Americans: Review of the literature. *Journal of Counseling Psychology, 33*, 196-206.

LeVine, E. S., & Franco, J. N. (1983). Effects of therapist's gender, ethnicity, and verbal style on client's willingness to seek therapy. *Journal of Social Psychology, 121*, 51-57.

Lopez, S. R., Lopez, A. A., & Fong, K. T. (1991). Mexican Americans' initial preferences for counselors: The role of ethnic factors. *Journal of Counseling Psychology, 38*, 487-496.

Luk, C. L., & Bond, M. H. (1992). Chinese lay beliefs about the causes and cures of psychological problems. *Journal of Social and Clinical Psychology, 11*, 140-157.

Merta, R. J., Ponterotto, J. G., & Brown, R. D. (1992). Comparing the effectiveness of two directive styles in the academic counseling of foreign students. *Journal of Counseling Psychology, 39*, 214-218.

Morten, G., & Atkinson, D. R. (1983). Minority identity development and preference for counselor race. *Journal of Negro Education, 52*, 156-161.

Murakawa, F. T. (1987). *Effect of race and generation level on Asian Americans' perceptions of therapist effectiveness and therapist preference (Japanese, Chinese, credibility).* Unpublished doctoral dissertation, California School of Professional Psychology, Los Angeles.

Narikiyo, T. A., & Kameoka, V. A. (1992). Attributions of mental illness and judgments about help seeking among Japanese-American and White American students. *Journal of Counseling Psychology, 39*, 363-369.

Pomales, J., Claiborn, C. D., & LaFromboise, T. D. (1986). Effects of Black students' racial identity on perceptions of White counselors varying in cultural sensitivity. *Journal of Counseling Psychology, 33*, 57-61.

Pomales, J., & Williams, V. (1989). Effects of level of acculturation and counseling style on Hispanic students' perceptions of counselor. *Journal of Counseling Psychology, 36*, 79-83.

Ponce, F. Q., & Atkinson, D. R. (1989). Mexican-American acculturation, counselor ethnicity, counseling style, and perceived counselor credibility. *Journal of Counseling Psychology, 36*, 203-208.

Ponterotto, J. G., Alexander, C. M., & Hinkston, J. A. (1988). Afro-American preferences for counselor characteristics: A replication and extension. *Journal of Counseling Psychology, 35*, 175-182.

Ponterotto, J. G., Anderson, W. H., Jr., & Grieger, I. Z. (1986). Black students' attitudes toward counseling as a function of racial identity. *Journal of Multicultural Counseling and Development, 14*, 51-59.

Poston, W. S. C., Craine, M., & Atkinson, D. R. (1991). Counselor dissimilarity confrontation, client cultural mistrust, and willingness to self-disclose. *Journal of Multicultural Counseling and Development, 19*, 65-73.

Reed, K. L. (1988). *The relationship of Black students' racial identity to counselor race preference and premature termination from counseling.* Unpublished doctoral dissertation, University of Wisconsin, Madison.

Rickard, H. C., & Clements, C. B. (1993). Critique of APA accreditation Criterion II: Cultural and individual differences. *Professional Psychology: Research and Practice, 24*, 123-126.

Ridley, C. R., Mendoza, D. W., & Kanitz, B. E. (1994). Multicultural training: Reexamination, operationalization, and integration. *The Counseling Psychologist, 22*, 227-289.

Ridley, C. R., Mendoza, D. W., Kanitz, B. E., Angermeier, L., & Zenk, R. (1994). Cultural sensitivity in multicultural counseling: A perceptual schema model. *Journal of Counseling Psychology, 41*, 125-136.

Rodriguez, M., & Blocher, D. (1988). A comparison of two approaches to enhancing career maturity in Puerto Rican college women. *Journal of Counseling Psychology, 35*, 275-280.

Sanchez, A. R., & King, M. (1986). Mexican Americans' use of counseling services: Cultural and institutional factors. *Journal of College Student Personnel, 27*, 344-349.

Sandhu, D. S. (1984). *The effects of mirroring vs. non-mirroring of clients' nonverbal behaviors on empathy, trustworthiness, and positive interaction in cross-cultural counseling dyads (NLP, Neuro-linguistic programming).* Unpublished doctoral dissertation, Mississippi State University, Mississippi.

Sattler, J. M. (1977). The effects of therapist-client racial similarity. In A. S. Gurman & A. M. Razin (Eds.), *Effective psychotherapy: A handbook of research* (pp. 252-290). New York: Pergamon.

Schinke, S. P., Orlandi, M. A., Botvin, G. J., Gilchrist, L. D., Trimble, J. E., & Locklear, V. S. (1988). Preventing substance abuse among American Indian adolescents: A bicultural competence skills approach. *Journal of Counseling Psychology, 35*, 87-90.

Shipp, P. L. (1986). *A comparison of Africentric and Eurocentric counseling approaches and Black and White clients' perceptions of counselor credibility.* Unpublished doctoral dissertation, University of Denver, Colorado.

Simons, H. W., Berkowitz, N. N., & Moyer, R. J. (1970). Similarity, credibility, and attitude change: A review and a theory. *Psychological Bulletin, 73*, 1-16.

Sodowsky, G. R. (1991). Effects of cultural consistent counseling tasks on American and international student observers' perception of counselor credibility: A preliminary investigation. *Journal of Counseling and Development, 69*, 253-256.

Strong, S. R. (1968). Counseling: An interpersonal influence process. *Journal of Counseling Psychology, 15*, 215-224.

Sue, S., Fujino, D. C., Hu, L., Takeuchi, D. T., & Zane, N. W. S. (1991). Community mental health services for ethnic minority groups: A test of the cultural responsiveness hypothesis. *Journal of Consulting and Clinical Psychology, 59*, 533-540.

Sue, S., & Zane, N. W. S. (1987). The role of culture and cultural techniques in psychotherapy: A critique and reformulation. *American Psychologist, 42*, 37-45.

Terrell, F., & Terrell, S. L. (1981). An inventory to measure cultural mistrust among Blacks. *Western Journal of Black Studies, 5*, 180-184.

Terrell, F., & Terrell, S. L. (1984). Race of counselor, client sex, cultural mistrust level, and premature termination from counseling among Black clients. *Journal of Counseling Psychology, 31*, 371-375.

Thompson, C. E., Worthington, R., & Atkinson, D. R. (1994). Counselor content orientation, counselor race, and Black women's cultural mistrust and self-disclosures. *Journal of Counseling Psychology, 41*, 155-161.

U.S. Bureau of the Census. (1992). *Population projections of the United States, by age, sex, race, and Hispanic origin: 1992 to 2050* (Current Population Reports, P25-1092). Washington, DC: Government Printing Office.

Wade, P., & Bernstein, B. L. (1991). Culture sensitivity training and counselor's race: Effects on Black female clients' perceptions and attrition. *Journal of Counseling Psychology, 38*, 9-15.

Watkins, C. E., & Terrell, F. (1988). Mistrust level and its effects on counseling expectations in Black-White counselor relationships: An analogue study. *Journal of Counseling Psychology, 35*, 194-197.

Watkins, C. E., Terrell, F., Miller, F. S., & Terrell, S. L. (1989). Cultural mistrust and its effects on expectational variables in Black client-White counselor relationships. *Journal of Counseling Psychology, 36,* 447-450.

Wetzel, C. G., & Wright-Buckley, C. (1988). Reciprocity of self-disclosure: Breakdowns of trust in cross-racial dyads. *Basic and Applied Social Psychology, 9,* 277-288.

20

Racial and Ethnic Variations in Help-Seeking Attitudes

FREDERICK T. L. LEONG

NICOLE S. WAGNER

SHIRAZ PIROSHAW TATA

AS FAR BACK as Hollingshead and Redlich's (1958) classic study of social class and mental illness, there has been a recognition that the help-seeking process is a complicated one. As recognized by Hollingshead and Redlich (1958) and others (e.g., Rogler, Malgady, & Rodriguez, 1989), the help-seeking process serves as an important filter such that only a portion of those who need professional mental health treatment actually seek such assistance. Clearly, there is a need to examine the help-seeking attitudes and behaviors of racial and ethnic minority groups as well as those who are economically disadvantaged in order to arrive at a fuller comprehension of mental health and mental illness among these groups. In discussing the complex process of help seeking for mental health problems under the rubric of "paths to psychiatrists," Hollingshead and Redlich (1958) observed that

> every person that follows a path that leads him eventually to a psychiatrist must pass four milestones. The first marks the occurrence of "abnormal" behavior; the second involves the appraisal of his behavior as "disturbed" in a psychiatric sense; the third is when the decision is made that psychiatric treatment is indicated and the fourth is reached when the decision is

implemented and the "disturbed" person actually enters the care of a psychiatrist. (p. 171)

Just as these authors observed in the 1950s that the help-seeking process was
intricately linked to social class, researchers now generally recognize that help
seeking for mental health problems is linked to cultural and ethnic factors.

In view of the importance of understanding the myriad ways in which
culture, race, and ethnicity can influence the help-seeking process, the current
chapter explores the literature on attitudes toward and use of Western mental
health services by ethnic minority group members, including Asian Americans, Hispanic Americans, and African Americans. Due to the page limitations, we decided not to include American Indians in this chapter. Including
American Indians would have resulted in rather superficial coverage of that
minority group. In general, research has shown that members of these groups
are at equal or greater risk for psychological problems than majority group
members due to stressors such as lower income, undereducation, and acculturation (Padilla, Ruiz, & Alvarez, 1975; Ruiz & Padilla, 1973). Thus, understanding help-seeking attitudes and behaviors is of great concern to
professionals as we attempt to meet the mental health needs of these underserved populations.

HELP-SEEKING ATTITUDES
AMONG AFRICAN AMERICANS

Unlike other ethnic minority groups such as Hispanic and Asian Americans, African Americans have been found to overutilize mental health services
relative to their proportion in the general population (Sue, Zane, & Young,
1994). This pattern of overutilization is not surprising given the fact that they
tend to experience disproportionately higher levels of social, occupational, and
economic stress than other groups. For example, in a national survey of over
2,000 African Americans (Neighbors, Jackson, Bowman, & Gurin, 1983), a
substantial majority of the respondents (63.6%) reported experiencing a serious personal problem, with 47% experiencing a problem at the "nervous breakdown level." However, concerns about the help-seeking process for African
Americans and other ethnic minority groups have been prompted in large part
by the fact that these minority groups tend to have differential experiences
within the mental health system relative to the majority group. For example,
Sue (1977) found that over 50% of African Americans failed to return for the
second session in comparison to 30% of White Americans. For African Americans, the double oppression of experiencing higher levels of stress and facing
a less than responsive mental health system points to the urgency of identifying barriers to service utilization among this minority group. An examination of African Americans' attitudes toward seeking professional help for their

mental health problems seems to be an important means of identifying these barriers.

Although there is evidence to suggest that African Americans are over-utilizing mental health services, there is also evidence that they may use the mental health system in a different manner. Wood and Sherrets (1984) found that African Americans, in comparison to White Americans, were more likely to seek help for administrative matters (e.g., problems with the law, social service agencies, and schools), medication, and questions about help sources in the community. If we could array the list of problems for which individuals would seek help along a continuum from very personal to very impersonal, African Americans tend to present more impersonal problems to mental health professionals. This pattern of African Americans' use of mental health professionals for less personal problems is further supported by Webster and Fretz's study (1978). In comparing Blacks, Asians, and Whites' preferences for different help sources, Webster and Fretz found that Black females and males who were rank-ordering help sources for educational/vocational problems gave the university counseling center a rank of 1 and 2, respectively, whereas Black females and males who were ranking help sources for personal/emotional problems gave the university counseling center a rank of 6 and 6.5, respectively.

Thus, it appears that many African Americans may be viewing the mental health system more as an ombudsperson or referral service than as a service for dealing with personal psychological problems. This pattern of using mental health professionals as resources for "practical" problems rather than "personal" problems seems to be related to a pervasive issue among African Americans, namely, the distrust of mainstream social institutions such as mental health clinics and hospitals as well as White mental health professionals. Maultsby (1982) discussed African Americans' distrust of psychiatry by reviewing the historical evidence of institutional and societal racism toward African Americans. She pointed to two enduring beliefs held by White Americans concerning African Americans: "(a) Black people are inferior and therefore have less mental capacity than White people, and (b) Whether by nurture or nature, the personality structure of Black Americans is hopelessly abnormal by White American standards" (p. 40). According to Maultsby (1982), mental health professionals, being primarily White and middle-class, held these same beliefs about the African American patients they encountered. Hence, like Thomas and Comer (1973), she argued that racism and the maintenance of this "deficit hypothesis" underlie much of the African American community's historical and contemporary distrust of mental health professionals.

Ridley (1989) provided evidence for a similar conclusion regarding the racism in the mental health system:

> Consider the following adverse outcomes in counseling and other mental health services. Compared to White clients, ethnic minority clients are more likely to receive inaccurate diagnoses; be assigned to junior professionals,

paraprofessionals, or nonprofessionals rather than senior professionals; receive low-cost, less preferred treatment consisting of minimal contact, medication, or custodial care rather than individual psychotherapy; be disproportionately represented in mental health facilities; show a much higher rate of premature termination; and have more unfavorable impressions regarding treatment. (p. 55)

It is not surprising, then, that Sussman, Robins, and Earls (1987) found that fear of the treatment itself was a significant barrier to treatment seeking among Blacks who were depressed. In their study comparing treatment seeking among depressed Black and White Americans, Sussman et al. (1987) also found that fear of hospitalization was another major barrier for help seeking. Data from Snowden and Cheung (1990) indicate that this fear of hospitalization among African Americans is realistic in that African Americans are disproportionately hospitalized. The higher level of hospitalization is problematic because studies have found no racial differences in the prevalence of psychological disorders among African Americans. The misuse of hospitalization for African Americans is probably due to clinician bias and/or problems in misdiagnosis (e.g., African Americans are more likely to be misdiagnosed as experiencing schizophrenia). Hence the problems of misdiagnosis and misuse of hospitalization for African Americans are another factor underlying their distrust of mental health professionals.

It should not be assumed that African Americans' distrust of mental health professionals and the mental health system is a simple unidimensional problem. For example, Ridley (1984) pointed out the need for clinicians to differentiate between functional and cultural paranoia in African Americans' patterns of self-disclosure within the therapeutic relationship. Ridley (1984) defined *cultural paranoia* as a healthy psychological reaction to racism and *functional paranoia* as an unhealthy condition that is itself an illness. Using these two dimensions, Ridley provided a four-mode typology that categorizes clients according to their type of paranoia and patterns of self-disclosure.

Mode one, the intercultural nonparanoiac discloser, includes clients who are low on both functional and cultural paranoia. This client can be expected to disclose in any therapy setting, regardless of the therapist's ethnicity. Mode two, the functional paranoiac, includes clients for whom the problem of nondisclosure lies primarily in their personal pathology. These clients are nondisclosing to both White therapists and therapists from their own ethnic minority group. Mode three, the healthy cultural paranoiac, includes clients whose nondisclosure is evidence of a protection against the negative consequences of racism and oppression. These clients are nondisclosing to White therapists but are likely to disclose to therapists from their own ethnic minority group. Mode four, the confluent paranoiac, includes clients whose problem is both a reaction to racism and part of a personal pathology. This is the most difficult client to treat because of the complex interaction of cultural and functional paranoia in the client. These clients, like the functional paranoiac, are nondisclosing in any therapy setting, regardless of the therapist's ethnicity. (Ridley, 1989, pp. 67-68)

Within Ridley's (1984) framework, it is the healthy cultural paranoiac and the confluent paranoiac that the previous authors were referring to when discussing African Americans' distrust of the mental health system. As pointed out by Ridley (1989), the distrust of mental health professionals is often created by these professionals' misclassifying the cultural paranoiac as a functional paranoiac, thus pathologizing an adaptive response to an oppressive environment. Within Ridley's framework, it is the healthy cultural paranoiac and the confluent paranoiac who are most ambivalent about seeking counseling and psychotherapy. But the cultural paranoiac is much more likely to seek help from mental health professionals than the functional paranoiac, who will consistently resist counseling and psychotherapy regardless of the therapist's race and ethnicity.

As another indication of the complexity of this issue of African Americans' distrust of mental health professionals, Terrell and Terrell (1984) examined premature termination from counseling among African American clients as a function of the therapist's race and the client's level of "cultural mistrust" (measured by Cultural Mistrust Inventory [CMI]; Terrell & Terrell, 1981). A sample of 135 outpatients was asked to complete the CMI at the time of the initial appointment at a community mental health center. Subjects' rates of premature termination (defined as not returning for the second or any subsequent sessions) were also recorded. Results indicated a significant main effect for counselor's race: 25% of the African American clients who were seeing a White therapist returned to treatment, as compared to 43% of those clients seeing an African American therapist. A significant interaction among counselor's race, level of cultural mistrust, and termination rates was found. However, a significant relation was also found between termination rates and the main effect of client's trust level, regardless of counselor's race. These findings seem to support Ridley's model in that it was probably the healthy cultural paranoiac clients who prematurely terminated from White therapists. On the other hand, it was probably the confluent and functional paranoiac clients who prematurely terminated from treatment regardless of the therapist's race. Probably the termination of these last two groups from treatment led the authors to conclude that "despite being assigned to a Black counselor, highly mistrustful clients discontinued treatment due to suspiciousness regarding the counseling setting" (Terrell & Terrell, 1984, p. 374).

Another major dimension influencing African Americans' attitudes toward seeking professional psychological help is set forth by the ethnic similarity hypothesis, which maintains that, everything else being equal, racial and ethnic minority clients will have a greater preference for a therapist of the same race and ethnicity. According to this hypothesis, ethnic similarity between client and counselor, besides being more comfortable for both parties, will also promote better counseling outcomes because a higher level of similarity will facilitate the social influence process inherent to the therapeutic process. Ethnically similar therapists will be experienced by their clients as higher on credibility, attractiveness, and influence (Atkinson, 1983).

Although the ethnic similarity hypothesis is quite controversial, it is none-theless important because the majority of counselors and therapists are White. If indeed ethnic similarity promotes better counseling outcomes, and ethnic dissimilarity results in premature termination and negative outcomes, then an ethnic matching approach to counseling may be necessary in order to reduce the level of underutilization of mental health services by African Americans who need such services. The ethnic similarity hypothesis has prompted a series of studies to examine African Americans' preferences for the race of their counselor. For example, in an early study examining the differential effects of therapists' race and social class on the level of exploration among clients, Carkhuff and Pierce (1967) found that those therapists who were most different from their clients in terms of race and social class had the most difficulty with effective constructive exploration among their clients. Not surprisingly, then, numerous studies have found that African American clients have a higher preference for African American therapists (e.g., Pinchot, Riccio, & Peters, 1975; Riccio & Barnes, 1973; Stranges & Riccio, 1970; Thompson & Cimbolic, 1978). As pointed out by Atkinson (1983) in his review, African American clients' greater preference for African American therapists seems to be consistent across a 11-year time span. With regard to implications of the ethnic similarity hypothesis for help-seeking behaviors, Atkinson (1983) concluded that "despite these limitations, the consistency with which Black subjects preferred racially similar counselors implies that for many Blacks, utilization of counseling services may be a function of the availability of Black counselors" (p. 82).

Counselors and therapists are by no means universal in their belief regarding the importance of ethnic similarity to counseling process and outcomes. Parloff, Waskow, and Wolfe (1978) concluded that ethnic matching of therapist and client is not clearly indicated by the research evidence. For example, Gambosa, Tosi, and Riccio (1976) found no differences in 40 White and 40 Black delinquent girls' preferences for the race of the counselor. Sattler (1977), in his review of the studies, noted that "other things being equal, many Black subjects prefer Black therapists to White therapists. However, a competent White professional is preferred to a less competent Black professional and the therapist's style and technique are more important factors in affecting Black clients' choices than the therapist's race" (p. 267). Griffith (1977), in his review, also concluded that the evidence did not support a clear race preference among Black clients. Relatedly, Peoples and Dell (1975) found that preference for counseling style was more important than racial match among Black and White clients.

Perhaps ethnic similarity effect is merely an overt manifestation of an underlying mismatch. Sue et al. (1994) called for an assessment of the effects of more proximal factors such as cultural values instead of normative ethnic group differences. One major factor that serves as a potential underlying contributor to African Americans' preferences for racially similar counselors is cross-cultural differences in worldviews. Sue and Sue (1990) defined *world-*

view as "how a person perceived his/her relationship to the world (nature, institutions, other people)" (p. 137). They also observed that "counselors who hold a worldview different from that of their clients and are unaware of the basis for this difference are most likely to impute negative traits to clients" (p. 137). Quite possibly, it is the clash of worldviews between racially and ethnically dissimilar counseling dyads that underlies much of the preference for ethnic similarity in counseling. For example, Millet, Sullivan, Schwebel, and James-Myers (1994) proposed that those clients adhering to an Afrocentric worldview may find that many mental health professionals do not share the same worldview and may therefore prematurely terminate treatment. Further support for the notion of within-group differences in attitudes toward counseling is provided by Jackson and Kirschner (1973), who found that it was the African American clients with the strongest African American identity who tended to prefer an African American counselor. Similar effects have been found by Helms and her colleagues (Helms, 1990).

One's racial, ethnic, and cultural identity seems to be a central component of one's worldview. Another important component in one's worldview is one's religious orientation. Given that many White therapists tend to view religiosity negatively (see Giglio, 1993), the spirituality of many African American clients may be ignored or minimized, a factor that in turn promotes further distrust of the therapist on the part of the client. Another aspect of African Americans' worldview is their attribution of causality for their personal problems. Sue and Sue (1990) referred to this as the "locus of responsibility" (internal or external): that is, whether persons hold that internal forces are responsible for their problems (e.g., "I lack the courage to ask for a pay raise") or that external forces are responsible for their problems (e.g., "Organizations tend to favor their own, and I am unlikely to be promoted because there is a glass ceiling for minorities"). Cheatham, Shelton, and Ray (1987) examined the relationship between causal attribution and help-seeking behavior among Black and White students. Although they found no relationships between the variables, they did find that Black students were much more likely to attribute personal problems to external causes, whereas White students were much more likely to make internal attributions. By extension, if White therapists are also much more likely to make internal attributions, many African American clients who lean toward external attributions will find their therapist's approach to problem solving quite alienating. Hence African Americans' recognition of these potential clashes in worldviews between themselves and psychotherapists seems to contribute further to their nonutilization of mental health services even when such services are needed.

As Brown (1978) pointed out, individuals may seek help for personal problems from both formal and informal help sources. Formal help sources include mental health professionals such as counselors, psychologists, and psychiatrists, whereas informal help sources include parents, relatives, friends, and neighbors. As pointed out above, African Americans tend to have a greater distrust of formal help sources. An important part of this distrust of formal help sources is the lack of culturally appropriate services offered by these help sources. For example, psychodynamic and insight-oriented psychotherapies represent a dominant approach within the field. Many authors have argued that such an approach is quite inappropriate for African Americans who are struggling daily with problems of social injustice rather than the intrapsychic problems of guilt and anxiety that seem to plague White middle-class Americans (e.g., Grier & Cobbs, 1968; Halleck, 1971; Thomas & Sillen, 1972). It should not be assumed that the psychodynamic approach is the only one that has been questioned as to its relevance and appropriateness for African American communities. Turner and Jones (1982) also pointed to African Americans' distrust of behavior modification approaches. They observed that such suspicions on the part of African Americans are quite understandable in light of the historical oppression of this group and their need to be cautious about issues of intrusive and external attempts to control African Americans. Hence mismatch of therapeutic approaches serves as an additional focal point for many African Americans' negative attitudes toward seeking professional psychological help.

Help seeking among African Americans may also be influenced by cross-cultural differences in coping resources. Studies with African Americans have consistently revealed the importance of spirituality and the central role of the church in their social lives (Lincoln & Mamyia, 1990). In a study of stress, adaptation, and depression within a southern Black community, Dressler (1991) found that of four coping or "resistance" resources, two involved religion. The first was religious attitudes or spirituality. Dressler (1991) observed that

> it was very clear that the institution of the church was essential in supporting the everyday coping of individuals. . . . The level of commitment to those beliefs was found to be very high indeed in the community. . . . A strong belief in God was seen as a foundation for dealing actively with day-to-day problems of the world. (p. 215)

The second resistance resource for dealing with stress was religious participation, which provided the Blacks in the community with much social support via a sense of belonging, attachment, and social involvement. Hence many African Americans do not seek professional psychological assistance precisely because of their high levels of cultural competence that provide them with viable and effective coping alternatives.

In a study illustrating the important role of religion in the coping responses of African Americans, Millet et al. (1994) hypothesized that the historically important function of the church in African American culture and the spirituality associated with it could well be "a factor in how African-Americans perceive mental health, the etiology of mental illness, and its treatment" (p. 6). To explore this hypothesis, Millet et al. asked Black and White university undergraduate students to answer questions concerning etiology and proper treatment in regard to a series of vignettes describing various mental illnesses (Mental Illness Vignettes Instrument). In support of their hypothesis, the results revealed that Black students attributed significantly more importance to spirituality in causing and treating mental illness than did White students.

In summary, African Americans, because of the high level of stress they experience, tend to overutilize mental health services relative to their proportion in the community. Despite this global pattern of overutilization, research studies indicate that many African Americans who do need mental health services will often forego such assistance due to racism and bias in the mental health system as well as the lack of therapists who are racially similar or who share their worldviews. In addition, many African Americans do not seek professional help because of the rich network of resources within their own communities in the form of churches and other social support groups.

HELP-SEEKING ATTITUDES AMONG HISPANIC AMERICANS

This section will explore Hispanic American attitudes toward seeking help and their influence on mental health service utilization. The term *Hispanic* will be used to include the various Spanish-speaking, Spanish-surnamed groups of diverse national origins, including Mexico, the countries of Central and South America, Cuba, Puerto Rico, and Spain. Although we will use the umbrella terms *Hispanic* and *Hispanic American* throughout this text, an attempt has been made to retain the authors' original terminology when referring to specific research. Much of the available research has been done with Mexican American subjects, so the reader should be tentative about generalizations until more research is done.

Hispanics are the second largest and fastest growing minority group in the United States today, including approximately 15 million people (Dworkin & Adams, 1987; Flaskerud, 1986; Padilla & Ruiz, 1976; Rogler, Malgady, Costantino, & Blumenthal, 1987). It is expected that by the year 2000 they will overtake Blacks and become the largest minority group in the United States due to a high birthrate and steady immigration from Mexico and the movement to the mainland by Puerto Ricans (Gaviria & Stern, 1980). Thus, attention to their mental health status, needs, and problems seems crucial.

Five factors have been hypothesized in the literature as influencing Hispanics' attitudes toward and use of Western mental health services. These factors have also been used to account for Hispanics' documented underutilization of Western mental health services (Becerra & Greenblatt, 1981; Bui & Takeuchi, 1992; Hough et al., 1987; Karno & Edgerton, 1969; Longshore, Hsieh, Anglin, & Annon, 1992; Sanchez & King, 1986; Sue, 1977; Wells, Golding, Hough, Burnam, & Karno, 1988; Wells, Hough, Golding, Burnam, & Karno, 1987). First, it has been suggested that Hispanics' negative attitude toward and underutilization of mental health services may be due to a lower incidence of mental illness in this ethnic population (Jaco, 1959). More recent researchers have dismissed this factor due to community surveys of prevalence (Swanson, Holzer, & Ganju, 1993) or studies of utilization that include needs assessment (Wells et al., 1987), which suggest that mental disorders are at least as common in the Hispanic American population as they are in the population as a whole. In fact, several authors have suggested that Hispanics in general are actually in need of greater mental health services than majority individuals because they are subjected to higher levels of stress due to their minority position (Padilla et al., 1975; Padilla & Ruiz, 1976). These stressors have been associated with mental disturbance and include difficulty communicating in English, poverty and low levels of education, unemployment, deteriorated housing, minimal political influence and low socioeconomic status, rural agrarian traits that are not adaptive in an urban technological society, and interactions in a prejudiced society (Padilla et al., 1975; Ruiz, 1993). Furthermore, under certain circumstances Hispanic Americans' utilization is equivalent to that of Anglos, indicating that Hispanic Americans' patterns of utilization are a function of relevance of services rather than lower rates of mental illness (Keefe & Casas, 1980).

Although there appears to be agreement that Hispanic American underutilization of mental health services cannot be explained by a lower prevalence rate of mental problems, studies of mental health prevalence among the Hispanic population have been criticized for utilizing biased instrumentation to determine prevalence (Woodward, Dwinell, & Arons, 1992). Also, some authors have suggested that Anglos and Hispanics may manifest different types of emotional problems and that this may account for the underutilization of Hispanic Americans. In particular, Mexican Americans have been found to have higher rates of drug abuse and lower rates of suicide than their Caucasian American counterparts (Keefe & Casas, 1980). In a more recent review, Chavez and Swaim (1992) pointed out that some studies have found that Hispanic Americans have higher rates of drug abuse, whereas other studies have found them to have lower rates relative to European Americans. They interpreted these conflicting results to be due to the heterogeneity of the Hispanic American population. Nevertheless, although most authors agree that Hispanics do not have an "ethnic immunity" to mental illness, more research is needed to verify prevalence rates and determine if different subpopulations of Hispanic Americans suffer from different rates of psychiatric disturbances. In total, it appears that underutilization of mental health services by Hispanic Americans cannot be explained away by lower rates of mental illness.

A second factor suggested to explain Hispanic underutilization is financial barriers that serve to limit Hispanics' access to care (Reeves, 1986; Ruiz, 1993; Wells et al., 1987; Woodward et al., 1992). One of the reasons why Hispanics wait until problems are severe before seeking mental health care (Barrera, 1978) may be their status as underclass citizens who lack the financial resources to pay for services out of pocket and who often lack any medical insurance. Thus, low income is both a direct financial barrier to payment and an indirect financial barrier that predisposes Hispanics to lack of insurance. Stefl and Prosperi (1985) found that of four types of barriers to mental health service utilization, affordability ranked as the dominant barrier to use, followed by availability, accessibility, and acceptability, respectively. Ruiz (1993) found that only 57% of Hispanic families with adult workers have private health insurance compared to 69% of African American families and 86% of White American families with adult workers. Furthermore, of those with health insurance, fewer Hispanic families receive mental health benefits than White families (Woodward et al., 1992). In terms of uninsured individuals, 35% of Hispanic families with adult workers lack insurance compared to only 13% of White families with adult workers (Ruiz, 1993). These alarming statistics could be the result of low-paying jobs that do not offer health insurance benefits, lack of income to buy private insurance, and/or the fact that Hispanics do not place high priority on health insurance benefits. Regardless of the reason, it is clear that Hispanics have less access to health care due to finances than Whites.

A third factor that has been proposed as influencing the utilization of mental health services by Hispanic Americans has been labeled *cultural barriers*. This set of barriers suggests that aspects of Hispanic American culture may conflict with the tenets of Westernized mental health and consequently may serve to limit the utilization of Western mental health services by Hispanics. The first and perhaps most important cultural barrier to mental health service utilization is language (Becerra & Greenblatt, 1981; Gaviria & Stern, 1980; Swanson et al., 1993; Wells et al., 1987). According to Gaviria and Stern (1980), it has been generally agreed upon that the ability of mental health workers to speak Spanish is crucial if they hope to increase Latino utilization. Padilla and Ruiz (1976) estimated that Spanish is the first language of approximately 70% of the Spanish-speaking, Spanish-surnamed population and that over 50% of this population speak Spanish "primarily" in the home. This same pattern of many Hispanics, especially those from lower socioeconomic classes, having limited English language proficiency, has been confirmed with recent data (e.g., see Bean & Tienda, 1987, pp. 130-131). It should not surprise us that Hispanic clients will be hesitant to receive services from an institution with which they are not able to communicate in their native tongue. Sue, Fujino, Hu, Takeuchi, and Zane (1991) found that for clients whose primary language was Spanish rather than English, matching therapists and clients on ethnicity and language was significantly related to reduced premature termination and greater number of sessions for Mexican American clients. Thus having staff members who are bilingual and signs that give information in both Spanish and English is important for initially bringing Hispanic Americans into mental health centers as well as for retaining this population once they have initiated contact.

Closely associated with the notion of bilingual therapists is the idea that to be truly helpful staff members must also be bicultural: That is, they must have grown up in a Hispanic community or have had some other direct contact with the values and beliefs of this population (Barrera, 1978). Hiring bilingual and bicultural therapists is important because these individuals should be knowledgeable about the values and beliefs of Hispanic Americans that predispose them to perceive emotional problems in such a way that they do not seek professional services. These beliefs, including the view that mental illness is caused by weakness of character and that the need for psychological help is a disgrace (Keefe, 1982), may result in Hispanic Americans putting off help seeking until symptoms become severe. Cultural barriers blocking help seeking are particularly detrimental to Hispanic males, who may feel their *machismo* (pride in manliness) is jeopardized by seeking assistance from any mental health service. Other traditional values such as *confianza* (trust), *personalismo* (trust in the immediate person rather than the institution), *respeto* (respect owed to older persons), *verguenza* (sense of shame), *orgullo* (pride), familism, fatalism, and present orientation have been linked to the mental health underutilization patterns of Hispanics because these values stress face-to-face relations and avoidance of impersonal, bureaucratic organizations (Rogler et al., 1989). Interaction of Hispanic clients with staff members who lack a cultural understanding of these values is likely to result in distrust and misunderstanding of mental health services by the Hispanic population, which will ultimately manifest itself in underutilization.

Another cultural barrier that may influence Hispanic utilization of mental health services is acculturation. Hispanic Americans with lower levels of acculturation tend to have lower socioeconomic status (SES), greater likelihood of primarily or solely speaking Spanish, greater stigma attached to mental illness, fewer social support systems, less familiarity with American culture, and less familiarity with U.S. public agencies (Keefe, 1982; Wells et al., 1987). Consequently, it has been suggested that lower acculturation results in lower utilization. In support of this hypothesis, Wells et al. (1987) found that non-Hispanic Whites were almost twice as likely as high-acculturated Mexican Americans and almost seven times as likely as low-acculturated Mexican Americans to have seen a mental health specialist. Rogler et al. (1987) found that making the therapy setting more culturally relevant to unacculturated Hispanics in terms of treatment, modality, approach, and setting increased utilization and effectiveness of treatment. Thus level of acculturation does appear to influence utilization patterns within this population.

A fourth factor influencing Hispanic utilization of mental health services is what has been called *alternative resource theory* in the literature (Dworkin & Adams, 1987; Reeves, 1986; Sanchez & King, 1986). This factor is based on the assumption that Hispanics have a number of resources other than the professional mental health system to which they can turn in order to relieve psychological distress. These resources include family, friends, folk healers, clergy, and general medical providers. In general, research has shown that given equal numbers of stressful life events, as social support systems increase, the likelihood of experiencing psychological distress and subsequently seeking counseling decreases (Goodman, Sewell, & Jampol, 1984). Thus, support systems do appear to at least partially mediate the relationship between stress and help seeking. Research has shown that Hispanics in general do tend to have strong extended family ties that are used to support members who are dealing with emotional problems (Flaskerud, 1982; Keefe & Casas, 1980; Padilla & Ruiz, 1976). Keefe and Casas (1980) cited research showing that Mexican American extended families persist in urban areas and across generations. Furthermore, they appear to be stronger among Mexican Americans who are more acculturated, are more educated, and have higher incomes. It appears that the family is the first and main source of help that Hispanics consult when dealing with emotional problems (Rogler et al., 1989). Although Hispanics do rely on the family as a primary mental health resource, studies show that when Western mental health facilities are culturally responsive to Hispanic needs, utilization increases (Reeves, 1986; Rogler et al., 1987). Thus, Hispanics do recognize mental illness and the need for special mental health services outside the family, but appear to be deterred from satisfying these needs by the lack of culturally responsive services.

Folk healers are probably most often cited as the alternative resource that Hispanics utilize rather than seeking help from the formal Western mental health system. Some researchers suggest that Hispanics prefer folk healers to Western mental health specialists because they share conceptualizations of mental health and illness, values, and beliefs with their clients (Padilla et al., 1975). However, the findings of studies addressing utilization of folk medicine have been equivocal. Many suggest that the utilization of folk healers is not common, particularly among urbanized, acculturated Hispanics (Barrera, 1978; Keefe, 1982; Keefe & Casas, 1980; Meredith, 1984). Becerra and Greenblatt (1981) found that only 2% of 234 Hispanic subjects utilized folk healers. Likewise, Edgerton, Karno, and Fernandez (1970) surveyed 500 Mexican American families and found less than 1% included folk healers in their responses to questions about treatment of illness or behavior. However, Martinez and Martin (1966) found that approximately 97% of the 75 Mexican American housewives they surveyed were familiar with folk remedies and more than 50% had been treated by a folk healer during their lifetime. Although specific prevalence rates cannot be determined at this time, researchers agree that use of folk healers cannot be used to explain underutilization of Western mental health services (Gaviria & Stern, 1980; Padilla & Ruiz, 1976; Wells et al., 1987) because in most cases traditional healers are used as adjuncts to Western healers rather than replacements (Gafner & Duckett, 1992; Krassner, 1986; Mayers, 1989).

Members of the clergy and general medical providers also serve as alternative resources for Hispanic Americans seeking help with psychological distress. A survey by Keefe (1982) found that clergymen and physicians were two of the four most common sources of support for emotional problems in Hispanic populations. Because Hispanics do not generally differentiate between physical and mental health, they are likely to use general medical care providers to help them deal with psychological problems. Barrera (1978) suggested that use of non-mental-health professionals is best understood as a result of in-adequate service rather than a cause of underutilization. Thus, although there does appear to be evidence to support the use of various alternative resources by Hispanic Americans, these sources alone do not account for underutiliza-tion of Western mental health facilities.

The final factor associated with Hispanic underutilization of mental health services is labeled *institutional barriers* in the literature (Keefe & Casas, 1980; Rogler et al., 1989; Sue, Allen, & Conaway, 1978). These barriers refer to aspects of the mental health system that keep Hispanics from using services, such as geographic inaccessibility, transportation difficulties, lack of child care, failure to use indigenous therapies and therapists, focus on intrapsychic prob-lems, adherence to formal procedures, adherence to strict time schedules, and absence of community input. Acosta (1980) found that for Mexican Ameri-cans, environmental constraints ranked second in reasons for leaving therapy prematurely. Thus, institutional barriers appear to be important not only in initial utilization of the mental health system but also in retention. Basically, these institutional barriers represent the failure of community mental health to address the needs of the Hispanic population, which in turn results in un-derutilization. Research supports the conclusion that when these needs are addressed, Hispanic utilization rates increase.

Overall, it appears that financial constraints, cultural barriers, and insti-tutional barriers are primarily responsible for Hispanic underutilization of Western mental health care. Recommendations for change that address these barriers hold the greatest promise for increasing Hispanic utilization and cre-ating services that focus more on responsiveness than simple equity.

HELP-SEEKING ATTITUDES AMONG ASIAN AMERICANS

Research has shown that members of non-Caucasian ethnic groups in general, and Asian Americans in particular, underutilize professional psycho-logical help services (Leong, 1986; Sattler, 1977; Sue, 1977; Sue & Sue, 1974; Yamamoto, 1978). This is particularly distressing in that studies have shown a great need for these services among Asian Americans to deal with a variety of problems including academic, interpersonal, health/substance abuse, dat-ing, bicultural and biracial issues, family difficulties due to emerging cultural differences, marginality, difficulties relating within various subgroups, and the experience of racism (Gim, Atkinson, & Whiteley, 1990; Solberg, Ritsma, Davis, Tata, & Jolly, 1994). The underutilization of such services by Asian Americans seems to be the result of an interaction between client and service provider variables (Leong, 1986). Cultural, social, language, and service bar-riers on an individual and institutional level affect attitudes that Asian Ameri-cans have toward service utilization (Root, 1985; Sue & Sue, 1977). These attitudes in turn may affect the act of seeking professional psychological help (Halgin, Weaver, Edell, & Spencer, 1987).

It is extremely important to note that there are differences both between members of different Asian American groups and within groups due to factors such as gender, acculturation, stage of ethnic/cultural identity (Sue, 1990), geographic location, immigration experience (Toupin, 1980), history of the group both in the United States and in the country in which the person's ancestors lived, values, social and economic class, education, ability, sexual orientation, religious beliefs, extent of social support systems, and age. Hence it is vital to note the interplay of a wide range of factors whenever one is working with an Asian American client and to try to understand the uniqueness of that individual while keeping in mind his or her cultural context.

Acculturation represents a very important influence in terms of Asian American attitudes toward seeking psychological help. Atkinson and Gim (1989) examined the relationship between the level of acculturation of Asian American college students and their attitudes toward seeking professional psychological help. Their sample included Chinese American, Korean American, and Japanese American students enrolled at a major West Coast university. They found that acculturation had a direct relationship with positive attitudes toward seeking professional psychological help. Tata and Leong (1994) also found that more highly acculturated Asian Americans had more positive attitudes toward seeking professional psychological help than Asians with lower levels of acculturation. On the other hand, belief that the system will change to meet their needs was higher among the less acculturated Asians than the more acculturated Asians. Overall, these studies speak to the importance of assessing and taking acculturation into account when counseling Asian Americans (Atkinson, Thompson, & Grant, 1993).

Factors that affect the rate at which Asian Americans make some initial contact with mental health service providers may differ from factors that help them to follow through and continue to receive these services. As Atkinson and Gim (1989) summarized so well, the conflict between cultural values of Asian Americans and the values inherent in the Western mental health system may be the main cause of lack of initial contact with the system, whereas the inappropriateness of services may account for the high dropout rate among Asian Americans. In the following paragraphs we first explore some of the value conflicts experienced by Asian Americans that keep them from entering the Western mental health system. Then we look at the inappropriateness of services that Asian Americans use if they are able to overcome the value conflicts and initiate treatment.

Collectivistic values that are traditionally held by Asian Americans (Triandis, 1988), particularly those who may be newer immigrants, oppose the values traditionally associated with counseling in the United States. The Western values emphasize the use of verbal communication, the presence of ambiguity, and a focus on the individual, which often involves encouraging

clients to put their own individual goals ahead of the goals of the collective
(Sue & Sue, 1977). Asian Americans, on the other hand, generally have more
allocentric values that involve some subordination of one's individual goals
to the goals of the collective. However, the extent to which Asian individuals
act out the values that define allocentrism and idiocentrism will differ depending on the situation (Triandis, Bontempo, Villareal, Asai, & Lucca, 1988). Generally, the collective for the Asian American will involve members of his or
her family and community. Lin and Lin (1978) suggested that Asian Americans
rely heavily on trusted intrafamilial resources. These authors described how
the sphere of privacy for Asian Americans, particularly Chinese Americans,
extends from the individual to the immediate family and then to the extended
family, which may include relatives by marriage or childhood friends of parents. Information that is private or problems faced by an Asian American
individual are expected to stay within this realm of privacy, with the sharing
of such information with outsiders being considered as an act that would bring
disgrace or loss of face for the whole family.

Tata and Leong (1994) provided empirical evidence that collectivist values
and familial support systems influence Asian Americans' views of Western
mental health. They examined the relationship of acculturation, gender, col-
lectivist-individualist values, and social network orientation with the criterion
variable of attitudes toward seeking professional psychological help among
219 Chinese-American students at a midwestern university. Each of the four
independent variables was found to be a significant predictor of attitudes toward seeking professional psychological help. The counseling implications of
this study include the importance of paying attention to acculturation, values
such as collectivism, and social support variables if we hope to make mental
health services culturally responsive to Asian Americans.

Another factor linked to the process of counseling in the United States is
the expectation that the communication between client and counselor will be
characterized by openness, intimacy, and verbal, emotional, and/or behavioral
expressiveness. Persons with roots in traditionally collectivistic cultures, such
as those in Asia, often do not have much interaction with out-group members.
Thus, they may have difficulty being open and intimate with a therapist who
is a stranger. The concern that Asian clients have about the impact of their
behavior on members of their in-group (Hui & Triandis, 1986) and their fears
about bringing shame upon their in-group by talking about problems make it
difficult for them to engage in traditional psychotherapy.

Such differences in values reduce the acceptability of professional psychological services in the eyes of members of the Asian American community.
Given their high involvement with their in-group members and the value
placed on the opinions of the in-group, especially by Asian Americans who
have maintained their allocentric values, the lack of acceptance in the Asian
American community of mental health services may keep individuals who
feel they need such services from seeking them out. On the basis of this values
conflict, it is not surprising that studies on preferences for help sources have

shown that Asian Americans do not indicate a preference to see counselors as a source of help (Pliner & Brown, 1985; Webster & Fretz, 1978).

We now turn to an exploration of the factors influencing the appropriateness of treatments once an Asian American individual begins the counseling process. Credibility of services and service providers qualifies as one dimension of the appropriateness of treatment for Asian Americans. Sue and Sue (1990) identified trustworthiness and expertness as the two components of credibility, and other researchers have suggested that the components of credibility include the therapist's race, his or her counseling approach, and his or her degree of cultural competence (Atkinson, Maruyama, & Matsui, 1978; Gim, Atkinson, & Kim, 1991). Whatever its specific components, *credibility* can be defined as "the constellation of characteristics that makes certain individuals appear worthy of belief, capable, entitled to confidence, reliable and trustworthy" (Sue & Sue, 1990, p. 87). The credibility of psychological service providers is fundamentally related to the beliefs that Asian Americans have about mental health (Sue, Wagner, Davis, Margullis, & Lew, 1976), the values they hold (Ho, 1976), and their preferences for different sources of support (Lin & Lin, 1978; Webster & Fretz, 1978). Perceived credibility of the particular service provider with whom Asian Americans make contact as well as the general degree to which Asian Americans may perceive counseling services to be credible are factors influencing the high dropout rate among Asian Americans. The lack of ascribed credibility/status, which involves the position that one is assigned by others, may be linked to the underutilization of counseling services among Asian Americans (Sue & Zane, 1987).

The literature is equivocal about whether Asian Americans necessarily perceive a counselor of the same race as more credible and have more positive attitudes toward counseling when they are matched with an ethnically similar counselor (Atkinson et al., 1978; Gim et al., 1991). Rather than focusing on ethnicity of the counselor as the main variable, Sue and Zane (1987) stressed that credibility can be achieved through effective therapist skills and culturally relevant interventions. Sue and Zane (1987) suggested that counselors can achieve credibility by paying attention to the three areas of counseling in which cultural issues may be most important: conceptualization of the problem, means for problem resolution, and goals for treatment. Incongruities between counselors and clients in any of these three areas can reduce credibility. They also suggested the use of cultural knowledge, not to make assumptions about all clients from a particular ethnic group, but rather as information that may help counselors understand the roots of certain incongruities if and when they arise. Sue and Zane also advocated "gift giving," or providing clients with some experience of direct benefit from therapy as early as possible in the process. The lack of such gift giving may increase an Asian American's skepticism about therapy, decrease the therapist's credibility, and lead to premature termination for Asian American clients.

Other therapist variables related to credibility also influence Asian American attitudes toward and likelihood of seeking counseling as well as the appropriateness of services once treatment is initiated. One study on the preferences for counselor characteristics among Asian American, Mexican American, and Caucasian American students found that similarity of ethnicity and attitudes between students and counselors, and higher education on the counselor's part, were preferred counselor characteristics by all subjects (Atkinson, Poston, Furlong, & Mercado, 1989). Thus, although a majority of the subjects preferred an ethnically similar counselor as opposed to an ethnically dissimilar counselor, they also gave considerable importance to other counselor characteristics. Preference for counselor characteristics will also vary depending on the stage of ethnic identity of the client. Unfortunately, little has been published on this relationship among Asian Americans, even though empirical research on the relationship between cultural identity and preferences for counselor characteristics has been done among other ethnic groups (Atkinson, Furlong, & Poston, 1986; Parham & Helms, 1981; Ponterotto, Alexander, & Hinkston, 1988).

Obviously, counselor characteristics such as credibility, ethnicity, education, and attitudes influence Asian American attitudes about seeking professional psychological help and consequently their service utilization patterns. Counselors who are willing to explore the role of cultural factors in a client's life and who remain aware of within-group differences are likely to promote more positive attitudes toward seeking help within the Western mental health system on the part of Asian American clients.

SUMMARY

Although the various ethnic groups differ with regard to their attitudes toward and use of Western mental health services, several common themes seem to characterize ethnic minority members' attitudes toward help seeking. First is the common need for mental health services exhibited by minority individuals. Although different groups utilize formal mental health facilities in different ways, most authors agree that minorities do not have lower prevalence rates of mental disorders than majority individuals. In fact, several researchers have suggested that minorities show greater prevalence rates of psychological disturbance than their majority counterparts due to the stressors associated with being a minority group member. These stressors have been linked to psychological disorders and include racism, prejudice and discrimination, lower SES, less education, and minimal political influence (Padilla et al., 1975; Padilla & Ruiz, 1976; Ridley, 1989). It is also crucial to realize that what is considered deviant behavior in need of treatment may vary from one culture to the next (Arkoff, Thaver, & Elkind, 1966; Lin & Lin, 1978; Sue et al., 1976) and will greatly affect an individual's likelihood of seeking professional mental health services.

Another common thread is the importance of intraethnic differences among subgroups as well as individuals in terms of mental health attitudes and behaviors. It is crucial for researchers and practitioners to understand the interaction between the unique individual and his or her common cultural characteristics whenever they work with ethnic minority individuals. For African Americans, racial identity and worldviews serve as significant moderators of the help-seeking process. Along the same line is the importance of acculturation for members of groups who are recent immigrants to the United States. For Asian and Hispanic individuals, in particular, acculturation will have an important impact on help seeking, and it needs to be assessed in counseling. Some of the aspects of acculturation that are particularly important include language, ethnic identity, friendship choice, knowledge about cultural heritage, attitudes toward members of one's own ethnic group and members of other ethnic groups, and cultural behaviors such as celebration of ethnic occasions and holidays (Padilla, 1980; Triandis et al., 1988). Counselors need to assess these factors while refraining from making the assumption that a bicultural or highly acculturated ethnic client subscribes to all the values that one may associate with the culture in which he or she currently resides (Tata & Leong, 1994; Toupin, 1980).

Finally, it is evident that all minority groups are in need of culturally responsive services if they are to maximally benefit from counseling (Sue, 1977). Recommendations for changing our mental health system have been provided by many researchers (Abad, Ramos, & Boyce, 1974; Flaskerud, 1986; Keefe & Casas, 1980; Leong, 1985; Padilla et al., 1975; Padilla & Ruiz, 1976; Ruiz, 1993; Sue, 1990; Sue & Zane, 1987; Tracey, Leong, & Glidden, 1986; Woodward et al., 1992). These recommendations focus on staff, service, Community Mental Health Centers (CMHC), and public policy changes that will help the mental health system meet the needs of all ethnic minorities. In terms of staff characteristics, employing bilingual/bicultural staff members, incorporating traditional cultural healers, having therapists put aside personal therapy biases in favor of treatment modalities that match minority values, and accepting somatic and spiritual complaints as legitimate areas of concern for mental health services promise to increase the cultural sensitivity of treatments. Mental health service providers also need to expand their prevention efforts by getting involved in community outreach that dispels stereotypes about minorities, confronts oppression, and provides role models from different careers for ethnic minority youth (Leong, 1985).

Changes in service characteristics should include focusing on preventive services and education and providing crisis, brief, and family counseling for minority clients. Reducing fees for disadvantaged populations and maintaining flexible hours and appointments are also crucial components of culturally responsive services. Recommended changes in CMHC characteristics involve defining *mental health* broadly so that help is provided for a variety of problems related to mental health, such as finances, housing, physical health care, and legal matters; collaborating with the community in developing services; locating mental health facilities in the communities that they hope to serve; arranging transportation and child care; and offering facilities for community needs such as youth activities and community meetings. Education of mental health professionals to increase their level of cultural sensitivity and to decrease ethnic minorities' historical distrust of the mental health system is crucial. Finally, suggested public policy changes focus on providing health insurance benefits to minorities via employer-based programs or universal insurance plans, increasing the representation of minorities in health and mental health occupations, and allocating funds for research on health and mental health needs of minorities. If these changes are implemented and evaluated, we believe that mental health services will serve minority populations more effectively.

REFERENCES

Abad, V., Ramos, J., & Boyce, E. (1974). A model for delivery of mental health services to Spanish-speaking minorities. *American Journal of Orthopsychiatry, 44*(4), 584-595.

Acosta, F. X. (1980). Self-described reasons for premature termination of psychotherapy by Mexican American, Black American, and Anglo-American patients. *Psychological Reports, 47,* 435-443.

Arkoff, A., Thaver, F., & Elkind, L. (1966). Mental health and counseling ideas of Asian and American students. *Journal of Counseling Psychology, 13,* 219-223.

Atkinson, D. R. (1983). Ethnic similarity in counseling psychology: A review of research. *The Counseling Psychologist, 11,* 79-92.

Atkinson, D. R., Furlong, M. J., & Poston, W. C. (1986). Afro-American preferences for counselor characteristics. *Journal of Counseling Psychology, 33,* 326-330.

Atkinson, D. R., & Gim, R. H. (1989). Asian-American cultural identity and attitudes toward mental-health services. *Journal of Counseling Psychology, 36,* 209-212.

Atkinson, D. R., Maruyama, M., & Matsui, S. (1978). The effects of counselor race and counseling approach on Asian-Americans' perceptions of counselor credibility and utility. *Journal of Counseling Psychology, 25,* 76-83.

Atkinson, D. R., Poston, W. C., Furlong, M. J., & Mercado, P. (1989). Ethnic group preferences for counselor characteristics. *Journal of Counseling Psychology, 36,* 68-72.

Atkinson, D. R., Thompson, C. E., & Grant, S. K. (1993). A three-dimensional model for counseling racial and ethnic minorities. *The Counseling Psychologist, 21,* 257-277.

Barrera, M. (1978). Mexican-American mental health service utilization: A critical examination of some proposed variables. *Community Mental Health Journal, 14*(1), 35-45.

Bean, F. D., & Tienda, M. (1987). *The Hispanic population in the United States.* New York: Russell Sage.

Becerra, R. M., & Greenblatt, M. (1981). The mental health-seeking behavior of Hispanic veterans. *Comprehensive Psychiatry, 22*(1), 124-133.

Brown, B. B. (1978). Social and psychological correlates of help-seeking behavior among urban adults. *American Journal of Community Psychology, 6,* 425-439.

Bui, K. T., & Takeuchi, D. T. (1992). Ethnic minority adolescents and the use of community mental health care services. *American Journal of Community Psychology, 20*(4), 403-417.

Carkhuff, R. R., & Pierce, R. (1967). Differential effects of therapist race and social class upon patient depth of self-exploration in the initial clinical interview. *Journal of Consulting Psychology, 31,* 632-634.

Chavez, E. L., & Swaim, R. C. (1992). Hispanic substance use: Problems in epidemiology. In J. E. Trimble, C. S. Bolek, & S. J. Niemcryk (Eds.), *Ethnic and multicultural drug abuse: Perspectives on current research* (pp. 211-230). New York: Harrington Park.

Cheatham, H. E., Shelton, T. O., & Ray, W. J. (1987). Race, sex, causal attribution and help-seeking behavior. *Journal of College Student Personnel, 28*, 559-568.

Dressler, W. W. (1991). *Stress and adaptation in the context of culture: Depression in a southern Black community.* Albany: State University of New York Press.

Dworkin, R. J., & Adams, G. L. (1987). Retention of Hispanics in public sector mental health services. *Community Mental Health Journal, 23*(3), 204-216.

Edgerton, R. B., Karno, M., & Fernandez, I. (1970). Curanderismo in the metropolis: The diminished role of folk psychiatry among Los Angeles Mexican Americans. *American Journal of Psychotherapy, 24*, 124-134.

Flaskerud, J. H. (1982). Community mental health nursing: Its unique role in delivery of services to ethnic minorities. *Perspectives in Psychiatric Care, 20*, 37-43.

Flaskerud, J. H. (1986). The effects of culture-compatible intervention on the utilization of mental health services by minority clients. *Community Mental Health Journal, 22*(2), 127-141.

Gafner, G., & Duckett, S. (1992). Treating the sequelae of a curse in elderly Mexican-Americans. *Clinical Gerontologist, 11*, 145-153.

Gambosa, A. M., Jr., Tosi, D. J., & Riccio, A. C. (1976). Race and counselor climate in the counselor preference of delinquent girls. *Journal of Counseling Psychology, 23*, 160-162.

Gaviria, M., & Stern, G. (1980). Problems in designing and implementing culturally relevant mental health services for Latinos in the U.S. *Social Science Medicine, 14B*, 65-71.

Giglio, J. (1993). The impact of patients' and therapists' religious values on psychotherapy. *Hospital and Community Psychiatry, 44*, 768-771.

Gim, R. H., Atkinson, D. R., & Kim, S. J. (1991). Asian American acculturation, counselor ethnicity and cultural sensitivity, and ratings of counselors. *Journal of Counseling Psychology, 38*, 57-62.

Gim, R. H., Atkinson, D. R., & Whiteley, S. (1990). Asian American acculturation, severity of concerns, and willingness to see a counselor. *Journal of Counseling Psychology, 37*, 281-285.

Goodman, S. H., Sewell, D. R., & Jampol, R. C. (1984). On going to the counselor: Contributions of life stress and social supports to the decision to seek psychological counseling. *Journal of Counseling Psychology, 31*(3), 306-313.

Grier, W. H., & Cobbs, P. M. (1968). *Black rage.* New York: Bantam.

Griffith, M. S. (1977). The influence of race on the psychotherapeutic relationship. *Psychiatry, 40*, 27-40.

Halgin, R. P., Weaver, D. D., Edell, W. S., & Spencer, P. G. (1987). Relation of depression and help-seeking history to attitudes toward seeking professional psychological help. *Journal of Counseling Psychology, 34*, 177-185.

Halleck, S. L. (1971). *The politics of therapy.* New York: Science House.

Helms, J. E. (1990). *Black and White racial identity: Theory, research, and practice.* Westport, CT: Greenwood Press.

Ho, M. K. (1976). Social work with Asian Americans. *Social Casework, 57*, 195-201.

Hollingshead, A. B., & Redlich, F. C. (1958). *Social class and mental illness.* New York: John Wiley.

Hough, R. L., Landsverk, J. A., Karno, M., Burnam, M. A., Timbers, D. M., Escobar, J. I., & Regier, D. A. (1987). Utilization of health and mental health services by Los Angeles Mexican Americans and non-Hispanic Whites. *Archives of General Psychiatry, 44*, 702-709.

Hui, C. H., & Triandis, H. C. (1986). Individualism and collectivism: A study of cross-cultural researchers. *Journal of Cross-Cultural Psychology, 17*, 225-248.

Jackson, G. G., & Kirschner, S. A. (1973). Racial self-designation and preference for counselor race. *Journal of Counseling Psychology, 20*, 560-564.

Jaco, E. G. (1959). Mental health of Spanish Americans in Texas. In M. F. Opler (Ed.), *Culture and mental health: Cross cultural studies* (pp. 467-485). New York: Macmillan.

Karno, M., & Edgerton, R. B. (1969). Perception of mental illness in a Mexican American community. *Archives of General Psychiatry, 20*, 233-238.

Keefe, S. E. (1982). Help-seeking behavior among foreign-born and native-born Mexican Americans. *Social Science and Medicine, 16*, 1467-1472.

Keefe, S. E., & Casas, J. M. (1980). Mexican Americans and mental health: A selected review and recommendations for mental health service delivery. *American Journal of Community Psychology, 8*(3), 303-326.

Krassner, M. (1986). Effective features of therapy from the healer's perspective: A study of curanderismo. *Smith College Studies in Social Work, 56,* 157-183.

Leong, F. T. L. (1985). Career development of Asian Americans. *Journal of College Student Personnel, 26,* 539-546.

Leong, F. T. L. (1986). Counseling and psychotherapy with Asian-Americans: Review of the literature. *Journal of Counseling Psychology, 33,* 196-206.

Lin, T., & Lin, M. (1978). Service delivery issues in Asian North American communities. *American Journal of Psychiatry, 135,* 454-457.

Lincoln, C. E., & Mamyia, L. H. (1990). *The Black church in the African American experience.* Durham, NC: Duke University Press.

Longshore, D., Hsieh, S., Anglin, M. D., & Annon, T. A. (1992). Ethnic patterns in drug abuse treatment utilization. *Journal of Mental Health Administration, 19,* 268-277.

Martinez, C., & Martin, H. W. (1966). Folk diseases among urban Mexican Americans. *Journal of the American Medical Association, 196,* 161-164.

Maultsby, M. C. (1982). A historical view of Blacks' mistrust of psychiatry. In S. M. Turner & R. T. Jones (Eds.), *Behavior modification in Black populations: Psychosocial issues and empirical findings* (pp. 39-55). New York: Plenum.

Mayers, R. S. (1989). Use of folk medicine by elderly Mexican-American women. *Journal of Drug Issues, 19*(2), 283-295.

Meredith, J. D. (1984). Ethnic medicine on the frontier: A case study in Wyoming. *Hispanic Journal of Behavioral Sciences, 6*(3), 247-260.

Millet, P. E., Sullivan, B. F., Schwebel, A. I., & James-Myers, L. (1994). *Afro-Americans' and Whites' views of the etiology and treatment of mental health problems.* Unpublished manuscript.

Neighbors, H. W., Jackson, J. S., Bowman, P. J., & Gurin, G. (1983). Stress, coping, and Black mental health: Preliminary findings from a national study. *Prevention in Human Services, 2,* 5-29.

Padilla, A. M. (1980). The role of cultural awareness and ethnic loyalty in acculturation. In A. Padilla (Ed.), *Acculturation: Theory, models, and some new findings* (pp. 47-84). Boulder, CO: Westview.

Padilla, A. M., & Ruiz, R. A. (1976). *Latino mental health: A review of literature.* Rockville, MD: U.S. Department of Health, Education and Welfare.

Padilla, A. M., Ruiz, R. A., & Alvarez, R. (1975). Community mental health services for the Spanish-speaking/surnamed population. *American Psychologist, 30,* 892-905.

Parham, T. A., & Helms, J. E. (1981). The influence of Black students' racial identity attitudes on preference for counselor race. *Journal of Counseling Psychology, 28,* 250-257.

Parloff, M. B., Waskow, I. E., & Wolfe, B. E. (1978). Research on therapist variables in relation to process and outcome. In S. Garfield & A. E. Bergin (Eds.), *Handbook of psychotherapy and behavior change* (pp. 233-282). New York: John Wiley.

Peoples, V. Y., & Dell, D. M. (1975). Black and White student preferences for counselor roles. *Journal of Counseling Psychology, 22,* 529-534.

Pinchot, N., Riccio, A. C., & Peters, H. J. (1975). Elementary school students' and their parents' preferences for counselors. *Counselor Education and Supervision, 15,* 28-33.

Pliner, J. E., & Brown, D. (1985). Projections of reactions to stress and preference for helpers among students from four ethnic groups. *Journal of College Student Personnel, 26,* 147-151.

Ponterotto, J. G., Alexander, C. M., & Hinkston, J. A. (1988). Afro-American preferences for counselor characteristics: A replication and extension. *Journal of Counseling Psychology, 35,* 175-182.

Reeves, K. (1986). Hispanic utilization of an ethnic mental health clinic. *Journal of Psychosocial Nursing, 24,* 23-26.

Riccio, A. C., & Barnes, K. D. (1973). Counselor preferences of senior high school students. *Counselor Education and Supervision, 13,* 36-40.

Ridley, C. R. (1984). Clinical treatment of the nondisclosing Black client: A therapeutic paradox. *American Psychologist, 39*, 1234-1244.

Ridley, C. R. (1989). Racism in counseling as an adversive behavioral process. In P. B. Pedersen, J. G. Draguns, W. J. Lonner, & J. E. Trimble (Eds.), *Counseling across cultures* (3rd ed., pp. 55-77). Honolulu: University of Hawaii Press.

Rogler, L. H., Malgady, R. G., Costantino, G., & Blumenthal, R. (1987). What do culturally sensitive mental health services mean? The case of Hispanics. *American Psychologist, 42*(6), 565-570.

Rogler, L. H., Malgady, R. G., & Rodriguez, O. (1989). *Hispanics and mental health: A framework for research.* Malabar, FL: Robert E. Krieger.

Root, M. P. (1985). Guidelines for facilitating therapy with Asian-American clients. *Psychotherapy, 22*, 349-356.

Ruiz, P. (1993). Access to health care for uninsured Hispanics: Policy recommendations. *Hospital and Community Psychiatry, 44*(10), 958-962.

Ruiz, R. A., & Padilla, A. M. (1973). *Latino mental health: A review of literature.* Rockville, MD: National Institute of Mental Health.

Sanchez, A. R., & King, M. (1986). Mexican Americans' use of counseling services: Cultural and institutional factors. *Journal of College Student Personnel, 27*, 344-349.

Sattler, J. M. (1977). The effects of therapist-client racial similarity. In A. S. Gurman & A. M. Razin (Eds.), *Effective psychotherapy: A handbook of research* (pp. 252-290). New York: Pergamon.

Snowden, L. R., & Cheung, F. K. (1990). Use of inpatient mental health services by members of ethnic minority groups. *American Psychologist, 45*, 347-355.

Solberg, V. S., Ritsma, S., Davis, B. J., Tata, S. P., & Jolly, A. (1994). Asian Americans' severity of problems and willingness to seek help from university counseling centers: Role of previous counseling experience, gender, and ethnicity. *Journal of Counseling Psychology, 41*, 275-279.

Stefl, M. E., & Prosperi, D. C. (1985). Barriers to mental health service utilization. *Community Mental Health Journal, 21*(3), 167-177.

Stranges, R., & Riccio, A. C. (1970). Counselee preference for counselors: Some implications for counselor education. *Counselor Education and Supervision, 10*, 39-46.

Sue, D. W. (1990). Culture-specific strategies in counseling: A conceptual framework. *Professional Psychology: Research and Practice, 21*, 424-433.

Sue, D. W., & Sue, D. (1977). Barriers to effective cross-cultural counseling. *Journal of Counseling Psychology, 24*, 420-429.

Sue, D. W., & Sue, D. (1990). *Counseling the culturally different: Theory and practice* (2nd ed.). New York: John Wiley.

Sue, S. (1977). Community mental health services to minority groups: Some optimism, some pessimism. *American Psychologist, 32*, 616-624.

Sue, S., Allen, D. B., & Conaway, L. (1978). The responsiveness and equality of mental health care to Chicanos and Native Americans. *American Journal of Community Psychology, 6*(2), 137-146.

Sue, S., Fujino, D. C., Hu, L., Takeuchi, D. T., & Zane, N. W. S. (1991). Community mental health services for ethnic minority groups: A test of the cultural responsiveness hypothesis. *Journal of Consulting and Clinical Psychology, 59*(4), 533-540.

Sue, S., & Sue, D. W. (1974). MMPI comparisons between Asian-American and non-Asian students utilizing a student health psychiatric clinic. *Journal of Counseling Psychology, 21*, 423-427.

Sue, S., Wagner, N., Davis, J. A., Margullis, C., & Lew, L. (1976). Conceptions of mental illness among Asian and Caucasian-American students. *Psychological Reports, 38*, 703-708.

Sue, S., & Zane, N. (1987). The role of culture and cultural techniques in psychotherapy. *American Psychologist, 42*, 37-45.

Sue, S., Zane, N., & Young, K. (1994). Research on psychotherapy with culturally diverse populations. In A. E. Bergin & S. L. Garfield (Eds.), *Handbook of psychotherapy and behavior change* (4th ed., pp. 783-817). New York: John Wiley.

Sussman, L. K., Robbins, L. N., & Earls, F. (1987). Treatment-seeking for depression by Black and White Americans. *Social Science and Medicine, 24*, 187-196.

Swanson, J. W., Holzer, C. E., & Ganju, V. K. (1993). Hispanic Americans and the state mental hospitals in Texas: Ethnic parity as a latent function of a fiscal incentive policy. *Social Science and Medicine, 37*(7), 917-926.

Tata, S. P., & Leong, F. T. L. (1994). Individualism-collectivism, network orientation, and acculturation as predictors of attitudes towards seeking professional psychological help among Chinese Americans. *Journal of Counseling Psychology, 41*, 280-287.

Terrell, F., & Terrell, S. (1981). An inventory to measure cultural mistrust among Blacks. *Western Journal of Black Studies, 5*, 180-185.

Terrell, F., & Terrell, S. (1984). Race of counselor, client sex, cultural mistrust level, and premature termination from counseling among Black clients. *Journal of Counseling Psychology, 31*, 371-375.

Thomas, A. P., & Sillen, S. (1972). *Racism and psychiatry.* New York: Brunner/Mazel.

Thomas, C. S., & Comer, J. P. (1973). Racism and mental health services. In C. V. Willie, B. M. Kramer, & B. S. Brown (Eds.), *Racism and mental health* (pp. 165-181). Pittsburgh: University of Pittsburgh Press.

Thompson, R. A., & Cimbolic, P. (1978). Black students' counselor preference and attitudes toward counseling center use. *Journal of Counseling Psychology, 25*, 570-575.

Toupin, E. S. W. A. (1980). Counseling Asians: Psychotherapy in the context of racism and Asian-American history. *American Journal of Orthopsychiatry, 50*, 76-86.

Tracey, T. J., Leong, F. T. L., & Glidden, C. (1986). Help-seeking and problem perception among Asian-Americans. *Journal of Counseling Psychology, 33*, 331-336.

Triandis, H. C. (1988). Collectivism and individualism: A reconceptualization of a basic concept in cross cultural psychology. In G. K. Verma & C. Bargley (Eds.), *Personality, attitudes, and cognition* (pp. 60-95). London: Macmillan.

Triandis, H. C., Bontempo, R., Villareal, M. J., Asai, M., & Lucca, N. (1988). Individualism and collectivism: Cross cultural perspectives on self-ingroup relationships. *Journal of Personality and Social Psychology, 54*, 323-338.

Turner, S. M., & Jones, R. T. (Eds.). (1982). *Behavior modification in Black populations: Psychosocial issues and empirical findings.* New York: Plenum.

Webster, D. W., & Fretz, B. R. (1978). Asian-American, Black, and White college students' preferences for help giving sources. *Journal of Counseling Psychology, 25*, 124-130.

Wells, K. B., Golding, J. M., Hough, R. L., Burnam, A., & Karno, M. (1988). Factors affecting the probability of use and medical health and social community services for Mexican Americans and non-Hispanic Whites. *Medical Care, 26*, 441-452.

Wells, K. B., Hough, R. L., Golding, J. M., Burnam, M. A., & Karno, M. (1987). Which Mexican-Americans underutilize health services? *American Journal of Psychiatry, 144*(7), 918-922.

Wood, W. D., & Sherrets, S. D. (1984). Requests for outpatient mental health services: A comparison of Whites and Blacks. *Comprehensive Psychiatry, 25*, 329-334.

Woodward, A. M., Dwinell, A. D., & Arons, B. S. (1992). Barriers to mental health care for Hispanic Americans: A literature review and discussion. *Journal of Mental Health Administration, 19*, 224-236.

Yamamoto, J. (1978). Research priorities in Asian-American mental health delivery. *American Journal of Psychiatry, 135*, 457-458.

PART VI

Critical and Emerging Topics
in Multicultural Counseling:
Section 1

PARTS VI AND VII of the *Handbook* present the latest thinking and research on important and emerging topics in multicultural counseling. The competent counselor working in a heterogeneous society will have a working knowledge of all of the areas discussed in this part.

In Chapter 21, Courtland C. Lee and Kathleen L. Armstrong examine the role of traditional healing practices abroad and in the United States. They describe some common features of traditional healing practices and associated belief systems. They also emphasize that Western-trained counselors need to familiarize themselves with culturally indigenous models and work with them in their own cross-cultural practice. Helpful guidelines for the practitioner are provided.

In Chapter 22, Clemmont E. Vontress, a pioneer in the field of multicultural counseling, tackles an important yet neglected construct in counseling young African American males—the breakdown of authority. The author presents a comprehensive analysis of the authority construct and examines reasons for the breakdown of authority among African American male youth. He then proceeds to discuss critical implications of the construct for counseling young Blacks.

Derald Wing Sue, the author of Chapter 23, discusses the need for the counseling profession to broaden its focus beyond individual and group counseling. Sue believes that the next frontier for the multicultural counseling movement is the "organization," whether it be industrial, educational, governmental, or professional. Using a revealing personal case study as a backdrop, Sue delineates the necessary prerequisites for organizational change along multicultural lines and presents his own model for diversity training in organizations.

Chapter 24 focuses on intelligence and personality assessment, certainly one of the most controversial topics in multicultural counseling. Lisa A. Suzuki and John F. Kugler tackle this issue in a concise and enlightening summary of key issues to consider in multicultural assessment. Using a multicultural lens, the authors review leading intelligence assessments as well as both objective and projective personality measures. They also present helpful guidelines for conducting assessments across cultures and highlight critical assessment issues through the incorporation of two revealing case studies.

The rapid demographic changes taking place in the United States are most readily seen among the country's youth and in elementary schools. A majority of school counselors have not been adequately trained to serve a culturally diverse clientele. Chapter 25, coauthored by Mark S. Kiselica, Jill C. Changizi, Va Lecia L. Cureton, and Betty E. Gridley, provides valuable information for counseling practitioners and administrators working in schools. The authors cover key issues for the school counselor, particularly family consultation, career development, and assessment, and provide well-reasoned, pragmatic suggestions to counselors working in today's schools.

21

Indigenous Models of Mental Health Intervention

Lessons From Traditional Healers

COURTLAND C. LEE

KATHLEEN L. ARMSTRONG

> The origins of shamanism predate recorded civilizations and lie beyond protohistory. Evidence of shamanic practices exists from the Paleolithic period, tens of thousands of years ago. The wellspring of shamanism may in fact be the rise of consciousness itself and could be inextricably bound to the necessarily first urge of consciousness, to explain itself.—*Shaman: The Paintings of Susan Seddon Boulet* (Boulet, 1989)

IN EVERY CULTURE, people, to varying degrees, face challenges associated with psychological distress or behavioral deviance. Throughout history, individuals worldwide have experienced stress that interferes with normal cognitive, affective, or behavioral functioning. Significantly, all cultural groups have traditional attitudes about behavior that seems to be outside the realm generally considered to be "normal." Such behavior usually exceeds culturally defined and accepted boundaries for optimal physical or psychological functioning.

When such boundaries are exceeded, cultures have traditionally found methods for dealing with the issues of psychological distress and behavioral deviance. For example, in the United States for the past century, the practices found in counseling have evolved into a formal profession whose basic purpose is to help individuals resolve both situational and developmental problems in various aspects of their lives. Counseling and related mental health professions in the United States, however, are merely the most recent manifestation of a long-standing worldwide helping tradition. Such an idea is underscored by the fact that in cultures predating that of the United States, people have for centuries found guidance to resolve personal problems from individuals who are acknowledged within their communities as possessing special insight and helping skills. These individuals have been commonly recognized as "healers" and are believed to possess awareness, knowledge, and skills that grow out of a timeless wisdom. The healers are the keepers of this wisdom and enlist it to help people solve problems and make decisions.

The purpose of this chapter is to provide a detailed examination of these traditional healers and the nature of their practices. The chapter expands on recent research into the nature and importance of traditional healing practices in a number of cultures that take place outside of what would be considered in the United States as formal counseling with trained mental health professionals (Lee, Oh, & Mountcastle, 1992; Vontress, 1991). These healing practices are part of the indigenous methods of responding to life challenges and are an ancient and integral part of many cultures (Lee et al., 1992). We first examine the nature and traditions of indigenous healing practices and some of the important commonalities that underlie traditional healing approaches throughout the world. Next, we compare these practices with so-called "Western" mental health practices. Finally, we consider implications of traditional healing for contemporary multicultural counseling.

THE UNIVERSAL SHAMANIC TRADITION: EXPLORING THE PSYCHOSPIRITUAL DOMAIN

For centuries traditional healers have been major sources for help with psychological distress and behavioral deviance throughout the world (Harner, 1990; Lee et al., 1992; Vontress, 1991). From a review of indigenous methods of mental and physical treatment in many countries (Lee et al., 1992), it is apparent that there is a centuries-old universal tradition of specially recognized individuals who offer help with problem resolution and decision making within their communities. This tradition will be referred to as *the universal shamanic tradition*.

Shaman is a term adopted by anthropologists to refer to people often called *witch*, *witch doctor*, *medicine man/woman*, *sorcerer*, *wizard*, or *magic man/woman*. A shaman is a man or woman who, at will, enters an altered state of consciousness to contact and utilize an ordinarily hidden reality in order to acquire knowledge and power and to help other people (Harner, 1990). Although there are important distinctions within the shamanic tradition, several salient characteristics appear to define the role and function of these indigenous helpers.

Holistic Approach

Within this tradition helpers make little or no distinction between physical and mental well-being. Instead, human beings are seen as interrelated entities in a synergistic relationship with their total environment. Any type of distress, therefore, is an indication that an individual is out of harmony or balance with forces either internal or external to his or her total being (Idowu, 1992; Mbiti, 1988; Torrey, 1986).

Nonordinary Reality

As a rule, the healers representative of this tradition possess a belief in different levels of human experience. In addition to the plane of reality on which daily existence takes place, practitioners in many indigenous helping traditions generally conceptualize a reality that transcends the "normal" world while still influencing it (Eliade, 1964; Harner, 1990). In many cultures, this nonordinary reality is referred to as the realm of spirits, and it is here that human destiny is often decided. For many helpers in this tradition, the goal is to enter this realm, in some fashion, on behalf of other people. The helpers then act as conduits of positive energy from this dimension. This energy is then translated into concrete insight or action leading to problem resolution or decision making.

Emphasis on the Psychospiritual
Realm of Personality

There has never been a people anywhere or at any time that has not been spiritual. It is natural, therefore, that within the universal shamanic tradition, helpers often have strong links with the religious or spiritual traditions of a community. In many instances, these helpers are religious or spiritual leaders. As such, their major efforts are in the psychospiritual domain of personality. Although there is no clear operational definition of this personality domain, various authors have suggested its existence (Allport, 1950; Assagioli, 1991; Batson & Ventis, 1982; Conn, 1978, 1981; Fran, 1977; Jung, 1933; Maslow, 1964; May, 1969; Sellner, 1990).

This is the realm of personality that goes beyond the mind and body. Although traditional concepts of personality encompass the cognitive, affective, and behavioral realms of existence, the psychospiritual transcends these realms while binding them together into an integrated whole. Ideas concerning the psychospiritual realm of personality assume that there is a state of being that transcends thoughts, feelings, and action, in which human beings are seen as part of a larger whole, interconnected through a universal force that binds all existence together (Assagioli, 1991). For some, this binding force is interpreted as the deity or "god-figure." With or without this interpretation, however, in many cultures, this realm of personality is perceived to be the seat of the spirit or the soul (Zukav, 1989). The existence of the psychospiritual realm of personality is given credence not only through the world's great religious traditions, but also by the importance placed in many cultures on such nonreligious phenomena as intuition, extrasensory perception, dream states, and meditation.

This universal shamanic tradition can be observed today in ancient helping practices of individuals in all parts of the world who are acknowledged as "healers" within their communities. Vontress (1991), for example, in research on traditional healing in Africa, discovered a variety of helping specialists still using centuries-old practices rooted in this tradition.

Lee et al. (1992) in a study of indigenous models of helping, found examples of healers currently practicing within this tradition in many other parts of the world. For example, in Korea, shamans called *mudangs* are traditional healers who use sorcery to chase out demons or evil spirits believed to be in possession of an individual. In many Islamic countries, *piris* and *fakirs* are religious leaders within the Moslem faith who use verses from the Koran to treat illness. *Sufis* are secular traditional healers in these same regions who use music to treat psychological distress. In Mexico, it was reported that this tradition is still carried on by *curandera(o)s,* female or male healers who use herbalism and massage to alleviate mental and physical suffering.

Lee et al. (1992) suggested that there are several assumptions about illness related to traditional healing practices. First, family relationship dynamics may play a causative role in illness. Second, fate may cause sickness: That is, one experiences health problems because one is predestined to do so. Third, illness is the result of possession by malevolent spirits. Taking these assumptions into consideration, then, in many societies ill health of the mind and ill health of the body are interrelated and may be the punishment imposed by spirit ancestors for breaking laws or customs. Behavior such as neglecting family duties or treating the land and its resources carelessly may be punished with sickness. Therefore, healers are consulted for problems of the body and mind as well as the spirit.

In the modern world, such traditional healing practices appear to be more prevalent in rural areas where there is often limited access to modern medical and psychological services. When considered in a contemporary "Western" context, these practices are generally considered to be backward, primitive, or unsophisticated. What is generally not considered, however, is that these indigenous services offered by traditional practitioners have effectively addressed physical and mental illnesses for millennia.

REFLECTIONS OF A MAORI HEALER

The Maori are the indigenous people of New Zealand. Their name for that country is *Aotearoa* or "Land of the Long White Cloud." The Maori trace their cultural origins to the Polynesian people who populated the islands of the South Pacific. Settling in Aotearoa nearly 1,000 years ago, the Maori developed a culture based on traditions that included communalism and a reverence for nature. Contemporary Maori culture still rests on a strong spiritual foundation.

Throughout their history, the Maori have had a tradition of individuals recognized within the community for their healing gifts. What follows is an account of one man who practices in an age-old Maori healing tradition. This account is a synthesis of an interview conducted at a Maori community center on the outskirts of Auckland, New Zealand, in August 1993. The healer's name is John, and he is of an unspecified age. The interview was conducted by the first author.

1. For what types of issues or problems do people come to see you?

John stated that people came to see him for a variety of physical and/or emotional problems. He said that people came to see him either before or after seeing a *Pakeha* (European) medical doctor or mental health professional. Sometimes people would come to seek his help while simultaneously seeing a *Pakeha* health professional. He maintained an office in a professional building and claimed to have a large clientele.

2. What types of diagnostic techniques do you use?

John stated that he generally talked with people to ascertain their problem. In many instances he would pray with individuals as a way to discern the nature of their affliction. In most cases he believed that people experienced stress because for one reason or another their lives had gotten out of synch with natural forces.

3. What specific healing methods/techniques do you employ?

John explained that after listening to a person in need of help, he usually went into the woods for a specified period of time and engaged in a form of prayer. Through this activity, he received information from spiritual forces about herbs and plants with healing powers that would be of help to the person with the problem. He would then search the woods for these plants and herbs, bring them back to his client, and direct the client to use these in certain ways, such as drinking them in teas or using them to make curative poultices. He said that he encouraged his clients to use these natural healing remedies in conjunction with the medications prescribed by *Pakeha* professionals. When pressed for more specificity about his healing methods, John stated that they could not be divulged to outsiders.

4. Did you receive formal training as a healer?

John claimed that his healing powers were a gift. Apparently this gift had been in his family for a long time. John's mother had also been a healer. He learned from her about herbalism as a way to combat illness. She also taught him how to use his gift by employing prayer as a meditative medium.

5. *What type of relationship do you have with* Pakeha *counseling professionals?*

John said that he believes in the power of *Pakeha* medicine and is willing to consult with health and related professionals at any time. However, he stated that a majority of *Pakeha* doctors do not wish to work with him and the other Maori healers. He senses that many *Pakeha* professionals think that his helping tradition does little for people.

TRADITIONAL HEALING AND CONTEMPORARY MENTAL HEALTH PRACTICES

The shamanic tradition still flourishes in many parts of the world, but in Western Europe and North America within the past century, cultural and theoretical revolutions have spawned the development of new ideas on mental and physical health. Part of this intellectual dynamism has been the evolution of a Western psychology that has helped define scientific notions of human behavior and personality (Freud, 1920/1955; Hall & Lindzey, 1970; Hilgard, 1948; Perls, 1947; Skinner, 1953). Out of these notions have developed professional mental health disciplines that focus primarily on the empirical study of and rational approaches to challenges associated with behavioral and personality dynamics. These professions include counseling, clinical psychology, psychiatry, and social work. Although they may differ qualitatively in their philosophies and approaches, they all focus in varying degrees on helping people to enhance their well-being, alleviate life stressors, cope effectively with crises, and solve problems and/or make decisions related to psychological or social functioning (Education and Training Committee of Division 17, 1984).

Upon close examination of the helping practices within these professions representative of Western psychology can be found both interesting differences and striking similarities to the universal shamanic tradition. Overriding the specific differences between Western psychology and this tradition appears to be a fundamental philosophical distinction. This distinction lies at the very heart of differences between Western and non-Western thought and can be seen as a conceptual thread running through any discussion of these two helping traditions. It is centered on differences in cosmology, or how people arrange, order, and perceive reality (Kattsoff, 1953; Torrey, 1986). Examples of this distinction can be seen when contrasting the universal shamanic tradition and Western psychology. These are exemplified by issues surrounding balance, the nature of logic, the importance of the spiritual dimension, and the essence of the helping role itself.

Holistic Balance Versus Intrapsychic Balance

As previously stated, one of the principles of the universal shamanic tradition is an emphasis on a holistic balance between the elements of human existence. However, in Western psychological traditions there are generally clear distinctions made between physical, mental, and spiritual existence and well-being (Sue & Sue, 1977). This can often lead to a disconnected approach to helping focusing exclusively on one dimension of human experience. For example, the legacy of Freud, one of the architects of Western psychology, is an emphasis on intrapsychic balance (Freud, 1920/1955). Simply, this is the notion that cognitive, affective, and behavioral functioning is dependent, in large measure, on a balance among intrapsychic forces. This suggests that mental well-being takes precedence over other dimensions of human experience. In other words, this notion generally negates the alternative concept of the total integration of mind, body, and spirit and their interconnectedness with the environment, which characterizes the universal shamanic tradition.

Linear Perspective Versus Circular Perspective

There is an evident epistemological distinction in the perspectives of Western psychology and the universal shamanic tradition. The helping principles in Western psychology are primarily ordered around the scientific method and are characterized by an emphasis on objectivity and rationality. Issues that interfere with human development are objectively analyzed in a quantitative manner, and a deductive reasoning process is engaged in to explain the issues.

Underlying the notion of the scientific method is a basic assumption that emphasizes a linear perspective on the dynamics associated with human behavior. Western notions of helping are therefore generally conceptualized within a discrete cause-and-effect framework. This framework implies a unidirectionality to problem etiology: "A" (some precipitating event) causes "B" (the present issue or problem). Implicit in this framework is the deeper notion that time is unidirectional: that is, that "A" *then* caused "B" *now* (Ornstein, 1972). Specifically, issues or challenges that interfere with optimal well-being can be traced to a distinct precipitating event, or a series of events, readily located in a specific time frame.

Conversely, helping concepts found within the universal shamanic tradition can generally be conceptualized within a framework that goes beyond mere objectivity and deductive reasoning. This tradition extends into a subjective realm characterized by intuitive reasoning and an emphasis on qualitative understanding. Human behavior and its consequences are viewed in a circular context, and models of helping are predicated on the notion that effects are multidimensional and that it may not be necessary to identify a single cause.

Within a circular perspective, therefore, it is often difficult to conceptualize true causality. This is because causality itself is unidirectional. Instead of causality, simultaneity, the notion of many things happening at once that may influence each other, must be considered (Ornstein, 1972).

Helpers with this circular perspective therefore employ more of an inductive reasoning process that reflects a different orientation regarding problem etiology. Although traditional healers may appear to frame a "diagnosis" in a linear manner (e.g., "You were possessed by an evil spirit; therefore, you are now sick"), the nature of the "causative" event may not necessarily lend itself to strict sequential understanding. Instead, that event may be merely an ingredient in a patterned whole that includes all dimensions of human experience. Rather than merely considering the relationship between cause and effect as a linear sequence of connected events, healers in the universal shamanic tradition transcend this reasoning process and view problem etiology in a manner that stresses interconnectedness and may go beyond a linear time-bound perspective.

Cognitive/Affective Basis Versus Spiritual Basis of Health and Well-Being

To a great extent, the helping practices inherent in the Western psychological tradition are based on an assumption that optimal mental health can be achieved through extensive examination of cognitive and affective functioning. The philosophy that underlies this helping tradition is that problem etiology is associated with separate mental or physical processes. These processes are often not considered in an integrated manner. In addition, most Western helping practices stop at the mental and/or physical boundary of human existence. Often ignored in Western psychological thought and practice is that domain considered to transcend the mental and the physical. As previously discussed, this is the realm of spirituality. Within this realm, the mental and the physical become interconnected and part of a larger cosmic whole. Most Western helpers are trained to offer their services in a manner that generally ignores or discounts these notions of spirituality.

Within the universal shamanic tradition, however, the spiritual aspect of life is assumed and provides the impetus for helping strategies. The concept of the psychospiritual domain of human existence is highly valued and provides the basis for the relationship between mental and physical health and well-being. Helpers within this tradition are always trained to intervene at some spiritual level to relieve the stress surrounding issues that affect body, mind, and spirit.

Active Versus Passive Helping Role

A final feature that appears to distinguish these two traditions is the role that the helper assumes during the helping process itself. In the Western tradition, as a general rule, helpers tend to assume a somewhat passive role during the intervention process. Helping is often predicated on the notion that clients hold within themselves the potential to bring about beneficial change. Therefore, helpers usually act as facilitators for, rather than instigators of, client change. In a general sense, the role of the Western helper is to provide the necessary and sufficient conditions in which the client can develop personal insight and motivation for attitudinal or behavioral change. Developing such insight or motivation may require a long-term relationship between helper and client. The helping relationship can be characterized as an equal partnership between the helper and the person in need of assistance, in which each uniquely contributes to client change.

However, within the universal shamanic tradition, helpers tend to assume a much more active role in the intervention process. Significantly, the entire helping process appears to be built on the notion that clients have problems or issues that are often beyond their control. Therefore, helpers generally assume the total responsibility for instigating client change. Clients are rarely expected to be able to "discover" answers within themselves; rather, they are often given specific, solution-oriented advice by the helper. Within this tradition it becomes evident that helpers play an active role in the process of problem identification and resolution. Because they provide the solution to client problems, the helping process may often be of shorter duration. Because the power to effect change rests primarily with the helper, the relationship between the two individuals is often not egalitarian.

Although there are significant differences in the cosmological nature of the two helping traditions, it is apparent that they share some important characteristics. These characteristics include similarities in the role of the helper and perceptions of the helper held by the person in need of help.

Helper as "Expert"

In both Western psychology and the universal shamanic tradition, the helper can be considered an "expert" within the community. Helpers in both traditions present themselves to people in need as specialists who have experience in dealing with the presenting issues. Whether he or she is a counseling professional in New York City or a *mudang* in Korea, the helper has received some specialized training that has included some type of supervised apprenticeship. Considered in a broad sense, this training and apprenticeship consists of key elements in each tradition. First, helpers in both traditions seem to engage in some process for developing self-knowledge. Such knowledge of self forms a necessary bridge for connecting with other people. Second, implicit in the training of each tradition is the importance of developing both objectivity and insight regarding client concerns. Acquiring the skill to hold oneself separately from a person in need and to assess his or her presenting issue in a compassionate or empathic manner appears to be an important aspect of training in both traditions. This objectivity and "clinical" insight then allows the helper to assist the person in need in defining the present problem or issue and intervening accordingly. This training and apprenticeship, therefore, also allows for the development of helping skills that then set individuals apart from the rest of their community. These individuals are considered to be the ones who have the skills to help alleviate life stressors and enhance well-being.

Helper as Primary Instrument of Change

In both traditions the intervention strategy includes the healer's use of himself or herself as a primary instrument for change on behalf of the person in need (i.e., the "client"). In both the shamanic and Western helping traditions, the helper forms some type of therapeutic alliance with the "client." This alliance is characterized by a degree of commitment on the part of the helper to challenge the issues that confront the person in need. In the universal shamanic tradition, this might entail the helper's undertaking a "spirit journey" on behalf of a person. In the Western psychological tradition, this might be an attempt on the part of the helper to "be there" for a client through the means of active listening, empathic understanding, and unconditional positive regard.

Belief in the Power of the Helper

A final similarity between these two traditions is the fact that successful practice rests on the assumption that the person in need of assistance believes in the power of the helper. In other words, "clients" must have an inherent faith that the helping process will benefit them (Frank, 1961). In both traditions, therefore, the helper is empowered because the person in need of help believes that change is possible and expects to change.

It is apparent that for centuries "counseling" or other forms of mental health intervention have taken place under many different names throughout the world. The helping tradition appears to be universal in its nature and seems to entail a fundamental process. First, an individual in distress seeks help from a person in his or her community who is recognized for having specialized skills. Next, the helper engages in a programmed process aimed at the alleviation of the distress. Although the intent of the process appears universal, there are major cultural distinctions in its content. Whereas some cultures view the helping process from a broad perspective that focuses on the interconnectedness of all aspects of human experience, other cultures view helping from a narrower perspective, choosing to emphasize a disconnected approach to addressing human experience. It is important to note, however, that both helping processes can be valid.

IMPLICATIONS OF THE
UNIVERSAL SHAMANIC TRADITION FOR
CONTEMPORARY MULTICULTURAL COUNSELING

With the growing impact of cultural diversity in contemporary American society, it is incumbent upon counseling professionals to understand all of the dynamics that shape the development of their clients. Culturally responsive counseling strategies and techniques must be predicated on an understanding of cultural dynamics and their crucial role in fostering optimal mental health. This is especially true for the growing number of clients from culturally diverse backgrounds who will be entering counseling in the coming years. Given this, counseling professionals need to find ways to incorporate cultural dynamics into the helping process (Lee, 1991).

Within the context of this chapter, psychospiritual influences in traditional helping may need to be considered as important aspects of intervention with clients from many cultural backgrounds. Within many cultural groups, there is often little distinction made between spiritual existence and secular life. The philosophical tenets inherent in spiritual beliefs influence all aspects of human development and interaction. Therefore, in many cultures the psychospiritual domain of personality is always preeminent in helping practices. Within the universal shamanic tradition, religious and/or spiritual leaders have often been expected not only to provide for spiritual needs but also to offer guidance for physical and emotional concerns.

Sue, Arredondo, and McDavis (1992) outlined a set of competencies and standards for multicultural counseling. These detail attitudes, knowledge, and skills necessary for culturally responsive counseling. One intervention strategy pertaining to attitudes and beliefs stresses counselor respect for client's religious and/or spiritual beliefs as well as respect for indigenous helping practices and intrinsic help-giving networks. Another strategy emphasizes the importance of counselor knowledge of indigenous helping resources available within a community. Out of this respect and knowledge, therefore, should come a willingness to seek consultation with traditional healers and religious/spiritual leaders and practitioners when appropriate.

Guidelines for Developing Consultative Relationships With Traditional Healers

In working with clients from diverse cultural backgrounds, contemporary counseling professionals are confronted with a variety of beliefs about health and well-being. For many of these clients, a central assumption of these beliefs may include the concept of an individual from their community who has the power and wisdom to alleviate distress. Unlike the counseling professional, however, this person may have a strong link to the historical and cultural worldview of the client and often represents a tradition with centuries of cultural credibility.

Successful mental health intervention by counseling professionals who are from outside of a culturally diverse community may rest upon the ability to locate such individuals and to incorporate their healing practices for the benefit of clients. This would necessitate consulting, as appropriate, with those individuals who practice traditional healing methods. Richardson (1991), in writing about using the indigenous resources of the African American church for the benefit of Black clients, for example, provides an excellent framework for understanding and developing consultative relationships with traditional healers:

- Begin by encouraging a client to explore his or her worldview and belief system. As with all counseling, a client should be invited to tell his or her story. During this process, a counselor should determine the importance of indigenous helping methods to a client's well-being. As a part of this, explore with a client the role that a traditional healer may play in his or her life. These traditional healers may range from shamans or fortunetellers to religious leaders (e.g., imams, ministers, priests, rabbis).
- This cultural storytelling should serve the purpose of validating the client's belief system.
- As part of the cultural exploration with a client, it is important for a counselor to suspend his or her own cultural beliefs. This may be particularly important with respect to a client's belief in the role and function of traditional healers. Cultural relativism requires that counseling professionals acknowledge and respect beliefs that differ from their own, but not that they necessarily subscribe to these beliefs.
- During the course of counseling, if it becomes apparent that the client may benefit from the services of a traditional healer, it may be necessary for a counselor to rely on the client to locate the appropriate helping source. Such healers may be well known within their own communities, but they may be difficult for someone outside of the community to find.
- When the traditional helper has been located, an exchange of information must take place. A counselor must be ready to explain his or her role and function as a helping professional. Likewise, he or she must be willing to learn about the roles and functions of the healer. A counselor should be prepared to appreciate the skill of a traditional healer even if he or she does not agree with a healer's interpretation of underlying factors that contribute to a client's issues, or why traditional helping practices work.
- A counselor must be willing to form a working partnership with a traditional healer, if necessary. As with all consultative relationships, the goal is to help the client. An integral part of such a relationship should be the establishment of treatment boundaries that respect both Western psychological traditions and the universal shamanic tradition.
- As part of the working partnership with a traditional healer, it might be appropriate or even necessary to observe a healer in ceremonial activities or practices that are engaged in for the benefit of a client. Observation of such activities or practices may afford a counselor a greater understanding of the worldview of the client.
- In order to strengthen professional ties and enhance credibility within culturally diverse communities, it might be important to consider developing a referral system with traditional healers. Then a counselor could, when necessary, refer clients to receive help that was rooted in cultural traditions. An important aspect to such a system should be accepting referrals from healers as well. This would indicate an acknowledgment of and respect for indigenous healing networks prevalent in many communities.

LESSONS FROM TRADITIONAL HEALERS:
THE LEGACY OF ANCIENT WISDOM FOR
CONTEMPORARY COUNSELING PRACTICE

As cultural diversity becomes a greater fact of life in American society, it is evident that counseling theory and practice is undergoing a major transformation. Pedersen (1991) suggested that multiculturalism has become the fourth theoretical force in counseling. Implicit in considering counseling theory from diverse perspectives is the notion that counseling practice must become inclusive of many worldviews and cultural beliefs.

The universal shamanic tradition appears to offer much that could expand the scope of contemporary counseling practice in a culturally diverse society. Counselors can learn important lessons from the ancient wisdom of traditional healers to improve their own practice as helpers.

A Transpersonal Approach
to Theory and Practice

As was discussed earlier, in the universal shamanic tradition, healers adopt a holistic approach to helping that stresses the interconnectedness of mind, body, and spirit with larger cosmic forces. This interconnectedness is the basis of the cosmology of many groups of people. An important lesson to be learned from traditional healers, therefore, is that counselors may need to adopt a transpersonal approach to theory and practice. Such an approach is both proactive and reactive and works with the whole person in terms of body, mind, emotions, and spirit in the context of the person's total environment (Peterson & Nisenholz, 1990). Adopting a fully holistic perspective such as that embodied in the universal shamanic tradition and the transpersonal approach may be a necessary philosophical transition for counseling professionals to make.

In attempting to offer services to clients who come from cultures in which such interconnectedness is valued, it is imperative that such a holistic approach be considered. Multicultural counseling practice, in particular, will be enhanced if the influence of the psychospiritual domain of personality is given greater credence as a dynamic in the helping process. Indeed, the success of the counseling relationship may rest on the ability to acknowledge and work from this perspective.

Expanded Notions of Helping

Pedersen (1987) admonished the counseling profession to be wary of assumptions that reflect a Western cultural bias in counseling theory and practice. Among these is an assumption that indigenous models of helping should be discounted because they are primitive, whereas counseling, in a Western context, is highly prized because it is "state of the art." A related assumption is that Western counselors know everything there is to know about helping because of this "state-of-the-art" status.

However, the belief held by many groups of people in the power of traditional healers to relieve distress calls into question these assumptions. The centuries-old traditional wisdom inherent in traditional healing practices makes it necessary to expand on ideas that counseling professionals hold about the nature of helping. Traditional healers teach counseling professionals that counseling, as practiced in the West, is only one way to help people cope with psychological distress or behavioral deviance. As clients from increasingly diverse cultural backgrounds enter counseling, it is perhaps necessary to reassess where counseling fits in a universal helping paradigm.

SUMMARY

Individuals experience stress that interferes with normal functioning in every culture. In many instances, they seek help outside of their families to cope with this stress. The helper therefore stands ready to bring a body of knowledge to bear on alleviating the stress. In the Western world, these helpers are referred to as counseling professionals. In other parts of the world they are generally considered to be "healers." Although on the surface these two types of helpers appear to be very different, they have much in common. In fact, in many ways, traditional healers can be considered "psychologists" or "counselors," but instead of calling on Freud or Rogers, they call on spirits or deities from a cultural past.

It is important, therefore, that counseling professionals trained in the traditions of Western psychology understand the importance of cultural relativism in the validity of helping resources. This is particularly important when working with clients who come from cultures in which the helping traditions emphasize the importance of the healer.

In developing the awareness, knowledge, and skills that promote culturally responsive mental health intervention, it is important for counseling professionals to appreciate the debt that they owe to traditional healers. Further, it is critical to understand the place of contemporary counseling within the universal shamanic tradition. Counselors must remember that within the context of this tradition they are, in reality, modern-day shamans.

REFERENCES

Allport, G. (1950). *The individual and his religion: A psychological interpretation.* New York: Macmillan.

Assagioli, R. (1991). *Transpersonal development: The dimension beyond psychosynthesis.* London: Crucible.

Batson, C. D., & Ventis, W. L. (1982). *The religious experience.* New York: Oxford University Press.

Boulet, S. S. (1989). *Shaman: The paintings of Susan Seddon Boulet.* San Francisco: Pomegranate Artbooks.

Conn, W. (Ed.). (1978). *Conversion: Perspectives in personal social transformation.* New York: Alba House.

Conn, W. (Ed.). (1981). *Conscious development and self-transcendence.* Birmingham, AL: Religious Education Press.

Education and Training Committee of Division 17. (1984). *What is a counseling psychologist?* Washington, DC: American Psychological Association.

Eliade, M. (1964). *Shamanism: Archaic techniques of ecstasy.* New York: Pantheon.

Fran, J. (1977). Nature and the function of belief systems: Humanism and transcendental religion. *American Psychologist, 32,* 555-559.

Frank, J. D. (1961). *Persuasion and healing.* Baltimore, MD: Johns Hopkins University Press.

Freud, S. (1955). Beyond the pleasure principle. In S. Strachey & A. Freud (Eds.), *The standard edition of the complete psychological works of Sigmund Freud* (Vol. 28, pp. 73-104). London: Hogarth. (Original work published 1920)

Hall, C. S., & Lindzey, G. (1970). *Theories of personality.* (2nd ed.). New York: John Wiley.

Harner, M. (1990). *The way of the shaman.* San Francisco: Harper & Row.

Hilgard, E. R. (1948). *Theories of learning.* Englewood Cliffs, NJ: Prentice Hall.

Idowu, A. I. (1992). The Oshun festival: An African traditional religious healing process. *Counseling and Values, 36,* 192-200.

Jung, C. (1933). *Modern man in search of a soul.* New York: Harcourt Brace.

Kattsoff, L. (1953). *Elements of philosophy.* New York: Ronald Press.

Lee, C. C. (1991). Cultural dynamics: Their importance in multicultural counseling. In C. C. Lee & B. L. Richardson (Eds.), *Multicultural issues in counseling: New approaches to diversity* (pp. 11-17). Alexandria, VA: American Counseling Association.

Lee, C. C., Oh, M. Y., & Mountcastle, A. R. (1992). Indigenous models of helping in nonwestern countries: Implications for multicultural counseling. *Journal of Multicultural Counseling and Development, 20,* 3-10.

Maslow, A. (1964). *Religion, values, and peak experiences.* New York: Viking.

May, R. (1969). *Existential psychology.* New York: Random House.

Mbiti, J. S. (1988). *African religions and philosophy.* London: Heinemann.

Ornstein, R. E. (1972). *The psychology of consciousness.* New York: Penguin.

Pedersen, P. (1987). Ten frequent assumptions of cultural bias in counseling. *Journal of Multicultural Counseling and Development, 15,* 16-24.

Pedersen, P. B. (Ed.). (1991). Multiculturalism as a fourth force in counseling [Special issue]. *Journal of Multicultural Counseling and Development, 70*(1).

Perls, F. S. (1947). *Ego, hunger, and aggression.* New York: Random House.

Peterson, J. V., & Nisenholz, B. (1990, March). *A comparison of transpersonal, holistic, and other major counseling theories.* Paper presented at the annual meeting of the American Holistic Counselors' Association, Cincinnati, OH.

Richardson, B. L. (1991). Utilizing the resources of the African American church: Strategies for counseling professionals. In C. C. Lee & B. L. Richardson (Eds.), *Multicultural issues in counseling: New approaches to diversity* (pp. 65-75). Alexandria, VA: American Counseling Association.

Sellner, E. (1990). *Mentoring: The ministry of spiritual kinship.* Notre Dame, IN: Ave Maria.

Skinner, B. F. (1953). *Science and human behavior.* New York: Macmillan.

Sue, D. W., Arredondo, P., & McDavis, R. J. (1992). Multicultural counseling competencies and standards: A call to the profession. *Journal of Counseling and Development, 70,* 477-486.

Sue, D. W., & Sue, D. (1977). Barriers to effective cross-cultural counseling. *Journal of Counseling Psychology, 5,* 420-429.

Torrey, E. F. (1986). *Witchdoctors and psychiatrists: The common roots of psychotherapy and its future.* New York: Harper & Row.

Vontress, C. E. (1991). Traditional healing in Africa: Implications for cross-cultural counseling. *Journal of Counseling and Development, 70,* 242-249.

Zukav, G. (1989). *The seat of the soul.* New York: Simon & Schuster.

22

The Breakdown of Authority

Implications for Counseling
Young African American Males

CLEMMONT E. VONTRESS

HUMANS TUMBLE HELPLESSLY into a ready-made world controlled by preceding generations. Having somebody on the scene to care for and instruct them in the ways of the group is basic to their survival (Degler, 1991). During dependency, they submit to the authority of adults who prepare them for future roles. Although there is an innate need for them to be free of external restraints, during their lifetime most of them learn that they must relinquish some personal freedoms in order to achieve greater goals (Doob, 1983). Among these are the security, fellowship, and fulfillment that come from living in a group (Neubauer & Neubauer, 1990). As Ollman (1971) pointed out, people who feel alone and afraid often yearn for direction from those they perceive to be more powerful and knowledgeable than they. However, there comes a time when authority figures must step aside for younger and stronger people to replace them (Sennett, 1980). They are most comfortable doing so when they feel that the replacements are qualified to continue the work that must be done in the best interest of the group.

Because of the historical events that have been triggered by individuals and groups refusing to submit to the will of others, authority is a concept that has been a source of interest to writers for many centuries. For example, Christ is often perceived to have been a revolutionist who refused to obey the authority of the Roman state. In the 16th century, Martin Luther resisted the authority of the Church and started a new religious movement. During the civil rights struggle of the 1950s and 1960s, African Americans challenged traditional authority that historically had denied them equal opportunity. According to Gergen (1991) and Harris (1976), authority is questioned today as never before. Institutions are no longer respected just because they are institutions. The family, school, church, and state are under attack. Individual authority figures such as parents, physicians, psychiatrists, economists, and professors are overtly disrespected and challenged. Alternative perspectives and explanations are proposed and submitted for equal validation (Gergen, 1991).

The purpose of this chapter is to (a) define authority, (b) describe its importance to the socialization process, (c) indicate the sources of authority that contribute to socialization, (d) posit reasons for the breakdown of authority among young African American males, and (e) discuss the implications of the breakdown for counseling young Blacks.

AUTHORITY DEFINED

Authority is a construct that defines command-obedience relations between people. According to Wrong (1988), it is successful ordering or forbidding, and anyone who is regularly obeyed is an authority. Significantly important to understanding human behavior, authority is closely related to power, as Benn (1967), Centerwall (1992), Peters (1960), Diggins (1981), and McIntosh (1969) explained. Wrong (1988) posited four types of power: (a) force, (b) manipulation, (c) persuasion, and (d) authority. *Force* refers to the creation of physical obstacles that restrict the freedom of a subject and that may inflict pain, injury, or death. *Manipulation* is any intended and productive effort to influence others by subterfuge to respond in a given way. *Persuasion* suggests one individual presenting arguments to another, who after reflection, accepts the reasoning of the first as the basis for personal action. *Authority* is the untested acceptance of the judgment of one or more individuals.

Wrong (1988) discussed five subtypes of authority: (a) coercive, (b) induced, (c) legitimate, (d) competent, and (e) personal. In the case of coercive authority, one or more individuals obtain compliance from another or others by threatening to use force against them. In order for such an authority to have an effect, the subject must be convinced that the person in whom it resides is capable and willing to use the force. Authority by inducement obtains compliance by rewarding the subject in some way. Legitimate authority is a relationship in which one person by virtue of office or appointment has the power to judge and reassure the subject (Bourricaud, 1969; Sennett, 1980). Competent authority is a power relationship in which subjects are willing to accede to the directives of another out of the belief in that person's superior competence or expertise to decide what is in their best interest. In the case of personal authority, individuals obey authority figures out of the desire to please or serve them because of their personal qualities. This type of authority is sometimes considered to be charismatic authority (Peters, 1960). Individuals generate a faith, following, and submission because of their perceived inherent qualities.

Authority is both individual and collective. According to Benn (1967), the best authority is derived from a compact or covenant whereby each member of society agrees to submit to the will of designated authority figures when it is beneficial to the group. For example, parents, teachers, police, judges, and other powerful people in society derive their mandate from the collectivity to "do their duty." They perform the assigned roles most effectively when subjects accept and submit willingly to their directives. The breakdown of authority refers to the progressive diminution of the force of traditional authority figures and systems to exert control over the comportment of individuals and groups.

AUTHORITY AND SOCIALIZATION

When individuals are born, they are socialized by members of their community to fit into the social order. It is in everybody's best interest that newcomers embody the collective identity of the group (Wilson, 1987). The embodiment enables recent arrivals to negotiate effectively the environment and to relate harmoniously to their cultural peers (Mucchielli, 1986). In all societies, the agents of socialization train, nurture, love, punish, and reward children for complying with their demands to conform to their expectations (Kilborne & Langness, 1987). They instill in young people the essential knowledge, values, and behaviors requisite for successful membership in the specific human group.

Socialization is holistic. At birth, it is primarily physical. Parents and others who attend children feed, change, bathe, and burp them. Gradually, attendants introduce social controls. They spank, scold, and instruct newcomers in the ways of the group. By responding to the special qualities of children, adults help them to develop an understanding of their individual uniqueness. Consequently children come to perceive their emotional, intellectual, psychological, and social dispositions. From contact with authority figures, they also acquire an intangible self that allows them to transcend the immediate environment and to connect spiritually with departed ancestors, powerful deities, and other inexplicable forces in their lives.

In general, the controls in the lives of children are external. As they mature in atmospheres charged with love, support, threats, rewards, and punishment, the external restraints gradually become internalized (Kilborne & Langness, 1987). The self system enables them to negotiate life with confidence, respect for others, and predictability.

Of course, societies socialize people differently. Authorities and the roles they play are culture specific. For example, in traditional West Africa, departed ancestors in villages are influential authority figures who continue to dictate thoughts, feelings, and behavior of the living from their tombs (Vontress,

1991). Fearful of incurring their wrath, individuals often live an existence more exemplary than that of people whose lives are not influenced by the deceased.

Whether the society is individualistic or collectivistic determines the roles played by authority figures responsible for socializing the young. In traditional collectivistic communities, fathers, uncles, elders, and other adults know each other and collaborate to monitor the behavior of children (Marsal, 1971). In individualistic societies in which parents value privacy and the freedom to rear children as they see fit, people external to individual nuclear families generally do not invade the sanctity of these units.

SOURCES OF AUTHORITY

The primary source of authority responsible for socializing people is the human group itself. The collectivity may be the neighborhood, community, village, city, state, or nation. It is in the interest of the group that young people be prepared to fit in with the previous generations. At birth, individuals become a part of that collectivity, which usually acts as one body to direct their behavior, thoughts, attitudes, and values directly or indirectly (Locke, 1947). In general, the group, by tradition, law, or helplessness, delegates or relinquishes its authority to socialize the young to various subgroups. Some of these are (a) the family, (b) school, (c) church, (d) government, and (e) celebrities.

The Family

Throughout human history, the family has been the primary vehicle for socializing the young. Hsu (1983) pointed out that it is the arena in which individuals develop feelings about and perceptions of themselves, others, and the world around them. Society cannot replace the family, no matter how good other institutions may be (Bennett, 1987). The externalized controls imposed by parents gradually become internalized by children (Mitscherlich, 1970). As children move through life, the dictates of parental authority figures put them in good stead as they relate to other authority figures, not only because of the conscience that they have acquired within the context of love and support, but also because they learn imperceptibly how to relate to other authority figures (Jenkins, 1976; McIntosh, 1969).

Although the family is where children internalize many attitudes and qualities that prepare them to fit into society, perhaps none of them is as important as the ability to feel, understand, and appreciate the feelings and needs of others. This ability suggests constructs such as empathy and sympathy. *Empathy* communicates the idea that people experience other people's inner selves as their own (Katz, 1963). According to Katz (1963), the ability to put oneself in another's shoes is dependent on parental practices. Fathers and mothers who help children to understand how their acts affect others contribute to their children's likelihood as adults to live and work effectively with their fellows.

Sympathy is usually differentiated from *empathy*. For example, Strauss (1964) defined it as the ability of one person to internalize the emotions of another. Clive (1965) pointed out that it is the introjection of the joys and sorrows of others. Katz (1963) indicated that people become deeply involved psychologically with others because they see in them a reflection of themselves. Indeed, sympathy is a deeply felt phenomenon that interconnects humans (Ochanine, 1988). Without empathy and sympathy, people are apt to be callous to the needs and rights of others. They therefore often become threats to interpersonal harmony, which is requisite to the cohesion of the human group.

The School

Next to the family, the school is the most important institution in society. According to Durkheim (1922/1980), each society communicates by official public statements and by its recognitions of heroes, public servants, and historical personalities what traits and characteristics it looks for in the ideal citizen. In large measure, it is this implicit model that is the basis of public education.

Education suggests teaching. What is taught is best taught under the careful eye of a competent authority who knows and insists on the fulfillment of the requirements of the group (Wrong, 1988). It is a tradition for commencement speakers to implore high school and college graduates to assume responsible roles in society. Their enthusiastic send-off is based on the assumption that the agents of educational institutions have prepared students to meet the expectations of the community, state, and nation (Lasch, 1984). Youth cannot be prepared to meet the expectations of the group unless the agents of the school have the authority to exact from their charges academic, social, and moral behaviors and values prerequisite to responsible membership in the social order.

Education and authority are inseparable. By establishing certification requirements for teachers, counselors, administrators, and other school agents, the community passes on the authority to teach the children under their care the ways of the group. The extent to which they carry out the dictates of the community is the extent to which the social order functions as envisioned by the group. If the school is remiss in its responsibility to educate each generation, citizens become progressively unable to fit into the social order as expected. If students drop out of school before they complete the established curriculum or if they challenge the academic and moral authority of their teachers, they simultaneously alienate themselves from the rest of society and very often establish enduring conflicting relationships with that society. As people who prematurely terminate society's orientation for ethical membership, they, as parents, are apt to rear children who imitate them, setting in motion a perpetual and worsening trend (Sheaffer, 1988).

The Church

According to Jaynes (1976), modern religion looks to a "higher authority" in an extended heaven, where presumably God or the gods reside. The church, temple, or mosque is where people assemble when they wish to get in touch with the authority. In prophetic religions, it is important for worshipers to "hear the word of God" as a medium of contact with the divine (Alston, 1972). The Word communicated through religious authority figures such as preachers, priests, and rabbis is a powerful moral force in the lives of believers (Jaynes, 1976). For regular churchgoers, sermons based on the holy scriptures amount to a moral code sanctioned by God (Alston, 1972). Sheaffer (1988) declared that people who internalize the code demonstrate love and consideration for their fellows that is not evident in individuals whose lives are not influenced by direct religious instruction.

Religion and religious practices are powerful forces in life because they are based in large part on the fear of death (Cassirer, 1972). The tacit collective fear brings people together in the House of God so that they can express reverence for the Almighty and ask for special dispensation when needed (Theunissen, 1984). Simultaneously, they enjoy the fellowship of "all God's Children" who are in the same existential fix. Although none of us will get out of life alive, we can all be with and help one another while we are in the world.

The Government

In the United States, ultimate authority belongs to the people who decide their system of government and who governs them. Although the authority is vested in governors, it must be acknowledged by the governed (Jenkins, 1976). People are not inclined to obey authority unless they feel that it is legitimate (Sennett, 1980). It is also important that citizens feel that laws are applied equally to all races and ethnic groups. Failure of the government to ensure equal opportunity in the application of laws runs the risk of causing the whole criminal justice system to collapse out of disrespect and hostility. Why should individuals subordinate themselves to the will of the government and its agents unless they can be assured of fair play and equal justice? (Groat, 1976).

People also lose faith in the government when public officials are exposed as corrupt and dishonest (Nisbet, 1976). If the perception of governmental deception is widespread, there is danger that law and order of the whole society will be undermined. Why should people abide by the rules when their officials ignore the laws they themselves enact? A government governs best when it has the patriotic support of all of its people. The support constitutes a spiritual cement that unifies people. Unless there is some way to nourish the shared experiences of Americans, there may be little or nothing to bridge the differences that separate us. Without that bridge, it is apt to become progressively more difficult to realize and maintain a collective authority, which is the embodiment of government (Christian, 1977).

Celebrities

The United States has become a celebrity-driven society. Business and industry use movie stars, sports figures, politicians, and entertainers to promote their goods and services. These and other celebrities access the airways and exert a nonstop influence on young people, who are often fascinated only by a Madison Avenue image, not the real person behind the image. In some cases, the images of celebrities continue to influence people long after the demise of the charismatic authorities. A case in point is Elvis Presley, whose image significantly influences millions of people around the world.

Many people respond to celebrities as if they were larger than life. They identify with their power, glamour, talent, success, money, and public acclaim. Because of the charismatic authority projected on-screen, onstage, or in person, they want to submit to them and be like them (Peters, 1960). They surrender their will to them because they identify with their perceived personal qualities (Wrong, 1988). Obviously, individuals who are so idolized exert inordinate influence over others. Citizens are usually pleased when the influence is positive and constructive to the well-being of the social order; they are concerned when it is negative and dangerous to the harmony of the group. In U.S. society, authoritative images and messages compete for devotees in the same communities. Whether individuals are influenced by celebrity "pitches" depends on the force of the charismatic authority and the audience's potential for seduction. The likelihood of one's being seduced by the presence, presentation, and endorsement of celebrities is determined by such factors as one's educational level, emotional maturity, and outlook on life.

AUTHORITY IN THE
AFRICAN AMERICAN COMMUNITY

According to West (1993), de Tocqueville (1851), Rushing, Ritter, and Burton (1992), and Massey and Denton (1993), a profound hatred of African Americans is the centerpiece of American civilization. It is reflected in the long years of slavery, lynchings, legal segregation, and the continued struggle to achieve rights and opportunities other Americans take for granted. From slavery days to the present, White Americans have refused to accept Black Americans as a part of their community (Hacker, 1992). The refusal has resulted in the development of two nations, one Black and one White, separate and unequal. At least one third of African Americans live under conditions of extreme racial segregation (Massey & Denton, 1993). The complex of ideas and attitudes toward Blacks is transformed into a set of policies and rules, traditional practices, and informal networks that operate in major institutions (politics, economics, and education) to keep them "in their place" (Majors & Billson, 1992). Denied access to the community to which they have contributed their blood, sweat, and tears, many Blacks express overt hostility toward those who reject and oppress them. Those who do so are in turn criticized by Whites as being "un-American" for declaring hatred of them. It is clear that the Black question divides the United States in the middle of the 20th century, as slavery did in the middle of the 19th century (Fohlen, 1965). Race significantly affects all aspects of the Black person's life (Rushing et al., 1992). It contributes to the breakdown of authority in the African American community.

The Family

Throughout history, the Black family has been affected directly by racism. During nearly 300 years of slavery, individual slaveowners exerted complete authority over the slave family (Fohlen, 1965). In case owners were unavailable to control the slaves they owned, any other White person was expected to act on their behalf. After the passage of the Emancipation Act of 1863, White landowners continued to control the lives of their Black sharecroppers. As individuals who imposed unilateral external controls on African Americans, they were ipso facto the source of internal restraints that Blacks imposed on themselves. Even though most African Americans have escaped the farms on which they worked for others, a large segment of them have not been able to elude the economic hardships that contribute to the dysfunction of their families (Gaudin, Polansky, Kilpatrick, & Shilton, 1993).

Perhaps nothing is more responsible for the breakdown of authority in Black families than the psychological castration of Black males (Majors & Billson, 1992). They are rendered impotent in the economic, political, and social arenas that Whites have dominated historically. No matter how exemplary their behavior, most of them cannot measure up to the standards set by White men. Many become despondent, depressed, and bitter fathers from whom their children derive superegos (Gay, 1988). According to Freud (Chein, 1972), the formation of the superego or conscience depends largely on identification. Children identify with their parents, who unconsciously internalize the values, attitudes, and expectations of the society at large. Because the society is shot through with pernicious racism, Black children internalize the dominant racial group's attitude toward African Americans. If White people are repelled by Black skin, kinky hair, big lips, and the recognition that Blacks were once the slaves of their ancestors, then Blacks unconsciously appropriate the same repulsion. They hate themselves for being Black. For example, in families in which there is a wide range of skin color among children, it is not unusual for light-skinned children to tease their darker skinned siblings about being "Black." In some cases, parents reveal by their behavior that they prefer their lighter skinned children over the darker ones. Darker skinned children growing up in such families often hate themselves and those who remind them of their color.

Historical hostility is also a contributing factor to the breakdown of authority in the Black family. It is the hatred for Whites who abducted Africans from their native continent, forced them into nearly three centuries of slavery, and reluctantly released them to conditions that they have been protesting to this day. Black Americans were traumatized so much by these experiences that few have been able to forgive and forget the people who subjected them to these horrors. Although members of the middle class in the mainstream workplace mask overt hatred, they often pay a terrible price for their psychological cover-up. Ulcers, drug abuse, and a host of psychosomatic problems rob them of fulfillment in life. Instead of overtly expressing hostility toward people who brutalized their ancestors and encumber their own existence, they are apt to internalize their anger.

Although lower class Blacks also try to conceal their hatred for Whites, they are more inclined to ventilate the hostility on people closest to them: family members, friends, strangers passing alongside them in cars, and other opportunistic targets. Historical hostility is a cultural phenomenon. It is an important part of the traumatic Black experience in the United States. Because the trauma is ongoing, it is transmitted from one generation to another. Few people who are continually traumatized by the dominant racial group are disposed to affiliate psychologically with that group.

Historical hostility, self-hatred, economic hardships, and stressed single mothers deprived of any real long-term adult love and affection combine to produce family environments contaminated with negative emotions that rob children of a sense of being wanted and loved (Gaudin et al., 1993). Youngsters from such homes are also apt to feel alienated. That is, they easily get the impression that they are not a part of the family. There is a feeling of disconnection between themselves and the rest of the world—their parents (Murchland, 1971). As they mature, the alienation is likely to extend to society at large, which has little meaning to them because it has failed to confirm their identity and existence. According to Mucchielli (1986), a large number of alienated people go through life trying to "get even," striking back at an amorphous "them." Some turn the hatred for others inward and commit themselves to a course of self-destruction by abusing drugs, leading reckless lives, and inflicting direct physical harm on themselves and others.

In lower class African American communities, the seeds of hostility and violence are sowed in economically hard-pressed single-parent families and cultivated in a society in which most Whites are unable or unwilling to understand the root causes of the alarming homicide rate in urban areas. Dupont (1993), Mucchielli (1986), Mercy (1993), and Laporte (1993) are among writers who have documented the extent of violence in Black communities. For those between the ages of 15 and 34, homicide is the primary cause of death. The rate is 11 times that of Whites in the same age group. In 1992, 2,829 minors were arrested for murder (Laporte, 1993), and no abatement of the carnage is

in sight. Undoubtedly, the social breakdown in African American neighborhoods is related to racism and its wide-ranging effects on the lives of their
inhabitants, especially young men who are dispirited by their inability "to be
a man" in a society that has historically put a lot of stock in "each man's
carrying his weight." Primary in carrying one's own weight is being able to
look after one's family. Denied economic parity, disillusioned Black men in
turn are ambivalent about socializing their children to aspire to and compete
in a society that rejects them because of their race.

The School

The home and the school have always been connected. Teachers act in
loco parentis during school hours. Parents relinquish their socialization roles
to agents of the school. The authority that parents exercise over their children
is transferred to the school. Children who obey their parents at home are also
the ones who obey their teachers at school, because authority is generalizable,
as Rigby (1986) pointed out. The reasons for the breakdown of authority in
the family are the same as those in the school. Children leave home and enter
school burdened with low-grade psychological depression, feelings of personal
worthlessness, social despair, and rage (Hacker, 1992; West, 1993), which keep
them "on edge" during the day and distract them in the classroom.

The places where young Blacks congregate have become war zones in urban areas (Laporte, 1993). Each day, over 270,000 pistols are introduced into
public schools in the United States, and gangs terrorize students who follow
the rules of the system. The lower class tradition of machismo, which frequently defines masculinity as brute force, causes achievement to be scorned
by many males as a feminine trait, because achievers are perceived to be tolerant of authority, whereas "real men" are supposed to be "wild" and antiestablishment. Students espousing the latter view of themselves resent academic
achievement. They display their resentment by cutting classes, committing
petty vandalism, slashing tires, breaking windows, harassing "White-acting"
students, and other actions taken to challenge the authority of those in charge.

Schools in deprived urban communities are in a "state of war with their
students," as Sheaffer (1988, p. 62) pointed out. Unfortunately, young people
hostile to authority appear to be winning the war. Children as young as 9 and
10 use the school as a marketplace to sell drugs, not to learn. Many of the
youngsters are filled with chronic rage, which makes them indifferent to learning, the authority of their parents and teachers, and life itself (Hacker, 1992).
As they mature, they strive to do whatever is necessary to offset an externally
imposed negative self-image (Majors & Billson, 1992). Some strike a "cool"
pose, designed to communicate to observers that they are sure of themselves
and therefore know where they are going in life. Majors and Billson (1992)
explained that the pose is a strategy for coping with the strain of living in a
racist society and their resulting rage that must be suppressed every day. In
order to avoid thinking about their future, they seek one activity after another

without completing any one of them. Overwhelmed by the mayhem that disrupts many schools, an increasing number of teachers trained to teach middle-class students have resigned themselves to sit out each day, afraid to try to restore their classrooms to conducive learning environments.

The Church

Sheaffer (1988) posited that every society has its own set of beliefs, assumptions, and practices, which are collectively referred to as its morality. A society's morality influences the behavior of its people and is responsible for shaping its way of life. The same observation can be made about a racial enclave in the society, especially if members of the group in question are cut off from participating as equals in the community of the larger group. Historically, Blacks have been rejected as full participatory members of the White community. The rejection created a moral dilemma for them. In due course, they established the Black church in order to help themselves sort out the contradictions in the religion that Whites reluctantly allowed them to practice.

From the beginning, the Black church was the centerpiece of a carefully concealed revolutionary movement. It was, as Kilborne and Langness (1987) argued, a cultural institution designed to satisfy a need. During slavery, the need of Africans was to liberate themselves from perpetual and barbaric bondage. Because the church was the only place slaveowners would let them assemble, they used the White man's religion to plot their liberation. Many of the spirituals sung today in Black churches are disguised messages detailing routes slaves used to escape to freedom (Hines & Boyd-Franklin, 1982).

During the civil rights movement, the church continued to be the institution committed to the liberation of African Americans from the oppression of racism. It was a place where Blacks of all ages went on Sunday morning to hear "The Word," and as Alston (1972) described it, the minister's role was that of a messenger of God. The message usually related to the oppression that Blacks endured at the hands of Whites. Dr. Martin Luther King Jr., and other ministers were so effective carrying the message to their people that Blacks were galvanized to pressure the local, state, and federal governments to "let my people go!"

Once the civil rights legislation of the 1960s and 1970s was passed, the demographics of church attendance in the Black urban community changed progressively. The church congregation was no longer a cross section of the community, but was composed mainly of Black women, who listened attentively to preachers advising them on how to get the men in their lives to "do the right thing." Black children, especially males, started "sleeping in" on Sunday morning, instead of going to church with their mothers. Even though church attendance plummeted for all young people during the 1960s and 1970s, the decline was especially acute in the lower class Black community (U.S. Bureau of the Census, 1993). The decline is important to recognize because there is a perceived relationship between religion and religious practices and human conduct (Alston, 1972). The voice carries authority (Jaynes, 1976). The Black preacher's voice is no longer heard by a large segment of lower class African American youth on Sunday morning, a fact that may help to explain the rise of irresponsible behavior in many parts of the Black community.

The Government

Ultimate authority rests with the people, who elect their governors (Jenkins, 1976). Elected officials legislate laws designed to ensure civil association. They also set up structures for administering the laws and establish procedures for hiring agents of the government. In discussing our democratic system of government, Guinier (1994) pointed out that in a homogeneous society, the interest of the majority and minority is likely to be the same. However, in a heterogeneous nation in which the White majority rejects the Black minority, it is unfair when that majority monopolizes all the power all the time. The laws passed are apt to favor the majority. The administrative structures are generally controlled by members of the majority group. For example, the police, judges, and other agents of the criminal justice system are White or allegiant to the racial majority.

The collective authority on which government is based assumes an equality of the people who submit themselves to the requirements of that government (Marsal, 1971). To many Black Americans, the rules of government are illegitimate, because they believe them to be boundaries and restrictions set by the White majority (Hacker, 1992). A century and a quarter after slavery, White America continues to ask of its Black citizens an extra patience and perseverance that Whites have never required of themselves. In the Black ghetto and to a lesser extent throughout the entire African American community, there is an erosion of faith in the authority of the government, because historically that authority has been used unjustly against people of color. The erosion intensifies when Blacks see TV images of police beating helpless Blacks and hear reports of their killing members of their group without cause. Agents of the government are often seen as extensions of White oppression, and therefore as authorities to oppose. Racism as reflected in the local, state, and federal governments contributes to the breakdown of authority in lower class Black America.

Celebrities

Down through history, African Americans have suffered a great deal (Fohlen, 1965). Despite the great strides that they have made since the civil rights revolution, their daily lives are filled with anxieties from which there is no escape. According to Hacker (1992), they get less sleep and are more likely to be overweight, to develop hypertension, and to suffer from mild depression than any other racial group in society. The more socioeconomically deprived individuals are, the more apt are they to experience these difficulties in life.

It is understandable that Black people, especially the young, identify with African American celebrities who represent achievement, success, power, and sometimes defiance. Identifying with sports figures, musicians, and movie stars enables lower class Blacks, in particular, to live lives remote from the realities of their bleak existence. Gangsta' rappers articulate the deep angry antiestablishment feelings of many young inner-city Black males better than any other individual or group today. Unfortunately, instead of benefiting from the messages explicit in the lyrics that the adolescents find so appealing, federal policy makers lambaste the rappers.

IMPLICATIONS FOR COUNSELING

Young African Americans experience many problems preparing for responsible adulthood in the American society. In large measure, the difficulties are related to the absence of an enduring, supportive, and instructive male authority in their lives. Without such a stable and consistent figure, the boy has no satisfactory male model with whom to identify and to follow into manhood. Usually, he is left only with a series of his mother's boyfriends, whom he resents as intruders in the family (Lidz, 1976). The mother's search for adult love and affection pits her children against her, especially the boys. She "gets no respect" when she tries to discipline them. In acquiring a masculine identity, the boy has to alienate himself from everything that is mother mediated, including abstract adult rules (La Barre, 1980). When he gets to school, he has mostly women teachers and administrators who impose more adult rules. These authorities also threaten the confirmation of his masculinity.

Young Black males are overwhelmed by a world they do not understand. Lacking fathers and grandfathers in their lives, they often feel that their manhood is beyond rescue. Frustrated in adolescence, they want to rush into adulthood; however, they have no real role models to direct them except the ones they see on television and in the movies, and these are "some bad dudes!" The youngsters and the adults they idolize are generally angry, hostile to authority, devoid of empathy for others, and indifferent to academic learning and the rules of society. In a sense, today's ghetto youth are not socialized to live responsibly with others. Their superegos are "stunted" because they have never had adults in their lives who imposed external restraints that could be internalized.

The problems presented by young African Americans cause some counselors to feel that they somehow must do for them what parents, teachers, and other authority figures have been unable to do. Often this commitment sets them up for failure. Clients who have not learned to relate constructively to authority may not find it any easier to relate to counselors, be they men or women. Moreover, counseling requires that clients introspect and self-disclose. Young African Americans are apt to be unable to do either. Introspection requires that the individual look within the self, become cognizant of its many-faceted content, and disclose to another person the perception of that self. This behavior is foreign to people who are ignorant of themselves and therefore unable to tell anybody who they are. Not only is the client a "closed" personality, but he is also apt to be hostile for reasons that he is unable to explain logically. Being closed may be a way of suppressing and concealing his hostility toward the outside world.

Counselors who want to assist in the resocialization of young Black males need to reconsider their role as therapeutic professionals. First, it is recommended that they use group guidance and counseling to instruct, advise, and counsel clients. The purpose of these groups is to socialize and resocialize individuals whose social formation is incomplete or distorted. Many lack the social skills to interact comfortably with others, a fact that may cause them to strike out at people who are different, because they do not know "where they are coming from." Second, it would seem advisable to separate clients by gender. Boys have been socialized primarily by women whose inconsistent, uncertain, and often unreasonable expectations threaten the development of their masculine identity. As a result, many of them exhibit a confused ambivalence toward their female peers. On the one hand, they are sexually attracted to them; on the other, they resent them because African American female adolescents seem to be more sure of themselves and to know how to manage their lives better. In single-gender groups, counselors are able to focus attention specifically on the real feelings of inadequacy that trouble many males. The presence of females usually inhibits frank exploration of these feelings.

Racism is an important concern of African American adolescents. Counselors who concede that it still exists are generally more successful working with them than those who deny its existence. It is important to help them understand that they must develop the strength and courage to continue to become all they can become despite possible racial roadblocks. Examples of other Black Americans who have achieved despite such adversity can be used to encourage them to persevere. In connection with this point, counselors should be agents of change. Instead of counseling clients to alter their perception of reality or behavior to adjust to the system (home, school, workplace, etc.), it may be feasible to get the system or its agents to modify their perception and/or behavior in the interest of the client's adjustment.

Finally, counselors need to concentrate on clients, not on the therapeutic techniques that they use with middle-class clients. The role that they must play to help the Black clients discussed here is unpredictable and therefore does not lend itself neatly to a particular counseling theory. Counselors should do whatever is necessary to rescue their clients from the morass of despair. They must teach, advise, cajole, and implore them to prepare themselves to negotiate a minefield of racism and their own hostility engendered by it. Although there is a great deal of similarity in the problems presented by Black adolescents, there are also many differences. Some clients are more vulnerable than others to the negatives that encumber their existence; some have learned to cope with racism better than others. Counselors expecting a modicum of success with Black adolescent male clients in urban ghettos need to view them as members of five cultures that influence their existence: (a) a universal culture, which makes them like all other human beings; (b) an ecological culture, which forces them to adjust to the physical environment to which others in their geographical zone must adjust; (c) a national culture, which forces on them unconscious beliefs, attitudes, and behaviors that they take for granted; (d) a regional culture, which often differentiates them from people in other parts of the United States; and (e) a racioethnic culture, which results from their isolation from the larger racial group. Despite the problems discussed in this chapter, counselors are more effective when they view their Black clients first as human beings who are molded more by the first four cultural influences than they are by the fact that they are members of the African American community (see Vontress, 1986).

SUMMARY

Authority is a construct that defines command-obedience relationships between people. It suggests power, knowledge, charisma, and control that one person has over another. It is an important part of the human condition. Without it, people cannot survive. Infants need the love and care of their parents until they are able to manage by themselves. By the imposition of controls on children, mothers, fathers, and other caretakers cause the restraints to become internalized. Individuals move through life with inner systems that monitor their behavior to ensure that it does not deviate too much from the expectations of society.

The sources of authority that socialize people are (a) the family, (b) school, (c) church, (d) government, and (e) celebrities. In this chapter the role that each plays in the lives of people is discussed. The argument is made that the authority systems have broken down in the Black community to such an extent that many young males are not able to internalize the usual controls necessary for life in a society of law and order. As adolescents, they strike out at what they perceive to be a hostile and unjust environment. Counselors working with such clients need to consider using group guidance and counseling to help them understand themselves and to relate more effectively to others. It is recommended that groups be segregated by gender, because African American males are generally unable to engage in a frank discussion in the presence of female peers. Racism is also a dominant theme in their lives. Therefore, counselors should help them understand how it affects their lives while also showing them how to succeed despite it. Finally, it is important for counselors to recognize that their clients are not just African American. They are also cultural products of the universe, the Western world, the United States, and the region in which they live. These cultures also influence their development and status in society.

REFERENCES

Alston, W. P. (1972). Religion. In P. Edwards (Ed.), *Encyclopedia of philosophy* (Vol. 7, pp. 140-145). New York: Macmillan.

Benn, S. I. (1967). Authority. In P. Edwards (Ed.), *Encyclopedia of philosophy* (Vol. 1, pp. 215-218). New York: Macmillan.

Bennett, W. J. (1987). The role of the family in the nurture and protection of the young. *American Psychologist, 42*(3), 246-250.

Bourricaud, F. (1969). *Esquisse d'une theorie de l'autorité* [Outline of a theory of authority]. Paris: Librairie Plon.

Cassirer, E. (1972). *An essay on man.* New Haven, CT: Yale University Press.

Centerwall, B. S. (1992). Television and violence: The scale of the problem and where to go from here. *Journal of the American Medical Association, 267*(22), 3059-3063.

Chein, I. (1972). *The science of behavior and the image of man.* New York: Basic Books.

Christian, J. L. (1977). *Philosophy: An introduction to the art of wondering* (2nd ed.). New York: Holt, Rinehart & Winston.

Clive, G. (Ed.). (1965). *The philosophy of Nietzsche.* New York: New American Library.

Degler, C. N. (1991). *In search of human nature: The decline and revival of Darwinism in American social thought.* New York: Oxford University Press.

de Tocqueville, A. (1851). *American institutions and their influence.* New York: Barnes.

Diggins, J. P. (1981). The three faces of authority in American history. In J. P. Diggins & M. E. Kann (Eds.), *The problem of authority in America* (pp. 17-39). Philadelphia: Temple University Press.

Doob, L. W. (1983). *Personality, power, and authority: A view from the behavioral sciences.* Westport, CT.: Greenwood Press.

Dupont, P. (1993). *La bannière étiolée: Voyage sur les traces de Tocqueville* [Faded flag: A trip to follow up de Tocqueville]. Paris: Edition du Seuil.

Durkheim, E. (1980). *Education et sociologie* [Education and sociology]. Paris: Presses Universitaires de France. (Original work published 1922)

Fohlen, C. (1965). *Les noirs aux États-Unis* [Blacks in the United States]. Paris: Presses Universitaires de France.

Gaudin, J. M., Jr., Polansky, N. A., Kilpatrick, A. C., & Shilton, P. (1993). Loneliness, depression, stress, and social supports in neglectful families. *American Journal of Orthopsychiatry, 63*(4), 597-605.

Gay, P. (1988). *Freud: A life for our time.* New York: Norton.

Gergen, K. J. (1991). *The saturated self: Dilemmas of identity in contemporary life.* New York: Basic Books.

Groat, H. T. (1976). Community and conflict in mass society. In A. G. Neal (Ed.), *Violence in animal and human societies* (pp. 49-77). Chicago: Nelson Hall.

Guinier, L. (1994). *The tyranny of the majority.* New York: Free Press.

Hacker, A. (1992). *Two nations: Black and White, separate, hostile, unequal.* New York: Scribner.

Harris, R. B. (1976). *Authority: A philosophical analysis.* University, AL: University of Alabama Press.

Hines, P., & Boyd-Franklin, N. (1982). Black families. In M. McGoldrick, J. K. Pearce, & J. Giordano (Eds.), *Ethnicity and family therapy* (pp. 84-107). New York: Guilford.

Hsu, F. L. K. (1983). *Rugged individualism reconsidered: Essays in psychological anthropology.* Knoxville: University of Tennessee Press.

Jaynes, J. (1976). *The origin of consciousness in the breakdown of the bicameral mind.* Boston: Houghton Mifflin.

Jenkins, I. (1976). Authority: Its nature and locus. In R. B. Harris (Ed.), *Authority: A philosophical analysis* (pp. 25-44). University, AL: The University of Alabama Press.

Katz, R. L. (1963). *Empathy.* New York: Free Press of Glencoe.

Kilborne, B. J., & Langness, L. L. (Eds.). (1987). *Culture and human nature: Theoretical papers of Melford E. Spiro.* Chicago: University of Chicago Press.

La Barre, W. (1980). *Culture in context: Selected writings of Weston La Barre.* Durham, NC: Duke University Press.

Laporte, B. (1993, December 31). États-Unis: Le cancer de la violence urbaine [United States: The cancer of urban violence]. *Le Point*, pp. 26-30.

Lasch, C. (1984). *The minimal self: Psychic survival in troubled times*. New York: Norton.

Lidz, T. (1976). *The person* (rev. ed.). New York: Basic Books.

Locke, J. (1947). *On politics and education*. Roslyn, NJ: Walter J. Black.

Majors, R., & Billson, J. M. (1992). *Cool pose: The dilemmas of Black manhood in America*. New York: Free Press.

Marsal, M. (1971). *L'autorité* [Authority]. Paris: Presses Universitaires de France.

Massey, D. S., & Denton, N. A. (1993). *American apartheid: Segregation and the making of the underclass*. Cambridge, MA: Harvard University Press.

McIntosh, D. (1969). *The foundations of human society*. Chicago: University of Chicago Press.

Mercy, J. A. (1993). Youth violence as a public health problem. *Spectrum, 66*(3), 26-30.

Mitscherlich, A. (1970). *Society without father*. New York: Schocken.

Mucchielli, A. (1986). *L'identité* [Identity]. Paris: Presses Universitaires de France.

Murchland, B. (1971). *The age of alienation*. New York: Random House.

Neubauer, P. B., & Neubauer, A. (1990). *Nature's thumbprint: The new genetics of personality*. New York: Addison-Wesley.

Nisbet, R. (1976). *Twilight of authority*. London: Heinemann.

Ochanine, D. (1988). *La sympathie et ses trois aspects: Harmonie, contrainte, déliverance* [Three aspects of sympathy: Harmony, restraint, release]. Paris: Librarie de Rodstein.

Ollman, B. (1971). *Alienation: Marx's conception of man in capitalist society* (2nd ed.). Cambridge, UK: Cambridge University Press.

Peters, R. (1960). *Authority, responsibility, and education*. New York: Eriksson-Taplinger.

Rigby, K. (1986). Acceptance of authority, self, and others. *Journal of Social Psychology, 126*(4), 493-501.

Rushing, B., Ritter, C., & Burton, P. D. (1992). Race differences in the effects of multiple roles on health: Longitudinal evidence from a national sample of older men. *Journal of Health and Social Behavior, 33*, 126-139.

Sennett, R. (1980). *Authority*. New York: Knopf.

Sheaffer, R. (1988). *Resentment against achievement: Understanding the assault upon ability*. Buffalo, NY: Prometheus.

Strauss, A. (1964). *George Herbert Mead on social psychology: Selected papers*. Chicago: University of Chicago Press.

Theunissen, M. (1984). *The other: Studies in the social ontology of Husserl, Heidegger, Sartre, and Buber* (C. Macann, Trans.). Cambridge: MIT Press.

U.S. Bureau of the Census. (1993). *Statistical abstract of the United States: 1993* (113th ed.). Washington, DC: Government Printing Office.

Vontress, C. E. (1986). Social and cultural foundations. In M. D. Lewis, R. Hayes, & J. A. Lewis (Eds.), *An introduction to the counseling profession* (pp. 215-250). Itasca, IL: Peacock.

Vontress, C. E. (1991). Traditional healing in Africa: Implication for cross-cultural counseling. *Journal of Counseling and Development, 70*(1), 242-249.

West, C. (1993). *Race matters*. Boston: Beacon.

Wilson, J. (1987). *A preface to morality*. Totowa, NJ: Barnes & Noble.

Wrong, D. H. (1988). *Power: Its forms, bases, and uses*. Chicago: University of Chicago Press.

23

Multicultural Organizational Development

*Implications for
the Counseling Profession*

DERALD WING SUE

MANY READERS may be wondering what a chapter on organizational development (OD) is doing in a handbook of multicultural counseling. After all, isn't counseling concerned with the direct delivery of services to people? Shouldn't multicultural counseling be more concerned with how to make counseling more responsive to the needs and life experiences of various racial, ethnic, and cultural groups in our society? Why should counselors be concerned about OD when its principal goal is institutional rather than individual change and development? Isn't OD more a "business sector" than a "human services" field?

If the multicultural movement is to truly become a "fourth force" in counseling (Pedersen, 1991), these questions and their premises need to be seriously challenged, for they serve as major barriers to a more liberated view of the counseling profession. It is my contention that the counseling profession has too long accepted an extremely narrow view of counseling, leaving us with tunnel vision and ill prepared to work with organizations and larger social systems. Yet it is precisely our ability to influence organizational dynamics that represents the next multicultural counseling frontier. Let us briefly look at the assumptions that seem to underlie these questions.

ORGANIZATIONAL DEVELOPMENT
AND COUNSELING: THE NEED AND RATIONALE

First, there is a common belief, supported by actual practices, that counselors work primarily with individuals in an office setting and in a one-to-one relationship (Atkinson, Morten, & Sue, 1993). Traditional Euro-American schools of counseling have implicitly or explicitly glamorized and defined the "professional counselor" as someone who works along these lines. The practice of counseling and psychotherapy has arisen from the study of individual differences and reflects the value of individualism in U.S. society (Sue & Sue, 1990). Although the development of individual intervention skills has been the main focus in counselor training programs, little emphasis is given to other roles, activities, or settings. Thus not only are counselors lacking in systems intervention knowledge and skills, but they are unaccustomed to and uncomfortable with leaving their offices (Sue, Ivey, & Pedersen, in press). Yet work with racial/ethnic minority groups suggests that out-of-office sites/activities (client homes, churches, volunteer organizations, etc.) and alternative helping roles (ombudsman, advocate, consultant, organizational change agent, facilitator of indigenous healing systems, etc.) may prove more therapeutic and effective (Atkinson, Thompson, & Grant, 1993; Sue & Sue, 1990).

Second, it is commonly believed that counseling should be concerned primarily with internal or intrapsychic dynamics and conflicts. When the focus of counseling is on the individual, however, there is a strong tendency to locate the problem solely in the person (Berman, 1979; Ivey, 1986; Ivey, Ivey, & Simek-Morgan, 1993; Pedersen & Ivey, 1994; Sue & Sue, 1990) rather than in the organization or social structures. As a result, well-intentioned counselors may mistakenly "blame the victim," seeing a problem as a deficiency of the person when in actuality it may reside in the environment. For example, African Americans who are unemployed are often perceived as lazy, unmotivated, or lacking in skills to acquire a job when the actual source of the problem may be prejudice and discrimination. When the practices of an organization/employer are biased against minority groups, shouldn't attempts at change be directed toward the "discriminating" organizational structures?

Third, training programs often imbue trainees with the belief that the role of counselors is relatively free of organizational influences or pressures. In the privacy of their offices, counselors may be under the illusion that they are free to help clients attain their full potential and that their allegiance is to the individual client seeking help. Yet it is becoming clear that what counselors can or cannot do is often dictated by the rules and regulations of their employing agencies (length of sessions, maximum number of sessions, types of problems treated, definition of counseling role, limits of confidentiality, etc.). The policies of an organization may conflict with the therapeutic help needed by clients. This is especially true in an organization that lacks sensitivity toward minority groups.

In addition, counselors may find themselves in conflict when the needs of their clients differ from those of the employer. The fact that a counselor's livelihood depends on the employing agency creates additional pressures to conform. How do counselors handle such conflicts? Who truly are their clients? Organizational knowledge and skills become a necessity if the counselor is to be truly effective.

Fourth, counseling continues to be oriented toward remediation rather than prevention. Although no one would deny the contributions of biological and internal psychological factors to personal problems, more research now acknowledges the important role of sociocultural factors (inadequate or biased education, poor socialization practices, biased values, and discriminatory institutional policies) in creating many of the difficulties encountered by individuals. As counselors, we are frequently placed in a position of treating clients who represent the "aftermath" of failed and oppressive policies and practices (Sue, 1991, 1994). We have been trapped in the role of remediation—attempting to cure clients once they have been damaged by sociocultural biases. Although treating troubled clients (remediation) is a necessity, our task will be an endless and losing venture unless the true sources of the problem (stereotypes, prejudice, discrimination, and oppression) are changed. Would it not make more sense to take a proactive and preventative approach by attacking the cultural and institutional bases of the problem?

Finally, many of us behave as if the main focus of counselors should be on individual or small group change; organizational change is the province of industrial/organizational (I/O) psychologists. The arguments presented thus far challenge this point of view; the need for counselors to acquire organizational knowledge and skills is a counseling necessity. Intraprofessional divisions (territorial turf) should not prevent us from developing and adopting OD strategies in our work. We can profit much from I/O work in the business world. Indeed, many counseling psychologists have recently advocated increasing roles for counselors in business and industry. As psychologists move into the areas of occupational health (Osipow, 1982; Toomer, 1982) and diversity training (Katz & Miller, 1988; Sue, 1991, 1994), the artificial distinctions between the roles of I/O and counseling psychologists may become outdated.

Furthermore, the multicultural movement has severely criticized graduate programs of education and psychology for being monocultural in their emphasis and approach (D'Andrea, Daniels, & Heck, 1991; Hills & Strozier, 1992). These programs represent subsystems within a larger organization (the university) that are responsible for the training of future mental health professionals. If we are to have meaningful impact in changing the curriculum and operation of the programs, OD principles will have to be employed.

Just as multicultural counseling has become a "fourth force" in individual and group counseling (Pedersen, 1991), so too will it increasingly influence organizational development. If our society is to truly value diversity and to become multicultural, then our organizations (businesses, industries, schools, universities, governmental agencies, and even our professional organizations, such as the American Counseling Association and the American Psychological Association) must move toward becoming multicultural.

In the remainder of this chapter, a description of multicultural organizational development (MOD) models will be presented to readers for their consideration (Adler, 1986; Barr & Strong, 1987; Chesler, 1994; Cross, Bazron, Dennis, & Isaacs, 1989; Foster, Jackson, Cross, Jackson, & Hardiman, 1988). Based upon work in MOD, some suggestions for institutional assessment and change will be offered (Sue, 1991, 1994). We begin with a case study.

A CASE STUDY ON
ORGANIZATIONAL INTERVENTION AND FAILURE

Several years after receiving my doctorate in counseling psychology, I accepted a position at a well-known private university on the West Coast. The university was located in an area with a large Latino population, but the student body was over 90% White. Having previously been employed at the University of California, Berkeley Counseling Center, I had been exposed to the aftermath of the Free Speech Movement and had been involved with the Third World Strike, a movement begun in the late 1960s aimed at multicultural curriculum reform and increasing representation of minorities in students, faculty and staff alike.

With these goals in mind, several colleagues and I confronted the university administration with the low numbers of Chicano students on the college campus. We (a) suggested there was bias in the admission criteria, (b) asked for a change in the standards used to admit students of minority cultural background, (c) demanded the placement of minority faculty members on admissions committees, (d) requested the formation of outreach groups to recruit minority students, and (e) asked for creation of an ethnic studies department.

Being a very conservative institution, the university resisted strongly all of our demands. I recall countless hours of meetings, debates and even community demonstrations concerning the underrepresentation of minority student admissions to the university. Academic Senate meetings became very emotional with the majority of faculty and administrators claiming that our group wanted to "lower the standards" of the university. We, in turn, took the position that current admission criteria were biased against minority applicants, and that what we sought was not a "lowering," but a "changing of standards" which could be fairly applied to a culturally different student population. Indeed, many of our other requests such as curriculum reform, increased minority faculty and staff, culturally relevant student services, etc., soon were dropped as the battleground was fought on the frontiers of traditional admission criteria (G.P.A., SAT scores, recommendations, extracurricular activities, etc.).

After nearly a year of sustained debate on this issue, the university administration yielded to community pressures and developed what was called a "special accommodated category," which allowed the admission of large numbers of primarily Latino students onto the campus. While many of us celebrated this development, our victory was short-lived. By the end of the first quarter, nearly 50% of the minority students admitted under the new standard were placed on academic probation. By the end of the academic year, many of those on probation had failed and even those students who had maintained a "C" average had decided not to return to the university. Fueled by these results, our opponents used them to buttress their arguments: "Minority students were not qualified to undertake college level work unless they met the same standards as their White counterparts." The next year, the university dropped the "special category" provision. I also left the following year, and accepted a position at another higher education institution.

This incident has always haunted me for several reasons. First, my own guilt at having started a movement which suddenly backfired and left all those involved (proponents and opponents alike) with negative feelings toward concepts of affirmative action and diversity. Second, for years after my departure, I could not fully understand what had happened to derail our movement. I was left with a bitter taste in my mouth; I was confused about what had gone wrong; and I was at a loss as to what else we might have done to effect a more positive outcome. It was only years later, as I became increasingly involved with OD, that I came to fully understand some of the reasons which led to our downfall. (Sue et al., in press)

LESSONS ON ORGANIZATIONAL CHANGE

Let me use the above case example to illustrate some important lessons I learned about multicultural organizational change.

Lesson 1: A Realistic Assessment of the Level of Multicultural Development Is Needed

Before advocating a change in admission standards at the university for prospective minority students, we should have conducted a thorough assessment of the institutional climate with respect to multiculturalism. All organizations differ in their receptivity to diversity concepts, and premature intervention may result in devastating consequences (D'Andrea et al., 1991). We should have known not only that institutions in general are conservative (resist change), but also that this institution was downright hostile to multicultural concerns. Indeed, most MOD models would have characterized the university as monocultural: (a) Cultural diversity issues were either ignored or purposefully undermined, (b) most workers (faculty and staff) were either ethnocentric or highly assimilated tokens, (c) hiring and admission practices were highly discriminatory, (d) the curriculum was taught from a Euro-American perspective without regard for other cultural views, and (e) there was a strong organizational belief that there was only one best way to run a university.

Under these conditions, it is little wonder that our attempts to implement change met with such devastating results. Our tunnel vision and narrow focus prevented us from seeing the larger picture. We were motivated by naive idealism without a full understanding of systems intervention. Our task was much larger than getting the university to adopt different admissions criteria. It was much greater than trying to convince key members of committees to accept our suggestions. As novices, we failed to realize that the effective introduction of change depends not only on how and what is introduced but also on the readiness and commitment of an organization. The MOD stage of an organization (to be presented shortly) often dictates the type of interventions deemed most effective.

Lesson 2: The Interrelationships of Subsystems Need to Be Understood

In family counseling, we often warn students that treating the "identified patient" without intervening in the family system may prove to be futile. The assumption is that the problem or pathology observed in one member of the family is not necessarily due to internal conflicts, but may be due to unhealthy values and pressures of family life (Sue, Sue, & Sue, 1994). Treating a child in individual sessions, for example, may appear to eradicate the symptoms as long as the child remains outside of the family. Once the child reenters the family, however, he or she may again be forced to play the "sick" role because the subsystems and rules of the family remain unchanged. Treating the child has unbalanced the family homeostasis, and family dynamics will again strive for balance.

Like a family system, organizations are also composed of many interacting subsystems (Levinson, 1994). Over time, these subsystems have worked out a homeostatic relationship held together by institutional policies and practices (formal and informal) governing their relationship to one another. These rules and regulations seemingly attain a "functional autonomy" that dictates what one can or cannot do in the organization (Sue, 1994). Changing only one aspect of a system does not guarantee change in others. For example, to put it very simply, the university can be seen as having three major functions: recruitment, retention, and graduation of students. Within each of these three functions are multiple systems that theoretically support the activities. Student support services, grading standards and processes, teaching and learning styles, curriculum content, and campus culture may all be seen as subsystems. One very important subsystem is that of the admissions process and criteria used to select students. Our attempt to get the university to change one of these subsystems (standards for admission) was doomed to fail because we did not have the understanding or foresight to recognize that the other systems did not change. Indeed, these other subsystems worked against the changes (attempting to reestablish equilibrium) and eventually succeeded in reinstituting the original subsystem. The low enrollment of Latino students at the university may have initially been due to biased admissions criteria (the recruitment system), but our failure to consider the influence of other university systems led to the loss of minority students. The subsequent high dropout rates were due largely to characteristics of a monocultural university: The curriculum alienated many minority students; the teaching styles were culturally biased; grading practices emphasized individual competition; the campus climate was hostile to minority students (they were also perceived as less qualified); support services (counseling, study skills, etc.) were not geared for nontraditional students; and there were few role models (minority faculty, staff, or administrators).

The large group of Latino students who were admitted were subjected to all these antagonistic systems, which eventually took their toll. What we should have done was somehow to make existing systems more sensitive and receptive to multicultural issues (curriculum reform and introducing varying teaching styles that would recognize diversity) or to create new subsystems that would support the students. Organizational change must occur throughout to be effective.

Lesson 3: Commitment Must Come From the Top

Diversity implementation is most effective when strong leadership is exerted on behalf of multiculturalism. For private businesses, the board of directors, CEO, and management team are the principals; for governmental agencies, the head of the service or unit (Secretary of Labor, Housing, etc.); for education, the school board, superintendent, principal, and so forth; and for our nation, the president of the United States, Congress, the judiciary, and local, state, and federal leaders.

In this case, the university administrators were either publicly or privately resentful and antagonistic to our goals. The deans and department chairs were usually adamant in their vocal opposition to proposed changes, and those in the higher echelons of the university (president, academic vice president, and governing board) kept silent. The old saying "silence can be deafening" was proved throughout. Even when the changed standards were adopted, many leaders in the university voiced only lukewarm support.

It also is important to note that faculty, staff, and students alike tend to watch the actions (not just the words) of their leaders. Commitment must be manifested in action. It is more than a written policy statement of affirmative action or statements that one is an "equal opportunity employer." What specific steps has the leadership taken to implement diversity goals at the university? It was clear that the university was not prepared to make any other adjustments in the operation of the university to accommodate minority students. The message was quite clear: "Minority students are not wanted on this campus." Such a message from the leadership gave permission for those in the lower ranks (faculty, staff, and even White students) to resist and/or sabotage proposed changes.

Lesson 4: Premature Introduction of Change May Only Support the Mistaken/Biased Beliefs of the Opposition

One of the greatest lessons learned from this incident was that lack of an overarching plan for change can backfire with devastating consequences. Many of our more well-meaning and receptive colleagues harbored grave doubts about changing admission standards. We felt that attempting to work on those who were adamantly opposed was a waste of time, so we concentrated our efforts on the former group. With such a high dropout rate among the minority students, the "we told you so" cry was used by the opposition in reaffirming three points: (a) The standards of the university had been lowered, (b) less qualified students had been admitted solely because of their race, and (c) these students were incapable of handling university work. All of these beliefs became reinforced, and even our "borderline" allies finally concluded that reinstituting traditional admission criteria was a necessity. Thus the negative beliefs regarding minority students and implementing diversity became more firmly entrenched as a result of our "good intentions." It might have been better if we had not attempted any intervention at all!

Lesson 5: White People Are Also Victims and Under Strong Institutional Pressures to Conform

Even the most well-intentioned White educators or administrators are not immune from inheriting the racial biases, stereotypes, and prejudices of the larger society. During the brief time I was in the Psychology Department, I had made a number of friends. When the issue of accepting more minority students came up, I was quite surprised to find that many of my faculty friends expressed biases toward various minority groups. I saw them as enemies and unfortunately grouped individuals as "good" or "bad" people. This artificial dichotomy failed to recognize a simple fact that I learned much later. Although minorities are often seen as the victims of prejudice and discrimination, White people may also be victims as well. Their victimization is different, however, because they were socialized into oppressor roles. It is my current belief that no one was ever born wanting to be racist, sexist, or prejudiced. White people are programmed into roles without their informed consent (Sue, 1992, 1993). Although this does not absolve them from taking responsibilities for their biases, this understanding may make it easier to avoid seeing them as "evil beings." Many of the educators I worked with might have been enlightened with some effort on our part, becoming allies. Yet our seeing those who expressed doubts about our goals as enemies led to a dismissal of them.

Furthermore, our failure to understand the power of institutional forces (forced compliance) led to continued loss of potential allies. For example, in many informal discussions, White faculty and staff said things that suggested their sympathies with our cause. When we asked for their support, they would often readily agree (in private). Yet when more formal meetings were held with committees and university representatives, these very same White faculty members would either say nothing or couch their responses in a very ambiguous or guarded manner. When votes were taken, they would vote against our proposal, abstain, or not show for the meetings (always with a very convenient excuse). We were enraged by their actions and saw this as "deceit," "insincerity," and "hypocrisy." Years later, I was able to gain greater clarity on such behaviors. Again, these were not "bad" people, but individuals exposed to a punitive system. They may personally have believed in our cause, but the institution had great ability to reward or punish them (promotion, tenure, treatment at the university, etc.). Indeed, the situation is not much different from that of a person who hears a racist joke told by a group of friends. Although it may be personally offensive, the person fails to voice any objections for fear of losing friends or being ridiculed. This indifference, fear, and lack of action on the part of well-meaning individuals is a major condition that has to be ameliorated if we are to deal honestly with our prejudices and biases.

MULTICULTURAL ORGANIZATIONAL DEVELOPMENT

The lessons I learned from this painful incident taught me the importance of developing organization knowledge and skills. The first steps toward effective systems intervention require not only a knowledge of OD but an understanding of its relationship to diversity goals. This requires us to first define *OD*. Chesler (1994) stated:

> Traditionally, OD: is a long range effort to introduce planned change; is based on a diagnosis that is shared by the members of an organization; involves the entire organization, or a significant subsystem; aims for increased organizational effectiveness and self-renewal; uses various strategies to intervene into ongoing activities to facilitate learning and choose alternative ways to proceed. (pp. 12-13)

Nowhere in this definition, however, is there a mention of issues pertaining to race, gender, class, or other aspects of discrimination and oppression. MOD is different from OD in that it (a) takes a social justice perspective (ending of oppression and discrimination in organizations); (b) believes that inequities that arise within organizations may be primarily due not to poor communication, lack of knowledge, poor management, person-organization fit problems, and so forth, but to monopolies of power; and (c) assumes that conflict is inevitable and not necessarily unhealthy. MOD is increasingly subscribed to by diversity trainers and consultants.

MOD is based on the premise that organizations vary in their awareness of how racial, cultural, ethnic, and gender issues affect their workers and the workplace. Institutions that recognize and value diversity in a pluralistic society will be in a better position to avoid many of the misunderstandings and conflicts characteristic of monocultural organizations. They will also be in a better position to fully tap a culturally diverse population, thereby improving services, productivity, and education. Because the needs and issues confronting different organizations vary considerably, it is important that interventions on behalf of diversity be geared to meet the characteristics of the organization or agency.

Moving from a monocultural to a multicultural organization requires the counselor or change agent to understand its characteristics. Businesses, for example, vary in their commitment to multiculturalism, and one's ability to determine where he or she stands on the continuum may dictate what strategies are most effective for change (Highlen, 1994). Ascertaining what the organizational culture is like, what policies or practices either facilitate or impede cultural diversity, and how to implement change is crucial.

Models of Multicultural Organizational Development

Some of the more helpful MOD models have arisen from a variety of areas including the business sector (Adler, 1986; Foster et al., 1988; Jackson & Holvino, 1988; Sue, 1991), education (Barr & Strong, 1987; D'Andrea et al., 1991; Highlen, 1994), and mental health agencies (Cross et al., 1989). Interestingly, nearly all of these models seem to describe a stage or process similar to the racial/cultural identity models for individual development (Atkinson et al., 1993a; Cross, 1971, 1991; Helms, 1984, 1986, 1990; Jackson, 1975; Parham & Helms, 1981) and for White racial identity development (Hardiman, 1982; Rowe, Bennett, & Atkinson, 1994; Sabnani, Ponterotto, & Borodovsky, 1991).

In comparing a number of these MOD models, Jensen (1992) noted some very strong similarities. First, most describe a developmental stage process by which organizations move from a primarily monocultural orientation to a more multicultural one. The labels or terms for the stages differ, but their descriptors are primarily the same (see Table 23.1). The following characteristics of organizations as they move toward diversity implementation have been distilled from Adler (1986), Katz and Miller (1988), Foster et al. (1988), Barr and Strong (1987), Cross et al. (1989), D'Andrea et al. (1991), Sue (1991), and Highlen (1994).

1. *Monocultural Organizations.* At the one extreme are organizations that are primarily Eurocentric and ethnocentric. They are characterized by the following premises and practices:

   - There is an implicit or explicit exclusion of racial minorities, women, and other oppressed groups.
   - Many organizations are rigged to the advantage of the dominant majority. In this case, Whites are privileged.

TABLE 23.1 Stages of Multicultural Development

Author			Stages			
Adler (1986)		Parochial		Ethnocentric		Synergistic
Foster et al. (1988)		Monocultural		Nondiscriminatory	Multicultural	
Barr & Strong (1987)	Traditional		Liberal, Managing Diversity		Radical	
Cross et al. (1989)	Cultural Destructiveness	Cultural Incapacity	Cultural Blindness	Cultural Pre-Competency	Cultural Competence	Cultural Proficiency
Characteristics typical of organizations at particular stages	Cultural diversity is either deliberately ignored or destroyed. Organization members are monocultural or highly assimilated "tokens." Hiring practices and services or products are discriminatory, and services or products are inadequate or inappropriate for cultural minorities. Organization believes there is only one right way to do things.			Organization acknowledges that diversity exists and has "good intentions," but operates from a sense that "our way is the best way." Focus is on meeting affirmative action and EEO goals, with legalistic approach to nondiscrimination. There may be attempts at cross-cultural sensitivity training for individuals, but no focus on organizational change. Staff may be culturally diverse but are judged by traditional (White male) standards.		Organization values diversity and views it as an asset rather than a problem. Staff diversity is evident at all levels, and staff are evaluated and promoted for meeting diversity criteria. Training focuses on personal and organizational dynamics of racism, sexism, etc. Planning is creative and flexible to accommodate ongoing cultural change.

- There is only one best way to manage, teach, or administrate.
- Culture does not affect management, mental health, or education.
- Workers or students should assimilate.
- Culture-specific ways of doing things are neither recognized nor valued. Everyone should be treated the same.
- There is a strong belief in the melting pot concept.

2. *Nondiscriminatory Organizations.* As organizations become more culturally aware and enlightened, they enter another stage often referred to as "nondiscriminatory." These organizations are characterized by the following premises and practices:

- The organization has inconsistent policies and practices regarding multicultural issues. Certain departments or managers/teachers/counselors are becoming sensitive to minority issues, but it is not an organizational priority.
- Leadership may recognize need for some action, but it lacks a systematic program or policy addressing the issue of prejudice and bias.
- There is an attempt to make the climate of an organization less hostile or different, but these changes are superficial and often without conviction. They are more for public relations or perception.
- EEO, affirmative action, and numerical symmetry of minorities and women are implemented grudgingly.

3. *Multicultural Organizations.* As organizations become progressively more multicultural, they begin to value diversity and evidence continuing attempts to accommodate ongoing cultural change. Their basic premises and practices reflect these values:

- They are in the process of working on a vision that reflects multiculturalism.
- They reflect the contributions of diverse cultural and social groups in their mission, operations, products, or services.
- They value diversity and view it as an asset.
- They actively engage in envisioning, planning, and problem-solving activities that allow for equal access and opportunities.
- They realize that equal access and opportunities are not equal treatment.
- They value diversity (rather than just tolerating it) and work to diversify the environment.

These models are helpful as heuristic devices, but they still beg the question of how best to move an organization toward multiculturalism. Sue (1991, 1994) proposed a model for incorporating cultural diversity in organizations. The model is based upon a $3 \times 3 \times 3$ matrix that analyzes the *functional focus,* or where the intervention should take place (recruitment, retention, or promotion), the *multicultural competencies* needed by the organization or individual (beliefs/attitudes, knowledge, and skills), and the *barriers to multiculturalism* (differences, discrimination, and systemic factors). Figure 23.1

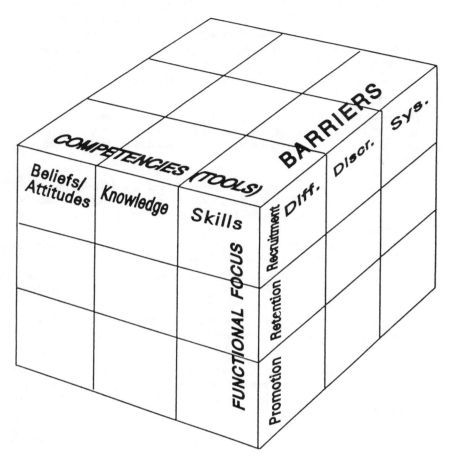

Figure 23.1. A Model for Cultural Diversity Training: Functional Focus, Barriers, and Competencies

SOURCE: Developed by Derald Wing Sue, Ph.D., A Psychological Corporation. Not to be reproduced without written consent.

depicts the model, which has both an assessment (stage of MOD) and an intervention component, and which incorporates the interaction of all three factors: functional focus, competencies, and barriers. In determining when and how to intervene in an organization, it is important to incorporate all three dimensions in the initial analysis. As can be seen, 27 cells are formed from the $3 \times 3 \times 3$ matrix. Each cell allows one to develop the appropriate training or intervention program.

For example, the first step might be to determine the functional focus for intervention. Extensive work in the area of organizational intervention points to three primary levels at which diversity training would be helpful (Morrison & Von Glinow, 1990): (a) recruitment (labor pool)—attracting minority applicants and expanding the pool of students, faculty, staff, or workers from which to recruit; (b) retention (educational or corporate culture)—keeping qualified minorities and women by accommodating cultural diversity and making minority individuals feel a part of the work or educational environment; and (c) promotion (career path) or graduation—improving racial/ethnic minorities' chances of promotion, advancement, and graduation in the organization or institution.

Second, numerous multicultural specialists have found it important to approach training on the basis of competency. The effective and culturally skilled multicultural counselor, educator, or manager must possess the following competencies (tools) in order to be successful in a multicultural environment: (a) beliefs/attitudes—changing false beliefs, stereotypes, and negative attitudes about minority groups; (b) knowledge—acquiring important knowledge regarding racial/ethnic minority history, lifestyles, cultural values, and so forth; and (c) skills—learning culture-specific strategies that moderate teaching, communication, management, and/or counseling styles. These characteristics of multicultural competencies have been described in detail elsewhere (Sue et al., 1982; Sue, Arredondo, & McDavis, 1992).

Third, MOD may be seriously impeded for a number of reasons. Because these will be discussed shortly, suffice it to say that understanding the source of the barriers or resistances is important prior to diversity intervention.

Barriers to Valuing Diversity in Organizations

Although many of us would eagerly embrace the vision of multicultural organizations, some major obstacles remain in our path. Some of these institutional barriers have already been described in the case study. They are also listed under "barriers" in Figure 23.1. Although understanding the functional focus and types of competencies needed by an organization is important, the major requirement for effective MOD is understanding organizational resistance.

1. *Differences in communication styles and differences in characteristics of racial/ethnic minorities* are often misunderstood by White counselors, educators, workers, and managers. For example, the orientation and leadership of most organizations are primarily masculine: They are organized by military, competitive, athletic, and sexual metaphors. To men, such language conveys

aggressiveness, competitiveness, and possible leadership qualities. It also represents a form of "bonding" among men (this may be one reason why many men often talk about sports at the worksite).

The communication styles of women may be more relationship oriented, fostering cooperation rather than competition. Such an approach may be perceived as passivity and dependence—qualities of poor leadership. Levinson (1994) stated, "The male orientation is described as penetration and thrust versus the female orientation of enveloping and surrounding. The whole psychology of management is that of aggressive attack and dominance, sexual in its imagery: screw or be screwed, to be on top or on the bottom—helpless, dependent, and victimized" (p. 430).

It is very important to point out several ironic aspects of studies of the characteristics of minorities and women as well. First, research does indicate that racial/ethnic minorities and women may possess certain traits, attitudes, behaviors, and values that are viewed by institutions as clashing with those required to achieve success (Morrison & Von Glinow, 1990). To operate under this assumption is to "blame the victim" and fail to recognize that institutional policies and practices may be at the heart of the problem. Second, even when minorities and women "act like White males," they are likely to be viewed negatively. A White male manager is often given credit for being a dynamic leader or manager when he exhibits a "no-nonsense" approach to others. However, an African American manager who is as verbally forceful as his White counterpart may be seen as "hostile," "angry," "prone to violence," "unable to control emotions," and "unreasonable"; a woman who exhibits similar behavior may be seen as a "bitch."

These differences are only impediments when viewed from a biased and monocultural perspective. In organizations in which differences are valued, understood, and utilized fully, productivity has increased beyond expectations (Adler, 1986).

2. *Interpersonal discrimination and prejudice (racism and sexism)* have been identified as one of the most serious impediments to the implementation of diversity into education and the labor force. It is important for all of us to realize that we all possess biases, prejudices, and stereotypes that can seriously impair cultural diversity goals. Unconscious stereotypes that African Americans are lacking in intelligence, prone to violence or impulsiveness, and hostile may unfairly deny them decision-making positions. Such biases and prejudices may operate on both a conscious and an unconscious level. A White manager may not recommend an outstanding Latino worker for a promotion because he or she speaks with an accent. The unconscious appraisal may be that the Latino worker is less intelligent because of "poor English." The conscious bias may reside in the White manager's rationalization that supervisors need to speak "clearly" to their workers (accents cause communication problems) and that because the Latino worker must fit into the management team,

"we need to feel comfortable working with him/her." This last argument is a common statement often made by management. It strongly implies that cultural/racial/gender differences will not fit into "the old boys' network."

Such discrimination can óperate at all levels of an organization. At the recruitment (labor pool) level, biased recruitment criteria (not fitting a White definition of qualification) are often reflected in statements from management or educators that "we can't find enough qualified minorities." At the retention (corporate culture) level, the institutional climate/culture is often hostile to minorities and women (from open expressions of racism and sexism to subtle behaviors that do not give credit to or recognize their contributions to the company, classroom, or agency), and this hostility may result in lower productivity, lower school performance, and burnout. Finally, at the level of promotion (career path) and graduation, the existence of a glass ceiling based upon hidden bias and discrimination unfairly allows only certain groups to graduate from schools or rise within an organization.

3. *The existence of systemic barriers* in an institution may mirror the nature of race and gender relations in the United States. For example, high-status positions are usually White dominated, whereas lower status positions are occupied by minority groups. The dominance of White men in management and executive positions poses a structural problem for nontraditional employees because evaluations of minority members are likely to be biased at best. Furthermore, the university or corporate culture may create culture conflicts for the minority employee or student, leading to alienation, loss of productivity, and retention/promotion/graduation problems. Formal institutional policies and practices may maintain exclusion of minorities, and powerful informal liaisons/mentoring arrangements ("the old boys' network") may be equally unfair.

Generally, discovering which rules, regulations, policies, and practices may show bias against the culturally different may prove very difficult for several reasons. First, once developed, management systems, communication systems, chain-of-command systems, promotion and tenure systems, and performance appraisal systems often attain "untouchable and godfather" status in an organization. Such systems are embedded in the corporate or university culture, and any attempts to tamper with them are resisted. As we have seen in the case example, changing one aspect of a performance appraisal system, for example, cannot be done in isolation from the entire organizational culture. A change in one system dictates a change in others as well. This is a major barrier in MOD. Second, policies and procedures are developed with the thought that everyone will be treated the same. Often equal treatment can be discriminatory, whereas differential treatment that recognizes differences is not necessarily preferential. Organizations often have great difficulty comprehending this statement. Indeed, the blind application of a single policy or standard to all populations may be unfair.

The Next Multicultural Frontier:
Organizational Development

MOD represents the next major frontier on which the issues of diversity will be fought. The counseling profession must realize that although individual change and development are important goals, true lasting change can occur in our society only if our organizations also change and develop. It matters little for counseling professionals to develop effective multicultural beliefs/ attitudes, knowledge, and beliefs when the very organizations that employ them are monocultural, working to negate the very multicultural competencies they have developed.

In this chapter, I have tried to (a) provide a rationale for why counselors must become involved in MOD, (b) share with readers the many pitfalls that await the unenlightened change agent, (c) pull together the conceptual models and characteristics of organizations as they move from monoculturalism to multiculturalism, (d) present a model for diversity assessment and intervention, and (e) discuss the types of institutional barriers that are most likely to block attempts at incorporating diversity.

Clearly, the task before us is immense. Being successful means getting organizations to review their policies, practices, and organizational structures to remove potential barriers. They may need to create new policies, practices, and internal structures that will support and advance cultural diversity. To truly value diversity, however, means altering the power relations in organizations to minimize structural discrimination. This may mean the following developments: (a) including minorities in decision-making positions and sharing power with them, and (b) constructing diversity programs and practices with the same economic and maintenance priorities as other valued aspects of the company.

More important, programs need to be implemented that directly attack the biases, prejudices, and stereotypes of employers and employees. Any diversity initiative that does not contain a strong antiracism component, for example, will not be successful. Eliminating prejudice and discrimination is not simply an acquisition of new knowledge and information (cognitive exercise). If that were the case, we would have eradicated racism years ago. White employers and employees need to realize that they have directly or indirectly benefited from individual, institutional, and cultural racism (Sue & Sue, 1990). Although many Whites may acknowledge that minorities and women are placed at a disadvantage in the current system, few realize or recognize "White privilege" (invisible systems that confer dominance on Whites) (McIntosh, 1989). Although no one was ever born wanting to be a racist, Whites have been socialized in a racist society; they need to accept responsibility for their own racism and to deal with it in a nondefensive, guilt-free manner. Movement toward valuing and respecting differences, becoming aware of one's own values and biases, and becoming comfortable with racial and cultural differences, among other characteristics, are essential.

Producing these conditions and changes is fundamental in meeting the challenge of cultural diversity. On a business level, how we meet the challenge foretells the economic viability of U.S. companies. On an educational level, our viability as a society depends on allowing equal access and opportunities for all by instilling a bias-free education. On a personal level, how we meet the challenge also foretells the legacy we will leave our children. Race, culture, ethnicity, and gender are fundamental aspects of each and every one of us. They are not just "minority issues" or "women's issues." Continuing to deny the impact and importance of these variables is to deny social reality itself. I encourage my counseling colleagues to meet the challenge honestly and with courage.

REFERENCES

Adler, N. J. (1986). Cultural synergy: Managing the impact of cultural diversity. *The 1986 annual: Developing human resources* (pp. 229-238). San Diego, CA: University Associates.

Atkinson, D. R., Morten, G., & Sue, D. W. (1993a). *Counseling American minorities: A cross-cultural perspective.* Dubuque, IA: Brown & Benchmark.

Atkinson, D. R., Thompson, C. E., & Grant, S. K. (1993b). A three-dimensional model for counseling racial/ethnic minorities. *The Counseling Psychologist, 21*, 257-277.

Barr, D. J., & Strong, L. J. (1987, May). Embracing multiculturalism: The existing contradictions. *ACU-I Bulletin,* pp. 20-23.

Berman, J. (1979). Counseling skills used by Black and White male and female counselors. *Journal of Counseling Psychology, 26*, 81-84.

Chesler, M. A. (1994, Winter). Strategies for multicultural organizational development. *The Diversity Factor,* pp. 12-18.

Cross, T. L., Bazron, B. J., Dennis, K. W., & Isaacs, M. R. (1989). *Towards a culturally competent system of care.* Washington, DC: Child and Adolescent Service System Program Technical Assistance Center.

Cross, W. E. (1971). The Negro-to-Black conversion experience: Toward a psychology of Black liberation. *Black World, 20*, 13-27.

Cross, W. E. (1991). *Shades of Black: Diversity in African American identity.* Philadelphia: Temple University Press.

D'Andrea, M., Daniels, J., & Heck, R. (1991). Evaluating the impact of multicultural training. *Journal of Counseling and Development, 70*, 143-150.

Foster, B. G., Jackson, G., Cross, W. E., Jackson, B., & Hardiman, R. (1988). Workforce diversity and business. Alexandria, VA: American Society for Training and Development. Reprinted from *Training and Development Journal,* 1988, April, pp. 1-4.

Hardiman, R. (1982). White identity development: A process oriented model for describing the racial consciousness of White Americans. *Dissertation Abstracts International, 43*, 104A. (University Microfilms No. 82-10330)

Helms, J. E. (1984). Toward a theoretical model of the effects of race on counseling: A Black and White model. *The Counseling Psychologist, 12*, 153-165.

Helms, J. E. (1986). Expanding racial identity theory to cover counseling process. *Journal of Counseling Psychology, 33*, 62-64.

Helms, J. E. (Ed.). (1990). *Black and White racial identity: Theory, research, and practice.* Westport, CT: Greenwood Press.

Highlen, P. S. (1994). Racial/ethnic diversity in doctoral programs of psychology: Challenges for the twenty-first century. *Applied and Preventive Psychology, 3*, 91-107.

Hills, H. I., & Strozier, A. L. (1992). Multicultural training in APA approved counseling psychology programs: A survey. *Professional Psychology: Research and Theory, 23*, 43-51.

Ivey, A. E. (1986). *Developmental therapy.* San Francisco: Jossey-Bass.

Ivey, A. E., Ivey, M. B., & Simek-Morgan, L. (1993). *Counseling and psychotherapy: A multicultural perspective.* Boston: Allyn & Bacon.

Jackson, B. (1975). Black identity development. *Journal of Educational Diversity, 2,* 19-25.

Jackson, B. W., & Holvino, E. (1988). Developing multicultural organizations. *Journal of Religion and the Applied Behavioral Sciences, 9,* 14-19.

Jensen, M. P. (1992). *Building multicultural competencies for mental health organizations.* Unpublished master's thesis, California State University, Hayward.

Katz, J. H., & Miller, F. A. (1988). Between monoculturalism and multiculturalism: Traps awaiting the organization. *O.D. Practitioner, 20,* 1-5.

Levinson, H. (1994). Why the behemoths fell: Psychological roots of corporate failure. *American Psychologist, 49,* 428-436.

McIntosh, P. (1989, July/August). White privilege: Unpacking the invisible knapsack. *Peace and Freedom,* pp. 8-10.

Morrison, A. M., & Von Glinow, M. A. (1990). Women and minorities in management. *American Psychologist, 45,* 200-208.

Osipow, S. H. (1982). Counseling psychology: Applications in the world of work. *The The Counseling Psychologist, 10,* 19-25.

Parham, T. A., & Helms, J. E. (1981). The influence of Black students' racial attitudes on preferences for counselor's race. *Journal of Counseling Psychology, 28,* 250-257.

Pedersen, P. (1991). Multiculturalism as a fourth force in counseling. *Journal of Counseling and Development, 70*(1), 1-250.

Pedersen, P., & Ivey, A. (1994). *Culture-centered counseling and interviewing skills.* New York: Greenwood.

Rowe, W., Bennett, S., & Atkinson, D. R. (1994). White racial identity consciousness: A social learning analysis. *The Counseling Psychologist, 22,* 129-146.

Sabnani, H. B., Ponterotto, J. G., & Borodovsky, L. G. (1991). White racial identity development and cross-cultural counselor training. *The Counseling Psychologist, 19,* 76-102.

Sue, D. W. (1991). A model for cultural diversity training. *Journal of Counseling and Development, 70,* 99-105.

Sue, D. W. (1992). The challenge of multiculturalism: The road less traveled. *American Counselor, 1,* 7-14.

Sue, D. W. (1993). Confronting ourselves: The White and racial/ethnic minority researcher. *The Counseling Psychologist, 21,* 244-249.

Sue, D. W. (1994, Winter). U.S. business and the challenge of cultural diversity. *The Diversity Factor,* pp. 24-28.

Sue, D. W., Arredondo, P., & McDavis, R. J. (1992). Multicultural competencies/standards: A pressing need. *Journal of Counseling and Development, 70*(4), 477-486.

Sue, D. W., Bernier, J. B., Durran, M., Feinberg, L., Pedersen, P., Smith, E., & Vasquez-Nuttall, E. (1982). Position paper: Cross-cultural counseling competencies. *The Counseling Psychologist, 10,* 45-52.

Sue, D. W., Ivey, A. E., & Pedersen, P. (in press). *A theory of multicultural counseling and psychotherapy.* Pacific Grove, CA: Brooks/Cole.

Sue, D. W., & Sue, D. (1990). *Counseling the culturally different: Theory and practice.* New York: John Wiley.

Sue, D., Sue, D. W., & Sue, S. (1994). *Understanding abnormal behavior* (4th ed.). Boston: Houghton-Mifflin.

Toomer, J. E. (1982). Counseling psychologists in business and industry. *The Counseling Psychologist, 10,* 9-18.

24

Intelligence and Personality Assessment

Multicultural Perspectives

LISA A. SUZUKI

JOHN F. KUGLER

THE TERM *ASSESSMENT* refers to a process through which a clinician obtains information about a client. The assessment process includes both quantitative information (e.g., test information) and qualitative information (e.g., information yielded in a clinical interview) that can be put together to provide a more comprehensive picture of the total functioning of a client. Although any person who can read and memorize instructions can administer a particular instrument, one's professional judgment is needed to integrate the information into a comprehensive and appropriate client conceptualization.

The complexities of the assessment process are evident given the need to integrate information obtained from various sources (e.g., client, family members, other professionals), observations, and the results of formal testing. The clinician may obtain what appears to be discrepant data, and making sense of these differences requires good clinical judgment and skills. These complexities are further compounded during a multicultural assessment given the potential differences in culture between the client, the clinician, the norm group upon which the test is based, culture-specific constructs being assessed, and related issues that may influence the assessment process and the interpretation of results.

This chapter highlights issues to be considered in conducting multicultural assessments. Some of these issues are general and may be applied to all testing circumstances; others pertain to multicultural populations. Particular attention is given to the use of standardized measures in the assessment process. The areas covered include concerns that have arisen about the assessment process with racial/ethnic minority groups, variables that may affect the assessment process, examination of the most popular intelligence (i.e., Wechsler Scales) and personality (i.e., MMPI, Rorschach) tests, and hints for the examiner in conducting and writing "sensitive" and accurate psychological reports. The chapter concludes with two cases that illustrate the multicultural issues presented.

Due to the brevity of this chapter, information is presented on only a few of the primary instruments used in assessment procedures in educational and clinical settings. For more in-depth information concerning a wider range of personality and intellectual instruments, the reader is referred to Brislin, Lonner, and Thorndike (1973), Dana (1993), Sattler (1988), and Suzuki, Meller, and Ponterotto (in press).

CONCERNS PERTAINING TO PERSONALITY AND INTELLECTUAL ASSESSMENT WITH DIVERSE POPULATIONS

Many questions have been raised by clinicians and researchers regarding the use of standardized intellectual and personality instruments and their application to different racial/ethnic groups. Do intellectual instruments underestimate the abilities of individuals from diverse populations? Do personality instruments "overpathologize" racial/ethnic minority group members? Do particular tests measure the same psychological constructs across diverse groups? What are the differences? What are the similarities? What are the variables that affect the obtained results of measures administered to different ethnic/racial groups? Questions like these have existed in the assessment literature for decades. Despite numerous attempts by researchers to provide answers, results remain for the most part inconclusive given assessment concerns.

The following are summaries of areas of concern highlighted by Reynolds and Kaiser (1990). Others have also posed similar concerns in their writings (Armour-Thomas, 1992; Dana, 1993; Sattler, 1988). These concerns include:

1. *Inappropriate Test Content:* Many tests incorporate items and procedures that reflect White middle-class values. Thus individuals from various racial/ethnic minority groups may not have been exposed to the test content, format, and task attributes.

2. *Inappropriate Standardization Samples:* Racial/ethnic minority groups are often underrepresented in standardization samples. National norms reflect predominantly White middle-class samples, for which results may be inappropriately applied to minorities. Separate racial/ethnic standardizations or pluralistic norms are not a favorable alternative, as they do not provide information regarding the complexity of issues that affect multicultural assessment or the reasons why discrepancies between different diverse populations exist.

3. *Examiner and Language Bias:* Clinicians who are unfamiliar with the culture and language of clients may inadvertently misjudge, stereotype, and/or intimidate their clients due to difficulties in verbal and nonverbal communication. A lack of rapport may also result, given cultural differences between clinician and client.

4. *Inequitable Social Consequences:* Due to histories of oppression and discrimination, members of racial/ethnic minority groups are already at a disadvantage in educational and vocational achievement. Therefore, score discrepancies between groups may reflect systemic problems rather than deficits inherent in the individual being assessed.

5. *Measurement of Different Constructs:* A test may measure different attributes when used with individuals from different cultural groups (see this chapter's section on concept equivalence).

6. *Differential Predictive Validity:* Many have raised questions as to whether tests accurately predict outcomes for racial/ethnic minority group members in comparison to White middle-class individuals. Part of this concern is also the selection of criteria to evaluate outcomes. Often variables such as academic and scholastic achievement (i.e., GPA, level of education) and occupational attainment are used as evidence of success. Reynolds and Kaiser (1990) noted that Black psychologists have raised concerns regarding these "biased" criteria.

7. *Differences in Test-Taking Skills:* Minority individuals may not be accustomed to taking tests as they are presented in current assessment practices (Sattler, 1988). Issues of motivation, test practice, and lack of understanding of the purposes of the testing may influence the accuracy of test results. An individual who is unfamiliar with test-taking strategies may opt not to guess at a response, thereby obtaining a lower score than someone who attempts to provide an answer using problem-solving strategies.

CULTURAL BIAS
AND CULTURAL LOADING

Differences in scoring patterns between racial/ethnic groups on both intellectual and personality tests have been used to indicate that the instruments are biased with respect to racial/ethnic minority groups. The differences in IQ scores and personality profiles have been attributed to deficits that are detected by particular instruments as certain racial/ethnic groups score differentially in comparison to Whites. However, psychometrists note that by definition, cultural bias refers to "systematic error in the estimation of some 'true' value for a group of individuals" (Reynolds, 1982, p. 186). When particular instruments are subjected to psychometric scrutiny, the results have often yielded inconsistent findings. In one attempt to "eyeball" items to determine which items would be more difficult for Black individuals, federal judges were found to have a hit rate no better than chance (Sattler, 1991). It appears that we do not know with confidence what culturally biased items on a test look like.

It is important to note that a test can be culturally loaded without being culturally biased. Cultural loading refers to the degree of cultural specificity present in a particular test. All tests in existence are to some extent based upon the unique aspects of the culture in which they were developed (Reynolds, 1982). Cultural loading may be present not only in terms of the content of the measure but also in terms of the testing procedures. Dahlstrom (1986) noted that "testing procedures may be viewed as part and parcel of the dominant society from which many of these individuals [racial/ethnic minorities] are deeply estranged and cut off" (p. 19).

There exists a potential for professionals to use *all* tests inappropriately with individuals from diverse racial/ethnic groups. Although it is true that some past attempts at multicultural testing have been based on improper assumptions and inappropriate test use, professionals should still be invested in making better attempts toward culturally sensitive assessment practices (De Vos & Boyer, 1989). Appropriate usage and interpretation in assessment are vital, as the results of these procedures are used to make decisions regarding diagnosis, educational and clinical placement, and psychological intervention.

ISSUES TO BE CONSIDERED
IN THE ASSESSMENT PROCESS

Several issues must be considered in the use of intellectual and personality instruments with different racial/ethnic groups. These include but are not limited to questions pertaining to concept and psychological equivalence, demographic and environmental factors, racial identity and acculturation, use of translated tests, and language issues.

Concept Equivalence

Concept equivalence or *cultural equivalence* refers to the question of whether the psychological construct or concept being measured has equivalent or similar psychological meaning within and across different cultural groups (Butcher & Pancheri, 1976; Helms, 1992). Particular behaviors may have different etiologies or meanings in different cultural contexts. Awareness of these issues is imperative, for inaccurate conclusions may be based upon differences in construct meaning or mistaken attribution regarding a particular response behavior.

Demographic and Environmental Variables

Demographic and environmental variables must be taken into consideration in making decisions about what tests to use with culturally diverse populations. These include but are not limited to language, socioeconomic status, educational level, acculturation status, and region of the country. For example, the discrepancies between racial/ethnic minority groups on both personality measures (i.e., MMPI) (Dahlstrom, Lachar, & Dahlstrom, 1986; Timbrook & Graham, 1994) and intellectual measures (i.e., Wechsler Scales) decrease when racial/ethnic minority samples are comparable on age, education, socioeconomic status, and other demographic variables. "Low-income, underemployed or unemployed, poorly educated, physically ill, or socially isolated individuals, particularly if they are also members of a minority group that lacks respect and full acceptance by the dominant group, show in their test responses the effects of such deprivations" (Dahlstrom et al., 1986, p. 202). Poverty, educational failure, malnutrition, lead poisoning, ear infections, and other health-related concerns, which may be more prevalent within certain racial/ethnic minority groups, can also affect test performance (Dahlstrom et al., 1986).

Racial Identity and Level of Acculturation

Acculturation and racial identity status are important components of the assessment process given that culture affects the nature and configuration of symptoms, the way in which problems are reported, strategies of problem solving, attributions regarding the origin of the presenting concerns, and appropriate interventions (Gaw, 1993). Given these issues, understanding the degree to which the individual being assessed perceives his or her identity is imperative.

Racial identity refers to stages within a dynamic process of development; members of the same racial/ethnic group may differ in terms of their racial/cultural identity. For example, some individuals may adhere strongly to the beliefs and values of the dominant White culture to the exclusion of their own racial identity. Others belonging to the same racial/ethnic group may value their own culture to the exclusion of the dominant culture. Extensive information regarding identity issues is provided in the eight chapters that constitute Part II of this book. Information regarding identity development and acculturation may be obtained through the clinical interview and/or standardized measures. Various scales assessing racial identity and acculturation have been developed (see Dana, 1986, 1993; Sabnani & Ponterotto, 1992).

Use of Translated Measures

It is not unusual to find clinicians utilizing translated versions of tests or including translators/interpreters during the assessment procedure. The dangers of these practices are clearly evident. Direct translations are often not possible, as psychological constructs may have relevance in one culture but not another. As Butcher and Pancheri (1976) reported, "As soon as a test is published, it is translated, often without validation in the target population and in some instances in the population of origin" (p. 28). Determining whether to use a translated measure in the assessment process involves consideration of the following questions (Butcher & Pancheri, 1976):

1. Do the constructs of interest exist in the culture of the client?
2. Is the format of the test (tasks presented) meaningful in the client's culture? For example, some respondents may find a true-false format to be completely foreign to them.
3. Is the test valid in the client's culture? Problems arise when examiners use translated versions of tests without proper exploration of validity issues and assume that the test is valid because it has been translated.
4. Has the test followed appropriate translation procedures? For example, the back-translation method is a way to translate verbal content into an equivalent form. The test is translated into the target language and then translated back to the source language to examine possible discrepancies between the original test and the translated version. This process does not ensure cultural equivalence, given that the items may have different meanings in varying cultural contexts.
5. Have the test translators and publishers kept the response format the same so that the scores can be interpreted accurately? For example, there are approximately 50 translated versions of the MMPI in existence. Some of the response formats are so different that they yield different profiles.

It is important to note that there is no specific monitoring body or code of ethics regarding test translation.

Language Dominance

Challenges become apparent when assessing individuals whose primary language is not standard English. This is especially clear for professionals testing immigrant and refugee children in the schools, who may be identified as limited-English-proficient (LEP). It is often recommended that bilingual individuals be evaluated in both languages, given legal and ethical guidelines regarding appropriate assessment procedures (Rogers, 1993). Scales are available to assist professionals in determining proficiency and dominance in various languages. It should be noted that individuals may demonstrate a lack of proficiency in standard English for a variety of reasons, such as limited exposure to standard English or some type of language disorder.

Concerns have been raised when language issues are not addressed. For example, colleagues have shared tragic stories of students classified as learning disabled because they could not communicate effectively in English. Mercer (1987) reported that individuals in the process of learning a new language may experience difficulty with academic concepts and language given their abstract nature. These same indivi

focusing on social interactions

ond-language learners may appea

dysfluencies common in the process

tant for professionals to be aware of thes

are designated as dominant in a language c

lingual.

INTELLECTUAL ASSESSMENT

The intellectual assessment of racial/ethnic minority pe
plagued with controversy concerning the consistent discrepancy
tween Blacks and Whites on IQ measures (e.g., Jensen, 1985; Shuey,
As early as 1958, Shuey reviewed approximately 72 studies incorporat
total of 36,000 Black children and concluded that Black children tended to
score one standard deviation below White children on standardized IQ measures. This discrepancy has been deemed by some as one of the most well-
documented phenomena in psychometrics today (Reynolds, 1982). Similar
differences are noted for the Hispanic and American Indian groups. Specific
methodological concerns have been raised with regard to the assessment of
intelligence. These include the lack of an agreed-upon definition of intelligence
and limitations of research studies.

The concept of intelligence has been defined in a variety of ways—for
example, "the ability to think abstractly, give a critical opinion, deal effectively
with reality, the art of adjusting, to be able to combine separate impressions,
working with abstract symbols" (Vroon, 1980, p. 29). Discussions regarding
the definition of intelligence have also noted the possibility that intelligence
may simply be what intelligence tests measure (Boring, 1923; Samuda, 1975;
Vroon, 1980).

Early cognitive theorists viewed intelligence as a cognitive construct; however, attempts at theory construction often resulted in failure to account for
complex abilities, so these theories were either "abandoned or attenuated"
(Das, Kirby, & Jarman, 1979, p. 29). Intelligence testing has evolved into a
"technology divorced from psychological theory" (Das et al., 1979, p. 29).

Research examining the intelligence of racial/ethnic minorities has suffered from other problems. For example, studies often incorporate samples of
referred subjects (e.g., referred for testing due to educational or behavioral
concerns) and nonreferred subjects, small sample sizes, unrepresentative samples, and failure to note within-racial/ethnic-group differences.

The following discussion focuses on the use of the Wechsler Scales and
nonverbal measures with multicultural populations. For more information
regarding the Wechsler Scales and other intelligence instruments, the reader
is referred to Sattler (1988), Kaufman (1990, 1994), and Dana (1993).

...sler Adult Intelligence Scale-Revised (WAIS-R) (Wechsler, 1981), ...echsler Intelligence Scale for Children-III (WISC-III) (Wechsler, 1991), and the Wechsler Primary Preschool Scale of Intelligence-Revised (WPPSI-R) (Wechsler, 1989) are some of the most frequently used individual intelligence measures in the United States (Anastasi, 1982). The tests are divided into two scales, Verbal and Performance, and yield an overall Full Scale IQ (FSIQ). Wechsler (1949) conceptualized intelligence as the capacity of an individual to understand and adapt to the world around him or her. His scales were designed to be representative of the ways in which human abilities were expressed, such as verbal reasoning and responding (Verbal scale), and spatial reasoning (Performance scale). The subtests of the scales reflect Wechsler's belief that intelligence is a multidetermined, multifaceted, composite, yet global entity (Kaufman, 1994). In general, the subtests assess general fund of knowledge, vocabulary development, abstract thinking, visual analysis, visual synthesis, visual discrimination, visual-motor speed, visual scanning, and so on. For each scale, attempts were made to include proportional representation of different racial/ethnic minority group members in the standardization sample. Numerous studies have been conducted addressing the reliability and validity of the Wechsler scales in relation to various ethnic/racial groups. In general, the Wechsler scales have been found to be valid and reliable (e.g., Kaufman, 1990; McShane & Cook, 1985; Sattler, 1988), though concerns continue to be raised regarding discrepancies in FSIQ between ethnic groups. These concerns are especially noteworthy given the use of IQ tests in determining educational placement (i.e., special education classification).

The most recent update of the Wechsler Scales was the WISC-III, published in 1991. Concern regarding multicultural issues led the test developers to use a panel of minority experts to review the scales for bias. In addition, the bias issue was addressed psychometrically through item analysis with a sample of minority children. The standardization sample of the WISC-III reflects the 1988 U.S. Census, and representative numbers of African Americans, Caucasians, American Indians, Hispanics, Asian Americans, Aleuts, Pacific Islanders, and so forth were included. Helms (1992) recommended that the procedures used to develop the WISC-III be used as a potential model for redevelopment of intellectual measures. However, she also raised concerns regarding the need for consideration of sociocultural experiences for various racial/ethnic groups.

System of Multicultural Pluralistic Assessment (SOMPA)

The System of Multicultural Pluralistic Assessment (SOMPA) (Mercer, 1979) was an attempt to adjust intellectual indicators (i.e., scores on the Wechsler Intelligence Scale for Children—Revised [WISC-R], Wechsler, 1974) in accordance with various demographic, social, cultural, and linguistic characteristics. The SOMPA was validated on samples of White, Hispanic, and Black children. This battery included medical assessments (physical dexterity, perceptual-neurological factors, nutritional and growth factors, visual acuity, auditory acuity, health history), the WISC-R, and a measure of adaptive functioning. As part of the SOMPA standardization interview, the mothers of the children in the sample were asked 38 questions concerning the social and cultural characteristics of the family. The SOMPA yields an Estimated Learning Potential (ELP) based upon comparison of the individual with others from the same sociocultural background. Questions still remain regarding the effectiveness of the SOMPA. For example, one evaluation of the SOMPA (Figueroa & Sassenrath, 1989) indicates that the ELP does not appear to predict or correlate with academic achievement for minority children as accurately as other standardized IQ scores (e.g., Verbal IQ).

Nonverbal Measures

Nonverbal measures have been identified as more "culture fair" because they depend less on language than verbal measures (Rogers, 1993). One popular group of nonverbal measures is Raven's Progressive Matrices (RPM) (Raven, 1989). These tests measure cognitive ability using visual matrices. The client must complete the matrix by identifying the missing symbol.

There are three forms of the Progressive Matrices: the Coloured version (children), the Standard version (all ages), and the Advanced version. The original Standard Progressive Matrices were standardized on children in England. Numerous norming studies have since been conducted in the United States. A review of the norming studies that included samples from various racial/ethnic groups yielded data indicating that the RPM "scales in the same way for children . . . from different ethnic groups in the 1986 U.S. standardization, and from different cultures" (Raven, 1989, p. 4). Variations in mean scores between ethnic groups within the United States are noted for the RPM. Raven reported that these differences correspond to variations between the same groups in terms of height, birth weight, and infant mortality. Raven also noted that height and birth weight have increased over the past 80 years in the United States. Thus he argued that the increases in RPM scores that he observed over time might be "due to the same variables as increases in height and birth weight and decline in infant mortality—that is, to improved nutrition, welfare, and hygiene" (p. 7).

Many criticisms have arisen regarding the usage of nonverbal measures as "culture-fair" instruments. Sattler (1988) referred to RPM as a "culturally reduced" test because it is "less dependent on exposure to specific language symbols" (p. 579). But he noted that this test does have some degree of cultural loading—it is "neither culture fair nor culture free" (p. 579). Rogers (1993) reported that "little evidence exists that suggests a relationship between performance on nonverbal tests of intelligence and academic success in the classroom" (p. 429). Helms (1992) reported that culture-fair tests "represent attempts to control the influences of different cultures rather than to measure them" (p. 1091). Research indicates that racial/ethnic minorities do not score higher on culture-fair tests in comparison to traditional measures of intelligence (Arvey, 1972, cited in Sattler, 1988). For example, Black children have similar difficulties with nonverbal and culture-fair tests in comparison to verbal measures (Sattler, 1988). Given these concerns, nonverbal measures should be used with caution and only in conjunction with other measures.

PERSONALITY ASSESSMENT

Questions have been raised regarding the "overpathologizing" of particular racial/ethnic groups on the basis of personality tests, given that many instruments do not include people of color in their norming samples (e.g., Gynther, 1972). Some studies have revealed scaled score differences between various racial/ethnic groups on traditionally used personality measures.

Minnesota Multiphasic
Personality Inventory (MMPI)

The Minnesota Multiphasic Personality Inventory (MMPI) has been cited as the most "useful psychological test available in clinical and counseling settings for assessing the degree and nature of emotional upset" (Walsh & Betz, 1990, p. 117). The MMPI is also one of the most well-researched instruments currently in use today.

Some have criticized the MMPI and encouraged the development of special norms for particular minority groups (Gynther, 1972). Application of the MMPI with diverse populations has yielded information indicating that higher F scales may be attributed to cultural factors (Butcher & Williams, 1992). Few members of racial/ethnic minority groups were recruited in the initial sampling procedures. Questions were raised regarding the appropriate usage of this test with various racial/ethnic groups given the absence of their inclusion in the norming sample. However, examination of empirical research on the MMPI has yielded inconsistent findings regarding racial/ethnic group membership and bias in MMPI profiles (e.g., Dahlstrom et al., 1986; Green, 1987).

The MMPI-2 was developed incorporating representative samples of only two racial/ethnic minority groups (i.e., Black and American Indian). Examination of scores and MMPI-2 profiles indicates no substantial mean differences between these ethnic group samples and the general normative sample on the MMPI-2 validity and standard scales (Butcher & Williams, 1992). Thus, some authors conclude that "these data indicate that the MMPI-2 norms apply equally well, regardless of ethnic group background, and that no special interpretive considerations need to be made with regard to race" (Butcher & Williams, 1992, p. 188). Despite these claims, it is interesting to note that the MMPI-2 Manual stated: "While the proportions are quite comparable to the Black and Native American minorities in this country, both Hispanic- and Asian-American subgroups are underrepresented in the restandardization sample" (Hathaway & McKinley, 1991, p. 5). Specific means and standard deviations of scale scores for each ethnic group and gender are provided in the MMPI-2 manual. A recent study by Timbrook and Graham (1994) comparing Black and White samples noted that the MMPI-2 scales appeared to "under-predict" the ratings of symptoms and problems of African Americans on the basis of five of the clinical scales. They concluded that the difference between the samples may have been due to differences in demographic information. When subjects were matched for age, education, and income, differences between the two groups decreased. Graham (1987) and Dana (1988) cautioned professionals in using the test with racial/ethnic minority individuals.

A note of caution to those who use computer-generated reports on the MMPI: In order to be sensitive to the complexities of the multicultural assessment process, it is imperative not to rely upon a computer report, which cannot possibly integrate all of the relevant cultural information (see the case of Tamiko at the end of this chapter).

California Personality Inventory (CPI)

The California Personality Inventory (CPI) (Gough, 1987) is an inventory that measures folk concepts—"concepts that arise from and are linked to the ineluctable processes of interpersonal life, and that are found everywhere that humans congregate into groups and establish societal functions" (p. 1). These concepts include responsibility, tolerance, sociability, empathy, and sense of well-being. The CPI is designed to assess overall well-adjusted individuals (Walsh & Betz, 1990) in relation to social, educational, vocational, and family issues.

The 1987 version of the CPI consists of 462 items (194 were taken from the MMPI), making up 20 scales. Megargee (1972) noted that although Gough's concept of folk cultures has stimulated "considerable cross-cultural and cross-national validational research, only recently have studies been undertaken to explore the validity of the CPI among Blacks, Chicanos or other domestic minority groups in the United States" (p. 33). De Vos and Boyer (1989) reported that they have used translated and renormed versions of the CPI in Taiwan and Japan. They noted that within these "literate, modern, but culturally different settings, the norms were different but the subscales differentiated as they do in the United States" (p. 440). They also summarized research indicating the effective usage of the CPI in India and Italy. Dana (1993) reported that currently "cross-cultural invariance is neither apparent nor believed to be necessary by CPI proponents" (p. 184).

Dana's review of the cross-cultural usage of the CPI indicates that there are item differences between various ethnic groups. For example, Davis, Hoffman, and Nelson (1990) found that there were differences in CPI response patterns between Native Americans and White samples equated on age, occupation, and education. They also noted scaled score differences due to an interaction between gender and racial/ethnic group membership. The authors concluded that ethnic background should be considered in usage of the CPI as a screening instrument.

Projective Methods

Projective methods refer to a classification of techniques in which ambiguous stimuli are presented to individuals, who then respond by projecting their inner needs. Ambiguous stimuli may include pictures (e.g., Thematic Apperception Test), inkblots (e.g., Rorschach), sentence completion exercises, and projective drawings (e.g., House-Tree-Person). "It is assumed that whatever structure is imposed on the stimulus material represents a projection of the observer's own individual perceptions on the world. It is also maintained that the more unstructured the task, the more likely the responses are to reveal important facets of personality" (Aiken, 1989, p. 306).

Projective methods have been used in cross-cultural studies for decades. Anthropologists have used various projective instruments "to characterize the modal personality of a given cultural group" (Butcher & Pancheri, 1976, p. 26). It was believed that usage of ambiguous stimuli would result in "purer" personal projections, and interpretations would be used to make inferences about the particular culture and the personality of its members. In addition, use of projectives has its roots in psychodynamic theories indicating that "there are universals in psychosexual maturation inherent in individuals rather than in culture" (De Vos & Boyer, 1989, p. 441). Projective methods have been criticized by those who state that projectives can be subject to "loose" interpretations given their ambiguity.

Dana (1993) provided a list of criteria for multicultural usage of projective measures, namely, picture-story and inkblot techniques (p. 147):

1. The stimuli should be culturally relevant.
2. The scoring should reflect variables that are culturally important for psychopathology and/or problems in living.
3. Normative data should be available for the intended population(s).
4. The interpretation of findings should make use of information available within the living contexts of intended assessees to amplify and verify the meanings of the scoring variables.
5. Culturally relevant personality theory should be used to ensure that the data provided by scoring variables constitute a sufficient basis for personality study.
6. There should be substantive validation literature, including case studies.

The Rorschach

The Rorschach (Rorschach, 1921) has been touted as the "pinnacle of the psychodiagnostic methods known as projective techniques" (Aiken, 1989, p. 329). It is made up of 10 inkblots that are bilaterally symmetrical in design. The first phase of administration is called *free association*. During this phase the client is presented with each card and asked to indicate what it might be. The examiner records the client's responses to each card verbatim. In the second phase, called the *inquiry phase*, the client is asked to elaborate upon how he or she arrived at his or her initial responses. The client's responses are scored according to the characteristics of the inkblot he or she identifies as salient perception(s). Determinants such as form, color, shading, animate/inanimate, and movement are scored and used in interpretation. It is beyond the scope of this chapter to provide information regarding the scoring and specific interpretation of the Rorschach technique. The current primary scoring system for the Rorschach is the Exner Comprehensive Rorschach (Exner, 1990), which is a synthesis of various scoring systems (Aiken, 1989). There are no special norms for different cultural groups in the United States incorporating this scoring system (Dana, 1993).

De Vos and Boyer (1989) noted that the Rorschach test can be used cross-culturally to examine modalities of thought and emotional control, citing usage of the Rorschach for Japanese Americans, Algerian Arabs, and Native Americans. They stressed the need for flexible interpretation in utilizing the Rorschach and claimed that they did not believe in quantitative analyses of percentages and mechanical determinations of ratios in interpretation.

> One must maintain a configurational approach and a flexibility in understanding the very great perceptual differences of members of different cultures. The danger to validity in using the Rorschach test cross-culturally is not that, once sufficient rapport with subjects is established, one obtains invalid material, but that individuals trained only in clinical practice may make overly rigid interpretations. (p. 52)

De Vos and Boyer highlighted the importance of understanding a "culture's normative percepts and patternings" (p. 55) in interpreting the Rorschach results. What is seen as "normative" in one culture may be "aberrant" in another. Responses must be interpreted within the social and cultural context in which the individual resides.

Thematic Apperception Test (TAT)

The second most popular projective technique is the Thematic Apperception Test (TAT) (Murray, 1943). Thirty picture cards and one blank card make up this measure. Generally only 10 to 12 cards are administered. The client is presented with a card and asked to tell a story about the picture. The story should include what is going on in the picture, what happened before, and what happens at the end. The client is also asked to provide a description of the emotions and cognitions of the characters in the picture. The clinician may request elaboration in a follow-up inquiry after each story. Interpretation is based upon a content analysis of the primary character, his or her motives and feelings, the press of the environment, outcomes, and overall themes.

A few variations of the TAT have been developed for different racial/ethnic groups. The Thompson TAT (1949) was developed for Black individuals and follows the same format as the Murray TAT. The test is made up of 21 of the original TAT pictures that were redrawn with Black characters. The test developers believed that Black people would respond more readily to pictures of Black characters in comparison to the White characters depicted in the original TAT.

More recently, the Tell Me a Story Test (TEMAS) (Costantino, Malgady, & Vasquez, 1981) was developed for urban Hispanics. The 23 picture cards depict the interaction of Hispanic characters and were designed to elicit culturally relevant themes. Studies have indicated that Hispanic children demonstrate greater verbal fluency in response to the TEMAS in comparison to the TAT.

The Children's Apperception Test (CAT) (Bellak & Bellak, 1949) has been examined for cross-cultural content (French, 1993). The CAT employs pictures of animals instead of humans. The administration and interpretation of the CAT is similar to the TAT's. French (1993) noted that the animals depicted in the cards may insult or mislead American Indian children whose culture places value on animal clans and fetishes. The animal themes may not have significance to Hispanic children in terms of their cultural lifestyle. French recommended a modification to incorporate the child's own drawings and then ask questions using the TAT format.

THE ASSESSMENT PROCESS

The preceding discussion highlights concerns with the use of various personality and intellectual measures in multicultural assessment. The following section outlines an assessment procedure for professionals to follow.

Preassessment Considerations

Although it is impossible to know all of the nuances about particular cultures, it is important that professionals continue to learn about assessment issues as they pertain to racial/ethnic minority groups. It is vital that one remain up to date regarding empirical findings that may affect usage of particular tests with various populations. A well-trained clinician will be aware of current instruments, restandardization procedures, revisions, and other state-of-the-art practices. Continuing education workshops regarding new and updated instruments often include information regarding multicultural populations. If the presenters do not include this information, be sure to contact the test publishers to find out.

Know the Referral Question

It is the practice of some professionals to enter into the assessment process with as little information regarding the client as possible: That is, they want to be "blind" to potential biases or preconceptions regarding the client. However, problems arise when vital information is disregarded due to neglect on the part of the clinician. Anecdotal records may yield important information that makes the process more efficient. If discrepancies are evident in the data, the clinician needs to spend time addressing these issues for clarification.

Gathering information through interviews, direct observations, and review of records pertaining to the individual's past and current functioning in diverse environments (e.g., homeland, school, home, social settings) is imperative. In the past, problems have arisen in the utilization of data gathered from a limited number of sources.

When testing clients from diverse backgrounds, it is important to obtain information regarding their histories to obtain a more comprehensive picture of clients' current functioning within a cultural context. For example, if an individual/family has recently relocated to the United States, it is important to obtain information about the conditions under which the move took place. For example, refugees to the United States may have experienced high levels of trauma prior to their arrival. These issues may affect the assessment process and the test scores obtained on personality and intellectual measures.

Selecting the Next Step

Based upon the information obtained regarding the referral question and information about the client, a determination must be made regarding whether the individual should be tested or whether an alternative process should be used. For example, if the individual is not English dominant and has recently immigrated to the United States, one may want to postpone testing to see how the individual adjusts to the new setting and monitor progress. Whether to test should be a conscious decision on the part of the clinician, taking into consideration the various factors affecting the individual client. Often consulting with colleagues regarding particular cases is invaluable.

Selecting Appropriate Instruments

If it is determined that testing is in order, then the selection of appropriate tests constitutes the next step. The selection process should include consideration of the test norms and any studies that have examined the use of the particular instrument with diverse populations. It may be necessary to research what tests are available and appropriate for use with a particular racial/ethnic group. Many professionals face a dilemma when dealing with clients who are monolingual or dominant in a particular language other than English. Unfortunately, the number of instruments that have been translated and validated with diverse populations is very limited.

Administering the Tests

It is always important to establish rapport with the individual you are testing. The client should understand the reason(s) for the testing. To facilitate this process, Williams (1987) suggested testing individuals in familiar surroundings (e.g., home) and using culture-appropriate reinforcers.

In many cases, the use of translators may be necessary. Translation does not ensure that the construct will be equally valid or even existent within the client's culture. As one translator explained while assisting a colleague in administering the WISC-R, "I don't think that concept is translatable into my language. I'll explain it as best I can." The notion of "explaining" the concept to the client will probably violate the already questionable adherence to the standardized test administration.

If a translator was used in the assessment process, this should be noted in the report. Feedback from the translator regarding observations of the client during this process may be incorporated in your report. Because culture is often translated through language, the translator may serve as a good cultural informant. The translator may be able to provide an informal evaluation of the client's proficiency in both languages.

Behavioral Observations

Behavioral observations can be utilized to put the assessment process within a context. Information regarding rapport with the client during the testing (e.g., level of cooperation, defensiveness, and verbal expressiveness) should be included. In addition, descriptive information about how the individual approached each task (e.g., frustration level, problem-solving abilities, trial-and-error learning, etc.) should be provided.

Putting It All Together

Any deviations from the standard test administration should be noted (Rogers, 1993). It is important that discrepancies within the test results be addressed on the basis of accurate information.

When the examiner is in doubt about an interpretive issue, it is always recommended that he or she consult with cultural experts and colleagues to ensure to some extent the "reasonableness" of the interpretation and recommendations. As noted previously, it is beneficial also to incorporate the feedback of everyone involved in the assessment process: client, parents, significant others, teachers, mental health workers, community agency personnel, cultural informants, and so forth.

CASE EXAMPLES

The following cases represent compilations of information obtained from various client profiles. They are designed to promote discussion regarding the importance of integration of cultural issues into the assessment process.

A Case Example: Katya

Katya is a 13-year-old African American student who was referred for a psychological evaluation by her teachers due to dramatic drops in achievement and motivation during the last 3 months of school. Prior to this time Katya appeared to be a well-adjusted student performing in the average to above-average range in all academic subjects, including reading, math, and social studies. Changes were evidenced in terms of poor attendance, poor personal hygiene, and lack of motivation. Katya has lived in the Midwest for approximately 3 years and was born in the United States. English is her primary language.

On the basis of the initial referral, it was determined that Katya would undergo an intellectual assessment. A psychometrician at the community agency to which Katya was referred was assigned to complete this evaluation using the WISC-III. His report indicated that Katya scored in the overall borderline range of intelligence (FSIQ = 77, 6th percentile, 95% confidence interval 72-84), with a Performance Scale IQ (PIQ = 84, 14th percentile, 95% confidence interval 77-93) in the low-average range and a Verbal Scale IQ (VIQ = 74, 4th percentile, 95% confidence interval 69-82) in the borderline range. Specific scores were as follows:

Performance Scale		Verbal Scale	
Picture Completion	8	Information	4
Coding	6	Similarities	7
Picture Arrangement	8	Arithmetic	5
Block Design	9	Vocabulary	6
Object Assembly	7	Comprehension	5
Symbol Search	6	Digit Span	6

No behavioral observations were included in the write-up.

An evaluation team at the agency reviewed the report to determine recommendations to be forwarded to the school. The team was alarmed by the borderline scores on the intelligence test and attributed the lack of motivation to Katya's low abilities and difficulties in meeting the expectations of those around her, namely, teachers. Katya's scores were then forwarded to the school with recommendations that she undergo a complete educational evaluation for possible change in placement to special education.

Considerations for Interpretation

A number of problems with this case are evident. First, there was a lack of regard for the initial referral question, namely, the recent change in Katya's behavior. The concerns regarding attendance, hygiene, and motivational problems would point to emotional factors as a primary area of concern. The administration of an intelligence test as the main investigative tool left important questions about the child's socioemotional functioning unanswered. The team neglected to note that Katya had been performing in the average to above-average range in all academic subjects for 3 years. Problems were noted approximately 3 months ago. This disparity between scores on the intelligence test and previous academic functioning was not addressed.

Second, the lack of behavioral observations in the intellectual report make it difficult to place the assessment within context. Was Katya motivated to complete the evaluation tasks as they were presented to her? What was her overall affect like? Was she agitated, anxious, or depressed? Were the importance of and reasons for the test communicated to Katya?

On the basis of these interpretive concerns, the school psychologist receiving the report noted the lack of information regarding Katya's socioemotional state. Therefore, the psychologist decided to complete a socioemotional assessment by administering the Rorschach and the TAT. Overall results indicated depressive themes and general indicators of anxiety. In a discussion of her findings with agency personnel, they attributed the depression and anxiety to Katya's low abilities and difficulties meeting the expectations of her teachers. They cited numerous cases of African American students who demonstrated similar problems.

It should be noted that up to this point, information from Katya's family was not integrated into the clinical picture. Katya's parents had given consent to the testing and had brought her to the agency for testing but were not interviewed as part of the assessment process.

When the psychologist shared the information she had obtained from the agency and from her testing, Katya's mother tearfully shared that Katya had undergone an abortion on the morning she was tested by the psychometrist. Katya had not wanted to share this information earlier because it brought "shame" upon the family. The specific circumstances of Katya's pregnancy were not explored at the time of the evaluation, but the psychologist recommended that Katya be seen for counseling to address issues surrounding the abortion, sexuality, and self-esteem. During the interview, it was revealed that Katya had been living in Nigeria from the age of 3 up until moving to the Midwest. The school personnel had assumed that she had lived in the United

States most of her life, given that she had been born here. This information has ramifications regarding language issues and cultural equivalence.

This case example highlights the importance of culturally sensitive assessment as a process of putting together a comprehensive clinical picture that accurately depicts the client. Identifying the presenting problem by integrating information from multiple sources (i.e., standardized tests, clinical interviews, projectives, observations, informal assessments, historical data) is imperative.

A Case Example: Tamiko

Tamiko is a 56-year-old, first-generation Japanese-American who has been referred for a psychological evaluation due to reported symptoms of depression and short-term memory problems noted by family members and a physician. Tamiko notes that she is "fine" and cites frequent headaches and backaches as the causes of her lack of activity, long periods of time spent in bed, and decrease in appetite. According to the family, Tamiko's symptoms started upon the death of her mother at the age of 91 approximately 1 year ago.

Given the presenting concerns, a decision was made to do a complete psychological evaluation including an in-depth clinical interview and intelligence (i.e., Wechsler Adult Intelligence Scale) and personality (i.e., MMPI and TAT) testing. Results of the WAIS-R (Wechsler, 1981) indicated that Tamiko's cognitive abilities fell within the average range. She obtained a Verbal IQ of 90 and a Performance IQ of 110 with a Full Scale IQ of 100. All subtest scores fell within the average to high-average range.

The MMPI revealed elevations on Scales 1 (Hypochondriasis), 2 (Depression), and 4 (Psychopathic Deviate). The psychometrist who scored the MMPI expressed concern regarding these elevations based upon the computer generated report. Specific items endorsed indicated a great deal of anger toward others.

On the TAT, themes regarding anger toward authority figures and feelings of inadequacy and loneliness were indicated. For example, in response to 1BF, a picture of a young boy sitting in a darkened doorway, Tamiko told the following story.

> The boy is sad. He has no friends because he is living in a new place. He misses his old home, his toys, and his neighborhood. His family was forced to live here and can't leave this place. There are fences all around it. His parents try to make the best of it but the boy knows that they are heartbroken.

(How does the story end?)

> The family gets to leave but things are never the way they used to be. People are never as happy as they used to be.

During the clinical interview, the psychologist delved into the feelings of anger evidenced in the psychological testing. Tamiko shared that she had a great deal of anger toward the U.S. government and revealed that her family was interned during World War II. She recalled seeing her father and mother having to sell all of their belongings during a "fire sale" when they found out that they would have to be relocated to Arizona. "We could only take one suitcase each. My father cried because he had worked so hard and had to give it all up just like that. He was never the same." She went on to share that her father died shortly after they were given their freedom. "He never achieved what he had before." Tamiko grew angrier as she indicated that her mother received her redress check from the government at a time when "she was so old, how could she enjoy it. The government thinks that everything is OK now that they have apologized and given out some money. But it's too late. The people who deserve it are no longer alive to enjoy it."

Considerations for Interpretation

Although some would express concerns regarding the 20-point discrepancy between Tamiko's VIQ and PIQ, this finding is congruent with research indicating the Japanese tend to score higher on visual-spatial abilities in comparison to verbal abilities. It is important to note that her scores fall within the average range on this test. The relative strengths in nonverbal abilities have been attributed to the nonverbal emphasis in communication within the Japanese culture.

The score elevations on Scales 1, 2, and 4 of the MMPI appear to be congruent with Tamiko's clinical picture. First, somatization of psychological symptoms is often common within the Japanese culture. It is more "acceptable" to identify physical complaints than psychological problems. The depressive symptoms are reflected in elevations on Scale 2. The elevation on Scale 4 is also a relevant part of this clinical picture given the information Tamiko shared during the clinical interview and the TAT. It is hypothesized that her TAT story reflects the feelings and perceptions she had of the internment experience. Her feelings of anger toward the government for the internment of her family had potentially increased upon the recent death of her mother.

SUMMARY

As noted in the preceding discussion, the process of conducting an assessment is a multifaceted procedure. The added complexities of understanding an individual who is culturally different from oneself is a challenging task, especially given the impact of the results and recommendations for clinical and educational practice. The concerns raised regarding the utilization of popular instruments in the field have been noted. The responsibility of selecting, administering, and interpreting test results in a culturally sensitive manner remains with the clinician. Although some would fault the tests as being "biased," when used appropriately these instruments yield important objective information that can be used in planning effective treatment and educational planning. When used inappropriately the results may be tragic. This chapter has attempted to briefly cover important issues for consideration in clinical practice and to present a procedure that incorporates multicultural issues in the assessment process.

REFERENCES

Aiken, L. R. (1989). *Assessment of personality*. Needham Heights, MA: Allyn & Bacon.

Anastasi, A. (1982). *Psychological testing* (5th ed.). New York: Macmillan.

Armour-Thomas, E. A. (1992). Intellectual assessment of children from culturally diverse backgrounds. *School Psychology Review, 21*(4), 552-565.

Bellak, L., & Bellak, S. S. (1949). *Children's Apperception Test*. New York: C.P.S.

Boring, E. G. (1923, June). Intelligence as the tests test it. *New Republic*, pp. 35-37.

Brislin, R. W., Lonner, W. J., & Thorndike, R. M. (1973). *Cross-cultural research methods*. New York: Wiley-Interscience.

Butcher, J. N., & Pancheri, P. (1976). *A handbook of cross-national MMPI research*. Minneapolis: University of Minnesota Press.

Butcher, J. N., & Williams, C. L. (1992). *Essentials of MMPI-2 and MMPI-A interpretation*. Minneapolis: University of Minnesota Press.

Costantino, G., Malgady, R., & Vasquez, C. (1981). A comparison of the Murray-TAT and a new thematic apperception test for urban Hispanic children. *Hispanic Journal of Behavioral Science, 3*, 291-300.

Dahlstrom, W. (1986). Ethnic status and personality measurement. In W. G. Dahlstrom, D. Lachar, & L. E. Dahlstrom (Eds.), *MMPI patterns of American minorities* (pp. 3-23). Minneapolis: University of Minnesota Press.

Dahlstrom, W. G., Lachar, D., & Dahlstrom, L. E. (1986). Overview and conclusions. In W. G. Dahlstrom, D. Lachar, & L. E. Dahlstrom (Eds.), *MMPI patterns of American minorities* (pp. 188-206). Minneapolis: University of Minnesota Press.

Dana, R. H. (1986). Personality assessment and Native Americans. *Journal of Personality Assessment, 50*(3), 480-500.

Dana, R. H. (1988). Culturally diverse groups and MMPI interpretation. *Professional Psychology: Research and Practice, 19*(5), 490-495.

Dana, R. H. (1993). *Multicultural assessment perspectives for professional psychology*. Boston: Allyn & Bacon.

Das, J. P., Kirby, J., & Jarman, R. F. (1979). *Simultaneous and successive cognitive processes*. New York: Academic Press.

Davis, G. L., Hoffman, R. G., & Nelson, K. S. (1990). Differences between Native Americans and Whites on the California Psychological Inventory. *Psychological Assessment, 2*(3), 238-242.

De Vos, G. A., & Boyer, L. B. (1989). *Symbolic analysis cross culturally: The Rorschach Test*. Los Angeles: University of California Press.

Exner, J. E. (1990). *A Rorschach workbook for the comprehensive system* (3rd ed.). Asheville, NC: Rorschach Workshops.

Figueroa, R. A., & Sassenrath, J. M. (1989). A longitudinal study of the predictive validity of the System of Multicultural Pluralistic Assessment (SOMPA). *Psychology in the Schools, 26*, 5-19.

French, L. A. (1993). Adapting projective tests for minority children. *Psychological Reports, 72*, 15-18.

Gaw, A. C. (Ed.). (1993). *Culture, ethnicity and mental illness*. Washington, DC: American Psychiatric Press.

Gough, H. G. (1987). *Manual for the California Psychological Inventory*. Palo Alto, CA: Consulting Psychologists Press.

Graham, J. R. (1987). *The MMPI: A practical guide* (2nd ed.). New York: Oxford University Press.

Green, R. L. (1987). Ethnicity and MMPI performance: A review. *Journal of Consulting and Clinical Psychology, 55*(4), 497-512.

Gynther, M. D. (1972). White norms and Black MMPIs: A prescription for discrimination. *Psychological Bulletin, 78*(5), 386-402.

Hathaway, S. R., & McKinley, J. C. (1991). *Manual for administration and scoring MMPI-2*. Minneapolis: University of Minnesota Press.

Helms, J. E. (1992). Why there is no study of cultural equivalence in standardized cognitive ability testing? *American Psychologist, 47*(9), 1083-1101.

Jensen, A. R. (1985). The nature of Black-White difference on various psychometric tests: Spearman's hypothesis. *Behavioural and Brain Sciences, 8*(2), 193-263.

Kaufman, A. S. (1990). *Assessing adolescent and adult intelligence*. Boston: Allyn & Bacon.

Kaufman, A. S. (1994). *Intelligent testing with the WISC-III*. New York: John Wiley.

McShane, D., & Cook, V. (1985). Transcultural intellectual assessment: Performance by Hispanics on the Wechsler Scales. In B. B. Wolman (Ed.), *Handbook of intelligence: Theories, measurement, and applications* (pp. 737-785). New York: John Wiley.

Megargee, E. I. (1972). *The California Psychological Inventory handbook*. San Francisco: Jossey-Bass.

Mercer, C. D. (1987). *Students with learning disabilities* (3rd ed.). Columbus, OH: Merrill.

Mercer, J. R. (1979). *System of Multicultural Pluralistic Assessment (SOMPA) technical manual*. New York: Psychological Corporation.

Murray, H. A. (1943). *Thematic Apperception Test*. Cambridge, MA: Harvard University Press.

Raven, J. (1989). The Raven Progressive Matrices: A review of national norming studies and ethnic and socioeconomic variation within the United States. *Journal of Educational Measurement, 26*(1), 1-16.

Reynolds, C. R. (1982). The problem of bias in psychological assessment. In C. R. Reynolds & T. B. Gutkin (Eds.), *The handbook of school psychology* (pp. 178-208). New York: John Wiley.

Reynolds, C. R., & Kaiser, S. M. (1990). Test bias in psychological assessment. In T. B. Gutkin & C. R. Reynolds (Eds.), *The handbook of school psychology* (pp. 487-525). New York: John Wiley.

Rogers, M. R. (1993). Psychoeducational assessment of racial/ethnic minority children and youth. In H. B. Vance (Ed.), *Best practices in assessment for school and clinical settings* (pp. 399-440). Brandon, VT: Clinical Psychology Publishing.

Rorschach, H. (1921). *Psychodiagnostik*. Bern: Bircher.

Sabnani, H. B., & Ponterotto, J. G. (1992). Racial/ethnic minority-specific instrumentation in counseling research: A review, critique, and recommendations. *Measurement and Evaluation in Counseling and Development, 24*, 161-187.

Samuda, R. J. (1975). *Psychological testing of American minorities: Issues and consequences*. New York: Harper & Row.

Sattler, J. M. (1988). *Assessment of children* (3rd ed.). San Diego: Author.

Sattler, J. M. (1991). How good are federal judges in detecting differences in item difficulty on intelligence tests for ethnic groups? *Psychological Assessment, 3*(1), 125-129.

Shuey, A. M. (1958). *The testing of Negro intelligence*. Lynchburg, VA: J. P. Bell.

Suzuki, L. A., Meller, P. M., & Ponterotto, J. G. (in press). *Multicultural assessment: Clinical, psychological and educational applications*. San Francisco: Jossey-Bass.

Thompson, C. (1949). The Thompson modification of the Thematic Apperception Test. *Journal of Projective Techniques, 13*, 469-478.

Timbrook, R. E., & Graham, J. R. (1994). Ethnic differences on the MMPI-2? *Psychological Assessment, 6*(3), 212-217.

Vroon, P. A. (1980). Intelligence on myths and measurement. In G. E. Stelmach (Ed.), *Advances in psychology 3* (pp. 27-44). New York: North Holland.

Walsh, W. B., & Betz, N. E. (1990). *Tests and assessment* (3rd ed.). Englewood Cliffs, NJ: Prentice Hall.

Wechsler, D. (1949). *Manual for the Wechsler Intelligence Scale for Children*. New York: Psychological Corporation.

Wechsler, D. (1974). *Manual for the Wechsler Intelligence Scale for Children—Revised*. San Antonio, TX: Psychological Corporation.

Wechsler, D. (1981). *Manual for the Wechsler Adult Intelligence Scale—Revised*. San Antonio, TX: Psychological Corporation.

Wechsler, D. (1989). *Manual for the Wechsler Preschool and Primary Scale of Intelligence—Revised*. San Antonio, TX: Psychological Corporation.

Wechsler, D. (1991). *Manual for the Wechsler Intelligence Scale for Children—Third Edition*. San Antonio, TX: Psychological Corporation.

Williams, C. L. (1987). Issues surrounding psychological testing of minority patients. *Hospital and Community Psychiatry, 38*(2), 184-189.

25

Counseling Children and Adolescents in Schools

Salient Multicultural Issues

MARK S. KISELICA

JILL C. CHANGIZI

VA LECIA L. CURETON

BETTY E. GRIDLEY

DEMOGRAPHIC STATISTICS regarding enrollments in our nation's elementary schools indicate that increasing numbers of ethnically diverse students are attending U.S. school systems. According to Hodgkinson (1985), approximately half of the elementary school populations in California and Texas consist of racial/ethnic minority students. Kellogg (1988) reported that minority students now constitute 70% to 96% of the student population in 15 of the nation's largest school districts. Furthermore, according to a 1988 report entitled *One-Third of a Nation*, commissioned by the American Council on Education (cited in Ponterotto & Casas, 1991), it is estimated that by the year 2000, 33% of all elementary school children in the United States will be racial/ethnic minorities, and by the year 2020, this percentage will rise to 39%.

In response to the growing cultural diversity of students attending our nation's schools, the American School Counselor Association (ASCA) has taken two major measures to ensure that the specific needs of all students are met. First, recognizing that cultural diversity is an important factor deserving increased awareness and understanding on the part of school counselors, ASCA (1988) prepared the following position statement on cross/multicultural counseling: "School counselors must take action to insure [that] students of culturally diverse backgrounds have access to appropriate services and opportunities which promote maximum development" (p. 4). Second, ASCA (1992) recently published the revised *American School Counselor Association Ethical Standards for School Counselors,* which now dictate that competency in multicultural counseling is an ethical obligation of school counselors: "The school counselor... recognizes that differences in clients relating to age, gender, race, religion, sexual orientation, socioeconomic and ethnic backgrounds may require specific training to ensure competent services" (p. 3).

These directives challenge school counselors to increase their sensitivity to cultural issues and to develop the skills necessary for enhancing the school environment and the personal development of culturally diverse students. In an effort to assist in these endeavors, this chapter highlights a variety of salient multicultural issues involved in counseling children and adolescents in schools. Specifically, it reviews critical multicultural considerations pertaining to several services offered by school counselors, including family consultation services, career development and placement services, and assessment services.

Although this chapter focuses on the multicultural counseling activities of school counselors, it will be of service to all school personnel, including school psychologists and social workers, teachers, and administrators, who are interested in expanding their skills for working in multicultural school settings. Woven throughout are recommendations for how school counselors and other school officials can adjust their practices in order to serve culturally diverse students and their families more effectively. This chapter also contains numerous suggestions for empowering ethnic minority families in their interactions with educational professionals.

Before we begin our review, however, three cautions are in order. First, we have restricted our discussion to issues pertaining to multicultural school counseling with racial/ethnic minority populations. We purposely focused on these groups because the needs of racial/ethnic minority clients historically have been neglected by the helping professions (see Ponterotto & Casas, 1991; Sue & Sue, 1990). Nevertheless, we recognize that there are important, unique, cultural considerations in counseling subgroups of White, majority populations, such as Anglo-Saxon Americans and White ethnic Americans, and we refer the reader to Axelson (1993) for a cogent discussion of the subject. Second, due to space limitations, we addressed multicultural issues pertaining to only three of the many services provided by school counselors, namely, family consultation, career development and placement, and assessment services. It should be noted that other domains of school counseling (e.g., pedagogical services, referral services, and accountability services; see Baker, 1992) not covered in this chapter also warrant a reconceptualization from a multicultural perspective. School counselors who wish to improve their multicultural competencies in these areas are encouraged to read Lee's (1994) excellent resource on the subject. For in-depth suggestions for addressing the emotional and personal needs of ethnic minority children and adolescents, the reader is referred to Ho (1992). Our third caution is that our counseling recommendations for particular racial/ethnic minority groups can be misused if they are applied in a stereotypic manner. It should be noted that there are large within-group differences for any racial/ethnic minority population. School counselors should use our recommendations to formulate tentative hypotheses about the potential cultural issues and problems faced by a particular client and then explore these hypotheses with the client. By proceeding in this manner, counselors will discover the unique cultural perspective of each individual client.

FAMILY CONSULTATION SERVICES

The family is an integral part of the American school system (Chapman, 1991; Nardine & Morris, 1991; Solomon, 1991). Studies have demonstrated that programs with a strong emphasis on parental involvement produce more successful students (Henderson, 1988). The importance of the family in counseling children in schools has been addressed by a number of authors (e.g., Atkinson, 1986; Golden, 1986; Ottens, May, & Ottens, 1986). Yet public schools have fallen short in their attempts to involve racial/ethnic minority parents (Chrispeels, 1991).

Historically, ethnic minority families have held educational attainment in high esteem, considering the potential benefits of educational advancement. Unfortunately, the educational system is not always sensitive to the needs and challenges faced by racial/ethnic minority children and their parents. Cultural beliefs and traditions established in the home are often devalued in the school setting (Cole, Thomas, & Lee, 1988). When ethnic minority students have problems adjusting, the student is often deemed inadequate, when in actuality the educational system itself may need adjustment (Lee, 1989).

The school counselor is in the position to serve as a liaison between the racial/ethnic minority family and the school (Atkinson & Juntunen, 1994). Casas and Furlong (1994), in their support of the role of the school counselor as a liaison, noted that "it is our belief that school counselors have the kinds of skills that place them in a unique position to work closely with teachers, administrators, and communities to facilitate and maximize parental participation in all aspects of the children's education" (p. 146). To be successful in this role, school counselors must understand the factors that influence the involvement of racial/ethnic minority parents in their children's education.

Factors That Influence Parental Involvement

Three factors influencing the involvement of racial/ethnic minority parents have been discussed in the literature: cultural value conflicts, racism and alienation, and poverty.

Cultural Value Conflicts

The customs and values of ethnic minority families often conflict with those of the American educational system. As a prerequisite for working with racial/ethnic minority parents, it is recommended that school counselors understand these potential difficulties.

School personnel and racial/ethnic minority parents often have differing expectations and ideas about the role of the family in the education of the child (Atkinson, 1986). For example, Yao (1988) explained that although Asian immigrant parents usually do not initiate contact with school personnel, they have a deep respect for teachers and do not believe in questioning the authority of school officials. The lack of involvement of some Asian immigrant parents in schools is due to traditional beliefs that their domain of influence is in the home, whereas it is the responsibility of school officials to take control in the school setting.

Morrow (1991) outlined a number of additional cultural factors that influence Southeast Asian parental involvement, including the emphasis on the family rather than the Western emphasis on independence, the educational level of the parents before they came to the United States, and English language fluency. He also pointed out that school officials often misinterpret the behavior of both Asian immigrant and Asian American parents as a lack of interest or desire to be involved in their children's education. When Asian American parents do have a problem with the schools, they are slow to challenge the system (Divoky, 1988).

Nicolau and Ramos (1990) pointed out that poor Hispanic parents also commonly view the educational system as an intimidating bureaucracy that they have no right to question. In addition, Hispanic parents tend to view the role of parents and the role of the school in relation to education as sharply differentiated. Parents have a duty to instill respect and proper behavior in their children, and it is the school's job to instill knowledge. These cultural influences make Hispanic parents appear uninterested in their children's educational progress, but this is not the case (Nicolau & Ramos, 1990). On the contrary, most Hispanic parents want their children to succeed in school (Casas & Furlong, 1994).

Lee (1989) also suggested that the cultural values of African Americans are often at odds with the American educational system. The structure of the African American family is often seen by school officials as having detrimental effects on adolescent development. As a result, African American parents often feel disregarded and disconnected from the schools that their children attend.

The traditional values of Native American families also clash with those espoused by school personnel from the majority culture. Traditional Native American parents feel that children are born with the power, ability, and rights to make important choices. Consequently, they generally prefer noninterfering styles of parenting that according to Kallam, Hoernicke, and Coser (1994) may be perceived as permissive or negligent by school officials within the majority culture.

Racism and Alienation

Another factor related to the involvement of racial/ethnic minority parents in schools is the racism and alienation experienced by racial/ethnic minority children and their parents. Faced with years of institutionalized racism and discrimination, many African American parents have grown to mistrust the educational system, doubting that the school system has their child's best interest in mind (Cole et al., 1988). Nicolau and Ramos (1990) explained that many Hispanic parents perceive the educational system as a symbol of their past failures and feelings of alienation. That is, these parents are uncomfortable with the thought of subjecting their children to the same U.S. educational system that brought them feelings of inadequacy and defeat. According to Kallam et al. (1994), one of the few universal beliefs among Native American peoples is a mistrust of the dominant culture's institutions, including schools, because throughout history those institutions have attempted to change the customs, practices, and beliefs of Native American populations.

In addition to these issues, racial/ethnic minority parents commonly report having a lack of understanding of the American educational system (Atkinson, 1986; Nicolau & Ramos, 1990; Yao, 1988). This lack of understanding often leads to feelings of powerlessness and alienation.

Poverty

Government statistics regarding socioeconomic conditions in the United States indicate that racial/ethnic minority families are overrepresented among the poor. For example, citing U.S. census data for 1987, Ponterotto and Casas (1991) reported that whereas only 11% of White families live in poverty, approximately 31% of African Americans, 28% of Mexican Americans, and 39% of Puerto Rican Americans are poor. Other government statistics summarized by Locke (1992) document that Native Americans have the highest unemployment and the lowest average income of any minority group in the United States.

The problems associated with the poverty experienced by racial/ethnic minority parents can have a significant impact on their participation in the educational system. For example, studies by Sullivan (1984, 1985) and

Williams (1991) chronicled the difficulties that poor, inner-city African American parents have in monitoring and partaking in their children's educational progress. Although the parents in these studies were concerned about their children's academic performance, a variety of responsibilities and hardships— caring for preschool children; one or both parents working in low-paying jobs located far from home, problems with housing, health, and crime; dealing with governmental agencies—made it nearly impossible for most of the parents to play an active role in their children's education or to provide older children with parental supervision during after-school hours.

Unless school counselors help racial/ethnic minority parents to manage these many stressors, parental involvement with the schools will be minimal. Yet according to McLaughlin and Shields (1987), most school districts have failed to implement programs targeted to increase the involvement of low-income families in schools by recognizing and assisting with problems related to poverty.

Strategies for Increasing Minority Parent Involvement

School counselors are in a position to serve as a resource for racial/ethnic minority parents (Lee, 1989). Specifically, it is recommended that school counselors work toward preventing and mediating cultural values conflicts and misunderstandings, taking measures to reduce feelings of alienation, and assisting parents in overcoming socioeconomic hardships.

One strategy for preventing cultural misunderstandings and reducing alienation has been to educate school personnel about the value systems and cultural experiences of racial/ethnic minority families. Lee (1989) argued that "acting in the role of student advocate, the counselor should function to facilitate an awareness among his or her educational colleagues of the systemic factors that impinge upon the development of Black students" (p. 304). Lee (1989) and Atkinson and Juntunen (1994) suggested that multicultural training sessions be conducted to help familiarize and sensitize school personnel to the issues faced by ethnic minorities. Nicolau and Ramos (1990) reported that such efforts have been successful in eliminating many of the negative feelings and misconceptions often encountered between school personnel and racial/ethnic minority parents.

A number of other recommendations have pertained to educating racial/ethnic minority parents about the U.S. educational system. The intent of these strategies has been to reduce parental hesitation about being involved in schools. For example, Atkinson and Juntunen (1994) reported that ethnic minority parents benefit from community awareness workshops and parent training programs designed to familiarize them with school policies, procedures, and goals. In regard to immigrant parents, First (1988) recommended that print and electronic media be utilized to inform immigrant parents about the American school system through community outreach programs.

According to Yao (1988), schools should utilize interpreters via parent orientation workshops to disseminate information about the school to non-English-speaking parents. Nieto (1992) suggested that ethnic/racial minority students be utilized to translate information from English to the languages spoken by the parents. Sending letters to parents (Liontos, 1992; Yao, 1988) and making home visits (Nicolau & Ramos, 1990) are other tactics that have been recommended for keeping racial/ethnic minority parents informed about school activities and for promoting parental participation in those activities.

Other strategies for reducing alienation from the school system include genuinely showing an interest in how the parents feel about the educational system and working to empower parents. For example, with many African American parents, school counselors should be prepared to empathize with the perception that the school has taken away their control over their children's destiny in school (Liontos, 1992). School counselors can empower parents to regain control by encouraging the parents to become leaders in their school communities (Casas & Furlong, 1994).

Herring (1991) discussed two critical considerations for building trust between Native Americans and school personnel and suggested that school counselors can play a lead role in achieving this goal. First, Herring recommended that school counselors demonstrate awareness of the tribal identity and familial pattern of Native American clients to gain their respect and trust. Second, Herring advised school counselors to be knowledgeable of three distinct family patterns among Native Americans:

> (1) the *traditional* family, which overtly attempts to adhere to culturally defined styles of living; (2) the *nontraditional* family, which retains only rudimentary elements of historical Native American family life, preferring to live within the majority culture; and (3) the *pantraditional* family, which desires to return to an ancestral culture of nomadism and isolation from non-Native Americans. (pp. 43-44)

Herring added that counselors need to be able to match their counseling strategies with the appropriate family pattern. For a more comprehensive discussion regarding this task, the reader is referred to Herring and Erchul (1988).

Nicolau and Ramos (1990) explained that an important element in enhancing the involvement of Hispanic parents is for school personnel to be committed to outreach, to communicate honestly, and to be respectful of the cultural values and concerns of Hispanic parents. They also encouraged a personal approach to the Hispanic family that might involve home visits by the school counselor.

Morrow (1991) argued that school personnel can promote the involvement of Asian parents by attempting to understand the cultural values of Asian people and by genuinely caring about the concerns of the parents. In addition, Morrow recommended taking the time to look at each family on an individual basis in order to refrain from responding to Asian Americans in a stereotypic manner.

Cole et al. (1988) proposed a comprehensive family consultation model to bridge the gap between home and school. They suggested that community awareness programs be conducted in the following areas: school curriculum, standardized testing and placement, parental participation and involvement, and the educational and administrative structure of the school. Within the home, counselors were encouraged to provide academic counseling, personal-social counseling, parent skills training, and information on community resources.

Finally, school counselors can work as advocates for broadening the mission of schools to make them more relevant to their surrounding communities. As Dryfoos (1994) argued, schools can no longer be viewed merely as places where children are educated. Consistent with this view, Murphy (1993) recommended that schools should develop partnerships with social and health agencies, remain open 7 days a week, 12 months a year, and provide parents and children struggling to overcome the untold hardships of poverty a safe haven for health care, socializing, and recreation.

CAREER INFORMATION
AND PLACEMENT SERVICES

As all children go through school, they must continually be provided with educational, occupational, and career information that is relevant and appropriate to their age and cognitive development (Gottfredson, 1981; Piaget, 1977). Information dissemination is not a one-time event but rather a process that should occur throughout a student's childhood and adolescence. Useful information helps students deal with developmental issues effectively (Baker, 1992). According to Hoppock (cited in Baker, 1992), information serves the following purposes: It (a) increases feelings of security, (b) encourages natural curiosity, (c) extends horizons, (d) encourages wholesome attitudes, (e) develops desirable approaches to decision making, and (f) is helpful when pragmatic decisions such as selecting school programs or courses, deciding which college to attend, and determining whether to drop out of school have to be made.

Despite the numerous advantages of new information, most children and adolescents are not aware of how helpful it can be. Therefore, it is the school counselor's responsibility to take a proactive role in providing and distributing educational, career, and placement information so that all students are prepared and encouraged to grow (Lee, 1989).

As was mentioned earlier in this chapter, there will be a substantial increase in the number of racial/ethnic minority students over the next several decades. Also, it should be noted that between now and the year 2000, 85% of new workers in the labor force will be racial/ethnic minorities and women (Herr & Niles, 1994). Because school counselors are responsible for providing information and preparing all students for their futures, it is crucial that they understand the career issues of racial/ethnic minority students in order to address the growing needs of a diverse student body.

Racial/Ethnic Minority Career Issues

For many years, any difficulties experienced by racial/ethnic minority students were thought to be due to deficits within the individual or his or her cultural upbringing (Cheatham, 1990; Solarzano, 1992). Racial/ethnic minorities were expected to conform to the norms of the White middle class (Lee, 1989). However, there is little evidence for the claims of the well-known cultural deficit model. Research findings have demonstrated that Black and Hispanic students have occupational aspirations as high as or higher than those of Whites on virtually every socioeconomic level (Arbona & Novy, 1991; Solarzano, 1992). Other findings suggest that Mexican American and Puerto Rican youth also have aspirations as high as those of Whites. However, their career *expectations* are not as high because they recognize the barriers ahead of them (Arbona, 1990). These barriers have caused many students to become discouraged about school and their future job outlook, hence negatively affecting motivation and self-esteem. This predicament has contributed to a mismatch between minority student aspirations and minority student educational and occupational attainment (Solarzano, 1992).

The reference groups utilized by racial/ethnic minority children for job information and standards also affect educational and occupational attainment. Children develop a reference group for job information and standards based on members of their social class and racial group. Lower class children, for example, tend to have knowledge only of the type of work they observe in their lower class community (Gottfredson, 1981; Sharf, 1992). In a study of urban children, Vondracek and Kirchner (1974) found that African American children had less knowledge than White children of the types of work adults do. Other research has shown that minority children often have a limited scope of occupational choice reasons such as lack of effective role models (Herr & Niles, 1994; Herring, 1990; Miller, Springer, & Wells, 1988; Sanders, 1987; Sharf, 1992).

Gottfredson's (1981) theory about the development of occupational aspirations is helpful in understanding the career aspirations and choices of racial/ethnic minority students. Gottfredson proposed that there is an important relationship between the self-concept and occupational pursuits. She suggested that the self-concept begins to develop in early childhood and that it represents how one identifies oneself, encompassing characteristics compatible with the self as well as acknowledging those characteristics that are incompatible with the self. According to Gottfredson (1981), by the age of 13, children have formed cognitive maps for their career pursuits based on the compatibility of a particular career with their image of themselves (Miller et al., 1988). The more externally visible the valued characteristic, the more it will influence one's job choice. Someone who values femininity, for example, may choose a traditionally feminine job, even if she has many interests in a traditionally masculine field, so that her career is compatible with her image of herself (Gottfredson, 1981). The same phenomenon may be occurring among African Americans who have been found to lean toward careers with a "social" environment (Miller et al., 1988). African Americans may gravitate toward "social" fields because others of their race tend to do so, and thus they may be experiencing a compatibility of self-concept with occupational choice.

Gottfredson (1981) also recognized that the perceived accessibility of a job is an important factor affecting career choice. Racial/ethnic minorities, for example, may foresee many obstacles, social or economic, as being in the way of their success in a desired field. Perhaps their desired occupation does not exist in their own community, or perhaps they are aware of job discrimination in that particular field. Many occupations, for example, have excluded individuals of racial/ethnic minorities to such a degree that a sense of disentitlement exists among employers and employees (Herr & Niles, 1994). This can create the cognitive set that only members of certain cultural groups are allowed in such positions, resulting in job discrimination. Rather than facing these types of barriers, racial/ethnic minorities may limit their career choices to those in which they will feel accepted and have a chance for mobility (Gottfredson, 1981; Sharf, 1992). They also make compromises based on the reality of the job market (Gottfredson, 1981). Negative career experiences that racial/ethnic minorities foresee greatly affect their self-concepts, ambition, motivation, and self-efficacy, all of which influence their personal and career development (Herr & Niles, 1994).

Suggestions for Counselors

Numerous counseling recommendations have been offered to mitigate the negative effects of racism, poverty, and oppression on the career development of racial/ethnic minority students. Pertinent recommendations have been focused on the following topics: (a) a life-planning approach to counseling, (b) work attitudes and values, (c) exposure to role models, (d) parent involvement in career planning, (e) group activities, and (f) career placement and testing skills. Each of these recommendations is highlighted here.

A Life-Planning Approach to Career Counseling

Lee (1989) recommended that counselors take a life-planning approach to career counseling with racial/ethnic minority students. Similarly, others have suggested that the process of information dissemination needs to begin in the primary grades because a racial/ethnic minority child starts to eliminate or circumscribe his or her career options at a young age (Gottfredson, 1981; Herr & Niles, 1994). In addition, throughout elementary, junior high, and high school, an emphasis needs to be placed on appreciation of and respect for cultural and individual differences (Herr & Niles, 1994).

Career development activities should vary according to different developmental periods. By providing a variety of career development activities for students at each age level, school counselors will help racial/ethnic minority students to "develop a sense of commitment to the career planning process as a means for overcoming racial and ethnic barriers" (Herr & Niles, 1994, p. 189). With young children in Grades K through 6, exposure to concrete and clear information regarding a wide range of traditional and nontraditional careers is recommended (Herr & Niles, 1994; Lee, 1989; Sharf, 1992). Once racial/ethnic minority students reach adolescence, they are better able to think abstractly and hypothetically, and thus can begin setting goals and planning their future. Because adolescents have higher intellectual capacities, school counselors should encourage them to begin identifying their personal, familial, and cultural values toward work and examining how these values compare with society's work ethic (Herr & Niles, 1994).

Work Attitudes and Values

As was discussed earlier, the parents and guardians of many racial/ethnic minority students are uninformed about the realities of the workforce and unaware that their own cultural values may not be congruent with the work ethic in U.S. society. Many children, therefore, are not learning the attitudes and values at home that are necessary to be successful in the workforce as it is in the United States today (Baker, 1992; Lee, 1989). Consequently, school counselors must help racial/ethnic minority students to develop attitudes and behavioral skills that will lead to success in the U.S. job market (Baker, 1992; Lee, 1989). Racial/ethnic minority children need to be taught that succeeding in school and in work takes a great deal of "mental strength and stamina" (Lee, 1989, p. 300). Assertiveness skills training is necessary to help students locate and compete for jobs and to counter possible discrimination in the workforce (Baker, 1992).

Besides learning these skills, racial/ethnic minority children can benefit from discovering sources of intrinsic motivation to work. Thomas (1986) noted that a student's source of motivation, whether intrinsically or extrinsically based, greatly affects attitudes toward school and work. An intrinsically motivated student enjoys working for its own sake: That is, work is interesting or meaningful, allowing for independence and autonomy. An extrinsically motivated student, on the other hand, views work as necessary in order to make money, gain prestige, or ensure economic security. Students with extrinsic motivation are unlikely to gain much internal satisfaction from their efforts, and thus will probably experience skepticism or discouragement upon entering the workforce. Therefore, it is recommended that school counselors identify and reinforce intrinsic motivation to work among racial/ethnic minority students to increase their sense of satisfaction with the work experience.

Role Models

The effectiveness of role models in the life-planning process has been well documented (Gottfredson, 1981; Herr & Niles, 1994; Miller, 1986; Sharf, 1992). Social modeling fosters curiosity, self-initiation, and information-seeking behaviors in students (Krumboltz & Schroeder, 1965; Krumboltz & Thoresen, 1965) and keeps racial/ethnic minority students from eliminating career possibilities that may outwardly appear incompatible with their social status or self-concept (Miller, 1986).

Racial/ethnic minority children should be provided opportunities to observe a diverse group of role models (Herr & Niles, 1994; Lee, 1989; Sharf, 1992), including older peers, former students, parents, teachers, community leaders and representatives, and professionals, preferably of the same ethnic group (Lee, 1989). Numerous activities such as field trips to worksites, work simulation activities, minicourses, hands-on workshops, career nights, and mentoring programs can effectively involve role models (Herr & Niles, 1994; Lee, 1989).

Parent Involvement

Involving parents or guardians in the career development process can benefit both the student and the parents. For example, Hispanic Americans typically have strong familial ties, and therefore, the family of an Hispanic student is likely to have a great influence on his or her development (Sue & Sue, 1990). Often minority parents/guardians have high educational aspirations for their children, yet at the same time know very little information about occupations or the education system with which their children are involved (Cole et al., 1988). If parents/guardians are educated about career options, job preparation strategies, strategies for dealing with discrimination, and the realities of the workforce, they will be better able to support and encourage their children (Herr & Niles, 1994). By using the strategies for promoting parental involvement that were described earlier in this chapter, school counselors can ensure that students are receiving consistent, accurate, and realistic information both at school and at home (Cole et al., 1988).

Group Activities

Opportunities for career exploration and development in group situations have proved to be successful with racial/ethnic minority students (Herr & Niles, 1994; Lee, 1989). This success is due, in part, to the preference among racial/ethnic minority individuals for activities that emphasize group cohesiveness and cooperation (Herr & Niles, 1994; Sue & Sue, 1990). Thus, working with racial/ethnic minority students in groups fosters a more culturally relevant environment in which to learn. In addition, group activities provide students with a support system in which cultural differences, frustrations, and challenges can be discussed. Group experiences also raise consciousness levels and increase educational and career expectations. Finally, group experiences allow for the development of pride in one's cultural heritage and increased confidence with one's individual differences (Lee, 1989).

Career Placement and Testing Skills

Racial/ethnic minority students may need special training in learning skills for career placement and for preparing for and taking career placement tests, because their parents may lack knowledge in these areas and therefore may be unable to teach them adequately (Baker, 1992; Lee, 1989). Some useful placement skills include the following: interviewing strategies and preparation, completing job and/or college applications, producing resumes and cover letters, and preparation for placement tests. For interview preparation, counselors can help students "learn to project expertness, trustworthiness, and attractiveness" (Baker, 1992, p. 151). Preparation for placement tests includes test-wiseness, test coaching, and dealing with test anxiety (Baker, 1992).

ASSESSMENT SERVICES

Issues of testing with racial/ethnic minority students are not limited to the confines of career development and placement. Racial/ethnic minority students are apt to encounter more academic, social, behavioral, and other difficulties than students from the mainstream culture (Gibbs & Huang, 1989). In these situations school counselors may be called upon to supply additional information about a particular student. This information often takes the form of results of various tests and other assessments. School counselors are asked to provide expertise in both the administration of these assessments and the interpretation of results of their own testing and that of others, such as school psychologists and diagnosticians. Many of the general issues important to counseling within a multicultural framework also apply to the choice, administration, and/or interpretation of such assessments. Because of the limited scope of this chapter, only general considerations are outlined below.

Because there is a real danger in approaching assessment in such a context from a cursory or surface viewpoint, school counselors have an ethical obligation to be well educated in the implications of using various assessments with racial/ethnic minority students. For example, much of the controversy about using tests with these students has focused on the concept of test bias. Researchers conducting the myriad of bias studies during the 1970s and 1980s failed to uncover substantive evidence of bias in modern tests (Kamphaus, 1993). But this is an extremely narrow focus that does little to recognize the many aspects of cultural differences, and consequently may result in injustices against the very students about whom we are most concerned. That test scores continue to be different for different groups of students should cause us concern. Test scores need to be examined from a societal point of view. Inappropriate test choice and interpretations are very likely when school counselors are unfamiliar with children's cultures. Within-group variability can be substantial, and classifying or comparing children within a particular racial, cultural, or language group may produce as much error as comparing them against a standard population. A school counselor may behave in a way that is insulting or intimidating to a child from a different culture merely because he or she has an overly simplistic view of a particular ethnic or cultural group. Each assessment situation should be approached on an individual basis.

Although many tests have information and norms available about diverse groups, a school counselor must make an evaluation of whether these apply to an individual child. Test results can never be interpreted without adequate information about the background, history, and testing situation for a particular youngster. Assessment and the subsequent interpretation of such assessments must take into account many factors such as language proficiency, acculturation, and differing cultural expectations whenever students are from a group that differs from the mainstream.

Kamphaus (1993) suggested an alternative to the usual paradigm of assessment when dealing with diverse groups. He recommended that all testing be considered tentative and short term, with its primary focus being on the development of alternative intervention plans. These plans should be reevaluated frequently and on an ongoing basis to determine their effectiveness. This allows for assessment in the long term in order to chart the trajectory of development and allows advances in language development and the acculturation process to occur. It resists long-term predictions made on data that are flawed or insufficient.

Because only a brief overview of assessment is provided in this chapter, the reader is urged to refer to excellent sources for more complete discussions of multicultural issues in assessment (e.g., Facundo, Nuttall, & Walton, 1994; Figueroa, 1990; Nuttall, DeLeon, & Valle, 1990). Each of these resources provides an excellent bibliography for readers truly interested in becoming educated about the ramifications of assessment within a multicultural framework.

SUMMARY

We have highlighted some key multicultural counseling issues for school counselors. Although it is our belief that the recommendations reviewed in this chapter will assist school counselors in their efforts to serve adequately an increasingly diverse student population in U.S. schools, we acknowledge that our suggestions cover only a limited scope of the vast array of knowledge and competencies required for effective multicultural counseling. In addition, because the United States is a dynamic society, we recognize that the roles of the school counselor will need to be redefined repeatedly in order for school counselors to respond effectively to the ever-changing needs of children, adolescents, and their families. Therefore, we encourage school counselors to incorporate our ideas into an ongoing effort to remain sensitive to a multicultural student population. Undoubtedly, achieving this goal will demand sustained work that will challenge even the most dedicated of school counselors. However, as Kiselica (1991) noted, the life-long task of becoming a competent, multicultural counselor is filled with profoundly fulfilling opportunities, such as clarifying one's own values, confronting one's fears and biases regarding the culturally different, developing new counseling skills, and experiencing the beauty of other cultures. School counselors who view multiculturalism in this manner are likely to embrace the experience as one of personal and professional enrichment.

REFERENCES

American School Counselor Association. (1988). *Position statements of the American School Counselor Association.* Alexandria, VA: Author.

American School Counselor Association. (1992). *American School Counselor Association ethical standards for school counselors.* Alexandria, VA: Author.

Arbona, C. (1990). Career counseling research and Hispanics: A review of the literature. *The Counseling Psychologist, 18,* 300-323.

Arbona, C., & Novy, D. M. (1991). Career aspirations and expectations of Black, Mexican American, and White students. *Career Development Quarterly, 39,* 231-239.

Atkinson, D. R. (1986). Cultural issues in school and family. In L. B. Golden & D. Capuzzi (Eds.), *Helping families help children* (pp. 237-244). Springfield, IL: Charles C Thomas.

Atkinson, D. R., & Juntunen, C. L. (1994). School counselors and school psychologists as school-home-community liaisons in ethnically diverse schools. In P. Pedersen & J. C. Carey (Eds.), *Multicultural counseling in schools: A practical handbook* (pp. 103-120). Boston: Allyn & Bacon.

Axelson, J. A. (1993). *Counseling and development in a multicultural society* (2nd ed.). Pacific Grove, CA: Brooks/Cole.

Baker, S. (1992). *School counseling for the twenty-first century.* New York: Macmillan.

Casas, I. M., & Furlong, M. J. (1994). School counselor as advocates for increased Hispanic parent participation in schools. In P. Pedersen & J. C. Carey (Eds.), *Multicultural counseling in schools: A practical handbook* (pp. 121-156). Boston: Allyn & Bacon.

Chapman, W. (1991). The Illinois experience. *Phi Delta Kappan, 72,* 355-358.

Cheatham, H. E. (1990). Africentricity and career development of African-Americans. *Career Development Quarterly, 38,* 334-336.

Chrispeels, J. H. (1991). District leadership in parent involvement: Policies and action in San Diego. *Phi Delta Kappan, 72,* 367-371.

Cole, S. M., Thomas, A. R., & Lee, C. C. (1988). School counselor and school psychologist: Partners in minority family outreach. *Journal of Multicultural Counseling and Development, 16,* 110-116.

Divoky, D. (1988). The model minority goes to school. *Phi Delta Kappan, 70,* 219-222.

Dryfoos, J. G. (1994). *Full-service schools: A revolution in health and social services for children, youth, and families.* San Francisco: Jossey-Bass.

Facundo, A., Nuttall, E. V., & Walton, J. (1994). Culturally sensitive assessment in schools. In P. Pedersen & J. C. Carey (Eds.), *Multicultural counseling in schools: A practical handbook* (pp. 207-223). Boston: Allyn & Bacon.

Figueroa, R. A. (1990). Best practices in the assessment of bilingual children. In A. Thomas & J. Grimes (Eds.), *Best practices in school psychology—II* (pp. 93-106). Washington, DC: National Association of School Psychologists.

First, J. M. (1988). Immigrant students in U.S. public schools: Challenges with solutions. *Phi Delta Kappan, 70,* 205-209.

Gibbs, J. T., & Huang, L. N. (1989). *Children of color.* San Francisco: Jossey-Bass.

Golden, L. B. (1986). Counseling children and families in the schools. In L. B. Golden & D. Capuzzi (Eds.), *Helping families help children* (pp. 245-257). Springfield, IL: Charles C Thomas.

Gottfredson, L. S. (1981). Circumscription and compromise: A developmental theory of occupational aspirations. *Journal of Counseling Psychology, 28,* 545-579.

Henderson, A. T. (1988). Parents are a school's best friends. *Phi Delta Kappan, 70,* 148-153.

Herr, E. L., & Niles, S. G. (1994). Multicultural career guidance in the schools. In P. Pedersen & J. C. Carey (Eds.), *Multicultural counseling in schools: A practical handbook* (pp. 177-194). Boston: Allyn & Bacon.

Herring, R. D. (1990). Attacking career myths among Native Americans: Implications for counseling. *School Counselor, 38,* 13-18.

Herring, R. D. (1991). Counseling Native American youth. In C. C. Lee & B. L. Richardson (Eds.), *Multicultural issues in counseling: New approaches to diversity* (pp. 37-47). Alexandria, VA: American Association for Counseling and Development.

Herring, R. D., & Erchul, W. P. (1988). *The applicability of Olson's circumplex model to Native American families* (RC 017 116). Ann Arbor: University of Michigan. (ERIC/CRESS AEL Document Service No. ED 308 050)

Ho, M. K. (1992). *Minority children and adolescents in therapy.* Newbury Park, CA: Sage.

Hodgkinson, H. L. (1985). *All one system: Demographics of education, kindergarten through graduate school.* Washington, DC: Institute for Educational Leadership.

Kallam, M., Hoernicke, P. A., & Coser, P. G. (1994). Native Americans and behavioral disorders. In R. L. Peterson & S. Ishii-Jordan (Eds.), *Multicultural issues in the education of students with behavioral disorders* (pp. 126-137). Cambridge, MA: Brookline.

Kamphaus, R. W. (1993). *Clinical assessment of children's intelligence.* Boston: Allyn & Bacon.

Kellogg, J. B. (1988). Forces of change. *Phi Delta Kappan, 70,* 199-204.

Kiselica, M. S. (1991). Reflections on a multicultural internship experience. *Journal of Counseling and Development, 70,* 126-130.

Krumboltz, J. D., & Schroeder, W. W. (1965). Promoting career planning through reinforcement and models. *Personnel and Guidance Journal, 44,* 19-26.

Krumboltz, J. D., & Thoresen, C. E. (1965). The effect of behavioral counseling in group and individual settings on information-seeking behavior. *Journal of Counseling Psychology, 11,* 324-333.

Lee, C. (1989). Counseling the Black adolescent: Critical roles and functions for counseling professionals. In R. L. Jones (Ed.), *Black adolescents* (pp. 293-308). Berkeley, CA: Cobb & Henry.

Lee, C. (1994). *Counseling for diversity: A guide for school counselors and related professionals.* Boston: Allyn & Bacon.

Liontos, L. B. (1992). *At-risk families and schools: Becoming partners.* Eugene, OR: ERIC Clearinghouse on Educational Management.

Locke, D. C. (1992). *Increasing multicultural understanding.* Newbury Park, CA: Sage.

McLaughlin, M., & Shields, P. (1987). Involving low-income parents in the schools: A role for policy? *Phi Delta Kappan, 69,* 159-160.

Miller, M. J., Springer, T. P., & Wells, D. (1988). Which occupational environments do Black youths prefer? Extending Holland's typology. *School Counselor, 36,* 103-106.

Miller, R. R. (1986). Reducing occupational circumscription. *Elementary School Guidance and Counseling, 20,* 250-254.

Morrow, R. D. (1991). The challenge of Southeast Asian parental involvement. *Principal, 70,* 20-22.

Murphy, J. (1993). What's in? What's out? American education in the nineties. *Phi Delta Kappan, 74,* 641-646.

Nardine, F. E., & Morris, R. D. (1991). Parent involvement in the states: How firm is the commitment? *Phi Delta Kappan, 72,* 363-366.

Nicolau, S., & Ramos, C. L. (1990). *Together is better: Building strong partnerships between schools and Hispanic parents* (Report No. UD 027 472). New York: Hispanic Policy Development Project. (ERIC Document Reproduction Service No. ED 325 543)

Nieto, S. (1992). *Affirming diversity: The sociopolitical context of multicultural education.* White Plains, NY: Longman.

Nuttall, E. V., DeLeon, B., & Valle, M. (1990). Best practices in considering cultural factors. In A. Thomas & J. Grimes (Eds.), *Best practices in school psychology—II* (pp. 219-223). Washington, DC: National Association of School Psychologists.

Ottens, A. J., May, K., & Ottens, A. (1986). The IEP school-parent problem solving. In L. B. Golden & D. Capuzzi (Eds.), *Helping families help children* (pp. 221-236). Springfield, IL: Charles C Thomas.

Piaget, J. (1977). *The development of thought: Equilibrium of cognitive structures.* New York: Viking.

Ponterotto, J. G., & Casas, J. M. (1991). *Handbook of racial/ethnic minority counseling research.* Springfield, IL: Charles C Thomas.

Sanders, D. (1987). Cultural conflicts: An important factor in the academic failures of American Indian students. *Journal of Multicultural Counseling and Development, 15,* 81-90.

Sharf, R. S. (1992). *Applying career development theory to counseling.* Belmont, CA: Brooks/Cole.

Solarzano, D. G. (1992). An exploratory analysis of the effects of race, class, and gender on student and parent mobility aspirations. *Journal of Negro Education, 61,* 30-43.

Solomon, Z. P. (1991). California's policy on parent involvement. *Phi Delta Kappan, 72,* 359-362.

Sue, D. W., & Sue, D. (1990). *Counseling the culturally different: Theory and practice* (2nd ed.). New York: John Wiley.

Sullivan, M. (1984). *Youth, crime and employment patterns in three Brooklyn neighborhoods.* New York: Vera Institute of Justice.

Sullivan, M. L. (1985). *Teen fathers in the inner city: An exploratory ethnographic study* (Report No. UD 024 536). New York: Vera Institute of Justice. (ERIC Document Reproduction Service No. ED 264 316)

Thomas, G. E. (1986). *Understanding the major field choice and career aspirations of Black college students.* Atlanta: Southern Education Foundation.

Vondracek, S. J., & Kirchner, E. P. (1974). Vocational development in early childhood: An examination of young children's expressions of vocational aspirations. *Journal of Vocational Behavior, 5,* 251-260.

Williams, C. W. (1991). *Black teenage mothers: Pregnancy and child rearing from their perspective.* Lexington, MA: Lexington Books.

Yao, E. L. (1988). Working effectively with Asian immigrant parents. *Phi Delta Kappan, 70,* 223-225.

PART VII

Critical and Emerging Topics in Multicultural Counseling: Section 2

THE FINAL PART of the *Handbook of Multicultural Counseling* continues with coverage of emerging subspecialties within multicultural counseling: health counseling, career counseling, group counseling, and family counseling.

Merle A. Keitel, Mary Kopala, and Ismini Georgiades open Part VII in Chapter 26 with a concise overview of multicultural health counseling issues. The authors carefully define the construct of health counseling and demonstrate the particular relevance of this specialty to multicultural populations. Major health areas such as coronary disease, cancer, substance abuse, and AIDS are examined from multicultural perspectives. The interaction of culture and socioeconomic status with regard to health is highlighted. Specific attention is devoted to health issues as they apply to women in general and minority women specifically. The chapter includes recommendations for health enhancement with minorities and specific recommendations for needed research.

S. Alvin Leung authored Chapter 27, which focuses on career development and counseling with racial/ethnic minority groups. The author reviews salient issues in career counseling with minorities in general, as well as culture-specific research and issues for Black Americans, Hispanic Americans,

Asian Americans, and American Indians. Leung introduces his own concise and understandable model of career intervention with ethnic minorities. The chapter concludes with helpful and quite specific recommendations for needed research in the area.

Chapter 28, written by Rod J. Merta, focuses on group counseling in a multicultural context. The author begins his discussion by placing group counseling in a clear historical framework. Important issues that the counselor must consider during all stages of the group process with culturally diverse persons are thoroughly addressed.

George V. Gushue and Daniel T. Sciarra coauthor Chapter 29, which focuses on family counseling from a multicultural perspective. In this final chapter of the *Handbook of Multicultural Counseling*, the authors review the family perspective in counseling and then present four conceptual paradigms for examining family counseling within a cultural context. Drawing on the latest theory and research in family psychology and multicultural counseling, the authors integrate the constructs of acculturation, racial identity, and bilingualism into a reasoned approach to counseling families. Key points are highlighted in a thorough case study.

26

Multicultural Health Counseling

MERLE A. KEITEL

MARY KOPALA

ISMINI GEORGIADES

GIVEN THE ENORMITY of health costs—both financial and in terms of human suffering—it is essential that preventive interventions be developed and/or enhanced. Psychologists, counselors, and other helping professionals are in a good position, by virtue of their training, to add to such preventive efforts. *Health psychology* has been defined by Matarazzo (1980) as the contribution of the "discipline of psychology to the promotion and maintenance of health, the prevention and treatment of illness" (p. 815) and as the identification of causes of health and illness.

Most of the writings and interventions used for health-related issues come from the work of health psychologists or other psychologists (e.g., counseling psychologists) who work in health-related facilities (Keitel & Kopala, 1994). The reader is directed to a special issue of *The Counseling Psychologist* (Alcorn, 1991a) entitled "Counseling Psychology and Health Applications" for a thorough discussion of what counseling psychologists can contribute in health-related matters.

Lewis, Sperry, and Carlson (1993) defined *health counseling* as an approach that recognizes the interactions among psychosocial and physical factors. Health counselors use psychoeducational methods to impart information and develop skills that help their clients to maintain or improve their health.

535

As opposed to health psychology, health counseling is in its infancy, with the first book on health counseling appearing in 1993 (Lewis et al.). Professional counseling journals increasingly are publishing articles related to health concerns (Keitel & Kopala, 1994). Health counseling draws heavily on the knowledge base of health psychology. Whereas health psychologists typically are employed in hospitals and work with individuals who have suffered from strokes, heart attacks, and so forth, health counselors may be employed in "schools, human service agencies, private practices, health-care organizations, businesses, and other environments" (Lewis et al., 1993, p. v). Currently, a national survey is under way to identify whether and in what ways counselors are working on health issues with their clients (Miller, Keitel, & Kopala, 1994). The fact that we can improve our health and extend our lives by changing our behaviors (i.e., eating well, exercising, not smoking, getting regular physical checkups, and reducing stress) supports the incorporation of health education, counseling, and prevention programs into a broad variety of settings.

STATUS OF MULTICULTURAL HEALTH

The promotion of health has been primarily a White middle-class phenomenon (Gottlieb & Green, 1987). It is critical that minority groups be included in preventive care, particularly because racial/ethnic minority group members are likely to suffer from higher mortality and morbidity than are White Americans.

> Although some differences in health status observed across groups can be directly attributed to characteristic lifestyles and habits of living, factors such as prejudice, fear, and stereotyping may further isolate certain groups from mainstream care. . . . Treatment planning may be flawed through simply failing to account for cultural and lifestyle influences that ultimately reduce the effectiveness of interventions or treatments. (Alcorn, 1991b, pp. 334-335)

The following statistics will highlight differences in mortality and morbidity for various groups with respect to different diseases and health risk factors. The terms *Black* and *African American* are used so as to be consistent with the specific studies being cited.

Coronary Disease

In the United States, the 1990 death rates for stroke were 28% for White males and 56% for Black males, 24% for White females, and 43% for Black females. In 1990, coronary heart disease death rates were 1.3% higher for Black males than White males and 29.4% higher for Black females than White females. It is important to note, however, that of those with coronary heart disease, 88.2% are White, 9.5% are Black, and 2.4% are of other races (American Heart Association, 1993).

With respect to adult risk factors for coronary heart disease (e.g., obesity and hypertension), Native Hawaiians (males and females), followed by Black females, have the highest rate of being overweight (i.e., 20% over desired weight), followed by American Indian females. Blacks, Puerto Ricans, and Cuban and Mexican Americans tend to be more hypertensive than Anglo Americans; 71% of non-Hispanic Blacks are hypertensive compared to 60% of non-Hispanic Whites. Death rates in 1990 from high blood pressure are reported as 6% for White males, 30% for Black males, 5% for White females, and 23% for Black females (American Heart Association, 1993).

Livingston (1993) noted that young Black American men are particularly vulnerable to high blood pressure: "Overall, more than 10% of Black American male children, 1% of Black American female children, and no White female children or male children had systolic BP [blood pressure] greater than 140 mmHg" (p. 134). Livingston focused primarily on the relationship between stress and hypertension and specifically on the sources of tension for young Black men in the United States. Racial differences in hypertension are clearly related to socioeconomic status (Kotchen, Kotchen, & Schwertman, 1974).

Cancer

Cancer rates differ dramatically among various races in the United States. Because Blacks are less likely to have early diagnosis and intervention, Whites have higher 5-year survival rates than Blacks when all types of cancer are considered. Blacks have significantly higher rates of incidence and mortality than Whites in multiple myeloma and in cancers of the esophagus, uterus, cervix, stomach, liver, prostate, and larynx. Hispanics have lower incidence and mortality rates than do White or Black Americans for all cancers (American Cancer Society, 1993). African Americans have a higher incidence of cancers that may be caused, in part, by smoking (i.e., cancers of the esophagus and larynx).

Substance Abuse

According to the U.S. Bureau of the Census (1993), there are differences by gender and race in the prevalence of substance abuse. Although much of the literature focuses on the disproportionate number of racial minorities that abuse certain substances, there are other substances that Whites abuse more than do racial minorities. There is also evidence that different racial groups metabolize substances at different rates, which may contribute to differential morbidity patterns. Cultures also vary with respect to the degree that they are willing to acknowledge substance abuse. Because some cultures view substance abuse as shameful, actual incidence may be underreported. The degree to which a specific culture provides alternatives to substance use and abuse may also influence the prevalence of abuse (Stimmel, 1984).

African Americans tend to become ill from cigarette smoking at younger ages than do Whites. Although African Americans smoke fewer cigarettes per day than do Whites and tend to begin smoking later in life, they have higher smoking mortality rates (Royce, Hymowitz, Corbett, Hartwell, & Orlandi, 1993). One of the reasons cited for this is that although African Americans smoke fewer cigarettes per day than do Whites, they prefer menthol cigarettes, which have higher tar and nicotine levels (Royce et al., 1993). Furthermore, African Americans have more trouble quitting, regardless of socioeconomic status, which may be related to differences in health attitudes such as health locus of control.

In 1991, 58.1% of U.S. males and 44.3% of U.S. females reported using alcohol at least once a month, with the total population figure being 50.9%. In terms of race, 52.7% of Whites, 43.7% of African Americans, and 47.5% of Hispanics used alcohol regularly. There is a very high incidence of alcohol abuse among Native Americans (Rowell & Kusterer, 1991). This has been viewed as one effect of a 500-year history of contact with and domination by Europeans. When the use of substances by Native Americans increased in response to disease, genocide, and relocation, the once very clear definitions of acceptable and unacceptable behavior became blurred. Widespread alcohol abuse weakened the concept of personal responsibility. Parents who were abusers found it difficult to hold their children responsible for their own problems with alcohol. A cultural standard of "taking care of one's own" and not seeking outside professional assistance contributed to a pattern of alcohol and drug use within entire families (Rowell & Kusterer, 1991).

With respect to marijuana use, in 1991, 6.3% of males and 3.4% of females abused marijuana, and 4.5% of Whites, 7.2% of African Americans, and 4.3% of Hispanics abused marijuana. Cocaine was also abused at different rates by different groups: 1.3% of men abused cocaine compared to 0.6% of women, and 0.7% of Whites, 1.8% of African Americans, and 1.6% of Hispanics abused cocaine. Although no ethnic/racial group abused all three drugs (alcohol, marijuana, cocaine) consistently more than any other group, men abused all three of these substances more than women.

In 1991, 1.5% of Whites, 4.3% of African Americans, and 2.1% of Hispanics abused crack. Whites were more likely than African Americans and Hispanics to abuse stimulants, sedatives, tranquilizers, and analgesics; 7.9% of Whites abused stimulants compared to 3.3% of African Americans and 4.8% of Hispanics; 3% of both African Americans and Hispanics abused sedatives compared to 4.6% of Whites; 6% of Whites, 3.1% of African Americans, and 3.9% of Hispanics abused tranquilizers. Finally, 6.5% of Whites, 4.7% of African Americans, and 3.9% of Hispanics abused analgesics in 1991 (U.S. Bureau of the Census, 1993).

AIDS

Inner-city males and females are at higher risk for HIV infection than non-inner-city dwellers due to the higher prevalence of IV drug abuse and unprotected sex (Mays & Cochran, 1988). According to the Centers for Disease Control and Prevention (1993), White males accounted for 54.6% of AIDS cases among men, African Americans accounted for 28.2%, Hispanics for 16.2%, Asians for .68%, and Native Americans for .21%. Among women, White women accounted for 50.8% of AIDS cases, African Americans for 31.4%, Hispanics for 16.7%, Asians for .67%, and Native Americans for .21%. Among African American men and women, most AIDS cases result from exposure to intravenous drug use. This also holds for White men and women, but among White men the majority of AIDS cases result from sexual contact with men (Centers for Disease Control and Prevention, 1993).

FACTORS INFLUENCING
MULTICULTURAL HEALTH

The factors that contribute to the high mortality and morbidity rates among minorities are complex. Socioeconomic status and cultural beliefs and practices including socialization and dietary patterns may influence the incidence and progression of disease.

Socioeconomic Status (SES)

Research has shown that socioeconomic status (SES) is related to incidence of illness and mortality rates. Albino and Tedesco (1984) discussed the conditions related to poverty that are associated with poor health: (a) stress due to noisy and/or overcrowded conditions, (b) lack of meaningful work, (c) prejudice and discrimination, (d) absence of social support, and (e) polluted and/or unsanitary environments.

The relationship between SES and health outcomes has traditionally been viewed as a result of the conditions of poverty described above. However, a recent study (Adler et al., 1994) suggested that the relationship between SES and health outcomes exists all the way up the socioeconomic ladder. In other words, the very wealthy have better health outcomes than members of the upper middle class, members of the upper middle class have better health outcomes than members of the middle class, and so on.

Nevertheless, minorities are overrepresented in the lower SES group. Because people of low SES tend to be less educated and lack insurance coverage, they are less likely to seek medical help, and when they do, the medical care they receive may be of poor quality. It is common for people who lack insurance coverage to utilize emergency rooms as their only source of health care. Consequently, health care is haphazard, and these individuals are less likely to be screened for diseases, less likely to receive preventive care, and more likely to ignore early symptoms of disease. Tanney (1991) reported that minorities underutilize appropriate health care services (e.g., they are less likely to use dentists). Therefore, it is difficult to determine whether high mortality and morbidity are the result of ethnicity and race, culture, low SES, or interactions among these variables. Given the seriousness of the increased health problems for minorities, there is a paucity of literature on multicultural health counseling issues. A notable exception is a recent issue of the *Journal of Multicultural Counseling and Development* that focuses on multicultural health (Harper, 1993).

Cultural Beliefs and Practices

In addition to SES, cultural values, beliefs, and practices may influence individuals' decisions to seek medical help (Gottlieb & Green, 1987; Uba, 1992). Uba (1992) reported that Southeast Asian refugees underutilize the American health care system despite the high, disproportionate numbers of health problems, including serious illnesses such as tuberculosis, malnutrition, intestinal parasites, and hepatitis B.

Cultural reasons may partly contribute to underuse of medical services. Suffering and illness are seen by some as unavoidable; therefore, medical interventions may be avoided because such care may be an "inappropriate response to physical pain" (Uba, 1992, p. 545). Others believe that death is predetermined and thus that life-saving interventions are useless. Further, the value placed on stoicism for some Southeast Asians may result in their not seeking health services.

How individuals perceive the cause of illnesses may be another explanation for underuse of Westernized medical services. Some individuals believe illnesses to be the result of supernatural causes or a failure to be in harmony with nature or punishment for immoral behavior. Herbal medicines or intervention by religious healers may be viewed as more appropriate than Western treatments (Uba, 1992).

Even when individuals seek medical treatment, there may be a lack of compliance or a failure to follow directions. Individuals may expect an instant cure or may mistake diagnostic methods, such as X-rays, for the intervention (Uba, 1992). Poor communication between health providers and patients also compromises medical care for racial/ethnic minorities. Deference to medical professionals, lack of bilingual health care providers, and desire to avoid embarrassment may inhibit people from asking necessary questions.

A lack of understanding of different cultures on the part of health care providers and a history of receiving inappropriate advice also may be barriers to seeking help. For example, a lack of understanding of the role of folk medicines may lead to undesirable consequences. Resulting marks from coining or cupping (healing practices that leave marks on skin) may be mistaken as child abuse (Kopala, Keitel, & Suzuki, 1994). Consequently, parents may avoid seeing physicians who might report them to Child Protective Services. Women who report symptoms may not be taken seriously by doctors who discount certain types of complaints as "female problems." Physicians may also make dietary recommendations that do not take into account cultural differences in eating habits (Uba, 1992). Dietary practices may vary across cultures. For example, some Asian cultures have low-fat, high-fiber diets that result in lower rates of colon-rectal cancer. Interestingly, as Asians become more Westernized and increase their consumption of fat, their rates of colon-rectal cancer increase (American Cancer Society, 1993).

Beliefs That May Foster Poor Health Practices

Many factors related to culture may prevent individuals from establishing good health habits. For example, women may not protect themselves adequately when having sex for fear of being rejected by men (Airhihenbuwa, DiClemente, Wingood, & Lowe, 1992). According to Airhihenbuwa et al., there are fewer marriageable men than women in the African American community. (*Marriageable* is defined as employed, not incarcerated, and heterosexual.) Further, women who depend on men for financial support may risk their own health and even their lives rather than insisting on their partners' using condoms. Insisting on condom use may imply that the woman believes that her partner has engaged in unsafe sexual behavior and/or other high-risk behaviors such as IV drug use. Women may fear that challenging men in this way may anger them and result in the termination of the relationship.

Mikawa et al. (1992) examined level of acculturation and cultural beliefs in relation to condom use by Hispanics. They found that Hispanics who were low in acculturation compared to those who were high in acculturation reported more *machismo* beliefs, less fear of AIDS, and more willingness to believe in fate. Surprisingly, acculturation was not directly related to the use of condoms for the sample as a whole.

Hispanic males in college were less likely to use condoms and were more acculturated than were noncollege males. Being religious and Catholic did not prevent Hispanics from using condoms. Hispanics placed high value on maintaining relationships and family cohesiveness, and men and women were willing to talk to family and peer groups about their sexual activities.

Aruffo, Coverdale, Pavlik, and Vallbona (1993) found that Hispanic and Black individuals had a higher external orientation than did White individuals. In other words, Whites were more likely to believe that they had personal control over their health. Research has shown that people who have high internal orientations are more likely to engage in health-promoting behaviors (Lau, 1982). Whites had the most knowledge about AIDS, followed by Blacks, and Hispanics had the least knowledge about AIDS.

According to Stimmel (1984), several beliefs may foster substance abuse within a particular culture. Different cultures have different outlooks on the role and use of substances in rituals, social customs, and religious activities. Furthermore, substance use in many cultures is differentiated from abuse and may not be seen as an individual's attempts to escape personal anxiety.

African Americans may be less likely to take steps to prevent illness because they distrust members of the White dominant culture who promote prevention programs (Airhihenbuwa et al., 1992). This mistrust has slowed progress toward AIDS prevention in particular.

WOMEN AND HEALTH

Women are likely to be treated differently by physicians than are men. Data support that women are less likely than men to receive complete medical workups when they present with symptoms and are more likely to receive prescriptions for tranquilizers than are men (Holt, 1990). Women who do not have the required skills of assertiveness and who see physicians as authority figures may be less likely to ask questions and challenge physicians.

Women on average live 7 years longer than men. If quality of life is taken into account, however, the female advantage is reduced to about 3 years. In other words, although females may live longer, their quality of life is not necessarily better. During the years they are alive, men are in better health, according to measures of health-related quality of life. Gender differences in reporting do not seem to account sufficiently for these differences. There are complex differences between the health outcomes of men and women, and more research is needed to understand these differences (Kaplan, Anderson, & Wingard, 1991).

Some conditions and illnesses affect women exclusively or primarily, and these conditions have been underresearched until fairly recently, when research on breast cancer and mammography screening (Aiken, 1993; Stein, Fox, & Murata, 1991), premenstrual syndrome, menstruation, pregnancy (Berkowitz, Lapinski, Wein, & Lee, 1992), and childbirth (Engle, Scrimshaw, Zambrana, & Dunkel-Schetter, 1990), menopause, and osteoporosis (Klohn & Rogers, 1991) increased.

Minority women experience higher infant mortality rates, are more likely to be diagnosed with diabetes, cardiovascular disease, and some types of cancer, and have a lower life expectancy than White women (Manley, Lin-Fu, Miranda, Noonan, & Parker, 1984). The interplay between race and gender in health research, therefore, will be the focus of the following section.

Breast Cancer and Mammography Screening

Mammography is the most effective and available technique for breast cancer screening, although there has been some suggestion that it is more effective for women over age 50 (Fletcher, Black, Harris, Rimer, & Shapiro, 1993). Stein et al. (1991) reported that Hispanic women have lower mammography screening rates than do Black or White women. Minority women, in general, are diagnosed with breast cancer at more advanced stages and, therefore, have higher mortality rates (Swanson et al., 1993). Rimer et al. (1992) found that minority women were less likely to benefit from a community-wide intervention to promote breast cancer screening than were White women. Even with reduced costs offered for mammography, cost was the primary barrier cited by minority women for not pursuing the screening.

Premenstrual Syndrome (PMS) and Premenstrual Symptoms

Women in different cultures vary according to their reports of intensity and/or type of premenstrual symptoms (Hamilton & Gallant, 1993). Although the reports are retrospective, Black women report PMS characterized by food cravings more than do White women. There is some support that in societies that celebrate menarche, and in which women and men have equal status, premenstrual symptoms are greatly reduced or absent. In the United States, Black women tend to report less severe cramping and irritability but more weight gain, swelling, and headaches than White women when they are menstruating (Woods, Most, & Dery, 1982).

HIV/AIDS

In recent years, women have demonstrated an increased risk for HIV infection. In 1988, HIV-related disease was one of the top 10 leading causes of death in women age 15 to 44, and it has been estimated that soon it will be one of the top 5 causes of death in this age group (Ickovics & Rodin, 1992). Because male-to-female transmission is 12 times more likely than female-to-male transmission, and because males in the inner city have a frighteningly high incidence of IV drug abuse and prison experience (i.e., higher exposure to HIV), the chances that inner-city women will be exposed to HIV are high.

In a study by Kalichman, Hunter, and Kelly (1992), 22% of their sample of urban women reported engaging in high-risk behavior. Nonminority women at high risk reported more concern about getting AIDS than did high-risk minority women, and minority women were less well informed about AIDS than were nonminority women. Minority women also estimated their personal risk of getting AIDS as lower than did nonminority women, even though they were engaging in high-risk behaviors. Disadvantaged women face a multitude of life problems, including concerns about employment, child care, and crime, that preclude them from making HIV and AIDS prevention a priority issue.

RECOMMENDATIONS FOR
HEALTH ENHANCEMENT OF MINORITIES

Health prevention and health care behaviors can be encouraged only through the implementation of culturally sensitive programs and behaviors by health care providers. Further, societal interventions are critical to the enhancement of minority health: For example, broad policy decisions that improve economic conditions for minorities must be implemented.

Health behaviors are likely to be compromised by limited knowledge and/or by cultural definitions that promote risky behaviors. For example, inner-city minority youth may have limited or incorrect information about health issues. For instance, they are two to three times as likely to believe that all gays and lesbians have AIDS as are their White counterparts (DiClemente, Boyer, & Morales, 1988). The cultural definition of appropriate male behavior centering around *machismo* may prevent some Hispanic and Black males from using condoms (Marin & Marin, 1992).

Kalichman et al. (1992) suggested that AIDS prevention messages must be more culturally sensitive than they have been in the past, given that the highest rates of AIDS are found in minority communities. One way this has been done in Hispanic communities is through the use of *fotonovelas*, or storyboards. *Fotonovelas* are commonly used in Hispanic communities and therefore are effective in promoting the healthy behaviors modeled by the characters they portray (Casas & Furlong, 1994).

Because Hispanics place high value on family relationships and are willing to discuss their sexual behaviors, prevention could focus on extended family and peer groups (Mikawa et al., 1992). The purchase and use of condoms in the Hispanic population is controlled by men, suggesting that education and prevention efforts should be strongly directed toward them. Capitalizing on the Hispanic belief that males should protect women, interventions should emphasize how using condoms helps them to fill that role (Mikawa et al., 1992).

Prevention methods directed at adolescents should include peer components. Adolescents may resist directives from authority figures and feel invulnerable to health threats.

Given the emphasis in the African American community on the values of cooperation, interdependence, and the concern for the welfare of others, health prevention efforts, rather than be directed at individual health benefits, should address the preservation of the African American extended family and the preservation of the race as a whole (Mays & Cochran, 1988).

Programs and clinics must include minority health professionals (e.g., counselors, doctors, nurses, health educators) given the reported mistrust of White majority culture by minorities (Airhihenbuwa et al., 1992). Minority professionals are likely to be more knowledgeable about the culture, speak the same language, and understand the vernacular. Therefore, they may have more credibility among their clients and patients. Because there are currently few minority professionals, it may be important to implement policies that mandate the education of majority professionals on cultural issues that affect health behaviors (Airhihenbuwa et al., 1992).

RESEARCH ISSUES
IN MULTICULTURAL HEALTH

Methodological Issues

A multitude of problems surround the study of multicultural health. Early research was criticized because ethnicity and race were not examined in study samples. More current research has included these variables. However, race has been discredited as a scientific construct because there is more variation within races than between races. Nevertheless, researchers continue to use it as an independent variable in health research (Sheldon, 1992).

The construct of ethnicity has been viewed by some researchers as preferable to the construct of race because rather than focusing primarily on biological differences, it includes cultural aspects, such as participant self-definitions of ethnicity, country of birth, and spoken language. However, this approach has also been criticized because there is little consistency across studies with respect to the method of determining ethnicity. Sheldon (1992) suggested that *ethnicity* is a euphemism for *race* and no better defines the categories used to study individuals.

In addition, little attention has been paid to acculturation level of participants, length of time living in the United States or other countries, and within-group cultural differences such as religion. Lack of a common definition of *ethnicity* across languages further complicates the study of multicultural health (Edwards, 1992).

Methodological concerns also exist for understanding the impact of SES on health. The majority of the research has controlled for SES instead of examining it. Adler et al. (1994) called for a more thorough examination of factors related to SES, such as health behaviors (e.g., smoking, physical inactivity, diet, and substance abuse), psychological characteristics (e.g., depression, hostility, and psychological distress), and the effects of social order—that is, "one's relative position in the SES hierarchy apart from the material implications of one's position" (p. 20). This may have tremendous implications for understanding health outcomes for minority individuals because oppression of minority groups automatically relegates them to a lower position in the social hierarchy.

Recommendations for Future Research

On the basis of criticisms of earlier health research and the status and current knowledge base in multicultural health, we recommend the following:

1. All groups and both men and women must be included in health research in order to increase external validity.

2. A standard method of determining ethnicity might be created and used consistently in all health research.

3. Differences in levels of acculturation and other within-group differences must be assessed.

4. Prevention and treatment efforts might be tailored to be maximally effective for the specific cultural group targeted.

5. The efficacy of intervention and prevention efforts must be evaluated.

6. Culture-specific beliefs about health behaviors must be examined to determine their impact on intervention efforts.

7. Factors that increase the salience and relevance of health education and prevention methods must be examined.

IMPLICATIONS FOR
TRAINING HEALTH COUNSELORS

In order for intervention and prevention efforts to be effective, health counselors must consider cultural issues. Counselor training programs must provide students with (a) knowledge about different cultures; (b) knowledge of how health behaviors are influenced by cultural norms and expectations; (c) opportunities to become more multiculturally sensitive through course work, practica, and internships; and (d) knowledge of culturally salient health counseling interventions. Programs that adhere to these recommendations may increase the likelihood of developing health counselors who are flexible and sensitive.

SUMMARY

Cultural beliefs and values affect how individuals maintain their health and respond to symptoms when a health problem arises, whether they seek treatment, and the type of treatment they seek. Communication between patients and health personnel and compliance with medical treatments and recommendations may be thwarted by cultural practices. Diet, sexual activity and practices, and the use of substances are also influenced by culture. Health counselors must be aware of the effect culture plays in health behaviors in order to (a) deliver effective services, (b) develop culturally sensitive health programs, and (c) engage in research that is generalizable to groups other than the dominant culture. Finally, training programs must emphasize the role culture plays in order to train culturally sensitive and aware counselors.

REFERENCES

Adler, N. E., Boyce, T., Chesney, M. A., Cohen, S., Folkman, S., Kahn, R. L., & Syme, S. L. (1994). Socioeconomic status and health: The challenge of the gradient. *American Psychologist, 49,* 15-24.

Aiken, L. S. (1993). Mammography screening guidelines, effectiveness, utilization, and a role for health psychology. *Health Psychologist, 15*(2), 8-9.

Airhihenbuwa, C. O., DiClemente, R. J., Wingood, G. M., & Lowe, A. (1992). HIV/AIDS education and prevention among African-Americans: A focus on culture. *AIDS Education and Prevention, 4,* 267-276.

Albino, J. E., & Tedesco, L. A. (1984). Women's health issues. In A. U. Rickel, M. Gerrard, & I. Iscoe (Eds.), *Social and psychological problems of women: Prevention and crisis intervention* (pp. 157-172). Washington, DC: Hemisphere.

Alcorn, J. D. (Ed.). (1991a). Counseling psychology and health applications [Special issue]. *The Counseling Psychologist, 19*(3).

Alcorn, J. D. (1991b). Counseling psychology and health applications. *The Counseling Psychologist, 19,* 325-341.

American Cancer Society. (1993). *Cancer facts and figures—1993.* Atlanta: Author.

American Heart Association. (1993). *Heart and stroke facts: 1994 statistical supplement.* Dallas: Author.

Aruffo, J. F., Coverdale, J. H., Pavlik, V. N., & Vallbona, C. (1993). AIDS knowledge in minorities: Significance of locus of control. *American Journal of Preventive Medicine, 9,* 15-20.

Berkowitz, G. S., Lapinski, R. H., Wein, R., & Lee, D. (1992). Race/ethnicity and other risk factors for gestational diabetes. *American Journal of Epidemiology, 135,* 965-973.

Casas, J. M., & Furlong, M. J. (1994). School counselors as advocates for increased Hispanic parent participation in schools. In P. Pedersen & J. C. Carey (Eds.), *Multicultural counseling in schools* (pp. 121-155). Boston: Allyn & Bacon.

Centers for Disease Control and Prevention. (1993). *HIV/AIDS surveillance report.* Atlanta: Author.

DiClemente, R. J., Boyer, C. B., & Morales, E. (1988). Minorities and AIDS: Knowledge, attitudes, and misconceptions among Black and Latino adolescents. *American Journal of Public Health, 1,* 55-57.

Edwards, N. C. (1992, January-February). Important considerations in the use of ethnicity as a study variable. *Canadian Journal of Public Health, 83,* 31-33.

Engle, P. L., Scrimshaw, S. C. M., Zambrana, R. E., & Dunkel-Schetter, C. (1990). Prenatal and postnatal anxiety in Mexican women giving birth in Los Angeles. *Health Psychology, 9,* 285-299.

Fletcher, S. W., Black, W., Harris, R., Rimer, B. K., & Shapiro, S. (1993). *Report of the International Workshop on Screening for Breast Cancer, February 24-25.* Bethesda, MD: National Cancer Institute.

Gottlieb, N. H., & Green, W. L. (1987, Summer). Ethnicity and lifestyle health risk: Some possible mechanisms. *American Journal of Health Promotion, 2,* 37-45.

Hamilton, J. A., & Gallant, S. (1993). Premenstrual syndromes: A health psychology critique of biomedically oriented research. In R. J. Gatchel & E. B. Blanchard (Eds.), *Physiological disorders* (pp. 383-438). Washington, DC: American Psychological Association.

Harper, F. D. (Ed.). (1993). Multicultural health issues [Special issue]. *Journal of Multicultural Counseling and Development, 21*(3).

Holt, L. H. (1990, October). *How the medical care system has failed to meet women's needs.* Paper presented at the Rush/North Shore Medical Center's Women and Mental Health Conference, Evanston, IL.

Ickovics, J. R., & Rodin, J. (1992). Women and AIDS in the United States: Epidemiology, natural history, and mediating mechanisms. *Health Psychology, 11,* 1-16.

Kalichman, S. C., Hunter, T. L., & Kelly, J. A. (1992). Perceptions of AIDS susceptibility among minority and nonminority women at risk for HIV infection. *Journal of Consulting and Clinical Psychology, 60,* 725-732.

Kaplan, R. M., Anderson, J. P., & Wingard, D. L. (1991). Gender differences in health-related quality of life. *Health Psychology, 10,* 86-93.

Keitel, M. A., & Kopala, M. (1994). Health counseling. In J. L. Ronch, W. Van Ornum, & N. C. Stilwell (Eds.), *The counseling source book* (pp. 403-423). New York: Crossroad.

Klohn, L. S., & Rogers, R. W. (1991). Dimensions of the severity of a health threat: The persuasive effects of visibility, time of onset, and rate of onset on young women's intentions to prevent osteoporosis. *Health Psychology, 10,* 323-329.

Kopala, M., Keitel, M. A., & Suzuki, L. A. (1994, February). *Resolving ethical dilemmas from a multicultural perspective: A symposium.* Paper presented at the Midwinter Multicultural Roundtable, New York, NY.

Kotchen, J. M., Kotchen, T. A., & Schwertman, N. C. (1974). Blood pressure distributions of urban adolescents. *American Journal of Epidemiology, 99,* 315-324.

Lau, R. R. (1982). Origins of health locus of control beliefs. *Journal of Personality and Social Psychology, 42,* 322-334.

Lewis, J. A., Sperry, L., & Carlson, J. (1993). *Health counseling.* Pacific Grove, CA: Brooks/Cole.

Livingston, I. L. (1993). Stress, hypertension, and young Black Americans: The importance of counseling. *Journal of Multicultural Counseling and Development, 21,* 132-142.

Manley, A., Lin-Fu, J. S., Miranda, M., Noonan, A., & Parker, T. (1984). Special health concerns of ethnic minority women. Commissioned paper. In U.S. Public Health Service (Ed.), *Report of the Public Health Service Task Force on Women's Health Issues* (Vol. 2, pp. II-37-II-47). Washington, DC: Government Printing Office.

Marin, G., & Marin, B. (1992). Predictors of condom accessibility among Hispanics in San Francisco. *American Journal of Public Health, 82,* 592-595

Matarazzo, J. D. (1980). Behavioral health and behavioral medicine: Frontiers for a new health psychology. *American Psychologist, 35,* 807-817.

Mays, V., & Cochran, S. (1988). Issues in the perception of AIDS risk and risk reduction activities by Black and Hispanic/Latina women. *American Psychologist, 43,* 949-957.

Mikawa, J. K., Morones, P. A., Gomez, A., Case, H. L., Olsen, D., & Gonzales-Huss, M. (1992). Cultural practice of Hispanics: Implications for the prevention of AIDS. *Hispanic Journal of Behavioral Sciences, 14,* 421-433.

Miller, K. S., Keitel, M. A., & Kopala, M. (1994). [Health survey]. Unpublished raw data.

Rimer, B. K., Resch, N., King, E., Ross, E., Lerman, C., Boyce, A., Kessler, H. B., & Engstrom, P. F. (1992). Multistrategy health education program to increase mammography use among women ages 65 and older. *Public Health Reports, 107,* 369-380.

Rowell, R. M., & Kusterer, H. (1991). Care of HIV-infected Native American substance abusers. *Journal of Chemical Dependency Treatment, 4,* 91-103.

Royce, J. M., Hymowitz, N., Corbett, K., Hartwell, T. D., & Orlandi, M. A. (1993). Smoking cessation factors among African Americans and Whites. *American Journal of Public Health, 83,* 220-226.

Sheldon, T. A. (1992). Race and ethnicity in health research. *Journal of Public Health Medicine, 14,* 104-110.

Stein, J. A., Fox, S. A., & Murata, P. J. (1991). The influence of ethnicity, socioeconomic status, and psychological barriers on use of mammography. *Journal of Health and Social Behavior, 32,* 101-113.

Stimmel, B. (Ed.). (1984). *Cultural and sociological aspects of alcoholism and substance abuse.* New York: Haworth.

Swanson, G. M., Ragheb, N. E., Lin, C. S., Hankey, B. F., Miller, B., Horn-Ross, P., White, E., Liff, J. M., Harlan, L. C., McWhorter, W. P., & Mullan, P. B. (1993). Breast cancer among Black and White women in the 1980s: Changing patterns in the United States by race, age, and extent of disease. *Cancer, 72,* 788-798.

Tanney, F. (1991). Counseling psychology and health psychology: Some suggestions for a burgeoning area. *The Counseling Psychologist, 19,* 392-395.

Uba, L. (1992). Cultural barriers to health care for Southeast Asian refugees. *Public Health Reports, 107,* 544-548.

U.S. Bureau of the Census. (1993). *Statistical abstract of the United States* (113th ed.). Washington, DC: Author.

Woods, N., Most, A., & Dery, G. (1982). Estimating the prevalence of premenstrual symptoms. *Research in Nursing Health, 5,* 81-91.

27

Career Development and Counseling

A Multicultural Perspective

S. ALVIN LEUNG

THE SYSTEMATIC STUDY and practice of career development began in the early 20th century as Frank Parson initiated the national vocational guidance movement in Boston (Whiteley, 1984). At that time, the goal of Parson was to help young persons, including many immigrants from the European nations, to identify vocational choices through a deliberate process of self- and occupational examination. Parson's approach has been further expanded and elaborated by many theorists (e.g., Rounds & Tracey, 1990) into what is today called a trait factor approach. Since the time of Parson, career development and counseling has evolved into a major discipline with many diverse theories and models. Although adolescents and young adults are still the groups that tend to receive the most attention, researchers and practitioners of career development and counseling have, in recent years, expanded the scope of the discipline to other age and social groups, such as older adults, women, individuals with disabilities, and ethnic/racial minorities. The purpose of this chapter is to examine the career development of ethnic minority groups in the United States and to offer a model of career intervention with culturally different individuals.

The study of the career behavior of ethnic minorities is a relatively new endeavor. Despite some recent research suggesting that some career development theories, such as Holland's (1985) theory of career choice, are valid for members of ethnic minority persons (e.g., Fouad & Dancer, 1992; Swanson, 1992), there are several reasons why a multicultural perspective of career

development is needed. First and foremost, current models of career development and counseling do not take into consideration the effects of social and
economic barriers such as economic hardship, immigration disruption, and
racial discrimination on the career behavior of ethnic minority individuals
(Brown, Brooks, & Associates, 1990; Smith, 1983). These barriers have restricted both the actual and perceived career alternatives available to these
individuals. Second, existing theories of career development are limited in
terms of their relevance for culturally different individuals (e.g., Smith, 1983).
Theories of career development are usually based on Eurocentric worldviews
that may be different from those of the minority groups. For instance, they
usually assume an individualistic and self-actualizing perspective regarding
career behavior and choices, whereas members of some minority groups may
favor a collectivistic orientation to choices and decisions (e.g., Leong & Leung,
1994). Third, many career assessment instruments commonly used in career
counseling were developed and normed for the White majority population
and may not be applicable to culturally different individuals (Fouad, 1993;
Hansen, 1987; Leong & Leung, 1994).

An examination of the career behavior and development of the different
ethnic minority groups in the United States revealed both areas of convergence
and areas of divergence. The first section of this chapter examines areas of
convergence by exploring the effects of two variables on the career behavior
of ethnic minorities: racial discrimination and social class. The limited literature on the career development of ethnic minorities suggests that the career
concerns of different ethnic groups are quite diverse (e.g., Axelson, 1993;
Smith, 1983). The divergence in career development issues among the four
main minority groups in the United States (African American, Hispanic
American, Asian American, and Native American) are examined in the second
section of this chapter, and selected issues salient to each group are identified
and examined. In the third section, a model of career intervention for ethnic
minorities is discussed. In the fourth section, some directions for future research on multicultural career counseling and development are proposed.

CONVERGENCE IN CAREER
DEVELOPMENT AMONG ETHNIC MINORITIES

Most theories of career development place a strong emphasis on the degree
of control an individual has on the career decision-making process, and the
psychological aspects of career development and choice that contribute to
career satisfaction. In this chapter, I argue that for all minority persons, the
degree of control over one's career satisfaction and attainment is impeded by
a set of long-standing social, institutional, and structural barriers (Hotchkiss
& Borow, 1984, 1990). These barriers are the result of racial discrimination
and have limited the quantity and quality of occupational opportunities available to minority persons. In addition, the career development of ethnic

minorities is inhibited by a disadvantaged socioeconomic background, as indicated by the overrepresentation of minorities in the lower socioeconomic echelon.

The Effects of Racial Discrimination

The effects of racial discrimination on the career behavior of ethnic minorities are elaborated in a sociological perspective of career attainment by Hotchkiss and Borow (1984, 1990). The sociological perspective suggested that occupational segregation based on race, gender, and social class is perpetuated by the structure of the economic system. The economy can be viewed as consisting of two segments, the *core* and the *periphery*. The core economy consists of large firms that have control over a large amount of resources. These firms offer attractive benefits and wages and opportunities for advancement. The periphery economy consists of small firms whose fate is very much controlled by the rules set by the larger firms in the core structure, and whose well-being is controlled by fluctuations in the economy. Entrance into the core system, especially for high-salary and prestigious positions, is restrictive. The sociological perspective suggests that institutions often set up formal and informal rules for making decisions on whether an individual is suited for certain positions. As Rosenbaum (1981) stated, they follow a process of elimination. Individuals who do not fit into a set of narrowly defined norms in terms of educational background, values, beliefs, and racial and gender characteristics are eliminated from contention for high-salary, prestigious positions. After reviewing results of research studies that examined the dual structure of the economy, Hotchkiss and Borow (1990) concluded that both women and racial minorities have limited access to key positions in the core section.

The sociological perspective offers a framework to understand the process of social discrimination and oppression against members of minority groups. Structural discrimination is at least partly responsible for the underrepresentation of racial minorities on professional and managerial occupations, which are usually positions that carry higher prestige and wages. According to the data from the U.S. Equal Employment Opportunity Commission (1991), the percentages of minority persons in the professional and managerial jobs are 13% and 10.1%, respectively. These percentages are much lower than the proportion of minority persons in the United States, which in 1990 was 30% of the total population.

Differences in education and training may be used to explain the differences in occupational attainment between Whites and the various minority groups. However, researchers have shown that disparity in income between Whites and members of minority groups exists when controlling for levels of training and education (e.g., Hirschman & Wong, 1984; Jiobu, 1976). For instance, in a study by Hirschman and Wong (1984) using survey data of income and education from the Bureau of the Census on representative samples of Black, Hispanic, Asian, and White Americans, the authors found that in

1975, Blacks and Hispanics earned about $4,000 less than Whites, and about $1,500 of that difference could be explained in terms of differences in educational level. The remaining differences could be attributed to other institutional factors, including racial discrimination. Hirschman and Wong (1984) also demonstrated that although the average earnings of Asian Americans were much closer to Whites' than those of other minority groups, this equality was accomplished through overachievement in education by Asian Americans. Even though Asian Americans are stereotyped as having achieved the same level of occupational attainment as Whites, Hsia (1988) showed that Asian Americans have consistently earned less than their White counterparts in professional careers even after education and years of experience have been accounted for. One can infer that these observed inequalities are the results of discrimination, although quantitative evidence of discrimination is rarely available (Hotchkiss & Borow, 1990).

In addition, the social experience of racial discrimination can cause some minority persons to restrict the range of occupations they consider. For example, some researchers have speculated that actual or perceived discrimination may discourage minority persons from choosing some occupations (Gottfredson, 1978; Leung, Ivey, & Suzuki, 1994). Racial discrimination can also cause minority persons to feel a sense of hopelessness about their occupational future. Racial minorities who have internalized a sense of inferiority because of the experience of racial discrimination may develop a poor or inaccurate vocational self-concept. The experience of being discriminated against racially also plays an important role in the formation of racial identity, a construct that has a significant influence on the psychological and social functioning of ethnic minorities (e.g., Helms, 1990).

Exactly how the experience of racial discrimination affects the career development of racial minorities has not been clearly delineated in the literature. The practical implication for psychologists and counselors is that career intervention to combat the effects of racism should target both the individual and system levels. Counselors can help individuals to explore how their vocational self is affected by racial oppression. The counselor can also work to effect changes in schools, organizations, families, and communities to create racially affirming environments for all individuals.

The Effects of Social Class

Researchers of career development have suggested that socioeconomic status (SES) is an important variable moderating the effects of ethnicity on career behavior (e.g., Arbona, in press; Smith, 1983). Most research studies on the career behavior of ethnic minorities have failed to control for the differences in SES among research participants, and as a result, it is not clear whether observed career attributes and behavior among members of a minority group can be attributed to either ethnic-related variables or SES. Exactly how career behavior is influenced by the interaction between ethnic-related variables and SES is still unclear. However, the fact that ethnic minorities are overrepresented in the lower SES levels suggests that low SES has an adverse effect on the career development of ethnic minorities.

Sociologists interested in the study of occupations have contended that parental SES is a good predictor of occupational attainment, as delineated by a framework called the status attainment model (e.g., Bielby, 1981; Blau & Duncan, 1967). A review of the sociological perspective of career development, including the status attainment model, can be found in Hotchkiss and Borow (1984, 1990). I would like to highlight a version of the status attainment model called the Wisconsin model (Sewell, Haller, & Ohlendorf, 1970), in terms of its implications for multicultural career development and counseling.

The Wisconsin model (Sewell et al., 1970) posited that three sets of intervening variables moderate between family SES and occupational status. The first set is called *cognitive variables*, referring to the mental and academic abilities of the individual. The second set is termed *social-psychological processes*. It includes educational and occupational aspirations, encouragement from significant others (parents and teachers) to attend college, and the aspirations of one's peers to attend college. The third set is *educational attainment*, or the level of education attained by the individual.

The Wisconsin model of status attainment does not assume a deterministic perspective. It explains how individual aspirations, the attitudes of significant others, and educational attainment moderate the effects of parental SES on occupational attainment. Accordingly, at least three areas of intervention could affect occupational attainment. First, individual aspiration is an important part of the social-psychological processes that motivates the person to attain occupational goals. Research about occupational aspirations suggests that minority youths do not necessarily have lower career aspirations than Whites, but they tend to have low expectations that their aspirations could be realized in the real world (Arbona, 1990; Smith, 1983). In order to facilitate the career development of ethnic minority youths, it is essential to elevate their educational and occupational aspirations and expectations and to set realistic goals based on these aspirations and expectations.

Second, the aspirations of disadvantaged minority youths are influenced by the expectations and attitudes of individuals around them, including parents, teachers, and peers. The implication for career counseling practice is that parents and teachers could be productively involved in the process of empowering disadvantaged youths in their educational and occupational pursuits.

Third, the association between educational attainment and occupational attainment has been noted not only by the Wisconsin model of status attainment but also by other studies (e.g., Arbona, 1989; Gottfredson, 1978). A major deterrent to the upward social mobility of ethnic minority groups, perhaps with the exception of Asian Americans, is the high school dropout rate. For example, according to the U.S. Bureau of the Census (cited in Axelson, 1993), in 1990 the high school dropout rate for Hispanics was about 50%, and for Blacks about 35%, as compared to about 22% for Whites. These figures indicate that facilitating the educational attainment of minority groups is as important as facilitating their career development, because without the appropriate education and training, the range of vocational choices available to them is very limited.

DIVERGENCE IN CAREER DEVELOPMENT AMONG MINORITY GROUPS

An extensive review of the literature on the career development of each of the four major minority groups in the United States is beyond the scope of this chapter. Accordingly, only selected career development issues are examined. It is important to note that Black Americans, Hispanic Americans, Asian Americans, and American Indians share some career development issues, but that the meaning of those issues varies because of the unique cultural, social, and economic circumstances surrounding each ethnic group.

Black Americans

The educational and career development of Black Americans has been affected by conditions such as poverty, racism, high rates of juvenile delinquency, and a high percentage of single-parent families (Parham & McDavis, 1987; Sue & Sue, 1990). The educational attainment of Black Americans, in terms of both school graduation rate and test scores, has been below the national average (Axelson, 1993; Sue & Sue, 1990). Despite these adverse conditions, Black Americans have made considerable gains in educational development since the 1960s (Smith, 1983). For example, the percentage of Black Americans who finished high school has gone from 60% in 1970 to 76% in 1989 (Axelson, 1993). The percentage of Black Americans who completed college has also gone from 4% in 1970 to about 12% in 1989 (Axelson, 1993). However, the gradual cutback in federal financial support to disadvantaged students since the 1980s has contributed to a reduction in college enrollment among Black students (Sue & Sue, 1990). Improving the educational attainment of Black American students at both the high school and college levels remains the most important career development issue for Black Americans.

The literature on the career development of Black Americans has identified considerable gender differences in the area of occupational aspirations and attainment. Black females tend to have higher educational and occupational aspirations than Black males (Smith, 1982). Gender differences, however, decline in the college years to the point that the aspirations of Black females are lower than those of Black males (Betz & Fitzgerald, 1987; Smith, 1982). Black females also perform better than Black males in terms of scholastic achievement (Smith, 1982) and are more likely than the latter to be employed in professional positions (Betz & Fitzgerald, 1987; Gottfredson,

1978). Yet the progress Black women have made in the educational and occupational arenas has not been translated into occupational status in terms of income. Black women still earn significantly less than Black males and White females (Betz & Fitzgerald, 1987). Although most Black women expect to work most of their lifetime (Betz & Fitzgerald, 1987; Smith, 1982), most of them choose occupations that are traditional for women and for Blacks (Gurin & Gaylord, 1976; Smith, 1982). The combination of racial and gender discrimination that Black females experience in the occupational world has been referred as "double jeopardy" (Beale, 1970; Betz & Fitzgerald, 1987).

The above analysis suggests that it is important to enhance the career aspirations and expectations of Black American youths (Smith, 1983). Career intervention programs can be offered in conjunction with other types of intervention programs to foster the career and educational development of Black students (e.g., D'Andrea & Daniels, 1992). It is especially important to maintain Black female students' career aspirations beyond the high school level. Career intervention programs that encourage Black women to explore occupations that are nontraditional for women and Blacks are needed.

The occupational choice pattern of Black Americans is quite narrow. An analysis of the 1970 census data by Gottfredson (1978) suggested that Blacks were overrepresented in low-paying Realistic and Social occupations (according to the Holland occupational classification system) and underrepresented in Investigative and Enterprising occupations. Although the numbers of Black Americans in professional and technical jobs have increased in the past two decades, the proportions of Blacks in occupational areas such as law, medicine, college teaching, and engineering are still below the proportion of Black Americans in the total population (Smith, 1983). Systematic career intervention programs that foster the interest of Black Americans in these nontraditional occupational areas are needed. The use of role models as part of an intervention can help Black American youths develop an expectation that they can attain their occupational goals.

Hispanic Americans

Hispanic Americans are a very diverse group of people of different cultural origins, including Mexico, Puerto Rico, Cuba, and South and Central America. The Hispanic population is one of the fastest growing ethnic minority groups in the United States and is also the youngest, with a median age of 23.2 years in 1980 (Axelson, 1993).

The career development status of Hispanic Americans is highly related to their status in educational attainment (Arbona, 1990). Hispanic Americans experience significant difficulties in the area of education. Efforts in the past 20 years to improve educational achievement of minorities have only produced a slight decrease in high school dropout rate from about 48% in 1970 to about 44% in 1990 (Axelson, 1993). In a review of the literature on the career development of Hispanics, Arbona (1989) suggested that the differences in educational attainment between Hispanics and Anglos are due to structural variables related to schooling background and SES, rather than cultural traits (e.g., family values). For instance, variables such as SES, participation in college preparation courses, and generational level were found to be related to levels of educational and occupational attainment among Hispanic youths (e.g., Ortiz, 1986).

One intervention program targeting Hispanic students is the creation of bilingual educational programs in many elementary school systems with a large Hispanic population. Research studies on the effects of these programs have found mixed results (e.g., Baker & de Kanter, 1981; Cummins, 1986). The literature seems to suggest that bilingual education by itself is not sufficient in reversing the educational attainment of Hispanics as a group. Cummins (1986) suggested the importance of adopting an empowering framework, in which the cultural characteristics (e.g., languages, values) of students are affirmed and incorporated into classrooms, and the school system works in collaboration with the cultural community of the students to enhance their development. The implication for educational and career intervention is that a comprehensive program that facilitates a sense of self-efficacy (e.g., Hackett, Betz, Casas, & Roca-Singh, 1992) among Hispanic students is preferable to isolated educational and career intervention programs.

The career needs of Hispanics vary depending on SES and levels of acculturation (Arbona, 1990, in press). There is a direct relationship between levels of acculturation, SES level, and educational attainment. Middle-class and college-educated Hispanic students are similar to Anglo students in terms of career attitudes and aspirations. Hispanics of lower SES, many of whom are first-generation families who immigrated to the United States for economic and political security, are likely to be in a disadvantaged position with regard to educational and career development. Low-SES, less acculturated Hispanic persons experience barriers that many middle-class, acculturated Hispanics do not, such as language deficiency, economic hardship, nontransferable credentials, problems with the U.S. Immigration and Naturalization Service, and social and emotional adjustment. Consequently, an assessment of the levels of SES and acculturation is especially important during career counseling with Hispanic clients. Career intervention that provides practical help in career and personal adjustment and adaptation would be appropriate for less acculturated and economically disadvantaged Hispanics.

Asian Americans

Asian Americans encompass a number of different Asian ethnic groups with some shared cultural characteristics (e.g., family structure, worldviews). There are also significant differences among Asian Americans in many areas, including cultural beliefs, acculturation, immigration history, and economic and occupational attainment (Hsia, 1988; Leong & Gim, in press; Leong & Leung, 1994; Sue & Morishima, 1982).

Asian Americans have been widely perceived as the high achievers in the educational system. The educational attainment of Asian Americans is reflected in a number of areas, including above-average school grades, quantitative scores in scholastic aptitude tests, and enrollment in higher educational institutions (Hsia, 1988). However, the educational attainment of Asian Americans has caused some educational needs to be neglected. First, Asian Americans consistently score lower than the national average in the verbal section of scholastic aptitude tests. Hsia (1988) showed that this verbal deficiency is true not only of Asian immigrant students but also of second- and third-generation Asian students. Hsia found that the deficiency of Asian American students in the verbal area has not been adequately recognized and remedied in the educational system. Lack of proficiency in written English may have caused some Asian students to stay away from educational and occupational areas requiring written communication skills. Second, there are variations within various Asian ethnic groups in terms of academic attainment. For example, in 1980, the percentage of males who graduated from high school ranged from about 70% for Asian Indians to about 18% for Vietnamese (compared to 21.3% for Whites). Among females, the range was from about 41% for Filipinos to 8% for Vietnamese (compared to 13.3% for Whites) (Hsia, 1988). The perception that Asian students are overrepresented in the higher educational system has restricted some Asian students, such as Vietnamese Americans, from getting important financial aid resources available to other disadvantaged ethnic groups.

Another popular perception of the career development of Asian Americans is that they tend to choose occupations in the technical and scientific areas. Leung et al. (1994) suggested that this career choice pattern could be due to unique personality characteristics of Asian Americans, such as intolerance of ambiguity and preference for structure (Leong, 1985; Sue & Kirk, 1972). Leung et al. (1994) suggested that Asian Americans may also choose technical and science occupations because of their preference for occupational prestige. Hsia (1988) showed that the career choice pattern of Asian Americans can be explained in terms of immigration status. After reviewing occupational data in the 1970s and 1980s, Hsia (1988) found that most Asians in the engineering field were actually foreign-born persons who came to the United States for an education and elected to stay permanently. In contrast to popular stereotypes, the percentages of native-born Asian Americans in engineering were consistent with what would be expected from the population count in the 1970s and 1980s. Also, native-born Asian Americans were more likely than foreign-born Asian Americans to be in the physical and behavioral sciences. Hsia, however, corroborated that the occupational choice pattern of Asian Americans is still narrow. Asian Americans are underrepresented in many important occupational areas such as law, politics, and teaching. From a counseling standpoint, it is important to encourage Asian American students to consider the full range of occupational alternatives available, including career choices nontraditional to Asians (Leong & Leung, 1994; Leung et al., 1994).

Immigrant status is an important variable for Asian Americans. Many Asian immigrants have educational and work credentials that are not being recognized in the United States. Recent immigrants also encounter barriers such as limited language proficiency, discrimination, social isolation, economic hardship, and inadequate knowledge about the U.S. occupational structure. These barriers often result in downward occupational mobility in terms of prestige level. Some new immigrants who are refugees from Indochina are also coping with adjustment issues related to psychological wounds from wars in their home country (e.g., Cook & Timberlake, 1989; Sue & Sue, 1990). Career counseling should offer practical help to immigrant clients who seek it, such as provision of information about resources available within the Asian community and training in language and job search skills. Supportive intervention that helps Asian immigrants deal with the frustrations of their social, psychological, and economic adjustment would also be desirable.

Finally, the image of being high achievers in the educational and occupational arenas has taken a toll on some Asian American youths (Leong & Gim, in press; Leong & Leung, 1994). Some students may experience intense shame when their performance does not meet their own or their family's expectations. Some students may experience vocational choice difficulties because they feel they are being pushed into occupational areas that are expected of Asian Americans. Counselors need to understand that these difficulties are rooted in the educational values and family structure of Asian Americans. In conducting career counseling with Asian American students, it is important to help the student clarify his or her cultural values and beliefs in making educational or career-related decisions.

American Indians

American Indians have been referred to as the most economically disadvantaged minority group in the United States (Epperson & Hammond, 1981). They suffer from a high unemployment rate of about 50% on reservations (Heinrich, Corbine, & Thomas, 1990; Martin, 1991). The rate of high school dropout has been estimated to be around 60% (Heinrich et al., 1990). The rates of suicide, economic poverty, and alcoholism are significantly higher than the national levels (Sue & Sue, 1990).

About 50% of American Indians currently live on reservations or lands surrounding them (Martin, 1991). The career issues confronting American Indians on the reservations are different from the issues of those who live off the reservations. For those who live on the reservations, career development is affected by a number of unique factors. First, the vocational opportunities in and around the reservations, most of them in rural areas, are limited. Many professional occupations of higher social status are available only in urban areas, and to gain access to those opportunities one has to leave the reservation. Second, the limited exposure to the world of work around the reservation has resulted in a general lack of occupational information among American

Indians (Martin, 1991; McDiarmid & Kleinfeld, 1986). Third, American Indians on the reservations who choose not to adopt the Anglo mainstream
cultural and occupational values may not have adequate job search and job
maintenance skills to survive in the occupational world. In view of these environmental constraints, Martin (1991) suggested that American Indians on
the reservations might have a restricted perception of their occupational possibilities, resulting in occupational choices that are unfulfilling. Martin (1991)
suggested that many commonly used career counseling intervention strategies, such as job try-out experience, computerized career exploration program,
informational interviewing, and shadowing experiences, could be used with
American Indian clients who are lacking in occupational knowledge.

Information about the vocational needs of American Indians who do not
live on the reservations is rather scanty. Heinrich et al. (1990) suggested that
many American Indians leave the reservations for urban areas for vocational
reasons. Their levels of acculturation and identification with traditional Indian
cultural values vary (Heinrich et al., 1990; Sue & Sue, 1990; Trimble &
Fleming, 1989). Many American Indians who have left the reservations may
feel torn between Anglo cultural values and traditional Indian values. Some
are burdened with a sense of guilt that they have abandoned their Indian heritage for economic and vocational gains (Sue & Sue, 1990). Some are disillusioned because of the discrimination and cultural conflicts they experience in
their work environment. Understanding the complex interaction between vocational development issues and acculturation is important in working with
American Indians who do not reside on Indian reservations.

The economic reality of the reservations and the contrast in work and life
values between American Indian culture and the Anglo culture (Heinrich,
1990; Martin, 1991; Trimble & Fleming, 1989) pose a challenge for career
counseling with American Indian clients. Martin (1991) suggested that a decision to leave the reservation for an urban area for economic and vocational
reasons should not be made hastily without fully considering how this would
affect the client's social network and how the decision fits with his or her
value system. Martin also suggested that the effects of vocational decisions
on the client's family system should be considered, and that family members
should be involved in making career-related decisions.

A MODEL OF CAREER
INTERVENTION WITH ETHNIC MINORITIES

Fretz (1981) defined career intervention as "any activity or program intended to facilitate career development" (p. 78). Although the outcomes of
career intervention are often related to the resolution of career concerns, there
is an increasing recognition that vocational and personal issues are often intertwined, and that effective career counseling often involves the use of a
holistic approach in which multiple life issues are explored (e.g., Hackett,

Career Intervention Outcome

		Career-Related	Education-Related
Mode of Intervention	System	1	2
	Group	3	4
	One-to-One	5	6

Figure 27.1. A Model of Career Intervention for Ethnic Minorities

1993; Rounds & Tracey, 1990; Subich, 1993). For minority persons, career issues are often embedded in other personal, cultural, and economic issues; thus, the use of a holistic model appears to be most appropriate. Regardless of what mode of career intervention is being considered, counselors who are involved in multicultural career intervention should be trained in cross-cultural competencies as defined by a number of cross-cultural training guidelines (e.g., Pedersen, 1988; Sue, Arredondo, & McDavis, 1992).

A model of multicultural career intervention is presented in Figure 27.1. This model of career intervention involves three modes of intervention and two outcome areas. The three modes of intervention are system intervention, group counseling, and one-to-one counseling. The two outcome areas are career-related and education-related outcomes. In this chapter, I have suggested that educational attainment is very important to the career development of ethnic minorities. Intervention programs that seek to enhance the educational attainment of minority students must be included as an integral part of a model of career intervention for ethnic minorities. An increase in educational competencies should expand both real and perceived occupational opportunities for ethnic minorities.

Although counseling psychology has been viewed as a discipline that emphasizes prevention (see Whiteley, 1984), most of the existing literature on career intervention has conceptualized career intervention in the context of one-to-one counseling. The concept of system intervention is related to the concept of primary prevention in community psychology (e.g., Caplan, 1964; Forgays, 1983). The purpose is to reduce the occurrence of certain psychological problems among "at-risk" individuals by seeking changes in the environmental system of the individuals. In career intervention with ethnic minorities, intervention at the system level involves activities that seek to change and modify the environments of minority persons so that obstacles to their career and educational development can be eliminated (Cells 1 and 2 in Figure 27.1). In working to promote changes in the social and organizational systems, counselors would have to work with other change agents within the systems in collaboration. System intervention can be used to enhance career-related outcomes. For example, psychologists and counselors can assist school teachers and administrators in their awareness of the special career development concerns of ethnic minority students and collaborate with school personnel to create an empowering multicultural environment in the school to develop and maintain the career aspirations of minority students. System intervention can also be used to facilitate education-related outcomes. A comprehensive approach to create an affirming and accepting multicultural school environment is more desirable than isolated educational intervention programs for minority students (Cummins, 1986). Such an environment would foster the development of a strong, positive self-identity, which is vital to the maintenance of educational aspirations among minority students. Intervention at the system level is seldom mentioned in the career development literature and is rarely used as a mode of career intervention. However, it may be the most effective and important approach, especially for ethnic minority individuals, because of its potential to establish long-lasting change in the system and to influence a large number of individuals within the system.

The second mode of career intervention is group counseling (Cells 3 and 4 in Figure 27.1). In an article about career intervention strategies for ethnic minorities, Bowman (1993) suggested that because minority persons often operate within a group orientation, group intervention could be an effective approach. Although group career intervention seems to be a frequently used strategy with ethnic minorities (e.g., Dunn & Veltman, 1989; Rodriguez & Blocher, 1988), its degree of effectiveness remains to be examined by research. Some minority persons may have more difficulty with group counseling because of the cultural inhibitions they experience when they are expected to disclose their private worlds to a group of strangers. To make group career counseling more attractive for minority persons, the counselor may consider the use of a structured rather than a nonstructured format, given that some minority persons tend to be more comfortable with a structured format of helping (Sue & Sue, 1990). Also, if a counseling group consists of members from a homogeneous ethnic background, the similarity in cultural beliefs and experience may foster group rapport building and may facilitate the occurrence of interpersonal learning. All in all, there is a need for carefully planned research to examine how group career counseling can effectively assist ethnic minorities in career development.

The third level of career intervention is one-to-one counseling (Cells 5 and 6 in Figure 27.1). One-to-one career counseling is the mode of intervention that has been addressed most in the literature on career and multicultural counseling. Individual counseling can be used to achieve both career-related and education-related outcomes. In the context of individual counseling, career issues of minority clients must be understood in terms of the cultural background and beliefs of the client. The overlap between career issues and other personal and emotional issues suggests that career counseling is no less complex than other forms of counseling and psychotherapy (Hackett, 1993); thus, the level of multicultural competencies expected of the counselor is no less than in other instances of cross-cultural counseling and psychotherapy. The counselor also needs to understand the array of variables that affect the process of multicultural counseling, such as acculturation, racial identity development, and worldviews.

RECOMMENDATIONS FOR RESEARCH

There is a strong need for more research studies about the career behavior of different ethnic minority groups. Most of the existing research studies about the career development of ethnic minorities are on Black Americans (Betz & Fitzgerald, 1987; Smith, 1983) and, to a lesser extent, on Hispanic Americans. Research studies on the career development of Asian Americans and American Indians are lacking (Leong, 1985; Smith, 1983). The area of multicultural career development and counseling cannot be advanced without an adequate research base.

Research studies about the career development of ethnic minorities are needed in a number of areas. First, exploratory studies should be conducted to obtain descriptive information about the career behavior of ethnic minorities. Descriptive information about variables such as career interests, occupational values, aspirations, and decision-making style are useful for both researchers and practitioners. For the researcher, these data would provide a starting point to determine if theories of career development are relevant for ethnic minorities. For practitioners, these data would provide useful information about their client populations and would assist the counselor in serving the career needs of minority clients.

Second, there is a need for research studies that are theory based. Theory-based research would allow the researchers to determine the extent to which theories of career development are valid for the minority populations; to examine systematically the relations among career development variables; and to revise existing models or develop novel models of career development that have relevance and applications for ethnic minorities. Recent inquiries on the cross-cultural validity of Holland's model of career interests (e.g., Fouad & Dancer, 1992; Haverkamp, Collins, & Hansen, 1994; Swanson, 1992) and Gottfredson's theory of career aspirations (e.g., Leung, 1993) are examples of research studies that are theory based. Given the importance of theories in guiding practice, more research efforts should be directed toward examining the validity of career development theories for ethnic minorities.

Third, researchers should carefully document career intervention strategies aimed at the system, group, and individual levels that have been implemented for ethnic minorities and systematically evaluate these strategies in terms of outcome and effectiveness. This is an area of research that has received very little attention in the literature (Bowman, 1993; Spokane, 1991). Career intervention strategies that work would serve as a model for practitioners in different settings. Career intervention outcome research would also provide information about the usefulness of various theoretical frameworks for minority populations.

Fourth, there is a need for research on the validity of career assessment instruments on minority populations. The problems of using standardized career assessment instruments with ethnic minority persons have been discussed by a number of researchers (e.g., Fouad, 1993; Hansen, 1987; Leong & Leung, 1994). Future research has to examine not only the reliability and validity of various career assessment instruments but also the process of utilizing test scores that would maximize their utility for ethnic minority clients.

Finally, it is important to diversify the methodological approaches used in multicultural career development and counseling research. For example, quantitative approaches seem to be the most commonly used, but qualitative approaches such as case studies can provide unique perspectives that cannot be reflected in quantitative data. Also, a majority of the existing research on the career behavior of ethnic minorities has utilized a cross-racial group comparison research design in which one or more minority groups are compared with a White sample along different variables. Padilla (1994) recently suggested that the priority of multicultural research should be to study intragroup variability. Padilla argued that because there is tremendous diversity within each of the major ethnic groups in the United States, the use of a cross-racial comparison design may mask important within-group differences (e.g., differences among Mexicans, Cubans, and Puerto Ricans). Also, the comparison of two racial groups could not advance our understanding of how the effects of ethnicity and culture are manifested in behavior. Thus, the study of intragroup variability should be a priority for researchers in multicultural career development and counseling.

REFERENCES

Arbona, C. (1989). Hispanic employment and the Holland typology of work. *Career Development Quarterly, 37*, 257-268.

Arbona, C. (1990). Career counseling research and Hispanics: A review of literature. *The Counseling Psychologist, 18*, 300-323.

Arbona, C. (in press). Theory and research on racial and ethnic minorities: Hispanic Americans. In F. T. L. Leong (Ed.), *Career development and vocational behavior of racial and ethnic minorities*. Hillsdale, NJ: Lawrence Erlbaum.

Axelson, J. A. (1993). *Counseling and development in a multicultural society*. Pacific Grove, CA: Brooks/Cole.

Baker, K. A., & de Kanter, A. A. (1981). *Effectiveness of bi-lingual education: A review of the literature.* Washington, DC: U.S. Department of Education, Office of Planning and Budget.

Beale, F. (1970). Double jeopardy: To be Black and female. In T. Cade (Ed.), *The Black woman: An anthology* (pp. 90-100). New York: New American Library.

Betz, N. E., & Fitzgerald, L. F. (1987). *The career psychology of women.* Orlando, FL: Academic Press.

Bielby, W. T. (1981). Models of status attainment. In D. J. Treiman & R. V. Robinson (Eds.), *Research in social stratification and mobility: A research annual* (Vol. 1, pp. 3-16). Greenwich, CT: JAI.

Blau, P. M., & Duncan, O. D. (1967). *The American occupational structure.* New York: John Wiley.

Bowman, S. L. (1993). Career intervention strategies for ethnic minorities. *Career Development Quarterly, 42,* 14-15.

Brown, D., Brooks, L., & Associates (1990). *Career choice and development* (2nd ed.). San Francisco: Jossey-Bass.

Caplan, G. (1964). *Principles of preventive psychiatry.* New York: Basic Books.

Cook, K. O., & Timberlake, E. M. (1989). Cross-cultural counseling with Vietnamese refugees. In D. R. Koslow & E. P. Salett (Eds.), *Crossing cultures in mental health* (pp. 84-100). Washington, DC: International Counseling Center.

Cummins, J. (1986). Empowering minority students: A framework for intervention. *Harvard Educational Review, 56,* 18-36.

D'Andrea, M., & Daniels, J. (1992). A career development program for inner-city Black youth. *Career Development Quarterly, 40,* 272-280.

Dunn, C. W., & Veltman, G. C. (1989). Addressing the restrictive career minority youth: A program evaluation. *Journal of Multicultural Counseling, 17,* 156-164.

Epperson, D. L., & Hammond, D. C. (1981). Use of interest inventories with Native Americans: A case for local norms. *Journal of Counseling Psychology, 28,* 213-220.

Forgays, D. G. (1983). Primary prevention of psychopathology. In M. Hersen, A. E. Kazdin, & A. S. Bellack (Eds.), *The clinical psychology handbook* (pp. 701-733). New York: Pergamon.

Fouad, N. A. (1993). Cross-cultural vocational assessment. *Career Development Quarterly, 42,* 4-13.

Fouad, N. A., & Dancer, L. S. (1992). Cross-cultural structure of interests. *Journal of Vocational Behavior, 40,* 129-143.

Fretz, B. R. (1981). Evaluating the effectiveness of career interventions. *Journal of Counseling Psychology, 28,* 77-90.

Gottfredson, L. S. (1978). An analytical description of employment according to race, sex, prestige, and Holland type of work. *Journal of Vocational Behavior, 13,* 210-221.

Gurin, P., & Gaylord, C. (1976, June). Educational and occupational goals of men and women at Black colleges. *Monthly Labor Review, 99,* 10-16.

Hackett, G. (1993). Career counseling and psychotherapy: False dichotomies and recommended remedies. *Journal of Career Assessment, 2,* 105-117.

Hackett, G., Betz, N., Casas, M. J., & Roca-Singh, I. A. (1992). Gender, ethnicity, and social cognitive factors predicting the academic achievement of students in engineering. *Journal of Counseling Psychology, 39,* 527-538.

Hansen, J. C. (1987). Cross-cultural research in vocational interests. *Measurement and Evaluation in Counseling and Development, 19,* 163-176.

Haverkamp, B. E., Collins, R. C., & Hansen, J. C. (1994). Structure of interests of Asian American students. *Journal of Counseling Psychology, 41,* 256-264.

Heinrich, R. K., Corbine, J. L., & Thomas, K. R. (1990). Counseling Native Americans. *Journal of Counseling and Development, 69,* 126-133.

Helms, J. (Ed.). (1990). *Black and White racial identity: Theory, research, and practice.* Westport, CT: Greenwood Press.

Hirschman, C., & Wong, M. G. (1984). Socioeconomic gains of Asian Americans, Blacks, and Hispanics: 1960-1976. *American Journal of Sociology, 90,* 584-607.

Holland, J. L. (1985). *Making vocational choices* (2nd ed.). Englewood Cliffs, NJ: Prentice Hall.

Hotchkiss, L., & Borow, H. (1984). Sociological perspectives on career choice and attainment. In D. Brown, L. Brooks, & Associates (Eds.), *Career choice and development* (1st ed., pp. 137-168). San Francisco: Jossey-Bass.

Hotchkiss, L., & Borow, H. (1990). Sociological perspectives on work and career development. In D. Brown, L. Brooks, & Associates (Eds.), *Career choice and development* (2nd ed., pp. 262-307). San Francisco: Jossey-Bass.

Hsia, J. (1988). *Asian Americans in higher education and at work.* Hillsdale, NJ: Lawrence Erlbaum.

Jiobu, R. M. (1976, October). Earnings differentials between Whites and ethnic minorities: The cases of Asian Americans, Blacks, and Chicanos. *Sociology and Social Research, 61,* 24-38.

Leong, F. T. L. (1985). Career development of Asian-Americans. *Journal of College Student Personnel, 26,* 539-546.

Leong, F. T. L., & Gim, R. H. C. (in press). Career assessment and intervention with Asian Americans. In F. T. L. Leong (Ed.), *Career development and vocational behavior of racial minorities.* Hillsdale, NJ: Lawrence Erlbaum.

Leong, F. T. L., & Leung, S. A. (1994). Career assessment with Asian Americans. *Journal of Career Assessment, 2,* 240-257.

Leung, S. A. (1993). Circumscription and compromise: A replication study with Asian Americans. *Journal of Counseling Psychology, 40,* 188-193.

Leung, S. A., Ivey, D., & Suzuki, L. (1994). Factors affecting the career aspirations of Asian Americans. *Journal of Counseling and Development, 72,* 404-410.

Martin, W. E., Jr. (1991). Career development and American Indians living on reservations: Cross-cultural factors to consider. *Career Development Quarterly, 39,* 273-383.

McDiarmid, G. W., & Kleinfeld, J. S. (1986, May). Occupational values of rural Eskimos. *Journal of American Indian Education,* pp. 23-29.

Ortiz, V. (1986). Generational status, family background, and educational attainment among Hispanic youths and non-Hispanic White youths. In M. A. Olivas (Ed.), *Latino college students* (pp. 29-46). New York: Teachers College Press.

Padilla, A. M. (1994). Ethnic minority scholars, research, and mentoring: Current and future issues. *Educational Researchers, 23,* 24-27.

Parham, T. A., & McDavis, R. J. (1987). Black men, an endangered species: Who's really pulling the trigger. *Journal of Counseling and Development, 66,* 24-27.

Pedersen, P. (1988). *A handbook for developing multicultural awareness.* Alexandria, VA: American Association for Counseling and Development.

Rodriguez, M., & Blocher, D. (1988). A comparison of two approaches to enhancing career maturity in Puerto Rican college women. *Journal of Counseling Psychology, 35,* 275-280.

Rosenbaum, J. E. (1981). Careers in a corporate hierarchy: A longitudinal analysis of earnings and level attainment. In D. J. Treiman & R. V. Robinson (Eds.), *Research in social stratification and mobility: A research annual* (Vol. 1, pp. 95-124). Greenwich, CT: JAI.

Rounds, J. B., & Tracey, T. J. (1990). From trait and factor to person-environmental fit counseling: Theory and process. In W. B. Walsh & S. H. Osipow (Eds.), *Career counseling: Contemporary topics in vocational psychology* (pp. 1-44). Hillsdale, NJ: Lawrence Erlbaum.

Sewell, W. H., Haller, A. O., & Ohlendorf, G. (1970). The educational and early occupational attainment process: Replications and revisions. *American Sociological Review, 35,* 1014-1027.

Smith, E. J. (1982). The Black female adolescent: A review of the educational, career and psychological literature. *Psychology of Women Quarterly, 6,* 261-288.

Smith, E. J. (1983). Issues in ethnic minorities' career behavior. In W. B. Walsh & S. H. Osipow (Eds.), *Handbook of vocational psychology* (Vol. 1, pp. 161-222). Hillsdale, NJ: Lawrence Erlbaum.

Spokane, A. R. (1991). *Career intervention.* Englewood Cliffs, NJ: Prentice Hall.

Subich, L. M. S. (1993). How personal is career counseling? *Career Development Quarterly, 42,* 129-131.

Sue, D. W., Arredondo, P., & McDavis, R. (1992). Multicultural counseling competencies: A call to the profession. *Journal of Counseling and Development, 70,* 477-486.

Sue, D. W., & Kirk, B. A. (1972). Psychological characteristics of Chinese-American students. *Journal of Counseling Psychology, 19,* 471-478.

Sue, D. W., & Sue, D. (1990). *Counseling the culturally different: Theory and practice* (2nd ed.). New York: John Wiley.

Sue, S., & Morishima, J. K. (1982). *The mental health of Asian Americans.* San Francisco: Jossey-Bass.

Swanson, J. L. (1992). The structure of vocational interests for African-American college students. *Journal of Vocational Behavior, 40,* 144-157.

Trimble, J. E., & Fleming, C. M. (1989). Providing counseling services for Native American Indians: Client, counselor, and community characteristics. In P. B. Pedersen, J. G. Draguns, W. J. Lonner, & J. E. Trimble (Eds.), *Counseling across cultures* (3rd ed., pp. 177-204). Honolulu: University of Hawaii Press.

U.S. Equal Employment Opportunity Commission. (1991). *1990 Report: Job patterns for minorities and women in private industry.* Washington, DC: Government Printing Office.

Whiteley, J. M. (1984). *Counseling psychology: A historical perspective.* Schenectady, NY: Character Research Press.

28

Group Work

Multicultural Perspectives

ROD J. MERTA

THE UNFULFILLED PROMISE

As director of MIT's Research Center for Group Dynamics, Kurt Lewin, a social psychologist and a German immigrant, became renowned for developing the T-group, also called the *training group, laboratory-training group,* and *sensitivity group* (Johnson & Johnson, 1994; Yalom, 1985). By interacting with the other members in a T-group and then receiving feedback from them, participants obtained insight into their interpersonal styles and assistance in developing more democratic leadership roles (Corey & Corey, 1992). With the passing of the Fair Employment Practices Act in 1946, the Connecticut Interracial Commission contracted with Lewin to train community leaders to work more effectively in reducing tensions among interracial groups and to facilitate changes in racial/ethnic attitudes (Gazda, 1978; Marrow, 1967; Yalom, 1985). When Marrow (1967), his colleague and close friend, challenged his decision to undertake still another project given Lewin's poor health, Lewin responded, "When you have to go to sleep each night, hearing the anguished screams of your mother as the brutal Nazis tortured her to death in a concentration camp, you can't think of 'taking it easy'" (p. 146).

Although the T-group became formalized in the summer of 1947, with the founding of the National Training Laboratories at Bethel, Maine, Lewin was not present to view the success of his efforts—he had died that February (Marrow, 1967). As leaders in business, education, government, and industry recognized the potential of this experiential learning method for developing human relations skills necessary for successful functioning in organizations, the popularity of the T-group mushroomed in the 1950s and 1960s (Corey & Corey, 1992; Johnson & Johnson, 1994; Yalom, 1985). Unfortunately, its initial mission of improving interracial relations and facilitating changes in racial/ethnic attitudes appears to have been more or less forgotten (Walker & Hamilton, 1973; Yalom, 1985).

Beginning in the mid- to late 1960s, the T-group was transformed into the encounter group as Rogerian and Freudian clinicians shifted from a training emphasis to more of a clinical one (Yalom, 1985). The contemporary growth group, also known as the *process group, experiential group,* or *consciousness-raising group,* is the present-day derivative of both the T-group and the encounter group (Johnson & Johnson, 1994). Gazda (1978) provided a possible explanation for why the initial mission of using group work to focus on multicultural issues was abandoned: "Most early applications of the T- and related encounter groups were in business management and higher education, thus limiting the participants considerably to middle- and upper-middle-class Whites" (p. 304).

Despite its auspicious beginning, it appears that the initial promise of group work for the advancement of multicultural counseling has not been fulfilled (Davis, 1981; DeLucia, Coleman, & Jensen-Scott, 1992; Greeley, Garcia, Kessler, & Gilchrest, 1992; Helms, 1990; Walker & Hamilton, 1973). Despite its potential for promoting greater multicultural awareness, group work has not been used widely in interracial situations (Davis, 1981; Walker & Hamilton, 1973), there is little mention in the literature on group work as it relates to race or ethnicity (Davis, 1981; Greeley et al., 1992; Helms, 1990), and I have observed that recent publications on multicultural counseling (see Pedersen, 1991; Stone, 1994) have made little, if any, mention of group work as a modality separate from individual counseling. Indeed, the focus in multicultural counseling has been on individual counseling models and interventions, and group work models and interventions have been largely ignored (Davis, 1981; DeLucia et al., 1992).

The objectives of this chapter are (a) to provide an overview of the potential effectiveness of multicultural group work, (b) to identify the major guidelines for conducting multicultural group work, and (c) to make recommendations for advancing multicultural group work in training and research. Before undertaking these objectives, terms need defining.

DEFINITIONS

Multicultural counseling can be defined broadly or inclusively to denote counseling between or among people differing on any one of a variety of cultural characteristics (e.g., gender, religious affiliation, age), or it can be defined more narrowly or exclusively to denote counseling involving individuals of any one or more of the four major racial/ethnic minorities (i.e., African Americans, Asian Americans, Hispanic Americans, and Native Americans) (Locke, 1990; Ridley, Mendoza, & Kanitz, 1994). In fulfilling the objectives of this chapter, only the exclusive definition will be used.

The term *group counseling* has been used to describe everything from task groups to therapy groups. In an attempt to organize systematically and label the various group types, the Association for Specialists in Group Work (ASGW) decided upon the term *group work*, defined it as "a broad professional practice that refers to the giving of help or the accomplishment of tasks in a group setting," and identified four group work specializations: task/work, guidance/psychoeducational, counseling/interpersonal problem solving, and psychotherapy/personality reconstruction (ASGW, 1990, p. 14). Although the focus of this chapter will be primarily on the latter two group specializations (i.e., counseling and psychotherapy groups), the term *multicultural group work* will be used to refer to any one or all of the four group specializations in which individuals of any one or more of the four major racial/ethnic minorities are participating.

In terms of group composition, a group may be classified as having either a homogeneous or a heterogeneous membership. In a homogeneous group, the members share some characteristic (e.g., a diagnosis, a demographic characteristic) (Johnson & Johnson, 1994; Unger, 1989), whereas members of a heterogeneous group differ or vary on that characteristic. Members of a racially heterogeneous group are drawn from one or more of the four major racial/ethnic minorities as well as possibly from the majority culture, but members of a racially homogeneous group, also referred to as a *culture-specific group* (see Fukuyama & Coleman, 1992), are drawn exclusively from the same racial/ethnic minority.

THE POTENTIAL EFFECTIVENESS
OF MULTICULTURAL GROUP WORK

Designations of heterogeneity and homogeneity have been based on the most prevalent presenting problem or diagnosis of the group members (e.g., substance abuse, psychosomatic problems), whereas demographic characteristics (i.e., age, gender, race, and socioeconomic status) have been less frequently mentioned in the literature (Unger, 1989). Homogeneous groups are perceived as having less conflict, being more cohesive, providing more support, being better attended, and providing more rapid relief of symptoms than heterogeneous groups, but are at risk for being superficial and less creative and productive (Johnson & Johnson, 1994; Unger, 1989; Yalom, 1985). In contrast, heterogeneous groups are characterized by greater in-depth work, individuation, character change, productivity, and creativity, but are at risk for excessive conflict and alienation of members (Johnson & Johnson, 1994; Unger, 1989; Yalom, 1985). More on the basis of anecdotal accounts than on empirical evidence, these same advantages and disadvantages have been generalized to racially heterogeneous and homogeneous groups.

Racially Heterogeneous Groups

Participants in racially heterogeneous groups are seen as having the potential to achieve better minority-majority group interaction and understanding (Avila & Avila, 1988). In contrasting group work to individual counseling, Gelso and Fretz (1992) claimed that the members of racially heterogeneous groups "are able to contact a wide range of personalities, and receive rich and diverse feedback" (p. 450). Corey (1990) believed that members also can benefit from the collective feedback of a heterogeneous group as well as from the modeling of other members as they challenge their biases and stereotypes and make positive changes. Walsh (1989) contended that "contact with others from different cultures in a group context often helps members become more aware of their racial feelings and has 'the healthy effect' of making them realize their ethnocentric assumptions and limiting beliefs" (p. 547). Greeley et al. (1992), like Kurt Lewin before them, contended that the unique properties of group work provide its members with the potential "for intervening in and changing racial or cultural attitudes and identities" (p. 196).

Not all racially heterogeneous groups realize these benefits. Gladding (1991) noted that some groups do not transcend their racial bias and prejudice and become bogged down in excessive conflict, whereas others are characterized by denial as racial issues are simply ignored. Johnson and Johnson (1994) identified three common barriers to conducting an effective racially heterogeneous growth group: "prejudice, blaming the victim, and culture clash" (p. 445). Although conflict characterizes the group process, especially in the transitional stage, Yalom (1985) contended that the intensity of that conflict should not be permitted to exceed the group members' ability to tolerate it. Greeley et al. (1992) cited the research of Burke (1984) as evidence that those groups that are intentionally led in exploring "racial or cultural identity serve to modify racial attitudes better than groups in which exploration is haphazard" (p. 196).

Even though Yalom (1985) did not directly address the topic of multicultural group work in the third edition of his widely acclaimed book *Theory and Practice of Group Psychotherapy*, his theory for group work provides a conceptual framework for understanding how a racially heterogeneous growth group can be utilized to increase multicultural awareness and reduce racial prejudice. Whereas some groups (e.g., most guidance or psychoeducational groups and some counseling and psychotherapy groups) are highly structured, leader centered, and content oriented (i.e., focused on what is being discussed in group), the growth group, used as a basis for both group counseling and psychotherapy, is only slightly structured, member centered or interactional, and process oriented (focused on how the group is functioning) (Johnson & Johnson, 1994; Yalom, 1985).

The focus of the group is to facilitate interpersonal learning by having members disclose and receive feedback from each other in response to here-and-now issues and interactions occurring within the group. Because the group is more interactional, the interpersonal behaviors that a member customarily exhibits outside of group become manifested within the group, which is referred to as a social microcosm (Yalom, 1985). Although the group leader does not assume a directive role, he or she certainly plays a very active one. By a variety of group techniques (i.e., culture building, process illumination, here-and-now activation, consensual validation, and conflict resolution), he or she helps to develop a cohesive group in which members feel safe to disclose and to give and receive feedback, and in which conflict is worked through rather than avoided or left to go unchecked (Yalom, 1985). Members enter the group harboring certain "parataxic distortions"—distorted perceptions or beliefs regarding interpersonal relations that they have not been able to correct during normal social relations (Yalom, 1985). By acknowledging their parataxic distortions at the outset of or any time during the group, members can establish their goals of correcting these distortions and improving their interpersonal relations.

For many, if not all, members of a racially heterogeneous growth group, the parataxic distortions are likely to take the forms of racial biases and stereotypes, ethnocentrism, and ignorance of various multicultural issues and perspectives (see Johnson & Johnson, 1994). In adding further conceptualization to a racially heterogeneous growth group, Johnson and Johnson (1994) provided four conditions that must be met for a group to be effective: (a) high levels of positive interdependence for achieving a common goal, (b) a superordinate group identity that unites the diverse members and is based on a pluralistic set of values, (c) a sophisticated understanding of the differences among members by means of personal relationships and candid discussions, and (d) clarification of miscommunications among members of different races and ethnicities. A racially heterogeneous growth group operating on the basis of Yalom's theory and Johnson and Johnson's extension of it appears to offer the means of fulfilling that initial promise of Lewin's T-group—the promise of increasing multicultural awareness and reducing racial prejudice.

A review of the literature on multicultural group work reveals a smattering of primarily anecdotal accounts of interracial growth groups. Johnson (1963) briefly related an account of a reportedly successful 2-year group experience involving two Chinese Americans, three Jewish Americans, two African Americans, an English American, and an Irish American (all male) and a female group leader, but provided little detail on how the group proceeded. Rubin (1967) reported on a T-group experience involving 10-member groups with 1 or 2 African American members among 8 or 9 Anglo American members that resulted in a lessening of racial prejudice. Walker and Hamilton (1973) reported in detail the success of a nondirective encounter group involving six Black, four Chicano, and four White university students as group members and two White student personnel deans as group leaders.

Racially Homogeneous Groups

In contrast to interracial groups, racially homogeneous groups, also referred to as culture-specific groups, are made up of members all from the same racial/ethnic group. As noted previously, homogeneous groups are perceived as having less conflict, being more cohesive, providing more support, being better attended, and providing more rapid relief of symptoms than heterogeneous groups, but they are at risk for being more superficial and less creative and productive (Johnson & Johnson, 1994; Unger, 1989; Yalom, 1985). Although acknowledging the potential effectiveness of racially heterogeneous groups, Fukuyama and Coleman (1992) noted that there are times when a culture-specific group may be desirable. It is widely recognized in the literature on multicultural counseling that although much of human nature and counseling is universal, members of a certain racial/ethnic group are likely to benefit more from a particular culture-specific counseling modality, theory, or technique (Locke, 1990; Sue, 1990; Sundberg, 1976).

Fukuyama and Coleman (1992) provided an example of a culture-specific group in which eight Asian Pacific American college students participated in an effective 5-week bicultural assertion training group led by a woman and a man, both Asian Pacific American. In bicultural training, treatment is provided within the context of two values systems (e.g., traditional Asian Pacific or Asian Pacific American and contemporary, urban, middle-class Anglo American), and the individual is allowed the freedom "to choose from two or more equally important values systems, depending on the appropriateness of the behavior" (Fukuyama & Coleman, 1992, p. 213).

In citing what he considered legitimate criticisms for using culture-specific modalities and techniques in counseling racial/ethnic minority students, Sue (1990) noted that by highlighting characteristics of a racial/ethnic minority (e.g., reticence or shyness among Asian Pacific Americans), stereotypes are likely to be reinforced. Sue (1990) contended that this danger can be minimized if "we realize that we are discussing general group differences that may be moderated by such factors as gender, acculturation, stage of racial-cultural identity, socioeconomic status, education, and so on" (p. 424). As if to comply with Sue's suggestion, Fukuyama and Coleman (1992) recommended that an individual's particular stage of racial-cultural identity (i.e., Pre-Encounter, Encounter, Immersion, or Internalization) be considered when recommending placement in a culture-specific group. These authors contended that at times in an individual's life, immersion in one's own racial/ethnic culture can result in a positive affirmation of one's own racial/ethnic identity (e.g., during the Encounter or Immersion stages).

Arredondo (1991) reported on a culture-specific group for Latina immigrants in which the within-group difference that they shared was acculturation level. This eight-session psychoeducational group averaged 10 to 15 Latina immigrants and was led by two women and a man, all of whom were Latino American and bilingual. The group met after Sunday mass and provided support and information on various topics (e.g., community resources and services, parenting, and self-care and support networks).

As is true with any of ASGW's four specializations, the growth or process group approach to group counseling and psychotherapy is not restricted to either racially heterogeneous or racially homogeneous groups. Baron (1991) described a 12-week growth group, led by two Chicano male counselors and composed of eight Hispanic members, in which a culture-specific approach consisted of providing members with additional structure to make them feel more comfortable. Rollack, Westman, and Johnson (1992) described in great detail a growth group for African Americans made up of three male and three female members and led by two Black leaders. The goals of the group, personal growth and continuing adjustment to a predominantly White university, were largely realized by a minimally structured, process-oriented approach that focused on such core themes as coping with racism, male-female relations, and life after college. Gainor (1992) outlined a culture-specific growth group in helping African American women to work through internalized oppression.

GUIDELINES FOR CONDUCTING
MULTICULTURAL GROUP WORK

Whether a group is racially homogeneous or heterogeneous with a composition based on racial equality (equal numbers of racial/ethnic groups), racial equity (societal proportions of racial/ethnic groups), or the inclusion of only one member from a racial/ethnic minority group, it is likely that for the foreseeable future the group leader will be of the majority culture (see Davis, 1981). To render such multicultural groups more effective, certain guidelines need to be considered and then followed by a group leader: (a) being multiculturally aware; (b) being aware of one's own cultural identity; (c) recruiting, screening, selecting, and preparing multicultural group members; and (d) intervening in behalf of multicultural group members during the group process.

Multicultural Awareness

Whether leading a racially heterogeneous or homogeneous group, the group leader must have a general understanding of and an appreciation for the range of cultural similarities and differences existing within a multicultural group and the impact that they are apt to have on group dynamics (Corey, 1990; Pedersen, 1988). A review of the literature on multicultural group work reveals various generalizations regarding the appropriateness of group work for the four racial/ethnic minorities. Although these generalizations warrant attention, they also warrant ongoing scrutiny because they are based more on anecdotal reports than on systematic research and because they often fail to consider within-group differences (e.g., socioeconomic status, acculturation level) and between-group differences (e.g., between Japanese Americans and Vietnamese Americans).

African Americans

Due to the compatibility of various African American values (e.g., group identity, interdependence, and cooperation) with group work, there is widespread support for the potential effectiveness of this modality with African Americans, from children to the elderly (Baruth & Manning, 1991; Gladding, 1991; Rollack et al., 1992; Shipp, 1983). Group work may be attractive to many African Americans because the "safety in numbers" principle makes it easier to disclose before a group than with an individual counselor, and because they then have the opportunity to have their personal experiences validated (Rollack et al., 1992).

Consistent with the position of Fukuyama and Coleman (1992) that an individual's particular stage of racial/ethnic identity be considered before placement in a group, Shipp (1983) contended that the research on group work suggests that many African Americans would be well advised to work through various issues related to race/ethnicity within a racial homogeneous group before venturing into a heterogeneous one. There appear to be conflicting views of how African American adult males and females may interact in group. Rollack et al. (1992) felt compelled to balance their group with an equal number of African American males and females to limit the scapegoating of males for an array of perceived grievances that many of the females hold, whereas Baruth and Manning (1991) reported that African American women are apt to be reticent in mixed-gender groups on issues such as gender equality and the difficulties of single parenting.

Asian Americans

Of the four racial/ethnic minority groups, Asian Americans are frequently perceived as the least receptive and responsive to group work (Baruth & Manning, 1991; Gladding, 1991; Leong, 1992). Commitment to protecting the family name and honor makes it difficult for Asian Americans to disclose personal information or to share family secrets in groups (Ho, 1984; Vander Kolk, 1985). Baruth and Manning (1991) reported that "Chinese students frequently refuse to participate in counseling; in a group setting, they are usually quiet and withdrawn" (p. 201). Kitano (1981) contended that group work should be used less often with Japanese Americans and, when used, should be more formal and less confrontational. Leong (1986) predicted the likelihood of negative outcomes for Asian Americans in group work because of the inherent conflicts between the group work values (e.g., openness, expression of feelings, directness) and the cultural values of Asian Americans (e.g., verbal nonassertiveness, reluctance to display strong emotions in front of strangers, and unwillingness to disclose personal problems to strangers). Many Asian

Americans will find the giving and receiving of feedback uncomfortable (Leong, 1992). Potential positive outcomes in group work with Asian Americans appear more likely when the group is a highly structured, problem-solving one rather than a free-floating, process-oriented interactional group (Kitano, 1989; Leong, 1992). Kitano (1989) reported more positive outcomes with Asian Americans when the group members had been selected homogeneously on such demographic variables as age, gender, socioeconomic status, and professional status. Leong (1992) contended that careful screening, selection, and preparation can result in positive outcomes for many Asian Americans participating in group work.

Hispanic Americans

Hispanic Americans may be reluctant to disclose information that may reflect negatively on their family or, in the case of males, that may threaten their perception of masculinity or *machismo* (Baruth & Manning, 1991; Gladding, 1991). Baron (1991) attested to the importance of "developing behavioral, goal-oriented, prescriptive, and structured activities," especially at the initial stage or stages of group work (p. 179). Although loyalty to family, traditional sex roles, and preference for structure should be considered, the group leader should also take into account the incredible diversity among Hispanic Americans, in terms of both between-group differences (e.g., Mexican Americans, Puerto Ricans) (Newlon & Arciniega, 1992) and within-group differences (e.g., acculturation level, ethnic identity development) (Baron, 1991). There is ample anecdotal support for the effectiveness of group work with Hispanic Americans on a variety of issues: academic skills, value clarification, problem solving, self-esteem, and pride in one's cultural identity (Baruth & Manning, 1991; Gladding, 1991). Avila and Avila (1988) advocated the use of group work with Mexican Americans because of their natural orientation to groups and because homogeneous groups are apt to result in better self-understanding, whereas heterogeneous groups will bring about better minority-majority group interaction and understanding.

Native Americans

Given the reluctance of many traditional Native Americans to share personal problems and to allow outsiders to intervene in their personal problems, Native Americans are often perceived as not being receptive and responsive to group work (Baruth & Manning, 1991; Lum, 1986). Differences in verbal and nonverbal communication between Native Americans and Anglo Americans may complicate or impede the group process, and a preference for group harmony and cooperative behavior may render group conflict totally unacceptable to many Native Americans (Newlon & Arciniega, 1992). For these reasons, Lewis and Ho (1989) doubted the benefits of Native Americans' participation in racially heterogeneous groups and warned against pressuring them when they are late to group or silent during group. Nevertheless, Native Americans tend to value a group orientation and may find group work the preferred modality of treatment, as evidenced by a series of anecdotal reports suggesting successful group experiences with Native Americans (see Baruth & Manning, 1991). Baruth and Manning (1991) emphasized the importance of the group leader's being perceived by the Native American group member as genuine, considerate, and nonmanipulative. Preparation for group, structuring the group experience, and controlling the intensity of group conflict are important considerations when performing group work with Native Americans.

Self-Awareness

By accepting untested stereotypes of racial/ethnic minority members as reality, by not detecting cultural variations within multicultural groups, and by not recognizing the culture-specific nature of one's personal values (e.g., individualism, nuclear family) and professional values (e.g., use of a nondirective counseling approach with a client preferring a more structured and directive approach), all counselors are vulnerable to succumbing to "cultural encapsulation" (Wrenn, 1985). By being so encapsulated, the group leader runs the risk of imposing his or her values on the group members and rendering him- or herself less effective in leading the group. As cited in Sue and Sue (1990), McRoy and Oglesby (1984) provided an example of a racially homogeneous, psychoeducational group in which five prospective African American couples were being evaluated as prospective adoptive parents. The group was led by both an African American and an Anglo American, but the approach used to evaluate the prospective couples had been developed for Anglo American couples. At one point in the group, the African American members began to object to the negative bias toward the use of physical punishment with children inherent in the parent effectiveness training component. Prior to the objection, had the group leaders anticipated this value difference or had they simply assumed that all members shared this value? If there had been only one African American couple in the group, would the value difference have been noted? Chung and Okazaki (1991) reported a similar preference for the use of physical punishment in parenting among Americans of Southeast Asian descent. Is it possible that there had been other couples in past groups regardless of race or ethnicity who had also valued the use of physical punishment?

Leong (1992) disclosed his experience as a graduate student in which a few of his professors expressed their concern over his reticence and passivity in their seminar classes and, in so doing, imposed upon him their culturally based assumption "that active vocalization was a universal sign of maturity and that they viewed that characteristic as a requisite to being a good psychologist" (p. 219). Leong began to doubt the appropriateness of his career choice until he came upon literature that validated his cultural perspective of what was appropriate group behavior.

I recall a similar situation in which I participated in a graduate supervisory group in which the lack of assertiveness of an Asian American female student was criticized by the supervisor and several students, all of whom were Anglo American females. Armed with good intentions but with unbridled ethnocentrism, these individuals had taken it upon themselves to "empower" this Asian American woman. While not overlooking cultural similarities, the group leader must anticipate and draw out cultural differences among group members and ensure that all are given equal time and treated in a respectful manner. As stated by Corey (1990), the group leader need not abandon or even conceal his or her values; instead, he or she "must avoid assuming a stance of superiority that leads you to unthinkingly impose your values on others" (p. 17). This task becomes particularly challenging when the group leader's most cherished values become the focus of the group (e.g., democratic parenting styles, assertiveness, education, a prochoice position on abortion). For group work to be effective, the group leader must consider both the multicultural makeup of his or her group and his or her own cultural identity (Corey, 1990).

Recruitment, Screening, Selection, and Preparation

Given the reported underutilization of counseling services by racial/ethnic minority groups (Corey, 1990), recruiting prospective members for a voluntary group can be very challenging. In recruiting Hispanic males for a university growth group, Baron (1991) advertised heavily in newspapers and other media, as well as relying heavily on word of mouth. In advertising groups, I have found outreach efforts, such as visiting university student organizations or the community and school equivalents, to be very effective. Arredondo (1991) used a Catholic church to recruit Latino American immigrants for her group. An occasional pro bono service to such an organization, utilizing one of Blustein's (1982) informal groups (e.g., street corner groups in urban neighborhoods, peer groups in schools, work groups, self-help groups, or church groups), or conducting a single-session workshop (see Gainor, 1992) provides the necessary visibility and credibility for future recruitment.

Baruth and Manning (1991) advocated a three-step approach in deciding on the appropriateness of group work for multicultural clients: (a) understand the culture of the client, (b) understand the client, and (c) understand the advantages and disadvantages of group work. Although Leong (1992) questioned the appropriateness of racially heterogeneous growth groups for many Asian Americans, he added that with proper screening and preparation, placement in such an ambiguous group may be effective. Baruth and Manning (1991) and Baron (1991) recommended using a pregroup interview to screen, select, and prepare individuals for group. This interview gives the group leader the opportunity to get to know the client and vice versa, and to assess for both within-group differences (e.g., the acculturation level or the racial/ethnic identity stage of an Asian American) and the client's comfort level with group work and self-disclosure (Baruth & Manning, 1991). A potentially useful resource in deciding whether an individual would be better served in individual or group counseling is a listing of considerations (e.g., presenting problem, personality traits, personal circumstances), prepared by Seligman (1990) and based on anecdotal accounts and some research, for deciding whether individual, group, or family therapy is the best modality for a client. This session also gives the group leader the opportunity to prepare the client for group by clarifying the purpose or goals of the group, explaining what is expected of a group member, and describing what is apt to occur in group (Leong, 1992).

Group Interventions

An initial and ongoing form of group leader intervention on behalf of multicultural group members is that of structuring the group sessions to reduce ambiguity and anxiety. Members of racial/ethnic minority groups who are unfamiliar and uncomfortable with group work may prefer groups that are problem focused, behaviorally oriented, and highly structured (planned exercises), with concrete goals (Baron, 1991; Leong, 1992). Various publications exist from which to select planned exercises for structuring groups for all ages (see Jacobs, Harvill, & Masson, 1994; Morganett, 1990). For groups requiring only minimal structuring, Baron (1991) and Arredondo (1991) were successful using core themes (e.g., life after college, parenting) with which to structure the sessions to a mild to moderate degree.

Another form of structuring is the group leader's interruption of the group process, when he or she senses that a member appears confused and anxious with that process, in order to provide the member with clarification and support. Taking time before or after a session to touch base with a racial/ethnic minority group member, especially a lone member, provides the opportunity to convey support as well as give and receive clarification. Leong (1992) contended that the major problem with racially heterogeneous groups is the failure of the group leader to detect value conflicts among racial and ethnic minorities and to address them early in the group process.

Although a stereotypically reticent Asian American may benefit vicariously from the group experience without ever directly participating (Lum, 1986; Yalom, 1985), it is generally conceded that silent members do not benefit as much as do the more active and influential members (Yalom, 1985). As part of the growth group process, the more talkative members will eventually notice their more reticent counterparts, become uncomfortable with their silence, and begin to exert group pressure or groupthink, a demand by group members for an individual to submit to the group's standards, values, and norms. As stated in ASGW's *Ethical Guidelines for Group Counselors and Professional Standards for the Training of Group Workers* (1990), the group leader needs to anticipate this scenario, distinguish between what is therapeutic pressure and what is groupthink, and act to ensure that the vulnerable member is not victimized by the group. Kaneshige (1973) identified a series of approaches and techniques for helping the reticent group member "to be more expressive in communicating his feelings and thoughts to the group without negating his cultural values" (p. 412). For example, the group techniques of "blocking" or "cutting off" a more talkative in-group member coupled with words of encouragement can allow the group leader to "draw out" the more reticent out-group member. For an overview of these and other group counseling techniques, see Corey, Corey, Callanan, and Russell (1988) and Jacobs et al. (1994).

Controlling the intensity of conflict in a group is a key determinant of its eventual success because excessive curbing of conflict can result in superficiality, whereas excessive conflict can result in alienation (Yalom, 1985). Thus, the group leader must be aware of cultural differences in communication style and tolerance for confrontation. As already noted, the Asian American stereotype may be more uncomfortable with confrontation than his or her Anglo American counterpart (Kaneshige, 1973), whereas the African American stereotype may be more demonstrative in his or her communication style than his or her Anglo American counterpart (Sue & Sue, 1990).

Sue and Sue (1990) described in a case vignette a Black professor who was perceived by his White colleagues as too emotional, demonstrative, and threatening. I led a group of midwives and obstetricians in which a White female obstetrician charged a Black female midwife with having demonstrated these same behaviors. I was able to help the group work through the conflict: first, by acknowledging the existence of the conflict; second, by soliciting feedback (i.e., perceptions and feelings) from the members in conflict; and third, by containing the conflict by means of consensual validation (seeking the reactions of other members). Davis (1984) contended that the group leader must be willing to take risks in developing a positive group culture, and an essential form of risk taking is to acknowledge rather than avoid conflict—especially, interracial conflict. Greeley et al. (1992) asserted that the leader must be willing to take a direct approach in resolving conflict, and the technique of consensual validation allows the group leader to address the conflict without losing group members' perceptions that he or she is neutral. Whereas many in the group did perceive this midwife as somewhat aggressive, the obstetrician was perceived by many as overly sensitive and somewhat manipulative. This feedback generated personal disclosures from both women and resulted in a better understanding of both individuals and in improved communication among everyone.

More important than the use of specific techniques for making the group culture safe for all its members is the overall manner in which the group leader conducts him- or herself and, in so doing, acts as a positive role model for the members (Kaneshige, 1973; Yalom, 1985). To develop a multicultural group in which all members feel understood and valued, group counselors need to have what Derald Wing Sue described as the capacity to share a client's worldview without critically judging this view (cited in Corey, 1990).

RECOMMENDATIONS FOR TRAINING AND RESEARCH

Training

After years of what can best be called "benign neglect," specialists in group work have awakened to the need for addressing multicultural perspectives in group work. Capuzzi and Gross (1992), Corey (1990), Gladding (1991), and Johnson and Johnson (1994) addressed multicultural perspectives in the most recent editions of their books on group work. Corey (1990) provided useful guidelines for leading multicultural groups as well as evaluating the major counseling theories in terms of their appropriateness for multicultural group work. As noted previously, Johnson and Johnson (1994) provided a conceptual framework for conducting racial heterogeneous growth groups. Baruth and Manning (1991) and Lee and Richardson (1991), in their books on multicultural counseling, addressed the use of group work with multicultural populations. Baruth and Manning (1991) described the effectiveness of group work with members of all four racial/ethnic minority groups across the life span. Several chapters in the edited book by Lee and Richardson (1991) are devoted to multicultural group work with various multicultural populations. Davis (1984) edited a book on social group work practice that may have been the first book devoted entirely to multicultural group work. Multicultural group work appears to have received even more attention in professional journals. A fair number of articles on multicultural group work were published in the *Journal for Specialists in Group Work* (*JSGW*) throughout the 1980s and into the 1990s. Of particular note is a special issue of *JSGW* edited by DeLucia et al. (1992) that focuses on both training and practice in multicultural group work.

The overdependence on didactic approaches and lack of experiential exercises in multicultural training are widely recognized as serious limitations (Gudykunst & Hammer, 1983, cited in Ridley, Mendoza, & Kanitz, 1994; Merta, Stringham, & Ponterotto, 1988; Ridley et al., 1994; Wehrly, 1991). Wehrly (1991) believed that experiential techniques may increase cultural knowledge, empathy, and sensitivity and also reduce misconceptions and stereotypes. To me, Wehrly appears to be echoing Kurt Lewin, and the racially heterogeneous growth group would appear to offer the ultimate experiential exercise for training in multicultural counseling.

As far as providing training in multicultural group work, Davis (1984) recommended the use of role play, rehearsal, and practice. He also recommended that in classes lacking an adequate multicultural composition, students be given the opportunity to role-play the roles of a member and leader in an interracial group. Classes in group work that actually have racial/ethnic minorities can be used as laboratories for actually experiencing the group dynamics and personal insights likely to occur in a multicultural group (Davis, 1984). Greeley et al. (1992) reviewed a variety of other experiential exercises that can be adapted to either role-play or rehearsal situations.

As an experiential group exercise for a class in cultural diversity or group work, I had students form five groups of seven or eight members. The ensuing group sessions were structured by providing each group with a case vignette depicting a situation laden with racial/ethnic stereotypes and ethnocultural value differences. Although Sue and Sue (1990) provided excellent case vignettes from which to select, it is very easy to devise one's own. At the time of this exercise, the local media had given much attention to the situation of a young Hispanic American female who was awarded a full scholarship to attend MIT but whose father did not want her to leave the family at such an early age. It took very little to transform this real life experience into a pro- vocative case vignette and ultimately a group experience in which both Anglo and Hispanic students were given the opportunity to disclose their own values, test stereotypes, and give and receive feedback within an increasingly mean- ingful group experience. Out-of-class resource people or advanced students can serve as group leaders, and initial leader and member anxiety can be re- duced by structuring the sessions with written instructions, such as "Identify the value differences present in the case vignette."

Given that many programs do not have adequate numbers of racial/ethnic minority students, the fishbowl technique can be used for improvising. If one uses only one group of six to eight students constituting the desired multicul- tural composition, the remainder of the students can form the audience. Sev- eral students can be selected from the minority and majority groups to act as process observers; their observations will be solicited after the group session. If there is not an ample number of students to represent one of the racial/ethnic minority groups, it is possible to bring in university or community resource people to fill the void. For example, the author has solicited the participation of staff members and students from university support programs for Native American and international students. Feedback from the resource people is that they greatly preferred this format to their past stints as guest speakers or panel members.

Finally, Davis (1984) urged that priority be given to placing students in practica settings in which they are likely to lead multicultural groups. Blustein (1982) advocated the use of another out-of-class group experience for studying multicultural group dynamics; he recommended that practitioners and stu- dents act as participant-observers within informal support systems (e.g., street corner groups in urban neighborhoods, peer groups in schools, work groups, self-help groups, and church groups). Sage (1991) described, as an example of such a group, an American Indian women's group that combines traditional and contemporary therapeutic practices and provides the members with sup- port and an alternative to drinking.

Research

Considering the methodological difficulties one experiences when con- ducting research in group work, Gelso and Fretz (1992) portrayed group work as slow to develop a research base and slow to gain respectability because of the absence of a research base, and predicted that the pace of future research would continue to be slow. This assessment is in strong contrast to Lewin's strong advocacy for and modeling of his action research (research by doing) in group work (Johnson & Johnson, 1994) and Yalom's (1985) equally strong recommendation that all specialists in group work adopt a research orientation. Given the current paucity of research on multicultural group work, the following general recommendations for future research would appear to be warranted:

1. Despite the difficulty in researching groups, specialists for group work need to research the overall effectiveness of group work with multicultural populations, and in so doing, go beyond what Yalom (1985) called the "traditional standardized (nomothetic) approach" to outcome research and utilize more individualized and qualitative approaches (p. 535).

2. Because the generalizations regarding the overall appropriateness of group work for the four major racial/ethnic minorities are largely based upon anecdotal reports and often do not consider within-group and between-group differences, these generalizations need to be empirically tested. Attempting to assess use of racial/ethnic identity developmental stages as a within-group difference (see Greeley et al., 1992) of group members and leaders would appear to be a potentially meaningful area for research.

3. Despite some empirical evidence in support of the effectiveness of racially heterogeneous, process-oriented groups (i.e., T-groups, encounter, and process) for increasing multicultural awareness and reducing negative racial/ethnic stereotypes and prejudice, this research is minimal and has largely been restricted to groups composed of Blacks and Whites (see Burke, 1984; Rubin, 1967; Walker & Hamilton, 1973). Additional research is needed to assess the effectiveness of interracial groups with all racial/ethnic minority groups, taking into account within-group and between-group differences.

4. The effectiveness of culture-specific group interventions for fostering greater pride in one's racial/ethnic identity and for resolving an array of presenting problems (e.g., lack of assertiveness, difficulties in cultural adjustment) needs to be researched for each of the racial/ethnic minority groups, taking into account within-group and between-group differences.

5. A variety of factors or recommended guidelines (e.g., racial/ethnic composition of group, race/ethnicity of group leaders, preparation of group members, structuring of group) that may influence the effectiveness of multicultural group work need to be empirically tested. The research of Davis (1979) has resulted in a better understanding of the potential effects of racial composition on group work, but more is needed, and the other factors and guidelines are based largely on anecdotal reports.

SUMMARY

Fulfilling the promise of multicultural group work as first envisioned by Kurt Lewin is long overdue. Group work needs to be recognized as a distinct therapeutic modality possessing its own potential effectiveness for working with multicultural populations. Whereas the values of some multicultural populations are congruent with group work, those that prove incongruent may be rectified by specialists in group work who have been trained in multicultural awareness; self-awareness; the appropriate recruitment, screening, selection, and preparation of group members; and the building and maintaining of a group culture that is beneficial for all multicultural populations. For group work to be culturally effective, the training of specialists in multicultural group work and the researching of this modality must be given far more attention than has been given in the past.

REFERENCES

Arredondo, P. (1991). Counseling Latinas. In C. C. Lee & B. L. Richardson (Eds.), *Multicultural issues in counseling: Approaches to diversity* (pp. 143-156). Alexandria, VA: American Association for Counseling and Development.

Association for Specialists in Group Work. (1990). *Ethical guidelines for group counselors and professional standards for the training of group workers*. Alexandria, VA: Author.

Avila, D. L., & Avila, A. L. (1988). Mexican-Americans. In N. A. Vacc, J. Wittmer, & S. DeVaney (Eds.), *Experiencing and counseling multicultural and diverse populations* (2nd ed., pp. 289-316). Muncie, IN: Accelerated Development.

Baron, A. (1991). Counseling Chicano college students. In C. C. Lee & B. L. Richardson (Eds.), *Multicultural issues in counseling: Approaches to diversity* (pp. 171-184). Alexandria, VA: American Association for Counseling and Development.

Baruth, L. G., & Manning, M. L. (1991). *Multicultural counseling and psychotherapy: A lifetime perspective*. New York: Merrill.

Blustein, D. L. (1982). Using informal groups in cross-cultural counseling. *Journal for Specialists in Group Work, 7*, 260-265.

Burke, A. W. (1984). The outcome of the multi-racial small group experience. *International Journal of Social Psychiatry, 30*, 96-101.

Capuzzi, D., & Gross, D. R. (1992). *Introduction to group counseling*. Denver, CO: Love.

Chung, T. C., & Okazaki, S. (1991). Counseling Americans of Southeast Asian descent: The impact of the refugee experience. In C. C. Lee & B. L. Richardson (Eds.), *Multicultural issues in counseling: Approaches to diversity* (pp. 107-126). Alexandria, VA: American Association for Counseling and Development.

Corey, G. (1990). *Theory and practice of group counseling* (3rd ed.). Pacific Grove, CA: Brooks/Cole.

Corey, G., Corey, M. S., Callanan, P. J., & Russell, J. M. (1988). *Group techniques* (Rev. ed.). Pacific Grove, CA: Brooks/Cole.

Corey, M. S., & Corey, G. (1992). *Groups: Process and practice* (4th ed.). Pacific Grove, CA: Brooks/Cole.

Davis, L. E. (1979). Racial composition of groups. *Social Work, 24*, 208-213.

Davis, L. (1981). Racial issues in the training of group workers. *Journal for Specialists in Group Work, 6*, 155-159.

Davis, L. E. (1984). *Ethnicity in social group work practice*. New York: Haworth.

DeLucia, J. E., Coleman, V. L., & Jensen-Scott, R. L. (Eds.). (1992). Counseling with multicultural populations [Special issue]. *Journal for Specialists in Group Work, 17*(4).

Fukuyama, M. A., & Coleman, N. C. (1992). A model for bicultural assertion training with Asian-Pacific American college students: A pilot study. *Journal for Specialists in Group Work, 17*(4), 210-217.

Gainor, K. A. (1992). Internalized oppression as a barrier to effective group work with Black women. *Journal for Specialists in Group Work, 17*(4), 235-242.

Gazda, G. M. (1978). *Group counseling: A developmental approach* (2nd ed.). Boston: Allyn & Bacon.

Gelso, C. J., & Fretz, B. R. (1992). *Counseling psychology*. Fort Worth, TX: Harcourt, Brace, Jovanovich.

Gladding, S. T. (1991). *Group work: A counseling specialty*. New York: Merrill.

Greeley, A. T., Garcia, V. L., Kessler, B. L., & Gilchrest, G. (1992). Training effective multicultural group counselors: Issues for a group training course. *Journal for Specialists in Group Work, 17*(4), 197-209.

Helms, J. E. (1990). Generalizing racial identity interaction theory to groups. In J. E. Helms (Ed.), *Black and White racial identity: Theory, research, and practice* (pp. 187-204). Westport, CT: Greenwood Press.

Ho, M. K. (1984). Social group work with Asian/Pacific Americans. *Social Work With Groups, 7*, 49-61.

Jacobs, E., Harvill, R. L., & Masson, R. L. (1994). *Group counseling: Strategies and skills* (2nd ed.). Pacific Grove, CA: Brooks/Cole.

Johnson, D. W., & Johnson, F. P. (1994). *Joining together: Group theory and group skills*. Boston: Allyn & Bacon.

Johnson, J. A. (1963). *Group therapy: A practical approach*. New York: McGraw/Hill.

Kaneshige, E. (1973). Cultural factors in group counseling and interaction. *Personnel and Guidance Journal, 51*, 407-412.

Kitano, H. H. L. (1981). Counseling and psychotherapy with Japanese Americans. In A. J. Marsella & P. P. Pedersen (Eds.), *Cross cultural counseling and psychotherapy* (pp. 228-242). Elmsford, NY: Pergamon.

Kitano, H. H. L. (1989). A model for counseling Asian-Americans. In P. Pedersen, J. G. Draguns, J. Lonner, & J. E. Trimble (Eds.), *Counseling across cultures* (3rd ed., pp. 139-151). Honolulu: University of Hawaii Press.

Lee, C. C., & Richardson, B. L. (Eds.). (1991). *Multicultural issues in counseling: Approaches to diversity*. Alexandria, VA: American Association for Counseling and Development.

Leong, F. T. (1986). Counseling and psychotherapy with Asian Americans: Review of literature. *Journal of Counseling Psychology, 33*, 196-206.

Leong, F. T. (1992). Guidelines for minimizing premature termination among Asian American clients in group counseling. *Journal for Specialists in Group Work, 17*(4), 218-228.

Lewis, R. G., & Ho, M. K. (1989). Social work with Native Americans. In D. R. Atkinson, G. Morten, & D. W. Sue (Eds.), *Counseling American minorities* (3rd ed., pp. 65-72). Dubuque, IA: William C. Brown.

Locke, D. C. (1990). A not so provincial view of multicultural counseling. *Counselor Education and Supervision, 30*, 18-25.

Lum, D. (1986). *Social work practice and people of color: A process-stage approach*. Monterey, CA: Brooks/Cole.

Marrow, A. J. (1967). Events leading to the establishment of the National Training Laboratories. *Journal of Applied Behavioral Sciences, 3*, 144-150.

McRoy, R. G., & Oglesby, Z. (1984). Group work with Black adoptive applicants. *Social Work With Groups, 7*, 125-134.

Merta, R. J., Stringham, E. M., & Ponterotto, J. G. (1988). Stimulating culture shock in counselor trainees: An experimental exercise for cross-cultural training. *Journal of Counseling and Development, 66*(5), 242-245.

Morganett, R. S. (1990). *Skills for living: Group counseling activities for young adolescents*. Champaign, IL: Research Press.

Newlon, B. J., & Arciniega, M. (1992). Group counseling: Cross-cultural considerations. In D. Capuzzi & D. R. Gross (Eds.), *Introduction to group counseling* (pp. 285-306). Denver, CO: Love.

Pedersen, P. B. (1988). *A handbook for developing multicultural awareness*. Alexandria, VA: American Association for Counseling and Development.

Pedersen, P. B. (Ed.). (1991). Multiculturalism as fourth force in counseling [Special issue]. *Journal of Counseling and Development, 70*(1).

Ridley, C. R., Mendoza, D. W., & Kanitz, B. E. (1994). Multicultural training: Reexamination, operationalization, and integration. *The Counseling Psychologist, 22*(2), 227-289.

Rollack, D. A., Westman, J. S., & Johnson, C. (1992). A Black student support group on a White university campus: Issues for counselors and therapists. *Journal for Specialists in Group Work, 17*(4), 243-252.

Rubin, I. (1967). The reduction of prejudice through laboratory training. *Journal of Applied Behavioral Science, 3,* 29-51.

Sage, G. P. (1991). Counseling American Indian adults. In C. C. Lee & B. L. Richardson (Eds.), *Multicultural issues in counseling: Approaches to diversity* (pp. 23-36). Alexandria, VA: American Association for Counseling and Development.

Seligman, L. (1990). *Selecting effective treatments: A comprehensive systematic guide to treating adult mental disorders.* San Francisco: Jossey-Bass.

Shipp, P. L. (1983). Counseling Blacks: A group approach. *Personnel and Guidance Journal, 62,* 108-111.

Stone, G. L. (1994). Multicultural training [Special issue]. *The Counseling Psychologist, 22*(2).

Sue, D. W. (1990). Culture-specific strategies in counseling: A conceptual framework. *Professional Psychology: Research and Practice, 21,* 424-433.

Sue, D. W., & Sue, D. (1990). *Counseling the culturally different: Theory and practice* (2nd ed.). New York: John Wiley.

Sundberg, N. D. (1976). Research and research hypotheses about effectiveness in intercultural counseling. In P. B. Pedersen, J. G. Draguns, W. J. Lonner, & J. E. Trimble (Eds.), *Counseling across cultures* (Rev. ed.), pp. 304-342). Honolulu: University of Hawaii Press.

Unger, R. (1989). Selection and composition criteria in group psychotherapy. *Journal for Specialists in Group Work, 14*(3), 151-157.

Vander Kolk, C. J. (1985). *Introduction to group counseling and psychotherapy.* Columbus, OH: Merrill.

Walker, J. R., & Hamilton, L. S. (1973). A Chicano, Black, White encounter. *Personnel and Guidance Journal, 51*(7), 471-477.

Walsh, R. (1989). Asian psychotherapies. In R. J. Corsini & D. Wedding (Eds.), *Current psychotherapies* (4th ed., pp. 546-559). Itasca, IL: Peacock.

Wehrly, B. (1991). Preparing multicultural counselors. *Counseling and Human Development, 24*(3), 1-24.

Wrenn, C. G. (1985). Afterward: The culturally encapsulated counselor revisited. In P. Pedersen (Ed.), *Handbook of cross-cultural counseling and therapy* (pp. 323-329). Westport, CT: Greenwood Press.

Yalom, I. D. (1985). *Theory and practice of group psychotherapy* (3rd ed.). Pacific Grove, CA: Brooks/Cole.

29

Culture and Families

A Multidimensional Approach

GEORGE V. GUSHUE

DANIEL T. SCIARRA

BOTH THE FAMILY and the multicultural perspectives in counseling and psychotherapy share the premise that no adequate understanding of a particular individual may be attained apart from an understanding of a larger context—family or culture, respectively—that shapes that person, as well as his or her understanding of the presenting problem for which treatment is sought. On the basis of this shared premise, family and multicultural theoretical constructs may be viewed not as mutually exclusive but rather as complementary approaches to treatment. For instance, Szapocznik and Kurtines (1993) suggested that the individual, family, and culture be seen as expanding rings of concentric circles that form a particular individual's context. After a brief review of the family (vs. individual) perspective in counseling, this chapter considers four conceptual paradigms that have been suggested for understanding families and culture and then applies them to a specific case. The first seeks to illuminate important intercultural differences. The next three (i.e., acculturation, racial/cultural identity, and bilingual theory) address the crucial dimension of intracultural differences. We suggest that consideration of these four dimensions and how they operate both between subsystems within the family and between particular subsystems and the counselor may provide counselors with a helpful way to understand the role played by culture in their treatment of a particular family.

586

FAMILY THERAPY

The psychoanalytic tradition situated the etiology of psychological difficulties in family dynamics, most especially in the relationship with the client's mother and father. If family was the cause, the reasoned solution was to work with an individual removed from his or her family. It was thought that the precipitant of the client's problems ought not to be present in the therapeutic sanctuary. The family therapy movement turned such thinking on its head. In the 1950s, therapists began to notice one of two phenomena with hospitalized psychiatric patients. When the patients returned to their families, either they decompensated or someone else in the family became ill. Thus, the idea of working with an entire family system was born because of the realization that some dynamic in the family system was maintaining the symptom.

In 1967, Salvador Minuchin and his colleagues published their well-known book *Families of the Slums* (Minuchin, Montalvo, Guerney, Rosman, & Schumer, 1967), the result of working with the poor families of delinquent boys. With this publication, Minuchin set the stage for therapists to see that the disorganization resulting from a life of poverty profoundly affected the family system. Minuchin's fundamental idea of restructuring a family so as to ensure a viable executive (parental) subsystem proved to be extraordinarily useful for therapists working with families stressed by a life of poverty.

According to Minuchin, family structure is the organized pattern in which family members interact (Minuchin, 1974; Minuchin & Fishman, 1981; Nichols & Schwartz, 1991). The first task of the therapist is to observe these patterns in vivo and then, through the use of enactments, alter the dysfunctional structure. Family structure is delineated by subsystems—members who join together to perform various functions (Nichols & Schwartz, 1991). The two most basic subsystems in any family are the parental subsystem, also known as the executive subsystem, and the sibling subsystem. Subsystems are demarcated by boundaries that regulate the amount of contact among individuals and subsystems (Nichols & Schwartz, 1991). Boundaries can be either too rigid, leading to "disengagement" among members, or too loose, leading to "enmeshment." According to Minuchin, a common dysfunction in families involves a lack of appropriate boundaries around the executive subsystem. Siblings and one or the other of the parents can form covert coalitions. When this occurs, the parents undermine each other's authority and are prevented from working together as effective executors of the family system.

CULTURAL PERSPECTIVES ON THE FAMILY

The following paragraphs briefly consider four models found in the counseling literature that seek to delineate the impact of culture on family systems and family counseling. The first of these is the intercultural perspective. The remaining three address the issue of intracultural differences and their consequences for family counseling.

Families: Intercultural Dimension

The dramatic shift of perspective signaled by the recognition of the "fourth force" of multiculturalism in individual counseling and psychotherapy (see Pedersen, 1991) was felt in the area of family counseling as well. Just as counselors working with individual clients attempted to reassess and critique the White, middle-class, heterosexual male assumptions that had guided their theory and practice, family counselors began to realize that for families, too, diversity was normative. Different cultures had differing ways of understanding "appropriate" family organization, values, communication, and behavior. Although the family perspective had revolutionized the individual view of the client by taking family context into account, it now needed to understand its own unit of analysis (i.e., the family) in light of an even larger context: culture.

After the notable work of Minuchin cited above, perhaps the earliest and the most influential of those who responded to the challenge were McGoldrick, Pearce, and Giordano (1982). Their classic work *Ethnicity and Family Therapy* is a compendium of portraits of family patterns for some 19 different ethnic groups in the United States. Countering assumptions of universality based on the experience of White middle-class families, McGoldrick and her colleagues emphasized between-group cultural differences in family patterns of organization. These authors highlighted the fact that the normative family experiences of Italian American, Black, Irish American, and Puerto Rican families are very different. Other authors have also drawn attention to these critical between-group differences (e.g., Ho, 1987). This intercultural dimension represents a necessary first level of analysis in any culturally appropriate approach to family treatment. Before assessing anything else, the counselor must know which behaviors, values, and modes of expression are normative within a given family's cultural framework. Otherwise, the counselor runs the risk of viewing as "pathology" anything that differs from his or her own experience or beliefs about families.

Although the intercultural dimension represents a necessary step in the cultural assessment of families, it is not in itself sufficient. If it is false to assume that all families are like White Anglo middle-class families, it is equally false to assume that all Mexican American families are culturally the same. Although the first set of attitudes may be monocultural, the second outlook represents stereotyping. Rather, any given family will approximate the cultural norm for their group in some ways, and in other ways it will not. McGoldrick (1982) was aware of this and noted that the ethnic family patterns suggested should be seen as "starting points" for understanding a particular family. She observed that a number of variables "influence the way ethnic patterns surface in families" (p. 12), including the reason for the family's migration, socioeconomic status, level of education, place where it settles, race, religion, political affiliations, and stage in the family life cycle at the time of the move.

Families: Intracultural Dimensions

Having established the general cultural parameters that might be expected to influence a particular family's behavior (and how these are similar to or different from the counselor's own), the counselor must turn to two crucial questions of within-group difference. First, to what extent does this particular family conform to or differ from the "typical" patterns of family functioning for its culture? Second, what cultural differences may exist within the family itself (i.e., among the various subsystems)? If cultural differences exist within the family, what consequences do these differences have for interactions both among the subsystems and between the various subsystems and the counselor? The paragraphs that follow consider three paradigms that we believe may assist counselors in their efforts to delineate intracultural differences present in a specific family: acculturation, racial/cultural identity, and bilingual theory.

ACCULTURATION

The construct of acculturation, borrowed from anthropology, has been used by psychologists in their efforts to describe within-group cultural differences. In the anthropological literature, *acculturation* initially referred to the potentially mutual influence that two cultures have on each other when they come into contact (Redfield, Linton, & Herskovits, 1936). Over the years however, it has more commonly come to refer to the interaction between a dominant and a nondominant culture in which one is affected much more profoundly than the other. Psychologists have considered acculturation along a number of dimensions.

One line of research has sought to understand the psychological impact of migration and acculturation (see Berry, 1980; Graves, 1967). What are the psychological consequences for individuals of the nondominant culture as they come into contact with the dominant culture? What predictable patterns of stress are encountered? What types of strategies for adjustment are psychologically healthy? Which ones are maladaptive? Sluzki (1979) suggested five stages through which a family passes during the process of migration (preparatory stage, the act of migration, period of overcompensation, period of decompensation or crisis, and transgenerational impact). According to Sluzki, each of these stages "has distinctive characteristics, triggers different types of family coping mechanisms, and unchains different types of conflicts and symptoms" (p. 380). Each stage presents a unique set of crises and challenges that the family must negotiate and to which the family system must adapt. Although a full description of Sluzki's model lies outside the scope of this chapter, it is clear that one dimension that a counselor must assess when working with a recently migrated family is: Where is this family in the process of cultural transition? How is the psychological impact of cultural adjustment currently affecting this family system?

A second line of research, more germane to the purposes of this chapter, has focused on "levels of acculturation" as a way of delineating within-group cultural differences. From this perspective, acculturation offers a snapshot of where a particular individual's worldview, values, and behaviors lie on a continuum between those of the nondominant culture and those of the dominant culture. Thus, one second-generation Dominican's outlook may be decidedly "more American" than another second-generation Dominican's. In its most simple expression, this paradigm suggests that a person arriving in the United States gradually moves along the continuum from the nondominant pole toward the dominant pole, although numerous factors, including age and gender (Szapocznik, Scopetta, Kurtines, & Aranalde, 1978; see also Landau, 1982; Landau-Stanton, 1990; McGoldrick, 1982), are thought to affect the rate at which this occurs.

Many theorists have suggested important modifications to the general "levels of acculturation" outline just presented. For instance, Ruiz (1981) suggested that acculturation may be situational. Thus, the same individual might behave in a manner more closely associated with the dominant culture while in the workplace, but act in a manner more consonant with the nondominant culture while at home. Keefe and Padilla (1987) confirmed and extended this insight by suggesting that acculturation is in fact multidimensional. They proposed that "the acceptance of new cultural traits and the loss of traditional cultural traits varies from trait to trait" (p. 16). Furthermore, their data, involving four generations of Mexican American families, call the standard unidirectional linear approach into question. They found that although it is true that some "Mexican" traits (e.g., Spanish language ability) do diminish progressively from generation to generation, other traits (e.g., the extended family and kinship network) actually seem to grow stronger from the first to the fourth generation. On the basis of a sample of second-generation Puerto Rican women, Inclán (1980) found that higher scores in "American-ness" were positively related to higher scores in "Puerto Rican-ness," leading him to prefer a four-quadrant model of acculturation (see McFee, 1968; Ruiz, Casas, & Padilla, 1977) that includes "bicultural" and "marginalized" as alternatives to the possibility of affiliation with either the dominant culture or the nondominant culture.

It was noted above that age was found to be a factor related to rate of acculturation (Szapocznik et al., 1978). Szapocznik et al. maintained that this differential rate of acculturation may serve only to exacerbate the ordinary intergenerational conflict between the parental and adolescent sibling subsystems in families in cultural transition (Szapocznik et al., 1978; Szapocznik & Kurtines, 1993; Szapocznik, Santisteban, Kurtines, Perez-Vidal, & Hervis, 1984). In a family that has recently migrated, parents are often more closely allied with the culture of the country of origin (i.e., the nondominant culture) than their children. The children—especially those with frequent contacts with the dominant culture—adapt to the dominant culture more rapidly than their parents. Thus, Szapocznik et al. suggested that what is presented as intergenerational conflict between subsystems may often be intercultural conflict as well. Accordingly, they proposed a strategy for working with these families that both acknowledges and uses the cultural gap between the subsystems (Szapocznik et al., 1984; Szapocznik & Kurtines, 1993). By identifying "cultural conflict" as the problem afflicting the family and stressing the benefits of intergenerational collaboration, clinicians working from this perspective encourage both subsystems to form an intergenerational alliance against this "common foe." This "detour" (i.e., viewing the presenting problem as one of intercultural conflict rather than intergenerational strife) enables parents and children to strengthen the alliance between them and gradually to establish a crossed alliance with the other's cultural point of view.

The construct of levels of acculturation provides an important way to begin to think about intercultural differences in families. Counselors cannot assume that a family represents a seamless exemplar of a given cultural family pattern. Rather, there may be distinct variations of the same general culture operating within the family, each of which must be taken into account. In addition, the counselor must consider the above-mentioned possibility of situational acculturation (Ruiz, 1981) or multidimensional acculturation (Keefe & Padilla, 1987). In such cases, it may be important to assess what cultural dynamic may be at work in the areas in which family conflict emerges. Are there other areas in which the "cultures" present in different subsystems may be more consonant with each other? What kind of situational cultural presentation is each subsystem likely to make in the consulting room?

RACIAL/CULTURAL IDENTITY

The racial/cultural identity models represent a different approach to the question of within-group cultural differences. Unlike the models of acculturation just discussed, racial/cultural identity theory does not endeavor to locate an individual's beliefs, values, and behaviors on a continuum between the dominant and nondominant cultures. Rather, the central focus of this paradigm is to describe an individual's psychological orientation to membership in both the dominant and nondominant cultures in the United States, the most salient—though not the only—marker of which is race. Given the context of racism and oppression that permeates U.S. society, how does one experience membership in either the dominant or the nondominant group? What are one's attitudes toward members of the other group? Racial/cultural identity theorists suggest that an individual's attitudes toward both of these two groups (i.e., dominant and nondominant) are linked, and that specific clusters of attitudes toward both groups will define the particular racial/cultural identity "status" (Helms, 1994) that predominates at a given point in a person's development.

Models of racial/cultural identity have been suggested for members of both nondominant and dominant cultures in the United States. The various models of nondominant racial/cultural identity development (Atkinson, Morten, & Sue, 1989; Helms & Carter, cited in Carter, Fretz, & Mahalik, 1986; Sue & Sue, 1990) are based on pioneering work in the area of racial identity (see Helms, 1990c), especially Cross's (1971) five-stage model of Black racial identity development. The racial/cultural identity models adopt the titles for the five stages suggested by Atkinson et al. (1979, 1989): Conformity, Dissonance, Resistance and Immersion, Introspection, and Synergetic Articulation and Awareness. The minority identity development model (Atkinson et al., 1979, 1989; see also Sue & Sue, 1990) suggests two additional parameters for each of the five clusters beyond those included in Cross's original model (i.e., attitudes toward self, attitudes toward other minority groups), although in at least one study (Fernandez, 1989), empirical confirmation has not been found for the second of these. All of the models of racial/cultural identity just mentioned follow the Cross model in tracing an individual's development from a socially learned idealization of the dominant culture and denigration of one's own (Conformity), through a growing awareness of societal and cultural racism and questioning of previous assumptions (Dissonance), to an outright and emphatic rejection of the dominant culture and idealization of one's own (Resistance and Immersion). This may be followed by another period of questioning this new set of rigidly held, externally defined attitudes (Introspection) and lead to an internally based valuing of one's own culture combined with a critical acceptance of some of the dominant culture's values. In their model, Helms and Carter (1986, cited in Carter et al., 1986) suggested that the empirical evidence does not support two separate transitional statuses, and consequently collapsed them into one that they called "Dissonance/ Introspection." This model of nondominant culture identity is outlined in Table 29.1.

A model of racial identity development has also been proposed for Whites (Helms, 1984, 1990d). Insofar as Whites form the dominant culture in the United States, one of the key dynamics in the racial/cultural identity models is one's experience, either as oppressor or as oppressed, of the inequity of social power (Helms, 1990a; Sue & Sue, 1990). Gushue (1993) suggested that Helms's model of White racial identity statuses can also be understood as a model of "dominant culture" identity statuses. Helms suggests two phases in White racial identity development, each made up of three statuses or clusters of racial identity attitudes regarding both Blacks and Whites. The task of the first phase of the Helms model is the abandonment of racism. The racial identity statuses inherent in Phase 1 suggest initial naivete about race (Contact), discomfort produced by growing awareness of racism (Disintegration), and defensive or angry attitudes about race (Reintegration). The task of Phase 2 of the Helms model is the establishment of a positive (nonracist) White

TABLE 29.1 A Nondominant Culture Identity Development Model

Conformity	Naive acceptance of dominant culture's values. Tendency to denigrate one's own culture and idealize the dominant culture.
Dissonance/Introspection	Beginning to question uncritical assimilation to dominant culture in self and others. Growing interest in one's own cultural heritage.
Resistance	Exclusive interest and pride in one's own culture. Outright rejection of the dominant culture's values. Awareness of and resistance to cultural and political hegemony of the dominant group.
Awareness	A critical interest and pride in one's own culture. A critical acceptance of certain aspects of the dominant culture, combined with continued efforts to resist political marginalization and cultural assimilation to "the mainstream."

SOURCE: Based on Helms & Carter, 1986, cited in Carter, Fretz, & Mahalik, 1986. Reprinted from Gushue, 1993.

identity. Statuses associated with this phase suggest intellectual acceptance of racial differences (Pseudoindependence), internalization of positive aspects of being White (Immersion/Emersion), and the affective valuing (vs. mere tolerance) of difference (Autonomy). As with the Black racial identity model, it is thought that attitudes representing each of these statuses are generally present in Whites, but that at different moments in an individual's life a particular status will predominate.

Insofar as movement from one status to another is predicated, to some extent, on cross-racial experience, Helms (1984) also suggested that as the socially dominant race in the United States, Whites are able to discontinue further contact with Blacks, settling for prolonged periods into one particular status (i.e., Reintegration). Reframing Helms's discussion of White identity, Gushue (1993) described the process from the perspective of dominant culture identity (see Table 29.2).

Helms (1984, 1990b) suggested a Black/White interaction model based on the racial/cultural identity models for both Blacks and Whites. For Helms, it is each participant's salient racial/cultural identity status (not his or her race per se) that will predict the quality of an interaction. According to Helms, this is true for both cross-racial and same-race dyads. Thus, for two Whites, it is the similarity or the divergence of their predominant attitudes about race (and the similar or divergent worldviews, beliefs, and predispositions associated with those attitudes) that determines the nature of their interactions. Helms (1984) originally proposed her model to illuminate the interactions that characterize the counseling process, in which one person (the counselor) is in a socially more powerful role than the other (the client). Accordingly, Helms suggested a number of "relationship types" based on differing configurations of racial/cultural identity statuses in the counseling dyad. For Helms, the align-

TABLE 29.2 A Dominant Culture Identity Development Model

Contact	Monocultural perspective. Assumes universality and validity of dominant group's values, attitudes, etc. Complete unawareness of other cultural points of view.
Disintegration	Initial multicultural contacts spark curiosity as person "discovers" other cultures. Naive enthusiasm for the "exotic" combined with initial consciousness of membership in dominant (oppressive) culture. Possible attempts to reconcile these two perspectives via paternalism or overidentification.
Reintegration	Retreat into and idealization of dominant culture. Denigration of and hostility (overt or covert) toward nondominant cultures.
Pseudoindependence	Intellectual awareness of the validity of differing cultural perspectives. Intellectual acceptance of membership in dominant group (and the consequences for self and for members of nondominant cultures) as starting point for intercultural contacts.
Immersion/Emersion	Introspective time of cognitive and emotional restructuring. Attempt to work out a nonoppressive dominant-culture identity. Search for dominant-culture role models who have achieved a multicultural perspective.
Autonomy	Multicultural perspective. Beyond acceptance to affective appreciation of difference. Values (rather than tolerates) diversity. Commitment to work for a society that reflects this perspective.

SOURCE: Based on Helms (1984, 1990d). Reprinted from Gushue, 1993.

ment of racial/cultural identity statuses can be "parallel" when the salient statuses for each participant are associated with roughly equivalent attitudes toward both Blacks and Whites. The relationship can be thought of as "progressive" when the cluster of racial/cultural attitudes exhibited by the counselor is less influenced by societal racism than that of the client. Such a relationship enables the counselor to play his or her natural role of mentor to the client. As Helms (1984) pointed out, a counselor "cannot move the client further than the counselor has come" vis-à-vis race (p. 159). Another configuration discussed by Helms, termed *regressive*, occurs when the counselor's racial/cultural identity status is less evolved (more influenced by societal racism) than that of the client. One would expect to find greater potential for conflict in this type of relationship, but not as great as in a "crossed" relationship in which the racial/cultural identity statuses that predominate for the counselor and the client are characterized by virtually polar opposite attitudes about race. In her initial exposition of the model, Helms (1984) predicted "common affective issues," "counselor/client strategies," and "counseling outcome" based on the various relationship types. More recently, Helms (1990a) speculated that the relationship types she suggested might contribute to understanding other "dyadic interactions in which the participants differ in social power and/or status due to role expectations" (p. 177).

Gushue (1993) proposed an extension of Helms's interaction model to family assessment and counseling. He suggested that the racial/cultural interaction paradigm might assist counselors in their consideration of culture and families by helping them to focus systematically on four crucial dimensions. First, according to Gushue, the model highlights important intragroup cultural differences both between families of the same culture and within individual families. Second, the model emphasizes the dynamic process of cultural change as different statuses become salient for the various family subsystems over time, changing the nature of the interactions between them. Third, the interaction paradigm underscores the racial/cultural identity of the counselor (too frequently overlooked), suggesting that his or her own racial/cultural identity status will have an important impact on how the counselor relates to each of the subsystems and will therefore have critical implications for treatment strategies. Fourth, the interaction model allows for a consideration of the cultural issues involved for a nondominant culture counselor treating a dominant culture family or for situations in which both counselors and families are from the same culture.

Gushue (1993) suggested that one way in which the racial/cultural interaction model might be applied to family assessment and treatment is through the creation of a "cultural map" that includes the counselor as well as the various family subsystems, noting the salient racial/cultural identity status of each. He suggested assessing the relationship type that exists between each pair of subsystems on the cultural map and evaluating the consequences that the differing relationship types may have for interventions by a particular therapist with a given family.

The racial/cultural identity paradigm provides a second important perspective on within-group cultural differences in families. Whereas the "levels of acculturation" model explores how differences in worldviews are represented in patterns of thought, behavior, and family organization, the racial/cultural identity paradigm considers how some of the same differences in worldview are expressed in differing psychological orientations to racial/cultural group membership in the context of social power and oppression. In the case of a family that has migrated to the United States, language itself may serve as a marker for discerning differing levels of acculturation and/or psychological orientation to race and culture. This third perspective on within-group cultural differences in families is the topic of the following section.

BILINGUAL THEORY

A third perspective on the question of intracultural differences in a given family can be attained by observing and understanding the function of linguistic differences within the family system. As immigration from non-English-speaking countries continues to rise, bilingual persons in therapy will become an increasing phenomenon. The bilingual client brings to the therapy room a special set of dynamics.

Ojemann and Whitaker (1978) studied the bilingual brain. They concluded that in the center of the language area of the brain there were sites common to both languages. However, peripheral to the center were sites with differential organization according to the two languages. Sites concerned with a particular language tend to cluster together, thereby stringing segments of the languages in different areas of the cortex. This differentiation provides the basis for the bilingual person's ability to separate the languages and switch between them. Lambert, Havelka, and Crosby (1958) and Lambert (1972) did linguistic research that indicated that the bilingual person operated two parallel encoding mechanisms whereby the same word in both languages was linked to different associations, meanings, and affective responses. Bilingual persons, then, do not simply have a double set of words for objects and experiences, but have alternative and not necessarily congruent experiential worlds (Perez-Foster, 1990). Marcos, Eisman, and Guiman (1977) discovered that bilingual persons have a dual sense of self accompanied by two views of the universe and consequently two sets of object relatedness. Thus, for the bilingual client, important assessment questions will include at what stage of development and under what circumstances the second language was acquired.

The Immigration Experience

Immigration is accompanied by the experience of two cultures coming together, that of the immigrant's homeland and that of the country to which he or she immigrates. Berry (1980) and Berry and Kim (1988) suggested that this cultural conflict can be resolved through adjustment, reaction, or withdrawal. In *adjustment*, the immigrant moves toward or with the dominant culture; in *reaction*, against the dominant culture; and in *withdrawal*, away from the dominant culture. Adjustment can take the form of either *assimilation*, in which a person's original culture becomes completely subsumed by the dominant culture, or *integration*, in which the person internalizes positive aspects of the dominant culture while retaining positive elements of his or her original culture (Sciarra & Ponterotto, 1991).

A major factor determining the acculturation process and the form it will take is language (Bluestone & Vela, 1982; Casas & Vasquez, 1989; Marrero, 1983; Mirsky, 1991; Ponterotto, 1987; Ruiz, 1981; Valdes, 1983). The stronger the resistance to learning the language of the dominant culture, the greater the chance that the cultural conflict will be resolved via withdrawal. The strength of the resistance will be determined by many factors, including personality structure, age, and the early experience of learning the language of one's mother. This last factor is explained by Mirsky (1991) as the experience of every child who feels excluded when he or she does not understand what grownups are saying. When the immigrant loses his or her language by not being able to understand the new language of the dominant culture, the childhood experience of exclusion through language is reevoked (Grinberg & Grinberg, 1989). Therefore, difficulties in the acquisition of a new language are dependent upon the quality and intensity of the childhood experience of exclusion (Mirsky, 1991).

The Bilingual/Immigrant Family

The immigrant family typically will consist of one or both parents who have little or no knowledge of the language of the dominant culture and children whose knowledge of that language far surpasses that of their parents. The facility for language acquisition differs greatly between parents and children. Because they are still in the process of identity formation, children and adolescents are more apt to practice imitation and identification, essential motivators for learning a language. In fact, for children, such learning can be fun. Without the ability to laugh at oneself, language learning will not occur; adults have greater difficulty laughing at themselves than children.

As family members differentiate according to ability levels of the language of the dominant culture, distinct forms and levels of acculturation begin to emerge. Children, having gained a knowledge of the language and wanting to be accepted by their peers, take on the ways of the dominant culture. Parents, more isolated because of language and perhaps suspicious of the ways of the dominant culture, enter into conflict with their children. Issues of racial/cultural identity also emerge because children and parents feel differently about their cultural heritage.

Different levels of acculturation can lead to structural disorganization within a family. Children can easily be placed in or assume executive functions in the family system because of their greater linguistic ability and understanding of the dominant culture. When parents cease to be effective executors in the family system, there is a greater risk that the children will begin to exhibit behavioral problems (Minuchin et al., 1967).

The Bilingual Family in Therapy

When different levels of linguistic ability are represented by different family members, the counselor is presented with an immediate dilemma. In which language will the session be conducted? If the therapist is bilingual, he or she might ask the family to agree to speak in the language that all can speak and understand—which usually means the language of the traditional culture. However, such an agreement is frequently difficult to uphold. If children speak the language of the dominant culture as well as or better than the language of their parents, they will in most cases do battle with the counselor's demands that they speak in the language of their parents. There are several reasons for this. First, language is a way children have to differentiate from their parents. Even in nonbilingual families, children speak in colloquialisms that their parents cannot understand. In the bilingual family, this can take the form of speaking the language that their parents cannot understand. Another reason may be identification with the counselo., especially if the counselor's linguistic ability parallels that of the children—the counselor is more proficient in the language of the dominant culture and less so in the language of the parents.

If the therapist is monolingual, he or she must avoid some immediate pitfalls. The use of a translator is always risky, especially if the translator is not trained (Vasquez & Javier, 1991). Untrained interpreters are prone to many distortions in the communications process, including "role exchange," whereby the interpreter assumes more the role of counselor (Vasquez & Javier, 1991). The monolingual counselor may also be tempted to ask the children to translate for their parents. This approach is misguided for two reasons. First, children will commit the same errors as untrained interpreters. Second, from a structural point of view, the counselor puts the children in the role of executors, perhaps replicating the family structure responsible for the identified problem. The monolingual therapist has no choice but to work with a well-trained interpreter and through nonverbal behavior establish a connection with the parents and avoid being seduced into a coalition with the children who speak the therapist's language.

The bilingual therapist need not enforce the one-language rule in the counseling session. As stated previously, this rule is difficult to maintain, and it is also therapeutically contraindicated. Rather, the bilingual therapist can use the different levels of language ability as an assessment tool (Sciarra & Ponterotto, 1991). Who speaks to whom, when, and in what language, along with other behaviors, can allow the therapist to formulate hypotheses regarding the family's functioning. Instead of seeing the two languages available as an impediment, the therapist can see them as an additional diagnostic tool. After the assessment phase, the therapist can continue to use the two languages in favor of the therapeutic process. The bilingual family therapist can switch languages to form coalitions with certain family members or to undermine coalitions among family members if they are responsible for family dysfunction. If there is a family member who does not understand either of the two languages, the therapist ought not to slip automatically into the role of translator. Rather, asking a certain family member to translate for a certain other should be understood as a clinical intervention. The therapist's goal for picking a particular interpreter may be to strengthen a boundary around a certain relationship. In any event, language switching and interpretation while working with the bilingual family should not be looked upon as an obstacle to the therapeutic process. Rather, the availability of two languages is an asset that can be used along with other strategic techniques to reorganize a family's structure and thus minimize the problem behavior.

The family therapy case presented below is intended to illustrate the multidimensional approach discussed in the previous pages. First, an analysis and assessment from the perspective of structural family therapy is presented. Second, because family members and the therapist are from different cultural backgrounds, the intercultural dimension is highlighted. Third, intracultural factors are discussed under the three dimensions of acculturation, racial/cultural identity, and language ability presented above. First and last names of family members have been changed to protect their confidentiality.

CASE EXAMPLE

The Lopez family (named after the mother) began family therapy in 1993. The mother, Angela, has a long psychiatric history and is diagnosed as suffering from major depression with psychotic features. She has two sons, José, age 14, and Efraín, age 12. The presenting problems are the sons' truancy from school, lack of respect for both mother and stepfather, and aggression toward each other. Felix, age 57, has been Angela's common-law husband for 4 years, and they have a son, Miguel, age 3. Figure 29.1 depicts the Lopez family genogramatically.

Angela was born in Puerto Rico and came to the mainland United States at age 14. She is proficient bilingually. Felix is from Ecuador and immigrated to the United States at age 35. He is monolingual Spanish. Both José and Efraín were born and raised in an urban setting in the United States. José reportedly understands Spanish but is unable to speak in Spanish. Efraín is monolingual English. The therapist is a White Italian American, proficiently bilingual in Spanish and subordinately bicultural (i.e., he is more attuned to the ways of mainstream North American society, yet has experience living among the Latino population in both the United States and other Spanish-speaking countries).

The above description of the Lopez family and their therapist reveals potential conflicts in the five dimensions discussed above. First, from the point of view of structural family therapy, the Lopezes are a blended family. Felix is not the natural father of all three children, but only of Miguel. In blended families, the stepparent's authority over the stepchildren depends in large part on the natural parent, in this case, Angela. The stepchildren, in most cases, will take their cues from the natural parent. If she signals to the children, even in the most subtle fashion, that the stepparent is not to be considered an equal executor, the stepparent becomes marginalized and disregarded by the stepchildren.

When the Lopez family had been assigned as a therapy case to the second author, they already had been in family treatment with another therapist. During this time, Angela attended family sessions along with her two sons, José and Efraín. Because Felix was not included in these sessions, his marginal position in the family seemed evident, and it was hypothesized that Angela as the sole executor of the family was ineffective. Thus, the first intervention was to engage Felix in treatment and to build a working coalition between

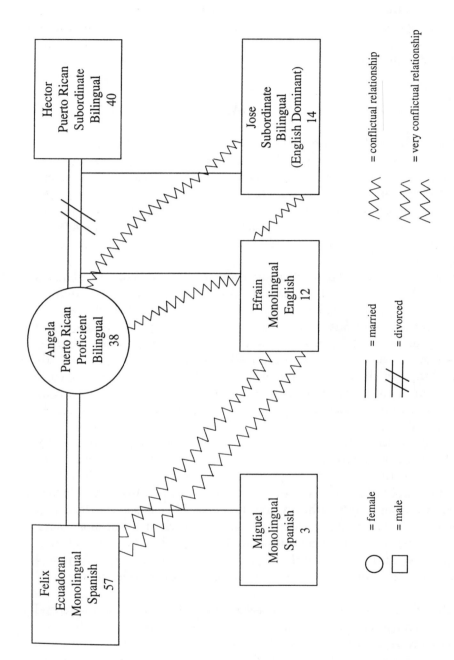

Figure 29.1. Genogram of the Lopez Family

himself and his wife to deal more effectively with the problematic behavior of José and Efraín. The therapist was able to use his language ability to connect with Felix. Furthermore, the therapist, sensitive to *machismo* issues in Latino culture, appealed to Felix as "head of the family" and stated that he needed Felix's help in order to be therapeutically effective. Felix became involved and cooperated in the early sessions by responding to the therapist's requests to enact interactions with his wife around how to deal, for example, with the boys' truancy.

A closer look at the Lopez family reveals other factors at work in creating Felix's marginal position in the family. The different levels of bilingualism among the family members easily enabled José and Efraín to connect with their mother while excluding their stepfather, who could not understand or speak English. In this situation, the therapist can be seduced to assume the role of translator for Felix, trying to alter his marginal position. Translation by the therapist may be indicated very early in the therapy as a way to engage Felix. However, the more structurally astute intervention would be to have Angela translate both (for Felix) what the stepsons are saying and (for the children) Felix's opinion concerning the problems at hand. This intervention serves a dual purpose. While lessening Felix's marginal position, it also communicates to José and Efraín that their mother is willing to work with their stepfather in solving the family's difficulties.

In the Lopez family, there are also different levels of acculturation. José and Efraín, born and raised in the inner city of the United States, identify with the dominant culture. Their mother, Angela, is bicultural and moves easily in Spanish-speaking and English-speaking environments. Felix, on the other hand, is minimally identified with the ways of the dominant culture. In several family sessions, Felix has often referred to his own upbringing in Ecuador, explaining that his father easily solved his children's opposition through physical punishment. He has indicated at times, though not explicitly, that this approach may be necessary in dealing with José and Efraín's truancy. Angela, on the other hand, often complains of Felix's harsh manner in talking with his stepchildren. She prefers a more "Americanized" conversational approach to solving family difficulties. From the point of view of structural family therapy, Angela and Felix's disagreement can be interpreted as different parenting styles that, with practice, can serve to complement one another. However, this difference in parenting styles has a cultural basis. A more culturally sensitive intervention would be to invite Felix to talk about what life was like growing up in Ecuador and how it differed from what he sees in the American inner city. The therapist would encourage Felix to accentuate the positive aspects of being raised in Ecuadoran culture as well as some of the negatives. In turn, the therapist would invite Efraín and José to share how their growing up contrasted with their stepfather's portrayal of life in Ecuador. The goal would be for both parties to appreciate the differences of life in such varied places as Ecuador and New York City. Furthermore, the intercultural dimension between the spouses could be acknowledged by having Felix and Angela talk about the differences between their childhoods in Puerto Rico and in Ecuador.

From a racial/cultural identity perspective, this case suggests a cultural map with four significant poles. First, the counselor's bilingual proficiency, ongoing interest in and appreciation of Latino cultures, and his acknowledgment of his own membership in the dominant culture suggest the salience of attitudes associated with at least Pseudoindependent status. The siblings seem to share similar racial/cultural identity attitudes. Their clear preference for the dominant culture linguistically and culturally and their distancing from the nondominant culture suggest Conformity status. The executive subsystem appears to be split in terms of their racial/cultural identity. Like his stepsons, Felix exhibits Conformity attitudes, but in a very different and more subtle way. Whereas their affirmation of the dominant culture is explicit, his is implicit. Felix's traditional cultural values of hard work and discipline dovetail with those of the "Protestant work ethic" espoused by the dominant culture. However, some of Felix's attitudes also suggest a uncritical acceptance of the ideology of the dominant culture. He is as yet either unaware or in denial of the full extent of institutional and societal racism, believing that the United States is the "land of equal opportunity." Felix maintains that if his stepsons will only work hard enough in this country, anything will be possible for them. Insofar as racism exists in the United States, it is directed toward Blacks, not Latinos. To some extent, Felix's isolation from the dominant culture helps him preserve his optimism about the benevolence of the exercise of social power in the United States. On the other hand, for Angela, attitudes associated with the Dissonance/Introspection status seem to predominate. Angela's feelings about the American system are more ambivalent. Although she shares a number of the values of the dominant culture regarding family organization, her bilingual ability has enabled her to interact with the system to a greater extent than Felix. This contact has led her to an incipient awareness of societal racism, certainly consistent with the feelings of hopelessness and lack of personal efficacy that figured in her initial diagnosis.

This cultural map suggests some hopeful indicators as well as areas that need attention. First, because the therapist is at a more advanced status than the various subsystems, he is well situated to assist the family as racial/cultural issues arise. Inasmuch as the subsystems are clustered around two adjacent statuses, one would not expect racial/cultural identity attitudes to form the central focus of family conflict at this moment. However, the split between the statuses that predominate in the executive subsystem suggests an important area for intervention. Rather than make the easy alliance with Angela, whose racial/cultural identity attitudes are more similar to his own, the therapist would be better advised to work at facilitating Felix's, José's, and Efraín's movement toward the Dissonance/Introspection status. For instance, the therapist might help them gain a critical perspective on the values of the dominant culture. In a way that mirrors the "detouring" suggested by Szapocznik and Kurtines (1993), a shared awareness of the racism inherent in the mainstream society to which they aspire may offer Felix and his stepsons the possibility of joining around their oppressed status. Similarly, if the therapist encourages Angela's continued racial/cultural development, this may lead to a greater predominance of Resistance attitudes, which may enable her to interact in a less strained way with Felix (the most traditional member of the system) as she comes to a greater valuing of her own Latino heritage. The therapist's own racial identity status suggests that he would be capable of tolerating and working with feelings of anger that might result as a consequence of Angela's move toward the Resistance status.

Although in a certain sense, as noted above, issues of racial/cultural identity may not be the most salient at this moment in the family's treatment, the therapist would make a serious mistake in ignoring them. Such an approach would provide a temporary "resolution" to the present crisis on the dimension of acculturation, while remaining oblivious to the potential "time bomb" ticking on the dimension of racial/cultural identity. As second-generation Latinos, José and Efraín will have the kind of constant contact with the dominant culture that will probably impel their continued movement through attitudes associated with the various racial identity statuses. Should they move "ahead" of their mother and stepfather so that the relationship with each of them becomes "regressive," family conflict around issues of racial/cultural identity will most probably become severely exacerbated, disorganizing this family for a second time. Thus, in the case example presented here, intervention on the dimension of acculturation would seem crucial to efforts to provide the family with a reduction in the presenting symptoms, while at the same time addressing the dimension of racial/cultural identity would seem critical for the family's ongoing adaptation and ability to handle future crises.

SUMMARY

The preceding pages have described some of the many issues in working structurally with a bilingual, bicultural family. The multidimensional approach presented here has emphasized the need to attend to both within-group and between-group cultural differences when working with families. Having an accurate picture of the general worldview and values of a given family's culture (and how these may differ from the counselor's own) is a sine qua non. However, the approach proposed also encourages counselors to consider both themselves and the families with which they work along three intracultural dimensions, taking into account differences in language ability, acculturation, and racial/cultural identity. Doing therapy from such a multidimensional perspective is a complex task in that the therapist must endeavor to be both linguistically and culturally attuned without losing sight of the basic structural dynamics of the family system. A family therapist who is unaware of these dimensions runs the risk of viewing the family who comes to therapy in either ethnocentric or stereotypical terms. Such a way of proceeding not only facilitates premature termination but overlooks the richness of representation in the bilingual, bicultural family and in the interactions that result. A family's different levels of acculturation and racial/cultural identity are not, from our perspective, to be seen as obstacles or impediments to the therapeutic process. Rather, they present unique opportunities to utilize intercultural and intracultural differences on behalf of facilitating the family's development to a higher level of functioning. It is hoped that insofar as the multidimensional perspective suggested in this chapter contributes to helping counselors gain a more accurate assessment of the families they serve and a better understanding of their own role and responses, it will also enable them to devise more appropriate and effective family interventions.

REFERENCES

Atkinson, D. R., Morten, G., & Sue, D. W. (1979). Proposed minority identity development model. In D. R. Atkinson, G. Morten, & D. W. Sue (Eds.), *Counseling American minorities: A cross-cultural perspective* (1st ed., pp. 32-42). Dubuque, IA: William C. Brown.

Atkinson, D. R., Morten, G., & Sue, D. W. (1989). *Counseling American minorities: A cross-cultural perspective* (3rd ed.). Dubuque, IA: William C. Brown.

Berry, J. W. (1980). Acculturation as variety of adaptation. In A. M. Padilla (Ed.), *Acculturation: Theory, models, and some new findings* (pp. 9-25). Washington, DC: American Association for the Advancement of Science.

Berry, J. W., & Kim, U. (1988). Acculturation and mental health. In P. R. Dasen, J. W. Berry, & N. Sartorius (Eds.), *Health and cross-cultural psychology* (pp. 207-236). Newbury Park, CA: Sage.

Bluestone, H., & Vela, R. M. (1982). Transcultural aspects in the psychotherapy of the Puerto Rican poor in New York City. *Journal of the American Academy of Psychoanalysis, 10*, 269-283.

Carter, R. T., Fretz, B. R., & Mahalik, J. R. (1986, August). *An exploratory investigation into the relationships between career maturity, work role salience, value orientations, and racial identity attitudes.* Paper presented at the 94th Annual American Psychological Convention, Washington, DC.

Casas, J. M., & Vasquez, M. J. P. (1989). Counseling the Hispanic client: A theoretical and applied perspective. In P. B. Pedersen, J. G. Draguns, W. J. Lonner, & J. E. Trimble (Eds.), *Counseling across cultures* (3rd ed., pp. 153-176). Honolulu: University of Hawaii Press.

Cross, W. E. (1971). The Negro to Black conversion experience. *Black World, 20(9)*, 13-27.

Fernandez, R. M. (1989). An empirical test of the Minority Identity Development Scale with Cuban-Americans (Doctoral dissertation, Teachers College, Columbia University, 1988). *Dissertations Abstracts International, 49/09*, 4035B.

Graves, T. D. (1967). Psychological acculturation in a tri-ethnic community. *Southwestern Journal of Anthropology, 23*, 337-350.

Grinberg, L., & Grinberg, R. (1989). *Psychoanalytic perspectives of migration and exile.* New Haven, CT: Yale University Press.

Gushue, G. V. (1993). Cultural identity development and family assessment: An interaction model. *The Counseling Psychologist, 21*, 487-513.

Helms, J. E. (1984). Toward a theoretical explanation of the effects of race on counseling: A Black and White model. *The Counseling Psychologist, 13*, 695-710.

Helms, J. E. (1990a). Applying the interaction model to social dyads. In J. E. Helms (Ed.), *Black and White racial identity: Theory, research and practice* (pp. 177-185). Westport, CT: Greenwood Press.

Helms, J. E. (1990b). Counseling attitudinal and behavioral predispositions: The Black/White interaction model. In J. E. Helms (Ed.) *Black and White racial identity: Theory, research, and practice* (pp. 135-143). Westport, CT: Greenwood Press.

Helms, J. E. (1990c). An overview of Black racial identity theory. In J. E. Helms (Ed.), *Black and White racial identity: Theory, research, and practice* (pp. 9-32). Westport, CT: Greenwood Press.

Helms, J. E. (1990d). Toward a model of White racial identity development. In J. E. Helms (Ed.), *Black and White racial identity: Theory, research, and practice* (pp. 49-66). Westport, CT: Greenwood Press.

Helms, J. E. (1994, February). *Helms' version of racial identity theory.* Paper presented at the 11th Annual Teachers College Winter Roundtable on Cross-Cultural Counseling and Psychotherapy, New York, NY.

Ho, M. K. (1987). *Family therapy with ethnic minorities.* Newbury Park, CA: Sage.

Inclán, J. (1980). Family organization, acculturation and psychological symptomatology in second generation Puerto Rican women of three socioeconomic groups (Doctoral dissertation, New York University, 1979). *Dissertation Abstracts International, 40/11,* 5407B.

Keefe, F. E., & Padilla, A. M. (1987). *Chicano ethnicity.* Albuquerque: University of New Mexico Press.

Lambert, W. (1972). *Language, psychology, and culture.* Stanford, CA: Stanford University Press.

Lambert, W., Havelka, J., & Crosby, C. (1958). The influence of language-acquisition contexts on bilingualism. *Journal of Abnormal Psychotherapy, 56,* 239-244.

Landau, J. (1982). Therapy with families in cultural transition. In M. McGoldrick, J. K. Pearce, & J. Giordano (Eds.), *Ethnicity and family therapy* (pp. 552-572). New York: Guilford.

Landau-Stanton, J. (1990). Issues and methods of treatment for families in cultural transition. In M. P. Mirkin (Ed.), *The social and political contexts of family therapy* (pp. 251-275). Boston: Allyn & Bacon.

Marcos, L. R., Eisman, J. E., & Guiman, J. (1977). Bilingualism and sense of self. *American Journal of Psychoanalysis, 37,* 285-290.

Marrero, R. (1983). Bilingualism and biculturalism. *Psychotherapy in Private Practice, 1,* 57-64.

McFee, M. (1968). The 150% man: A product of Blackfeet acculturation. *American Anthropologist, 70,* 1096-1103.

McGoldrick, M. (1982). Ethnicity and family therapy: An overview. In M. McGoldrick, J. K. Pearce, & J. Giordano (Eds.), *Ethnicity and family therapy* (pp. 3-30). New York: Guilford.

McGoldrick, M., Pearce, J. K., & Giordano, J. (Eds.). (1982). *Ethnicity and family therapy.* New York: Guilford.

Minuchin, S. (1974). *Families and family therapy.* Cambridge, MA: Harvard University Press.

Minuchin, S., & Fishman, H. C. (1981). *Family therapy techniques.* Cambridge, MA: Harvard University Press.

Minuchin, S., Montalvo, B., Guerney, B., Jr., Rosman, B. L., & Schumer, F. (1967). *Families of the slums: An exploration of their structure and treatment.* New York: Basic Books.

Mirsky, J. (1991). Language in migration: Separation individuation conflicts in relation to the mother tongue and the new language. *Psychotherapy, 28,* 618-624.

Nichols, M. P., & Schwartz, R. C. (1991). Structural family therapy. In M. P. Nichols & R. C. Schwartz (Eds.), *Family therapy: Concepts and methods* (pp. 445-480). Boston: Allyn & Bacon.

Ojemann, G. A., & Whitaker, H. A. (1978). The bilingual brain. *Archives in Neurology, 35,* 409-412.

Pedersen, P. B. (1991). Multiculturalism as a generic approach to counseling. *Journal of Counseling and Development, 70,* 6-12.

Perez-Foster, R. (1990). *Psychoanalytic treatment of the bilingual patient.* Unpublished manuscript.

Ponterotto, J. G. (1987). Counseling Mexican-Americans: A multimodal approach. *Journal of Counseling and Development, 65,* 308-312.

Redfield, R., Linton, R., & Herskovits, M. J. (1936). Memorandum for the study of acculturation. *American Anthropologist, 38,* 149-152.

Ruiz, R. A. (1981). Cultural and historical perspectives in counseling Hispanics. In D. W. Sue (Ed.), *Counseling the culturally different* (pp. 186-215). New York: John Wiley.

Ruiz, R. A., Casas, J. M., & Padilla, A. M. (1977). *Culturally relevant behavioristic counseling* (Occasional Paper No. 5). Los Angeles: University of California, Los Angeles, Spanish Speaking Mental Health Research Center.

Sciarra, D. T., & Ponterotto, J. G. (1991). Counseling the Hispanic bilingual family: Challenges to the therapeutic process. *Psychotherapy, 28,* 473-479.

Sluzki, C. E. (1979). Migration and family conflict. *Family Process, 18,* 379-390.

Sue, D. W., & Sue, S. (1990). *Counseling the culturally different: Theory and practice.* New York: John Wiley.

Szapocznik, J., & Kurtines, W. M. (1993). Family psychology and cultural diversity. *American Psychologist, 48,* 400-407.

Szapocznik, J., Santisteban, D., Kurtines, W., Perez-Vidal, A., & Hervis, O. (1984). Bicultural effectiveness training: Treatment intervention for enhancing intercultural adjustment in Cuban American families. *Hispanic Journal of Behavioral Sciences, 6,* 317-344.

Szapocznik, J., Scopetta, M., Kurtines, W., & Aranalde, M. (1978). Theory and measurement of acculturation. *Interamerican Journal of Psychology, 12,* 113-130.

Valdes, M. R. (1983). Psychotherapy with Hispanics. *Psychotherapy in Private Practice, 1,* 55-62.

Vasquez, C., & Javier, R. A. (1991). The problem with interpreters: Communicating with Spanish-speaking patients. *Hospital and Community Psychiatry, 42,* 163-165.

Introduction to Appendices

FOLLOWING ARE THREE APPENDICES that serve as important supplements to the chapter contents of the *Handbook*. Appendix I presents the Guidelines for Providers of Psychological Services to Ethnic, Linguistic, and Culturally Diverse Populations. These guidelines, published in 1993, affirm the commitment of the American Psychological Association to issues of diversity within the profession. Although brief, the guidelines are required reading for all mental health practitioners and researchers.

Appendix II presents the Advisory Principles for Ethical Considerations in the Conduct of Cross-Cultural Research. First published in 1973, these guidelines are considered by some *Handbook* authors (e.g., Pedersen in Chapter 3) to be far superior and inclusive than the present guidelines of the American Counseling Association and the American Psychological Association. The guidelines provide useful and pragmatic direction for researchers in multicultural counseling.

Appendix III presents what is probably the most referenced conceptual article in the multicultural literature over the past 3 years. Written by Derald Wing Sue (author of Chapter 23), Patricia Arredondo, and Roderick J. McDavis, the Multicultural Competencies and Standards document presents a comprehensive status report on the field. The article outlines specific training competencies that have been endorsed by the Association for Multicultural Counseling and Development (for measurement of these competencies, see Pope-Davis and Dings, Chapter 14).

Collectively, this set of appendices provides an important supplemental foundation for the study and practice of multicultural counseling.

Appendix I

Guidelines for Providers of Psychological Services to Ethnic, Linguistic, and Culturally Diverse Populations

INTRODUCTION

There is increasing motivation among psychologists to understand culture and ethnicity factors in order to provide appropriate psychological services. This increased motivation for improving quality of psychological services to ethnic and culturally diverse populations is attributable, in part, to the growing political and social presence of diverse cultural groups, both within APA and in the larger society. New sets of values, beliefs, and cultural expectations have been introduced into educational, political, business, and health care systems by the physical presence of these groups. The issues of language and culture do impact on the provision of appropriate psychological services.

Psychological service providers need a sociocultural framework to consider diversity of values, interactional styles, and cultural expectations in a systematic fashion. They need knowledge and skills for multicultural assessment and intervention, including abilities to

- recognize cultural diversity;
- understand the role that culture and ethnicity/race play in the sociopsychological and economic development of ethnic and culturally diverse populations;

NOTE: "Guidelines for Providers of Psychological Services to Ethnic, Linguistic, and Culturally Diverse Populations" by the American Psychological Association, 1993, *American Psychologist*, *48*, 45-48. Copyright 1993 by the American Psychological Association. Reprinted in Appendix I by permission for the general information of the membership. Correspondence concerning this article should be addressed to L. Philip Guzman, American Psychological Association, 750 First Street NE, Washington, DC 20002-4242.

- understand that socioeconomic and political factors significantly impact the psychosocial, political, and economic development of ethnic and culturally diverse groups;
- help clients to understand/maintain/resolve their own sociocultural identification; and
- understand the interaction of culture, gender, and sexual orientation on behavior and needs.

Likewise, there is a need to develop a conceptual framework that would enable psychologists to organize, access, and accurately assess the value and utility of existing and future research involving ethnic and culturally diverse populations.

Research has addressed issues regarding responsiveness of psychological services to the needs of ethnic minority populations. The focus of mental health research issues has included:

- the impact of ethnic/racial similarity in the counseling process (Acosta & Sheehan, 1976; Atkinson, 1983; Parham & Helms, 1981);
- minority utilization of mental health services (Cheung & Snowden, 1990; Everett, Proctor, & Cartmell, 1983; Rosado, 1986; Snowden & Cheung, 1990);
- relative effectiveness of directed versus nondirected styles of therapy (Acosta, Yamamoto, & Evans, 1982; Dauphinais, Dauphinais, & Rowe, 1981; Lorion, 1974);
- the role of cultural values in treatment (Juarez, 1985; Padilla & Ruiz, 1973; Padilla, Ruiz, & Alvarez, 1975; Sue & Sue, 1987);
- appropriate counseling and therapy models (Comas-Diaz & Griffith, 1988; McGoldrick, Pearce, & Giordano, 1982; Nishio & Bilmes, 1987);
- competency in skills for working with specific ethnic populations (Malgady, Rogler, & Costantino, 1987; Root, 1985; Zuniga, 1988).

The APA's Board of Ethnic Minority Affairs (BEMA) established a Task Force on the Delivery of Services to Ethnic Minority Populations in 1988 in response to the increased awareness about psychological service needs associated with ethnic and cultural diversity. The populations of concern include, but are not limited to, the following groups: American Indians/Alaska Natives, Asian Americans/Pacific Islanders, Blacks/African Americans, and Hispanics/Latinos. For example, the populations also include recently arrived refugee and immigrant groups and established U.S. subcultures such as Amish, Hasidic Jewish, and rural Appalachian people.

The Task Force established as its first priority development of the Guidelines for Providers of Psychological Services to Ethnic, Linguistic, and Culturally Diverse Populations. The guidelines that follow are intended to enlighten all areas of service delivery, not simply clinical or counseling endeavors. The clients referred to may be clients, organizations, government and/or community agencies.

GUIDELINES

Preamble: the Guidelines represent general principles that are intended to be aspirational in nature and are designed to provide suggestions to psychologists in working with ethnic, linguistic, and culturally diverse populations.

1. Psychologists educate their clients to the processes of psychological intervention, such as goals and expectations; the scope and, where appropriate, legal limits of confidentiality; and the psychologists' orientations.

   a. Whenever possible, psychologists provide information in writing along with oral explanations.

   b. Whenever possible, the written information is provided in the language understandable to the client.

2. Psychologists are cognizant of relevant research and practice issues as related to the population being served.

   a. Psychologists acknowledge that ethnicity and culture impact on behavior and take those factors into account when working with various ethnic/racial groups.

   b. Psychologists seek out educational and training experiences to enhance their understanding and thereby address the needs of these populations more appropriately and effectively. These experiences include cultural, social, psychological, political, economic, and historical material specific to the particular ethnic group being served.

   c. Psychologists recognize the limits of their competencies and expertise. Psychologists who do not possess knowledge and training about an ethnic group seek consultation with, and/or make referrals to, appropriate experts as necessary.

   d. Psychologists consider the validity of a given instrument or procedure and interpret resulting data, keeping in mind the cultural and linguistic characteristics of the person being assessed. Psychologists are aware of the test's reference population and possible limitations of such instruments with other populations.

3. Psychologists recognize ethnicity and culture as significant parameters in understanding psychological processes.

   a. Psychologists, regardless of ethnic/racial background, are aware of how their own cultural background/experiences, attitudes, values, and biases influence psychological processes. They make efforts to correct any prejudices and biases. *Illustrative Statement:* Psychologists might routinely ask themselves, "Is it appropriate for me to view this client or organization any differently than I would if they were from my own ethnic or cultural group?"

   b. Psychologists' practice incorporates an understanding of the client's ethnic and cultural background. This includes the client's familiarity and comfort with the majority culture as well as ways in which the client's culture may add to or improve various aspects of the majority culture and/or of society at large. *Illustrative Statement:* The kinds of mainstream social activities in which families participate may offer information about the level and quality of acculturation to American society. It is important to distinguish acculturation from length of stay in the United States and not to assume that these issues are relevant only for new immigrants and refugees.

   c. Psychologists help clients increase their awareness of their own cultural values and norms, and they facilitate discovery of ways clients can apply this awareness to their own lives and to society at large. *Illustrative Statement:* Psychologists may be able to help parents distinguish between generational conflict and culture gaps when problems arise between them and their children. In the process, psychologists could help both parents and children to appreciate their own distinguishing cultural values.

   d. Psychologists seek to help a client determine whether a "problem" stems from racism or bias in others so that the client does not inappropriately personalize problems. *Illustrative Statement:* The concept of "healthy paranoia," whereby ethnic minorities may develop defensive behaviors in response to discrimination, illustrates this principle.

e. Psychologists consider not only differential diagnostic issues but also the cultural beliefs and values of the client and his/her community in providing intervention. *Illustrative Statement:* There is a disorder among the traditional Navajo called "Moth Madness." Symptoms include seizure-like behaviors. This disorder is believed by the Navajo to be the supernatural result of incestuous thoughts or behaviors. Both differential diagnosis and intervention should take into consideration the traditional values of Moth Madness.

4. Psychologists respect the roles of family members and community structures, hierarchies, values, and beliefs within the client's culture.

a. Psychologists identify resources in the family and the larger community.

b. Clarification of the role of the psychologist and the expectations of the client precede intervention. Psychologists seek to ensure that both the psychologist and client have a clear understanding of what services and roles are reasonable. *Illustrative Statement:* It is not uncommon for an entire American Indian family to come into the clinic to provide support to the person in distress. Many of the healing practices found in American Indian communities are centered in the family and the whole community.

5. Psychologists respect clients' religious and/or spiritual beliefs and values, including attributions and taboos, since they affect world view, psychosocial functioning, and expressions of distress.

a. Part of working in minority communities is to become familiar with indigenous beliefs and practices and to respect them. *Illustrative Statement:* Traditional healers (e.g., shamans, curanderos, espiritistas) have an important place in minority communities.

b. Effective psychological intervention may be aided by consultation with and/or inclusion of religious/spiritual leaders/practitioners relevant to the client's cultural and belief systems.

6. Psychologists interact in the language requested by the client and, if this is not feasible, make an appropriate referral.

a. Problems may arise when the linguistic skills of the psychologist do not match the language of the client. In such a case, psychologists refer the client to a mental health professional who is competent to interact in the language of the client. If this is not possible, psychologists offer the client a translator with cultural knowledge and an appropriate professional background. When no translator is available, then a trained paraprofessional from the client's culture is used as a translator/culture broker.

b. If translation is necessary, psychologists do not retain the services of translators/paraprofessionals who may have a dual role with the client, to avoid jeopardizing the validity of evaluation or the effectiveness of intervention.

c. Psychologists interpret and relate test data in terms understandable and relevant to the needs of those assessed.

7. Psychologists consider the impact of adverse social, environmental, and political factors in assessing problems and designing interventions.

a. Types of intervention strategies to be used match the client's level of need (e.g., Maslow's hierarchy of needs). *Illustrative Statement:* Low income may be associated with such stressors as malnutrition, substandard housing, and poor medical care; and rural residency may mean inaccessibility of services. Clients may resist treatment at government agencies because of previous experience (e.g., refugees' status may be associated with violent treatments by government officials and agencies).

  b. Psychologists work within the cultural setting to improve the welfare of all persons concerned, if there is a conflict between cultural values and human rights.

8. Psychologists attend to, as well as work to eliminate, biases, prejudices, and discriminatory practices.

  a. Psychologists acknowledge relevant discriminatory practices at the social and community level that may be affecting the psychological welfare of the population being served. *Illustrative Statement:* Depression may be associated with frustrated attempts to climb the corporate ladder in an organization that is dominated by a top echelon of White men.

  b. Psychologists are cognizant of sociopolitical contexts in conducting evaluations and providing interventions; they develop sensitivity to issues of oppression, sexism, elitism, and racism. *Illustrative Statement:* An upsurge in the public expression of rancor or even violence between two ethnic or cultural groups may increase anxiety baselines in any member of those groups. This baseline of anxiety would interact with prevailing symptomatology. At the organizational level, the community conflict may interfere with open communication among staff.

9. Psychologists working with culturally diverse populations should document culturally and sociopolitically relevant factors in the records. These may include, but are not limited to the following:

  a. Number of generations in the country
  b. Number of years in the country
  c. Fluency in English
  d. Extent of family support (or disintegration of family)
  e. Community resources
  f. Level of education
  g. Change in social status as a result of coming to this country (for immigrant or refugee)
  h. Intimate relationship with people of different backgrounds
  i. Level of stress related to acculturation.

REFERENCES

Acosta, F. X., & Sheehan, J. G. (1976). Preference towards Mexican American and Anglo American psychotherapists. *Journal of Consulting and Clinical Psychology, 44,* 272-279.

Acosta, F., Yamamoto, J., & Evans, L. (1982). *Effective psychotherapy for low income and minority patients.* New York: Plenum Press.

Atkinson, D. R. (1983). Ethnic similarity in counseling psychology: A review of research. *The Counseling Psychologist, 11,* 79-92.

Cheung, F. K., & Snowden, L. R. (1990). Community mental health and ethnic minority populations. *Community Mental Health Journal, 26,* 277-291.

Comas-Diaz, L., & Griffith, E. H. (1988). *Clinical guidelines in cross-cultural mental health.* New York: Wiley.

Dauphinais, P., Dauphinais, L., & Rowe, W. (1981). Effects of race and communication style on Indian perceptions of counselor effectiveness. *Counselor Education and Supervision, 20,* 37-46.

Everett, F., Proctor, N., & Cartmell, B. (1983). Providing psychological services to American Indian children and families. *Professional Psychology: Research and Practice, 14,* 588-603.

Juarez, R. (1985). Core issues in psychotherapy with the Hispanic child. *Psychotherapy, 22,* 441-448.

Lorion, R. P. (1974). Patient and therapist variables in the treatment of low income patients. *Psychological Bulletin, 81,* 344-354.

Malgady, R. G., Rogler, L. H., & Costantino, G. (1987). Ethnocultural and linguistic bias in mental health evaluation of Hispanics. *American Psychologist, 42,* 228-234.

McGoldrick, M., Pearce, J. K., & Giordano, J. (1982). *Ethnicity and family therapy.* New York: Guilford Press.

Nishio, K., & Bilmes, M. (1987). Psychotherapy with Southeast Asian American clients. *Professional Psychology: Research and Practice, 18,* 342-346.

Padilla, A. M., & Ruiz, R. A. (1973). *Latino mental health: A review of literature* (DHEW Publication No. HSM 73-9143). Washington, DC: Government Printing Office.

Padilla, A. M., Ruiz, R. A., & Alvarez, R. (1975). Community mental health for the Spanish-speaking/surnamed population. *American Psychologist, 30,* 892-905.

Parham, T. A., & Helms, J. E. (1981). The influence of Black students' racial identity attitudes on preferences for counselor's race. *Journal of Counseling Psychology, 28,* 250-257.

Root, Maria P. P. (1985). Guidelines for facilitating therapy with Asian American clients. *Psychotherapy, 22,* 349-356.

Rosado, J. W. (1986). Toward an interfacing of Hispanic cultural variables with school psychology service delivery systems. *Professional Psychology: Research and Practice, 17,* 191-199.

Snowden, L. R., & Cheung, F. K. (1990). Use of inpatient mental health services by members of ethnic minority groups. *American Psychologist, 45,* 347-355.

Sue, D., & Sue, S. (1987). Cultural factors in the clinical assessment of Asian Americans. *Journal of Consulting and Clinical Psychology, 55,* 479-487.

Zuniga, M. E. (1988). Assessment issues with Chicanas: Practical implications. *Psychotherapy, 25,* 288-293.

Appendix II

Advisory Principles for Ethical Considerations in the Conduct of Cross-Cultural Research

Fall 1973 Revision

PREFACE

This guide is addressed primarily to those investigators, whether senior or junior, responsible for establishing and sustaining a research relationship in a host community. In total the guide contains thirteen advisory ethical principles: 6 in the area of responsibilities to the individuals and communities studied, 4 in the area of responsibilities to collaborators and colleagues in the host community, and 3 in the area of responsibilities to the discipline and the research enterprise. These thirteen principles articulate the obligations and responsibilities of the investigator; what he/she should and ought to do in establishing ethical conditions for the conduct of research. Each of the advisory principles is amplified by a series of corollaries. These lettered substatements operationalize the principles. The expository change in format from the principles to the corollaries purposefully underscores how the investigator can use this set of guidelines to specify ethical principles, respond to choice points, and handle ambiguous issues in the research enterprise.

NOTE: "Advisory Principals for Ethical Considerations in the Conduct of Cross-Cultural Research: Fall 1973 Revision" by J. L. Tapp, H. Kelman, H. Triandis, L. Wrightsman, & G. Coelho, 1974, *International Journal of Psychology*, 9(3), 240-249. Reprinted in Appendix II by permission of the International Union of Psychological Science.

A. RESPONSIBILITIES TO THE
INDIVIDUALS AND COMMUNITIES STUDIED

1. Ethical evaluation: The investigator should be personally responsible for evaluating the ethical acceptability of each study in terms of guidelines governing research in general as well as those governing trans-cultural relations.

   a. Engage only in activities abroad that are ethically acceptable at home. Decisions must be guided by the values and norms operative in one's own culture and community. For example, for members of the American Psychological Association these norms are articulated in the Ethical Principles in the Conduct of Research with Human Participants.

   b. Avoid actions ethically unacceptable to the host community, though within the norms of one's own community. In applying ethical guidelines to concrete situations, consider the cultural meaning of various actions and experiences. For example, protecting subjects from mental stress or invasion of privacy involves knowing what experiences culturally are considered degrading, embarrassing, or intrusive—no matter how harmless they may be elsewhere. Seek consultation with host members in making these assessments.

2. Respect for the host culture: The investigator should respect the cultural integrity of the research site and avoid actions that violate cultural expectations or reveal a culturally-biased perspective in formulating the research problem, executing the study, and reporting the findings.

   a. Become knowledgeable about and appreciative of the culture, language, history, social structure, and other aspects of community life before starting research. Since the research relationship involves an implicit social contract between the investigator and members of the host community, sensitivity to cultural expectations regarding social conduct and the maintenance of interpersonal trust is particularly important.

   b. Seek frequent guidance and cooperation from members of the host community, including scholars from related disciplines, other professional personnel, policy-makers, and local leaders.

   c. Avoid oversaturation of a particular community. Assess significance of the research and its potential value to the host community, relative to its costs in terms of the community's sense of exploitation and reduced readiness for future cooperation.

   d. Attend systematically to the technical problems of equivalent measurement across cultures. Failure to attend to the equivalency problem may result in inaccurate interpretations and potentially damaging consequences to the community studied. Consider multiple measurements to minimize methodological problems and unwarranted conclusions.

3. Open communication: Openness and honesty, conducive to the creation and maintenance of trust, should characterize the relationship between the investigator and the individuals and communities studied. The purposes, sponsorship, and funding source of the research project should be communicated clearly and accurately. Since the meanings of words and actions differ across cultures, the investigator should be sure communications are understood within the host community.

   a. Inform subjects of all features of the research that reasonably might influence willingness to participate, including the research auspices. When research conditions prevent providing full information to subjects before observing their behavior, exert even greater care to maintain confidentiality to protect the welfare and dignity of the subjects (see section A5).

b. Convey truthful communications to subjects throughout the research process. Mild concealment or deception in presenting research procedures may be justified only after consultation with members of the host community, only if non-impairment of subjects' welfare or dignity is assured, and only if full disclosure vitiates the validity of data obtained. Such procedures later require taking culturally adequate measures to ensure that subjects understand the scientific reasons for their use and to restore the quality of the relationship with the subjects.

c. Provide willingly information to the members or official representatives of the host community about professional qualifications and competencies, sponsorship and funding of the research, and the study's nature and goals. Only protecting the welfare or confidentiality of the subjects justifies withholding such information.

d. Resist efforts by sponsoring or funding agencies to keep the purposes and auspices of the research from the individuals or communities studied. If the sponsor insists on secrecy, refrain from participation, at least in the name of scientific research (see section C2).

4. Respect for subjects' rights: The rights and responsibilities of the investigator and subjects should be defined by an agreement that is contextually both clear and fair within the host culture. The investigator should honor all promises and commitments included in that agreement. The most basic right of subjects is free choice to participate or not, and to discontinue participation at any time. If this freedom is in any way limited (e.g., when the subjects are young children, or when data are obtained from official records), the research agreement should specify what steps will be taken to protect the subjects' welfare and dignity.

a. Identify and avoid subtle coercive elements to protect the subject's right to choose or refuse participation. Establish what influence tactics in effect constitute coercion within the host culture and refrain from using such tactics. Consider also the power imbalance that often characterizes the relationship of investigator and subjects. In some cultures, potential subjects may feel obliged to assent to requests from a scientist or from a representative of a richer, more powerful society. Even when requests for participation are transmitted through community authorities, their positions or tactics may exercise subtle coercion. Thus, in addition to obtaining formal permission from local authorities, consider contacting potential subjects directly.

b. Obtain explicit permission to observe in settings intended to be private or to probe into areas considered personal. Seeking informed consent is particularly important when subjects' right to privacy is at stake. Keep in mind that definitions of private and personal vary culturally; therefore, what may seem routine may be highly intrusive in the host community. Informed consent is less important when observations focus on ongoing behavior in public situations. Beware, however, that subjects have the right to "cultural privacy," and behavior that is public within the community may not be intended for public viewing by non-community members.

c. Solicit subjects' participation only if confident that the research problem is significant (scientifically and/or socially), that the methods are suited to the problem, and that the cultural context is sufficiently familiar to permit meaningful, valid interpretations. Trivial and methodologically unsound research violates subjects' rights in that it elicits cooperation under false pretenses and extracts costs without returns in the form of contributions to knowledge and human welfare.

5. Protection of subjects' welfare and dignity: The investigator should take responsibility for the welfare and dignity of the individuals and communities participating in the research. This responsibility includes protecting subjects from undue physical and psychological discomfort, harm, or risk as well as detecting and correcting procedures likely to have damaging or undesirable consequences for subjects or community. Recognizing cultural differences in what is experienced as stressful, embarrassing, or humiliating, the investigator should consult members of the host community about the potential for such reactions and the special areas of vulnerability for the host community and its members.

   a. Inform subjects in a clear, understandable way and secure their free consent before proceeding with research involving potentially stressful experiences or damaging consequences. Take all possible measures to minimize distress or damage to subjects.

   b. Clear research activities with appropriate authorities in the host community, whenever such clearance is necessary to protect the interests and safety of subjects and to maintain access and good will for future researchers. Refrain from involving members of the host community in the research if such participation is likely to jeopardize them (e.g., in relation to the authorities or other groups within the community), unless they thoroughly understand the risks involved and have consented freely to accept these risks.

   c. Keep confidential all information obtained about individual subjects and treat the data in ways ensuring anonymity. As part of the procedure for obtaining informed consent, explain to the participants any known possibility that others may obtain access to the information and plans for protecting confidentiality. Inform subjects and relevant community representatives of the extent to which the community and its subgroups will be identified in published research reports.

   d. Make every effort in reporting findings to forestall misinterpretations that may be damaging to the population studied. Interpret data within appropriate historical and cultural contexts (see section A2). Advance comparisons with other populations cautiously, attending to the problem of cultural equivalency of measures (see section A2-d) and to the possibility that both the measuring instruments and the comparative dimensions may be culturally biased in ways that unfairly present the host community. Address appropriate caveats to readers to avoid unwarranted or culturally biased policy implications from the data. To detect and prevent likely misinterpretations, consult with the subjects or their representatives before publication, providing an opportunity for critique.

   e. Prevent or counteract, wherever possible, the misuse of research findings in ways likely to be harmful to the population studied, particularly in the formulation of public policy. Help members of the host community to counteract damaging uses of the findings and to develop the resources for protecting their future interests.

   f. Ascertain the purposes of potential sponsoring or funding agencies in supporting research and their intended uses for the findings, particularly when financial support is from military, political, or commercial organizations. Refuse support from a sponsor whose intended use of the findings is likely to be damaging to the population studied or inconsistent with professional and personal values.

g. Recognize that both the process and the products of research may have implications for individuals and groups within the host community, enhancing the power position of some at the expense of others. Take responsibility for such effects, acknowledging or correcting for them if possible and desirable, rather than avoiding the issue by claiming that the research is neutral or that it serves the entire (undifferentiated) community.

6. Benefit to the participants: The total research experience should enrich and benefit in some way the individual subjects and the host community. A major source of potential benefit is generating knowledge that may enhance the welfare of the population studied and the development of the community. To maximize these potential benefits, members of the host community should be involved in all phases of the research.

a. Consider, in setting research priorities, not only theoretical problems of the discipline but also needs of the host community for research related to its welfare and development. In part determine the selection of culture to be sampled by the principle of maximizing social as well as scientific benefits. In soliciting local cooperation, recognize the possibility of diverting limited human resources away from the priorities of the host community (see section B3-e).

b. Make the results of the research available to the host community by publishing in local outlets, writing in the vernacular and in an understandable form. Provide direct feedback of the findings to subjects, their representatives, and other relevant groups in the community. During such feedback, actively explore the implications of the findings for the population studied, focusing both on the welfare and development needs of the community and on damaging misuses of the data (see section A5-e). Solicit and seriously consider community members' interpretations of the results.

c. Contribute something of lasting value to the host community after completion of a research project. Determined jointly, this may be in the form of increased capabilities and resources for independent research within the community (see section B4-a).

B. RESPONSIBILITIES TO COLLABORATORS AND COLLEAGUES IN THE HOST COMMUNITY

1. Local participation: There should be significant involvement of colleagues from the cultures studied during all project phases, particularly during formulation of the problem and interpretation of the results. The investigator should seek inputs from diverse cultural and intellectual perspectives to reduce the danger that problem setting and data interpretation may be culturally biased and uninformed by social and historical contextual influences. Participation of local colleagues in planning and executing the project should be arranged to ensure that the research does not exploit or damage colleagues and other members of the host community.

a. Collaborate, whenever feasible, with one or more local colleagues as full partners in the entire research enterprise, from defining the problems to publishing reports. Explore and arrange fully the nature of the collaborative relationship before activating the project and making major, irreversible decisions.

b. Share, totally and accurately, with local colleagues the purposes of the research as well as its sponsorship and sources of funds. Refrain from involving local colleagues as collaborators if such participation is likely to jeopardize them, unless they are clear about the risks involved and have chosen freely to accept them.

c. Select local collaborators with an eye, not only to complementing scientific skills and knowledge, but also to balancing cultural, historical, and socio-political perspectives. A major function of local participants is to question basic assumptions, correct for cultural biases, and bring another cultural perspective and conceptual orientation to the research.

2. Quality of collaborative relationship: The investigator, to act with integrity, should recognize the subtle expressions of exploitation and slight, possible between collaborators in a complex research relationship. The investigator, intervening in an ongoing professional community and making demands on its resources, has a special responsibility to local collaborators that should reflect an awareness of cultural differences in social expectations and in attitudes toward the research enterprise.

a. Establish the collaborative relationship so that complementary skills are used fully and actively in all important research decisions. Balance experience in research or proficiency in certain technical skills with wisdom, knowledge, and skills of a different variety. Avoid using the power derived from research funds and/or association with a prestigious institution to dominate the research unduly.

b. Recognize cultural differences in work habits, in professional goals, and in personal relations. Aim for mutually satisfying arrangements and refrain from imposing standards unilaterally.

c. Establish a pattern of regular, frequent and open communication through-out the course of the research (including its write-up), in order to resolve grievances, verify perceptions, and review expectations.

3. Benefit to collaborators: The investigator should ensure that research is mutually beneficial and that the participation of local collaborators is ade-quately reciprocated. Special attention should be paid to the impact of the project on local colleagues' professional status and career development. Par-ticipation on the project should constitute a significant net gain for colleagues in the host community by contributing to their professional advancement or experience and by yielding visible products, whenever possible.

a. Discuss financial arrangements explicitly and clearly with local collabora-tors, arriving at a mutually satisfactory understanding before the research begins. Establish the fairest and most favorable formula for financial remuneration, consistent with the policies of relevant host institutions and sensitive to possible resentments. Seek guidance from local and inter-national agencies experienced with cross-cultural working agreements.

b. Work out as early as possible and review periodically agreements on pub-lication plans and authorship credits. Recognize by joint authorship major contributions to a publication particularly in conceptualization, research design, and writing. Since definitions of a major contribution may vary culturally, clarify the criteria for joint authorship at the outset. Consider the interests of local collaborators in deciding on mode and place of publica-tions. Publishing reports in local channels (in the local vernacular, where relevant) as well as in international or other outside channels is often advisable. These reports may differ in emphasis, authorship, or order of authors' names. Acknowledge fully and visibly contributions to the research and publication not warranting joint authorship but worthy of public recognition.

c. Establish explicit, advance agreements on the location and ownership of the data, on later access to them, and on alternative uses of them—either collaboratively or independently. To maximize using the data to reflect the interests and perspectives of local colleagues and their community, leave copies of the raw data in the host community so that local investigators can freely draw on them for further analyses and publications after the original collaborative study has been completed.

d. Be sensitive to the danger that involvement of local colleagues in a large-scale, long-term, cross-cultural study may result in professional isolation and exclusion from local career opportunities. After completion of the project, maintain professional and personal communication with host collaborators, taking an interest in their career development, and actively involving them in relevant follow-up activities.

e. Consider the possible coercive, manipulative, or diversionary effects of an invitation to local colleagues. Funding availability and international contacts may make an invitation difficult to refuse, thus allowing priorities to be determined by other's needs rather than their own needs and those of their own communities (see section A6-a). Although local colleagues must decide if participation is in their own and/or their community's best interest, refrain from using resources to manipulate this decision.

4. Benefits to the local research community: The investigator should make contributions to the training and career development of local scholars and the advancement of the discipline within the host community.

a. Contribute to the local research community by increasing its capabilities and resources for independent research. Lasting contributions may take the form of greater technical skills and broader perspectives among local personnel; of institutional structures and mechanisms for carrying out independent research; and of data that local researchers can use in professional work and in addressing community problems.

b. Continue a relationship with the local research community beyond the period of the research project, governed by the principle of reciprocity. Explore possible exchanges of personnel or resources between institutions and facilitate the efforts of colleagues or students from the host community to conduct research in one's own community.

C. RESPONSIBILITIES TO THE
DISCIPLINE AND THE RESEARCH ENTERPRISE

1. Competence: The investigator should maintain high standards of professional competence by not undertaking research without the necessary skills and knowledge, including sophistication in cross-cultural methodology and familiarity with the cultural context of the research setting. The investigator should exercise care in the selection of measuring instruments, particularly when these are to be used for cross-cultural comparisons and in the interpretation of cultural differences.

a. Recognize the boundaries of one's personal competence and the limitations of psychological techniques in dealing with funding agencies and with authorities in the host community. Avoid inaccurate and inflated claims about knowledge and experience, keeping in mind that familiarity with the culture to be investigated is a crucial element of the competence required for cross-cultural research. Avoid excessive and unrealistic claims about the power of psychological techniques, particularly if inexperienced in applying them within the constraints of the host culture.

b. Refrain from undertaking research in a different culture without adequate preparatory work (see sections A2-a and A2-b). For example, do not routinely administer instruments developed for one culture without first exploring their meaning and validity in a different cultural context. Such practices are scientifically unsound and also may constitute an undue imposition on subjects (see section A4-c) or a potential source of damage to subjects (see sections A2-d and A5-d).

2. Publication: The investigator should recognize that free and open publication is a central feature of scientific research and that production of public knowledge legitimizes requests for cooperation and assistance. A cross-cultural study should be undertaken only with the expectation that it will eventuate in full publication. If publication may jeopardize or damage the population studied, the investigator should delay publication or disguise identifying information, refraining from publication altogether only as a last resort. Publication should be sufficiently detailed and explicit to enable scientific peers to evaluate findings and place them in perspective, including clear and accurate information about the original purposes of the research, its sponsorship, and source of funds.

a. Make clear to potential sponsors and funding agencies that there can be no interference with the freedom to publish research or with the interpretation placed on findings. Refuse support from any sponsor or funding agency that, as a condition of support, seeks to limit the right to publish, wants to keep its sponsorship secret, or expects confidential or classified information. Be especially careful to arrive at a clear, mutual understanding regarding publication and classification of results before accepting sponsorship from military, political, or commercial organization (see section A5-f).

b. Present as scientific research only an investigation that can be published without classified or proprietary findings. Clarify sponsorship, purposes, and utilization of the data. Scientific research cannot rightfully be used to cover activities that have a different and hidden purpose, such as the gathering of military or political intelligence, of market information for commercial decisions, or of personal data for the evaluation of employees or other groups.

c. Communicate, where appropriate or desirable, research findings in media that reach wider audiences, in addition to disseminating them in scientific journals, monographs, and meetings. Although often such communications are less technical and complete, be fully consistent with the data obtained and avoid distortions, over-generalizations, and exaggerated claims. In writing for popular media (or monitoring the work of professional writers based on the research), guard especially against misinterpretations of the data and against the danger that unwarranted policy implications may be drawn from them (see section A5-d).

3. Scientific community: The investigator should always keep in mind that he or she is part of a scientific community, international in scope, which includes

colleagues, assistants, students, and other investigators—both present and future. The investigator should consider the often unintended, direct and indirect consequences of research activities for various members of this community. From a long-run perspective, the investigator has the responsibility to maintain the integrity of the research enterprise.

a. Provide instruction and guidance to students and assistants in the ethics of cross-cultural research. Sensitize associates to ethical issues involved and be prepared to advise and supervise them in this domain. Assume final responsibility for maintaining ethical practice in a research project.

b. Maintain the trust and good will of the host community, thus increasing the likelihood of continued future access and cooperation. Avoid actions that pollute the research environment, such as exploiting a community that has already been oversaturated by outside research (see section A5-b), deceiving subjects (see section A3-b), breaking promises and commitments (see section A4), or showing insensitivity to cultural norms (see section A2).

c. Avoid pursuit of parochial interests in research, teaching, and professional activities, being mindful that one is a part of the larger, international scientific community. Maintain active communication with colleagues from different parts of the world and share in the responsibility of protecting the integrity and promoting the advancement of the scientific enterprise on a worldwide basis.

Appendix III

Multicultural Counseling Competencies and Standards

A Call to the Profession

DERALD WING SUE

PATRICIA ARREDONDO

RODERICK J. MCDAVIS

In April 1991, the Association for Multicultural Counseling and Development (AMCD) approved a document outlining the need and rationale for a multicultural perspective in counseling. The work of the Professional Standards committee went much further in proposing 31 multicultural counseling competencies and strongly encouraged the American Association for Counseling and Development (AACD) and the counseling profession to adopt these competencies in accreditation criteria. The hope was to have the competencies eventually become a standard for curriculum reform and training of helping professionals.

Originally accepted for publication in the *Journal for Multicultural Counseling and Development*, this document was considered so important that many recommended its publication in the *Journal of Counseling & Development* to reach the largest audience possible. As a result, we are pleased to announce that both journals have decided to publish the document jointly as a service to the profession.

RATIONALE AND DESCRIPTION

Despite the long history of warnings and recommendations concerning the need to develop a multicultural perspective in the counseling profession and the need to develop multicultural competencies and standards, it is ironic that the Association for Multicultural Counseling and Development (AMCD) finds itself continuing to justify these concerns. Numerous conferences held by the American Association for Counseling and Development (AACD), the American Psychological Association (APA), and other government-sponsored events have noted the serious lack and inadequacy of training programs in dealing with racial, ethnic, and cultural matters (ACES Commission on Non-White Concerns [McFadden, Quinn, & Sweeney, 1978]; Austin Conference 1975, Dulles Conference 1978, National Conference on Graduate Education in Psychology 1987, and President's Commission on Mental Health 1978 [Sue, 1990, 1991]; Vail Conference [Korman, 1974]).

Since the early 1970s, it has been gratifying to witness the increase in both literature and graduate training programs addressing the need to develop multicultural awareness, knowledge, and skills. For example, an early curriculum survey (McFadden & Wilson, 1977) of graduate education programs revealed that fewer than 1% of the respondents reported instructional requirements for the study of racial and ethnic minority groups. Subsequent surveys (Arredondo-Dowd & Gonzales, 1980; Ibrahim, Stadler, Arredondo, & McFadden, 1986; Wyatt & Parham, 1985) have revealed an increasing emphasis in this area. The most recent survey, to be published shortly (Hills & Strozier, in press),[1] revealed that 89% of counseling psychology programs now offer a multiculturally focused course. These surveys, however, fail to give us any indication about (a) their integration in the overall counseling curriculum, (b) the multicultural perspective of the courses, and (c) the degree of commitment by the department to multicultural issues. Indeed, the greatest fears among multicultural specialists are (a) that program professionals continue to see multicultural courses as less legitimate than other counseling requirements, (b) that they are taught primarily by junior-level faculty or adjuncts, (c) that they are haphazard and fragmented without a strong conceptual framework linked to specific competencies, and (d) that they tend to deal with cultural differences from a purely intellectual perspective without reference to the sociopolitical ramifications of counseling (oppression, discrimination, and racism) (Ponterotto & Casas, 1991; Sue, 1990; Sue & Sue, 1990; Sue et al., 1982). In reality, most counselors do not have enough practical experience in training, nor in their daily lives, with racial and ethnic minorities.

The purpose of this article is threefold. First, we explore the need and rationale for a multicultural perspective in our society, particularly in counseling and education. We advocate the need for a multicultural approach to assessment, practice, training, and research. Second, we propose specific multicultural standards and competencies that should become part of what can be defined as a culturally competent counselor. Last, we advocate specific strategies and issue a call for action regarding the implementation of multicultural standards in AACD.

The multicultural competencies and standards proposed in this report refer primarily to four groups in our society: African Americans, American Indians, Asian Americans, and Hispanics and Latinos. Many of these standards, however, have had useful relevance to other oppressed groups as well. Before we continue, it is imperative to clarify some terms and issues likely to be raised in this report. One of these is the controversy surrounding the inclusiveness or exclusiveness of the term *multicultural counseling* (Fukuyama, 1990; Lee & Richardson, 1991; Locke, 1990). There are those who would like to define *culture* broadly to include race, ethnicity, class, affectional orientation, class, religion, sex, age, and so forth. As such, multicultural counseling would include not only racial and ethnic minorities, but also women, gays and lesbians, and other special populations. There are those who prefer to limit the discussion of multicultural counseling to what has been referred to as "Visible Racial Ethnic Minority Groups" African Americans, American Indians, Asian Americans, and Hispanics and Latinos. Those who hold this point of view acknowledge that to some extent all counseling is cross-cultural, but that the term can be defined so broadly that it dilutes the focus on racial and ethnic concerns (a primary one being racism) and allows counseling professionals to avoid and omit dealing with the four major minority groups in our society.

We believe that the "universal" and "focused" multicultural approaches are not necessarily contradictory. Both offer legitimate issues and views that can enrich our understanding of multicultural counseling. On the one hand, we believe strongly that all forms of counseling are cross-cultural, that cultural issues need to be seen as central to cross-cultural counseling (not ancillary), and that by focusing just on ethnic minority issues, we may be "ghettoizing" the problem. Yet, we believe that multicultural counseling is a specialty area as well. Although all of us are racial, ethnic and cultural beings, belonging to a particular group does not endow a person with the competencies and skills necessary to be a cultural skilled counselor. After all, does a person who is born and raised in a family make that individual a competent family counselor?

THE RATIONALE AND NEED
FOR A MULTICULTURAL PERSPECTIVE

Multiculturalism has been referred to as psychology's "fourth force" (Pedersen, 1988, 1989, 1990) and is seen as "the hottest topic" in the counseling profession (Lee, 1989; Lee & Richardson, 1991). Much of this is driven by our recognition that we are fast becoming a multiracial, multicultural, and multilingual society (Sue, 1991; Sue & Sue, 1990). In the past, society has operated primarily within a monocultural and monolingual perspective reflected in what has been referred to as the "encapsulated counselor" (Wrenn, 1962). The changing "complexion of our society" and the "diversification of America (U.S.)" as reflected in the 1990 U.S. Census makes it imperative for the counseling profession to take a proactive stance on cultural diversity.

The Diversification of the United States

The 1990 U.S. Census reveals that the United States is fast undergoing some very radical demographic changes. Projections show that by the year 2000, more than one third of the population will be racial and ethnic minorities, with even higher numbers (45%) in our public schools. By the year 2010, fewer than 20 years from now, racial and ethnic minorities will become a numerical majority, with White Americans constituting approximately 48% of the population (Sue, 1991). The current population trend can be referred to as the "diversification of America" and is the result of two notable trends: (a) current immigration patterns and (b) differential birth rates among the White and racial and ethnic minority populations (Atkinson, Morten, & Sue, in press).[2]

1. The current immigration rates (documented immigrants, undocumented immigrants, and refugees) are the largest in U.S. history. Unlike their earlier European counterparts who are oriented more toward assimilation, the current wave consists of primarily Asian (34%), Latino (34%), and other visible racial and ethnic groups. These

groups are not readily assimilated, as many prefer to retain their cultural heritage. For example, the Asian American population is the fastest growing group in the United States (nearly an 80% increase in the 1980s) because of the large increase of Indochinese refugees since the 1965 changes in immigration laws. The Latino population will reach 55 million by the year 2000, and they will constitute the largest group by the year 2025.

2. Along with becoming an aging population (the mortality rate of Whites is declining, and people are living longer), White Americans are experiencing a declining fertility and birthrate (1.7 children per mother). This is in marked contrast to racial and ethnic minorities who are also showing birth declines, but continue to have a much higher rate (African Americans = 2.4, Mexican Americans = 2.9, Vietnamese = 3.4, Laotians = 4.6, Cambodians = 7.4, and Hmongs = 11.9 per mother).

The implications concerning the dramatic increase in the non-White population are immense. Already 75% of the entering labor force are racial and ethnic minorities and women. By the time the so-called "baby boomers" retire (those born between 1946 and 1961), the majority of people contributing to the social security and pension plans will be racial and ethnic minorities. Business and industry already recognize that in the United States the minority marketplace equals the GNP (gross national product) of Canada, and projections are that it will become immense as the shift in demographics continues. To remain economically competitive, businesses now recognize that they must learn how to utilize fully a diverse work force.

Likewise, counselors and teachers in our schools have already encountered these demographic forces in their work. Educational institutions are most likely to be first affected by the changing student population. In California, for example, the number of White students has already dropped below 50% enrollment. Last year, one in every four students in California lived in a home in which English was not spoken. One in every six students was foreign-born (Atkinson, Morten, & Sue, in press). Increasingly, working with minority constituents will become the norm rather than the exception. To be fully competent in working with minority populations or those clients culturally different from ourselves, it is imperative that AACD take a proactive stance in incorporating standards of practice that reflect the diversity of our society.

Monocultural Nature of Training

A body of literature exists that documents the widespread ineffectiveness of traditional counseling approaches and techniques when applied to racial and ethnic minority populations (Bernal & Padilla, 1982; Casas, 1982; Casas, Ponterotto, & Gutierrez, 1986; Ibrahim & Arredondo, 1986; President's Commission on Mental Health, 1978; Smith, 1982; Sue, 1990; Sue & Sue, 1990; Sue et al., 1982). It is apparent that the major reason for therapeutic ineffectiveness lies in the training of mental health professionals (Sue, Akutsu, & Higashi, 1985). Even in graduate programs where a course or courses on multicultural counseling exist, it is often still treated as ancillary and not an integral part of counseling (Arredondo-Dowd & Gawelek, 1982). Counseling professionals need to recognize that race, culture, and ethnicity are functions of each and everyone of us and not limited to "just minorities" (Sue & Sue, 1990). For example, a review of the AACD *Ethical Standards* (1988) and the AACD *Bylaws* (1989) by this committee leads us to three conclusions: (a) Not much, if anything is said about multicultural and cross-cultural issues, (b) not a single statement about multicultural and cross-cultural courses or preparation is included under Section H: Preparation Standards in the *Ethical Standards* (AACD, 1988), and (c) multicultural and cross-cultural competence is still seen in isolation (and as unnecessary) from the overall standards of the profession. Likewise, APA ethical guidelines (1991b) have been severely criticized by Pedersen (1989) who stated:

> . . . existing (APA) guidelines suggest that competence in the cultures of persons being studied or served should be included "when necessary." As long as that phrase is allowed to stand, cultural factors and the expertise in being responsive to them rest with the complainant, not the psychologist. In view of the present state of our knowledge about the presence of cultural factors in all forms of psychological functioning, we conclude that psychologists individually and collectively cannot justify the inclusion of the conditional phrase "when necessary." (p. 649)

There are hopeful signs, however, that APA has begun the process of revising the *Bylaws* and *Ethical Principles* to reflect an affirmation of cultural diversity. In the spring of 1990, a subcommittee on cultural and individual differences was created to review Criterion II of the APA "Criteria for Accreditation." A number of recommendations were proposed with new phrases "must be imparted," "must be developed," and "in all phases of the program's operation" (APA, 1991a).

Sociopolitical Reality

Another important factor that we need to recognize is that the profession of counseling, oftentimes, reflects the values of the larger society (Katz, 1985; Sue & Sue, 1990). References to counseling as "the handmaiden of the status quo" and "transmitters of society's values" indicate the potential sociopolitical nature of counseling. There are two political realities that counseling professionals must acknowledge and address.

First, the worldview of both the counselor and client is ultimately linked to the historical and current experiences of racism and oppression in the United States (Atkinson, Morten, & Sue, 1989; Helms, 1990; Parham, 1989; Sabnani, Ponterotto, & Borodovsky, 1991). For the minority client, he or she is likely to approach counseling with a great deal of healthy suspicion as to the counselor's conscious and unconscious motives in a cross-cultural context. For the White counselor or helping professional, he or she is likely to inherit the racial and cultural biases of his or her forebears (Corvin & Wiggins, 1989; White & Parham, 1990). In all cases, the counselor, client, and counseling process are influenced by the state of race relations in the larger society. That the counselor is "supposed to help" or that counseling is "supposed to encompass" values and assumptions that reflect democratic ideals such as "equal access to opportunity," "liberty and justice for all," and "pursuit of happiness" may not be realistically reflected in the actual practice of counseling. Indeed, these lofty goals have often been translated into support for the status quo. When used to restrict rather than foster the well-being and development of individuals from ethnic and racial minority groups, it may entail overt and covert forms of prejudice and discrimination (Sue & Sue, 1990).

Second, counseling professionals need to recognize that counseling does not occur in isolation from larger events in our society. All of us have a responsibility in understanding the political forces and events that affect not only our personal but professional lives as well. For example, the changing demographics cited earlier are having a major impact upon our educational, economic, social, political, legal, and cultural system (Sue, 1991). With the increased visibility of racial and ethnic minorities in the United States, it seems that racial intolerance is on the rise. The increase in so-called "hate crimes" (murder, physical attacks, threats, racial epithets, destruction of property, and so forth) against minority groups is well documented. These reports are even more disturbing in light of the apparent erosion of the nation's civil rights law and President Bush's vetoing of the Civil Rights Act of 1990 and his opposition to the democratic version of the 1991 proposal.

Likewise, the "English-only movement" seems to have major political ramifications on the nature of race relations in the United States and directly to education and counseling. In a perceptive article concerning the "English-only movement" and language use, specialists (Padilla et al., 1991) concluded that (a) linguistic assimilation is already occurring rapidly among racial and ethnic minorities, (b) promoting second language learning for English speakers fosters positive interethnic relations, (c) maintaining bilingualism enhances positive identity, (d) high-quality bilingual education programs can promote higher levels of academic achievement and language proficiency, and (e) the movement contains a strong racist flavor. These authors concluded further that the English-only movement can have negative consequences for the delivery of psychological, educational, psychometric, and health services for linguistic minorities. Promoting bilingualism rather than monolingualism should be a major goal to the provision of mental health services; it is an expression of personal freedom and pluralism.

Multicultural Conceptualizations and Research

White middle-class value systems are often reflected in counseling and social psychological research regarding racial and ethnic minorities. Historically, three very harmful models have been used to guide and conceptualize research on racial and linguistic minorities (Casas, 1985; Katz, 1985; Ponterotto, 1988; Sue & Sue, 1990). The first of these is the inferiority or pathological model. The basic premise is that minorities are lower on the evolutionary scale (more primitive) than are their White counterparts and, thus, are more inherently pathological. The second model assumes that Blacks and other racial and ethnic minorities were deficient in desirable genes and that differences between Whites and minorities were the reflection of biological and genetic inferiority (genetically deficient model). The culturally deprived (deficient) model blamed the culture for the "minority problem." Ironically, it was well-intentioned White social scientists who were attempting to reject the genetically deficient model who talked about "cultural deprivation." Unfortunately, these social scientists were as much prisoners of their own cultural conditioning as those of an earlier decade (Sue & Sue, 1990). Instead of blaming genes, they blamed the culture. The cultural deficit notion does not make sense because everyone inherits a culture. What proponents of this view were really saying was that racial and ethnic minorities do not possess "the right culture." Thus, the underlying data and research base regarding racial and ethnic minorities have (a) perpetuated a view that minorities are inherently pathological, (b) perpetuated racist research and counseling practices, and (c) provided an excuse for counseling professionals not to take social action to rectify inequities in the system (Baratz & Baratz, 1970; Katz, 1985; Sue & Sue, 1990; Thomas & Sillen, 1972).

Within the last 10 years, a new and conceptually different model has emerged in the literature. Oftentimes referred to as the "culturally different model" (Katz, 1985; Sue, 1981), multicultural model (Johnson, 1990), culturally pluralistic model, or culturally diverse model (Ponterotto & Casas, 1991), the new model makes several assumptions. First and foremost is the explicit belief that to be culturally different does not equate with "deviancy," "pathology," or "inferiority." Second, there is strong acknowledgment that racial and ethnic minorities are bicultural and function in at least two different cultural contexts. Third, biculturality is seen as a positive and desirable quality that enriches the full range of human potential. Last, individuals are viewed in relationship to their environment, and the larger social forces (racism, oppression, discrimination, and so forth) rather than the individual or minority group may be the obstacles.

If AACD and other professional organizations take a strong stand in adopting the new model and all its implicit assumptions, then research and counseling may become a proactive means of correcting many of the inadequacies and problems that have plagued us for ages. For example, adoption of such a model would mean that (a) graduate programs could no longer present a predominately White Anglo-Saxon Protestant orientation, (b) racial and ethnic minority issues would become an integral part of the curriculum and internship requirement, (c) research would become a powerful means of combating stereotypes and correcting biased studies, (d) studies would begin to focus on the positive attributes and characteristics of minorities as well as biculturalism, (e) recruitment, retention, and promotion of racial and ethnic minorities in counseling would increase, (f) interracial and interethnic relations would be improved, and (g) we would refocus research and practice toward the environment though systems intervention.

Ethical Issues

> The provision of professional services to persons of culturally diverse backgrounds by persons not competent in understanding and providing professional services to such groups shall be considered unethical. (Korman, 1974, p. 105)

> A serious moral vacuum exists in the delivery of cross-cultural counseling and therapy services because the values of a dominant culture have been imposed on the culturally different consumer. Cultural differences complicate the definition of guidelines even for the conscientious and well-intentioned counselor and therapist. (Pedersen & Marsella, 1982, p. 498)

Both of these quotes make it clear that professionals without training or competence in working with clients from diverse cultural backgrounds are unethical and potentially harmful, which borders on a violation of human rights. In 1981 both AACD (1981) and APA (1981) published ethical guidelines making imperative for counselors and therapists to have some sort of formal training on cultural differences. Yet, declarations such as these do not automatically improve counselor sensitivity and effectiveness, nor do they mean that training programs will on their own volition infuse cross-cultural concepts into the curriculum (Ibrahim & Arredondo, 1986, 1990). Too often, lip service is given to multicultural concerns, without the commitment to translate them into ethical standards and see that they become part of the accreditation criteria. If we truly believe that multiculturalism is central to our definition of a competent counselor, then monoculturalism can be seen as a form of maladjustment in a pluralistic society (Szapocznik, Santisteban, Durtines, Perez-Vidal, & Hervis, 1983).

It seems that a major obstacle in getting our profession to understand the negative implications of monoculturalism is that White culture is such a dominant norm that it acts as an invisible veil that prevents people from seeing counseling as a potentially biased system (Katz, 1985). Counselors who are unaware of the basis for differences that occur between them and their culturally different clients are likely to impute negative characteristics. What is needed is for counselors to become culturally aware, to act on the basis of a critical analysis and understanding on their own conditioning, the conditioning of their clients, and the sociopolitical system of which they are both a part. Without such awareness, the counselor who works with a culturally differ-ent client may be engaging in cultural oppression using unethical and harmful practices.

CROSS-CULTURAL
COMPETENCIES AND STANDARDS

It is clear to us that the need for multiculturalism in the counseling profession is urgent and necessary for ethical practice, an integral part of our professional work. These realities and philosophies should underlie AACD's mission and purpose. Yet, a study of AACD's *Bylaws* (1989) and the *Ethical Standards* (AACD, 1988) reveals serious shortcomings and casts doubt upon the organization's awareness and commit-ment to the concepts of multiculturalism. Reviews of the *Ethical Principles* (1981) of AACD have continued to indicate that it falls short in addressing racial and ethnic matters across all professional activities (Casas, Ponterotto, & Gutierrez, 1986; Cayleff, 1986; Ibrahim & Arredondo, 1986; Ponterotto & Casas, 1991). Our critical analysis of the bylaws, for instance, indicates only one place in which reference to racial and ethnic groups is made (Article XIV—Nondiscrimination). The *Ethical Standards* (AACD, 1988) contains nothing in the Preamble regarding multiculturalism and mentions racial, ethnic, national origin, and/or minority groups only four times (one under Section B: Counseling Relationship, Article 19; two under Section C: Measurement & Evaluation, Articles 1 and 12; and one under Section G: Personnel Administration Article 11). Sections on General, Research and Publication, Consult-ing, Private Practice, and Preparation Standards contain nothing on multiculturalism. Omission in the Preparation Standards, in our eyes, is inexcusable and represents a powerful statement of the low priority and lack of commitment to cultural diversity.

Furthermore, we find it difficult to accept two prevailing reasons given for the lack of multicultural statements in the standards and guidelines. The first is that additions and revision of the standards would make the document too cumbersome and lengthy. The second explanation is that although there is a failure to address minority groups explicitly, the guidelines do so implicitly (Ponterotto & Casas, 1991). Behind this last statement is the belief that the standards are developed from a universal humanistic perspective and that they underscore the dignity and worth of all persons. The first reason suffers from structural bias in that it considers racial and cultural statements less worthy than other statements. The issue of length is a convenient excuse not to make needed changes. Furthermore, we are not recommending simple changes in the standards that would tack on more articles to the *Ethical Principles* (AACD, 1981). What needs to occur is a philosophical change in the premise of counseling that incorporates a movement toward inclusiveness, altruism, community, care, and justice (Hillerbrand, 1987; Ivey, 1987; LaFromboise & Foster, 1989; Ponterotto & Casas, 1991). The second reason is simply another form of "universalism" in which "People are people" and "should be treated the same." Such beliefs are ethnocentric and have been documented to be highly destructive to racial and ethnic minority constituents (Sue & Sue, 1990).

Cross-Cultural Counselor Competencies

Although the AACD *Ethical Standards* (1988) makes reference to counselors not claiming professional qualifications exceeding those they possess and recognizing their boundaries of competence (Section A: General, Articles 4 and 9), it fails to define competence in the multicultural sense. We believe this represents one of the major shortcomings of our profession. Although many individual authors and groups have proposed cross-cultural counseling guidelines, skills, and competencies, AACD and its numerous divisions have failed to enact such standards. The only formal statement adopted by a division of AACD is seen in a position paper: ACES Commission on Non-White Concerns (McFadden, Quinn, & Sweeney, 1978). As a result of these glaring deficiencies, AMCD, under the Presidency of Dr. Thomas Parham, requested the Professional Standards Committee to (a) outline multicultural issues facing our profession, (b) develop tentative minimal cross-cultural counseling competencies for adoption by AMCD and AACD, and (c) explore means of implementing these standards into official documents of AACD and in the accreditation process.

In developing cross-cultural competencies, we have relied heavily upon the works of the Division of Counseling Psychology—*Position Paper: Cross-cultural Counseling Competencies* (Sue et al., 1982) and the *Guidelines for Providers of Psychological Services to Ethnic and Culturally Diverse Populations* (APA, 1991b). These competencies and standards have been widely endorsed and currently represent the best that various groups and organizations have to offer. If these principles are to be adopted by AACD, they need to be appropriately translated into meaningful statements for the profession. At this time, attempts to add to or refine them would require massive investment of time and energy. Because of time constraints, we have chosen to (a) provide a conceptual framework from which these competencies can be organized and developed and (b) leave the task of tangible translations for future urgent work.

The culturally competent counselor. In their review of the literature dealing with characteristics of the culturally skilled counselor, Sue and Sue (1990) have been able to organize these characteristics along three dimensions. *First, a culturally skilled counselor is one who is actively in the process of becoming aware of his or her own assumptions about human behavior, values, biases, preconceived notions, personal limitations, and so forth.* They understand their own worldviews, how they are the product of their cultural conditioning, and how it may be reflected in their counseling and work with racial and ethnic minorities. The old adage "counselor, know thyself" is important in not allowing biases, values, or "hangups" to interfere with the counselor's ability to work with clients. Prevention of ethnocentrism is a key ingredient to effective cross-cultural counseling.

Second, a culturally skilled counselor is one who actively attempts to understand the worldview of his or her culturally different client without negative judgments. It is crucial that counselors understand and share the worldviews of their culturally different clients with respect and appreciation. This statement does not imply that counselors have to hold the worldviews as their own, but can accept them as another legitimate perspective.

Third, a culturally skilled counselor is one who is in the process of actively developing and practicing appropriate, relevant, and sensitive intervention strategies and skills in working with his or her culturally different clients. Studies consistently reveal that counseling effectiveness is improved when counselors use modalities and define goals consistent with the life experiences and cultural values of clients. It is recognized that extrapsychic as well as intrapsychic approaches may be more appropriate and that differential helping strategies may be needed.

In summarizing these three characteristics, Sue and Sue (1990) stated:

These three goals stress the fact that becoming culturally skilled is an *active process*, that it is ongoing, and that it is a process that *never reaches an end point*. Implicit is recognition of the complexity and diversity of the client and client populations, and acknowledgements of our own personal limitations and the need to always improve. (p. 146)

Dimensions of cultural competency. Most attempts to identify specific cross-cultural counseling competencies have divided them up into three dimensions: (a) beliefs and attitudes, (b) knowledge, and (c) skills (Carney & Kahn, 1984; Sue et al., 1982). The first deals with counselors' attitudes and beliefs about racial and ethnic minorities, the need to check biases and stereotypes, development of a positive orientation toward multiculturalism, and the way counselors' values and biases may hinder effective cross-cultural counseling. The second recognizes that the culturally skilled counselor has good knowledge and understanding of his or her own worldview, has specific knowledge of the cultural groups he or she works with, and understands sociopolitical influences. The last deals with specific skills (intervention techniques and strategies) needed in working with minority groups (it includes both individual and institutional competencies). A more thorough description of these three dimensions can be found in the previous two cited references.

Cross-Cultural Counseling Competencies: A Conceptual Framework

Given the aforementioned discussion of cross-cultural counseling competencies, it is possible to develop a 3 (Characteristics) × 3 (Dimensions) matrix in which most of the cross-cultural skills can either be organized or developed. For example, the characteristics (a) counselor awareness of own assumptions, values, and biases; (b) understanding the worldview of the culturally different client; and (c) developing appropriate intervention strategies and techniques would each be described as having three dimensions: (a) beliefs and attitudes, (b) knowledge, and (c) skills. Thus, a total of nine competency areas are identified in Appendix A. We tentatively offer what we believe to be important competencies under each area.

COUNSELOR AWARENESS OF OWN ASSUMPTIONS, VALUES, AND BIASES

Beliefs and Attitudes

1. Culturally skilled counselors have moved from being culturally unaware to being aware and sensitive to their own cultural heritage and to valuing and respecting differences.
2. Culturally skilled counselors are aware of how their own cultural background and experiences, attitudes, and values and biases influence psychological processes.
3. Culturally skilled counselors are able to recognize the limits of their competencies and expertise.
4. Culturally skilled counselors are comfortable with differences that exist between themselves and clients in terms of race, ethnicity, culture, and beliefs.

Knowledge

1. Culturally skilled counselors have specific knowledge about their own racial and cultural heritage and how it personally and professionally affects their definitions and biases of normality-abnormality and the process of counseling.

2. Culturally skilled counselors possess knowledge and understanding about how oppression, racism, discrimination, and stereotyping affect them personally and in their work. This allows them to acknowledge their own racist attitudes, beliefs, and feelings. Although this standard applies to all groups, for White counselors it may mean that they understand how they may have directly or indirectly benefitted from individual, institutional, and cultural racism (White identity development models).

3. Culturally skilled counselors possess knowledge about their social impact upon others. They are knowledgeable about communication style differences, how their style may clash or facilitate the counseling process with minority clients, and how to anticipate the impact it may have on others.

Skills

1. Culturally skilled counselors seek out educational, consultative, and training experiences to enrich their understanding and effectiveness in working with culturally different populations. Being able to recognize the limits of their competencies, they (a) seek consultation, (b) seek further training or education, (c) refer out to more qualified individuals or resources, or (d) engage in a combination of these.

2. Culturally skilled counselors are constantly seeking to understand themselves as racial and cultural beings and are actively seeking a nonracist identity.

UNDERSTANDING THE WORLDVIEW OF THE CULTURALLY DIFFERENT CLIENT

Beliefs and Attitudes

1. Culturally skilled counselors are aware of their negative emotional reactions toward other racial and ethnic groups that may prove detrimental to their clients in counseling. They are willing to contrast their own beliefs and attitudes with those of their culturally different clients in a nonjudgmental fashion.

2. Culturally skilled counselors are aware of their stereotypes and preconceived notions that they may hold toward other racial and ethnic minority groups.

Knowledge

1. Culturally skilled counselors possess specific knowledge and information about the particular group that they are working with. They are aware of the life experiences, cultural heritage, and historical background of their culturally different clients. This particular competency is strongly linked to the "minority identity development models" available in the literature.

2. Culturally skilled counselors understand how race, culture, ethnicity, and so forth may affect personality formation, vocational choices, manifestation of psychological disorders, help-seeking behavior, and the appropriateness or inappropriateness of counseling approaches.

3. Culturally skilled counselors understand and have knowledge about sociopolitical influences that impinge upon the life of racial and ethnic minorities. Integration issues, poverty, racism, stereotyping and powerlessness all leave major scars that may influence the counseling process.

Skills

1. Culturally skilled counselors should familiarize themselves with relevant research and the latest findings regarding mental health and mental disorders of various ethnic and racial groups. They should actively seek out educational experiences that enrich their knowledge, understanding, and cross-cultural skills.

2. Culturally skilled counselors become actively involved with minority individuals outside the counseling setting (community events, social and political functions, celebrations, friendships, neighborhood groups, and so forth) so that their perspective of minorities is more than an academic or helping exercise.

DEVELOPING APPROPRIATE INTERVENTION STRATEGIES AND TECHNIQUES

Attitudes and Beliefs

1. Culturally skilled counselors respect clients' religious and/or spiritual beliefs and values about physical and mental functioning.

2. Culturally skilled counselors respect indigenous helping practices and respect minority community intrinsic help-giving networks.

3. Culturally skilled counselors value bilingualism and do not view another language as an impediment to counseling (monolingualism may be the culprit).

Knowledge

1. Culturally skilled counselors have a clear and explicit knowledge and understanding of the generic characteristics of counseling and therapy (culture bound, class bound, and monolingual) and how they may clash with the cultural values of various minority groups.

2. Culturally skilled counselors are aware of institutional barriers that prevent minorities from using mental health services.

3. Culturally skilled counselors have knowledge of the potential bias in assessment instruments and use procedures and interpret findings keeping in mind the cultural and linguistic characteristics of the clients.

4. Culturally skilled counselors have knowledge of minority family structures, hierarchies, values, and beliefs. They are knowledgeable about the community characteristics and the resources in the community as well as the family.

5. Culturally skilled counselors should be aware of relevant discriminatory practices at the social and community level that may be affecting the psychological welfare of the population being served.

Skills

1. Culturally skilled counselors are able to engage in a variety of verbal and nonverbal helping responses. They are able to *send* and *receive* both *verbal* and *nonverbal* messages *accurately* and *appropriately*. They are not tied down to only one method or approach to helping but recognize that helping styles and approaches may be culture bound. When they sense that their helping style is limited and potentially inappropriate, they can anticipate and ameliorate its negative impact.

2. Culturally skilled counselors are able to exercise institutional intervention skills on behalf of their clients. They can help clients determine whether a "problem" stems from racism or bias in others (the concept of healthy paranoia) so that clients do not inappropriately blame themselves.

3. Culturally skilled counselors are not averse to seeking consultation with traditional healers or religious and spiritual leaders and practitioners in the treatment of culturally different clients when appropriate.

4. Culturally skilled counselors take responsibility for interacting in the language requested by the client; this may mean appropriate referral to outside resources. A serious problem arises when the linguistic skills of the counselor do not match the language of the client. This being the case, counselors should (a) seek a translator with cultural knowledge and appropriate professional background or (b) refer to a knowledgeable and competent bilingual counselor.

5. Culturally skilled counselors have training and expertise in the use of traditional assessment and testing instruments. They not only understand the technical aspects of the instruments but are also aware of the cultural limitations. This allows them to use test instruments for the welfare of the diverse clients.

6. Culturally skilled counselors should attend to as well as work to eliminate biases, prejudices, and discriminatory practices. They should be cognizant of sociopolitical contexts in conducting evaluations and providing interventions, and should develop sensitivity to issues of oppression, sexism, and racism.

7. Culturally skilled counselors take responsibility in educating their clients to the processes of psychological intervention, such as goals, expectations, legal rights, and the counselor's orientation.

We believe that these cross-cultural competencies represent AMCD's first formal attempt to define the attributes of a culturally skilled counselor. They are not meant to be "the final word" in establishing cross-cultural standards for the profession; rather, they represent what we consider to be very important criteria for counselor practice in working with racial and ethnic minorities. Many will, no doubt, undergo further revision, and other new competencies will be added. We propose these competencies in the spirit of open inquiry and hope they eventually will be adopted into the counseling standards of the profession.

A CALL FOR ACTION

In light of the foregoing analysis and discussion, the Professional Standards Committee of AMCD makes the following recommendations and requests the following actions.

1. In keeping with Goal 11: Professional Standards, Objective C—"To promote and encourage the highest standards of ethical and professional conduct for multicultural counseling and development"—(Strategic Plan for the Association for Multicultural Counseling and Development, 1990, p. 6), we propose that the executive committee of AMCD immediately appoint an ad hoc committee to review, advocate, and work to implement a major change in the AACD *Bylaws* (1989) and *Ethical Standards* (1988). The direction of these changes should be consistent with the position and analysis outlined in this article and other detailed recommendations found elsewhere (Casas, Ponterotto, & Gutierrez, 1986; Cayleff, 1986; Ibrahim & Arredondo, 1986, 1990; Ponterotto & Casas, 1991; Sue & Sue, 1990). We believe that enough analysis and discussion has taken place and that the time for action is *now*.

2. We ask that AACD's governance and leadership actively endorse the spirit of the proposed competencies with the knowledge that further refinement, revisions, and extensions will occur. These competencies can serve to pace the movement of the profession because they are grounded in the realities of our culturally diverse populations.

3. We further propose that AMCD and AACD immediately set up a mechanism that will advocate the adoption of these competencies in accreditation criteria and eventually become a standard for curriculum reform in graduate schools of counseling and other helping professions. Perhaps a miniconference devoted to developing strategies for implementation of the standards and competencies would be helpful.

4. A change in the bylaws and ethical standards may be meaningless unless the goals of multiculturalism are put into practice. Strong (1986) has defined a multicultural organization as the following:

   . . . one which is genuinely committed to diverse representation of its membership; is sensitive to maintaining an open, supportive, and responsive environment; is working toward and purposefully including elements of diverse cultures in its ongoing operations; and one which is authentic in its response to issues confronting it. (p. 7)

We propose that AMCD serve a proactive role in doing a critical analysis of how AACD can become a more multicultural organization. This may entail altering the structure of the organization. We are aware, however, of the difficulty inherent in this task, but believe such actions are well worth the effort.

In closing, we urgently appeal to the leadership of AACD and all of its divisions to consider the infusion of multiculturalism throughout their organizations. We hope this commitment will be reflected in education, training, research, and practice of counselors everywhere. Multiculturalism is inclusive of all persons and groups. Continuing to deny its broad influence and importance is to deny social reality.

REFERENCES

American Association for Counseling and Development. (1981). *Ethical principles.* Alexandria, VA: Author.

American Association for Counseling and Development. (1988). *Ethical standards.* Alexandria, VA: Author.

American Association for Counseling and Development. (1989). *Bylaws.* Alexandria, VA: Author.

American Psychological Association. (1981). Ethical principles of psychologists. *American Psychologist, 36,* 633-681.

American Psychological Association. (1991a, July). *Capsule.* Washington, DC: Author.

American Psychological Association. (1991b). *Guidelines for providers of psychological services to ethnic, linguistic, and culturally diverse populations.* Washington, DC: Author.

Arredondo-Dowd, P., & Gawelek, M. (Eds.). (1982). *Human rights training manual.* Boston, MA: Association for Counselor Education and Supervision.

Arredondo-Dowd, P. M., & Gonzales, J. (1980). Preparing culturally effective counselors. *The Personnel and Guidance Journal, 58,* 657-662.

Atkinson, D., Morten, G., & Sue, D. W. (1989). *Counseling American minorities: A cross-cultural perspective.* Dubuque, IA: William C. Brown.

Atkinson, D., Morten, G., & Sue, D. W. (in press). *Counseling American minorities: A cross-cultural perspective.* Dubuque, IA: William C. Brown.

Baratz, S., & Baratz, J. (1970). Early childhood intervention: The social sciences base of institutional racism. *Harvard Educational Review, 40,* 29-50.

Bernal, M. E., & Padilla, A. M. (1982). Status of minority curricula and training in clinical psychology. *American Psychologist, 37,* 780-787.

Carney, C. G., & Kahn, K. B. (1984). Building competencies for effective cross-cultural counseling: A developmental view. *The Counseling Psychologist, 12,* 111-119.

Casas, J. M. (1982). Counseling psychology in the marketplace: The status of ethnic minorities. *The Counseling Psychologist, 37,* 780-787.

Casas, J. M. (1985). A reflection on the status of racial/ethnic minority research. *The Counseling Psychologist, 13,* 581-598.

Casas, J. M., Ponterotto, J. G., & Gutierrez, J. M. (1986). An ethical indictment of counseling research and training: The cross-cultural perspective. *Journal of Counseling and Development, 64,* 347-349.

Cayleff, S. E. (1986). Ethical issues in counseling gender, race, and culturally distinct groups. *Journal of Counseling and Development, 64,* 345-347.

Corvin, S., & Wiggins, F. (1989). An antiracism training model for White professionals. *Journal of Multicultural Counseling and Development, 17,* 105-114.

Fukuyama, M. A. (1990). Taking a universal approach to multicultural counseling. *Counselor Education and Supervision, 30,* 6-17.

Helms, J. (1990). *White identity development.* New York: Greenwood Press.

Hillerbrand, E. (1987). Philosophical tensions influencing psychology and social action. *American Psychologist, 42,* 111-118.

Hills, H. I., & Strozier, A. L. (in press). Multicultural training in APA approved counseling psychology programs: A survey. *Professional Psychology.*

Ibrahim, F. A., & Arredondo, P. M. (1986). Ethical standards for cross-cultural counseling: Counselor preparation, practice, assessment, and research. *Journal of Counseling and Development, 64,* 349-352.

Ibrahim, F. A., & Arredondo, P. M. (1990). Ethical issues in multicultural counseling. In B. Herlihy & L. Golden (Eds.), *Ethical standards casebook* (pp. 137-145). Alexandria, VA: American Association for Counseling and Development.

Ibrahim, F. A., Stadler, H. A., Arredondo, P., & McFadden, J. (1986, March). *Status of human rights in counselor education: A national survey.* Paper presented at the American Association for Counseling and Development Convention, Los Angeles, CA.

Ivey, A. E. (1987). The multicultural practice of therapy: Ethics, empathy, and dialectics. *Journal of Social and Clinical Psychology, 5,* 195-204.

Johnson, S. D. (1990). Toward clarifying culture, race, and ethnicity in the context of multicultural counseling. *Journal of Multicultural Counseling and Development, 18,* 41-50.

Katz, J. (1985). The sociopolitical nature of counseling. *The Counseling Psychologist, 13,* 615-624.

Korman, M. (1974). National conference on levels and patterns of professional training in psychology: Major themes. *American Psychologist, 29,* 301-313.

LaFromboise, T. D., & Foster, S. L. (1989). Ethics in multicultural counseling. In P. B. Pedersen, W. J. Lonner, & J. E. Trimble (Eds.), *Counseling across cultures* (3rd ed., pp. 115-136). Honolulu, HI: University of Hawaii Press.

Lee, C. (1989). Editorial: Who speaks for multicultural counseling? *Journal of Multicultural Counseling and Development, 17,* 1-3.

Lee, C., & Richardson, B. L. (1991). *Multicultural issues in counseling: New approaches to diversity.* Alexandria, VA: American Association for Counseling and Development.

Locke, D. C. (1990). A not so provincial view of multicultural counseling. *Counselor Education and Supervision, 30,* 18-25.

McFadden, J., Quinn, J. R., & Sweeney, T. J. (1978). *Position paper: Commission on non-White concerns.* Washington, DC: Association for Counselor Education and Supervision.

McFadden, J., & Wilson, T. (1977). *Non-White academic training with counselor education rehabilitation counseling, and student personnel programs.* Unpublished research.

Padilla, A. M., Lindholm, K. J., Chen, A., Duran, R., Hakuta, K., Lambert, W., & Tucker, G. R. (1991). The English-only movement: Myths, reality, nd implications for psychology. *American Psychologist, 46,* 120-130.

Parham, T. A. (1989). Cycles of psychological nigrescence. *The Counseling Psychologist, 17,* 197-226.

Pedersen, P. (1989). Developing multicultural ethical guidelines for psychology. *International Journal of Psychology, 24,* 643-652.

Pedersen, P. B. (1988). *A handbook for development multicultural awareness.* Alexandria, VA: American Association for Counseling and Development.

Pedersen, P. B. (1990). The constructs of complexity and balance in multicultural counseling theory and practice. *Journal of Counseling & Development, 68,* 550-554.

Pedersen, P. B., & Marsella, A. J. (1982). The ethical crisis for cross-cultural counseling and therapy. *Professional Psychology, 13,* 492-500.

Ponterotto, J. G. (1988). Racial/ethnic minority research in the *Journal of Counseling Psychology:* A content analysis and methodological critique. *Journal of Counseling Psychology, 35,* 410-418.

Ponterotto, J., & Casas, M. (1991). *Handbook of racial/ethnic minority counseling research.* Springfield, IL: Charles C Thomas.

President's Commission on Mental Health. (1980). *Report from the President's Commission on Mental Health.* Washington, DC: Government Printing Office.

Sabnani, H. B., Ponterotto, J. G., & Borodovsky, L. G. (1991). White racial identity development and cross-cultural training. *The Counseling Psychologist, 17,* 76-102.

Smith, E. J. (1982). Counseling psychology in the marketplace: The status of ethnic minorities. *The Counseling Psychologist, 10,* 61-67.

Strong, L. J. (1986). *Race relations for personal and organizational effectiveness.* Unpublished manuscript.

Sue, D. W. (1981). *Counseling the culturally different: Theory and practice.* New York: Wiley.

Sue, D. W. (1990). Culture specific strategies in counseling: A conceptual framework. *Professional Psychology, 24,* 424-433.

Sue, D. W. (1991). A conceptual model for cultural diversity training. *Journal of Counseling & Development, 70,* 99-105.

Sue, D. W., Bernier, Y., Durran, A., Feinberg, L., Pedersen, P. G., Smith, E. J., & Vasquez-Nuttal, E. (1982). Position paper: Cross-cultural counseling competencies. *The Counseling Psychologist, 10,* 45-52.

Sue, D. W., & Sue, D. (1990). *Counseling the culturally different: Theory and practice.* New York: Wiley.

Sue, S., Akutsu, P. D., & Higashi, C. (1985). Training issues in conducting therapy with ethnic-minority clients. In P. B. Pedersen (Ed.), *Handbook in cross-cultural counseling and therapy* (pp. 275-280). Westport, CT: Greenwood Press.

Szapocznik, J., Santisteban, D., Durtines, W., Perez-Vidal, A., & Hervis, O. L. (1983, November). *Bicultural effectiveness training: A treatment for enhancing intercultural adjustment in Cuban American families.* Paper presented at the Ethnicity, Acculturation, and Mental Health Among Hispanics Conference, Albuquerque, NM.

Thomas, A., & Sillen, S. (1972). *Racism and psychiatry.* New York: Brunner/Mazel.

White, J. L., & Parham, T. A. (1990). *The psychology of Blacks.* Englewood Cliffs, NJ: Prentice Hall.

Wrenn, C. G. (1962). The culturally encapsulated counselor. *Harvard Educational Review, 32,* 444-449.

Wyatt, G. G., & Parham, W. D. (1985). The inclusion of culturally sensitive course materials in graduate school and training programs. *Psychotherapy, 22,* 461-468.

APPENDIX A

Proposed Cross-Cultural Competencies and Objectives

I. Counselor Awareness of Own Cultural Values and Biases

A. Attitudes and Beliefs

1. Culturally skilled counselors have moved from being culturally unaware to being aware and sensitive to their own cultural heritage and to valuing and respecting differences.

2. Culturally skilled counselors are aware of how their own cultural backgrounds and experiences and attitudes, values, and biases influence psychological processes.

3. Culturally skilled counselors are able to recognize the limits of their competencies and expertise.

4. Culturally skilled counselors are comfortable with differences that exist between themselves and clients in terms of race, ethnicity, culture, and beliefs.

B. Knowledge

1. Culturally skilled counselors have specific knowledge about their own racial and cultural heritage and how it personally and professionally affects their definitions of normality-abnormality and the process of counseling.

2. Culturally skilled counselors possess knowledge and understanding about how oppression, racism, discrimination, and stereotyping affect them personally and in their work. This allows them to acknowledge their own racist attitudes, beliefs, and feelings. Although this standard applies to all groups, for White counselors it may mean that they understand how they may have directly or indirectly benefited from individual, institutional, and cultural racism (White identity development models).

3. Culturally skilled counselors possess knowledge about their social impact on others. They are knowledgeable about communication style differ-

ences, how their style may clash or foster the counseling process with minority clients, and how to anticipate the impact it may have on others.

C. Skills

1. Culturally skilled counselors seek out educational, consultative, and training experience to improve their understanding and effectiveness in working with culturally different populations. Being able to recognize the limits of their competencies, they (a) seek consultation, (b) seek further training or education, (c) refer out to more qualified individuals or resources, or (d) engage in a combination of these.

2. Culturally skilled counselors are constantly seeking to understand themselves as racial and cultural beings and are actively seeking a nonracist identity.

II. Counselor Awareness of Client's Worldview

A. Attitudes and Beliefs

1. Culturally skilled counselors are aware of their negative emotional reactions toward other racial and ethnic groups that may prove detrimental to their clients in counseling. They are willing to contrast their own beliefs and attitudes with those of their culturally different clients in a nonjudgmental fashion.

2. Culturally skilled counselors are aware of their stereotypes and preconceived notions that they may hold toward other racial and ethnic minority groups.

B. Knowledge

1. Culturally skilled counselors possess specific knowledge and information about the particular group they are working with. They are aware of the life experiences, cultural heritage, and historical background of their culturally different clients. This particular competency is strongly linked to the "minority identity development models" available in the literature.

2. Culturally skilled counselors understand how race, culture, ethnicity, and so forth may affect personality formation, vocational choices, manifestation of psychological disorders, help-seeking behavior, and the appropriateness or inappropriateness of counseling approaches.

3. Culturally skilled counselors understand and have knowledge about sociopolitical influences that impinge upon the life of racial and ethnic minorities. Immigration issues, poverty, racism, stereotyping, and powerlessness all leave major scars that may influence the counseling process.

C. Skills

1. Culturally skilled counselors should familiarize themselves with relevant research and the latest findings regarding mental health and mental disorders of various ethnic and racial groups. They should actively seek

out educational experiences that foster their knowledge, understanding, and cross-cultural skills.

2. Culturally skilled counselors become actively involved with minority individuals outside of the counseling setting (community events, social and political functions, celebrations, friendships, neighborhood groups, and so forth) so that their perspective of minorities is more than an academic or helping exercise.

III. Appropriate Intervention Strategies

A. Attitudes and Beliefs

1. Culturally skilled counselors respect clients' religious and/or spiritual beliefs and values, including attributions and taboos, because they affect worldview, psychosocial functioning, and expressions of distress.

2. Culturally skilled counselors respect indigenous helping practices and respect minority community intrinsic help-giving networks.

3. Culturally skilled counselors value bilingualism and do not view another language as an impediment to counseling (monolingualism may be the culprit).

B. Knowledge

1. Culturally skilled counselors have a clear and explicit knowledge and understanding of the generic characteristics of counseling and therapy (culture bound, class bound, and monolingual) and how they may clash with the cultural values of various minority groups.

2. Culturally skilled counselors are aware of institutional barriers that prevent minorities from using mental health services.

3. Culturally skilled counselors have knowledge of the potential bias in assessment instruments and use procedures and interpret findings keeping in mind the cultural and linguistic characteristics of the clients.

4. Culturally skilled counselors have knowledge of minority family structures, hierarchies, values, and beliefs. They are knowledgeable about the community characteristics and the resources in the community as well as the family.

5. Culturally skilled counselors should be aware of relevant discriminatory practices at the social and community level that may be affecting the psychological welfare of the population being served.

C. Skills

1. Culturally skilled counselors are able to engage in a variety of verbal and nonverbal helping responses. They are able to *send* and *receive* both *verbal* and *nonverbal* messages *accurately* and *appropriately*. They are not tied down to only one method or approach to helping but recognize that helping styles and approaches may be culture bound. When they sense that their helping style is limited and potentially inappropriate, they can anticipate and ameliorate its negative impact.

2. Culturally skilled counselors are able to exercise institutional intervention skills on behalf of their clients. They can help clients determine whether a "problem" stems from racism or bias in others (the concept of health paranoia) so that clients do not inappropriately personalize problems.

3. Culturally skilled counselors are not averse to seeking consultation with traditional healers and religious and spiritual leaders and practitioners in the treatment of culturally different clients when appropriate.

4. Culturally skilled counselors take responsibility for interacting in the language requested by the client and, if not feasible, make appropriate referral. A serious problem arises when the linguistic skills of a counselor do not match the language of the client. This being the case, counselors should (a) seek a translator with cultural knowledge and appropriate professional background and (b) refer to a knowledgeable and competent bilingual counselor.

5. Culturally skilled counselors have training and expertise in the use of traditional assessment and testing instruments. They not only understand the technical aspects of the instruments but are also aware of the cultural limitations. This allows them to use test instruments for the welfare of the diverse clients.

6. Culturally skilled counselors should attend to as well as work to eliminate biases, prejudices, and discriminatory practices. They should be cognizant of sociopolitical contexts in conducting evaluation and providing interventions and should develop sensitivity to issues of oppression, sexism, elitism, and racism.

7. Culturally skilled counselors take responsibility in educating their clients to the processes of psychological intervention, such as goals, expectations, legal rights, and the counselor's orientation.

Derald Wing Sue is a professor in the Department of Counseling Psychology at California State University, Hayward, and is president of Cultural Diversity Training in Oakland, California. **Patricia Arredondo** is director of Empowerment Workshop, Brookline, Massachusetts. **Roderick J. McDavis** is dean of the College of Education at the University of Arkansas, Fayetteville. The committee acknowledges the helpful comments of many individuals too numerous to name. The authors express special appreciation, however, to Thomas A. Parham, who as president of the AMCD had the foresight to appoint the committee and encourage its work throughout his presidency. Correspondence regarding this article should be sent to Derald Wing Sue, Department of Counseling Psychology, California State University, Hayward, CA 94542.[3]

EDITOR'S NOTES

1. This article was published in 1992. Hills, H. I., & Strozier, A. L. (1992). Multicultural training in APA-approved counseling psychology programs: A survey. *Professional Psychology: Research and Practice, 23*, 43-51.
2. This book was published in 1994.
3. Dr. Sue is presently also affiliated with the California School of Professional Psychology in Alameda.

Name Index

645

Subject Index

About the Editors

Joseph G. Ponterotto, Ph.D., is Professor of Education within the Division of Psychological and Educational Services, Fordham University at Lincoln Center, New York City. Prior to arriving at Fordham in 1987, he was an assistant professor in the Department of Educational Psychology at the University of Nebraska, Lincoln. He received his Ph.D. in counseling psychology from the University of California at Santa Barbara in 1985. His recent coauthored and coedited books include *Multicultural Assessment: Clinical, Psychological, and Educational Applications* (in press), *Preventing Prejudice: A Guide for Counselors and Educators* (1993), *Handbook of Racial/Ethnic Minority Counseling Research* (1991), and *Affirmative Action on Campus* (1990).

J. Manuel Casas, Ph.D., is Professor of Education in the Combined Counseling/Clinical/School Psychology Program at the University of California, Santa Barbara. He is also President of JMC & Associates, a consulting firm specializing in diversity training for corporations. Prior to joining the Santa Barbara Program in 1977, he was a psychologist in the UCLA Psychological and Counseling Services Center. He received his Ph.D. in 1975 from Stanford University. He is coauthor of the *Handbook of Racial/Ethnic Minority Counseling Research* (1991).

Lisa A. Suzuki, Ph.D., is Assistant Professor, Counseling Psychology Program, College of Education, University of Oregon. Prior to joining the Oregon faculty in 1993, she was assistant professor in the Division of Psychological and Educational Services at Fordham University. She is the senior editor of *Multicultural Assessment: Clinical, Psychological, and Educational Applications* (in press).

Charlene M. Alexander, Ph.D., is Assistant Professor, Division of Psychological and Educational Services, Fordham University at Lincoln Center. Born in Trinidad and educated for some time in England, she received her Ph.D. in 1992 from the Counseling Psychology Program, University of Nebraska, Lincoln. Her research specialty is in creative approaches to the practice of multicultural counseling.

Editors' and Contributors' Affiliations and Addresses

EDITORS

Joseph G. Ponterotto, Ph.D.
Professor
Division of Psychological and
    Educational Services
Fordham University—Lincoln Center
113 West 60th Street, Room 1008
New York, NY 10023-7478

J. Manuel Casas, Ph.D.
Professor
Counseling/Clinical/School Psychology
    Program
Graduate School of Education
University of California
Santa Barbara, CA 93106

Lisa A. Suzuki, Ph.D.
Assistant Professor
Counseling Psychology
Division of Special Education and
    Rehabilitation
College of Education, Room 270
University of Oregon
Eugene, OR 97403-5251

Charlene M. Alexander, Ph.D.
Assistant Professor
Division of Psychological and
    Educational Services
Fordham University—Lincoln Center
113 West 60th Street, Room 1008
New York, NY 10023-7478

CONTRIBUTORS

Kathleen L. Armstrong, M.Ed.
Counselor, Region Ten Community
    Services Board
413 E. Market Street
Charlottesville, VA 22902

Donald R. Atkinson, Ph.D.
Professor
Counseling/Clinical/School Psychology
    Program
Graduate School of Education
University of California
Santa Barbara, CA 93106

John T. Behrens, Ph.D.
Assistant Professor
Division of Psychology in
    Education
Arizona State University
Tempe, AZ 85287-0611

Linda Berg-Cross, Ph.D., A.B.P.P.
Director of Clinical Training
Howard University
525 Bryant Street
CB Powell
Washington, DC 20059

Elise Berryhill-Paapke, M.A.
Doctoral Candidate
Department of Educational Psychology
University of Oklahoma
820 Van Vleet Oval, Room 321
Norman, OK 73019-0260

Michael T. Brown, Ph.D.
Associate Professor
Counseling/Clinical/School Psychology
    Program
Graduate School of Education
University of California
Santa Barbara, CA 93106

Robert T. Carter, Ph.D.
Associate Professor
Psychology and Education
Teachers College, Columbia University
Box 102
525 West 120th Street
New York, NY 10027

Jill C. Changizi, M.A.
Graduate Student
Department of Counseling Psychology
    and Guidance Services
Ball State University
Muncie, IN 47306

Ruby Takushi Chinen, Ph.D.
Assistant Professor
Howard University
525 Bryant Street
CB Powell
Washington, DC 20059

Sandra K. Choney, Ph.D.
Assistant Professor
Department of Educational Psychology
University of Oklahoma
820 Van Vleet Oval, Room 321
Norman, OK 73019-0260

William E. Cross Jr., Ph.D.
Professor, Psychology Department
Penn State University
417 Moore Building
University Park, PA 16802

Va Lecia L. Cureton, B.A.
Graduate Student

Department of Counseling Psychology
    and Guidance Services
Ball State University
Muncie, IN 47306

Michael D'Andrea, Ph.D.
Associate Profesor
Counselor Education
College of Education
University of Hawaii at Manoa
Wist Hall Annex 2, Room 222
1776 University Avenue
Honolulu, HI 96822

Judy Daniels, Ph.D.
Associate Professor
Counselor Education
College of Education
University of Hawaii at Manoa
Wist Hall Annex 2, Room 222
1776 University Avenue
Honolulu, HI 96822

Jonathan G. Dings, M.A.
Doctoral Candidate, Measurement and
    Statistics
University of Iowa
361 Lindquist Center
Iowa City, IA 52242
    and
Kentucky Department of Education
19th Floor, CPT Building
500 Mero Street
Frankfort, KY 40601

Ismini Georgiades, M.A.
Doctoral Candidate
Division of Psychological and
    Educational Services
Fordham University—Lincoln Center
113 West 60th Street, Room 1008
New York, NY 10023-7478

Betty E. Gridley, Ph.D.
Professor
Department of Educational Psychology
Ball State University
Muncie, IN 47306

Ingrid Grieger, Ed.D.
Director
Counseling Center
Iona College

715 North Avenue
New Rochelle, NY 10801

George V. Gushue, M.Phil.
Doctoral Candidate
Counseling Psychology Program
Teachers College, Columbia University
Box 102
525 West 120th Street
New York, NY 10027

Janet E. Helms, Ph.D.
Professor
Department of Psychology
University of Maryland
College Park, MD 20742

Allen E. Ivey, Ed.D., A.B.P.P.
Distinguished University Professor
School and Counseling Psychology
    Program
University of Massachusetts, Amherst
352 Hills South
Amherst, MA 01003

Morris L. Jackson, Ed.D.
Director, Return to School Programs
The American University
4400 Massachusetts Avenue, NW
Washington, DC 20016-8113

Merle A. Keitel, Ph.D.
Associate Professor
Division of Psychological and
    Educational Services
Graduate School of Education
Fordham University—Lincoln Center
113 West 60th Street
New York, NY 10023-7478

Christine Kerwin, Ph.D.
School Psychologist
12A Dailey Drive
Croton-on-Hudson, NY 10520

Mark S. Kiselica, Ph.D.
Assistant Professor
Department of Counseling and
    Personnel Services
Trenton State College
Hillwood Lakes, CN 4700
Trenton, NJ 08650-4700

Mary Kopala, Ph.D.
Assistant Professor
Educational Foundations and
    Counseling
Hunter College
695 Park Avenue
New York, NY 10021

John F. Kugler, Ph.D.
School Psychologist
New York City Board of Education
District 20
6323 7th Avenue
Brooklyn, NY 11220

Kwong-Liem Karl Kwan, M.A.
Doctoral Candidate
Department of Educational Psychology
University of Nebraska
116 Bancroft Hall
Lincoln, NE 68588

Joycelyn Landrum-Brown, Ph.D.
Coordinator, Education Program for
    Culture Awareness (EPCA) and
    Lecturer, Department of Black
    Studies and Education
University of California
2330 Phelps Hall
Santa Barbara, CA 93106-9490

Mark M. Leach, Ph.D.
Assistant Professor
Department of Psychology
University of Southern Mississippi
S.S. Box 5025
Hattiesburg, MS 39406-5025

Courtland C. Lee, Ph.D.
Professor and Director
Counselor Education Program
School of Education
University of Virginia
169 Ruffner Hall
Charlottesville, VA 22903

Frederick T. L. Leong, Ph.D.
Associate Professor
Department of Psychology
The Ohio State University
1885 Neil Avenue Mall
Columbus, OH 43210-1222

S. Alvin Leung, Ph.D.
Associate Professor
Department of Educational Psychology
University of Houston
491 Farish Hall
Houston, TX 77204-5874

Susana M. Lowe, M.A.
Doctoral Candidate
Counseling/Clinical/School Psychology
    Program
Graduate School of Education
University of California
Santa Barbara, CA 93106

Rod J. Merta, Ph.D.
Assistant Professor
Counseling and Educational Psychology
New Mexico State University
Box 3 CEP
Las Cruces, NM 88003-0001

Raji Pannu, M.A.
Doctoral Candidate
Department of Psychology
University of Maryland
College Park, MD 20742

Thomas A. Parham, Ph.D.
Director, Counseling Center and Career
    Planning and Placement Center
University of California
Irvine, CA 92717

Paul B. Pedersen, Ph.D.
Professor
Counselor Education
School of Education
260 Huntington Hall
Syracuse, New York 13244-2340

Donald B. Pope-Davis, Ph.D.
Associate Professor
Department of Counseling and
    Personnel Services
University of Maryland
3208 Benjamin Building
College Park, MD 20742

Scott D. Pytluk, M.A.
Doctoral Candidate
Counseling/Clinical/School Psychology
    Program

Department of Education
University of California
Santa Barbara, CA 93106

Adil Qureshi, Ed.M.
Doctoral Student
Department of Counseling
University of Southern California
500 Waite Phillips Hall
Los Angeles, CA 90089-0031

Amy L. Reynolds, Ph.D.
Assistant Professor
Division of Psychological and
    Educational Services
Fordham University—Lincoln Center
113 West 60th Street, Room 1008
New York, NY 10023-7478

Rockey R. Robbins, M.A.
Doctoral Candidate
Department of Educational Psychology
University of Oklahoma
820 Van Vleet Oval, Room 321
Norman, OK 73019-0260

Wayne Rowe, Ph.D.
Professor Emeritus
Department of Educational Psychology
University of Oklahoma
820 Van Vleet Oval
Norman, OK 73019-0260

Daniel T. Sciarra, Ph.D.
Psychologist
Sunset Park Mental Health Center of
    the Lutheran Medical Center
1220 8th Avenue
Brooklyn, NY 11215

Gargi Roysircar Sodowsky, Ph.D.
Associate Professor
Department of Educational Psychology
University of Nebraska-Lincoln
116 Bancroft Hall
Lincoln, NE 68588-0345

Derald Wing Sue, Ph.D.
Professor
California School of Professional
    Psychology
1005 Atlantic Avenue
Alameda, CA 94501

and
Professor
Department of Educational Psychology
California State University, Hayward
Hayward, CA 94542

Lynn Sussman, M.A.
Doctoral Candidate
Division of Psychological and
    Educational Services
Fordham University—Lincoln Center
113 West 60th Street, Room 1008
New York, NY 10023-7478

Shiraz Piroshaw Tata, Ph.D.
Psychologist
Counseling and Student Development
    Center

Northern Illinois University
Dekalb, IL 60115

Clemmont E. Vontress, Ph.D.
Professor of Counseling and Director of
    the Counseling Program
Department of Human Services
George Washington University
Washington, DC 20052

Nicole S. Wagner, M.A.
Doctoral Student
Department of Psychology
The Ohio State University
1885 Neil Avenue Mall
Columbus, OH 43210-1222